1 MONTH OF
FREE
READING

at

www.ForgottenBooks.com

By purchasing this book you are eligible for one month membership to ForgottenBooks.com, giving you unlimited access to our entire collection of over 1,000,000 titles via our web site and mobile apps.

To claim your free month visit:

www.forgottenbooks.com/free505649

ISBN 978-0-331-66217-7
PIBN 10505649

ΚΥΡΙΑΚΗ᾽ ῾ΗΜΕ᾽ΡΑ.

A DISCOURSE

IN

SIX DIALOGUES

ON THE

Name, Notion, and *Observation*

OF THE

LORD'S DAY.

WITH

An Account of several Canons, Decrees, and Laws, *Foreign* and *English,* for the keeping it holy.

The Way of Worship in the Church of *England,* vindicated. And,

An *Office,* or *Collection* of DEVOTIONS, proper for the Day.

By THO. MORER, *Rector of the United Parishes of SS.* Ann *and* Agnes, *within* Aldersgate, *and S.* John Zachary, London.

῾Ημεῖς μὴ ἓν τιμῶμὴ Κυριακὴν διὰ τὴν ἀνάστασιν. Athanaf. de Sem.

LONDON,
Printed for *Tho. Newborough,* at the *Golden Ball* in St. *Paul's* Church-yard, 1701.

THE
PREFACE.

Reader,

YOU may expect perhaps to be told, according to custom, that the Authority of some of my friends or the Importunity of others forced me to the publication of what you find in the following sheets; But I offer no such Apology, nor will I use my friends so ill as to hazard their Reputation to secure thereby my Own. This only I say, That if you receive any benefit by what is here written, Let your Charity suppose that to be the true reason; and if this reason be wanting, I am afraid no other will excuse me.

But waving this, 'Tis necessary I should lay before you the summ of this Book, which consists of a Controversie between the Church and these Five sorts of Men. First, Libertines,

bertines, who allow no Set-days for the Service of God, but would be left to their own Will to worship as their humour and fancy lead 'em. Secondly, Sabbatarians or such as contend for the Jewish Sabbath, and stand to the perpetual obligation of the Fourth Commandment, both as to the day itself and the manner of Keeping it. Thirdly, Those who reject the Saturday-Sabbath, yet take up the Morality of the Seventh-day, and will have it to be the appointment of God and Nature. Fourthly, Such as consider the Lords-day de Jure Divino strictly, and make it the institution of Christ or his Apostles; and on that account, of the same influence on Christians under the Gospel, as the Sabbath had over the Jews by the Law of Moses. Fifthly the Prophaners of the Festival who by their misbehaviour or neglect of holy duties to be done on this day, too openly declare they lay no stress on it, and think they incur no Spiritual danger if they do not observe it. All these with some other mistakes concerning the manner of Our Churches-Service on the day are examined in their Turns, and the Names and Notion

of

of the Lord's-day fully explain'd and directions added to keep it well.

The Office may seem impracticable for proposing more than a man is well able to do. And as to this exception I might excuse myself by the number and authority of those pious Divines out of whose devotions I made the Collection. But I only say, I intend an help and not a rule: And if the Votary comes not up to it, I Judge him not; yet give me leave to apply those words of our Lord, He that is able to receive it, let him receive it---And if a man's Will and Strength be such as to attempt the work, I was loath he should want directions; And let such a one use me as his guide and not his Master.

I speak very much in the language of the Authors I had occasion to consult; partly in Justice to them, and partly with regard to myself, who have cause enough to distrust my own performances: And therefore for fear any thing relating to this Argument should suffer by my words, I chose rather to borrow theirs, who are admired for their Learning or Piety in this or other ages.

ages. *So that*, if in multiplicity of citations there appear Vanity, Often-
tation or Digreffion, Modefty and
Honefty muft make my excufe, who
acknowledge, with *Pliny*, that to
chufe rather to be taken in a theft than
to give every Man his due is *obnoxii*
Animi & infœlicis Ingenii. And herein I
follow the example of * St. Jerom, *who*
profeffes that in a great meafure he made
only a Collection *of what others before him*
had faid on the fame Subject. And if I
fay what has bin often faid, I do it on St.
Auguftine's *reafon, That 'tis for the Good*
of Chrift-Church *that the fame things be*
written by diverfe Men that fo the Truth
may fpread the further. But the Apoftle
has a better warrant for me (Heb. **1. 1.**)
God at fundry times and in diverfe
manners hath fpoken (*the fame thing*)
to the Fathers *and us.*

If any fhould call this an unfeafonable
difpute, and think I contribute to the propha-

---

* *Cautior atq; timidior imbecillitatem virium mearum*
fentiens Origenis commentarios fum fecutus, &c. Prœm: in
Ep. ad Galat.

nation of the day, (which all good Men are labouring against) by lessening the Obligations laid upon 'em to reverence and observe it; I answer, that to set every thing on its right Foot, I have always thought it the likeliest way to keep it standing. Sure I am the Lord's Day has such and so many Authorities to gain it Veneration, that it does not want any Writer's Art to support and recommend it: And therefore either to prevent, or remove all the Cavils, the Prophaners of the Day do, or may catch at, to colour their Remisness, is to leave 'em more excuseless before God and Man. But we shall meet with this in the Body of the Discourse, so I dismiss it here.

The Discourse is by Dialogue, as a more natural, familiar, and easie way: And if any doubts arise, they are better thus proposed, and more intelligibly answered, than they could otherwise be. However, the Method is pleasant, and People are sooner invited to read a Subject delivered in this manner. I have great Examples of this kind, whose Figure and Number

ber

ber are able to excuse me. And this *muſt be my Apology for thoſe many Excurſions from the main Subject throughout this Piece, againſt the ſtrict Rules of Argument and Art:* For it is in conformity *to the way of People in common Diſcourſe,* † *wherein new Queſtions are apt to ſtart from the Anſwers made to what goes before.* And this might have appeared a *a piece of* Art, *if I had imitated* Nature *well.* Yet I hope nothing has intruded, *but what may be ſerviceable to an unprejudiced Reader; whoſe inſight in this Controverſie I ſhall not ſo far ſcruple, as to ſuppoſe he will think the Digreſſions ſo many, or ſome Matters ſo impertinent, as at firſt ſight they ſeem to be.*

I have made the Debaters Men of Moderation and Temper, becauſe Paſſion *and* Eagerneſs *ſeldom diſcover* Truth; *And when Diſputants are bitter and violent (which they miſcall* Zeal) *all they aim at, is* Victory, *and to ſettle an* Opinion, *without conſidering whether they be in the right*

---

or no. *The Opponent therefore makes one of our Congregation, tho' he be not well satisfied with all the Instances of the Publick Service:* Yet notwithstanding his dislike of divers Particulars in it, he believes Separation *an ill Remedy; and therefore, according to the way of Charitable and Prudent Men, he chuses rather to bear a great deal, than to distract the Church, and disturb the Peace of it:* For he dreads the Sad Effects and Consequences of Schism; and remembers the Maxim of Old and New Rome, Divide and we shall master 'em. *The Subject I am upon, puts us in mind, That as God created us all in one Nature, so he redeem'd us to be all of one Name. Difference of Stiles are apt to divide Men.* To be sure, when their Notions are not the same, their Affections will stand at a distance; *and then beginning to dispute and quarrel, while each Party contends for the right way, we are all of us in danger to lose it.* This let us remember, that Jesus our Saviour (whose Resurrection we weekly celebrate on this day) died upon the Cross, To gather together in one the

Children

Children of God, *that so there might be* one Fold, *and* one Shepherd. *The first Christians were of* one heart, *and* one mind; *They worshipped God in* one way, *and in* one Place; *They had* one Lord, *and* one Faith.——*May we follow* them *as they did Christ, that our Creed and Practice being the very same, we may all of us get to the same Glory, and that* Eternal Rest, *of which this day is the* Emblem.

Amen.

Note, *That* [A] *means him who likes, and defends the Constitution of the Church as it is at present.* [B] *Him who complies, but not without finding Fault with it.*

E R-

ERRATA.

Pag. 24. Lin. 19. r. *visible Son of God.* p. 129. l. 31. r. *and the week been made.* p. 133. l. 12. r. *owed* Job *a spite.* p. 142. l. 24. r. Seder Olam Rabba. p. 247. l. 1. r. *Nations.* p. 248 l. 19. r. *rejoicing.* p. 249. l. ult. r. *attending.* p. 253. l. 10. r. *oftner.* p. 276. l. 4. r. *to worship God.* p. 320. l. 35. r. *House of the Lord* p. 330. l. 4. r. *promised it.* p. 391. l. 21. r. *and was worn out in the following Ages.* p. 428. l. 8. r. *every thought.* In the Notes, p. 132. r. desumpta. p. 534. r. Psallentiam Græcorum.

THE

A DISCOURSE,

By Way of DIALOGUE,

ON THE

𝕷𝖔𝖗𝖉'𝖘=𝕯𝖆𝖞.

DIALOGUE I.

The CONTENTS.

Too much thoughtfulness injurious to health. The reason of it. The Body not to be neglected. The Sympathy between Body and Soul. How they mutually act on one another. The word [Sabbath] not proper for the Lords-Day. How the word is to be understood in the Fathers. Altar and Priest not improper. The Lords Supper a Sacrifice. What kind of Sacrifice. The Question in Minucius Felix *cleared about Temples and Altars. Q.* Maries *Statute about Altars. Whether repealed.* Queen Elizabeth's *injunction for Tables instead of Altars.* Sunday, *why the Lord's-Day so called. Whether it*

B   be

be a Gentile Name. *The Myftical and Natural reafon of that Name. The Order of the Planets according to* Ptolemy. *Their Influence and Prefidentſhip over the days of the Week. Objections of* Scaliger *and* Selden *anſwer'd.* Ptolemy's *Order very ancient. The names of the Days of long ſtanding, but only among the Aſtronomers, and not admitted into the Civil account to conſtitute a Week till the times of* Dionyſius Exiguus. Cicero's Hebdomada Quarta. *The Seventh Day Critical among the Phyſicians. Saxon Names for the Days of the Week. The word* [Feria] *referrs to the Heathens, as* Sabbath *to the Jews.* ❧. John's *Lords-Day, what? Whether Eaſter-Day or ſome other Great Feſtival, or the Day of Judgment. The Apocalypfe examined. Authorities and Reaſons for and againſt it. The uſefulneſs of Tradition. It may explain St.* John, *but is no infallible Proof. The Lords-Day by whom appointed. Why it is not called Chriſts-Day, as appropriated to him.*

A. MY good Neighbour, I am glad to fee you in this place, after your long confinement by Sicknefs.

B. Sir, I thank you. I have been a Prifoner for a great while; and, which was the fting of my confinement, not only denied Liberty, but kept to my Bed and Chamber in a great deal of mifery; which makes me the more defirous to go abroad, having fome low degree of Strength given me, to try what effect the *Air* will have towards my Recovery.

A. You do well: For the *Air* not only *refreshes,* but may be faid to *feed* the Body, provided it be good, as this is, and that you take *convenient hours* for your walk, b
late, at both wh

with feveral *Vapours*, which may rather injure
than help you. And one thing more, let me
caution you of ; Your Looks befpeak you *ferious*
and *thoughtful,* and you feem to me a greater Stu-
dent than fuits your prefent condition.

B. I muft confefs, my Thoughts were not idle,
though not in fo deep a Meditation as to give me
the character of a *Philofopher* or a *Pharifee :* And
one end I propofed to my felf in it, was, to make
my Walk the eafier, by employing the Mind, and
keeping it from attending to the complaints and
wearifomnefs of the Body.

A. 'Tis true, Meditation fhortens the way :
But the end, you fay, of your going abroad is for
the Air's-fake, to help your Recovery. Now this
defign is fruftrated by fo much Thoughtfulnefs ;
becaufe *to Think,* is to limit the Soul to the Subject
you are upon, and fo in a great meafure you withdraw it from the fervice it owes the Body, which
thereupon fuffers more than you are aware of, and
is much expofed to the reliques of your Diftemper.
Befides ———

B. Pray, Sir, hold a little. I do not underftand you.

A. You muft needs know, that the *Body* hath
neither life nor motion without the *Soul :* And
therefore at death, when the *Soul* is gone, the
Body becomes a mere Carkafs, and breaths no
more. Now then, if the *Soul* be fo neceffary to
enliven and quicken the *Body,* whenever you call
the *Soul* from that part of its miniftry (which is
done by much *Meditation.*) by this means you bring
a *numbnefs* on the Faculties, and hinder the good
improvement they might make of the *Air,* or any
thing elfe which would be ferviceable to the
Body.

B. I believe this to be the reafon, why many
of your *great Scholars* are fo *fpare and thin,* becaufe
they

they hardly admit the leaft refpite from their Studies, but will, with *Aquina's*, be drawing Conclufions at the very *Table*; fo that what they eat and drink doth 'em little good, for the Reafon you give, namely, the retirement of the Soul, which being fo very intent on other matters, it cannot communicate to the Stomach fo much Heat and Motion as is neceffary to digeft it.

A. I think they are to blame for it : *Extremes* are dangerous, and ought to be avoided. I muft confefs, a pamper'd Body is not eafily govern'd, it affects and difables the Mind, cafts a cloud on the Underftanding, clogs the Brain, and is a great enemy to the practice of Piety, (for which and the like Reafons it muft be fubdued, and the *Afs* kept under, as St. *Bernard* fpeaks, to keep it from kicking ;) yet after all, I muft needs fay, it is a thing not to be defpifed or neglected : -The *Make* of it was enough to aftonifh *David*, and difpute *Galen* into the belief of a Deity. In truth, it deferves part of our care ; nor are we to look on it fo vile a thing, but that for its *own* and the *Creator's fake* it ought to be valuable to us, and in a moderate way we are to cherifh and feed it.

B. The Apoftles, *John* and *Paul*, warrant what you fay ; yet I have often heard our *Minifters* teach us the contrary, who think they can never enough commend the *Soul*, unlefs they difparage the *Body*, and make it one of the moft contemptible things in the world, calling it *Clay*, and I know not what ; whereas we may obferve, that the Lord *Chrift* had an honourable notion of it, and made it the fubject of almoft all his Miracles which he wrought for the *preferving, fuftaining and healing the Body of Man* (*a*).

(*a*) Lord Bacon's Advancement of Learning, B. 2. pag. 41.

A. He

A. He that would ftraighten a crooked Stick always bends it the other way (*b*). Our *Minifters* take notice how much we indulge the *Flefh* to the prejudice of the *Spirit*, and that we beftow much more Coft and Care on the *one* than on the *other*; and therefore there lies a neceffity on 'em to ufe this method, thereby to bring us, not fo much into a difefteem of the *Body*, as to a greater refpect for the *Soul*, which feems flighted, and never thought on. And as for thofe vile Characters you object, they are occafionally offer'd for fome *Perfons* and *Times*. In the Primitive Ages *fome* were forced to plead for the *Body*, as *thefe* do for the *Soul*, that fo they might keep the ancient Chriftians from expofing themfelves needlefly to the fury of their Perfecutors, out of a rafh and unfeafonable Zeal to be accounted *Martyrs*; and our Teachers would do the fame, but that they find we love the *Flefh* more than our *Religion*.

B. It may be fo. Well, Sir, be pleas'd to purfue your Argument.

A. I fay then, *To Think*, is *Action* : But *Action* continued, ends in *Wearinefs*, which on a double account is bad for the *Body* ; firft, becaufe the *Soul* is made *dull* by it, and becomes incapable to difcharge its duty to the *Body*; and, fecondly, it communicates that Languor to its part'ner, and concurs with the Difeafe to make the Body weaker than before.

B. I conceive not, how either of thefe can be true. For, as to the *firft*, that a thing is *weary*, proceeds from the *grofsnefs* of Matter wherewith it is incumbred and clogg'd ; but the *Soul* has no *Matter*, being like the *Angels* and *Spirits* above, who

---

(*b*) *Solent hortulani*, &c. *Saunderfon. prælect.* 2. *de bona intentione, N.* 21. *Rivet. Critic. Sacr. c.* 11. *Contraria contrariis curantur, Extrema extremis.* Aphor. Medic.

hourly

hourly contemplate the Divine Nature, yet neither are nor can be *weary*, for that would deſtroy the Notion of *Bleſſedneſs* in the other State.

A. The ſtate of the Soul in *this* World and *that* to come is not the ſame : *There* indeed its condition is ſuch, that, comparatively ſpeaking, it may be called *Actus Purus*, becauſe of no impediment or hindrance to its operation. But *here* it is not ſo : For though in it ſelf it be not *material*, yet it is tied to *Matter*, which is no ſmall weight to it, and makes it act with ſome repugnance and difficulty, and is the reaſon why a Man is ſo often *tired* with *thinking*.

B. If this be the reaſon, then the Soul would be under no better terms in Heaven, becauſe the the *Body* as well as the *Soul* ſhall be bleſſed above, and conſequently there will be the ſame *impediment* in both Places.

A. Not ſo neither : For *there* our Bodies are to be refined and glorified ; all the dullneſs and groſsneſs of Matter will be done away. In compariſon of what they now are, they are named *ſpiritual* ; not that ſtrictly they are turned into *Spirits* ; for if ſo, they would be no longer *Bodies* ; but they are guided by the Bleſſed *Spirit*, and ſo prepared and ordered that the Souls act as freely, as if altogether abstracted or ſeparated from 'em.

B. Well, allowing the *Soul* to be ſomewhat *tired* with much *thinking*, yet how can this Languor be communicated to the *Body* ? What Commerce or mutual Affection can there poſſibly be between things of ſuch different Natures as *Spirit* and *Matter* ?

A. *Heat* and *Cold* as much differ, yet they affect one another.

B. But theſe are bare *Qualities*, having one and the ſame Subject or Matter between 'em, and by this *medium* they may eaſily ſucceed, and in

ſome

ſome degree conſiſt together : But there is no
ſuch *ſubject* here, and therefore by what *mean* or
conveyance can the *Body* and *Soul poſſeſs* each
other ?

A. Tho' *Body* and *Soul* are Subſtances very *unlike,* if conſidered in *themſelves,* yet *both* concurr to
make a *Man* ; and as *one conſtitution,* they ſubſiſt,
rejoyce and ſuffer together. Now the *copula* between 'em (whatever name it has) is the common
paſſage to *both,* and becomes the ſame thing to the
Body and *Soul,* as the Matter is to the aforeſaid
Qualities.

B. But again ; (*c*) As to *Heat* and *Cold,* or
other Inſtances of that kind, they cannot move
without their own *alteration,* and ceaſing to be
what they were before, as *Cold* ſpends it ſelf by
acting on the *Fire,* and ſo on the contrary ; either
then the *Union* between *Body* and *Soul* is not ſuch as
to admit this *Sympathy,* or elſe becauſe of it, they
remain not as they were.

A. As to things ſubject to *change,* every ſuch
Union cauſes a *change* in 'em, as in the mixture of
Elements and their Qualities : But in *Intelligent
Beings,* ſuch as the *Soul* is, it holds not good. For
though it be united to the *Body,* yet its Subſtance
is too pure to admit alteration, and that is the
reaſon of its *Immortality.* And this we may take
for a good illuſtration of that inexplicable *Union*
of the *Two Natures* in the Perſon of *Chriſt* without
confuſion or *change.*

B. But then this confirms my conceit, That
there cannot be that mutual *acting,* you propoſe,
between the *Body* and *Soul* ; becauſe to *affect* any
thing, is to *alter,* and render it not the ſame.

(*c*) *Ignis & aqua —— ſi cominus venerint, alterutrum quod
ſuperaverit, conficiat alterum, neceſſe eſt.* Lactant. de Orig.
Error. n. 9.

A. If

A. If by *Alteration* you mean a *Physical Change*, it cannot be in the *Soul*, becaufe it has no *Matter*, and *Matter* is the Subject of fuch *Alteration :* Yet as to its *Efficacy* and *Operation* it is not the fame, becaufe it acts not with that *freedom* it did before, and on that account it is faid to fuffer. But to explain this better by your own experience : How often, during your Sicknefs, were you under a *Delirium?* And what was this, but a piece of violence on your Reafon, by the rage and malignity of your *Fever*, when not only the *Body* but the *Mind* fuffer'd by the excefs of the Diftemper ?

B. I confefs it, but believe this to proceed from the *Organs*, difabled by the Difeafe, and made unfit for the *Soul* to act by, not that the *Soul* or *Mind* it felf was affected with the Pain.

A. You are in the right : And hence it is that after a long and violent Sicknefs, there follows in fome People fuch a *Stupidity*, *Forgetfulnefs* and *Childifhnefs* for the future, that they retain little elfe befides the *Shapes* and *Faces* of Men, their Memory and Underftanding being taken quite away upon the difability of the Inftruments, which the contagion and force of the Difeafe has made ufelefs and incapable to ferve 'em. But then this very *Obftruction* is a continual acting and refifting the Soul, and this Action or Refiftance powerfully affects it. Let me ask you another Queftion ; Were you not fometimes extremely *dry* in your late Illnefs, and withal very *impatient* if you were not fatisfied ?

B. I muft needs own it, and was frequently *angry* with my *Nurfe* upon the leaft delay of bringing the Drink to me.

A. Do you fee, how the violence of your *Drought* influenced your *Mind*, put you into *Paffion*, and fo far debauched your *Reafon* as to make you drink againft the Phyfician's *order* and your own *fafety?* Now what occafioned this *Drought*, but

the

the vigour of your Diſtemper, which though properly and ſtrictly belonging to the *Body,* yet the *Soul* was moved with it, and ſhared in the Fever?

B. I remember it well, and you have put me in a way to improve the overſight: I ſhall give you no further trouble concerning this affair, unleſs you pleaſe to add a word or two about the *Soul,* and how it *affects* the *Body.*

A. That will be quickly diſpatch'd, provided we conſider, That as the *Soul* acts the *Body,* ſo this muſt be done in ſuch a way as ſhe is qualified for it; otherwiſe (which cannot be in Nature) the Cauſe would outdo it ſelf in the Operation. So that the *Soul* being the *Principle* of *Life* and *Motion* to the *Body,* the *Body* cannot have theſe things in other ſort than as the *Principle* gives 'em. And conſequently, if the *Soul* be diſturbed, and the *Spirits* oppreſs'd, which are the means of every Action, it muſt neceſſarily follow that the *Body* will be caſt down, languiſh and decay.

B. Inſtances of this kind are too often ſeen in the *wild Looks* of People diſcontented in Mind, and who, by the confuſion of their *Face, pale Viſage, want of Stomach,* a general *decay,* and in the end downright *Sickneſs,* loudly publiſh the *Diſtraction*

as to hurry 'em to fatal deſigns againſt themſelves, by *drowning, hanging, ſhooting, cutting the Throat,* and the like, of which we have moſt Weeks in our Bills ſome lamentable Examples. But may not all this be charged on the abundance and dominion of *ill humours* in the *Body,* without any regard to the *Mind* or *Soul* ?

A. It is not rarely ſo: And this proves what was ſaid before concerning the Power of the *Body* over the *Mind, and is one reaſon* (d) *of thoſe many*

_____

(d) Sir *Francis* Bacon, *loc. cit.*

ſcruples

scruples and superstitions, of diet and other regiment
of the Body in the Sect of the Pythagoreans *and in the*
Law of Mahomet: *and was the occasion of the Ordi-*
nances of the Ceremonial Law of Moses *interdicting*
the eating of blood and the fat ; distinguishing between
Beasts clean and unclean, and the like ; and argues
for our present practice under the Gospel in retaining
the use of Fastings, Abstinencies, and other Macera-
tions and Humiliations of the Body. The root and
life of all which prescripts is, besides the Ceremony,
the consideration of that dependance which the affections of the Mind are submitted unto upon the state
and disposition of the Body——However the motive
very often proceeds from the *Soul,* and the wound
is begun in *Conscience* upon the apprehension of
disgrace or other misfortune in *this* World, or
the foresight it has of its deplorable Condition in
the *other.* So that in short, we (*e*) both ways
discover the *Sympathy* we are speaking of ; and
which we need no more doubt than we do the
fellow-feeling or mutual concern the inferiour
parts of the Body have for one another. And
therefore the *passions* which come from the *Body*
are given the *Soul* and called by *its name* ; and according to the different complexions and tempers
of the *one,* the *other* discovers it self with more or
less vigour (*f*).

B. I yield to what you say, Sir, and I stand
indebted to you for this care of my *health,* yet the
Subject I was upon will excuse me, being a *Point*
wherein *Body* and *Soul* have an equal interest, and
which not only imployed my thoughts when *you*

(*e*) Pf. 105. 18. Nehem. 2. 2. (*f*) *Physicæ rationes*
docent nos esse Sympathiam inter corpus & animam. Solet enim
anima verè affici pro temperatura corporis, nam qui abundat flava
aut atra bili animo solet esse iracundo aut mœsto. P. Mart.
Loc. Com.

came

came to this place, but which indeed much exer-
ciſed my *Mind* all the time of my Sickneſs; looking one while on my danger as a Divine Puniſhment for my negligence *that way*, and anon taking
it as a gracious alarm from God, to make me put
on new Reſolutions of better diligence for the future, to anſwer the end of my being here. It is
the *Sabbath* I mean, which our Miniſter *yeſterday*
made the *Theme* of his Sermon, and took no little
pains to explain and preſs us to obſerve it.

A. I ſuppoſe you intend the *Lords-Day*, becauſe
the *Miniſter* you ſay, was earneſt to have you
keep it. For as to the *Sabbath*, or day called by
that name, it was the day *before*; and tho' it was
the great Feſtival among the *Jews*, yet now 'tis
exploded by *us*, and we lie under no obligation to
give it particular honour.

B. Right, but I called it *Sabbath* (*g*) by way
of alluſion to *that Holiday* of the *Jews* ſtrictly ſo
named, in conformity to ſome of the *Ancients* who
uſe the ſame language. For ſo (*h*) *Auguſtine* calls
Thurſday the *fifth of the Sabbath*. And (*i*) *Jerom*,
Tueſday the third of the Sabbath. (*k*) And *Tertullian*, *Friday the Preparation* — So *Origen*, and
others.

A. Tho' the word *Sabbath* be ſometimes met
with in the Writings of the *Fathers*, yet it means
either *that day* conſtantly appropriated to the
Jewiſh Sabbath, namely *Saturday*, or the *Spiritual*
and *Myſtical Sabbath* typed and repreſented by the
Sabbath of the 4th *Commandment*. But when they
diſtinguiſh and give the *proper* names to the *days* of
the *Week*, they call *Saturday* Τὸ Σάββατον, and our
Sunday, *Dominicum*; unleſs ſometimes in their Diſ-

(*g*) *Quaſi ab ejus parente Sabbato Judaico*—Young, *de die Dom.*
(*h*) *Quintum Sabbati*, Aug. Ep. 118. (*i*) *Tertium Sabbati*,
Hieron. Epitaph. Paul. (*k*) *Paraſceve.* Adv. Marc.

putations

putations with the *Jews* they accommodate themselves to the way of their Adversaries, and so
term the *Lords-day* μίαν τῶν σαββάτων, one of the
Sabbaths, or the *first Day of the Week*, as *Justin
Martyr* doth in the Dialogue between *him* and
Tryphon. But elsewhere he saith it is ἡμέρᾳ τῇ ἡλίε—
or *Sunday*, in more congruous Language, when in
his Apology he addresses to the *Gentiles.* But admit the *Fathers* spake in that manner, yet this is
very seldom, and for that Reason (*l*) *Alexander
Hales* gives, because *Sabbath-day* taken at large is
said to be a *day* of *leisure*, i. e. of *rest* from all
other works to serve God the better. And on this
account indeed the *Lords-day* may have that name
without scandal or prejudice to the Christian Religion.

B. I lay no stress on the *word*, but consider the
thing. And to call the *Lords-day* by the *name of
the Sabbath may I suppose on several accounts be allowed the Christian Church without any great incon-
veniency; and therefore Men otherwise sober and moderate ought not to be censur'd with too much severity, neither be charged with Judaism if they so
speak.*

A. Yet as your (*m*) Author saith, *for sundry
respects too, it were perhaps much more expedient, if
the word Sabbath were not at all, or more sparingly,
used.* But that which makes me take notice of it,
is, because *those Persons* who of late years have
pitched on the *word*, and from *whose* custom you
borrow it, will not give other people the same *liberty* which themselves take, but charge us with
Popery and I know not what, for calling the Minister *Priest*, and the Communion-Table *Altar*;

(*l*) P. 3. Q. 3². *Quælibet dies statuta ad divinam culturam
dici potest Sabbatum*—Johan de Burgo—
(*m*) Bishop *Sanderson*'s Case of Conscience of the Sabbath.

whereas

whereas, this way of arguing flies back into their own Faces, and more effectually proves them *Jews* for using the word *Sabbath*, than it makes us *Papists* for entertaining the names of *Priest* and *Altar.* However, I think the way of Speech innocent enough in all Cases but where *Christianity* may suffer, and *weak Brethren* be offended by it, which the *Old Doctors* had a special regard to, and therefore on such occasions forbore all *Jewish* and *Heathenish* words, that they might not be suspected to lean to either side.

B. It was a good reason to make *them* cautious. But there is not, I conceive, any such danger *now*, and so we need not speak with that preciseness.

A. I think the *reason* in a great measure still continues, because we have to deal with a *sort* of *Men* who rigorously insist on the *Saturday-Sabbath*, and will observe no *other.* So that as St. *Augustine* faith, because of the *ambiguity* of the word, which is not always explained in our ordinary discourse, we may sometimes seem to mean *that* which will be very offensive to our Christian liberty; and by naming the word *Sabbath*, when we should say the *Lords-day*, we may be suspected to be of their *mind* who so much stickle for the *Jewish* Notion.

B. But then is not the Objection full as strong against *Priest and Altar*, which may create some jealousie that we are leaning to *Popery*, because these terms naturally suppose a *real Sacrifice* to justifie the language, otherwise the words are irrelative and improper; and where there is no *Sacrifice*, it cannot be said there is either *Altar* or *Priest.*

A. You say well, these words do certainly depend one upon the other. If so be therefore we allow *Sacrifices* in our Church, we must in the consequence have *Priests* and *Altars.*

B. Do

B. Do not we *Proteſtants* except againſt *that* language, and find fault with thoſe of the *Romiſh* perſwaſion for retaining this Doctrine?

A. That which we object againſt the *Church* of *Rome* conſiſts not in *words*, but in the *ſenſe* of 'em. They call the Lords-Supper a *Sacrifice*, and ſo do we, but with this difference, that whereas *they* mean by it *an external, viſible, true and proper Sacrifice, a literal, propitiation for the living and the dead*, (which the One and Thirtieth Article of Religion calls *a blaſphemous, dangerous Fable.*) *We* on the other ſide uſe the word in *a Figurative, Spiritual* manner, and conſider the *Sacrament* as the (*n*) *repreſentation* and *remembrance* of what was literally done ſo many years *before*; a *memorial* of that *Sacrifice* once made on the *Croſs*, but *daily* ſet before us in the miniſtration of the H. *Myſteries*; wherein, if we ſay *Chriſt* is *offered*, we do it on St. *Auguſtine's* Reaſon; (*o*) becauſe *if the Sacraments had not the likeneſs of what they repreſent, they could not be called Sacraments*; and from this *likeneſs* they uſually carry the names of the *things* themſelves; as when in Pictures we ſay *Cæſar* and *Cicero*, yet none miſtake us, or think we mean *either* of thoſe Perſons as *now* living or *preſent* in the place. But 'tis enough to excuſe the language, that there is a *reſemblance* of thoſe Perſons anciently ſo called, tho' *dead* above 1700 years ago. (*p*) So the *Sacrament* of Chriſts Body is by a form of Speech the *Body* of *Chriſt*, becauſe the *Print* or *Image* of his Body, but then being in ſtrictneſs the *Sign* only of his Body, if we offer it in the Sacrament, it is but to *emblem* forth his paſ-

---

(*n*) Chryſoſt. Serm. 17. *in* Heb. 10. *Vid.* Forbes *Iren.*l.2. &c.
(*o*) *Ea eſt Scripturarum conſuetudo ut ſimilitudines appellant nomine ipſarum rerum quas repræſentant.* Auguſtin *ad* Simplic. *Si enim Sacramenta*, &c. (*p*) Thus *Ælian* wrote over his Pictures. Τᵶ ὁ βᵶς, Ἐκεῖ ὁ ἱππ⊙, τᵶ τὸ δένδρον, l. 10. c. 10.

sion on Mount *Calvary*, when the *Jews* Crucified
and slew him. For there must needs be an *accommodation* in sense between the *Body* and the *Sacrifice*. And therefore if it be not his real *Body* and
Blood proposed in the Elements, the Action of the
Minister makes it no more than the *commemoration*
of the former Sacrifice. And if it bears the same
name, it must be, as in the case of *Pictures* and
Images, because it lively *represents* what was once
in being, and really true. (*q*) If the *Romanist*
could be reduced to this notion of Christs Body in
the Sacrament, we would never contend with him
about its being a *Sacrifice*. For we readily grant
him the *memory* of a Sacrifice in this *mysterious
Supper*, but we cannot grant that Christ made of
Bread becomes a *literal Sacrifice* as often as he
thinks fit to bring him on the Altar. But besides
this *commemorative Sacrifice* of Christs death, we
have *other* Sacrifices of *Prayers* and *Alms-deeds*;
we have our Sacrifice of *Praise* and *Thanksgiving*;
we are taught to present our *Bodies*, as a *Sacrifice*
pure, holy and acceptable to God, and to offer
up to him the burning *Oblations* of our hearts, and
the *Calves* of *our lips*. These, I say, are *Sacrifices*
of *our Church*; and the *Place* where these are
offer'd according to the way of Antiquity, and the
Language of *Fathers* and *Councils*, we call (†) *an
Altar*, and *He* who *offers* 'em and officiates at the
Altar we call a *Priest*; (*r*) *and all this while we
are farther off from Popery in this practice than
others from Puritanism, or any Puritan from true
Popery.*

(*q*) *Tollantur hi & similes his abusus*, &c. Casaub. *ad Card.*
Perron. Ep.   (†) *Quid est altare nisi sedes corporis & sanguinis Christi?* Optat. cont. Parm. l. 6. *Altare Ecclesiæ est
ubi quotidiè consecratur Corpus Dom.* Primas. ad Heb. c. 13.
(*r*) Mountague. *Apello Cæsarem.*

B. If this was the language of the *Ancients,* as you affirm, how comes it to be objected in the days of *Origen,* and *Minucius Felix,* that *Christians* had no (*s*) *Temples* nor *Altars,* there being no such *thing,* and probably no such *language* in those days, whichcaused the objection?

A. Those who talked thus were profest *Pagans,* and their design was to run down Christianity because of its *Poverty,* and the little Figure it made in the World, and thereupon demanded why we had no *Temples* or such *magnificent Structures* as were built by them, and dedicated to their false *Gods;* which, under persecution, as then, had been a ridiculous attempt in our *Fathers,* who either had not *Money* to raise such *Fabricks,* or not sufficient *Authority* to secure·their standing. However there were *places·* for the Divine Worship, tho' very short of that outward magnificence which was the matter of the Objection. They had such as suited their Condition; whether called *Temples, Churches* or *Oratories,* and when the times would bear it, they were not wanting in those instances of *Grandure,* and after-Ages taught the Adversary that there was little room for such an exception. (*t*) Or we may say, *That whereas by Temples the Heathens understood such Buildings whereunto their Gods by the power of Spells or Magical Consecrations were confined and limited, and for the presencing of whom a Statue was thought necessary; Places wherein they dwelt, shut up as Birds in a Cage, or as the Devil restrained within a Circle, that so they might be ready at hand when Men had occasion to address 'em. Christians indeed had no such dwellings for their God as these, for he dwells not in Temples made with hands: Yet they had their Wor-*

(*s*) *Cur non aras habent, nulla Templa?*
(*t*) Vid. Mr. *Mede* in his Treatise of Churches.

shipping-places, Houses of Prayer, and Churches, for such the Histories and Monuments of those Times expresly inform us they had; and the Gentiles themselves who objected this defect knew it too well, as may appear by their Emperors Rescripts for demolishing 'em, and sometimes for restoring 'em when the Persecutions were over. Then as for *Altars*, they had not indeed *any* either of *Wood* or *Stone* to slaughter and Sacrifice *Beasts* on, which made up a great part of the *Jewish* and *Pagan* Religion; yet still they had *their Altars* for the offering up of the *Christian Sacrifices, Altars* not polluted with real *blood*, but *such* as we *now* imploy to *remember* that great *Sacrifice* of the *Lamb* of God which was once effectually made *for the Sins of the whole world.* So that you may perceive in what sense the Objection of *Celsus* and *Cecilius* is to be taken; not to prove that *Christians* had no *Altars*, no more than to prove they had *no God*, because they refused to worship their *Idols*; and upon that reason we may observe, that at the same time as they denied 'em to have *Altars*, they also charged 'em with downright *Atheism.* (*u*) Yet it is very probable the *first Christians* were very sparing in the use of these words, [*Temple, Priest* and *Altar*,] while the notion and practice of the *Aaronical Sacrifices* were still fresh in their Memories, and they took great care to keep themselves at a distance from the *Jews* in all respects whatever; which is the reason, that almost to the times of *Irenæus* the term *Presbyter* was used instead of *Priest.* But the danger

---

(*u*) Dico primos . *Christianos propter recentem memoriam Sacerdotii Aaronici abstinuisse, non solum à vocabulo templi, sed etiam Sacerdotis, nè viderentur adhuc durare Judaicæ Ceremoniæ. Itaq; Apostoli in suis Epistolis pro Sacerdotibus, Episcopos & Presbyteros, pro Templo Ecclesias dicunt, Et similiter loquuntur Irenæus, Justinus, Ignatius, & cæteri antiquissimi patres——Bellarm. de cult. sanct.* c. 4. *Vid.* Durant. *de ritib. Eccl. Cath.* l. 1.

and

and fufpicion of complying with them being well
over, the *Fathers* refumed the old Names, as very
innocent and fignificant.

B. But do not our *Laws* reject *Altars*, both
thing and *name*, by repealing a Statute made in
Popifh times to protect the ufe of 'em?

    A. The Statute is that of Queen *Mary*,
1 *Mar.* wherein it is faid, 𝔍𝔣 𝔞𝔫𝔭 𝔰𝔥𝔞𝔩𝔩 𝔲𝔫𝔩𝔞𝔴=
𝔣𝔲𝔩𝔩𝔭, 𝔠𝔬𝔫𝔱𝔢𝔪𝔭𝔱𝔲𝔬𝔲𝔰𝔩𝔭 𝔬𝔯 𝔪𝔞𝔩𝔦𝔠𝔦𝔬𝔲𝔰𝔩𝔭
𝔬𝔣 𝔱𝔥𝔢𝔦𝔯 𝔬𝔴𝔫 𝔭𝔬𝔴𝔢𝔯 𝔬𝔯 𝔞𝔲𝔱𝔥𝔬𝔯𝔦𝔱𝔭 𝔭𝔲𝔩𝔩 𝔡𝔬𝔴𝔫,
𝔰𝔭𝔬𝔦𝔩 𝔬𝔯 𝔟𝔯𝔢𝔞𝔨 𝔞𝔫𝔭 𝔄𝔩𝔱𝔞𝔯 𝔬𝔯 𝔄𝔩𝔱𝔞𝔯𝔰, 𝔰𝔲𝔠𝔥
𝔓𝔢𝔯𝔰𝔬𝔫 𝔬𝔯 𝔓𝔢𝔯𝔰𝔬𝔫𝔰, &c. they were to be punifhed.——Queen *Mary* who made this Law, repealed another of *Edward* VI. for the Au-
1 *Eliz.* thorizing of the *Common-Prayer*; but
    Queen *Elizabeth,* who fucceeded, to re-
eftablifh that Law of King *Edward, repealed* fo
much of the *repeal* of Queen *Mary*'s as concern'd
the *Liturgy,* but left *that* part concerning *Altars,*
as before, (*w*) and fo it may be faid to continue in force to this day. However it appears,
the Law was not fo well underftood at *that* time,
but that according to the different fentiments of
the Perfons then in being, *fome Altars* were removed, and *others* kept their *ftanding.* So that the
    Queen was engaged to make an *Injunction.*
1559. 𝔗𝔥𝔞𝔱 𝔱𝔥𝔬' 𝔦𝔱 𝔰𝔢𝔢𝔪'𝔡 𝔱𝔬 𝔥𝔢𝔯 𝔞 𝔪𝔞𝔱=
𝔱𝔢𝔯 𝔬𝔣 𝔫𝔬 𝔤𝔯𝔢𝔞𝔱 𝔪𝔬𝔪𝔢𝔫𝔱 𝔴𝔥𝔦𝔠𝔥 𝔥𝔞𝔡
𝔱𝔥𝔢 𝔭𝔯𝔢𝔣𝔢𝔯𝔢𝔫𝔠𝔢, 𝔴𝔥𝔢𝔱𝔥𝔢𝔯 𝔗𝔞𝔟𝔩𝔢𝔰, 𝔬𝔯 𝔄𝔩𝔱𝔞𝔯𝔰,
𝔭𝔯𝔬𝔳𝔦𝔡𝔢𝔡 𝔱𝔥𝔢 𝔖𝔞𝔠𝔯𝔞𝔪𝔢𝔫𝔱 𝔴𝔞𝔰 𝔡𝔲𝔩𝔭 𝔞𝔫𝔡 𝔯𝔢=
𝔳𝔢𝔯𝔢𝔫𝔱𝔩𝔭 𝔄𝔡𝔪𝔦𝔫𝔦𝔰𝔱𝔯𝔢𝔡, 𝔭𝔢𝔱 𝔣𝔬𝔯 𝔘𝔫𝔦𝔣𝔬𝔯𝔪𝔦𝔱𝔭
𝔰𝔞𝔨𝔢, 𝔖𝔥𝔢 𝔴𝔬𝔲𝔩𝔡 𝔥𝔞𝔳𝔢 '𝔢𝔪 𝔞𝔩𝔩 𝔬𝔣 𝔬𝔫𝔢 𝔨𝔦𝔫𝔡.
And thereupon Commanded all the *Altars* to be
taken down, and *Tables* fet in their ftead; and

(*w*) *Altare Chriftianum*——Arch Bifhop *Laud*'s Speech in
the Star-Chamber, at the Cenfure of *Prynne, Baftwick* and
Burton, June 16, 1637. *Rufhworth.*

thefe

these the rather to be used, because better *suiting* the notion then of the *Sacrament,* which the *Papists* considered as a *real Sacrifice,* and consequently the *Place* whereon it was offered a *real Altar*; *neither* of which the *Reformers* allowing, it was thought adviseable to remove the *One,* that the sight of it might not countenance the *other Error.*

B. Well, for my part, I am not offended at the *word,* but believe it proper and conformable enough to Antiquity and the Gospel; and all the use I would make of the Objection, is only to perswade Men to *Charity* and *good temper,* and not make such a-do about innocent *terms;* when they all agree in the *sense* and *reason* of 'em.

A. I subscribe to that Design, and do wish all People so unaffected and moderate as not to catch at *words,* and *thence* force *inferences* to disturb our *Peace,* and prejudice the *Truth.* By this means among other things, the dispute of the *Sabbath* might have an end, except in such Cases where endeavours are used to introduce the *old Day* as well as the *old Name.* But when Men are fond to shew their parts in disputing us into *Popery,* because we sometimes call the *Minister Priest,* and the *Table an Altar,* it ought not to be ill taken, if we retort the Argument; and by putting them in mind of the *word Sabbath,* they are so much in love with (and which they so earnestly contend for) we discover to 'em what haste themselves are making towards *Judaism,* from the proof they manage against us, which is full as strong for *this* relapse, as it is for the *other;* my meaning is, it concludes against *neither.*

B. But there is *another* word commonly used, which I am more offended with, and that is *Sunday,* because it seems to lessen the veneration we ought to have for this *Christian Festival.* And

tho'

tho' there is no danger on this account of our re-
lapſing to *Gentiliſm,* (*x*) yet methinks-we honour *their* way too much in retaining the Language, and by fixing on our great *Holiday* the
Stile of that *Planet,* we may be thought to neglect the *Saviour of the World* to whoſe Service we
Conſecrate it, and whoſe *Name* certainly it ought
to bear, out of a grateful remembrance of the Redemption he wrought for us. And thus far I cannot but commend the Zeal of *Philaſtrius* who
charges this ill cuſtom with the odious name of
Hereſie, and looks on it a very great Error in
thoſe who uſed it.

A. The *Days* of the *Week* derive their *names*
from the *Heathen-Deities,* but in theſe Ages we
uſe 'em only for *diſtinction-ſake,* without any relation to their firſt Original. *Superſtition* indeed
began and *Cuſtom* continues 'em, but we deal
with *theſe* words as with *Money,* which uſe makes
proper and paſſible. (†) *And truly it looks peeviſh
and froward to refuſe a piece of Coin that is currant
thro' the World, becauſe it is not ſtamp'd after our
own fancy.* As it was the way of the *Gentiles* to
call every *day* of the *Week* by the *names* of *their
Gods,* ſo they likewiſe dealt with ſome of the
Months ; and if we keep *theſe* without any regard to *Janus* or *Mars,* why may not *Saturday* be
ſo called without thinking of *Saturn ;* and *Sunday*
without relation to the *Sun ?* Yet I could wiſh with
(*y*) St. *Auguſtine, that Men were more careful in*

(*x Pudendum eſt ſimulq; dolendum deos gentium inter Chri-
ſtianos & quidem Evangelicos tam memorabile monumentum habere.* Hoſpinian. *de feſtis Chriſt.* (†) Biſhop *Bramhal*
againſt *Hobbs,* about Liberty and Neceſſity. (*y*) *Nolumus
ut dicant, & utinam corrigantur ut non dicant—Melius de ore
Chriſtiano ritus loquendi Eccleſiaſticus procedit.* Aug. *in*
Pſalm.

their

*their forms of Speech ; and that they would be pre-
vailed on to express themselves more agreeably to the
way of the Church.* Yet seeing by *Custom,* they
speak otherwise, and that it is no more than a
Civil and *Popular* term used for a long time in most
parts of the World without any *Religion* or *Mystery* in it, I my self am ready to comply with
the general practice, and think them too severe,
who call it *Prophane, Heathenish and unlawful.*

B. My Charge against 'em goes not so far ;
yet I should be better pleas'd, if they always
called the *Day* by a more reverend and its proper name.

A. I read of the *Hebrews,* (*z*) That when they
meet with the word *Jehova,* they pass it over with
a silent respect, or depute some other name of
God, *viz. Adonai, Elohim,* or the like, to fill up
the Text, being of opinion that it is not fit for any
Person below (*) the *High-Priest,* and for *him*
seldom to pronounce *it,* because it is God's *more
peculiar and proper Name,* which no flight of *Rhetorick* can communicate to the Creature. I hope it
proceeds out of a principle of reverence, that
we do not make the *Lords-day* familiar in our
mouths at all times and upon all occasions. And
altho' we mostly give it its right name, whenever
we or the *Subject* be *serious,* yet at such times as
we are less thoughtful, or our minds imploy'd
about secular Matters, perhaps a more ordinary
stile may appear suitable, especially in Discourse,
where there may be reason to mention the *Day,*
without any regard to the *Solemnity* or *Worship of it.*

(*z*) *Quoniam divina essentia secundum proprium ejus esse,
mente nullatenus excogitari potest, &c.* Vid. Pet. Galat. *de
Arcanis Cath.* Verit. l. 2. c. 7. &. 10. (*) *Solis summis
pontificib. quotannis permissa erat ejus pronuntiatio in diebus je-
juniorum & propitiationis.* Reuchlin. de Arte Cabbalist. l. 3.

B. I doubt the *reaſon* of this habit is quite contrary, and the ill Cuſtom is kept up for want of Religion in People, whoſe behaviour and language too much agree, and who make as bold with the *Day* it ſelf as they do with the *name* of it.

A. Pray God their hearts be *right*, who conſtantly uſe more ſanctified Phraſes. However the word *Sunday* has not that ground, but began and is retained upon better Reaſons than what you mention.

B. I ſhall be glad to hear you ſpeak on that Subject.

A. I ſay then it is not to be denied but we borrow the name of this Day from the ancient *Greeks* and *Romans,* and we allow that the old *Egyptians* worſhipped the *Sun,* and as a ſtanding *memorial* of their veneration, dedicated *this Day* to him. And we find, by the influence of their Examples, *other* Nations, and among them the *Jews* themſelves, doing him Homage [2 *King.* 23. 5. *Jerem.* 43. 13.] yet theſe abuſes did not hinder the *Fathers* of the Chriſtian Church ſimply to repeal or altogether lay by the *Day* or its *name,* but only to ſanctifie and improve *both,* as they did alſo the Pagan *Temples* polluted before with idolatrous Services and other inſtances wherein thoſe good Men were always tender to work any other change than what was evidently neceſſary, and in ſuch things as were plainly inconſiſtent with the Chriſtian Religion; ſo that *Sunday* being the day on which the *Gentiles* ſolemnly adored *that Planet,* and called it *Sunday,* partly from *its* influence on *that day* eſpecially, and partly in reſpect to its Divine Body (as they conceived it) the Chriſtians thought fit to keep the *ſame day* and the *ſame name* of it, that they might not appear cauſeleſly peeviſh, and by that means hinder the converſion

of

of the *Gentiles*, and bring a greater prejudice than
might be otherwiſe taken againſt the *Goſpel.* They
kept therefore the ſame day, and ſpent it in Religious Worſhip, tho', with very great difference
both in the *manner* of Worſhip, and the *Objects*
of it, the *one* party ſerving the *Creator*, the *other*
the *Creature.* And this they might ſafely do
without any regard to the *Sun*, becauſe it was the
Day on which the *Lord Chriſt* aroſe from the
Dead; a *Miracle* of that virtue and of ſo great
concern for the welfare of Chriſtians, that it was
very ſeemly to ſet apart ſome particular time for
the commemoration of it; and certainly no better time than the *day it ſelf* on which the thing
was done, tho' falling in with *that* which the *Infidels* ſpent in their Superſtition. And then as for
the name which they promiſcuouſly uſed and by
common conſent called it *Sunday.* This did not
in the leaſt derogate from the honour of our Feſtival, becauſe the *Gentiles* obſerved and called it
ſo as well as *we.* For altho' with them the *reaſon*
of the name was (1) becauſe on *that* day they
adored the *Sun* for his more beneficial aſpect at
that time; yet this motive made no impreſſion on
the Chriſtian, who indeed adored the *Sun*, but it
was *that Sun,* ſaith St. *Auguſtine,* which the Scripture
calls the *Sun of Righteouſneſs, who aroſe with healing
in his wings* [Malachi 4. 2.] and on this account
it is called *Sunday,* (2) becauſe on *this* day *Chriſt
was raiſed from death to life to inlighten the Chil-*

---

(1) *Secundum gentes dies Dom. primus eſt, cum principio
illius diei incipiat dominari principalis Planeta Sol, propter quod
vocabant eum diem ſolis.* Bonaventura. (2) φωῖὸς ϰ᷉ ζω᷉ης
ἐπώνυμον——Euſeb. de laud. Conſtant. c. 9. *Dominica dicitur
quia in ea Dominus victor aſcendit ad patrem. Quod ſi à gentilibus dies ſolis vocatur, & hoc nos libentiſſime confitemur. Hoc
enim die lux mundi ortá eſt.*——Hieron. in Pſalm. Vid. Maxim.
Turon. *Homil. de* Pen.

dren

dren of this world, and by his *Triumphant Reſurre-*
ction cauſe the heavenly light of truth and grace to
appear in full luſtre to them, who before ſate in darkneſs and the ſhadow of death. And hence it is that
this word is ſo often found in the *ancient* Writings,
to ſignifie *this* great Holiday which we *now* Celebrate, and was always kept from the beginning
of *Chriſtianity* in honour of our *Redeemer* the *Sun*
of the Prophet *Malachy*, and not the *ordinary Star*
which the *Heathens* worſhipped, and from whom
we ſeem to derive the name, but is much improved beyond the reach of their Religion.

B. This is but Metaphor and Alluſion.

A. True, yet an alluſion ſo neceſſary, that the
Prophets and other Holy Men of God conſidering
the Majeſty of Chriſts Perſon, and the excellency
of his Kingdom, they had no ſimilitude or compariſon to expreſs themſelves by but the glory of *this*
Creature, which *Plato* calls the *viſible Sun of God*,
and we the *Image of the inviſible one.*

B. However this is only *Figurative.* But in our
enumeration of the days of the Week, and the
names they go by, we are underſtood to adhere
to the *letter*, and the *firſt* day of the Week being
called *Sunday*, we may be reaſonably ſuppoſed to
referr   name of *this day*,
as well as to the *Moon* and the reſt of the *Planets*
in the other *ſix*, which in their order follow it.

A. In the ordinary account of time, as I ſaid,
we take this method, and uſe the old names as of
the *Months*, ſo of the *Days*, without much ſcruple.
And being we are contented to make the *Aſtrono-*
mers our Maſters in the diviſion of time, we are
not over-nice in accepting the terms of this diviſion, and thoſe words *they* lend us to diſtinguiſh
one time from another. However this is done
without the leaſt remain of the old ſuperſtition;
and as for the *particular day*, which by the conſent

fent of all Parties was and is now *holy*, tho' we keep the name it before went by, that we might not fhew our felves a captious quarrelfome People, yet you fee we have refined the word into a nobler fenfe than what it originally had. And fince by the allowance (we may fay the Authority) of the Bleffed Spirit, the *Object* of our Worfhip has the *fame denomination* with that of the *Gentiles*, why we fhould not have the *fame name* likewife for *the day* we do him fervice in, I fee no reafon, at leaft none ftrong enough to make us explode it.

B. This improvement of the word, I muft confefs, doth not a little foften it, otherwife (if not fanctified) the found might be harfh to pious ears, as it often is to many who confider not this reafon, and who, out of a godly jealoufie, are fearful to admit any thing that feems to reflect on our Chriftian profeffion.

A. It is the caution of Scripture that we be not *over-wife*, becaufe all extreams are bad. A Man may be too Religious, and that *excefs*, not to give it a worfe name, is called *precifenefs*, which inftead of making a *Saint*, often ends in *hypocrifie.* But put the cafe we had not this refuge, nor that we were able by the *Spiritual fignification* of the word [*Sunday*] to juftifie this language among us, and had no mind to be beholding to the (3) *Saxon* or (4) *Danifh Etymologifts* to render it excufable, yet the Cuftom might be fupported by the *natural reafon* of it; and fince the *Aftronomers* affure us, that the *Sun begins* this day with a more peculiar influence, what *more proper name* can there be to diftinguifh it by than *that* of the *Planet* which prefides and governs it?

---

(3) *Sonen* to judge, *qu.* the day of the Judge——
(4) *Sone pacare, qu. dies pacationis*—Pontanus——wherein we appeafe God.——

B. I thought all the *Planets* claim'd an interest in *every day* of the Week; and that the *Moon*, *Mars*, *Mercury* and *the rest* had, in their capacity, a *common* influence on things below.

A. It is so said by those who are most exact in this Study, but then they have their several turns and hours, which is the reason why *Astrologers* are so curious, when Questions are put 'em, to know the *precise time* of the Birth, *&c.* that so they may be the better able to satisfie their inquisitive Clients, by finding what *Planet* had the dominion of that *hour* relating to the *Question*.

B. How then doth your Reason hold concerning *Sunday*?

A. Tho' the *Seven Planets* govern *every day*, yet it is *successively* and in their courses, and their *efficacy* is appropriate chiefly to their *peculiar hours*; and in this constant revolution of hours, the *Planet* which happens to *begin* the day, whatever it be, is said to *preside* and *intitle* himself to that day, as it falls out in many other Examples, for the more excellent *part* to denominate the *whole*, (5) so that the *Sun* being the *Lord* of the *first hour* of *this day*, the *Moon* Mistress of the first hour of the *next*, and so on ; this occasion'd the *Astronomers* to distinguish the parts of the Week in that manner, and the Method continues to the present Age: And this agrees with the Doctrine of the Jewish *Rabbins*, as appears by *Rabbi Gedaliah Ben Jechei* — (*) *The Planet, saith he, which begins to Rule the first hour, whether day or night, he claims that whole day and night as the supreme*

---

(5) *Philosophi quod Sol Regnabat prima hora diei Dom. ideo illum diem denominarunt à sole. Et quod Luna regnabat prima hora secundæ feriæ ideo diem illum denominarunt à Luna, & sic de cæteris.*—Durand Rational.

(*) *In Sepher Shalsheleth*——

Lord

Lord of it, yet the other *Planets* which *in their order have charge of the following hours, are as it were the Ministers and Assistants of that Superiour Planet, and with him rule the day, tho' being Lord of the first hour he takes place, and the day is called by his Name.* ·So that tho' the *rest* have an interest in each *day* or *night,* yet they act in a *subordinate way,* and as so many *Ministers* to him——As for instance in *Saturday, Saturn* is *Lord* of *this Day,* and possesses the whole Day. But tho' as *Lord* he influences and governs the *first* hour, yet he leaves the *second* to *Jupiter.* And we say tho' *Saturn* be Lord of the *second* hour as well as the *first* hour, yet *Jupiter* is his *assistant,* whose Ministry he uses in it.

B. And is it certain that this revolution of hours gives every *Planet* its particular day by those names and in that *order* we have 'em?

A. So it is affirmed, especially if we follow *Ptolemy*'s System, where the Planets are set in this *Order. Saturn, Jupiter, Mars, Sun, Venus, Mercury, Moon.* And therefore according to this Scheme, we will begin with *Saturn,* and the rather, not only because the *Ancients* had a great veneration for him in remembrance of the *golden Age* when he is said to Reign, but because he is the reputed *God of Time,* and on that account *Time* ought to *begin* with *him.* The *first* hour then of the day (called by his Name) is allotted to him, the 2*d* to *Jupiter,* the 3*d* to *Mars,* the 4*th* to the *Sun,* the 5*th* to *Venus,* the 6*th* to *Mercury,* the 7*th* to the *Moon,* the 8*th* to *Saturn* again, and so forwards as before to the 24*th* hour, which concludes the natural day, and is assign'd to *Mars.* Thence begins the *first* hour of the *next* day, and the *Planet* next in order to *Mars* being the *Sun,* he is said to· govern *that* hour, and is president of the *following day,* which therefore goes by his Name.

Name. This method if we take in all the reft, we fhall find every 25*th* hour, or the 1*st* hour of every *natural day* to have a *new Planet* to rule and name it, in that manner as we commonly take it——'Tis true, this dominion of the Planets to intitle to themfelves the days of the Week doth not pleafe either (6) *Scaliger* or *Selden* for this reafon, becaufe this naming of the *days* is of longer ftanding than the divifion of the *day* by *hours,* and therefore 'tis thought more likely that thefe names were not given the days of the Week on the account of the *Planetary hours,* or becaufe *fuch* or *fuch hours are* influenced by *this* or *that Planet,* but on the contrary, this Superftition is derived rather from the *days,* which being called after the *names* of the *Planets,* they afterwards fixed thefe *names* on the *hours* likewife. And Mr. *Selden* conceives that thefe names of the days, and the order they are in, proceeded from the dignity and preeminence which the *Sun* and *Moon* have among the Stars. For the *Indians* and *Perfians* call the *firft* the *King,* and the *other* the *Queen* ; and the *Egyptians* compared the *Sun* to the *right Eye,* and the *Moon* to the *left,* and the other 5 *Planets* were confidered as the ῥαβδοφόροι or *Officers* to thofe who were deem'd the *Sovereigns* of Heaven, as indeed *Ptolemy* himfelf calls 'em ; for, faith he, ὁ μὲν ἥλιΘ῾ κỳ ἡ σελήνη διατάκτικοι ὥσπερ ἡγέμονες εἰσὶ τῶν ἄλλων—the *Sun* and *Moon* are as it were the *Governours* and *Princes* of the reft. And hereupon probably *Anaximander, Metrodorus* and *Crates* placed the *Sun* in the *firft Orb,* and next to him the *Moon,* and fo from their fuperiority and excellency they are made to lead the Van in giving names to the days of the Week----and the Style

---

(6) Scaliger. *Prolog. ad Emendat. Temp.*

of ἑβδομηγέτης is ſuppoſed to be given to *Apollo*, becauſe he is *hebdomadæ dux*, the *preſident of the Week*, which Mr. *Selden* thinks to be the meaning of the word in *Æſchylus* and *Proclus*, thoſe Authors having an eye not to his *Birth*, but the *dominion* and the *prerogative* he has in the *ſeptenary* account of time. I diſpute not this matter with him, but ſhall only obſerve that himſelf owns the notion we propoſe to be the Tenet of *Vettius Valens* an ancient Aſtronomer of *Antioch*, and from *Dio* reports it as the opinion of former Ages, and withal confeſſes that it is much approved by thoſe Learned Moderns who treat of theſe Affairs ; ſuch as *Nicolaus Cardinalis Cuſanus, Johannes Garcæus, Franciſcus Maurolycus, Johannes Lucidus, Chriſtoph. Clavius, Johannes Kepler*, and others, which I take to be Authority enough to excuſe, if not juſtifie, a thing of this kind. *Selden de jure Nat.* l. 3. c. 31. Then as to *Scaliger*, tho' we are not ſo credulous as to believe with ſome People that the names of the *Week* bear date with the *Creation*, yet plainly the Cuſtom is very ancient, as appears from St. *Auguſtine*, who on the title of *Pſalm* 93, delivers himſelf thus----*Pſalmus ipſi David. in quarta Sabbati*---this fourth of the Sabbath, ſaith he, *is the fourth day of the Week, which by the Pagans and many Chriſtians is called Mercurii dies*----St. *Jerom* teſtifies the ſame thing, Every Week is called a *Sabbath*, and is diſtinguiſh'd into the 1, 2, 3, 4, &c. *of the Sabbath*, which the *Heathens* call after the names of their *Idols*. But before them *Clement* of *Alexandria* ſpeaking of *Wedneſday* and *Friday*, ſaith, ἡ μὲν Ἑρμῆ, ἡ δὲ Ἀφροδίτης ἐπωνυμίζονται, the *one* is the day of *Mercury*, the *other* of *Venus, Stro.* l. 7. And both *Tertullian* and *Juſtin Martyr* in their reſpective Apologies expreſly name *Saturday*, and *Sunday*. It is reported of *Apollonius Tyaneus* that *Jarcha* preſented
him

him with ſeven Rings after the names of the *ſe-*
ven Planets, which he wore one after another ac-
cotding to the *names* of the *days.* But before his
time *Oracles* ceaſed ; yet in añ old one of *Apollo*
we read theſe Verſes.

Euſeb.de Præp.
Evang. l. 5.

Κλνίζειν Ἑρμὴν ἠδ᾽ Ἥλιον κα᾿α ταῦ᾽α
Ἡμέρη Ἡελίῳ, Μήνην τό᾿ε τῆς δε παρείη
Ἡμέρη, ἠδὲ Κρόνον ἠδ᾽ ἑξείης Ἀφροδίτην—

Invocate Mercury and the Sun on Sunday, and the
Moon when her day comes, and after the ſame
manner Saturn and Venus.   But they ſtill go higher,
this invention being fathered on the Schools of
Zoroaſtres and *Hyſtaſpes* among the *Chaldeans* and
*Egyptians---*Οἱ μεν πρὶ Ζωροάσρην κ᾿ Ὑσάσπην χαλδαῖοι
κ᾿ Ἀγύπ᾿ιοι ἀπ᾽ ἀριθμῦ τῶν πλανη᾿ῶν ἐν ἑβδομάδι τὰς ἡμέρας
ἀπέλαβον—*vid.* Rivet. *de Orig. Sab.*   From all which
it appears, ſaith *Scaliger,* that the calling of the
days by the names of the *Planets* is very ancient a-
mong the *Greeks,* and this Evidence confutes thoſe
who ſay that the uſage (concerning *Sunday,*
Monday, &c.) hath no footſteps in the Writings
of *Old Authors.*   But then it muſt be remembred
that theſe Names were taken up by the *Aſtrono-*
mers and their Diſciples, and not admitted by
either the *Civil* or *Religious* Government of the
Greeks or *Romans.*   And ſuppoſe that *Zoroaſtres*
or his Scholars either began or advanced this
Cuſtom, yet if it be true that *Jupiter* and the reſt
of ’em were not accounted or worſhipped as Gods
’till the reigns of *Cecrops* or *Theſeus,* as *Pauſanias*
and *Athanaſius* aſſert, then Religion at firſt had
nothing to do with theſe Names which *Aſtrono-*
mers invented to diſtinguiſh the *Stars* and their
Influences ; and then why might not the *hours* be
introduced in the ſame way, and have the ſame
reaſon to be intituled to theſe Names? When in-
                                                    deed

deed this division of *hours* began, may be, for
ought I know, as hard to determine, as it is to resolve how and when the days came to be called
by the Planets. 'Tis plain *Homer* and, *Hesiod*
speak of 'em; the Scripture tells us of the *Dial of
Ahaz*, and *Anaximenes* was a famous *Dialist* at
Lacedæmon; and by this means was discovered
every day the ascent and declension of the Sun,
and the shadow the *Gnomon* cast on the Plate or
Stone, let 'em see how many degrees he past,
and thence they found a way to judge of time by
hours. The first mention of an *hour* in Scripture
by that term is in the Prophet, *Daniel* 3. 6. but
whether it is meant in the vulgar acceptation for
the 24*th part* of the natural day is a little uncertain, seeing the word is used more largely for a
Season, and *day* as well as an *hour* strictly so called;
and we cannot but own that the *Greeks* and *Romans* heretofore contracted the number, or say
rather had not subdivided their *hours* into so many
as we use this day. Yet without contradiction,
before Christs time this Custom was well known,
as we find *Jo.* xi. 9. *are there not twelve hours in the
day?* by which he means the *Civil day*, when the
Sun by his presence giveth light to the World.
So that this *division by hours* has its gray hairs as
well as the days of the Week; and seeing both are
owing to the *Astronomers*, it is not absurd to think,
but that the date may be near the same for the
names of the days and hours; and we may suppose the *Planets* may influence both alike, and
with equal exactness. I do not mean that we are
not subject to the power of the *Heavenly Bodies*,
daily experience abundantly confirms it, but it
may be *every Planet* has its particular presidentship
as truly over every *hour* of the day and night, as
over the *day* and *night* themselves in the progress
of the Week, if we limit 'em precisely to their

Order

Order and Courſes. However, be this Doctrine true or falſe, we may uſe the *Hypotheſis* as a piece of Art, and ſince we diſcover whence we have and how we are to underſtand it, what need is there to be offended if it be a miſtake, ſeeing we lay no more ſtreſs upon't, than on other *artificial* inſtances we embrace to make the things we are imploy'd about, the more intelligible and eaſie.

B. The account you have given concerning the antiquity of the names on the days of the Week (which I conſent to) contradicts what ſome affirm, That namely we owe it to the *Egyptian Ptolemy* who liv'd near a *Century* and half after *Chriſt's Nativity*, and yet others date it lower, and bring it down to the times of *Dionyſius Exiguus* or thereabouts, which I wonder at in a Caſe ſo plain as this is, and where the Evidence is ſo ſtrong againſt 'em.

A. I find you miſtook me, the *names* of the *days*, and the reducing the *days* to that *form* and *number* as conſtitute a *Week*, are different things. For ſhou'd it be true that the names were full as old as *Zoroaſtres*, yet it follows not but the *Week* may have its *birth* after *Ptolemy* or *Dionyſius*; and you may remember I ſaid before, that the uſage was *Aſtrological* and not *Civil*, known and conni-ved at, but never inſtituted by the *Greeks* or *Romans* while they continued *Pagan*, as Mr. *Selden* himſelf owns, and declares that the dividing of time by Weeks doth not appear to be receiv'd till their Converſion to Chriſtianity, *de Jure Nat.* l. 3. c. 19. And this interprets *Joſephus*, who confidently gave out τὸ ἔθΘ. τῆς ἑβδυάδΘ., that *this Septenary Account was Celebrated throughout the whole World*——True, but with this limitation———παρὰ τοῖς δοκιμοτάϊοις Ἑλλήνων κ᾿ Βαρβάρων οἱ τὴν μαθημα-τικὴν ἐπισήμην διαπονῦσιν—*it was among ſuch both Greeks and Barbarians who were well ſkilled in the Mathe-maticks,*

maticks, faith *Philo de Mundo.* We read indeed,
that at the long run this Science fo far prevailed,
and the *Aftrologers* gain'd fo much credit among
the Vulgar, as to be reputed the *Priefts* and *Se-
cretaries of the Gods*; yet this was only by way of
Science, not by *publick Appointment* : However it
became matter of complaint to *Sextus Empiricus*,
that *they brought great mifchief to the World*, and
advanced Superftition among the Credulous, Adv.
Mathem. l. 5. And an inftance we have of this
Opinion currant then among fome of the *Gentiles*,
who believed they had their *Soul* from the *Sun*,
their *Body* from the *Moon*, the *Blood* from *Mars*,
Wit from *Mercury*, good *Temper* from *Jupiter*, from
Venus Pleafantnefs, *Dulnefs* from *Saturn* : A
Notion which incouraged *Friar Bacon* to fay, That
Chriftians erred much in not refting on *Saturday*
after the manner of the *Jews*, becaufe *it was a
Day leaft of all proper for the difpatch of Bufinefs.*
But ftill no *Chuich* or *State* fetled this *Account* till
the period before mention'd. For as to *Cæfar's
Kalendar*, the terms of Art therein ufed are too
barbarous for the Age of *Julius* or *Auguftus*, as
Petavius argues——*I make no doubt of it*, faith he,
*but the Kalendar going by Cæfar's Name is very fhort
of the date pretended*; *for it appears modern with
refpect to them*, and was made by fome *Chriftian* ——
de doctr. temp. l. 6. and *Scaliger* faith the fame---
de Emend. temp. l. 4. So that tho' the *Greeks* and
Romans were well acquainted with the *Planets* and
their *motions*, yet they might not divide their
Kalendar into *Weeks* (which is what is afferted) as
now they do, 'till about the times of *Dionyfius
Exiguus*, nor in all probability had they then receiv'd it, but that then *Chriftianity* was admitted
throughout the *Empire*, and therewith the knowledge of the Holy Scripture, where the *account
by Weeks* was exceeding obvious. And 'till then

D   they

they reckon'd the Month by *Kalends*, *Nones* and
Ides, and the other Days reducible to these
Names.

, *B.* I know this was their more familiar Custom;
yet it appears from *Cicero* that the *Latins* sometimes used another way. For in one of his Letters
to *Tiro* his Freeman, we have the (6) 4th *Week*
exprefly, and this near 200 years before *Ptolemy*
was Born, who was yet much older than *Dionysius.*

A. The word *hebdomas* or *hebdomada* tranflated
Week, in ftrict propriety fignifies no more than
the *seventh* or *seventh day*; tho' by custom of
Speech now, we deal with the term, as the *Jews*
heretofore by their *Sabbatum*, which was in reality
the *Name* of their *principal Day* only, but to give
it honour, they made it include the *whole Week*,
and all the *seven Days* were called the *Sabbath.*
And in this sense, as a word meaning such a
number, we take the expreffion of that Orator,
who by his *quarta hebdomada*, which you English
the *fourth Week*, intends nothing else befides the
fourth seventh Day; and that is the periphrafis of
the 28*th*, which he cautions *Tiro* to be fure to
remember. The truth is, if we confider well the
Letter, we shall find the word directed to the
Condition that Man was in. That he had been
very ill for a great while, is evident from the
next (7) Epiftle; and therefore his Mafter wifhes
him to confider his Cafe, and beware of the *seventh Day*, which the *Phyficians* call κρίσιμον ἡμέραν,
a *Critical Day*, when *Nature* and the *Difeafe* being
in their greateft conteft, they can better judge
how it will go with the Patient, by obferving

_____

(6) *Ne in quartam hebdomadam incideres*—Ep. 9. lib. 16—
(7) *Graviffime ægrotafti*—Ep. 10.

which

which of the two at that time gets the upper hand. The 14*th*, the 21*ft* and the 28*th* were noted after the fame manner, and this laft being favourable to the fick Party, 'tis thereupon hoped that the danger is over. So that *Tully's* Advice was this, That *Tiro* fhould have a care how he did eat, drink, or do any thing which might add ftrength to his diftemper, and expofe himfelf to a new conflict with it on the 28*th Day*, wherein, if *Nature* had the Victory, he might do well, if not, it would retard if not altogether hinder his recovery. Whereby you fee, the Orator had no regard to any *Weekly* fupputation of time, but only the *Critical Days* among the (8) *Phyficians* which they divided into *Sevenths*, to be better able to provide for the Cure. And to inforce the likelihood of this his meaning, we find he never ufes the word elfewhere, as I know of, in all his Works. And in this very Epiftle giving us an *Ephemeris* or *Diary* of his Voyage, he doth it in the *old Roman Stile* by the *Kalends* and *Ides* without our notion of *Weeks*, or fo much as mentioning one *Planetary Name* in it.

B. 'Tis not improbable but this *hebdomada quarta* may be fuch as you have explained it. However methinks, the *natural Reafon* for the Names of the *Planets* to be given the Days of the *Week* (which you have taken notice of) I mean their *influences*, and the impreffions they make on the inferiour Creatures, fhould prove this way of Calculation to be exceeding *ancient*. And as foon as the *Aftrolo-*

---

(8) *Galenus docet febres ardentiffimas primo die folvi. Si non primo, fecundo, i. e. decimo quarto. Si non fecundo, tertio. i. e. vigefimo primo, ut omnes labores & moleftiæ feptenario numero conquiefcant—*Hieronym. —*Vid.* Aul. Gell. Noct. Att. l. 3. c. 10. Et Pezelium *in* Melancthon. *de efficacia Stellarum.*

gers, whether *Egyptian, Chaldean* or others, discovered the power and efficacy of these *Heavenly Bodies,* they might be well thought to appropriate to
each *Planet* its particular *Day.* And because all
time depends on the revolution of these Heavenly
Bodies, they might divide it into so many *periods,*
and use the Number *seven* to form the *Weeks* as
we now have 'em. *Quia ordo Planetarum ultra
numerum Septenarium non procedit, sed ad primum
revertitur, ideò tantum septem dies in septimana
sunt à sapientibus constituti* —— Durand. Ratio.

A. Some indeed, have been persuaded, that
the days of the Week had these Names of the
Planets (9) by God's own appointment ever since
the beginning of the World. An Error defended
by the Authority of *Hermes,* a Man of great Reputation among the old *Egyptians.* But that reflection of (10) St. *Augustine* is a sufficient confu-
tation of any such Doctrine. That namely, tho'
the *Stars* themselves had certainly a Being from
the very Creation, yet the *Persons* whose Names
they bear, were not known, nor indeed born
'till many Ages after. Such as *Saturn, Jupiter,
Mars, Mercury,* &c. (11) who being *Princes* or
otherwise *Great Men,* who had deserved well of
the World, they were thro' the *flattery* of some,
and *credulity* of others advanced to Heaven, and
said to be turn'd into *this* or *that Star,* existent
long before, but unobserv'd by the *Vulgar,* who
were taught to believe and receive them as their

(9) *Nomina dierum Solis, Lunæ, Martis,* &c.—*à Deo ita
posita ab origine mundi, non hominum vana præsumptione nuncupata,
ut refert* Philallrius.   (10) Aug. *in Ps.* 93——
(11) *Perseus, Zenonis auditor eos dicit habitos deos à quibus
magna utilitas ad vita cultum esset inventa,* Cic. l. 1. *de nat.
Deorum.* vid. Lactant. *de falsa Relig.* N. 10, 11.—vid. pag. 34.
63. 76. 80. 84. Edit. Spark.

admired *Heroes.* However all this was Modern
in comparison of the time supported by that opinion; and tho' each of these *Stars* so named, had
its Proselytes, and in all likelihood special Days
assign'd and consecrated to 'em; yet as for the
reducing them to that *Order* they are at present
in, and bringing them all within the compass of a
Week, it doth not appear by any credible Author
that this was done 'till *Ptolemy* went about it;
and the Account was so slowly carried on, and
admitted with so much indifferency, that St. *Augustine* affirms of his Age (12) two hundred years
after *Ptolemy,* that many Nations, retained other
measures, and had *different. Names* to distinguish
their *Days* by.

B. This is made good in our own Case. For
what relation have our *Tuesday, Wednesday, Thursday* and *Friday* to the *Planets,* or to *Mars, Mercury, Jupiter* and *Venus,* from whom in Latin
they take their Names?

A. We have these Names from our (13) *Ancestors* the *Saxons,* who in memory of their Founders *Woden* and *Thor* his Son, allotted them these
two Days *Wednesday* and *Thursday,* and did 'em
divine honours.

B. It may be so, yet your last words seem to
contradict the words of (14) *Cæsar,* who affirms
that *Germany* (of which *Saxony* is a considerable

---

(12) *Multæ gentes aliæ atque aliæ aliter vocant.* loc. cit.
(13) *Rex* [Vortigernus] *ab in* [Horso & Hengisto] *quæsivit,
quam fidem, quam religionem patres eorum coluissent. Cui Hen-*
giftus: *Deos Patrios,* viz. Saturnum, Jovem *atque cæteros, qui
mundum gubernant, colimus;* maximè *autem* Mercurium *quem
lingua nostra* Woden *appellamus. Huic patres nostri veteres dedicaverunt quartam feriam Septimanæ quæ in hunc hodiernum
diem* Wodens-day *appellatur.* - (14) *Deorum numero eos
folos ducunt quos vident,* Solem, Vulcanum & Lunam; *reliquos
ne fama quidem acceperunt—*De Bello Gall. *l, 6.*

Branch) acknowledged no other Gods besides those whose influence was serviceable to 'em, as *Sun*, *Moon*, and *Fire*; but for *other gods*, they had not so much as the *Names* of 'em.

A. Cæsar, as I take it, meant that the *Germans* then had no more gods *in common* with the *Romans* besides the *Sun*——tho' they might abound with others peculiar to their own Country. Yet it appears afterwards in the days of (15) *Tacitus* that *Mars* and *Mercury* were added; not I think to increase their number, but to signifie their conformity to the Victorious *Romans*, whose way of Worship they followed in a great measure, and by an obsequious analogy ascribed the virtues and operations of the *Latin Deities* to their own, and frequently called 'em as we do now. So that 'tis no great surprize if we sometimes find 'em Saluting *Woden* with the Name of *Mercury*, and *Thor* with *Jupiter*'s, and the like, as *Paulus Diaconus* and *Pontanus* tell us. As for *Friday* they deduce it from *Friga* the Wife of *Woden*, which comes from a *Saxon* Word made to signifie *Love*, that so there might be the better resemblance between her and *Venus* the Goddess of Love with the *Romans*, to whose Patronage the *fifth* Day of the *Week* was assigned under both these Names. The reason of *Tuesday* is much more uncertain. For some take it from *Tuisco* the Son (the Grandson say others) of *Noah*, supposed to be the Head and Leader of a distinct Colony after the confusion of Tongues at *Babel*; who taking his way *North-West*, Peopled all that tract of Land called afterwards by the *Romans Germany*, from the word *Germanus*; meaning that the People of this

---

(15) *Deorum maximè Mercurium colunt, cui certis diebus humanis quoque hostiis litare fas habent Herculem, & Martem concessis animalibus placant.* Tacitus de morib. Germ.

Country were in Manners and Cuſtoms Brethren to the *Gauls.*

B. The Story of this *Tuiſco,* is, in the opinion of many, very Fabulous; and I think *Aventinus* has reaſon enough to call him a *Gyant,* becauſe the account given of him exceeds belief, and appears *monſtrous* in divers reſpects.

A. That there was ſuch a Man, Named *Tuiſco,* or ſomething in ſound like it, whom the *Germans* had in ſpecial veneration and adored as a God, *Cæſar* and (16) *Tacitus* both witneſs, and we cannot deny it. But that he was ſo nearly related to *Noah,* and that he came into *Germany* one hundred thirty one Years after the Flood, when the confuſion of Languages (if St. *Jerom, Toſtatus, Lyranus* and the *Hebrews* may be credited) did not fall out 'till 200 Years after: And moreover that in 25 *Years* he ſhould not only People that vaſt *Country,* but withal ſettle divers *Kingdoms* and *Principalities,* is ſo impoſſible, that we cannot aſſent to any Hiſtorian who reports theſe particularities. However, ſince we find by good Authority that there was a *Tuiſto* or *Tuiſco* who was Worſhipped by the *Germans* as the Father of that vaſt Country, a Famous *Warriour,* (and thereupon probably called a *Gyant* from his great Strength and Spirit, bearing in this reſpect the Image of *Mars* the reputed God of Battles among the *Latins,*) they might think fit to dedicate a Day to him, the very ſame ſet apart for *Mars* whom they likened him to; and ſo in their Language,

---

(16) *Opinantur viri docti à* Tuiſtonis *ſeu* Teutatis (*quorum alterum habetur apud Lucanum pro deo Barbarorum qui ſeptentrionales regiones incoluere,* Pharſal. 1. *Alterum apud* Tacitum *pro* Gentis German. *conditore, de* morib. Germ.) *Nomine diei prænomen in linguas illas cognatas pariter defluxiſſe.* Selden de Jure Nat. l. 3. c. 22—

D 4   by

by the help of a *Syncope*, ſtiled it *Tueſday*, a Name we ſtill retain in compliance with 'em; yet this account diſpleaſes others, who rather referr the Day to *Teutates*, one very much celebrated among the *Gauls* and *Britains* before the *Saxons* invaded this Nation, as the *Inventer of Letters*, and was looked upon to be the *Patron* of *Buſineſs* and *Journeys*.

B. This deſcription of him better ſuits *Mercury*, and little intitles him to *Tueſday* or *Mars's-*Day, who has in Writers another complexion and character.

A. True; and accordingly *Livy* makes it the Sirname of *Mercury*, and calls him *Mercurius Teutates.* And being by Office the *Meſſenger* and *Interpreter of the Gods*, from the excellent Skill he had in Arts and Languages; therefore from him comes *Tuiſten* to *Interperet*, and *Tuiſto* an *Interpreter*, a word they afterwards uſed to call him by, inſtead of *Tuet*, and *Teutates*; and gave him *Tueſday*, that he might be remembred with Honour.

B. But then, as I was ſaying, this has no reſemblance to *Mars*, who is *Preſident* of *Tueſday.*

A. I confeſs it, and indeed the Characters of theſe two Perſons ſeem to be tranſpoſed. *That* of *Woden* which ſignifies *Furious* better becoming *Mars*, and *Tuet*, *Mercury.* Yet not to offend the *Romans*, whom being once acquainted with, they induſtriouſly flatter'd in the inſtances of Worſhip, they cloſed with 'em in the main; and as they admitted *their Gods* under *German Names*, ſo they did the *Days* too, tho' not with that preciſeneſs and order as was obſerved at *Rome.* Yet ſome not ſatisfied with this reaſon of the word, give it another Original, and draw it from *Thyſa* the Wife of *Thor*, who was thought as fit to have

her

her place among the *Goddesses* as *Friga* the Wife
of *Woden*, and therefore created her the *Patroness*
of Justice.

B. I take all this to be meer conjecture; and
therefore would it not be much safer to use such
Names for our Days, as we can support by better
Authority, and not honour after this sort a par-
cel of *Non-Entities*, to be sure Men or Things
far short of this Credit we now give 'em.

A. Be it so, yet where is the harm? There can
be no greater absurdity in this practice, than entertaining the Names of those imaginary Creatures
in the *Zodiac*, which 'twould be very ridiculous
to think were ever translated thither. All these
are *Terms of Art*, invented by the Learned to a
good purpose, tho' abused by Credulity and Ignorance. And seeing we explode the *Superstitious*
part, and regard no more than the *Natural use*
of 'em, as a convenient means to give the Sense
of things, and communicate our Conceptions to
one another, I see no danger to retain still a ra-
dicated Custom; and so little do I love unnecessary Novelties, that I should not be the first to
make an alteration.

B. Methinks the word *Feria* would do better,
as *Constantine* required, to distinguish us by that
means from *Jews* and *Gentiles.*

A. It was the way of the Church to Count the
Days of the Week after that manner, as appears
from * St. *Augustine* in the same place, where he
dislikes the other Language, and wishes Men
would speak in the Ecclesiastical way; for there he
uses that Form you mention, and it is observed
by those of the *Roman Communion* to this day,
which might be reason enough for some among us

---

† *Præfat ad* Psalm. 93.

to

to except againſt it. However, it ought to be remembred without any reflection on them or the Fathers, that even this word is *(a) Heatheniſh* as well as others, and is derived from flaughtering the Sacrifices they on thoſe Days made their fictitious Gods; which referring to the bloody Worſhip then in uſe, we ought to forget it as well as the Objects; and if we are not to retain any *Name,* to put us in mind of thoſe *vain Deities;* ſo neither are we to be fond of ſuch *words* as will keep in memory the *abominable Service* ordinarily done 'em in thoſe Days.

B. Suppoſe then we follow the Example of *Moſes,* who reckons the Week by the 1ſt, 2d, 3d Day, *&c.* as they ſay the *Arabians* do, and is lately put in practice by ſome among us. *(b)* Some think this the way God himſelf appointed; and to this ſenſe is expounded, that *Remember* in the 4th Commandment, *(c)* which R. *Iſaac* and *Abarbinel* make a reflection on that Cuſtom taken up among the Nations of calling the Week by the Names of the *Planets;* and therefore, as I am told, is laid aſide by the *Polanders, Bohemians* and *Hungarians.*

A. I have no exception againſt what *Moſes* began, and is continued by *other People,* provided no principle of pride or oppoſition to an innocent Cuſtom invites 'em to it. I only obſerve from Scripture, that not the *Days* alone, but the *Months* of the Year went originally in that Numerical Order; yet in progreſs of time all the Months had Names given 'em, and we read of *Niſan, Abib,* and *Adar,* without any offence to the bleſ-

---

(a) A ferendis victimis. *(b) Dierum numerus,* 1, 2, 3, 4, 5, 6, 7, *à deo primo appellatus fuit.* Philaſtrius *de Hæreſib.* *(c) In* Piraſh Tora. *Non numerabis more quò numerare ſolent alij, ſed numerabis per nomen Sabbati.*

ſed

fed Spirit who allow'd this Account, tho' he was
pleafed to Prefcribe another. If then we ufe artificial Words to compofe our *Week;* as well as
Year, why fhould we trouble our thoughts about
it, much lefs from hence take occafion to quarrel
and defpife each other?

B. I would not have Difputes about *words* fo
far ingage the Paffions of Men : Yet if I could
prevail, whatever liberty they thought fit to take
as to the ordinary Days of the Week which God
allows for Civil Affairs and the common bufinefs
of Life (and therefore no great harm if they ufe
Names fuitable to thofe defigns) yet I would have
'em treat the *Lords-Day* with more referve, always confider whofe Day it is, and thereupon
give it its *peculiar and proper Name.*

A. I wifh it as well as you, but would be glad
withall to fee fo much Honour and Reverence
given in other refpects to *this Day,* as might perfwade the World we took it for what it is. And
that there is no Name more fitting than what you
propofe, I eafily allow ; however, that this is
truly its *neceffary Name,* a Name fo effential and proper, that we offer it violence if we do not always
call it fo, and feem to unfanctifie it if we give it
any *other,* I muft needs fay, I do not admit it
with that exactnefs, nor do I look on the Proof
fo ftrong for it, but it leaves me after all a little
uncertain.

B. Is not this the Language of Antiquity? Is it
not thus named by the *Doctors* of the Church, by
Councils, by *Laws* and *Edicts,* in *Hiftory,* and all
manner of *Writings.*

A. The Cuftom is not of that extent as you
take it. For our own ancient *Parliaments* till the
Reign of King *Charles* I. and thofe States-Men
and Prelates who were concerned in making our
Statutes, and compiling our *Liturgy* did frequently
                                          decline

decline this appellation, and called it *Sunday* after
the way of ſome Fathers both in the *Greek* and
Latin Church ; yet I deny not but it is ſo read, as
you ſay, in the *Canons* of the Apoſtles, in *Clements
Conſtitutions,* and in his *Epiſtle* to the *Corinthians,*
cited by *Dionyſius* Biſhop of *Corinth* in (1) *Euſebius,*
as alſo in (2) *Ignatius*'s Epiſtles, who being Scho-
lar to St. *John,* may be judged able to inform us
what his Maſter meant by the *εν τη ημερα κυριακη,*
whereon he was in the Spirit.' (3) Probably he
intended *Sunday* ; but how doth this Text infallibly prove it ? ſince the very emphaſis which
ſome lay ſo great a ſtreſs on in the Article [*τη*]
ſpeaks louder for the *Anniverſary* of Chriſts Reſurrection at *Eaſter,* which is always a *double Feſtival,* than it doth for *Sunday,* when indeed we
Weekly commemorate that great act of our Redeemer, but do it at *Eaſter* in a more ſolemn manner; and much more agreeable to the excellency
of the Particle. There are (4) thoſe who apply
it to the day of the *Nativity, Aſcenſion* and *Pentecoſt,* as days not inferiour to the *Reſurrection* in myſtery, *value* and *benefit* to *Man.* But (5) many aſſert
the *ημερα κυριε* and *ημερα χριςε,* to mean the ſame
Day, and that is the *Day* of *Judgment,* (6) which
St. *Paul* calls the *Lords-Day,* and which St. *John* in
an extaſie is ſuppoſed to ſee as already come.

B. But *Ignatius,* as you ſaid, has the ſame Name,
and queſtionleſs he took it either from the authority of *John* in this place (and may be preſumed
to take it in his ſence) or he referrs to the inſti-

(1) *Eccleſ. Hiſt.* l. 4. c. 23. (2) *Ep. ad Magneſ. ad
Philip.* (3) *Ubi dies reſurrectionis intelligi certum eſt, licet
quidam in dubium revocent an is qui ſingulis anris, an vero qui
ſingulis bebdomadibus recurrit.* Curcellæus de Relig. Chriſt. Inſtit. l. 7. c. 16 (4) Dr. Potter *Epiſt. Dedic.* about the
Sabbath. (5) Gomarus *de Sabbato.* (6) 1 *Cor.* 5. 5.

tution of *Chriſt*, or the practice of the *Apoſtles* whom he had ſufficient opportunity to be converſant with, and to diſcourſe about matters of Religion, to which he was ſo much and ſo zealoufly devoted, that at laſt he died a Martyr, to Seal it with his blood.

A. Had there been any ſuch *Inſtitution* of our *Lord*, or that the *Apoſtles* made it a cuſtom to call *this Day* by that Name, I wonder to find St. *Paul* paſſing it by, who every where in his Writings ſtiles it *the firſt Day of the Week* whenever he had occaſion to ſpeak of the day as a day of meeting and divine Worſhip. It is not to be conceived that this Zealous Man who always conſulted his Maſters honour, ſhould be profoundly ſilent in a thing which ſo much concern'd him ; and that he who writ ſo many Epiſtles to the *Gentiles*, and treated of ſo many points reſpecting Chriſtianity, ſhould never once mention the *Lords-Day* in all thoſe places, wherein tho' he takes notice of the Day; yet he ſets it down under another Name, and doth it when there was no ſhadow of Reaſon for conforming himſelf to that Language, becauſe his Letters were directed to the *Greek*, *Roman* and *Aſiatic* Converts, to whom the *Lords-Day* had been more proper and welcome than the *firſt Day of the Week*, which was too *judaizing* in a Perſon who after his Converſion appear'd ſo great a ſtickler againſt *Judaiſm*. Thus in one of his Epiſtles, he gives theſe directions to them at *Corinth*, (7) *On the firſt Day of the Week let every one of you lay by in ſtore as God hath proſper'd him*. This was writ to a Church remote enough from the *Jews*, and as is ſuppoſed about the Year 57. yet no hint of the *Lords-Day* but under the old Name. And in the *Itinerary* of the Apoſtles which St. *Luke* penned

_____

(7) 1 Cor. 16. 2.

ſome

ſome Years after, the ſame form of words is uſed.
as it was commonly known to the Churches.
(8) *And upon the firſt Day of the Week when the
Diſciples came together to break bread, Paul preach'd
unto 'em.* The Apoſtle was at *Troas* an whole
Week as we find by the context. *We came to
Troas in five days, where he abode ſeven days,* one
only of which was ſolemnly kept, and it is called
the *firſt Day of the Week*; ſo that either the *Lords
Day* was not obſerved at all within this time, or
not being known by that Name, it was obſerved
in the periphraſis of the *firſt Day of the Week.*
'Tis true, the *Syriac* Tranſlation inſtead of the
firſt Day, ſaith, (9) *on every Lords-Day*; and
where the Apoſtle ſpeaks thus, [(10) *when you
come together therefore into one place, this is not to
eat the Lords Body*] that verſion alters, or rather
adds to it, *you do not eat the Lords Body as becomes
the Lords Day.* And *Beza* tells us, that he found
in an ancient Greek Copy, after *the firſt Day of
the Week* theſe words, (11) *the Lords-Day,* as
exegetical, and by way of explanation. I might
perhaps ſubjoin more Authorities of this kind,
but after all they amount but to an high probability, grounded on Tradition, and them who
call it an *uſage* from the Apoſtles times, tho' we
diſcover no Apoſtle uſing the word, but barely
St. *John,* and he but once in the place cited.

B. I hope you are not of *Marcion*'s mind and
the *Alogi,* to queſtion this Book, becauſe you
ſeem to lay little ſtreſs on the Teſtimony of
John recorded in it.

A. Marcion and the *Alogi* were pernicious *Hereticks who denied the Eternal word;* and among

---

(8) Acts 20. 7.   (9) *Quâque Dominicâ.* 1 Cor. 16. 2.
(10) Chap. 11. 20. *Non ut decet diem domini noſtri.*
(11) Τὴν Κυριακήν.

many other Errors, this of rejecting the *Apocalypse*
was one. However they are not all *Hereticks* who
are of this Opinion; for not only Men of great
Figure in these later Ages, such as *Erasmus, Lu-
ther* and *Calvin*, had little esteem for this Book,
but among the Ancients, (12) St. *Jerom* saith,
that some Churches of the *Greeks* would not accept
it. *Gregory Nazianzen* has omitted it in his Poem
about Authentick Scripture. The (13) Council
of *Laodicea*, held about 364, giving a list of Canonical Books hath left it out. (14) *Amphilo-
chus* co-temporary with St. *Basil*, saith, that
tho' some inserted it in the legitimate Writings,
yet the majority did slight it as a spurious piece.
(15) *Caius* an old Orthodox Author in *Eusebius*
fixes it on *Cerinthus*, the notorious Millennary whom
he believes the penner of it, and who to give the
Book greater Authority, had it called by St. *John*'s
Name. *Dorotheus Bishop* of *Tyre*, and a Martyr,
owns that St. *John* writ his *Gospel* at *Patmos*, but
not a word of *this Book*, tho' the first Chapter lets
us know that he was in *that Isle* when he had his
Visions. (16) *Dionysius* of *Alexandria* conceives
it written by another holy Man whose Name was
John, not the *Apostle*, but a *Presbyter* so called,
and for distinction sake Sirnamed the *Divine*,
(17) as in the inscription of the Greek Copies:
and the *Æthiopic* Translation makes him Bishop
of *Constantinople* when he suffered persecution.
(18) And *Beza* who takes great pains to vindicate
the Book, and solve the Arguments against it,
cannot well tell, whether this (19) *John* might
not be St. *Mark*, whose Name was also *John*, be-

---

(12) Ep. 129. *ad Dardanum.* (13) Can. 59. (14)
Euseb. *Eccl. Hist.* l. 3. c. 28. (15) *Eccl. Hist.* l. 7. c. 25.
(16) *Loc. jam citat.* (17) Ἀποκάλυψις Ἰωάννε τῦ Θεολόγε.
(18) *Prolegom. in Apoc.* (19) Acts 12. 25. 15. 37.

cause

caufe the words and forms of Speech in this Revelation agree very much with thofe in his Gofpel. Notwithftanding all which, I do not in the
leaft hefitate about the honour of this Sacred
Work, but take it for Canonical and Authentick,
partly in conformity to our own Church which
affords it the fame veneration as the other portions of Scripture, and partly becaufe therein fhe
follows the greateft Authorities of the Churches
before her. In the Council of *Ancyra* convened before that of *Nice*, Can. 24. In the 3*d* Council of
Carthage, Can. 47. and 4*th* of *Toledo*, Can. 16.
we have it exprefly, as appears from thefe Words
of the Canon. 𝕬𝖘 𝖋𝖔𝖗 𝖙𝖍𝖊 𝕬𝖕𝖔𝖈𝖆𝖑𝖞𝖕𝖘𝖊, 𝕿𝖍𝖊
𝕬𝖚𝖙𝖍𝖔𝖗𝖎𝖙𝖞 𝖔𝖋 𝖉𝖎𝖛𝖊𝖗𝖘 𝕮𝖔𝖚𝖓𝖈𝖎𝖑𝖘, 𝖆𝖓𝖉 𝖙𝖍𝖊 𝕾𝖞-
𝖓𝖔𝖉𝖎𝖈𝖆𝖑 𝕯𝖊𝖈𝖗𝖊𝖊𝖘 𝖔𝖋 𝖒𝖆𝖓𝖞 𝕳𝖔𝖑𝖞 𝕻𝖗𝖊𝖑𝖆𝖙𝖊𝖘
𝖍𝖆𝖛𝖊 𝖉𝖊𝖈𝖑𝖆𝖗𝖊𝖉 𝖎𝖙 𝖙𝖍𝖊 𝖂𝖔𝖗𝖐 𝖔𝖋 𝕾𝖙. John 𝖙𝖍𝖊
𝕰𝖛𝖆𝖓𝖌𝖊𝖑𝖎𝖘𝖙, 𝖆𝖓𝖉 𝖙𝖍𝖊𝖗𝖊𝖋𝖔𝖗𝖊 𝖙𝖔 𝖇𝖊 𝖗𝖆𝖓𝖐𝖊𝖉 𝖜𝖎𝖙𝖍
𝖙𝖍𝖊 𝖗𝖊𝖘𝖙 𝖔𝖋 𝖙𝖍𝖊 𝕾𝖆𝖈𝖗𝖊𝖉 𝖁𝖔𝖑𝖚𝖒𝖊. 𝕬𝖓𝖉 𝖇𝖊-
𝖈𝖆𝖚𝖘𝖊 𝖙𝖍𝖊𝖗𝖊 𝖆𝖗𝖊 𝖘𝖔𝖒𝖊 𝖜𝖍𝖔 𝖉𝖔𝖚𝖇𝖙 𝖎𝖙𝖘 𝕬𝖚𝖙𝖍𝖔𝖗𝖎𝖙𝖞, 𝖆𝖓𝖉 𝖙𝖍𝖊𝖗𝖊𝖚𝖕𝖔𝖓 𝖋𝖔𝖗𝖇𝖊𝖆𝖗 𝖙𝖍𝖊 𝖚𝖘𝖊 𝖔𝖋 𝖎𝖙 𝖎𝖓
𝖙𝖍𝖊 𝕮𝖍𝖚𝖗𝖈𝖍 𝖔𝖋 𝕲𝖔𝖉, 𝖂𝖊 𝖉𝖔 𝕽𝖊𝖘𝖔𝖑𝖛𝖊, 𝖙𝖍𝖆𝖙
𝖎𝖋 𝖘𝖚𝖈𝖍 𝕻𝖊𝖔𝖕𝖑𝖊 𝖈𝖔𝖓𝖙𝖎𝖓𝖚𝖊 𝖎𝖓 𝖙𝖍𝖊𝖎𝖗 𝖔𝖇𝖘𝖙𝖎𝖓𝖆𝖈𝖞,
𝖆𝖓𝖉 𝖓𝖔𝖙𝖜𝖎𝖙𝖍𝖘𝖙𝖆𝖓𝖉𝖎𝖓𝖌 𝖜𝖍𝖆𝖙 𝖂𝖊 𝖘𝖆𝖞, 𝖗𝖊𝖋𝖚𝖘𝖊
𝖙𝖔 𝖆𝖉𝖒𝖎𝖙 𝖎𝖙, 𝖑𝖊𝖙 '𝖊𝖒 𝖇𝖊 𝕰𝖝𝖈𝖔𝖒𝖒𝖚𝖓𝖎𝖈𝖆𝖙𝖊𝖉.
thus the Canon, which as it is an Ecclefiaftical
Law in it felf, fo it contains an antecedent Declaration of what many *Councils* and *Bifhops* had
done in behalf of this Book. And tho' it was rejected by feveral Perfons at the very time when
this Council fate, yet we find 'em punifh'd with
the fevereft cenfures of the Church, and they
were to be Excommunicated for their Error, if
they perfifted in it. So again we have it recommended by *Innocent* I. in an Epiftle to *Exuperius*
Bifhop of *Tholoufe*, wherein however he takes care
to caution him againft many Tracts, which then
went abroad under the venerable Names of
St. *Matthew*,

St. *Matthew*, St. *James*, St. *Peter*, St. *John*, St. *Thomas*, and St. *Andrew*, but had for their Authors the Philoſophers *Leutius*, *Nexocharides*, *Leonidas*, &c. The ſame honourable regard (20) St. *Auguſtine* and *Iſidore* had for it, with divers others who had occaſion to ſet down the Canon of Scripture. And that it is of equal credit with the other Divine Treatiſes, appears from the citations of *Cyril*, *Chryſoſtom*, *Athanaſius*, *Baſil*, *Clemens Alexandrinus*, *Irenæus*, *Cyprian*, *Ambroſe* and *Juſtin Martyr*. And *Epiphanius* eſpouſed its intereſt with ſo much warmth, that he ſtigmatized them with the opprobrious Name of Hereticks who had the confidence to refuſe it. The *Syriac* Tranſlation calls him *John the Evangeliſt*, *baniſhed to Patmos by Nero*. The *Arabick*, *John the Apoſtle and Evangeliſt*. And tho' in the Greek Copies he is ſtill repreſented by *John the Divine*, yet they all mean this holy Man who was called the *Theologue*, becauſe he treated of the Eternal Word, or God the 2*d* Perſon of the Trinity, in a more lofty and heavenly manner than the other Evangeliſts before him. And hence *Dionyſius* the *Areopagite*, one of St. *Paul*'s Auditors (whom *Euſebius* and *Nicephorus* make Biſhop of *Athens*, and *Baronius* tranſlates afterwards to *Paris*) has this inſcription in one of his Epiſtles, *To John the Divine*, *the Apoſtle and Evangeliſt*. Which Stile, tho' firſt uſed by him, was continued by *Origen*, *Athanaſius*, *Chryſoſtom*, *Cyril* and others, as we read in *Baronius*. 'Tis true (21) " as *Dionyſius* objects, " the ſtile of this Book is very different from " that in his Goſpel, or what he uſes in his three " Epiſtles; wherein things are delivered not only " correctly and with that exactneſs as becomes the

___

(20) *De doctrina Chriſt.* (21) Euſeb. *Eccl. Hiſt.* l. 7. c. 25.

E " Greek

" Greek Tongue, but there is so much elegancy
" and politeness throughout the whole composure,
" so much majesty in the words, and strength in
" the argument, that they are not to be charged
" with any of those Barbarisms, Incongruities and
" Idioms too frequently met with in the Book of
" *Revelations.*———So he. But why should we expect such neatness and correspondence of language
in Subjects so unsuitable? In his Epistles and Gospel, tho' inspired by the Holy Ghost for the
materials of the writing, he was left at liberty to
express himself in such words as he thought proper to set forth his meaning by. Whereas in the
Apocalypse he was tied to stricter Rules, and commanded to Pen, not only *what*, but *as* it was told
him. In the *first* he delivers matter of fact or
points of Doctrine in what manner he thought
best. But *here* he treats of things to come, and
therefore must use *Prophetick*, i. e. *mysterious* Language, (23) very odd uncouth words, yet such
as were prescribed him. In short, not only *things*
were revealed, but the *Phrase* also dictated to
him, and (24) many of those things in the same
forms of expression as were observed by the Elder Prophets, *Ezekiel*, *Daniel*, *Isaiah* and *Zachary*,
by whom the holy Spirit before spake on those
Subjects; and therefore no wonder his stile is so
harsh and rough, when he was to shew himself a
Prophet and not an *Oratour*; especially in some
instances which he put into *Greek* from *Hebrew*
Originals, and which he durst not vary one tittle
from, lest he might be suspected to impose on the
Churches. Yet to assert simply, as some do, that
there is no affinity or resemblance between this
Piece and the others of this inspired Pen-Man,

---

(23) Ἰδιώμασί μεν Βαρβαρικοῖς χρώμενον κỳ πȣ κỳ συλλοͱ
γιζόμενα, loc. cit. (24) Beza *Proleg. ad Apocalypsin.*

one

one Example may ſuffice to weaken this Objection, and if we compare *Rev.* i. 7. with the *Goſpel* Ch. xix. 37. we ſhall find 'em agreeing as well between themſelves as they both do with the Prophet *Zachary*, from whom the expreſſion is borrowed, *They ſhall look on him whom they have pierced*, Zach. 12. 10.

B. I think, the ſtrongeſt exception againſt this Book is, becauſe it favours the *Millennary Doctrine*, which gave occaſion for ſome to attribute it to *Cerinthus* the *Abettor* of that Notion.

A. It cannot be denied, but the *Chiliaſts* uſe the credit of this Book to ſupport their fancy of reigning with Chriſt a thouſand Years here upon Earth. But it would be very unreaſonable to make ill Men the Authors of every part of Scripture which they wreſt to defend their Errors by: Yet the ſame misfortune befell the Epiſtle to the *Hebrews*, which ſome a long while rejected on the like ſcore, becauſe it ſeem'd to countenance the *Novatian* rigour, denying the poſſibility of true Repentance to them who ſinned *after Baptiſm*. And therefore the Diſciples of this Sect were called *Cathari* or *Puritans*, a Name well known among our ſelves, without conſidering from whence it came. But to return to *Cerinthus* and his Followers. Suppoſe Men miſtake that paſſage of St. *John* in Chapter 20. 5, 6. and uſe it for a proof for Chriſts Reigning a thouſand Years in this World ; can this be thought reaſon enough either to reject this Book, or aſſign it to *Cerinthus* the great promoter of that Doctrine ? The *Heretick* had other very groſs Tenets, beſides the *Millennium*, (25) ſuch as denied God to be the *Creator*, with many other bold aſſertions which reflected on the Son of God. So that were he the

_____
(25) Auguſt. *de Hæreſ.*

Penner of this Book, why do we not find *thefe Herefies* Recorded there as well as the other? How came *this* to be fet alone? and fo worded, that the *Treatife* it felf overthrows that to which it feems to give foundation. It mentions indeed the *Thoufand Years*, (26) but where is one tittle of the way of Life in it which *Cerinthus*, and after him *Mahomet*, promifes thofe who adhere to him? Where the leaft hint of that Luxury, that *Eating* and *Drinking*, thofe *Sports* and *Marriages*, thofe *Sacrifices* and *Feafts* to be celebrated at *Jerufalem*, which he talks of? Plainly the Book it felf confutes all thefe Dreams, and the folid and lofty Subjects of it, argues it to be the more Divine. Its Language is dark and intricate, but that is not ftrange where the Matter is *Prophecy*. The more obfcure it is, the more it calls for our pains, which being after all, not able to fatisfie us, let us treat it with veneration, expect *Elias*, and wait for, with patience, the ftated times, when all fhall be fulfilled, and every part of it be made eafie and plain. And having faid thus much in favour of that Book, I hope you do not queftion but that I take it for what it is, *Canonical*, and a Sacred Writing.

B. I am forry my rafh Queftion fhould put you to this trouble. I perceive you deny not the *authority* of the Text, but only fcrupled the *validity* of the Proof as it is *applied* to this Occafion.

A. You fay well; I allow thefe words written by St. *John*, yet doubted whether we took em in the right fence; and whether his *Lords-Day* did infallibly mean St. *Paul's* and St. *Luke's firft Day of the Week*, and that it is the fame Day we now Celebrate in the Exercifes of Religion.

B. Tradition faith it.

_____

(26) Eufeb. Ecclef. *Hift.* l. 3. c. 28.

A. It doth, and I much reverence *this way* of conveyance, and wish that all People would confider it an *instrument* or mean to bring many things to our Knowledge, which otherwise muft needs have been buried in Eternal Oblivion. Nor do I ever except againft the word, but when Men use it to colour *Novelty*, and impofe on our Confciences points of Doctrine which have no warrant from the Apoftles or the Gofpel. I include not this Article of the *Lords-Day* within that number. It has a more unqueftionable, becaufe an *univerfal Tradition* accepted at *all times* and in *all places* where Chriftianity has been or is profefs'd. Without all manner of doubt, the Cuftom is very ancient. St. *John* is a good precedent for us to admit the Stile, and we do admit it. I only boggle at the *Divine Inftitution* of it; nor can I readily allow that the *Apoftles* themfelves either by *Precept* or *folemn Confent* gave it that Name. This Authors words doth not inferr any fuch thing; all proofs ought to be plain, and many times a good Caufe fuffers extremely, when Arguments are offer'd to fupport it which are liable to Cavil. That St. *John's Lords-Day* intends *the firft Day of the Week*, and that he ufes this Name as well known among the Churches is highly *probable*, but is no more than *probable*, and fair appearances are not grounds for infallible and divine Credit. It might be our *Lords-Day* St. *John* fpeaks of, becaufe *Ignatius*, his Pupil, follows him in that Language, and Pofterity fubfcribes to it, yet it *may not* be the fame Day, becaufe St. *Paul* and St. *Luke* give it another *Name* in their Writings to the *Gentiles*. Nay this Apoftle himfelf who penned his Gofpel two years later than the *Apocalypfe* (27) and after

---

(27) *Vid.* A Lapid. *Proleg. ad Apocal.*

　　　　his

his return from *Patmos,* as St. *Auguſtine,* St. *Jerom*
and *Euſebius* affirm, complies with St. *Paul* in
this Character, and calls the Day of Chriſt's Reſurrection *the firſt Day of the Week*; yet this was
above twenty five years after the deſtruction of
Jeruſalem by *Titus,* and for that Reaſon he was
not obliged to conform himſelf to the way of calculation among the *Jews,* who were now no more
a National People.

B. However, he might continue their mode of
account with regard to the time while their conſtitution laſted, and when the paſſages fell out
which he records in his Goſpel.

A. Well; yet ſeeing that *Government* was now
diſſolved in *Church* and *State,* and that he went
about this Work at the motion and intreaties of
the *Aſiatick Biſhops,* and for the benefit of the
Chriſtian Church, it ſeems a little ſtrange he ſhould
always omit the *Chriſtian Name* of this Day
throughout his Goſpel; and having ſo fair an opportunity, not call it the *Lords-Day* inſtead of
the *firſt Day of the Week,* or at leaſt, after thoſe
words [*the firſt Day of the Week*] not add [*now
the Lords-Day*] according to the manner of Scripture in other caſes; which was natural enough,
and had thereby ſhown the veneration he had for
it, and taught them the ſame reverence to whom
and for whoſe ſake he writ that excellent Piece.
And this the rather, becauſe he brings in a *new
Term* for the honour of his Maſter, I mean [λόγ☉]
the word, to prove *Jeſus Chriſt* to be the Eternal
Son of God. And therefore it might be expected, he ſhould ſome how or other have given
us the *new Name of that Day* whereon the *Reſurrection* fell out, which more effectually demon-
ſtrated the Divinity of our Saviour, than λόγ☉
(which

(which we find (28) in *Plato*'s Writings as well as in the *Gospel*) possibly could, and to the remembrance of which it was shortly after dedicated, I mean in a little time after the Resurrection, but long before he writ this account of it.

B. He had indeed fair Opportunities to mention it; yet his not doing so concludes little. Herein he complied with the way of the other Evangelists who writ before him, and who call it *the first Day of the Week,* according to the supputation of the *Country* which was the *Scene of our Lord's* Actions.

A. This concurrence of all the Sacred Writers confirms the Doubt. But that I confess which stumbles me most, is the Authority of St. *Paul,* who appears so zealous against the *Jewish Sabbath,* calls it a meer *Shadow,* denies the obligation of it in the *Christian Church,* and yet so far revives and so much honours it as still to call the Week by its Name, and the *first Day* [μίαν τῶν σαββάτων,] *one* or *the first of the Sabbath,* when he was speaking religiously of that Day, and had a better and fitter Name for it, if indeed the Name was in use at that time.

B. What then is your Judgment and Sense of it?

A. My present Opinion is, That the *Lords-Day* was observed very early in the Church; and that St. *John's* ἡμέρα κυριακὴ, is the same with what we call by that Name; That probably the Apostles themselves (at least some of 'em) spake in that

---

(28) *Hinc & Gentilium Philosophi & Theologi, ut Trismegistus, Orpheus, Plato, aliique Græci, Chaldæi & Ægyptii Patrem vocarunt νῦν*—i. e.—*mentem : Filium verò* λόγον, qu. *mentis prolem,*teste Augustino l.7. Confes. c. 9. Theodoreto l. 2. de Curand. Gr. affect. & aliis. A Lap. in Johan. 1.

manner,

manner, because *Ignatius* who lived either with
or very near 'em, has the same denomination.
And we find it, in the *Ecclesiastical Canons*, sometimes for their Antiquity called the *Canons of the
Apostles*, tho' it may be short of their time; That
the *Fathers* took it up on the Credit of these Precedents, and from the conveniency of the Stile it
self, so respectful to our *Lord*, and so agreeable to
the business of the *Day*, being a grateful and
pious commemoration both of the honour our
Blessed Redeemer did himself, and the Benefits he
brought us by his *rising* from the Grave; and
that all the Churches in succeeding Ages have for
these Reasons conformed to the Language, which
is warrant enough for us, in a thing of this nature, to follow their Examples, and give the Day
this venerable Name rather than any other, at
least in our more serious thoughts and discourses.

B. What then sticks with you?

A. I would have nothing accounted *more* a
Truth, than it really is. Nor should we, as I
said, offer any proofs which may shake the thing
they are brought to confirm. I allow, nay I affirm it highly reasonable for *one Day in seven* to
be set apart to remember the Glory and Advantages of *Christs Resurrection*. I can conceive *no
Day* more proper than what we use, to make good
that Design. I acknowledge in it both the Sense
and Warrant of Antiquity; and I wonder at
those that are apt to cavil at the *Custom*. Yet I
approve by no means the other extreme; nor can
I imagine it a *Divine Institution*, or be yet perswaded to think that Text of St. *John* clear e-
nough to show it *an Apostolical Appointment,
and a Sacred Rule*. Because we may observe in
the Books of the Ancients it is variously called,

(29) *the firſt day, the firſt day of the Week,* (*the eighth day, Sabbath, Chriſtian Sabbath, Sunday,* &c.) So that [*Dominica* or] the *Lords-day,* tho' its moſt emphatical Name was never generally, abſolutely and preciſely uſed, as it certainly had been, if of *divine Inſtitution.* For we are not left to this latitude in things where *Chriſt and his Apoſtles* have ſet us a Rule. Nor would the Church have preſumed to take this Liberty, had the *Lords-day* been altogether its neceſſary Name, as it muſt needs be on that ſuppoſition. (30) And tho' I am not of *Metaphraſtes*'s Mind to make it the Invention of *Sylveſter* I. ſeeing we read the word many years before him, yet 'tis very likely that the ſolemn and more publick uſe of it was not obſerved 'till about his time, when by *Conſtantine*'s Command it became an *Injunction,* and was afterwards more generally noted in Converſation and Writings, Religious and Civil. And perhaps this might be that Authors Mind, who could not be ignorant of the word, tho' till that *Emperor* and *Prelate*'s time, it had never commenced an *Eccleſiaſtical Conſtitution,* which agrees with the Notion of the preſent Church, looking on it to be [τὸ ἔθΘ τὸ πρεπὸν,] a very decent and laudable Cuſtom, yet ſtill a *Cuſtom* which we continue from Univerſal Tradition; a Cuſtom of the Church, and not a Divine Ordinance, begun and kept up for the honour of the Lord Chriſt, that we might never forget the Miracle of his Reſurrection. So *Bede,* and *Rabanus Maurus* ſay *Cuſtom and Conſent.* Iſidore *and* Heſychius *an Apoſtolick Tradition,* and an inſtance of the Authority of the Church. The

---

(29) *Vid.* Cypr. *Ep.* 59. Baſil *de Sp.* S. Aug. *in Pſ.* 93. Concil. Forojulien. *Can.* 13. (30) Suri) *Tom.* 6. *de Vit. Sanct.*

(31) Councils

(31) Councils of *Paris*, *Friburg* and *Erpford*, a *Canonical Inftitution and Ordinance of the Fathers.* Alcuinus *and* Aquinas, *a Chriftian Ufage, a Conftitution of the Church*, and *Cuftom of Chriftian People.* Toftatus, Bellarmine, Azorius *and* Eftius among the Papifts *a Canonical, Humane Appointment.* (32) Among the Reformed, Chemnitius, Calvin, Peter Martyr, Bullinger *and* Rivet, *a Token of Chriftian Liberty.* Amefius *a pofitive Law*, Brentius *a Civil Inftitution and alterable*, and our own Homilies call it *The choice of Godly Chriftian People immediately after the Refurrection of our Lord.* To all which I add but one Authority more, and that is the *Royal Martyr*, who on this Principle argues for the obfervation of *Eafter*. His words are thefe. " I conceive, faith he to the New " Reformers, in his Reign, the Celebration of " this Feaft [*Eafter*] was Inftituted by the fame " Authority which changed the *Jewifh-Sabbath* " into the *Lords-day*, or *Sunday*. For it will not " be found in Scripture where *Saturday* is dif- " charged to be kept, or turn'd into *Sunday*; " wherefore it muft be the Churches Authority " that Changed the one, and Inftituted the other. " Therefore my Opinion is, That thofe who " will not keep this *Feaft*, may as well return to " the obfervation of the *Saturday*, and refufe the " Weekly *Sunday*: When any body can fhew me " that herein I am in an Error, I fhall not be a- " fhamed to confefs and amend it. *C. Rex.*

B. If this be fo; that it is not of *Divine Appointment*, and that it is on all hands agreed, the reafon of this ufage is in remembrance of Chrift,

---

(31) *Quia Chriftus-Dominico die mundum recreavit; Concilium Laodicenfe diem Sabbati in diem Dominicum mutavit nè Judaifmum imitari videremur.* Synod. Parif. apud Bochellum.

(32) *Novum Sabbatum pendet ex arbitrio Ecclefiæ, &c.* Urim. Catech. de Sab.

would not *Chriſts-day* be as proper for this end, and perhaps in some reſpect, more to his honour than the *other :* Becauſe this ſtile limits and makes *the Day* peculiar to himſelf, whereas the word *Lord* has a greater latitude, and means the other *Two* Perſons of the Trinity as well as *Him*, and *Him* with regard only to his *Divine Nature ?*

A. The words *Jeſus Chriſt* are words of *Office.* The *laſt* reſpects *God* the Father, the *other us.* *Chriſt* beſpeaks him the *anointed of God*, and *Jeſus* ſignifies *Saviour.* And being on this Errand ſent into the World, from hence he takes that Name. And in acknowledgment of the Time when he came hither to execute this Office, we call it *Chriſtmas, and Chriſt*'s *Nativity*, as having an eye to what was then done ; He at that time appearing in a Body of Fleſh, and thereby taking on him the condition and form of Man. But then this was a debaſement of his Divine Perſon, and a State below his Infinite Nature, tho' not below his Mercy. Beſides, under this Name he was expoſed to all the Miſeries and Infamies we are liable to, and was in the Prophet's Language, during his Sojourning here, *a Man of Sorrows, and acquainted with Grief.* In which, humanly ſpeaking, there could be little ſatisfaction or honour done him. Add further, that this was a ſtile communicable to others, as *Kings, Prieſts* and *Prophets,* for *Cyrus* the Heathen was a *Chriſt*, and *Joſhua* a *Jeſus.* But the term *Lord*, the conſtant Tranſlation of *Jehovah* in the Old Teſtament, is of a more ſublime and incommunicable excellency ; it has always a regard to his Divine Part, and every where both ſignifies and owns his *Dominion, Soveraignty* and *Power*; and hence *this word* was more in the mouths of the Ancients than that of *Chriſt*, according to the way of the Goſpel and the Holy Apoſtles who generally gave him that Name, *a Name*

he

he was pleased to diftinguifh himfelf by, as we may fee in *Matth.* xxi. 3. where he bids the two Difciples whom he fent for the *Affes* on which he intended to ride in Triumph to *Jerufalem*; *And if any man fay unto you ought, you fhall tell 'em, The Lord hath need of 'em*, &c. (33) infinuating thereby, that he was *Lord* of the Creatures, and of thofe who feem'd to own 'em. A knowledge of him he thought very neceffary for his Friends and Followers to be inftructed in; that as on the one fide, when he fpake mean things of his Perfon, he thereby propofed to 'em the Example of his *Humility and Patience*; (34) So when he fometimes magnified himfelf, it was to raife their Thoughts, and invite 'em to expect great things of him. So that from thefe warrants the Fathers took the Language, and every thing that was Sacred, Venerable and Great they called (35) *Lordly*, as *the Lords Banquet* and *Lord's Body* for the Eucharift. The *Dominic* for the Church. *The Lords Scripture*, and *Lords-word* for the Bible. *The Lords-People* for Chriftians, conformable to the Phrafes we find in the H. Book, *the Cup of the Lord*, *the beloved of the Lord*, *the word of the Lord*; and fo the *Altar* or *Communion-Table* is faid to be the *Lords-Table*; and therefore this day likewife the *Lords-day*, rather than by any other Name, as more fignificant, more noble in it felf, and more tending to his glory from whom the Name is derived.

And here I find I muft conclude, becaufe it grows late, and fo I bid you good Night.

(33) Jo. Gerhard Continuat. Harm. Evang. c. 144.
(34) *Ut nos doceret de fe credenda quæ magna erant.* Gerhard loc. cit.   (35) *Convivium Dominicum.* Κυριακὸν σῶμα. Κυριακόν, Dominicum. Κυριακὴ γραφή. Κυριακὸς λόγ⊙. Κυριακὸς λά⊙.

The End of the First Dialogue.

A DISCOURSE,

By Way of DIALOGUE,

ON THE

𝕷𝖔𝖗𝖉'𝖘=𝕯𝖆𝖞.

DIALOGUE II.

The CONTENTS.

Deep Meditation indisposes the Senses for their proper Objects. Students fix or shut their Eyes. Why Blind-men seem to have better Memories. The Notion of the Lords-day. This Controversie very ancient. The Authors and Abettors of the Sabbatarian Doctrine. The other Extreme denying all Festivals. Their Reasons. Coloss. ii. 16. Explained. Galat. iv. 10. Examined. The Original of Festivals among all Nations. Such Appointments no injury to our Christian Liberty. What is meant by an Holiday. Rom. xiv. 5, 23. clear'd. Sabbath not simply Moral. The Notion of a Moral Law. Why the fourth Precept was placed among Laws confessedly Moral. Authorities for the
Morality

; *fidered.* *Intermixture of Moral and Ceremonial
Laws frequent.* Tindal *and* Calvin *affert the*
Lords-day *to be alterable, abfolutely not practically alterable.'* The Englifh *Liturgy and Homily*
*explain'd as to the 7th Day, and reconciled to the
Statute of* Edw. VI. *Reafons for the* Jus Divinum
of the Lords-day *anfwered.* Acts xx. 7. *and*
1 Cor. xvi. 2. *how underftood.* *The* Lords-day
how Inftituted. *St.* Jerom's *Example of* Paula's
working on the Lords-day. *No Work allow'd on
this Day, but thofe of Neceffity and Charity.* To
*ftate the Day rightly, rather ftrengthens the vene-
ration belonging to it, and it ftops the mouths of*
Gain-fayers.

A. HOW now, my Friend, was it by
miftake or *defign* that you were
turning afide? *Would* you not or
did you not fee me coming?

B. The latter to be fure, becaufe I came pur-
pofely hither in hopes to meet you.

A. I impute it then to (*a*) your *Thoughtfulnefs*;
and excufe you by my own experience, it being
ordinary with me to pafs by People whom I well
know and have a kindnefs for, without taking the
leaft notice of 'em, when I am in a fit of thinking: And the reafon of it is, becaufe the Mind
being at fuch a time very bufie on fome particular
Subject, tho' the Senfes are open and at liberty to
receive their proper Objects, yet the Soul not attending and confidering what is *feen* or *heard,* 'tis
almoft the fame-thing, as if the Eyes and Ears
were fhut.

(*a*) *Cum intenti ad cogitandum fumus, & cum mens occupata
in altum fe abdiderit, neque audire quæ circumfonant, nec videre
quæ obftant folemus*—Lactantius de Opific. Dei. N. 16.

B. I confeſs I was very induſtrious to keep òut all Objeȼts that might divert my Mind from what I was thinking on, and therefore all the uſe I at preſent made of my *Sight* was only to keep me from ſtumbling, and that is the reaſon I did not diſcover you ſooner.

A. You took the right way to ſecure your Meditation. Becauſe *variety* of Objeȼts continually and tumultuouſly crowding in through that Senſe to the Brain, hinder the thoughts from being ſerious on any *One* particular thing. And therefore your Students when they are very intent on what they *read* or *compoſe*, they either *ſhut* or *fix* the Eye, to be able to comprehend and digeſt it the better. And hence it is that *Blind-Men* are ſaid to have better Memories than other People. Not that it is really ſo, and that they have brains fitter to receive or retain the Ideas or Images of things than what is commonly found with other Neighbours, but the *impreſſions* are *fewer*; and becauſe they ſee not at all, and hear little in comparison of others who converſe abroad, what they get they conſtantly chew, and as occaſion requires, can readily diſcourſe on. But pray, if it be fitting for me to ask, What were your Thoughts imploy'd on? that being made ſenſible of the matter of your Meditation, I may find my ſelf more oblig'd to beg your pardon for offering to diſturb you.

B. The Subjeȼt is, what I deſign'd to mention at our laſt Meeting, but that the Night prevented me. I mean the *Sabbath* or *Lords-day*, which our Miniſter lately Preach'd on, and whoſe Diſcourſe I have been indeavouring to bring into as little compaſs as poſſibly I can, that I might not be over-tedious to you.

A. Pray begin.

B. The

B. The Summ was this. That the *Sabbath* of the fourth Commandment was partly *Ceremonial*, and partly *Moral*; That as far as it is *Moral* we still continue it under the Gospel; but for the *Ceremony*, we explode it as a *Type* and *Shadow*; and tho' we keep a *Seventh-day* in common with the *Jews*, yet it is not the *same Seventh-day*, because that was a circumstance of *positive Religion* we are not now oblig'd to, and is *alterable* by the Church as She shall see occasion for it. And if she doth not think fit to change that *Number*, it is not upon any *Moral* or *Natural* account, but out of pure respect to the *example* of God, who, as She reads in Scripture, *rested the Seventh-day* from his Works, and therefore she will have her Children to rest from theirs, in conformity to that Divine Pattern; yet it shall be *that Seventh day* whereon she may remember the great work of our *Redemption* by the *Resurrection* of the Lord Christ, to whom she devotes it, and calls it by his *Name*. This, as I remember, is the substance of what he delivered, and which with the Proofs and Authorities he cited made up the *Doctrine* of his Sermon. And I lay it before you, Sir, to see how it suits your Opinion, and that we may take this opportunity to clear the Question.

A. This *Controversie* about the *Sabbath* is very early, and has as much conduced to disturb the Church of God as any other point of Religion. " (*b*) The starting needless Questions about the " *Morality* of it, occasioning such Disputes and " Heats as will not easily be allay'd. And while " one Party *raised* the obligation of the fourth " Commandment to a pitch that was not practi- " cable, it provoked others to *slacken* it too

---

(*b*) Hist. of the Reformation.

" much;

" much; and this produced many sharp refle-
" ctions on both sides, and has concluded in too
" common a neglect of the *Day*, which instead of
" being so great a Bond and Instrument of Reli-
" gion, as it ought to be, is become generally a
" Day of Looseness and Idleness.

It was begun by *Cerinthus* and *Ebion*, who gave
the Apostles St. *Peter* and St. *Paul* very great disturbance in the execution of their Ministry, and
were the occasion of that Famous Council at *Jerusalem* under St. *James* Bishop of the Place, wherein
it was *Decreed* that *Christians*, especially the Gentile Converts, were not obliged to *Circumcision*,
nor any rite of the *Law* of *Moses*, in opposition to
the Doctrine of those Men who held and taught,
that (c) *except all were circumcised after the manner
of Moses, they could not be saved.* Here indeed no
mention is made of any point besides *Circumcision*;
but they gave out, not only that Men ought to be
Circumcised in the Flesh, but, as appears from the
context, they were bound to the (d) *whole Law*,
and some name the *Sabbath* in particular. After
these followed the Sectaries, the Disciples of
Ebion, whom *Isidore* calls *Semi-Judæos*, and who
made the *Legal Ceremonies* necessary to Salvation, and
were *half Jews*, and *half Christians*. Of the same
stamp were the *Nazaræi* who retained the *Sabbath*;
and tho' they pretended to believe as *Christians*,
yet they practised as *Jews*, and so were in reality
neither *one* nor *other*. From them sprung the
Symmachiani, great *Sabbatizers*, making an odd
Miscellany of both Religions, and offering the

· (*c*) Acts 15. 1.   (d) *Non solum carne circumcidi sed
etiam alia hujusmodi legis præcepta servari.* Aug. de Heræf.
*Sola quidem circumcisio hic nominatur, sed ex contextu patet eos
de tota lege movisse controversiam.* Calv. -

grofs

grofs Sacrifices of *Beeves* and *Sheep*, as well as
the Spiritual ones of *Prayers* and *Praifes*. About
the fame time were the *Hypfiftarij* who clofed
with thefe as to what concern'd the *Sabbath*, yet
would by no means accept *Circumcifion*, as too plain
a teftimony of ancient Bondage. All thefe were
Hereticks, and fo adjudged to be by the *Catholick
Church*. Yet their Hypocrifie and Induftry was
fuch, as gain'd 'em a confiderable footing in the
Chriftian World. So that tho' the *Lords-day* had
got a very great figure, and was well fupported
by thofe who prefided in Religious Matters, yet
for a long while the *Sabbath* kept its ground, and
both together were refpected as *two Sifters*. And
when in procefs of' time the *Sabbath-day* grew
fomewhat feeble, and was at length forced to
give way to her Rival, the Abettors and Patrons
of it, by a *Pythagorean* or *Marcion* Spell, recovered it in *our Feftival*, and changing now and
then the *Name* of the Day, revived the *obfervation*
of it, and made it as folemn and rigorous in *Sunday*, as ever it had been in the *Day before*. This
appears from the 3*d.* Provincial Council of *Orleans*, Can. 21. made on purpofe to encounter this
Error, and allowed many forts of innocent *Work*
to be done upon the Day. This was in the Reign
of *Childebert*. About which time, the *Romans*
gave the *Goths* a memorable Defeat, who having
Married *Jewifh* Women, and learnt their way of
keeping the *Sabbath*, which they applied to the
Lords-day, they would not fo much as lift up their
hands in their own defence, and the Enemies being aware of it, took that Day to affault 'em,
and in a few hours utterly routed them. The
Contagion had, it feems, fpread it felf as far as
France, and fucceeded fo well, that the People
were grown very fuperftitious in their notion of
the *Chriftian Sabbath*, which occafion'd that Coun-

cil

cil to oppôfe the growth of it, and thereupon
gave that Indulgence I before fpake of, permit-
ting all bufinefs to be done which did not hinder
their coming to the Church and ferving God in
the hours of publick Worfhip. Yet ftill the others
went on in their way; and to induce their Profelytes to fpend the Day with greater exactnefs and
care, they brought in the old Argument of *(e)*
compaffion and charity to the Damned in Hell, who,
during the day, have fome refpite from their torments, and the Eafe and Liberty they have is
more or lefs, according to the zeal and degrees
of keeping it well. And now the *Morality* of the
fourth Commandment grew into great requeft;
which is the reafon that *Clotaire* and *Charlemaign*
publifhing Edicts for the ftricter obfervation of the
Lords-day, they fo worded 'em as to make *(f)*
Scripture the ground of what they required, fuppofing what was commanded concerning the *Sabbath* equally related to *this other Feftival*; and tho'
the *Day* was changed in remembrance of the *Refurrection,* yet in other refpects, the *Ceremonial*
part continued, and *Chriftians* were enjoyn'd to
obferve it with the fame precifenefs, as the *Jews*
did, and ftill do after the Law of *Mofes.* And
for fear the Doctrine fhould not take without *Miracles* to fupport it, *Gregory* of *Tours* furnifhes us
with feveral to that purpofe. And *Euftathius* a
Norman Abbot, Affociate to *Fulco* a French *Sabbatarian* in the Thirteenth Century, comes into
England with a *(g) Mandate* touching the *Lords-
day,* which he pretended was found on the Altar
at *Golgotha,* wherein God is faid to declare, that

(e) *Refrigerium pænarum habuerunt.* Pet. Dam.
(f) *Statuimus fecundum quod in lege Dominus præcepit.* Car.
Mag. in Leg. Aquifgr.   (g) Tom. 7. Binij. *Conc. in
Scotia celebrat.* An. 1203.

the *Famine* and fome other *Calamities* then raging, was, *becaufe they had not kept holy the Lords-day,* &c. So that we fee by what fort of Men the *Sabbatarian* Doctrine began, upon what foundation they built, and by what means and arts they kept it in repair. And notwithftanding this, after the *Reformation* here, upon a *fhew* of Piety by the pains and induftry of a few Men, it came abroad again with more vigour than before, and has not a little helped to diftract and divide us. I do not fay this was *intentionally* their End, but fo it has fallen out. Charity fuggefts better things; and I hope this Zeal was primarily directed againft another Extreme, and to check that party of Men who are fo far from admitting the Old *Sabbath*, that their notion of *Chriftian Liberty* is, to obferve henceforward *no Days* at all. And altho' both forts, as far as the *Jew* is concern'd, allow the *Divine Authority* of the fourth Commandment; yet, as to themfelves, they very much difagree in the interpretation and fence of it. For the *Latter* fo underftand it as to make it fimply and wholly *Ceremonial*; and therefore argue, That under the *Gofpel* we ought to have no *Set times* to Worfhip God in, but every Man is to be left to his own difcretion, to *time,* as he pleafes, the exercifes of his Religion. In the number of which *Libertines* were the (*h*) *Petrobrufians* of old, and in latter Ages the Error is charged on the *Anabaptifts* and *Family of Love.*

B. A wild Opinion furely, and without ground for it.

A. Yet they offer Scripture, and from thefe words of St. *Paul* [*Let no Man judge in meat or in drink, or in refpect of an holiday, or of the new Moons,*

(*h*) Vit. Bernardi. Hofpin. de feftis Chrift. c. 1.

or

or the Sabbaths---Coloſs. ii. 16. inferr, That there is now no more reaſon to tie our ſelves to *ſtated times* in the performance of Religious Service, than to make a difference between *meats* and *drinks* as the *Jews* did, and therein placed no low degrees of Holineſs.

B. I ſuppoſe the Apoſtle means the *Jewiſh Feſtivals,* ſuch as the *Paſsover* and *Pentecoſt,* becauſe he joyns 'em with the *New-Moons* and *Sabbaths* peculiar to that People.

A. In all likelihood he does. For the whole Epiſtle was purpoſely writ againſt the *Simoniani* and other falſe Teachers who made it their ſtudy to bring into the Church many Rites belonging to the *Jews,* as St. *Chryſoſtom, Ambroſe* and *Auguſtine* expounded it. And that they might put a better face on the matter, (*i*) They did not think it proper to preſs the *intire* and rigorous obſervance of the *Moſaic* Cuſtoms on theſe Converts at *Coloſſi* (*a Yoke they were not able to bear*) but moderating the uſe of 'em, they did not much care how little they were ſubmitted to, provided they gain'd ſo far as to be able to ſay, That they had reduced that People to *Judaiſm;* and this they did, either out of a deſire of *Novelty,* or thro' a mortal hatred of the Chriſtian Religion, which yet, in ſome Caſes, they would be thought to favour. This ſhows it ſelf from their own practice, which St. *Paul* twits 'em with in another Epiſtle, wherein he cautions the *Galatians,* and ſets before 'em the deſign of theſe Doctors. *For neither they themſelves, being circumciſed, keep the Law, but deſire to have you circumciſed, that they may glory in your*

(*i*) *Satis illis erant ſi cum circumciſione reliquam legem à Gentilibus ſaltem ex parte obſervari, facerent, ut ſic eos ad ritum ſuum Judaïcum ſe traduxiſſe gloriari poſſint.* Eſtius in Coloſs. 2. 16.

fleſh,

flefh, Gal. vi. 3.] They were contented to be circumcifed according to the Law, yet laid no ftrefs on- their obedience to the Law which they became Debtors to by the very act of Circumci- fion ; and provided the *Coloffians* wou'd be Cir- cumcifed as they were, they might live as they pleafed, their *Circumcifion* being enough to expofe the *Gofpel* Liberty. This feems to be the impor- tance of that Expreffion, Ἐν μέρει ἑορτῆς, which we render *in refpect of an Holy-day,* but more ftrictly fignifies *part of an Holiday.* For thefe *Hereticks* taught that there was no need to celebrate *all* the old Feftivals, nor any one of them fo *precifely,* as the *Jews* kept 'em, but if *(k) in part,* they ob-' ferved 'em it was fufficient, and even *this* was a mitigation of the *Legal* Severity, fo that there was no need to boggle at it in the ftate of *Chriftianity.* But the Apoftle will not allow the *Coloffians* to comply in the leaft tittle ; and bids 'em have a care how they lent an Ear to fuch Men who en- deavour'd, all they could, to impofe this Doctrine on 'em, and bring 'em back into thraldom.

B. I think I have read that this Phrafe [*ex parte diei fefti*] referrs to the *Talmud* divided into fe- veral *Sections* or Chapters, one whereof treats of this Subject about *Holidays, New-Moons,* &c.

A. Some take the words in that Sence, and Pa- raphrafe 'em thus: *(l)* " Let no Man intrude on " you thofe things which are fet down by the " *Rabbins* in their Section of Feafts——However it amounts to the fame thing, becaufe it is agreed on all fides, that the word [*Holiday*] eyes the *Jew*: and St. *Paul's* defign in it was to inform the People at *Coloffi* that they were not bound to the

---

(*k*) A Lapide in loc. (*l*) Dr. Hammond.

F 4 *Mofaick*

Mosaick Festivals, which were only (*m*) *Prophetick Ceremonies,* faith St. *Augustine,* leading to Chrift and the Gofpel, but of no further ufe fince the *Antitype* it felf was come. And therefore to fay there are to be no *fixed times* for the Service of God, under the Gofpel, and that every Man is now left to his own leifure and fancy, *when* and *how* to do it, This is to make Chrift the Author of great confufion, and very little comports with the mind of St. *Paul,* who would have all things done (of Religion efpecially) *decently and in order,* 1 Cor. xiv. 40.

B. Methinks the Exception againft our *Holidays* is much ftronger from the words of this Apoftle elfewhere. For he blames the *Galatians* after their Converfion (*n*) *For obferving days, and months, and times, and years,* and tells 'em that *he is afraid he has beftowed on 'em labour in vain.* Now here is no mention made of the *Jewifh Feftivals,* and yet it is plain they obferved fuch after their leaving *Paganifm,* and 'tis as plain *Paul* cenfures 'em for it, and thereby gives countenance to the Opinion of thefe Men.

A. The common Judgment is, faith *Calvin,* that St. *Paul* in this place means the (*o*) *Aftrological Days* of the *Chaldeans,* which the Heathens fuperftitioufly obferved in the tranfacting of all Bufinefs, and expected the Events of Life to be good or bad, according to the *afpect and fituation* of the Stars, or as *this* or *that Planet* favour'd or look'd askew on 'em. *One* Man would not begin his Journey, becaufe it was an *unlucky Day*; *Another* refus'd to Merchandize *this Month,* becaufe a *Star*

(*m*) *Prænunciativæ obfervationes contra Fauftum.* Ambrof. in Colof. (*n*) Galat. 4. 10. (*o*) *Vid.* Aug. Ep. 119. Hofpinian, *de Feftis Ethnic.* Calvin *in loc.* Rivet.

was then *Afcendant* which promifed him little Succefs. And a *Third* put off Planting his Vine-yard 'till *Leap-Year* was over. Thus *Lycurgus* made a Law, that the *Lacedæmonians* fhould never engage in Battel 'till the *Full-Moon.* And *Ammianus* reports of *Valentinian,* that being Elected Emperor he durft not appear abroad on the *Biffextile,* as an *unfortunate* Day every fourth Year, Among the ancient *Romans* the next Day after the *Kalends, Nones* and *Ides* of each Month was always fufpected; and fo was the whole Month of *Daifios* [*June*] by the *Macedonians.* The (p) Sea-Men have an ill opinion of feveral Days in *February, March* and *April,* becaufe, as they affirm, there is on them an alteration of the Sea, and a greater difpofition than at other times to Calms or Tempefts, and fo continue in Harbour 'till thofe Days are over. The like Cuftom is ufed by many who profefs *Chriftianity,* efpecially on *Childermas-day*; whereon, it is faid, *Lewis* XI. of *France* would not Debate any matter, but accounted it a *Sign* of fome great Misfortune attending him, if any Man, *at that time* troubled him with Bufinefs. Thefe, faith (q) St. *Auguftine,* the Apoftle chides, and is urgent with them to forbear their idle Fancies. And that Father much lamented, that People otherwife Pious, could not be perfwaded to lay afide thofe Superftitious Conceits which did not a little reflect on their *Chriftian* Principles. But if we examine the *Scope* and *Defign* of this Epiftle, we fhall find it much the fame with that in his other Epiftle to the *Coloffians*; and that St. *Paul* cenfures thefe Converts for being too favourable to thofe Teachers

---

(p) Cœlius. lib. 8. c. 9. *Vid.* Selden *de jure Nat.* l. 3. c. 17.
(q) Ad Januar.

who made it their bufinefs to fupport *Judaifm*, or at leaft by a compofition or *mixture* of both 'Perfwafions, confound *Chrift* and *Mofes* together. By *his Days* then are meant the *Sabbaths*, by *his Months* the *New-Moons*, and the *Seventh Month*, which for the variety of Feafts in it was almoft *(r) Holy*, by *his times*, are intended the *great Holidays* of the Four Seafons : [at *Spring*, the *Pafsover*, at *Summer*, *Pentecoft*, at *Autumn*, the Feaft of *Expiation*, at *Winter* the *Encœnia* or Feaft of *Dedication*] and by *his years* the *Sabbatum Sabbatorum*, the *Seventh* or *Sabbatic Year*, and the *fiftieth Year* the *Jubilee*. Or poffibly *by times*, as St. *Jerome* thinks, may be underftood the three folemn Times of the Year, when they were all to meet at *Jerufalem*, all the Males at leaft, as we fee *Exod.* xxiii. 14, 17. Now as it feems, the *Galatians* were infected with this Doctrine about *Days* and *Times*, and thereupon the Apoftle expreffes himfelf very much difpleas'd with 'em, and the rather, becaufe being *Gentiles*, and by confequence not related to the *Jews* or their Ceremonies; they fo readily fubmitted to a *Yoke* which their *Baptifm* fecured 'em from, and thro' a dangerous eafinefs ran from *one* Superftition of Days, which they were born and bred in, to *another* Superftition of Days, which they had been hitherto ftrangers to, and which was as unfafe for them, as what they left when they renounced *Gentilifm*. So that this concludes no more than the proof foregoing: And tho' the Apoftle blamed them for obferving the *Mofaical Sabbaths*, *New-Moons*, and the reft, yet his words condemn not the *(s) reafonable* and

---

(r) A Lap. ex Orig. in Nu. (s) *Prohibetur Chri-ftianis dierum difcrimen, non fimpliciter fed cum opinione neceffitatis obfervatum*—Urfin. Catech. de Sab.

equitable

equitable part of thofe Days, it being very fit that *fome times* fhould be alotted to honour God, and acknowledge his Mercies in, tho' void of that Superftition and Ceremony which made the *Jewifh* fo very burthenfome.

And certainly, as (*t*) St. *Auguftine* fpeaks, it is very *juft* that the Creature fhould magnifie his Creator, for he made us to praife him, tho' he ftands in no need of it. This is the great Errand we were fent into the World for; and here we find God doing fo many things for us, that we ought to fay with the Pfalmift, *praifed be the Lord daily, even the God that helpeth us, and poureth his benefits on us,* Pf. lxviii. 19. But tho' every minute of Life hath fome intereft and fhare in the inftances of kind Providence, and therefore we fhould be ingaged in a conftant acknowledgment of what we receive from God, and have our *whole time* confecrated to his Service, according to that of *David, my praife fhall be always of thee,* *Pfal.* lxxi. 5. (*u*) Yet becaufe our weaknefs will not admit this, and that our uninterrupted Hallelujahs are referved to a better Life, where there will be no Temptations to carry us afide, it hath pleas'd our Divine Benefactor to content himfelf with a *few days* and times for us to Celebrate thereon fuch Works of his as feem to have larger Characters either of Mercy or Power. *All the Works of God are fo done that they ought to be had in remembrance,* Pf. cxi. 4. But feeing it is very hard, if not impoffible, to be particular in our thanks for *every one of 'em*; and that God has not made *all* his Mercies alike, to call for a like Devotion; and that we have not leifure to reflect diftinctly and

---

(*t*) Medit. c. 28. Sect. 32.   (*u*) Calvin Inftit. l. 2. c. 8.

severally on 'em all, 'Tis a piece of holy difcretion to pitch on *fuch* for our beft and moft folemn acknowledgments as God hath diftinguifh'd and ftamp'd with fome *extraordinary* Figures. This is in few words, the reafon of all Feftivals throughout the World, whereon are Recorded the moft beneficial and furprizing Actions of God *to be ftanding Memorials of Gods Mercies to future Ages, and that they might not hide 'em from the Children of the Generations to come, but fhew forth the honour of the Lord, his mighty and wonderful works that he hath done.* And this is the ground of the Holi-days in ufe among us, (*w*) *To be commemorations of the myfteries, means and witneffes of our Redemption, to preferve a folemn memory of thofe high benefits which either by himfelf or any of his bleffed Inftruments God hath beftow'd on Mankind.*

The Heathens had *many* fuch Feafts or Days of *remembrance* ; and tho' they miftook the *Objects* which at fuch times they directed their Devotion to, yet they were *not* miftaken in the *reafon* of the Service; and they chofe rather to commit an Error in giving the honour of a Bleffing to a *wrong* Benefactor, than not to be grateful in celebrating the Bleffing it felf, which made them *fafe* or *happy*. It would be too tedious to go thro' em all, but briefly thofe Titles commonly given to *Jupiter*, of *Inventor, Feretrius, Stator, Victor, Servator* and *Confervator* ; *Sofpitatrix* to *Juno*; *Medicus, Palatinus, Actiacus* and *Navalis* to *Apollo*; σωΐηρ fo often added to the Names of *Neptune, Diana, Æfculapius, Caftor* and *Pollux*, &c. ——Thefe, I fay, were Teftimonies to fhew the great motive of all fuch Appointments ; and that both the *Wor-*

(*w*) St. Aug. de Civit. Dei, l. 10. c. 4. *Vid.* Hook. Eccl. Pol. l. 5. c. 71.

fhip

ſhip and the *Solemn Times* they ſet apart to expreſs
it in, were a kind of *Record* to Poſterity, to keep
a foot thoſe Benefits which the Almighty Power
and Infinite Wiſdom of the Deity convey'd to
'em by ſuch or ſuch hands. And this they were
taught by the *light of Nature,* which we call the
Equity and *Moral* of all the *Jewiſh* Feſtivals, and
which certainly reaches us ſtill, tho' we explode
the tyrannical part, and by virtue of our *Chriſtian Liberty* reject what made the obſervation of
their Days nauſeous and uneaſie. However it is a
thing altogether neceſſary that *ſome times* ſhould
be aſſigned for the Divine Worſhip; and no Man
ſurely is ſo licentious in his perſwaſion, but will
admit this neceſſity, only he would be left at liberty to appoint *ſuch* as pleaſe him beſt, which in
ſtrictneſs by the liberty he is recovered to thro'
the Goſpel he can and may. Yet in St. *Paul's* language, (*x*) *all things are lawful, but all things are
not expedient ; all things are lawfull, but all things
edifie not.* (*y*) It is not convenient for Piety-
ſake, that this ſhould be, becauſe if every Man
was thus left unto himſelf, and that *Peter* would
worſhip *this day and hour,* and *John that,* what diſtraction would there be in the Church of God ?
whereas by conſenting, as we may ſay, to ſome
particular and certain times, we make our Devotion, not leſs hearty, but more remarkable in the
eye of the World, and by that means more conducive to the honour of him whom publickly and
in *common* we adore at *ſuch an hour of this or that
Day.*
   B. Is not this a kind of *reſtraint,* and an
abridgment of our *Chriſtian Liberty wherewith*

(*x*) 1 Cor. vi. 12. c. x. 23.   (*y*) Calv. Inſtit. l. 2.
c. 8. Sect. 32.

Chriſt

Chrift has made us free? If we do not as we will,
(z) where is *Liberty?*

A. 'Tis no reftraint at all, but what tends to
our conveniency. For illuftration fake let us confider our felves in the *Civil Capacity.* We are all
Free by Nature; and it is a piece of our Birth-right
to be fubject to no Perfon, nor be obliged in any
thing. But who is there (able to think) that
would wifh himfelf in this State, which expofes
him to the Law of every Mans *Will?* Where each
one is left to the Empire of himfelf, it cannot be
poffibly thought that his Ambition will fix there;
and if he extends it beyond his own Perfon, as
every Man on Earth has a ftrong inclination to it,
then that which you call *Liberty,* is nothing but a
ftate of War, and a few days would bring us all
to confufion and flaughter. So that to be fubject
to wholfome Laws, is not *Slavery,* but a *Protection* from our Neighbours, who would, each in
his turn if he can get ftrength for it, make us *Slaves*
indeed, and quickly bring our Liberty to nothing.
Laws and Government are curbs to *Licentioufnefs,*
no deftroyers of *Liberty*; and where we do not
act the Slaves to our Vices, but live according to
the dictate and influence of better reafon, by
virtue of thefe Laws we act with more freedom,
and more like our-felves; becaufe in the mean
while they tie the hands of thofe who would otherwife opprefs us. Thus as to our *Chriftianity*; it
puts us into a ftate of *Liberty* as to what concerns
the *rigour* and *flavery* of the *Jewifh Conftitution*;

(z) *Quid eft libertas ? Poteftas vivendi ut velis.* Cicero in
Paradox. *Eft naturalis facultas quod cuique facere lubet.* Ju-
ftinian. Τις φυσικὴ εὐχέρεια συγχωρᾶσα πράτ]ειν ἃ βύλέ]αι—
or τῦ ποιεῖν ὅπερ τις βύλέ]αι. Τὸ ἐλεύθερον τὸ μηδενὸς ὑπη-
κοὸν ἀλλὰ πράτ]ειν ἁπλῶς τὰ δοκῦν]α ἑαυτῷ——Chryfolt.
Orat. 14.

and

and in particular we ftand not obliged to the tedioufnefs and troublefome obfervation of *their*
days, times and *years*. But doth this argue againft
any *fet times* for the Service of God, becaufe we
are freed from their *Superftitions*? Can we imagine
that our *Liberty* extends fo far, as not to worfhip
God, or not worfhip him in a way which better
anfwers the end we propofe in fo doing, and
which is to magnifie him the more in our unani-
mous and concurrent devotions? (1.) St. *Peter*'s
Advice is good, that we fhould *look on our felves as*
free, but not fo free as *to ufe our liberty for a cloke*
of malicioufnefs, but *as the Servants of God.* We
are freed from *legal Bondage,* yet ftill we are *God's*
Servants, and we ought to honour him in a *way*
that makes moft for his Glory. Which being beft
done at *fet times* and in *fet places,* it proves the
conveniency of fuch Inftitutions, wherein we
ferve him with a comparative freedom, and we
may call it *liberty* with refpect to the *ceremony* and
feverity of the *Mofaick* injunctions.

B. But do we not by the very terms attribute
fomething extraordinary to fuch *ftated Times*; and
by calling them *Holy-days,* fix the fame Sanctity on
'em as the *Jews* conceited to be in *theirs?*

A. (2) *Sanctification* is nothing elfe but a *Seque-*
ftration of any thing from a *common* to a *religious*
purpofe; and all we mean by *confecrating* things,
is to *fet 'em a-part* for facred ufes. And if we diftinguifh *one* Day from *another,* it is not to *alter*
the nature of the Day, or make it *fimply holy,* but
that the difference being known, People might be

---

(1) 1. Pet. ii. 16. (2). Τί ἐςιν, ἠγίασεν αὐτὴν;
ἀφώρισεν αὐτήν. Chryſ. Hom. 10. in Gen. Πᾶς χρόνῷ ἱερὸς
ἐν ᾧ τε τ θεε ἐπίνοιαν λαμβάνομεν. Clem. Alex. Strom.
l. 2.

invited

invited to come together, to do in a publick manner the Duties of Religion, the performance
whereof makes *any* Day or *any* Place *holy*, while
such things are doing. And so the Law of *England* explains it. (3) 𝕨𝕙𝕚𝕔𝕙 𝕎𝕠𝕣𝕜𝕤, 𝕒𝕤 𝕥𝕙𝕖𝕪
𝕞𝕒𝕪 𝕓𝕖 𝕨𝕖𝕝𝕝 𝕔𝕒𝕝𝕝𝕖𝕕 𝔾𝕠𝕕𝕤 𝕊𝕖𝕣𝕧𝕚𝕔𝕖, 𝕤𝕠 𝕥𝕙𝕖
𝕥𝕚𝕞𝕖𝕤 𝕖𝕤𝕡𝕖𝕔𝕚𝕒𝕝𝕝𝕪 𝕒𝕡𝕡𝕠𝕚𝕟𝕥𝕖𝕕 𝕗𝕠𝕣 𝕥𝕙𝕖 𝕤𝕒𝕞𝕖, 𝕒𝕣𝕖
𝕔𝕒𝕝𝕝𝕖𝕕 𝕙𝕠𝕝𝕚𝕕𝕒𝕪𝕤, 𝕟𝕠𝕥 𝕗𝕣𝕠𝕞 𝕥𝕙𝕖 𝕞𝕒𝕥𝕥𝕖𝕣 𝕠𝕣 𝕥𝕙𝕖
𝕟𝕒𝕥𝕦𝕣𝕖 𝕖𝕚𝕥𝕙𝕖𝕣 𝕠𝕗 𝕥𝕙𝕖 𝕥𝕚𝕞𝕖 𝕠𝕣 𝕕𝕒𝕪; 𝕗𝕠𝕣 𝕤𝕠 𝕒𝕝𝕝
𝕕𝕒𝕪𝕤 𝕒𝕟𝕕 𝕥𝕚𝕞𝕖𝕤 𝕒𝕣𝕖 𝕠𝕗 𝕝𝕚𝕜𝕖 𝕙𝕠𝕝𝕚𝕟𝕖𝕤𝕤, 𝕓𝕦𝕥 𝕗𝕠𝕣
𝕥𝕙𝕖 𝕟𝕒𝕥𝕦𝕣𝕖 𝕒𝕟𝕕 𝕔𝕠𝕟𝕕𝕚𝕥𝕚𝕠𝕟 𝕠𝕗 𝕤𝕦𝕔𝕙 𝕙𝕠𝕝𝕪 𝕨𝕠𝕣𝕜𝕤
𝕨𝕙𝕖𝕣𝕖𝕦𝕟𝕥𝕠 𝕤𝕦𝕔𝕙 𝕥𝕚𝕞𝕖𝕤 𝕒𝕟𝕕 𝕕𝕒𝕪𝕤 𝕒𝕣𝕖 𝕤𝕒𝕟𝕔𝕥𝕚-
𝕗𝕚𝕖𝕕, *i. e.* separated 𝕗𝕣𝕠𝕞 𝕒𝕝𝕝 𝕡𝕣𝕠𝕡𝕙𝕒𝕟𝕖 𝕦𝕤𝕖𝕤,
𝕒𝕟𝕕 𝕕𝕖𝕕𝕚𝕔𝕒𝕥𝕖𝕕 𝕥𝕠 𝔾𝕠𝕕 and his Worſhip. In all
this we conſult only (4) (*Order* and *good Government*, and our Opinion is, that every Day of the
Week and Year hath the ſame efficient Cauſe of
Divine Creation. And as Chriſt ∙is Lord of the
Sabbath, ſo likewiſe all Days and Times are ſubject to his Providence and Dominion ; and whenever our Language may ſeem to make *one Day*
more *holy* than *another*, we muſt not be underſtood
as if we infuſe any real ſanctity into it, but as
we apply it to a Sacred and Religious Uſe.
" (5) And *as Altars, Garments and Veſſels are*
" *ſaid to be holy becauſe typically ſo, and with re-*
" *lation to the things ſignified by 'em, but not in*
" *the things themſelves ; ſo times are holy, not*
" *ſtrictly and properly, but as they are the meaſure*
" *of holy actions.* Thus far the Apoſtle warrants
our practice, who tho' cenſuring the *Galatians*
for obſerving times, yet himſelf (without reſpect
to the *Jew*) had his *ſet day*, or *firſt Day of the*

---

(3) 5 & 6. Edw. VI.　　(4) *Reſpectus habetur politiæ
& ordinis, non dierum.* Marl. *Sabbatum æſtimamus non propter
ſe, ſed propter cultum dei*—Curcell. de eſu Sanguinis.
(5) *Biſhop of* Ely de Sab.

Week,

Week, whereon he and his Converts met for the exercises of their Religion, and 'tis continued in use to this Day. Which shows plainly, that tho' he exploded the *Sabbath as such,* it was not in his mind that all Days should be made so much alike as to leave no mark of distinction between 'em, because the *first Day of the Week* was solemnly kept, tho' solemnized and considered in a way more agreeable to the temper of the Gospel. So that I conclude with the words of *Zanchy*; " The Apostle in these places doth not forbid " certain Days, whereon the faithful might af- " semble to pray and communicate together; for " the Apostles and others did usually meet on " the Lords-day, and would that all things " should be done orderly in the Church. And " therefore unless we would affirm that St. *Paul* " contradicted himself, it must needs be con- " fess'd that in those Epistles to the *Galatians* " and *Colossians,* he did nothing less than teach, " that Days were not to be observed now in the " Church of Christ.

B. Well; but if a Mans perswasion be a- gainst it, and that according to the notion he has of *Christian Liberty* he believes he is not bound to such *stated Days,* would you have him comply against his Conscience? *Paul* in general denies this conformity, for, saith he (6) *whatever is not Faith is Sin.* And in particular, which is more to our present purpose, he tells us that one *Man esteemeth one Day above another, another esteemeth every Day alike.* What then? which of 'em is to blame, *They* that did, or *They* who did not make this distinction?

---

(6) Rom. xiv. 5, 23.

It feems *neither,* for *both* Parties were in the right, becaufe *both* acted according to Confci-ence. *Let every man be perfwaded in his own mind,* and then by virtue of this *perfwafion, he that regardeth the Day, regardeth it to the Lord, and he that regardeth not the Day, to the Lord he doth not regard it.* So that here is a *Rule* to walk by, *Confcience* is left the *Judge,* and ac-cording to her conduct we are to fquare our actions. *Concilio fuo remittatur,* are *Ambrofe's* words, and every Man is to fatisfie his own mind in what he is going to do, or elfe what he doth becomes a Sin.

A. The Place you referr to is brought for a third proof againft the inftitution of *certain Days* to worfhip God in. And fo far the Ar-gument holds good, that we are to do nothing with a doubtful mind, and while Confcience boggles againft the doing of it, and the Autho-rity of St. *Paul* in thofe two Texts of Scripture confirms the Doctrine. But altho' a Man is obli-ged in point of fafety to act or fpeak accord-ing to the influence of his *Confcience* or *inward perfwafion,* yet he is to take fpecial care that his *perfwafion* be well grounded, that he has ufed all honeft means to *inform* himfelf, and that he doth nothing out of *fingularity* or *wil-fulnefs,* but purely by the motions and dire-ctions of his Confcience, which he is certainly to follow, whether the thing be true or falfe, which at prefent fticks with him.

To explain then thefe words of the Apoftle, *whatfoever is not of Faith is Sin ;* and again *one man efteemeth one day above another.* It is evi-dent from the Law of *Mofes* that the People of the *Jews* were bound to make a difference between

tween *Meats* and *Days.* (7) *Thefe are the Beafts
which you fhall eat, and thefe fhall you not eat,
they are unclean.* And fo as to *times.* (s) *Three
times fhalt thou keep a Feaft unto me,* and remember the Sabbath-day. Now fome *Jews,* and
not a few *Gentiles,* being made Profelytes to
the *Chriftian* Religion, they had for a confiderable time *different* notions of many Points relating to their new profeffion ; and *this* difference
was like to occafion not only warm difputes,
but ftrong animofities among 'em, which the
Apoftle was aware of, and willing to prevent,
and fo for the confervation of *Charity* and
Peace he thought fit to let 'em know, that notwithftanding their *feeming* difagreement in
thefe and the like matters, yet they might reft
fatisfied with this Confideration, that they *all
confented* in the main, and in reality meant the
fame thing, which was to fubmit to *Confcience,*
and be guided every Man by his *perfwafion.*
Allowing then the *Jews* (in conformity to the
way they had been Educated in) ftarted at the
eating of *Swines flefh,* becaufe the *Law* forbid it,
and would ftill obferve the *Old Feftivals,* becaufe the fame *Law* required it, which *Law*
they had a great veneration for, and the repeal of it did not fo evidently appear, but fome
Scruples ftill remain'd, and during thofe Scruples, 'twas neceffary to comply with it, If
thefe Men (9) *being weak in the Faith* as he reprefents 'em, and as yet not fufficiently underftanding the *liberty* the Gofpel gave 'em, would
ftill retain the *Jewifh Feafts,* and forbear *Swines-
Flefh,* becaufe yet they were not *otherwife per-*

---

(7) Levit. xi. 2, 4.   (8) Exod. xxiii. 14.
(9) Rom. xiv. 1.

ſwaded, there was no harm in all this, they might do it, ſeeing in both theſe inſtances there was no diſhonour to God, but that on the contrary, their honeſt deſign was not to offend him. But for the *Gentiles,* who, it may be, had no ſuch Leſſons taught 'em in their youth, at leaſt not ſupported with that Authority which the *Jews* could offer for what they held and did, and perhaps were greater Proficients in the buſineſs of Chriſtianity, becauſe they had none of thoſe deep impreſſions to eraſe, nor ſtrong prejudices to remove; which made the *Jews* ſo ſlow and timorous; *theſe* Men made no diſtinction of *Meats* and *Days,* but without any reluctancy, enjoy'd and aſſerted the Privileges of the *Goſpel.* And *theſe* as much honour'd God in *refuſing* thoſe diſtinctions, as the *Jews* did in *keeping* 'em a-foot. And *both* did well, becauſe *both* were fully perſwaded in their own minds; and if *either Party* had behaved themſelves contrary to this *perſwaſion,* they had been guilty of Sin.

B. This therefore inforces the Argument. That their *Perſwaſion* was to guide 'em; and tho' their Opinions were contrary to one another, as to *Meats* and *Days,* yet all was well, becauſe in this difference their *Conſcience* it ſeems pleaded for 'em.

A. I hope you remember what I ſaid, that one ſort of the Perſons here ſpoken of were *Novices,* late Converts, and *weak in the Faith.* They muſt therefore be indulged and tenderly uſed, leſt they ſhould ſtart back and relapſe to the Errors they had renounced at their *Baptiſm.* And this is the Reaſon, (10) " Tho' the A-

---

(10) Hiſt. of the Reformation.

" poſtles

" poftles by the gift of Miracles had fufficient
" means to convince theWorld of their Autho-
" rity, yet they did not all at once change the
" Cuftoms of *Mofes* Law, but proceeded by
" degrees; and Chrift forbid the pulling up
" of the Tares, left the Wheat fhould be pul-
" led up with 'em. So it was fit to wean
" People by degrees from their former Super-
" ftition, and not run too faft. St. *Paul* was
willing to be (11) *all things to all Men to gain.
fome.* He knew their Condition would not yet
bear a *thorough Reformation.* He will therefore
judaize a little with thofe, who otherwife had
he carried himfelf ftiff, might return to *Judaifm.* Without doubt he difliked this *Medly*;
Nor did he fpare other Perfons better grounded, and for a longer time inured to the Principles of Chriftianity, witnefs his Carriage towards the *Galatians* on this account, whom he
fharply reprov'd for the very thing he excufes
in this Chapter. But he muft be *Prudent* as
well as *Zealous*, his *Zeal* fhall be according to
Knowledge, in due time he may make *them* as
fenfible of their Errors as *thofe of Galatia*, but
they muft be taught by degrees, and according
to their Capacities. The Grace of God and the
Apoftles inftruction might at length alter their
perfwafion, but until this be done, they ought
to act by it, and it was dangerous for thefe
Converts to abjure any part of their Creed,
'till they were well convinced they had been
miftaken in it.

The Summ is this: That Chriftians are not
obliged to the *Jewifh* diftinction of *Times* and

---

(11) 1 Cor. ix. 22.

Meats,

Meats. And for far thefe Proofs ftand good. But to inferr from thence, that becaufe we are not held to obferve the *Sabbath,* and other Feafts of the Old *Law,* we are not to fet apart *certain Times* for Gods Service under the *Gofpel* (-as being a *Ceremony* terminated by Chrift) this is very remote from the defign of the Holy Writer, whom we fo often find mentioning and preaching on *the firft Day of the Week.* As God is to be Worfhipped, fo he muft have *Set Times* and *Places.* for the doing of it, or elfe we fhall exprefs a very *wild* and *confufed* Devotion. And tho' as I faid, we are under no Superftitious Slavery or Opinion of Holinefs inherent to Times or Places, according to the Sentiments and Practice of the *Jews,* yet both *Times* and *Places* are very convenient to be fet apart and well known, that every body may ufe 'em for the honour of God, and thereby exhibit *Chriftian Communion* and *Charity* between themfelves. However, if any Scripture has fo much impreft fome People as to make 'em doubt whether any fuch Times ought to be obferved or no; To forbear is fafe 'till they be better informed; And as I would not have 'em comply as long as the Doubt remains, becaufe I would not have 'em offer violence to Confcience, yet let 'em not be obftinate and peevifh, when Satisfaction is tender'd 'em, for even this is an *offence* to Confcience, to *reject* a Truth when fufficient *Evidence* for it is laid before them. But if a Man will fhut his Eyes when the *Sun* fhines, upon no other reafon, but becaufe he will not fee, let him have a care the Judgment of God (the ufual lot of fuch People) never meets with him, to be in the iffue made fo blind, that he cannot thenceforward fee if he would.   But

But leaving this Extreme, which makes the *Sabbath* a Ceremony altogether, to elude in all respects the obligation and obſervance of it. Let us now go on to the other, which as much over-does, and by giving that *Law* of the 4th Commandment a greater degree of *Morality* than it can well bear, by this exceſs run themſelves into no leſs Error.

Theſe Men are of two ſorts: Whereof ſome look on this *Precept* with the ſame Eye as the other *Nine*, and thereupon keep not only *one Day in ſeven*, but the very *ſame Seventh-Day*, and in the *ſame manner* as the *Jews* before 'em; which indeed they ought to do, on the Suppoſition they eſpouſe, there being no room left for *alteration*, where Laws are *Perpetual*, and ſimply *Moral.* The Authors and Abettors of this Doctrine you had before; and it coſt St. *Paul* great pains to anſwer and confute it; And in particular thoſe places which we juſt now took notice of, are directed againſt that Notion; and their proper End was to ſilence the Controverſie, or ſtop the progreſs of it. Yet a few there are to this day who *Judaize* in this inſtance; And tho' I dare not play the Judge and uſurp on their Conſcience, yet they would do well to conſider St. *Paul* ſeriouſly, who among other things, makes the Sabbath a Shadow, and Chriſt the Body; and conſequently to continue the *Sabbath* now, indirectly denies that Chriſt is *come*.

Others therefore dare not venture ſo far, but do allow it ſo much *Ceremony* as to make good that Character the Apoſtle gives of it. And tho' on that account they explode the *Saturday-Sabbath* and the circumſtances of *reſt* writ down in the Commandment, yet conclude,

not

not only that *appointed Days* are neceſſary for divine Worſhip, but the very *ſame* proportion of time ought to be conſecrated to God, and will have the *Seventh Day* to be *Moral*, as well as the *Service* of it. And hence have proceeded many harſh Sayings, " *That to do any Buſineſs* " *on the* Lords-day, *is as great a Sin as to* mur- " ther *a Man, or, commit* Adultery ; *Or to* " *Feaſt on it is of as ill a complexion in Gods* " *ſight, as if a* Father *ſhould take a Knife and* " *cut his* Childs *Throat, and the like.* The rea- ſon of all which is, That they look on the *Pre-cept* about the *Sabbath* equally binding with the reſt, and equally puniſhable in the Old Teſta-ment, where they read that (12) *whoſoever doth work thereon ſhall be put to death,* (13) as the Man who *gathered ſticks* on that Day was *ſtoned with ſtones;* which they apply to the preſent Caſe, and believe the ſame *Law* ſtill in force, tho' the execution of it be ſuſpended by the *Magiſtrate's* neglect or indulgence. An Er-ror I think, confuted by its own practice. For if the keeping of the *Sabbath-day* and puniſh-ment for tranſgreſſing of it be *both Moral,* how come they ſo far to preſume on the Day as to *change* it into another? In ſhort, why do they not obſerve *that Sabbath-day?* Whatever *Rea-ſons* they offer for this liberty, deſtroys the *Mo-rality* of the *Sabbath;* and if they believe they have ſufficient power to alter the Day without danger, then the puniſhment it ſelf ceaſes of courſe; and either the *Law* is not in force, or themſelves are expoſed to the Penalty for tranſ-greſſing it in ſuch a groſs manner, as the *altera-tion* of the Day amounts to, and is a piece of

---

(12) Exod. xxxv. 2.   (13) Numb. xv. 36.

Boldneſs ſomewhat more unaccountable, than what they are guilty of who by ſome little ir-reverence do not keep it ſo religiouſly as they ought.

But without taking this advantage againſt ſome few indiſcreetly zealous on this Subject, Let us examine the *principle* and ground they *all* go upon concerning the Obligation of the Day, and conſider whether in truth the *Sabbath* be *Moral,* or the *Law ſuch,* which is brought for an Argument to prove it ſo. The notion of a *Moral Law,* which with reſpect to the way of having ſuch Principles convey'd to us, is alſo called *Natural,* I take to be this.

B. Pray give me leave to interrupt you. You make the *Moral Law* and the *Law of Na-ture* the ſame. And if ſo, what occaſion was there for God ſo ſolemnly to divulge thoſe Doctrines which by the light of Nature were known before ?

A. It was to ſhow by this new Publication, that he was the Author of thoſe 1*ſt.* Notions implanted in the Soul, and that *Nature* was no-thing but *himſelf* under another Name. And 2*dly,* (14) Becauſe after the fall of *Adam,* ſo great a darkneſs had invaded the Underſtand-ing of Man, that it very much obſcured the Knowledge of *Natural Laws,* and rendred the Aſſent more difficult, becauſe of the oppoſition in the inferiour Faculties continually made a-gainſt it, it pleas'd God in this formality to diſpel thoſe Clouds, and renew the impreſſion of all thoſe Laws, and make 'em more regarded than in that degeneracy they had otherwiſe been. As alſo to let 'em commence more *certain Rules*

---

(14) Bucan. Inſtit. Theolog. de Lege Loc. 19. ç. 11.

for the future to frame their Behaviour by. But notwithſtanding this *promulgation*, they do not ceaſe to be, nor are they *leſs the Laws of Nature* inſpired into the Soul from the very beginning, yet this Solemnity from Mount *Sinai* reſtores and improves them; and it is to let the World know that under what Name ſoever they place 'em, they are to be held Divine.

B. I am ſatisfied, be pleas'd to go on.

A. The notion of ſuch a *Law* then, I take to be this. That the *Matter* of it is diſcovered by the light of *Reaſon*; That it is *always* binding, *Univerſally own'd*, and there is no exception or *excuſe* for not obſerving it. The *Subject* of it is *good* or *evil* in it ſelf without the impreſſion of any *poſitive Precept* whether Divine or Humane; and the *one* Law and the *other*, differ in this; That the *poſitive* Law proceeds from the *Reaſon* and *Will* of our Governors, and the *matter* of it is *good*, becauſe *commanded*, or *evil* becauſe *forbidden*; whereas the *Moral* Law depends on *natural impreſſions*, and was not made for *certain Times, Places* or *Perſons*; but *was* and *is* to be for *ever*; and is not *good* or *bad*, becauſe made ſo by any *after-Law*, but *before* any ſuch *Law* was made, 'twas ſo by *Nature*. As for Example, *To worſhip God*; *To forbear taking his Name in vain*; *To honour Father and Mother*; *Nor to Kill, Steal, commit Adultery, bear Falſe Witneſs, Covet*, &c. Theſe were *Duties* well known *before* the Revelation of Scripture, or *before* there was any *Law* to mention or inforce 'em. And tho' we Read, that Men did ſometimes worſhip Idols and Images, yet that this was contrary to the better Reaſon of the Heathen-World, we have in the Confeſſions of *Thales, Pythagoras, Socrates, Chryſippus*

Chryſippus and others who laught at the folly of
their Countrymen in that kind of Service, tho'
they had in thoſe days the *Roman* Refuge ; That
they did not adore the *Image* it ſelf, but *this* or
that God lodged in it. Now becauſe theſe and
the like Doctrines were (15) generally received all over the Earth without any other A-
poſtle or Teacher, than barely their own Underſtanding, therefore *ſuch Laws* as theſe are
called *Natural* and *Moral,* and they are in *all
Places* and at *all Times* obliging.

· But the *Law* concerning the *Sabbath* is not ſo ;
that is, It is not underſtood *neceſſary* by the
light of *Nature,* that every *Seventh Day,* or e-
very· *Saturday* muſt be Dedicated · to the· Worſhip of God, rather than any other. For *ſeveral, Nations* had their *ſeveral Days,* and ſet-
Times : for Devotion, ſome *one Day,* and ſome
another, according to the appointment of their
Superiours whether Religious or Civil. (16)
The *Greeks* and *Romans* obſerved the *Eighth* or
Ninth ; The *Mexicans* the *Thirteenth* ; and the
Seventh or *Sabbath* was ſo appropriated to the
Jews, that either by way of *Proverb* or *Sarcaſm*
they were called (17) *Seventh-day-Men,* as a
note of diſtinction to make 'em known from ·

---

(15) *Jus naturale eſt illud quod ex ipſius naturæ inſtitu-
tione provenit, & hoc eſt omnibus commune.* Alphon. de **Caſtro**
de leg.——The *Rabbins* call theſe Laws *Præcepta intelle-
ctiva & manifeſtiſſima apud omnes gentes.* Παν]αχῦ τὴν
αὐτὼ ἔχει δύναμιν, Ariſt. Ethic. It is Κοινὸς νόμ☉ κ̓
ἄνιχη]☉. *Jus naturale eſt commune omnium nationum*——
Iſidore & Gratian. *Vid.* Pet. Gelat. de Arcan. Cath. Ver.
l. 11. c. 10. Lact. de ver. Sap. l. 4. c. 2. Chryſoſt. ad
Pop. Antioch. (16) *Satis liquet dierum ſive* 9. *ſive* 8.
non ſeptim. periodi uſum fuiſſe veteribus Romanis. Selden de
jure Nat. (17) *Septimi viri, Sabbatarij Quaſi à connotato
proprio,* Abulenſ. in Exod.

other

other People; and their Worſhip (18) *Septi-ma Sacra,* as *peculiar* to that Nation, and which the *Chaldeans* derided them for, † *they mocked at their Sabbaths,* or they ſcoffed at their reli-gious obſervation of the *Seventh-day,* as many (19) other Heathen Writers did; among whom (20) *Seneca* wondred that *they could ſpend the ſe-venth part of their time in idleneſs, and doing no-thing,* as he thought; Which ſhows that appoint-ments of this nature are of *poſitive* Religion; and tho' the *Worſhip* it ſelf is *Moral,* the *Time* is *not,* nor was ever look'd on as ſuch by the ſeveral Countries of the World, which yet had all of 'em their *ſet,* tho' *different Days* and *Hours* for their publick devotions. So that we may well look upon the *Inſtitution, Rule* and *Reaſon* of the *Sabbath* to be purely from the *Authority* of *Scripture.* *There* it had its *riſe* and *force;* *There* 'tis made a *Day* for holy per-formances; *There* 'tis a *ſign* between God and his People the *Jews,* a *peculiar ſign* to them, not heard or minded by *others* unleſs on their account; and as it is ſuppoſed, not obſerved by the *Patriarchs* themſelves before the Age of *Moſes.* And therefore it muſt follow, that the *Law* of the *Sabbath,* being only *poſitive,* and conſequently *temporary* (as moſt of the Laws of *Moſes* were) it might be ſafely laid aſide with all other *Types* when the *fulneſs of time was come:* No Law of his being to be accounted *perpetual,* but what is in it ſelf *ſimply Moral.* But tho' we deal with this Feaſt as a *Figure* of

---

(18) Ovid de Arte Amandi. (†) Lament. 1. 7.
(19) *Septima quæque Lux ignava fuit.* Juvenal. Satyr. 14.
(20) Auguſtin. de Civ. Dei. l. 6, c. 11.

something to come, (21) and thereupon to cease in the presence of *Chriftianity* of which it was the *Type,* yet we have still a refpectful Eye to the *Fourth* Commandment: And notwithstanding the *repeal* of the *Ceremonial* and *positive* part of the *Day,* we retain it hitherto in its *natural Equity.* Becaufe we do and muft think it highly *reasonable* to *consecrate* or set apart *some Days* for God's Service, that so he may be prevail'd on to affift and bless us in all our honeft undertakings on the reft alotted for our selves, and wherein we confult our prefent necessities. This is *naturally juft* and needful, and has been thought so all over the Earth, tho' particular Nations have varied, as you heard, in the time, according to their own conveniency and difcretion. And we do also confider it very fit to appoint *one Day of Seven* for this Service; not out of any Superftitious conceit of that *Climacterical* Number, but in conformity to the blessed *Example* of God himfelf who *refted* on such a Day. *This Day* therefore we judge *convenient,* tho' not so *neceffary,* as to admit no *alteration.* For that God, on this Day, refted from all his Labours, we have it by *special Revelation,* and difcovered but to a *few* of the World, and on that account cannot be reputed *moral* and *unchangeable,* becaufe not *universally* received and known. 'Tis true, it carried a great Authority with it as to the People of the *Jews,* to whom it was made a Reafon, why *they* fhould reft the *Seventh-day* from their Works, becaufe on a *Seventh-day* God refted

---

(21.) Ελθόντ⊕ δε τε διδασκάλε κατηργήθη ὁ Πηδαίζων⊕, χ ηλίε ανατείλαντ⊕ ὁ λύχν⊕ επανσα]ε. Athan. de fem. Urfin Car. de Sab.

from

from *His.* But tho' it was a Reason in the Commandment, the *Reason* was not so necessary, as *Obedience* to the Commandment was, because if so, how came it about that it made so little impression on the *Fathers* before the Law, who could not be strangers to the account of the Creation, yet did not hold themselves obliged (as we can learn) to the *Seventh-day,* 'tho without doubt they were by the Law of Nature bound to some *certain Times* for holy Performances. And if this reason did not sway the *Jews* but with respect to the *Precept* which contains it, and *his* Authority who made it a *Law,* much less can it be said to affect us either with respect to the *Day* it self, or the *Weekly* return of it. And yet we do accept it rather than the *8th,* *9th* or *10th,* because we have in holy Writ the example of God who finished the Creation at the end of the Sixth-day, and *rested the Seventh-day,* and by that rest *sanctified* and blest it.

This will help to explain *our Churches* practice in still reading the *Fourth* Commandment, and making it a part of our *Weekly Office.* She considers it in its *Natural Justice,* and thereby puts us in mind, how *decent* and *righteous* it is to alott *Days* for the Worship of God, and particularly *One in Seven,* yet without any regard to the *Jewish* Oeconomy, but having an Eye to the common reason both to them and us ; *viz.* the Example of the Creator, who on the *Seventh-day* rested from all his Labours. And in this sence it is, that the reading of the Precept is as requisite on *other Holidays,* as on the *Lordsday* it self, To remember us on all occasions when Service is performed, that we ought to allow and observe *such Times,* and not be so intent on our ordinary Business as to forget our

great

great Work which concerns our Soul, and the Maker's honour. A thing we are too often guilty of, and therefore stand in need of frequent *Memento*'s to keep us within compass.

And this peradventure was the reason why God was pleased to place *this Precept* among the Commandments absolutely *moral* (tho' it self be not so,) because of the hard hearts of the *Jews* who were a stubborn disobedient People, and with great difficulty to be brought from *Earthly* Things to *Divine*; and therefore this Commandment was often repeated to 'em, and the transgression of it punished with the greater severity, that they might be sure to do him that homage which otherwise had been neglected: And by that Emphasis *remember* which ushers in the Law, impresse such a Character of it in their Hearts, as *Nature* had done of the other *Nine*. And in reality the loudness of the caution [*Remember the Sabbath-day,*] doth not a little insinuate, that *this* Precept had not naturally the same force and dignity with the *others*. However that for a time it might be so to them, it was Prefaced with a *remember*, &c. and had the same Sanction or Penalty to support it, as *those* against *Murther*, *Theft*, *Adultery* and *Atheism*.

And if this were not the meaning of that Commandment under Christianity, and that it binds us in the *Equity* only and not in the *Letter*, it had been very dangerous for our Forefathers and for us to *alter* the *Sabbath-day*. And equally perilous would it be to *ride* on Horse-back or in a Coach, *dress Meat*, or do many other things which undoubtedly we have liberty now to do without the breach of our *Sabbath*. And this we owe to our Gracious Redeemer who is the
Lord

Lord of the Sabbath, the *body* and *substance* of all those legal *Ceremonies* which at his coming were to vanish away. Yet tho' we annul those Observances as to the intolerable burden of 'em, we still continue their *moral*; and because it is our duty to adore God, we accept the *equitable* part of the *Sabbath* to do this Duty in. And that we may discharge our selves the better in this great Affair, as soon as we hear the Commandment read, there immediately follows this short Petition, *Lord, have mercy on us, and incline our hearts to keep this Law*---to keep it, not *literally* with the *Jew*, but in that common *Equity* which reaches us and all Nations whatever. And in more words our meaning runs thus, (22) That God would be pleased at these *set Times* dedicated to him, to send his grace into our hearts to over-rule and soften 'em, that while we pretend to worship him, we do it as we ought; and as at *all times*, so more especially in *these*, behave our selves holy and blameless before him.

And as it is of ordinary Justice, and by the instinct of Natural Religion, that God should have some *Stated-times* for his Glory and Service; And as *One Day in Seven* was pitch'd on, partly in veneration to God's Example, and partly to let the *Jews* and the World see, that our *Christianity* has not impaired the Divine Worship: So, tho' we change the *Numerical Day* observed by the *Jews* as a testimony of our Liberty, we have made the *first Day of the Week* the eminent Day to express our acknowledgements in, because on *this Day* fell out a remarkable Blessing, which the *Sabbath* of the *Jews,*

---

(22) Bishop *Sanderson's* Cafe of the Sabbath.

and *their Deliverance* out of Egyptian Bondage
was the *Emblem* of, I mean our *Redemption* by
Chriſt, who, to prove the Victory he had got
over *Death* and *Sin*, return'd *this Day* from the
Grave.

That *ſuch Deliverance* was the occaſion of
their Sabbath, is clear from *Deut.* c. v. 15. And
therefore the ſubſtituting of this Holy-day, as it
juſtifies our Change upon a ſtronger Motive
than what the *Jews* had to keep it, ſo it ſhows
we could not aſſign a more proper Day of the
Week to glorifie God in, who has been more
gracious to us than he had been to thoſe before
us. Well then might *that Day* which remembred only a *Civil Ranſom*, reſign all its *Sanctity*
and Solemnity to *this other* whereon our *Lord and
Saviour* aroſe from the Dead, and by that *riſing*
wrought a more excellent, an *Eternal Redemption* for us. So that you ſee from what has been
ſaid, how proper the diſtinction is which your
Miniſter uſed. For as the *Fourth Commandment* is not altogether *Ceremonial* on the one
ſide, ſo neither on the other ſide is it *wholly Moral*; but there being in it (23) a *mixture* of
both, we partly retain and partly explode it.
The *Moral* of it continues, and will continue
for ever, becauſe to worſhip God is of the
Law of Nature; and if God had never required it in the other Law, we muſt have done
him Service at ſome certain times, becauſe reaſon will have it ſo. But for the *Seventh-day*
which the *Jews* obſerved, and the other Circumſtances that make up the Commandment,
theſe we lay by as *poſitive Points*, which oblige
no longer than the Law-giver deſign'd they
ſhould, and that was until Chriſt's coming;

---

(23). Aqui. 22. de Qu. 122. Art. 4. *ad* 1.

H   and

and to keep 'em now, is much the same as to say
He is not come. Yet as a thing of *Choice* we
have a *Seventh-day*, and we make it the *Day* of
our meeting in publick to make solemn Profeſ-
ſion of our Religion. But this we do without
conſulting the *Jews*, or conſidering it a *Sign* between *God* and *them*, but reſpect it as the *Day of
Chriſt's Reſurrection*, which happening on that
Seventh-day we now keep, we do and ſhall ever
obſerve it as the *memorial* of that Bleſſing.

B. Your Diſcourſe much agrees with what
the Miniſter ſaid. But pray give me leave to
except againſt ſome particulars; as when you
ſay, the *Patriarchs* before *Moſes* did not obſerve
the *Sabbath*, and the *Seventh-day* was ſo peculiar to the *Jews*, that no Nation elſe regarded
and hardly knew it. Somewhat to this purpoſe the Preacher affirmed, which made me
next Morning to examine ſome few Authors
which my Common-place Book directed me to,
to ſee what account they could give of the
Queſtion about theſe two Points; Becauſe if true,
That neither the *Fathers* between the *Creation*
and *Moſes*, nor the *Gentiles* took notice of the
Seventh-day Feſtival, this would much weaken
the *Morality* of the *Sabbath*, and make us no o-
therwiſe receive it than a bare *Law of Moſes*,
which with his other Ordinances Religious or
Civil, were upon the Coming of Chriſt to be
done away; but inquiring into the Matter I do
not find it ſo.

And *firſt* for the Patriarchs,

(24) *Tertullian* then repreſents it a current
Doctrine among the *Jews*, that *God from the
beginning* ſanctified the *Seventh-day* by reſting
from his Works. And thence it was that *Mo-*

_____

(24) Adv. Jud.

ſes

fes said unto the People *Remember the Sabbath-day to keep it holy.* Again, (25) *Chrift* faith he, *then fulfilled the Law, when the Sabbath, which his Father made holy by his blessing, he made more holy by his own.* —So that in both places *Tertullian* allows the Day to be no fooner made, than that it was fanctified or fequeftred to an holy purpofe. *Auguftin* faith the fame thing, as a Tenet among the *Jews*; and in a Letter to *Cafulanus*, avouches it as his own Opinion, that as God refted the *Seventh-day* from all his works, fo he commanded the *Hebrews* to take care to obferve it. That the *Jews* own it fo appears from *R. Juda* and *R. Solomon Jarchi*, who cite *Simpfon*, *Aben Ezra*, *D. Kimchi*, *Manaffeh-ben-Ifrael*, and more of the like Authorities. And we may obferve in the *Chaldee Paraphrafe* or *Targum of Jonathan*, who is fuppofed to live about half a *Century* before Chrift, that they carried the Tradition as high as *Adam*; for on the 1*ft* Chapter of the Book of *Canticles* there is mention of *Adam*'s finging a Pfalm on the *Sabbath*, And the Title of the 92*d* Pfalm is, *a Pfalm or Song which Adam faid on the Sabbath-day*; or (as Dr. *Lightfoot* faith) *which he made for the Sabbath.* *Philo* and *Jofephus* both fubfcribe to this, For the (26) *former* faith, *the Sabbath had a Privilege by Nature from the very time the World began*; *and therefore Mofes thought it reafonable that all his People following the Law of Nature fhould celebrate this Day*---meaning by *the Law of Nature*, the *early inftitution* of it, which was as old as *Nature* her felf. And as for *Jofephus*, he tells us, that God having refted from all his works on the *Seventh-day*, *on that account the Jews kept the Day by a ceffation of all Bufinefs*,

---

(25) **Adv. Marcion.** (26) *De vit. Mofis.*

and called it the Sabbath. (27) *Theophilus An-tiochenus* faith, that *God on the* 7th *Day finished all the works that he had made, and thereupon blest and sanctified it*--And adds, that the *Seventh-day was famous among all People, the Hebrews calling it Sabbath, and the Greeks the Seventh-day, because they were not acquainted with the reason of the Name,* i. e. the reſt of *God on that Day, which occasion'd him to pronounce it holy.* (28) *Cyprian* confeſſes that the number *Seven* was made Sacred by the order obſerved in Creating the World, *because in fix Days he did all his works, and the seventh he dedicated to reſt, as a Day holy in it self, and making other things holy, honour'd by a ceſſation from all buſineſs, and aſſign'd to the B. Spirit, the Sanctifier.* (29) Of the ſame mind is *Lactantius, That God finiſh'd this admirable work of Nature in the ſpace of 6 Days, and the 7th whereon he reſted, he decreed it holy, and this is the Sabbath.* (30) *Athanasius* ſaith, *That when God had perfected the firſt Creation he gave himself to reſt, and on this reaſon the Men of that Generation kept the Sabbath or* 7th *Day :* By which word [*Generation*] he intends all that ſpace of time from the *Creation* to *Chriſt,* and during all that time they kept the *Sabbath. Behold,* (31) ſaith Greg. Nyſſene, *a Sabbath bleſſed from the infancy of the World. By that Sabbath take an eſtimate of this ; a Day of reſt which God hath bleſſed above all other Days whatever. God bleſſed and ſanctified that Day,* (32) ſaith Chryſoſtom *what means that word* [Sanctified] *why, it diſtinguiſhes it from other Days.* And then ſubjoining the reaſon, *He did this to the Seventh-day, because on it he reſted from his*

---

(27) Ad Autolychum. (28) De Sp. Sancto. (29) De div. Præm. l. 7. c. 14. (30) De Sab. & Circ. (31) De Reſur. Chriſti. (32) Homil. 10. in Geneſ.

works ;

works ; *infinuating this Doctrine from the very be-*
ginning, that in the compafs of a Week we fhould
fet a-part one whole Day, and fpend it in Religion.
Inftead of making the Seventh-day remarkable by
any inftance of Creation, he made it moft remark-
able by beftowing his bleffing on it, faith (33) *Theo-*
doret, that it might not be the only Day without
fpecial honour ; and 'tis faid he did not barely
diftinguifh, but *fanctifie* it--And adds, *In bleffing*
the 7th Day in that manner, he fhow'd it was not
to be thought a vain and unprofitable Day, for
by his own appointment it was accommodated to
reft. And then asking the Queftion, (34) why
God did not command the *Sabbath* to be kept
as well on fome other day ? he anfwers, *Be-*
caufe the God of all things Created the Univerfe
in 6 Days, but did nothing on the 7th, and there-
fore dignified it with a fpecial benediction; as it is
recorded, in fix Days the Lord made Heaven and
Earth, and refted the 7th Day, &c. And *Celfus*
demanding Whether God was weary that he
needed reft, (35) *Origen* replies, that *God refted*
to the intent, that We refting from our works fhould
celebrate that Day. By all which it doth appear, that *from the very Creation* this *Day* was
fet a-part for *Reft* and *Holinefs* ; both from Gods
Example, and his *folemn Act* of *Bleffing* it. And
to this *Alexander Hales* and other School-Men
fubfcribe ; and *A Lapide* among the Jefuits,
with an infinite number of Authors of all Perfwafions, both Foreigners and Englifh, who
conclude as I do, *That the Sabbath was obferved*
before the times of Mofes. And among thefe,
that Remark of *Zanchy* is not to be omitted :
(36) *The word* Remember, *faith he, points back-*

---

(33) Quæft. in Exod. (34) Qu. in Gen. (35) l. 6.
(36) In quart. Præcept.

wards

wards to the *Generations foregoing*, and *puts them
in mind,* that *this Precept sets forth no new Duty,
but what was observed ever since the making of the
World.* So that tho' *Moses* put it into the Body
of his Laws, and made the observation of it
very rigorous; and the neglect more severely
punishable than in former Ages, yet still it was
kept by the *Patriarchs* and others from the very
beginning ; which overthrows the notion of that
low date, some are apt to give it, to strengthen
the Argument against its *morality.*

Then as to the *Second* Thing, the *Gentiles.*

That the *Seventh-day* was neglected by 'em,
is so far from being true, that they not only
knew, but own'd and *celebrated* it, as we find in
their own Writings, wherein they mention and
speak honourably of it. This (37) *Homer*
doth, and *Hesiod* and *Callimachus,* as we may
see in their Verses, in which they call it an *Holiday,* a *perfect day,* and *whereon all things were
made :* so exactly correspondent to the Character we have of it in the Book of Sacred Scripture. And not only the *Poets,* but (38) *Clemens* of *Alexandria* informs us, that *Solon* had a
great veneration for it. And hence probably
arose that conceit of the *Pythagoreans* about the
number *Seven* which they stiled the *Virgin, holy
and venerable, most agreeable to God and things*

---

(37) Ἑβδομάτη δ᾽ ἤπεια κατήλυθεν ἱερὸν ἦμαρ·

Ἕβδομον ἦμαρ ἔην κỳ τῷ τετέλεσο ἅπαντα.

Ἑβδέμη ἦν ἱερή.

Ἑβδομάτη δ᾽ ἠοῖ λέπομεν ῥόον ἐξ Ἀχέροντ⊙.

— Καὶ ἕβδομον ἱερὸν ἦμαρ.

Ἑβδομάτη δ᾽ αὖθις λαμπρὸν φα⊙ ἠελίοιο.

Ἑβδόμη ἐιν ἀγαθοῖσι κỳ ἑβδόμη ἐςι γҡνέθλη.

Ἑβδόμη ἐν πρώτοισι κỳ ἑβδόμη ἐςι τελείη.

Ἑβδομάτηδὴ ἧ τετελεσμένα πάντα τέτυκ]αι.

Ἑβδομάτη δ᾽ ἠοῖ τετύκοντα ἅπαν]α.

(38) Stromat, l. 5.

Divine ;

Divine ; upon which account the *Greek* word ἐπ]ὰς, was by the Ancients called σεπ]ὰς [ὑπὸ τῶ σιβασμῶ,] from *Worſhip* ; the *Seventh* being the *Day* whereon God is more ſolemnly adored ; for ſo the aſpirate, as *Priſcian* obſerves, is very frequently turned into σ or *s,* of which we might afford you many Examples. We further read what *Lampridius* ſaith of *Alexander Severus,* That *on the* 7th *Day he reſorted to the Temple,* as looking on it without doubt a very ſolemn time dedicated to Religion. So that upon the whole, it was not very bold in (39) *Joſephus* to aſſert, *That there were no Nations, Greek or Barbarous, but what reſpected this Day* ; which jumps with what *Philo* ſaith, who calls it ᾿Εοϛὴν πάνδημον, the *general Feſtival* of the World ; Holy to the *Greeks* as well as *Hebrews,* as *Clemens* ſpeaks, (40) and which all Mankind Celebrate with Decency and Honour. And *Philoponus,* by way of reaſon for this univerſal conſent, adds, *That all agree in this, That the conſtant revolution of ſeven Days conſtitutes all time :* And if the *Greeks* aſſign'd theſe Days to the Seven Planets, it was becauſe they knew not the real occaſion of that number ſet down by *Moſes* concerning Gods working on the *Six* and reſting on the *Seventh-day* ; which had they underſtood, the conſent might have been greater between the *Jews* and them. Thus far I go ; but thoſe who are better read may offer more Authorities of this kind, to prove, That both the *Patriarchs* and *Gentiles* had the knowledge of *this Feſtival,* which is what you and the Preacher ſeem to deny. If I am under any miſtake, as to the ſence of what I produced, pray ſet me right, and to that end I ſhall now deſire your anſwer.

---

(39) Adv. Apion. (40) Steuchius in Gen.

A. To

A. To deal roundly and sincerely with you, I muſt ſay, that the *Teſtimonies* you name, have not, to my thinking, that ſtrength you ſuppoſe, to convince me or any body elſe, That the *Patriarchs* or *Heathens* had any reſpect for the *Sabbath-day.* And 1ſt. For the *Patriarchs* and thoſe *Authors* you produce to make it credible that the Ancients before *Moſes,* knew and obſerv'd it. They ſay, That *on the Seventh Day God ended his work, and reſted the Seventh Day from all his works which he made; and God bleſſed the Seventh Day and ſanctified it, becauſe that in it he had reſted from all his work which God created and made.*——No body denies this, becauſe *Moſes* ſaith it, *Gen.* ii. 2, 3. But what is this to the *Patriarchs* before *Moſes?* what Scripture elder than the Law, gives us any account of that matter? - and where were the Fathers commanded to keep the Day, and does any one Text ſay they kept it? (41) *Zanchius,* one of your Witneſſes, confeſſes, that tho' *he will not go about to contradict the Opinion, yet it cannot be eaſily proved out of the Sacred Writings.* And ſo *Hoſpinian,* a diligent Searcher into the Antiquity and Reaſon of all *Feſtivals,* declares, that the *Patriarchs obſerving the Sabbath, is not to be made good by the word of God*---and that ſurely ought to be done to give it the credit of a *Conſtitution.*

But what if in reality, there was no ſuch *diſtinction of Days* at the Creation, tho' *Moſes* makes it to comply with the capacities of the People, and inable 'em to diſtinguiſh into parts, what *Siracides* teſtifies was done at (42) *Once. He that liveth for ever Created all things together.* It was *Moſes's* uſual way to ſpeak of things,

---

(41) In quart. Præcept. ——— (42) *Simul.* Vulg. Lat. Ecclu. 16. 1.

[*more*]

[*more humano,*] not as they *really* are, but as, the *Vulgar* underſtand 'em; as when he calls the *Moon* one of the *two great Lights*, becauſe ſhe ſeems to an ordinary Eye bigger than the other Stars, which yet in bulk and compaſs far exceed her. And ſo God is ſaid to *reſt*, which is a word applicable only to *Men* and other *Animals*; who after they have labour'd *Six Days*, take the benefit of the *Seventh* to refreſh and eaſe themſelves. But it would be abſurd to imagine that any ſuch (43) wearineſs could touch God on the account of thoſe Works he did. Yet in this alluſion 'tis ſignificant enough; and God may be thought to *reſt*, when he only *forbears* doing what he was before *imploy'd* in. Beſides, it would reflect on the notion we ought to have of the infinite Wiſdom and Power of God, to think he needed ſo many Days to produce the works of Nature, when the firſt Chapter of *Geneſis* repreſents all done with a bare *fiat*, and *his willing* this or that thing to be done, was ſufficient of it ſelf to give it being. (44) *He ſpake the word and they were made, he commanded and they were created.* (45) Yet it was convenient for the H. Pen-man to deſcribe the Creation by theſe *diſtinctions and ſteps*, that we might better comprehend the *Order* of what his Almighty word did *in an inſtant*; becauſe otherwiſe had they been all ſet before us (46) *in common*, as the Son of *Sirach* ſpeaks, That which the Creator did in a few moments by a moſt compendious and exquiſite method, according to the Eternal *Ideas* in his mind, would to us have ſeem'd *confuſion*; neither had we ſo well

---

(43) *Nec cum creavit defeſſus, nec cum ceſſavit refectus.* Aug. in Gen. ad lit. (44) Pſ. 33. 9. & 148. 5. (45) *Plures dies numerantur propter plura rerum genera—* Aqui. (46) Ἐν κοινῇ πάντα.

known

known the dignity of the Creatures, and how the Maker was pleas'd to preferr the exiſtence of *one* before *another.*

The likelihood of this further ſhows it ſelf, from the deſcription given of the *three firſt days,* as well as of the reſt, *the evening and the morning were the firſt day,* &c. Whereas it is evident the *Sun* was not made 'till the *fourth day,* whoſe revolution and motion *divides Time,* and *makes Days and Years;* and when the *Sun ſets,* 'tis *Evening,* and when he *riſes* 'tis *Morning.* And ſo 'tis expreſly ſaid, that as ſoon as the *Sun, Moon, &c.* were Created, *God ſet 'em in the firmament of Heaven to give Light on the Earth, and to rule over the day and over the night, and to divide the light from darkneſs.* To ſay that God appointed a *bright Cloud,* or ſome *miraculous light* to ſhine in the Day, the *retiring* of which cauſed *Darkneſs;* Or, (47) as St. *Baſil* ſaith, that the *Days* and *Nights* proceeded from the *emiſſion* and *retraction* of Light, and not by the *motion* of the Heavenly Bodies, is very unſeaſonable, when we find he was ordering and ſetling the *courſe of Nature.* Or to conceit he made *one Light* the firſt Day, and a *better* on the fourth; Or that he contracted the *firſt Light* into the *Body of the Sun, Moon and Stars* and the like, is not this a *reflection* on his *Almighty* and *moſt wiſe* contrivance, to *undo* thus his *firſt Days work,* and render it *vain,* by *altering* or making it better?

I am not alone in this conjecture. For you heard before what *Siracides* ſaid. Whoſe (48) Book, tho' it be not of that Credit with us, as among other Churches abroad where it is ad-

---

(47) Tho. p. 1. q. 67. Art. 4. ad tertiam.
(48) Dr. *Reynolds.* cenſ. de lib. Apocr.

mitted

mitted into the *Canon* of Scripture, yet furely
it calls for as great veneration as any common
Authority, and deferves as much honour, if
not more than any Writing whatever, below
what is confeffedly Sacred, and dictated by the
B. Spirit. *He that liveth for ever hath Created
all things* [κοινῆ faith the Greek, *fimul* the Latin]
in common, in grofs, at once and altogether.
(49) So *Philo* the Learned Jew underftands that
place, and calls it *filly to think that the World
was made in the compafs of fix Days.* And St. *Auguftine,* a Man of excellent infight into the fence of
Scripture, is of the fame Opinion, and faith that
there was but *one time* (you may call it *Day*)
*wherein God produced the World, tho' it be re-
peated* (50) *fix or feven times to difcern the
works of the Creation,* and by thofe imaginary
intervals or fpaces to diftinguifh them the better. All which works being *finifhed,* God is
faid to *reft,* becaufe then he had nothing more
to do, but by his ordinary Providence to con-
ferve thofe Species to which he had given a
Being. And whereas it is often faid by *Mofes
the Evening and the Morning were the firft Day,
the fecond Day,* and fo on, his language is fuited to
the divifion of that time in which the Creation
was carried on, yet means no more (as that
Father conceives) than that the *Ending* of one
piece of his *Work* may be called (51) *Evening,*
and the *Beginning* of another *Morning,* which
being difpatched, produced as it were another
Evening, and fo a third till all the Creatures
were made. And becaufe nothing remain'd to

---

(49) 'Ευηθὲς πάνυ τὸ οἴεϑαι ἐξ ἡμέραις κόσμον γεγονέναι.
l. Alleg. (50) *In feptimo die,* i. e. *eodem fepties repetito.*
de Civ. Dei, l. xi. c. 31. *Significat omnia fimul fuiffe
creata,* faith *Ludovicus Vives* on that of St. *Aug.* Vid. Auguft.
in Gen. ad lit. l. 1. c. 7. (51) Aug. in Gen. l. 4. c. 8.

be done after the laſt Creature *Man*, therefore God *reſted* in that he went no *further.* (52) Or more myſteriouſly by *Morning and Evening* (which he applies to every work of the Creation) he underſtands the *two* ſorts of knowledge we have of things. The *One* in the *eſſence of God* wherein the *Angels* diſcover all *ideas* diſtinctly and clearly as by *Morning-light*, and thus we ſhall ſee hereafter when we arrive at their Condition ; The *other* more obſcurely, as in the *Evening*, from the *natures* of the things themſelves, which we get with more difficulty and labour, and after all our pains may be miſtaken, according to that of St. *Paul, now we ſee thro' a glaſs darkly* [or in a riddle] *but then face to face: now I know in part, but then I ſhall know even as alſo I am known.* Thus St. *Auguſtine*; and if he gueſſes right, it is no wonder that the Ages before *Moſes* give us not a word of Gods *ſix days work,* and his *reſting on the ſeventh day,* ſeeing the time alotted the Creation will not admit that diſtinction ; yet the Prophet uſed it, that by this means we might better diſcover, as I ſaid, how God digeſted all the Creatures which he produced in a moment by his irreſiſtible power.

But take the literal interpretation, which in duty to Scripture I adhere to, that God was pleas'd to allow himſelf *Days* for the doing of that which he could have done as well in a *moment*; yet how does it appear that God *reſted on the ſeventh Day?* (53) St. *Jerom* will have it, that the *Woman* was made on the *Seventh day* ; and for the probability of it, *Steuchius* tells us, that at the concluſion of the *Sixth day* the Crea-

_____

(52) *Vid.* Coquæum in Aug. de Civ. Dei. l. xi. c. 7, 9.
(53) Adv. Jud.

tures were brought unto *Adam* to be named; which was a work of no little time, and being at length wearied with it, he fell into a found *Sleep,* and on the *Seventh-day morning* God took out his *Rib* and formed it into a *Woman.* And if fo, the (54) *whole Seventh day* was not fpent in *reft*; nor indeed doth the Text affirm it, becaufe in faying that God *finifhed* his work on that Day, it is implied, that *part* of the work was done on it; which the (55) Seventy Interpreters, with the *Syriac* and *Samaritan* Tranflators perceiving, they thought it the beft way to read it thus, *He ended his work on the fixth Day.* So that (56) St. *Jerom* obferving this difference between the *Greek* and the *Hebrew,* he faftens on it to expofe the rigorous *Sabbatizing* of the *Jews,* who pretended to reft in imitation of God, and yet God himfelf did not fo *ftrictly reft,* as to give them an Example to keep the *Sabbath* in that manner.

Yet granting this too, Gods reft could only be from the works of the *Creation* without any addition or increafe of new Species, yet his bufinefs of *Providence* ftill went on, and as (†) *Origen* fpeaks, we may fee God *every day* and *every Sabbath-day working, in making his Sun to fhine, and his rain to defcend upon us.* So that as (57) St. *Auguftine* tells the *Manichee,* the Jews needed not to have been affronted when *Chrift* told 'em *my Father hitherto worketh,* feeing he hath now as much care and labour upon him to

---

(54) *Dies tota non fuit quiete tranfacta, fed perfecto opere ejus deinceps quievit ut Hebræus contextus habet.* Steuch. in Gen. (55) Ἐν τῇ ἡμέρᾳ τῇ ἕκτῃ. *Et hoc eft unum de verbis quæ mutaverunt Sapientes Ptolemæo regi.* Galat. l. xi. c. 10. (56) Qu. Heb. in Gen. (†) Orig in Num. (57) Adv. Fauftum.

preferve the courfe of Nature, as it coft him at the firft to put it in motion.

But to proceed yet further; fuppofe God took up *fix Days* in making the Univerfe, and *refted the feventh,* and thereupon *bleft* and *fan-Etified it,* yet perhaps it is not fo eafie to fhow what date thefe words bear, and *when* the In-ftitution commences. 'Tis evident *Mofes* writ the Book of *Genefis,* as well as the *Decalogue* or two Tables of the Law ; and in *both places* he ufes the fame expreffion of *Gods refting and fan-Etifying the Seventh Day*; but it does not ap-pear how he had this account of what was done at the Creation, whether by *immediate revela-tion* of the Spirit at the very time he was pen-ning that Sacred Hiftory, or by *Tradition* from *Adam,* or fome other of the *Patriarchs* before him. If the *former,* and that the difcovery was firft made to him, then the Fathers are excufed for not putting in practice an *Inftitution* they knew nothing of, and which did not *begin* 'till they were laid in their graves. If the *latter,* that this account came by *Tradition,* does it not feem ftrange that *Mofes* who made the obferva-tion of the *Sabbath* into fo ftrict a Law, and in-ferted a reafon to ftrengthen it from the exam-ple of God who *refted, bleft and fanElified* it, fhould give no (58) footftep of this in all the Book of *Genefis,* wherein he prefents us with the occurrences of above 2000 years, and yet not one word of the *Sabbath.* Moft likely then it is, that there was no fuch thing known be-fore the times of *Mofes.* But if known, it made no figure, much lefs had it the force of a *Con-ftitution,* or became practicable till the *Jews* grew into a *Politick Body,* and had all forts of

---

(58) Curcellæus Inftit. l.iv.c. II.

Statutes

Statutes and *Ordinances Sacred* and *Civil* to guide
and govern them by; and then *this* among other
things commencing a *Law*, to make it; if poffible, more folemn and binding, there was fet
before 'em *the reft* of God, &c. that fo the *Divine Example*, as well as *Mofes's Authority*,
might influence them to celebrate *that* Day
which God himfelf was pleas'd to obferve as
foon as the Creation was over. And as foon as
they had all the inftances of Worfhip prefcrib'd
'em, then they had alfo *a Day* fet 'em to do that
Worfhip in, a Day originally fanctified by the
reft of God, and by a *Sacred Decree* that it fhould
be obferved by all his Servants when the *Time*
came wherein they appear'd a very great
Nation.

And until this time arrived, it is very obfervable from Scripture, that God gave 'em
very few Precepts, but left 'em for the moft
part to *Natural Religion*, and as their *Reafon* directed 'em. *Adam* had *one* only Commandment
about the *Tree*; *Noah Two*, *to forbear Murder*,
and to *eat no blood*; *Abraham Three*, *To leave
his Country*, *To walk before God* (but how is not
faid, unlefs in what the light of *Nature* fhow'd
him) and *To circumcife himfelf and his Family*:
And, for the *trial* of his Obedience, *To Sacrifice his Son*. As to all other things, he and they
were left to their own judgment, and they ferved God in fuch a manner as their underftan-
ing taught 'em. Thus we find *Cain and Abel*
Sacrificing, but no mention of the time, nor
any command of God to worfhip in fuch a way;
(59) yet Reafon fuggefted it as a proper inftance of gratitude and homage to their divine

---

(59) *Hoc ratio naturalis dictat ut de donis fuis honoretur inprimis ille qui dedit.* Rupert in Gen. & Burgenf.

Benefactor,

Benefactor, whereby they tender'd their *First-Fruits*, or some part of that Substance God had blest 'em with, and in that Act own their subjection to him after the example of *Tenants* who make Presents to their *Lords* to recognize and *own* their *Tenures*, and the dependance they have upon him. And being thus naturally taught, we find it the Doctrine and practice of all Ages, and in all Places; Accordingly *Porphyry* informs us out of *Hermippus*, that one of the Laws made for the *Athenians* by *Triptolemus* was *to Feast their Gods with Fruits*. And *Draco* puts this among his Laws, *to honour the Gods with First-Fruits*. And *Plutarch* saith, that many of the *Grecians* in their ancient Sacrifices did use Barley, *the First-Fruits being offered by the Citizens*. So *Horace* tells us, that *the ancient Husbandmen Sacrificed a Pork to Vesta, and Milk to Sylvanus*. And *Ovid*, that *They gave the First fruits of their Corn to Ceres*, and *Wine to Bacchus*; which was also done to the *Hours*, *Diana*, *Appollo*, &c. as we see in *Meursius*'s *Gr. Fer.* So that *Cain and Abel* did no more than what *Nature* directed all sorts of People; but that it was then done with little *Solemnity*, and perhaps without any *certain Rule*, partly appears from that of *Gen.* iv. 6. *then began Men to call upon the Name of the Lord*---or about that time, People began to *Pray*, saith the *Chaldee* Paraphrase, (60) *to Pray in common* or *by way of Congregation*; *publickly* and by *consent* doing that which *privately*, and *by Families*, in a *different manner* and on *different Days* was done before. But no news of the *Sabbath*, tho' here was a good Op-

---

(60) *Tunc cœptum est popularuer coli Deus.* Maria. *Invocare*—i. e. *Palam colere.* Eman. Sa. *Tunc cœptum publicè & per cœtus invocari.* A Lap. Publickly, and in a numerous Assembly. *Primeros in Sab. sic Perer. Junius,* &c.

portunity

portunity for *Moses* to speak of that *solemn Time*, as well as of a more *solemn Worship* Men then expreſſ for the honour of God, the Generality of the World before this, giving themſelves over to the adoration of the *Stars*, as the Hebrew Doctors report the ſtate of that Generation. And tho' in theſe days *Noah* is ſaid to be a zealous *Preacher of Righteouſneſs*, yet we have no account of *ſet times* for his Sermons, but he took any opportunity fairly offer'd him to Convert and Edifie thoſe who were to be improved by what he taught, without regard to any diſtinction of Days, as afterwards, of which in that Age there is a profound ſilence. And of him it is further to be noted, that he had no more than thoſe *ſeven Precepts* which we have by Tradition, and which the *Rabbins* do ſay were given by God, *firſt* to *Adam* and *then* to *Noah*, as, *That they ſhould worſhip one God, and abſtain from Idolatry ; That they ſhould not take God's Name in vain ; That they ſhould not kill, Nor ſteal, Nor admit inceſtuous Marriages ; that they ſhould not eat blood, and That they ſhould ordain Magiſtrates and Judges to puniſh ſuch Offenders* —— But as for *remember to keep holy the Sabbath*, not one tittle of it, notwithſtanding that in after Ages *Moſes* plac'd it within his two Tables ; yet it was not it ſeems worthy that *Patriarchs* notice, tho' it cannot be reaſonably expected that *He* or the *Rabbins* would have omitted it on ſuch an Occaſion, had there been ſo great a ſtreſs laid upon it, and that they were commanded to keep it holy. (61) On the contrary, *Maimonides* delivers himſelf thus. " The " Men and Women-Servants who are com- " manded to keep the Sabbath, are Servants

---

(61) **Maimon.** *de Sab.*

I

" that

" that are circumcifed; but Servants not cir-
" cumcifed nor baptized, but only fuch as
" have received the Seven Precepts given to
" the Sons of *Noah*, they are as fojourning
" Strangers, and may do works for themfelves
" openly upon the Sabbath. Where we fee
he diftinguifhes between the condition of Religion under *Noah* and *Mofes*; and tho' the *latter*
required the obfervation of the *Sabbath*, yet
thofe who followed the way of *Noah* were not
obliged to it, his Laws reaching no further
than the Particulars before-named; which inferrs, that *Noah* was a ftranger to the *Sabbath*,
or at leaft neglected it. Becaufe otherwife,
had it been an inftance of Religion, fo great
and neceffary, as fome would have it, the People muft have fhew'd refpect to *this* as well as
to the *reft* of his Ordinances, and had kept the
Sabbath whether *Circumcifed* or no.

B. 'Tis much indeed *Noah* fhould be fo very
filent in this Point; yet the obfervation of
(62) *Hofpinian*, touching what that Patriarch
did, is very material; and his fending out the
Dove on the *feventh-day*, was (as *He* and *Sim-
lerus* thinks) on the account of the *Sabbath*.

A. I muft confefs, (63) fome fuppofe from
hence, that *Noah* on *that Day* performed his
moft folemn Devotion to God with Prayers for
good news to be brought him concerning the a-
batement of the Flood. But certainly (64) *Toftatus*
better refolves it thus. That *Noah* by that
means was defirous to learn whether the *Waters*
decreafed: For *Water* being a moift Body, it is
influenced by the *Moon*, to whofe motion the

---

(62) *In Hiftoria Diluvij columbæ ex Arca emiffa Septe-
nario dierum intervallo ratione Sabbati videntur.* De Feft. Jud.
(63) Affembly in loc. (64) Abulenf. in Gen.

Patriarch

Patriarch had a fpecial regard at this time.
Becaufe, as She is either in *Oppofition* or *Conjunction* with the *Sun* in her *increafe* or *wane*, there is proportionably an *increafe* or *decreafe* of the Waters. So that *Noah* confidering the *Moon* in her feveral *Quarters*, which you know confifts of fo many *feven days*, he fent forth the *Dove* to bring him tidings, and this he did for four *times*; and the *4th* time the *Moon* being in her *laft Quarter*, when by the ordinary courfe of *Nature* the Waters ufually are, and by the will of God were then much abated; the *Dove* which was fent out had found footing on the Earth, and fo returned to the Ark no more—And this is all can be drawn from that paffage, which has more of *Philofophy* than (65) *Religion* in it.

B. You were fpeaking of *Cain and Abel.* It is faid of them, that *in procefs of time they brought their Offerings unto the Lord*, fo we render it, but in the Hebrew it is (66) *at the end of days*, which befpeaks a *fet time* for Sacrifice, and in all likelihood the *Sabbath*. For as by *Days* are meant the *Days of the Week*, fo the *end of thofe Days*, or the *laft of 'em* may well fignifie *that* which concludes the Week, I mean *the time* confecrated to the fervice of the *Creator*. And of this mind are the *Affembly of Divines*, who conceive the Phrafe intends the *Sabbath* as *a Day* fpecially *fanctified from the beginning*.

A. The words of thofe *Divines* are, " That " by *the end of Days may be meant the Sabbath—* but they deliver themfelves doubtfully, and therefore in the fame place confefs—" that

---

(65) *Quæ religio in ifta actione apparet? Nonne potuit illud facere refpectu curfus lunæ fingulis feptem diebus novam faciem nobis exhibentis, &c.* Curcellæ. de efu fang. c. 6.
(66) מֵקֵץ יָמִים, Gen. 4. 3.

" ufually

" *ufually the words are taken for a diftance of*
" *time of greater extent than the compafs of a*
" *Week, yet it might be a certa'n time by cuftom*
" *or conftitution; which now being compleat and*
" *run to a period, they both make their Oblations*
" *to God as followeth*—Wherein we are agreed,
that probably it might be fome *fet time ;* But
that it was the *Seventh-day,* or *every Seventh-
day* the expreffion does not prove it. The
(67) Tranflations of greateft figure render it,
after fome days. A Lapide, *after fome years ;*
(68) and St. *Ambrofe* inclines that way, and
on this account charges *Cain* with a double
fault; *one* that he was *fo long* before he came,
the other that he did not offer the *choiceft* of
his Flock. Becaufe that which recommends a
Sacrifice is, To offer what we fet a value on,
and to do it quickly and without hefitation.
Mr. *Ainfworth,* a Perfon of good infight into
Hebrew idioms, turns it *at the end of the Year,*
at which time it was cuftomary among many
Nations in moft folemn manner to Sacrifice
unto God, and give him thanks for bleffing
the *Fruits* which they had gather'd in. So
the Law of *Mofes* commanded ; and
thence was the [*Feftum Meffis,* or *Feftum Collecta,*] *the Harveft Feaft* among the
Jews ; an Order, as by this inftance appeareth, obferved by the Patriarchs from
the very beginning ; and the ufage at laft
prevail'd with the *Gentiles ;* the *Ancient Sacrifi-*

---

(67) The Targ. of *Onkelos,* the *Samaritan* and *Syriac*
fay *poft aliquot dies.* The *Arabick, cum aliquot dies pra-
teriiffent.* *Junius* and *Tremellius* referr to St. *Mark's* δι'
ημέρων, c. 21. The 70 μεθ' ημέρας. (68) L. 1. c. 7.
de Cain—

tes, (69) faith Ariſtotle, *and Aſſemblies to that end being after the gathering in of the Fruits.* For further confirmation of this, he ſhows us, that very frequently in Scripture, *Years* go by the name of *Days*, and a *full Year* is called *a Year of Days.* So that the ſence is, That at a *certain Time about the end of the Year*, *Cain and Abel*, according to the Inſtructions they had from their Father, brought their Offerings, as their acknowledgments of the Divine Good. neſs in bleſſing and increaſing their Flocks and Fruits. But to ſay that this was on the *Seventh-day* or *Sabbath*, tho' it were ſo, yet to be ſure this Text doth not much contribute to prove it, and therefore I wonder to find it inſiſted on.

Levit. 25. 29, 30.
1 Sam. 1. 20.
Exod. 34. 22.
Numb. 9. 22.
Amos 4. 4.
Deut. 14. 28.
Exod. 13. 10.
1 Sam. 1. 3.

B. I cannot deny but the word [*Days*] very often ſignifies *Years*, as ſoon as that way of computation by *Years* began; but I am per-ſwaded, that in the *Infancy* of the World they reckon'd only by *Weeks*, or a *ſeptenary* revolu-tion of Days according to the Rule God him-ſelf ſet 'em, *Gen.* 2. *on the ſeventh day God reſted*, &c. making thereby every *ſeventh day* a full *period.* So that as I ſaid before, *the end of days* might be well conſtrued into the Sabbath, or that *Holiday* which concluded the Week, and on which it is probable *Cain and Abel* made their Oblations. And according to this way of account, we find, that when *Jacob* took it ill, that after *ſeven years Service Laban* ſhould ſo im-poſe on him as to give him *Leah* inſtead of *Rachel*, *Laban* pacifies him with this Promiſe, that if he would be content to *fulfill Leah's*

_____

(69) Ethic. l. 6.

Week, or proceed to confummate the 1ſt Mar‑
riage by continuing the Wedding-feaſt, and
Bedding *Leah* for the term of a Seven-night ac‑
cording to cuſtom, that then he ſhould have
Rachel likewiſe ; conditionally that he ſerved
him *ſeven years* longer. *Fulfill her Week and we
will give thee this alſo. And Jacob did ſo, and
fulfilled her Week, and he gave him Rachel,* Gen.
xxix. 27.

A. If by *Week* you mean a conſtant *revolu‑
tion* and return of 7 *days,* which ended make
that period of time we call by this name, 'twill
be hard to ſhow, that the Patriarchs diſtin‑
guiſhed the year in that manner, but rather di‑
vided it by *Months* and *Days.* But if by *Week*
you underſtand the term of *ſeven days* as a pro‑
portion of time obſerved for the celebration of
Nuptials, we will not quarrel with you about a
word wherein Tranſlators *anticipate,* and
which they borrow from *after Ages* to repre‑
ſent the ſame number of days *our Week* conſiſts
of, tho' *then* among them there was no ſuch
notion. Plain it is that the cuſtom (70) of
the *Jews* called for *as many days* as make the
Week at preſent, to ſolemnize a Wedding in ;
and if a Man married a *Maid, ſeven* were ſpent
in Mirth and Feaſting, but if a *Widow three.*
And ſo by way of explanation the *Syriac* ſaith,
fulfill her Feaſt. But *Junius* and *Tremellius* more
fully, ſuffer the *ſeven days feaſt, now begun, to be ful‑
filled by accompanying Leah, and after that thou
ſhalt have her alſo whom thou deſireſt.* This is con‑
firmed by what *Sampſon* propoſed to his Bride-
Men ; *I will,* ſaith he, *put forth a Riddle to you, if
you can certainly declare it to me within the ſeven
days of the Feaſt,* Judg. xiv. 12. This was agree-

---

(70) *Maimonid.* Treat. of Wives. c. x. Sect. 12, 13.

able to the practice of all Nations; which at their *Marriages*, *Births* and *Burials* have set a-part *certain times* to express their *joy* or *grief* in, and that for a *longer* or *shorter* date as the *Occasion* and *Country* required. *Heretofore*, saith A Lapide, *Seven Days were alotted to consummate a Marriage, as now three*; yet the *Hebrew* saith no more than שָׁבֻעַ *Seven*; and upon the uncertainty of what that *Seven* signifies, whether. *Days* or *Years*, Interpreters differ. (71.) For *Josephus* affirms it to be *seven Years* between the two Marriages; *and when the other seven Years were expired he Married Rachel.* And if he be in the right, (who was a very Learned *Jew*, and well versed in the Language and Customs of his Country) then there is not in this Scripture the least shadow of a *Weekly* period, such as is meant in the Question. But I must own I dissent from *Josephus* in this Particular; and, (72) with St. *Augustine*, think it very unjust to put off *Jacob seven years* longer; and therefore *Laban* must be rather understood, that he would perswade his Son-in-Law to have patience only for *seven days* to finish the other Marriage, and then he should be sure to have her Sister. The Original indeed with the *Targum* of *Onkelos*, the *Samaritan* and *Arabick* Versions say no more than *fulfill the seven.* (73) But the Supplement of the Vulgar Latin is necessary, and it is rightly Englished *fulfill her Week.* Or after the (74) Greek, *compleat all her Sevenths*; *i. e.* every instance of the Marriage Solemnity, both as to *time* and *all things* else. This doubtless must be the sence of that

---

(71) Antiq. l. 1. c. 19.　　(72) Aug. in Gen. *Valde iniquum* Jacob *fallaciter deceptum,* &c.　　(73) *Imple hebdomadam dierum.*　　(74) Συντέλεσον ἐν τῇ ἑβδόμα ταύτης.

place,

place, as appears from the Story it felf, if we confider it. For *Jacob* abode with *Laban* 20 Years, as we read *Gen.* xxxi. 38, 41. at the 14*th* of which *Jofeph* was born, and before which time *Rachel* having been a good while Barren, and fo defpairing of Iffue, gave her Maid *Bilha* to her Husband, who had by her two Sons, before fhe her felf had any, as we fee *Ch.* 30. And therefore it muft follow that *Rachel* was Married before the *fecond feven years* after his Service was expired; which proves it to be no more than *a Week of days,* at the end of which *Jacob* Married *Rachel* like-wife. But how far does this operate to make good what you propofe? The *Hebrews* were wont to allow fometimes *feven,* fometimes *three* days for the celebration of a *Wedding;* Therefore the *Patriarchs* computed Time as we do, by *Septenaries* or *Weeks,* within the compafs of which they always obferved a *Sabbath.* We read in *Tully*'s Epiftles (before cited) the word *hebdomada,* which is the Tranflation of the He-brew *Seven,* and our Englifh *Week,* but no oft-ner than we find it here in the Book of *Genefis.* And we read moreover, that it was the way of the *Jews* to folemnize their *Marriages,* as alfo to *mourn* for *feven days* together: So there was a Cuftom among the *Romans,* at the death of their Friends, to meet in the Houfe of the De-ceafed for *feven days* before *Burial,* (75) to make great lamentations and outcries, to the end, that if the Party were not really dead, but only in a *Swoon* or deep *Sleep,* the noife might awake and recover him. Yet I think this Argument does not demonftrate any fuch *Weekly fupputation* among the ancient *Romans,*

(75) Ad conclamandum.

who reckon'd their *Years* by *Months*, and their *Months* by *Kalends*, *Nones* and *Ides*, as I before noted to you; and as to the reft, I leave you to apply it.

B. The Expreffion barely in it felf, and limited to this cuftom, may not commence an argument to fecure the Hypothefis; but confider'd as a *Comment* on the prime inftitution of the *Sabbath*, *when God refted and bleffed the Day*, this practice fuppofes the Inftitution obferved in thofe early Times; and probably the Patriarchs appointed fo many Days for their *Nuptials* on the fame Reafon the *Rabbins* give why *Circumcifion* was to be the 8th *Day* after the Birth of the Child, that fo *one Sabbath* might be fure to pafs over it, to fanctifie the Ceremony when they went about it. And in this fence I take that of *Job* (76) *There was a Day when the Sons of God came to prefent themfelves before the Lord.*--Again, (77) *There was a Day, &c.* Which evidently fhows that the Patriarchs had their *ftated Days* for Religious Worfhip. For this *Job* lived fome Generations before *Abraham*, and is look'd upon to be that (78) *Jobab* in *Genefis* who was the *fixth from Noah*. And in great likelihood thofe Days were *Weekly*, according to *Laban's* Language, and the Divine Leffon which God taught *Adam*, and *Adam's* Pofterity. " *And to be fure, had the 2d Meeting* " *of the Sons of God in this Book been at a greater* " *diftance than a Week from the firft, Satan had* " *loft all his patience; and thereupon had addrefs'd* " *God to inlarge his Commiffion, and lengthen his* " *Chain.*

---

(76) Job i. 6. (77) Job ii. 1. (78) *Septimum diem volunt aliqui Jobum Sacrificiis celebraffe.* Aben-Ezra. *Vid.* Gen. Chron.

A. The

A. The *Prolapſarian Doctrine* doth more fully
explain what you call the *prime Inſtitution* and
Original of the Sabbath, than thoſe practical
Comments you uſe to confirm it.   And in that
way of reſolution, there is no more abſurdity
in this than (79) in other Examples, and
particularly in that aſſertion which makes *Chriſt
the Lamb of God ſlain from the foundation of the
World.* For tho' he was not actually Sacrificed
'till the *fulneſs of time was come* under *Pontius
Pilate* the Roman Deputy ;   yet we give his
Sufferings an earlier date, (80) *and Michael the
Arch-Angel is ſaid to overcome the Dragon by the
blood of the Lamb,* becauſe it was virtually ſhed,
and he ſlain in the Eternal purpoſe of his Father. " *For when things are once put into a*
" *Divine Promiſe they are ſaid to be, becauſe*
" *tho' they do not attain to actual exiſtence 'till*
" *long after, yet the Promiſe gives 'em a real*
" *Being, a metaphyſical Eſſence, as a Roſe in*
" *Winter.* God *bleſſed* and *ſanctified this Day ;*
True, no Man gainſays it, becauſe we find it
ſo in *Geneſis,* a Book written by *Moſes,* who
was inſpired to pen it.   But how ſhall I be
aſſured that this diſcovery of God's ſanctifying
the Day was not made by the Holy Ghoſt to
that Prophet? To ſay, God taught it *Adam*
begs the Queſtion. For how do we come to
learn this Secret, when we have not one Syllable concerning the *Sabbath,* or the obſervation
of it 'till the *days of Moſes.* Yes, *Laban* has his
Week, and *Job* his ſolemn Days of Devotion.
I take this to be dealing with Scripture, as *Chy-
miſts* do with ſome ſorts of Bodies, which they
torture and ſqueeze, to extract Eſſences or Spi-

(79) *Vid.* Exod. xvi. 32. *in eo loco commemorat quod
poſtea factum eſt,* Aug.   (80) Rev. xii. 11.

rits

rits which were never in 'em: The Interpreters are not few who take pains to veil the cleareſt light ; and if the Text ſhould be hard in it ſelf, they make it ten times harder. But to come to this paſſage concerning *Job* ; wherein there are ſo many perplexities about his *Perſon, Condition,* and *Age* he lived in ; as alſo *what* is meant by the *Sons of God,* and *how* and *when they preſented themſelves before the Lord,* that we have little incouragement to draw any concluſion from him or thoſe words you quoted to clear the Doctrine we are now upon ; Yet Tho' ſome doubt whether there was ever ſuch a Perſon as *Job* in the World, and look on his *Book* (81) as a piece of *Poetry,* and a *Theme* to diſcourſe on *Providence* ; yet we muſt needs allow him a *real Being,* becauſe the Prophet *Ezekiel* and the Apoſtle St. *James* both mention and make him ſtand on the ſame *certainty* with *Noah* and *Daniel* ; and withall propoſing him as an *Example* of Patience, it ſufficiently proves that there was ſuch a Man.

The Book was divinely writ, and is of excellent uſe to confirm the notion of *Providence.* For it has been a Queſtion in all Ages, both *within* and *without* the Church, *Why Good Men are afflicted, and Ill Men flouriſh* : *Events* which ſeem ſo inconſiſtent with the Care and Conduct of a juſt and gracious God ; and which being miſunderſtood, have adminiſtred occaſion for ſeveral People to deny the Deity, and attribute all either to *Chance* or *Deſtiny.* But the Hiſtory of this Holy Man, his Sufferings, and the Diſputes thereon between him and his Friends, do

---

(81) *Ut parabolam confictam & thema diſputationis de Divina Providentia.*—Antonin. Florent. Chron. P. 1. C. 8. Tit. 3. Sect. 12.

very much conduce to folve the Riddle. For *Job* being fo feverely handled by *Satan*, as we find in the two firft Chapters; tho' his Wife could not on that account perfwade him to *curfe God and die*, yet he forbore not to difgrace *the day of his Birth*, and to wifh the (82) *Night had perifhed, wherein it was faid, there is a man-child conceived*. Upon this *Eliphaz, Bildad* and *Zophar* his 3 Friends, charge him with *want* of Religion: And being Perfons who own'd *Providence*, they juftifie the proceedings of God, and accufe him of fome *wickednefs* (tho' not openly known) which provoked the All-wife Judge to give him this ufage. This makes *Job* ftrain a little to vindicate himfelf, and convincing the 3 Difputants, That *Sin* is not always the *Caufe* of Mens *misfortunes*, he happens to let go fome words, which *Elihu* a Stander by, thought pinched too much on the *divine Juftice*, and fo rebukes him for it. In the conclufion, God was pleas'd (83) *out of a Whirl-wind* to fet 'em all at rights, and checks *Elihu* for judging too hard of *Job*; as he chides alfo the Holy Man himfelf for not being more *wary*, tho' *innocent*, in his expreffions, which gave the Hearers reafon to think amifs of his *Juftice:* But is very angry with the other Three, for calling his Servant an *Hypocrite*, and believing him to deferve all thofe pains and loffes, whereby he intended only to *try* his patience and fubmiffion; having a defign to reward him with a *double portion* of *Temporal Happinefs*, as well as afterwards with *Eternal Life.* And therefore he commands 'em to go immediately and offer *Sacrifice* to atone for this *Uncharitablenefs* towards their good Friend, and the

---

(82) Job iii. 3. (83) Job xxxviii. 1.

wrong

wrong Opinion they had of his own Conduct and Providence. This is the Substance of that Book which (84) some conceive purposely writ by *Moses*, to keep up the Spirits of the *Israelites* under their bondage in *Egypt*, and make 'em hope for an happy issue, as *Job* had, out of all their streights and troubles. (85) Yet others consider it a work of *Solomon*, or one of the *Prophets*, and many will have *Job* himself to be the *Author* of it, or one of his Companions. But this is uncertain; we imploy our minds rather on the Book it self, which as it contains an Heroick instance of *Religious Fortitude* and *Patience*, so it is Recorded to give us a right sence of what God designs in these Events, and to incourage us to follow an *Example*, so honourably remembred, and so well requited for his present Sufferings. But of this by the by.

The Point in Debate is *who, what* and *when* he was. You place him before *Abraham*, and if so, he may be that *Jobab* who was the Son of *Jocthan* in *Genesis* x. 29. But this Opinion does not find much countenance from the Interpreters of that place. Several indeed own him for *Jobab* the Son of *Zera* in *Bozra*, and for this we have the Authority of the 70, who at the conclusion of the Book make this Supplement. " *And these are the Kings that go-* " *verned in Edom, first Balak the Son of Beor,* " *and after him Jobab called also Job*—So that He was the 2d King in *Edom*, and Successor to *Balak*, or as he is named in the Book

---

(84) *Sunt qui opinantur Mosem Historiam Job apud Jethro socerum suum in terra Madian reperisse, &c.* Chemnic. Exam. Conc. Trident. (85) Anton. Chron. de Job loco cit.

(86) of *Chronicles, Bela the Son of Beor, who being dead, Jobab the Son of Zera in Bofra, Reigned in his ftead.* Whence it appears, faith *a Lapide,* that *Job* was a *King* in *Idumea,* and the 2d in order; and He cites *Philo, Origen, Athanafius, Chryfoftom, Auguftine, Eufebius* and others of the fame Mind, (87) as was alfo *Ifidore,* who makes him the 4th from *Efau.* That he was a great *Prince,* perhaps a *King,* we fee Chapter 29. For when *he went to the gate* (the place of Judicature) *the Princes refrained talking, and laid their hands on their mouths, and the Nobles held their peace. I fate as a King,* which *Cajetan* excepts againft, as not being truly a King, but like one, *as a King.* But the word does not always fignifie *fimilitude,* but confirms the *adjunct,* as in *John* i. 14. *as of the only Begotten of the Father,* which without an *Arrian* glofs does not weaken the reality and truth of Chrift's being the Son of God. However more plainly, Chapter xix. 9. *He hath ftrip'd me of my glory, and taken the Crown from my head.* — And this Quality made him a more agreeable Companion for *Eliphaz* and the reft, whom the (88) *Seventy* make *Kings* as well as *Him.* Yet it is objected that *Job* and *Jobab* cannot be the fame, becaufe thofe Names begin with different (89) Letters, the firft with *Aleph,* and the other with *Jod;* and tho' *Pinedas* would willingly reconcile 'em, by making *Job* (90) *Binominis,* as in many other Examples, yet this is meer conjecture, and not fufficient to fatisfie the fcrupulous.

---

(86) 1 Chron. i. 44.   (87) *De Vita Sanct.*
(88) Ελιφάζ Θαιμανῶν Βασιλεύς. Βαλδὰδ ὁ Σαυχαῶν Τύραννͻ. Σωφὰρ ὁ Μιναίων Βασιλεύς.   (89) יוֹב אִיּוֹב
(90) *Adah and* Judeth, *Aram and* Ram, *&c.* A Lap. Cau. 19, *in* Pent.

And therefore if this Objection be of any effect to difprove *Job* to be the *Son of Zera* notwithftanding the Authority of fo many Fathers and other Learned Men, I think it concludes as ftrongly againft *Jobab the Son of Jocthan* who lived a great while *before Abraham*, as the other a great while *after him.*

And as his *Perfon* is not well diftinguifh'd, fo neither his *Lineage.* For to pafs by the fancy of R. *Solomon*, who makes him a *Chanaanite*, and confequently of the Pofterity of *Cham*, the Authors of beft efteem derive him, fome from *Abraham*, *others* from (91) *Nachor Abrahams Brother* by his Wife *Melcha*, whofe Son *Uz* gave name to that *Region* of which *Job* is faid to be; which however is very doubtful, becaufe it might be fo called from another (92) *Huz*, the Grand-Son of *Noah* by *Sem*. Neither can they who draw him from *Abraham* agree among themfelves, whether he defcended from *Jacob* by his Son *Iffachar*, or from *Efau Jacob's Brother*, and the 3d or 4th of that Family, as *Origen*, *Chryfoftom*, *Ambrofe* and an whole Jury more affert, cited by *Pinedas*, and all of 'em fupported by the (93) *Seventy* who exprefly fay of him that *He was a Son of the Sons of Efau*, from whom defcended all or moft of thofe Friends of his who came to vifit him in his Diftrefs. And fo his Pedigree runs thus; *Efau* begat *Rahuel*, and *Rahuel Zera*, and *Zera Jobab* or *Job*. And in this they all confent, that he was long *after Abraham*, tho' 'tis very uncertain by what Branch he came from him.

---

(91) Hier. Heb. Qu.   (92) Gen. X. 23.
(93) 'Εκ.τῶν 'Ησαυ υἱῶν υἱός.   (94) A Lap. Loc. Cit.

The

The *Date* of his Reign is as doubtful as all the reſt. *Iſidore* makes him *cotemporary with Moſes.* *Stone* the Jeſuit ſaith, that *he lived* 70 *Years before Moſes was Born, and died about five before the Deliverance of the People of Iſrael.* And this cloſes with *Sulpitius Severus,* who gives him being about the time when *Moſes* dwelt with *Jethro* his Father-in-Law. *Burgenſis* brings him into the World *after* the Peoples departure out of *Egypt,* and *Gregory* yet *lower* to the days of the *Judges.* St. *Jerom* with ſome others, make him as *old* as *Jacob,* ſuppoſing (95) *that Eliphaz* to be the ſame with *him* who was the (96) Son of *Eſau.* *Genebrard* ſuppoſes him to flouriſh, when *Jacob* and his Family went down into *Egypt* ; and others ſome time *after* when *Jacob* died. . But 'tis reaſonable to think that he lived a conſiderable while *after Eſau,* as appears from the Names of his Aſſociates and Friends. For *Eliphaz* is ſaid to be a *Temanite,* the place borrowing its Name from *Teman,* the (97) Son of that *Eliphaz,* who was the Son of *Eſau* by his Wife *Adah.* *Bilda* was a *Shuite,* very likely from *Shua Abraham*'s Son by (98) *Keturah.* *Zophar* was a *Naamathite,* from (99) *Timna* (by a Metatheſis, as *Junius,* *Tremellius* and the Aſſembly conjecture) a Duke of that Name the Offspring of *Eſau.* *Elihu* is called a *Buzite,* from (100) *Buz* the Son of *Nahor.* So that the Account on all hands makes him *younger* than *Abraham,* and the generality bring him down to *Moſes.* And after all we muſt acknowledge this piece of Chronology very *un-*

---

(95) Job iv. 1. (96) Gen. xxxvi. 4. (97) Gen. xxxvi. 10, 11. . (98) Gen. xxv. 1, 2. (99) Gen. xxxvi. 4. (100) Gen. xxii. 21.

certain,

certain, and therefore of little force to prove any thing.

But to come to the words of the Text you propose, wherein we must incounter so many difficulties, that I cannot see what can be brought from thence to our present purpose. *There was a time when the Sons of God*—or as you say, *There was a day,* and you take it for the *Sabbath,* yet our Translators are justified from the latitude of the word, signifying *time* at large, as *Day* in the Writings of *Justin Martyr,* and *Plato* means *time* without determining or defining it by such a number of *hours.* And so the word being exposed to this uncertainty, it imports no more, than that it so fell out *on a time,* without saying *what time* it was. *Junius* and *Tremellius* limit it to *one of the days* whereon *Jobs* Children were Feasting; and affirm that on *one of these days* it happen'd that *the Sons of God likewise met,* and *Satan* among 'em. But as it is not resolved which of the days it was, so neither can it be inferred that it was *one of seven.* And tho' it be true, that the Feast lasted for *seven days,* yet this period had no eye to any *Weekly Revolution,* but only to the *number* of *Jobs Sons* which were *Seven,* and we are told that *they Feasted in their Houses every one his day,* ver. 4. So that if he had had *more* or *fewer* Sons, perhaps the time of the Feast had held the same proportion, and the Week made *longer* or *shorter* according to their *number.* All that a Man can well argue from the passage is, That this *Seven days Feast,* so ill spent in Rioting and Pleasures, that the good Father thought himself obliged to offer Sacrifices in behalf of his Children, did not well suit the *Patriarchal Sabbath,* if every *Seventh day* was necessarily distinguished

by

by actions of Devotion and Piety: And therefore inftead of Oblations, *Job* had been bound
in Confcience and Duty to ufe the Authority
of a *Magiftrate*, as he certainly was, and hindred the continuance of a *Revel* fo long and fo
fcandalous to Religion. And if this Sacrifice
was really offer'd on the 8th *Day*, when the
full time of the Feaft was over, then it muft
follow, that either the young People began
their Mirth on that *very day* when they ought
to have been at their Prayers, or elfe *Job*'s
Service had no refpect to the *Day*, or the *fame
number of Days* (*a*) afterwards in ufe among
the People of the *Jews.*

But let them behave themfelves as they
thought fit, There were *others* it feems of a
better Mind, who met together for *Ends* more
anfwerable to the *Principles* which guided *Job*
and them. *There was a day in which the Sons of
God came to prefent themfelves before the Lord.*
The Sons of God, is [*anceps nomen*] very ambiguous; and fo *many* lay claim to that Stile,
that it muft be hard to diftinguifh 'em one
from another. *Great Men* are called the *Sons
of God,* as *great Trees* are the *Trees of God,*
and *great Mountains,* the *Mountains of God*;
and fo *Symmachus, 'Vatablus* and *Pagnine,* what
we litterally render *Sons of God, they* tranflate
(*b*) the *Sons of the Mighty.* The Arabick, *Sons
of the Illuftrious.* The Targum of *Onkelos,* the
Sons of Princes. The Samaritan, *Sons of Men
in Power.* And oppofite to *this,* they turn [*the
Daughters of Men*] into the *Daughters of the
Common People, Plebeians,* or *Men* without any
Title or mark of Honour. Again, *Good Men*

(*a*) Selden *de Jure Nat.* l. 3. c. 14. (*b*) *On*
Gen. vi. 2.

have

have likewife the fame Periphrafis, and are
Sons of God by Adoption and Grace; and fo
(*c*) St. *Paul* afferts, that *as many as are lead by
the Spirit of God, are the Sons of God.* (*d*) And
St. *John* herein magnified the love of the· Father, *that we fhould be called the Sons of God*——
And in this fence doubtlefs is to be underftood
that of *Genefis, the Sons of God faw the Daughters of Men*; *i. e.* the *Sons* of *Seth* were ena-
mour'd of the *Daughters* of *Cain*, and at length
Married 'em. And as *Good Men* are the *Sons
of God*, fo are alfo the *Good Angels*; and the
rather becaufe being *Spirits* they approach
nearer the *Divine Nature,* and never univerfally fell, as *Man* did, to difpleafe their Maker.
And fo, when (*e*) King ·*Nebuchadnezzar* had
called the 4*th* Perfon in the Fiery Furnace, *the
Son of God,* he immediately explains himfelf,
while he blelfes God, *who had fent his Angel to
preferve his Servants that trufted in him.* If
therefore the Phrafe be of fuch extent in the
Holy Book, and fignifies either *Angels or Men*;
and *Men* of *different qualities* on the account of
Vertue or *Fortune,* I think there can be no better way to find out the meaning of the particular Text you name, than to examine this Author himfelf (who muft be fuppofed to underftand the fame thing in the fame Language)
and what he defigns in another place, where
he ufes the fame expreffion. In Chap. xxviii. 7.
we hear God challenging *Job* to anfwer this
Queftion, *Where waft thou when I laid the Foundations of the Earth*—*When the Morning ftars
fung together, and all the Sons of God fhouted for*

(*c*) **Rom.** viii. 14. (*d*) 1 Joh. iii. 1. (*e*) **Dan.**
iii. 25, 28.

joy?

joy? All Translations conspire in rendring these *Sons of God* by *Angels*; because no other Sons of God were then in Being before the Creation was *finished*. And who saith St. *Chryfostom*, " *Beholding the multitude of Creatures, the Beau-* " *ty, the dispositions, the Usefulness, the Va-* " *riety, the Order and other Qualities of 'em,* " *were amazed at the sight, and so brake out* " *into a Divine Hymn in Commendation of the* " *Creator.* So that 'tis very likely, that whatever *Moses* or other Writers mean by this form of words, yet *Job* or whoever else Penned the Book, must by this Periphrasis, be supposed to denote the *Holy Angels* in both these *Places* alike, as Commentators generally take it. And the drift was this, That because our Infirmities cannot comprehend God in his Majesty, he is set forth to us as (*f*) an Earthly *Prince*, or some *Great Man* sitting on his Throne or Chair of State, that so our Capacities might be able to reach what is spoken of him. And his *Angels* are compared to *Ministers*, or Officers in the Government, who *at certain times* present themselves before their Master to give an *account* of what they have done in their respective Imployments, by virtue of the *Commissions* he gave 'em.

How this was done is hard to say; and therefore different ways are taken to make us understand it. For some have their *Prosopopœia*, and think it no more than an *artful introduction* of Persons and Things to represent somewhat to ground a *Moral* or *Application* on. Others conceive it a *Vision*, and that the *Idea* or Characters of this passage were so lively impress'd

---

(*f*) Sunt hæc humanitus dicta & a terrenis regibus desumpta. Jun. & Trem. in 1 K. xxii. 29.

on the Mind of the Writer, that it feem'd to him as if he had really feen it. And thus (g) *Micah* faw God on his Throne, (h) and *Zachary Jofhua* the *High-Prieft, before the Angel of the Lord, and Satan ftanding at his right hand to refift him.*

Moft Conclude, That this is *Hiftorically* related, and contains matter of Fact about the *Angels* meeting together to prefent themfelves before God, and account for their feveral Charges ; and that *Satan* (who owed *Job* a fpleen) took the opportunity ; and while the *Angels* were making favourable reports in behalf of this devout Man ; He on the other fide, ufed all his cunning to *leffen* his Vertue, and defired a Warrant from God to proceed, as he did afterwards, to demonftrate, (as he pretended) the *hypocrifie* of *Job*. One only Exception there is againft this Expofition, and that is, If by the *Angels prefenting themfelves before the Lord,* is meant *Gods Throne* in Heaven, then it cannot be imagined that *Satan* being once caft out, fhould ever be again admitted thither. This is refolv'd and anfwer'd, by fuppofing that this Convention was *not in Heaven,* but in fome other place, probably in *Job's* Country, where the *Guardian Angels* of *Job's* Kingdom, Perfon and Family came together, to Difcourfe (in their way of communicating thoughts) concerning the Patriarch's Behaviour and Conduct ; and that the Devil having liberty to appear among *good Angels* as well as *good Men,* took this time to flur the *Saints* Reputation, and to Petition for Power to put his Piety to trial. Now among thefe, for Orders fake a *Superiour Angel* prefided ;

(g) 1 Kings xxii. 19.   (h) Zach. iii. 1.

who

who being in *Gods stead*, and acting in *his Name* he might carry his *Lord's stile* without offence; and God himself might be said to talk to *Satan*, tho' only by him, who was *President* at this Meeting. And thus we may consider that appearance of the *Lying Spirit* (who was to deceive King *Ahab*) before God's Throne; which ought not to be strictly taken, but as his Throne and Presence was elsewhere; or as *Personated* by one of the Angels.

This Assembly of *Angels* was it seems *twice*, and you fancy *six days* between them. Yet St. *Chrysostom* was of another Mind, and sets the *second Meeting* the *next day* after the first; and *Aquinas* the very *same day*, tho' called (*i*) *another* from the *new business* of it, as we read in *Genesis*, saith he, *that there were* (*k*) *several days in the Creation, from the variety of the Creatures, the better to discern one from another.* And this Conjecture is bottomed upon your own reason, *Satan's* (*l*) *impatience*, which would not admit of any delay; and therefore as soon as the Angels came together, he intruded among them, and presented himself to the *Prolocutor*.

But in reality, all this amounts no higher than bare Opinion, and the only Scripture in the History of *Job*, which gives any colour for the *Seventh-day*, is in Chapter ii. 13. *So they sate down with him upon the ground seven days and seven nights, and none spake a word unto him*—Yet this was no more than according to the manner of (*m*) *Physicians* in Cases of desperate Diseases; and they waited in expecta-

---

(*i*) *Propter novum factum.* (*k*) *Propter plura rerum genera.* Aqui. (*l*) *Illud certum videtur non refriguisse Dæmonis Sævitiam neque multum temporis expectasse,* &c. Pined. in Job. (*m*) *Medicorum more,* Pined. in loc.

tion that his grief might aſſwage when that term of Days was over. Or rather, their Deſign in this Viſit being to condole with him, they obſerved the *ſet Days* allotted on that Occaſion, and would enter on no Diſcourſe 'till he thought fit to give an opportunity for it, as we find he did, in the beginning of the third Chapter.

B. Well, but to argue from *Reaſon.* (*n*) Can it be imagined that God would leave the World at this *uncertainty,* and ſeeing he expected the *Homage* of their Devotion, would he not preſcribe them a *time* to do it in, to avoid that *confuſion and diſorder* which muſt neceſſarily attend the want of ſuch an *Inſtitution.* And tho' 'tis true, we do not read in expreſs terms that *Adam,* or the reſt of the *Patriarchs* obſerved the *Sabbath,* yet that ſilence doth not diſprove it, no more than in other Caſes, which certainly were, tho' they do not occurr in the Holy Writings. We no where read that *Adam* Worſhipped God, yet can we once imagine that he did not Worſhip? There is no hint of the *Sabbath* throughout the Book of *Judges;* nor do we find *Sampſon,* or *Deborah,* or *Joſhua* keeping it. Was it therefore not kept all that time? You were obſerving out of the *Rabbins,* that from the very beginning the World was devoted to Idolatry and Falſe Worſhip; and ſo indeed (*o*) *Maimonides* aſſerts, that *the Wiſeſt Men then, ſuch as the Prieſts themſelves, thought there was no God, ſave the Stars, for whoſe ſake, and in whoſe like-*

(*n*) *Naturali æquitati conſentaneum eſt tam tempus ad cultum peragendum quam cultum ipſum definire.* Dies Dom. l. 1. c. 8.　　(*o*) Loc. ſupra citato.

neſs

nefs they *made many Images; but for the Rock Everlafting, there were very few to acknowledge him 'till Abraham our Father was come.* No wonder then that *this Day* was exploded, when the Worfhip it felf ceafed, and I am not furprized at all to find that there is no mention made of it in *that Age* no more than during the Bondage of the People of *Ifrael* in *Egypt,* when it is not likely their fevere *Task-Mafters* could be induced to let 'em *reft* every *Seventh-day* for the hindrance of fo much bufinefs. (*p*) Hear how *Philo* defcribes their Condition. " *The* " *Overfeers of the Work were the moft cruel and* " *unmerciful Men in all the Country, who laid* " *upon 'em greater Tasks than they were able to* " *indure; inflicting on them no lefs Punifhment* " *than death it felf, if any of 'em (yea tho by* " *reafon of Infirmity) fhould withdraw himfelf* " *from his daily labour. Some were commanded* " *to imploy themfelves in the Publick Structures,* " *others to bring Materials for mighty Buildings,* " *never enjoying any reft Day or Night, that in* " *the end they were even fpent and tired with* " *continual travel*—So that in this woful State, it cannot be expected that they fhould have either *leave* or *leifure* to keep their *Sabbath,* or folemnly worfhip God. Yet fome *Jews* are otherwife perfwaded, and fay, *That even in their Slavery, they were Circumcifed and obferved the Sabbath;* and add, (*q*) *That this Obedience to the Holy Ordinance, was the motive which induced God to work out their deliverance.* Which, tho' (*r*) *Maimonides* contradicts, yet

---

(*p*) *De vit. Mof.* (*q*) *Redempti funt Ifraelitæ ex Ægypto ob obfervatam illic circumcifionem & Sabbatum.* Baal Turim in Exod. 1. Dr. *Lightfoot.* (*r*) *Neque quiefcere neque Sabbatum agere potuerunt.* Apud Rivet. in Decalog.

that they held Sacred Affemblies under that Condition, The *Tabernacle*, which *Mofes* calls (*s*) the *Tabernacle of the Congregation*, placed without the Camp, and brought along with 'em from *Egypt*, doth not a little prove. For as to that *Tabernacle*, whofe Pattern was received in the Mount, 'tis very evident that it was not yet made; and an account we have of it in the Chapter following. And therefore as this fhows they worfhip'd God in their Servitude, fo 'tis reafonable to fuppofe that they did it on *this Day*, which is the matter of difpute between us. But be it otherwife, in this and the like Cafes, there is a yielding to neceffity; and on this account it might fall out, what *Jofephus* faith happen'd at another time; (*t*) " When " *Antiochus* would not permit the *Jews* to " Celebrate the Sabbath, but obliged 'em to " do on it all Labour and Bnfinefs they were " accuftomed to do upon any other day. And " fo urgent he was, that in a fhort time the " Sabbath was not neglected among them of " *Antiochia* only, but alfo in other places, " and in the Cities round about.——But all this inferrs not that there was no Sabbath, becaufe the obfervation of it was fufpended for a while, and during that *fufpenfion*, might not be named for want of opportunity to do it.

A. That God did not appoint *Days* for the Duties of Religion, is no more to be admired than that he did not prefcribe the *Duties* themfelves, but left it to *natural light* to guide 'em in their Worfhip as *often* and *in what manner* they thought good, except in fome very few inftances, and many years after the World was made. And as for that deluge of *Impiety*

(*s*) Exod. xxxiii. 7. (*t*) *De Bello Jud. l.* 7. c. 21.

before

before the Flood, or the *Slavery* of the People *after* it, which for its Cruelty was indeed compared to *(u) an Iron Furnace.* In both these Cafes there might be a *fufpenfion* of keeping the *Sabbath*, yet there could not be wanting opportunities to name it, which was not done 'till *(w) Mofes* was Commiffion'd for it. Tho' when all's done, it feems very odd, that of fo many hundred thoufand Souls in *Egypt*, not *One* fhould have fo much *Zeal* and *Courage* as to hazard the utmoft difpleafure of *Pharaoh's* Officers for the Obfervation of *a Day* Divinely Inftituted, if it truly were, and they thought it to be fo. And if any Man or Woman had fuffer'd and died a *Martyr* in that Caufe, I am perfwaded the Prophet would not have forgot him, if only for their incouragement to whom he was recommending the *Sabbath*, and making a *Law* to keep it. Courage certainly they did did not want, *(x)* " For the miferies which
" they afterwards underwent under *Antiochus*
" rather than they would prophane the *Sab-*
" *bath*; and thofe Calamities which they chofe
" to fall upon them by the hands of the *Romans*
" rather than to make refiftance on *that Day*,
" are fufficient Proofs, that neither force nor
" fear could *now* have wrought upon 'em not
" to keep the fame, had fuch a Duty been
" commanded. Queftionlefs, *Jofeph* for his
" part, who did preferr a loathfome Prifon
" before the unchaft Embraces of his Mafter's
" Wife, would no lefs carefully have kept
" the *Sabbath* than he did his *Chaftity*, had
" there been any *Sabbath* then to be obferved

(*u*) Jerem. xi. 4.   (*w*) *Ad Mofis ufque tempora cæterorum dierum fimilis erat, i. e. dies Sabbati.* Bede.
(*x*) *Heylin's* Hift. of the Sabbath. *P.* 1. *c.* 3. *Sect.* 10.

" either

" either as dedicated by *Nature*, or prescribed
" by *Law*. And surely either the *Sabbath* was
" not reckon'd all this while as any branch of
" the *Law of Nature*, or else it finds hard mea-
" sure in the *Book of God*, that there should be
" particular Proofs how punctually the rest of
" the *Moral Law* was observed and practised
" among the Patriarchs, and not one word or
" item that concerns the observation of the
" *Sabbath*.

The *Tabernacle* you propose is a very uncertain medium to prove their *Worship*, much less
the *Sabbath*. For first *Calvin* and others say,
that this Tabernacle is the same with what God
commands to be erected in the Chapters following, and which they suppose made already.
And whereas in the beginning it was *within* or
(*y*) *in the middle of the Camp*, now he removed it *far from the Host*, with design to admonish them thereby, that they had made themselves unworthy the Divine Presence; and
tho' he left them still an opportunity of access, yet he would not give 'em the honour of
Co-habitation. But I think this too gross a *trans-
position*, and the circumstances of the History
will hardly admit so much time between *Moses*'s
coming down from the Mount, and the building of a *Tent* so glorious and costly. Nor am
I fond of a *Prolepsis* here to represent that *done*,
which *was to be done* some time after. Most
likely it is, what you take it to be, a *distinct*
Tent from that (*z*) which God commanded to
be built, and which being built, the Use this
was put to might cease for the future. The
Syriack and *Seventy* call it *Moses*'s *own Tent*;

(*y*) Numb. ii. 17.　　(*z*) Exod. xxv. 8.

and

and if fo, your Argument is loft. The *Arabick* faith it was the *Tabernacle of the Affembly*, the *Targum* of *Onkelos*, the *Tabernacle of the Houfe of Doctrine*, fignifying the *Bufinefs* it was put to, namely, to meet together for the exercife of Religion, as alfo to confult about Civil Matters. And tho' it might not be *Mofes's-Tent* strictly taken, as an ordinary apartment for himfelf and Family, which *Calvin* difallows, yet probably it was †a *Room of State* wherein the *Elders* met to conferr with *Mofes*. 'Tis doubtful *when* it was made, yet 'tis credible that its date bore about that time when the *Pillar of Cloud* appear'd in the Camp, ‖ out of which God difcourfed *Mofes*; for we never hear of it before that occafion. *Junius* and *Tremellius* affirm, that the erecting of this Tabernacle was a fign of Gods difpleafure, who would no longer vouchfafe to dwell among 'em, as he did before this Tabernacle was made. But were it fo, that they brought it out of *Egypt*, and put it to a Religious Ufe, (neither of which fhows it felf in the Hiftory of *Mofes*) yet it concludes no more for the obfervation of the *Jewifh Sabbath*, than the *Temples* of the Heathens do for a *Seventh-day*, to which they had little refpect, as we fhall fee anon. For tho' *both* had *their fet-places* and *fet times*, yet they very much *differed* from one another.

As to *Adam*, Tho' no mention is made of his *Worfhip*, (*a*) yet 'tis not to be thought but he did it, becaufe this was agreeable to the *Law of Nature* to adore the Deity at fome time or

---

† *Tentorium Mofis quatenus ipfe dux populi—Quo convenire folebant feniores acturi confilium cum Mofe.* A Lapide.
‖ Exod. xiii. 21.　(*a*) *Adam primus obtulit juvencum.* So the *Rabbins*. Vid. Reuchl. de arte Cabal. l. 1.

other,

other. But as we do not find that He had any
Rule set him besides that *one Precept* of forbearing the *Tree of Knowledge* (which by the bare
light of reason had never become a Duty, and
therefore called for a special Prohibition) so
it is more reasonable to believe that he had no
time named him; because if so, it must have
been remark'd as the other *positive Precepts*
were, and distinguish'd by some extraordinary
way to ingage the Memory, and keep it from
being forgotten. But to come at length to
those *Testimonies* of the Christian *Fathers* which
you laid before me, and which you desired my
thoughts of, concerning the Old *Patriarch's* observation of the *Sabbath-day*.

Tertullian then, and St. *Augustine*, as we see
in their own words, offer only the Opinion of
the *Jews*, who in stretching this point of the
Sabbath, are not to be wondred at, because the
Celebration of it was one of their most distinguishing Articles; and by magnifying it,
as they did, they would invite other Nations
to close with 'em in it, and bring a greater
odium on *Christianity* for abrogating an *Institution* (as they said) of the same date with the
World, and made by God himself, for People
to Worship him. And yet let me tell you,
Josephus is so ingenuous as to fix this account
wholly on *Moses*, the first Author and Disco-
verer of the Secret. His words run thus.
(b) " *Moses* saith that the World and all that
" is therein was made in *Six* whole *Days*, and
" that on the *Seventh* God took *rest* and ceased
" from his labours—So that this was unknown,
" till *Moses* said it. The same *Mercerus* reports from many of the *Rabbins*. And in par-

_____

(b) Antiq. l. 1.

ticular *Solomon Jarchi* commenting on *Moses's* words, underſtands him in a *Prolepſis*, as a way that holy Writer frequently uſes. *He bleſſed it*—i. e. the 7*th Day, when* ? *in the Manna*, God having never declared himſelf in that matter ſo clearly before. " He bleſſed it by " the *Manna*, becauſe on the *other Days* of " the Week, each of 'em had no more than " an *Omer*, but on the *Sixth Day* the propor- " tion was *double*. He ſanctified it alſo by the " *Manna*, becauſe on that, *i. e.* the 7*th* they " found none. And what is here written, re- " ſpected the time to come. Again, " He " bleſſed it in the *Manna*, becauſe on the *Se-* " *venth day* there was none on the ground.— The ſame ſaid *Moſes Bar Nachman*, and *R. Iſh-mael*, who taught that the Sanctifying of the 7*th* Day was by the *Manna*. And we read it in the Dialogue called *Sepher Cozri*, " *Can the* " *Original of the Sabbath be fetch'd from any* " *place but Sinai or Aluſh where the Manna de-* " *ſcended? In Aluſh* (the 10th Stage) *they re-* " *ceived the Sabbath, and there they firſt Cele-* " *brated it*——And in the Book called *Seder Olam*, they ſay, that " *The firſt Precept gi-* " *ven 'em after their departure out of Egypt,* " *was what was commanded in Mara*——He means the Sabbath. And this old Tradition often occurs, " *The Sabbath and other Laws* " *were enjoyn'd in Mara.* In ſo many words *R. Abraham, Levi Ben Gerſom* and others deli- ver themſelves. And *Abarbinel* expounding the *Memento* of this Precept, ſaith " *Remember* " *the Sabbath-day,* that is, *remember what I* " *commanded you in Mara.* And to ſay no more, *Manaſſeh Ben Iſrael* who ſlights the *Tra-dition*, confeſſes it a very *ancient one*; *what,* *tho' ſome of the Ancients ſay, that this Precept*

about

about the Sabbath was given in Mara? yet these *some* say no other thing than what is in their *Talmud* and Books of Chronology, of great Authority and veneration among 'em. And so in the Comment on the Hymn about the Sabbath. " *The Sabbath was ordain'd in Mara,* " *and made a Precept on Mount Sinai ; its fan-* " *tification was from the Beginning, but the* " *first* [actual] *Sabbath was in after Ages.* Which shows, that if the *Jews* had had any good ground for a greater Antiquity of their Sabbath, they would have made use of it to magnifie a thing they so much adored and valued themselves for. But to return to our two Authors. What St. *Augustine's* own judgment was, you had before, wherein he allows no distinction of Days in the Creation, but conceives *one time* (or Day) enough for the Almighty God to produce all things in. And for *(c) Tertullian,* he denies that *Noah, Enoch* or *Melchisedech* had any regard for it. " *God,* " faith he, *delivered Noah from the Flood with-* " *out the Sabbath. He translated Enoch to Hea-* " *ven without the Sabbath or Circumcision. He* " *made Melchisedech Priest without the Sabbath,* " without minding, perhaps without knowing " the *Sabbath.* And this he urges, to prove the *Institution* of it by *Moses,* a temporary thing, because *Adam* and the Fathers did not keep it. And before him *(d) Justin* the Martyr tells his Adversary, a Jew, that *in the days of Enoch People observed not Circumcision or the Sabbath, and that Melchisedech was accepted without it.* *(e)* And *Irenæus* faith, that *Abraham believed God, and it was imputed to him for righteousness,* before he was *Circumcised* and without the *Sab-*

(c) *Adv.* Jud. (*d*) *Adv.* Trypho. (*e*) L. iv. c. 30.

bath.

bath. And again, *The Company of juft Men before Abraham, and all the Patriarchs before Mofes were juftified without thefe things, and without the Law of Mofes.* So likewife (*f*) *Eufebius, There was no Circumcifion, nor obfervation of the Sabbath among them, as there is none among us.*

B. All this is true; neither *Abraham* nor the other *Patriarchs* were *juftified* by the *Sabbath* or by *Circumcifion*; and fo far *Juftin Martyr* and *Irenæus* fay well, that the *Fathers fine his juftificabantur,* for *Faith* did that work, and not the *Ceremony.* And fo the Martyr fpeaks, that the afore-named Holy Men pleafed God, [μὴ σαββατίζοντες,] *without Sabbatizing*—that is, as *Tertullian* well interprets it, not obferving the *Sabbath*; [*qu. Salutis medelam*] with that Superftition and Formality of the Jews afterwards, and without any opinion of *Merit,* or confidering it as the means to *juftification.* Indeed the Patriarchs had not this Notion of the *Sabbath,* nor was the Day fo abufed by them, as to keep it in that fence, nor by *us* no more than by *them,* as you faid out of *Eufebius.* But then this does not invalidate the former affertion, or prove that the *Sabbath* was not known to the Patriarchs, or Solemnized as a Day alotted Religion. For they might keep *that Day,* as we do *ours,* a Day holy to God, tho' not fuch as *Mofes* made it when the Law was given from Mount *Sinai*; or fuch at leaft as Pofterity fanfied it, which is what thofe (*g*) Authors cenfured and ex-

---

(*f*) Ecclef. Hift. L. i. c. i.   (*g*) *Non de omni obfervatione, loqui eum* [Tertul.] *dicere poffumus, fed de illa ægida tantum quietis & ceffationis exactione quàm apud Judæos in ufu fuiffe fcimus.* Hofpin. de Feft. Jud. c. 3.

cepted

cepted against, and will not have the Patriarchs take any notice of. And as for *Abraham* in particular, it's said in *Genesis* xxvi. 5.
Because Abraham obey'd my voice---Hence some
(h) *Jews* conclude, as *Mercerus* tells us (who
himself inclines to that Opinion) that *Abraham*
kept the *Sabbath* as well as *Circumcision*, and
other rites of the Law.

A. It was a very great Character and Commendation God was pleas'd to bestow on *A-
braham*, that *He had obey'd his voice*---" Right,
" saith St. *Chrysostom*, for God said unto him,
" *Get thee out from thy Fathers House, and
" from thy Kindred, and go unto the Land that
" I shall show thee.* And *Abraham* went, lea-
" ving a *certainty* for *hope*, and this not wa-
" vering, but with all cheerfulness and readi-
" ness imaginable. Then followeth his expe-
" ctation of a Son in his Old Age when Nature
" was decay'd in him, because the Lord had
" promised one; His casting out of *Ishmael*, as
" the Lord commanded him ; His readiness to
" offer *Isaac* as the Lord directed him, with
" many other things of that kind, enough to
" give occasion for that applause, but with-
" out regard to the *Sabbath*, for which this
place is so little proof, that *Rabbi Johanan* and
Galatinus from the Book they call *the lesser Exposition* on *Genesis*, assure us, *That Abraham did
not keep the Sabbath*: And as for *Justin*, let
him explain himself. " *Before Abraham there
was no use of Circumcision, nor before Moses of
keeping the Sabbath. Before Moses, none of the
Righteous observed the Sabbath, neither received
they any commandment to observe it*——They did
not keep it at all, nor hitherto was there any

(h) *Quo loco custodia Sabbati intelligitur.* Manasseh ben Israel. L, de Creat.

L   Precept

Precept for it, no more than for *Circumcifion*, which was not in ufe till *Abraham*. And to fancy they kept the *Sabbath* without the ufe of it, is a nicety I underftand not, no more than I can apprehend how *Circumcifion* was ufed without the *Ceremony*. (*i*) *Damafcen* is clofe, *Before Mofes's Law and Scripture given by Divine Infpiration, the Sabbath was not confecrated to God; But when the Scripture Divinely Infpired was given by Mofes, the Sabbath was made Sacred to God, that the People might be exercifed in the meditation of Scripture.* Thefe Expreffions are full and familiar; God did not actually confecrate a Day to be religioufly obferved, 'till *Mofes* was infpired to Pen thofe things he had got by *Revelation* or *Tradition*, whereby the People might have fomewhat *certain* before 'em to fpend the Day in by holy reading and meditation. And thus far the (*k*) Schoolman you fpoke of goes along with us. For tho' the keeping of the Sabbath might be propofed before *Mofes*, (*l*) *as a thing fit to be done*, yet there was no Command for it, nor does it appear that it was look'd on as a thing that (*m*) *ought to be done* or *was done*, until the Law made it a *Duty*. I might lay before you more evidences of this fort. But to be free with you, they ferve more to perplex than clear the Queftion. But then the inference is on my fide, That fince the Subject is *Problematical* and doubtful, and may adminifter frefh matter to continue the Difpute, what room is there left for the *morality* of the *Sabbath*? and how do thefe Arguments fo prove the ufe of it among the Patriarchs, as to be able to give it that

---

(*i*) *De fid. Ortho.*   (*k*) Alex. Hales, p. 3. Q. 32.
(*l*) *Secundum rationem honefti.*   (*m*) *Secundum rationem præcepti.*

Character?

Character? *Morality* is a Doctrine taught by the Light of Nature; and no sooner do we hear the several Lessons of it, but our Understanding assents immediately, without disputing or distrusting the Truth of 'em. But you see the different Sentiments of the Learned World make this Doctrine very *uncertain,* and that is a Condition nothing *moral* is or can be liable to. For to say, *I think,* is in other words *not* to be *perswaded;* and all the Quotations of this kind amount to very little more; the best is *conjecture,* because it has neither undeniable Reason nor Sacred Revelation to Seal what is proposed to us.

But I will humour the assertion, and call it True, that the *Patriarchs* kept the *Sabbath;* yet, this granted, the *Sabbath* is as far from *morality* as it was before; because all it can pretend to is *a positive Institution* of God, such as was the prohibition in Paradise about the *Tree of Knowledge;* abstinence from the *Blood* of Beasts; the difference between *clean* and *unclean* Creatures; the Sacrament of *Circumcision* and the like. " And to call these things (*n*) " *natural,* because the Fathers had regard to " 'em, is as much as to say, we are now obli- " ged to 'em. And if so, we must not only " keep the *Sabbath,* because they kept it, but " we must Sacrifice as they did, and be *Cir-* " *cumcised* as they were. For the Argument " holds good in the *latter* instances as well as " the *former,* and if one Law be of Nature, " the other must be so too; so *Zanchius.* And therefore plainly what is *positive* is *not moral.* And that I may conclude my Answer to this

---

(*n*) Zanch. *in quart. Precept.*

part

part of your Objection; Suppofing, as I faid, the Patriarchs had the *Sabbath* in great veneration, and kept it as a Day fet apart for Religious Ufes; and fuppofing withal that God commanded the Obfervation of it (which is the utmoft you contend for, and which is not demonftrable from any Text of Scripture, neither by way of *Doctrine* nor *Practice* before the times of *Mofes*) all this can go no higher than a *pofitive Precept*; and that very Language as it deftroys the notion of a *moral Law*, fo it fhows it was to laft and bind no longer, than he pleas'd, who made it a *Law* for a *particular People.*

Secondly, As to the *Gentiles*;

How far their Teftimony is concerned in this matter, we are to examine in the next place. And to begin with *Solon's-Week,* and what is meant by it. (*o*) To this Mr. *Selden* makes anfwer, that *it fignifies no more than the Climacterical Years* or *Stages of Humane Life: So it is confider'd by Ariftotle*; and in this fence it was very famous, as we find by *Plutarch*, *Cenforinus* and others. Again, *The very School-Boys know well enough that thefe Weeks of Solon were nothing elfe but the Climacterick-years.* So that *Solon's-Week* is as little to the purpofe as that of *Cicero's,* and contains *Years* and not *Days,* of which our common *Week* is conftituted. Then for *Alexander Severus*; 'tis not to be much doubted, but he had a great inclination either to *Judaifm* or *Chriftianity*, and on either account had refpect to the *Day*; becaufe, as Mr. *Selden* obferves, it immediately follows in *Lampridius,* that *he would willingly have erected a Temple to Chrift, and brought him within*

(*o*) De *Jure Nat.* L. iii. c. 17.

the

the number of his Country-Gods. And accordingly in a *jeer*, some were wont to call him the *Syrian Prieſt*, from the pleaſure he took in the *Jewiſh Rites*. But that all this was *Foreign*, and no otherwiſe regarded at *Rome* than as related to the Jews, appears from *Ovid*, in that Book of his before-cited, who calls 'em *Peregrina Sabbata*, which had not been proper, if the *Romans* and other Nations had kept the *Sabbath*, as the *Jews* among 'em did. And the words *Peregrina Sabbata*, *Peregrina Sacra*, and the like, import not ſo much a *Religious Rite* belonging to *Aliens*; (or as *Feſtus* ſaith, brought to *Rome* from ſome other Country, and obſerved in the ſame manner as in the places from whence it came,) as a *way of Worſhip* not allowed by *Authority* without Legal Eſtabliſhment, and had no more than bare *connivance* to keep it in being. As for the *Poets* who call the *Seventh-day Holy*, *Perfect*, and on *which all things* were *finiſhed*——Their *Seventh-day* doth not intend *that* which (*p*) *Weekly* occurs, and hath its revolution or return *four times* each Month, but *the* (*q*) *Day* of the twenty eight, which in order bears that name, and was ſaid to be *Holy*, becauſe it was thought to be the (*r*) *Birth-day* of *Apollo*, whom the Prieſts therefore ſtiled [Ἑβδομαγενῆ] *Seventh-day-born*. And ſo *Heſiod*, who calls it [ἱερὸν ἦμαρ,] or the *Holy-day*, ſubjoins this Reaſon for his ſaying ſo, *Becauſe on it* Latona *brought forth* Apollo. And elſewhere he joins the *Seventh* with the *Firſt* and *Fourth* Day of every Month,

---

(*p*) *Septimana, ſeptem dierum Syſtema.* (*q*) *Hi autores non loquuntur de diebus Septimanæ, ſed diebus Menſis Lunaris.* Hoſpinian. de Feſtis Ethnicis. (*r*) *Septimus dies menſis Apollinis natalibus ſacer fuit.* Selden de jure Nat.

and

and dedicates 'em all alike to *Jupiter.* But there were many other Days in the Month *holy* besides the *Seventh.* For the *Third* was confecrated to *Minerva,* the *Fourth* to *Mercury,* as Born on that Day; the *Eighth* to *Neptune* and *Thefeus;* the *Ninth* to *Jupiter* and the *Sun,* the *laft* to *Pluto.* And if at any time the Poets give an Emphafis to the *Seventh-day,* they are excufable for their *Zeal,* becaufe *Apollo* was the *Patron* and Prefident of Poefie; and that Principle led 'em to treat his *Birth-day* with a more particular honour. Befides, the *Seventh* is a *compleat Number,* becaufe whatever is perfect and moft excellent in its kind is fignified by 'that Number faith (*s*) *Grotius.* (*t*) The Reafons are various why it has this Figure from *Arithmetick, Phyfick* and *Scripture;* and the inftances are too many to lay 'em all before you; but this is not to be denied, that the World has all along looked on it as a *Myfterious, Sacred and perfect Number.*

But tho' the Number *Seven* bears a great Name in Writings of all forts, yet this is certain, that it is not the *only* Number that has the Character of *Perfect* and *Holy,* as we may eafily perceive in the following Particulars.

(*s*) *In Lib. Evang.* (*t*) *Vid.* Epiphan. Tom. 2. Cicero. in Som. Scip. Pet. Martyr. Loc. Com. c. 5. n. 43. Mafium *in* Jofh. 6. Aul. Gel. Noct. Attic. l. 3. c. 10. Pezelium *ex* Melanchton. p. 2. Franc. Georg. de Hift. Sacr. Tom. 1. Sect. 2. A Lapid. *in* Deut. v. 12. Philo. lib. Alleg. Curcel. *de Efufang.* c. 6. Quintilian. l. 1. c. 1. Ifidor. Hifp. l. 6. Orig. Dr. *Pridenax* fafcic. contro. Chryfoft. Orat. 5. in Jud. Bafil. Hom. 11. Hexam. Aug. de Civ. Dei. c. 31. Clem. Alex. Stro. 6. Ambr. de Noah, *&c.* Befides many inftances in the Old and New Teftament, as, 7 Spirits, 7 Stars, 7 Deacons, *&c.*

. ,O N E: (*u*) *Macrobius* not only makes *this* the beginning of all Number, but faith, that it has a fpecial reference or refemblance to God, the Caufe and Creator of the Univerfe. And fo we find it in St. *Jerom* much commended, and in the Speech *Eufebius* made in the praife of *Conftantine.*

T W O: (*w*) *This Number* is Celebrated in *both* the Books of God, *Nature*, and *Scripture.* All things confift of *matter* and *form.* There are *Two* great Lights in the Firmament. *Two* Eyes, Ears, Hands and Legs in Man. There are *Two* Teftaments; *Two* Tables, *Two* Commandments to which all Laws are reduced. *Two* Turtles, Pidgeons and Lambs for Sacrifice; *Two* Witneffes, and Chrift fent out his Difciples *Two* and *Two.*

T H R E E: (*x*) *This Number*, faith *Origen*, was made for *Myfteries.* *Athanafius* equals it to the *Seventh* as reprefenting the *Trinity.* And *Servius* Reports that the *Pythagoreans* accounted it a *perfect Number*, and liken'd it to the Deity; not becaufe of the *Three Perfons*, but as there is from him *beginning, middle*, and *end.* *Macrobius* difcovers in it the *Three* great *Faculties* of the Soul, *Underftanding*, *Memory*, and *Will.* And the *Arithmeticians* call it the *perfect Number*, becaufe, fay they, it hath *beginning, middle*, and *end*, which make up the *perfection* of a Number, and is a Condition moft peculiar to the Number *Three.* It is in the firft place *full and perfect*, faith *Cornelius Muffus*; and there is

---

(*u*) Vid. Hieron. in Amos. Eufeb. de laud. Conft. ch. 6.
(*w*) Vid. Lactant. de Opif. Dei. N. 10, 12. Eliam in Greg. Naz. Orat. 4. Chryf. Hom. in Gen. Ecclu. 33. 15. 42. 24. (*x*) Vid. Origen. Hom. in Gen. Servium in Virg. Ecclo 8. Eliam. loc. cit. Corn. Muff. de div. Hift. l. 3. c. 13. Eufeb. de laud. Conft. c. 6.

no Creature in the World which has any fhadow, or footftep of the Deity, wherein this
Trias does not fome way or other contribute to
its perfection.

FOUR: (*y*) *This* is the *Perfect, Holy* and
Laudable Number, faith *Philo*.. The Name of
God in Hebrew, Greek and Latin is made out
of *four Letters*. The Difciples of *Pythagoras*
honour'd the *Fourth* as the Jews the *Seventh-day*,
and on that *Swore*, if there was occafion for it;
and the *Oath* ran in this form. *I Swear by him
who taught us the fecret of the Number Four, the
Spring of ever-flowing Nature, or Fountain of all
things* — Meaning, faith *Nicetas*, the *Four* Elements, out of which all Creatures are produced.

FIVE: *This* is not without fome extraordinary fignification, if only becaufe it is the *half*
of the *Sacred Number. Ten*. Nature commends
it in the *Five* Senfes, *Five* Fingers, and *Five*
Toes; and Scripture in the *Five* Talents, *Five*
Loaves, and *Five* Virgins.

SIX: (*z*) *This* is a *perfect Number*, faith
Bede, nay it is the *firft of the Perfect*, as *Philo,
Bodin*, and *Clemens Alexandrinus* from the *Py-
thagoreans* tell us.

EIGHT: (1) *Hefychius* will have *this*
Number to be a *Figure* of the other World;
and that the *Pythagoreans* made it an *Hierogiy-
phick* of *Juftice*. It confifts of *even Numbers*,
and is the *double of the fquare*, which reprefenting *ftedfaftnefs*, it was therefore Dedicated to
Neptune.

(*y*) Vid. Philo. de opificio Mundi. Clem. Alex. Stro. l. 5.
Greg. Naz. Orat. 4. μα᾽ τὸν τετρακτὺν, ὅρκ☉ τιμιώτατον.
(*z*) Vid. Bede in Gen. Philo. de Mundi Opif. Clem.
Alex. Stro. l. 4. (1) Vid. Macrob. Plutarch in
Thefeo.

NINE:

NINE : (2) *This* was an *illustrious* Number among the Poets, as we find by their *Nine Muses*; and was solemn with the *Romans*, witness their *Nones*. It had a *Charm against Theft*, assisted *Flight*, and was *Holy to the Sun*, as *Dionysius Halicarnassus* informs us.

TEN : (3) Now we are come to the *most absolute and compleat Number*, as comprehending all Numbers, *the most perfect and holy*. The *Tenth Day Virgil* much applauds; and his *Septima post decimum* does not mean that the *Seventeenth-day* is prosperous; but as *Servius* explains him, the *Tenth* is a very *Fortunate Day*, and next to it the *Seventh*. Or, as *Hospinian* speaks, the Poet magnifies *Two* Days, the *Seventh* and *Tenth*; but *this last* rather than the *other*. *This* Number has two Privileges; *One* that it is *perfect in it self*,' and when we come to it we must begin again : The *Other*, 'that it is the *Mother of Perfection*, for Ten times Ten produce an *Hundred*, the *most perfect Number* of all. And the *Tenth* being so compleat a Number, it is sometimes made to signifie *ever*; *Deut.* xxiii. 2, 3. A Number consecrated to *Tythes*, not only by the *Law of Moses*, but by the *Law of Nature*, as appears from *Abraham* and *Jacob*, the (4) *former* paying that proportion to *Melchisedech* King of *Salem*, and *Priest of the high God*; (5) and the *latter* ingaging to set apart the *Tenth of all he should possess*, in case God would be pleased to bring him home to his Fathers House in safety. This was also the practice of divers Infidels, as we see in *Livy*,

---

(2) *Nona fugæ melior, contraria furtis.* Virg. (3) *Vid.* Greg. Naz. Orat. 42. Euseb. de laud. Conft. l. 6. Reuchlin. de Arte Cabal. l. 2. Hofp. de Feft. *Montague* againft *Selden, de decimis. decumanus fluctus.* (4) Gen. xiv. 20. (5) Gen. xxviii. 22.

Xenophon,

Xenophon, and *Laertius*, who were wont to dedicate a good portion of Money taken from the Captives to *Apollo* or *Diana* (6) [*decimæ nomine*] under the name of *Tythe*. And *Agesilaus*, as I take it, in two years time offer'd an Hundred Talents and more to the God at *Delphos*, that he might not be wanting in discharging the *Tythe*. And the Custom was so prevalent, that *Pisistratus* the Tyrant writes thus to *Solon*; (7) *All the Athenians do separate the Tythe of their Fruits, not to be spent in our use, but for the Publick Sacrifices and common profit.* So the Old *Latins* paid Tythes to their God *Hercules*; as did also *Posthumius* and other Roman Captains. From which, and the like Examples, a Man might very well argue, That if any one Day be consecrated by the Light of Nature, to the Service of God rather than another, then most likely it must be the *Tenth*, the *same* proportion of *time* better answering that part of our *Goods* and *Fruits* which by the dictate of *Natural Reason* was consecrated to Divine Uses.

TWELVE: *This* is a Number very Famous in Scripture, from the *Twelve* Patriarchs in the Old Testament, and *Twelve* Apostles in the New. And the Mystery of this, *Rabanus*, and out of him *Thomas* [in *Catena*] gives us, because *Twelve* arises out of the Numbers *Three* and *Four* multiplied in themselves, and signifies that they were to Preach the Doctrine of the *Trinity* in the *four Quarters of the World*. We read likewise of the *Twelve* Fountains in *Elim*; the *Twelve* Precious Stones in the Pectoral of the High-Priest; the *Twelve* Loaves of Shew-Bread; the *Twelve* Spies; the *Twelve* Tribes;

---

(6) Xenoph. in Cyro.   (7) Laert. in vit. Solon.

the

the *Twelve* Oxen; the *Twelve* Stars in the Crown of the Bride; the *Twelve* Gates, and *Twelve* Foundations of the Heavenly *Jerusalem.* So in the Heavens we have *Twelve* Signs; and in History the (8) *Twelve* Governours among the *Egyptians.* And in a word, 'tis a Number so necessary, that if we give any credit to the Doctrine of *Pythagoras,* (9) God made use of it to *settle* the Universe.

The (10) Politicians make the Numbers *Thirty, Hundred, Two Hundred and Fifty, Five Hundred,* and *Seven Hundred* very remarkable periods, and frequently attended with great Revolutions and Changes.

And for the Number *Fifty, Philo* calls it *the most Holy, the most Natural* of all Numbers; and (11) *Origen* durst not attempt to open the Secrets of it.

But I have dwelt too long on a Subject, out of which, as St. *Chrysostom* speaks, Curiosity hath produced many *Fictions,* and whence many Heresies had their beginning. Indeed *Marcion, Valentinus* and *Basilides* were the Men that borrowed these Lessons of the Schools of *Pythagoras* and *Plato,* on purpose to puzzle and amuse People with Mysteries in Religion. And if the Ancient Doctors of the Church took any notice of 'em, 'twas to make 'em able to talk with the Hereticks in their own Language; But for their Usefulness, (12) St. *Augustine* thought there was more affectation and *Pride* than *Profit* in this Study; and his advice was, to have regard not only to *Number,* but also to

---

(8) δωδεκαρχία, i. e. *duodecam virorum principatus apud Ægyptios.* Herodot. l. 2. (9) τῷ δὲ δωδεκαέδρῳ εἰς τὸ πᾶν ὁ θεὸς κατεχρήσατο. Plut. de placit. Philof. (10) *Axiomata Politica collecta à* Greg. Richtero. (11) Homil. 8. in Num. (12) de Civ. Dei, l. 11. c. 31.

Measure

Meafure and Weight, in difcourfes of this Nature. However, from what I have faid, we may partly difcover the little ftrefs there is to be laid on the *Sacrednefs* and *perfection of the Number Seven,* when *other Numbers* have thofe Commendations and Characters as well as the *Seventh,* and in particular the Numbers *One, Three,* and *Ten* feem to excell it.

But how it came by its laft Character, or that it is the *Day* on *which all things were finifhed,* This indeed feems more difficult to account for, unlefs we do allow (as we muft) that many of the Infidels were no ftrangers to the Book of God; but as they were curious to dive into *all* forts of other Learning, fo they were not altogether wanting in *this,* as appears by *Ariftotle,* or rather his *Mafter* who was fo converfant in *Mofes*'s Works, that he is hereupon often called the (13) *Athenian Mofes.* (14) *Ariftobulus* fpeaks this loud enough, that *Hefiod* and *Homer* fuck'd their Knowledge out of the Bible, which is not an improbable thing, becaufe *Homer* lived fome hundreds of years after *Mofes,* and *Callimachus* more after *Homer.* And it is evident the Poets took their *Deucalion's-Flood* from *that* of *Noah.* (15) The *Giant*'s Scaling *Heaven,* was drawn from that bold attempt of building the *Tower of Babel.* Their *Vulcan* was our *Tubal Cain* abbreviated, and both of the fame Profeffion. Their Sacrifice of *Iphigenia* comes from the Story of *Jeptha's* Daughter, and *Their* mighty (16) *Jove* from *our Almighty*

---

(13) Plato, Mofes *Attica lingua loquens, fic* Numenius. Pythag. apud Reuchlin de art. Ca. (14) Ἐκ τῶν ἡμετέρων βιβλίων μετειληφότες. Apud Eufeb. de præp. Evang. (15) *Vid.* A Lapide in Gen. vi. 4. & xi. 4. (16) *Quidam ex noftris aiunt, hoc nomen in noftris literis fonare* Jova: *à quo nomen* Jovis. Galat. de Arcan. Cath. Verit. l. 2. c. 10.

Jehovah.

Jehovah. And therefore, if the better to Celebrate the Birth-day of their *Apollo*, the *God of Wisdom*, they ſtole that account of Scripture concerning the Creation's being finiſhed on that Day (the ſtupendous work of Nature which nothing but an *Infinitely Wise* Deity was able to produce) and aſſign'd it to his Birthday, this is no more than what they did in other Caſes, aping *Moſes* and the People of *Iſrael* in many things which could never be thought of, if they had not had recourſe to thoſe places where the *Jews* were, and conſulted the Books they found among them, wherein theſe Particulars were revealed, and recorded. And for the greater credibility of this, we may obſerve that their moſt refined Wits went down at firſt from *Greece* to *Egypt*, which was in thoſe days the Nobleſt *Academy* and School in the World, where all ſorts of Arts and Sciences flouriſhed ; and there you know our Fathers reſided for many Generations ; and from *them* and *that Country* ſeveral *Cuſtoms*, ſuch as *Circumciſion* and ſome other Rites, were convey'd to the remoteſt parts. And if we ſometimes meet with the *ſame Notions* and the *ſame Words* too in their *Books* which we find in *Scripture*, we need not be ſurprized at it, ſince it is the affectation and humour of moſt People to publiſh any thing they have got abroad, leſt the World ſhould think they have travelled for nothing. And thereupon, as a token of improvement, they are apt to Diſcourſe in a *Language*, and perhaps in a *Sence* alſo remote from the capacities of the Vulgar.

B. How does this agree with *Lactantius*, (17) who admires that *Pythagoras* and *Plato*

---

(17) *Lactant. de vera Sap. l. 4. c. 2.*

ſhould

fhould fo much neglect the Nation of the *Jews*, as not to enquire into *their Cuftoms*, as they did into *thofe* of other Countries, which could not fo well anfwer the expence and fatigue of their Journey.

A. That thofe Philofophers went down to *Egypt Lactantius* himfelf confeffes; and there the *Jews* left many of their Cuftoms behind 'em; and thofe Cuftoms might be well enough called *Jewifh* tho' learnt in another Kingdom, becaufe they were *Originally* fo. But whether inftructed in *Egypt* or *Judea*, plain it is from thefe following Teftimonies that they were not ftrangers to the ways of the *Hebrews* in many inftances of Religion and Learning. (18) For *Ariftobulus*, whom I juft now mention'd, *Preceptor* to *Ptolemy Philometor*, 2 *Maccab.* i. 10. and who Flourifhed about 200 Years after *Plato*, faith of *Pythagoras*, That *He borrowed many things from the Jews.* Which (19) *Jofephus* alfo affirms, That *He knew our way*, and in many Cafes complied with it. The other Author faith the fame thing of *Plato*, That *He followed our Laws and Inftitutions after he had carefully examined and difcuffed each part of 'em.* And it is moreover added, that the (20) *Peripatetick Philofophy*, of which *Ariftotle* was the firft Introducer, depended on the Law of *Mofes*, and other Prophets. As for the Story among fome of the *Jews*, That (21) *Ariftotle* at the point of death, according to the Leffons he had learnt of the Pofterity of *Sem*, taught his Scholars the *Immortality* of the Soul, and the Doctrine of *Rewards* and *Punifhments* after this Life; and

---

(18) Clem. Alex, Stro. 5.　　(19) *Adv.* Apion. (20) Clem. Stro. fupra.　　(21) Comment. ad Sepher Cozri.

being

being inſtructed by *Simeon the Juſt* (then High-
Prieſt) he retracted many Points, and ſhow'd
himſelf quite another Man in all matters whatever, wherein he had been oppoſite to the Law
and Principles of the *Hebrews.* Tho' I ſay,
we lay no great ſtreſs on this *Tradition,* yet we
muſt not reject that prevailing Opinion among
the *Rabbins,* that there was a very cloſe Correſpondence between *themſelves* and the *Greek
Philoſophers* in many inſtances of Knowledge
and Diſcipline; and therefore it ſeems not
ſtrange in *Clement* and *Theodoret* what is ſaid
concerning *Pythagoras,* That he was *Circumciſed* in *Egypt* after the manner of the *Hebrews,*
which is in general terms vouched by (22)
Laertius, That *He was initiated into all the Myſteries both of the Greeks and Barbarians.* And
Jamblicus ſaith, That conferring with the
Phœnician and other Prieſts, *He was admitted
into the moſt Secret and Sacred Things then uſed
in Biblus, Tyre, and throughout all Syria.* St. *Ambroſe* ſaith little leſs, and affirms it to be the
judgment of very many before his time.
Then for *Plato,* (23) *Clement* calls him [τὸν ἐξ
Ἑβραίων Φιλόσοφον,] one whom the *Hebrews* furniſh'd with Philoſophy, as they did divers
others, who were little better than *Thieves and
Robbers, becauſe they were ſo ungrateful and diſ-
ingenuous as not to own their Maſters.* *Juſtin*
and *Philoponus* concurr with *Clement* concerning
Plato; and *Theodoret* is poſitive that he drew
his beſt water out of (24) *Hebrew Ciſterns;* and
whenever he ſaid well of *God* or his *Worſhip,*
it was owing purely to the *Theology* of the *Jews.*
Some will have him to be an Auditor of *Jeremy,*

---

(22) De Vir. Philoſ. l. 8.   (23) Strom. l. 1. & 6.
(24) Ἐκ τῶν Ἑβραίων ναμάτων.

which

which Chronology will hardly allow, that Prophet being above an hundred fifty years his Senior, and much nearer the times of *Pythagoras*, who Flourish'd about the *Overthrow* of the Temple, whereas *Plato* appear'd not in the World 'till about the *Reftoration*, or Rebuilding of it. But not to be curious of the *Date*, we are fure of the *Thing* we were fpeaking of; fo fure that *Tertullian* in his Apology demands, *What Poet or Sophifter among you has not drunk at the Fountain of the Prophets? thence your Philofophers have quench'd their thirft, or defire to improve their Wit*——And left it fhould be fufpected that Chriftians are partial in giving this account, (25) hear what *Hermippus* an ancient Pagan faith of *Pythagoras*, That *He borrowed many things of the Jews concerning the Soul, Blafphemy, &c.* and adds, *Thefe things he did and faid in imitation of the Jews and Thracians, whofe Doctrines he affumed, and made 'em one body with his own Writings.* This Teftimony (26) *Origen* remembers, and faith, *We read how Hermippus in his Firft Book about Law-Makers, afferted that Pythagoras derived his Philofophy from the Jews to the Grecians.* And *Porphyry* owns that he not only went to the *Arabians* and *Egyptians*, but alfo to the *Hebrews* and *Chaldeans* to learn what might be had from 'em; and *fo by his Travels into thefe Countries*, faith he, *he got the better part of his Philofophy.* And for *Plato*, 'tis, as I told you, little lefs than a Proverb, (27) That *Plato* was *Mofes in Greek.* And it may be juftly affirmed of him, that *he* ftole from *Mofes* what he faid of God

---

/ (25) Apud Jofephum.   (26) Adv. Celfum, L. 1.
(27) Τίς γάρ εςι Πλατων ἢ Μωσῆς Ἀττικίζων.

and

and the World. To thefe Authorities may be added that of *Clearchus* of *Cyprus*, who reports that he had feen a certain *Jew* with whom *Ariftotle* was very familiar. But above all, the Oracle of *Apollo* cannot furely be miftaken, which gave out, *That the Hebrews were well acquainted with many ways of the Gods; Wife-Men Worfhipping in an holy manner the Eternal Deity.* And elfewhere *Apollo* calls the *Hebrews* [ἀριζηλάντες,] very *Learned Men*; and therefore that it was the Cuftom of thofe Times to apply to 'em, is no marvel, fince they found 'em fo well able to be their Tutors. And this the great agreement between the (28) *Pythagorean* and *Cabaliftical* way among the *Jews* of *difguifing* Doctrines further fhows. They had their *Symbols, Notes* and *Proverbs, Numbers* and *Figures, Letters, Syllables* and *Words,* wherein both Parties were equally Superftitious; and it may be prefumed that they learn'd of one another; which is enough I think to anfwer your Objection out of *Lactantius,* who was not, it feems, throughly informed in what concern'd *Pythagoras* and *Plato.* For thefe two Philofophers, tho not exclufive of others, yet above all the reft were beholding to the *Hebrews*; altho' upon a Principle which too much governs, they were not willing to leffen their own parts, and give thofe *Originals* their due praifes. And of this his Commentator was aware, and thereupon faith, that *the Suffrages or Votes of the Fathers go againft Lactantius in this Point,* and he referrs you to feveral Authors who contradict his Opinion.

Thus as to the *Greeks*; Then for the *Romans,* you know it was *their Way* to incorporate *all-*

---

(28) Vid. Reuchlin de Arte Cabbalift. L. 2.

Religions

Religions into their *Own*, and Worſhip thoſe *Gods* whom before they Conquered. So that the *Jews* at laſt becoming Tributary to the *Romans*, they not only found acceſs into the Empire, but in a little time they began to plant and fill whole Towns with their Families. Scarce any City of good Note in *Syria* and the *Leſſer Aſia*, wherein the *Jews* were not conſiderable for their Numbers, and in which they had not *Synagogues* for their Devotion ; and the manner of their Lives, wherein *their diſperſion* had made 'em very circumſpect, and the forms of their Worſhip being once obſerved, many of the Roman People became well affected to the *Jewiſh Rites* ; were *Circumciſed*, forbore *Swine's-Fleſh*, and obſerved the *Sabbath*. (29) Of which *Seneca* complain'd, and cenſured his Countrymen for it. And this clears what you offer'd out of *Philo* ; That *the whole World had regard to the Sabbath.* Not that they knew the *Sabbath* by the *Light of Nature*, or had reſpect to it in the Ages paſt ; but that it was ſo generally admitted in the days of that Author both at *Rome* and *elſewhere*, that on that ſcore it might in ſome meaſure deſerve the Character ; for ſo (30) *Joſephus* explains him. " *The Laws eſtabliſhed among us have been fol-* " *lowed by all Nations ; yea the Common People* " *have long ſince drawn our Piety into imitation,* " *neither is there any Country, Greek or Barbarian,* " *to which the Reſt of our Sabbath-day hath not* " *reached.*—So that according to him, tho' many of the Heathens honour'd the *Sabbath* and ſome other particulars of the *Jewiſh Worſhip*, yet it was not as recommended by the *Law of*

---

(30) *Eo uſque ſceleratiſſimæ gentis conſuetudo invaluit, &c.* Apud Aug. de Civ. Dei. L. 6. c. 11.
(31.) Adv. Apion.

Nature, but as taught by the *Law of Moses*, which they followed and drew into practice. And for the *long since* he speaks of, he means the *time* between *him* and *Augustus Cæsar*, who was very favourable to them and their Sabbath, as we see by several *Decrees* made on their behalf. (31) " Augustus Cæsar Pontif. Max. " *Forasmuch as the Nation of the* Jews *hath always* " *been trusty to the* Romans, *not only at* this " Day, *but also in* former Ages, *and especially* " *in the time of our Father* Cæsar *the Emperor,* " *under* Hircanus *the High-Priest, I have or-* " *dain'd according to the common judgment of the* " Senate, *that they shall live* after their Country " Laws *under which they lived in the time of* " Hircanus *the High-Priest of God*; *and that* " *their Temple shall retain the privilege of a San-* " *ctuary, and that they shall not be compelled to* " *appear before any Judge upon their* Sabbath- " days, *or the Day* before *their* Sabbaths *after* " *Nine a Clock.* Again, " Cæsar *to* Norba- " nus Flaccus *Health. Let the* Jews *where-ever* " *they live, carry their Sacred Money to* Jerusa- " lem *according to their old Custom, and let no* " *Man presume to hinder 'em. Agrippa* also writ to the Magistrates, Senate and People at *Ephesus* on the same subject. " *I will that the* " Jews *living in* Asia *keep their Sacred Money—* And to the *Cyrenean* Magistrates and Senate: " *The* Jews *Inhabiting among you, I command* " *that they be permitted to live after their* Cu- " stom. And to *Syllanus,-* " *That the* Jews *be* " *not constrain'd upon their* Sabbaths *to appear* " *before any Judge—*And hereupon *Norbanus Flaccus* Proconsul, sends these Instructions to the Magistrates of *Sardinia*; " *That no Man*

(31) Joseph. Antiq. l. 16. c. 10.

" *hinder*

" *hinder the* Jews *to live according to* their Cu-
" ftom. And *Junius Antonius* another Pro-
Conful, difpatches Orders to the Governors
of *Ephefus,* " *That the* Jews *be allowed to ufe*
" their Country Cuftoms, *according to the De-*
" *crees, and Ordinances of* Cæfar *and* Agrippa,
" *and do all things as they pleafe according to*
" their Cuftoms.——I take the more notice of
thefe Indulgences and Decrees which tolerate
the *Jews* to exercife their Religion *out* of the
limits of the Land of *Paleftine,* becaufe we
may obferve from 'em, that *Auguftus, Agrippa*
and the *Proconfuls* call 'em *their Sabbaths, their*
Cuftoms, their Country-Cuftoms, as peculiar to
them ; and which if known to other Nations,
it was chiefly owing to this Favour of the *Ro-*
man Princes, whereby they had freedom of
Worfhip, and an Opportunity to gain Profelytes in thofe Provinces where they lived upon
the temptation and motive of *Novelty* to which
Humane Nature is much addicted. But yet
whatever their affection was to the *Roman* Government about the Reign of *Auguftus,* who
gave thefe Teftimonies of the Efteem he had
for 'em ; They were reckon'd by *Seneca* and
others a *Prophane* odd People on the account
of their Religion ; and in particular, becaufe
of the *Sabbath,* He and They very much derided 'em ; which had not been, were the *Sab-*
bath or *Seventh-day* Solemnity the *common Tenet*
of all Nations.

I cannot tell what impreffion this makes on
you, but to me it feems more than likely, That
neither the *Patriarchs* kept the *Sabbath,* becaufe
we have not one word of it in Scripture, nor
that the *Greeks* minded it any further than
barely to talk of it, as a thing they had met
with in their Travels *abroad,* or in their reading
at

at *home.* And if some of the *Roman Empire*
look'd on it with a favourable Eye, it was no
earlier than about the *Incarnation* of Chrift;
and their more Learned Citizens laughed àt
their Neighbours for refpecting *that* or any
other of the *Jewifh Cuftoms.* And tho' the Ancient *Poets* fpake very honourably of a *Seventh
Day,* it was not purely on its *own* account, but
with regard to their *Apollo,* whofe *Birth* they
Celebrated *on it.* And if others did the fame,
they defign'd no Reverence for the *Sabbath-day,*
but confider'd it only as a *Myfterious Number,*
made remarkably by *Nature,* but no Divine
Inftitution fanctifying and requiring it for the
Worfhip of the *Creator,* which is the Sence we
muft take it in, or elfe their knowledge of it,
if well proved, will fignifie little.

 B. But does not the *Manna* in the Wildernefs, before the Law was given, fhow the *Sabbath*
to have an earlier *Inftitution* than what you are
willing to allow it? For it is faid, (32) *The
People gather'd it Six Days, but on the Seventh-
Day, they could not find it.* And the Reafon
was, *becaufe the Seventh-Day was an Holy Sabbath unto the Lord. Six Days you fhall gather it,
but on the Seventh Day which is the Sabbath, in it
there fhall be none. See, the Lord hath given you
the Sabbath, therefore he giveth you on the Sixth
Day the bread of two Days.* So that in *this place*
at leaft, there is exprefs mention of the *Sabbath.* And the miraculous *Dew* on the ground
for all the *Six Days* together, and none on the
Seventh, plainly demonftrates that God diftinguifhed *that Day* as a time of *Reft* to the People,
*in which every Man was to abide in his place, and
none to ftir out of his Tent.*

---

(36) **Exod.** xvi. 23, 26, 29.

     M 3   *A.* This

A. This Miracle of the *Manna* is confider'd as a *Preface* to the promulgation of the Law from Mount *Sinai,* and intended to imprefs the People with the notion of the *Sabbath,* that they might not be furprized afterwards to find it within the *Two Tables.* (33) And peradventure it might ferve to *difcover* that Day of which the Precept fpake, and on which God was faid to *reft* from the works of *Creation.* But that it was an Obfervation altogether *new* we find in *ver.* 22. For notwithftanding the interpretation *Mofes* made on the Miracle in behalf of the *Sabbath,* yet the *Princes* and *Rulers* feeing fome of the People gathering twice as much *Manna* on the *Sixth Day* as they had got on the Days before, *they came and told Mofes,* reprefenting it as a tranfgreffion of what was before commanded them; which certainly they would not have done, had they known any thing of the *Sabbath-Day.* And again, *it came to pafs there went out fome of the People on the Seventh Day to gather, and they found none, ver.* 27. which alfo befpeaks very little notice of the *Sabbath,* or elfe the *Day,* as well as *Mofes's Order* had hindred their going abroad. And admit the *People* forgetful and negligent in fuch cafes, and that their Bondage in *Egypt* had obliterated or defaced this Doctrine of the *Seventh Day,* yet the *Great Men* and *Chiefs of Families* cannot be fuppofed ftrangers to fuch a Tradition, but muft be privy to thofe *Archives.* and Records all Nations preferve of the *ancient times.* and *things* concerning themfelves, and from which *Mofes* is thought to Pen this Book of *Genefis*; and yet thefe Princes were ftumbled at the *Sabbath,* as a thing altogether unknown

---

(33) Philo *de vit.* Mofis. l. 1.

to 'em. And further it is faid, *ver.* 1. that *they came to the Wildernefs on the* 15*th Day of the* 2*d Month.* (34) " Now the next Morn-
" ing to this it rained *Manna*, and fo conti-
" nued every Morning until the 22d, which
" being the 7th Day, it rained none, and that
" Day they were commanded to keep the *Sab-*
" *bath.* Now then if the 22d Day of the
" Month were the *Sabbath*, therefore the 15th
" muft be the *Sabbath* too, for that was the
" *Seventh* before it. But the Text faith ex-
" prefly they marched on that Day a long wea-
" rifome March, which fhows they did not
" obferve it, and this neglect proves it not
" kept before. And it is worth our notice,
" that the day of the Month is never named,
" unlefs it be once, for any Station but *this*,
" where the *Sabbath* was ordained, otherwife
" it could not have been known, that *That Day*
" was ordain'd for a *Day of Reft*, which be-
" fore was *none.* And it is not unlikely, but
the word *Remember* afterwards fet at the front
of the Precept about the *Sabbath*, might be occafion'd by that little concern *Mofes* found the
People had for it, even at this time, becaufe
they ftill took it for a *late appointment*, tho'
afferted by Miracle. And the infinuation of it
was, That they were to keep in mind that a-
ftonifhing fupply of Bread from Heaven given
'em by an Almighty and kind Power; and
withal *remember* that part of the wonder which
related to the Obfervation of the *Sabbath-Day*,
and which that *Law* prefcribed 'em.

B. Methinks the moft natural meaning of this
word, [*Remember*] argues for me; becaufe to
remember a thing, fuppofes it *known before*; and

_____

(34) Mr. *Mede* on Ezek. xx. 20.

therefore

therefore when God Commanded the Children of *Israel* to *Remember the Sabbath-Day*, the very Language declares it an *ancient Ordinance*, but *forgotten* for some time, and so the *Jews* are hereby quicken'd to the stricter observance of it for the time to come.

A. Undoubtedly the word often referrs to the *time past*; as when *Joseph* was in *Egypt*, he *remembred* the Dreams which he had dreamed of his Brethren while he was a Child, and living in *Canaan*, *Gen*. xlii. 9. But this is not the constant use of it, for it sometimes looks *forward*, as in the *Institution* of the *Passover*, and of the Blessed *Sacrament* of the *Lord's-Supper*, both which were appointed *before* the things fell out of which they were to be the *Memorials* to future Ages. This frequently appears in the ordinary Commands we lay on our Servants and Children ; when as a sign of our resolution to be obey'd, we bid 'em *remember this* or *that* thing; by which expression our meaning is to *charge their Memories* with what we expect them to do, and to take special care to do it. But then this is no recalling to their minds what they understood before ; but, as I said, to make 'em more *heedful* in that particular, be it what it will, or whether we ever heard of it before or no. And so in this place the *Æthiopick* Version renders it pertinently enough, *Observe the Sabbath-Day*; designing by the word *Remember*, nothing more than to *keep it holy*. Yet accepting your interpretation, that it means *looking back*, or a reflection on what was before, it is not necessary the word should signifie any great *Antiquity*, or what had been said or done in the Generations of Old ; all that can be pretended is, that it casts an eye on what is *past*. And if so, a Man may be said to
remember

remember as well what was done within a *few days* or a *few hours*, as what happen'd in the *Years* or *Ages foregoing*. And so St. *Peter* remembred the *words of Jesus* [*before the Cock Crow thou shalt deny me thrice*;] yet those words were utter'd not many hours before his Apprehension and Trial. And therefore should we in this Case take the *antecedent time*, we can go no higher than the Miracle of the *Manna* by which the *Sabbath* was notified, and the *remembrance* of it used as a Motive to make 'em diligently and faithfully keep it.

B. To consider the Subject of the *Seventh-Day*. It is a reflection on the *Wisdom*, *Power* and *Goodness* of God in the Works of the Creation; and *this* being always *necessary*, 'tis necessary to *keep the Day* which God himself made the *Memorial* of that *Power*, and was appointed a *Day of Rest* for us the better to reflect on those many Wonders he has done on our accounts. Besides, as it is a peculiar Day Sanctified by God, he has made it the *means* of the Divine Blessing; and to lay aside the *means* of Blessings, is to deprive our selves of those Blessings, because we reject the *way* of conveying 'em to us.

A. A thing is *necessary* when we cannot be *without it*. But tho' to remember the Creation be very necessary, in order to raise in us an admiration of those infinite attributes we must needs discover in God from his producing the World; yet this may be done without the *Seventh-Day*, and therefore this inferrs no *necessity* to have it continued, because this *end* may be had *without it*. We have many other *Memorials* of the Divine Power, and the many Objects which from the Books of *Nature* and *God*, every minute crowd thro' our Senses to
the

the Understanding, afford us Lessons enough to teach us this great Truth; and if we had never heard of a *Seventh-Day*, we must have been convinced of the Being of a *Creator*. Yet with regard to the *Jews*, who were to be distinguish'd from the *Gentiles*, besides the *Commandment*, there was an Emphasis laid on the *Day* as a practical Comment on their *Creed*, to signifie what they meant by their God, namely *Him* who *in six Days made Heaven and Earth*, &c. But then this was no more than a Ceremony of distinction which we have no occasion for, and as a Ceremony 'tis in no wise necessary, but we have free liberty either to retain or discharge the use of it.

As to the other thing, That God has made it an *instrument* and *conveyance* of his Blessings. Tho' I confess God uses *means* to bless his People by, yet those *means* are not always the same; and tho' *necessary* at *one* time, they are not so at *another*. *Sabbath* and *Circumcision* were certainly the *instruments* of Gods blessing to the People of *Israel*; But as we do not take our selves obliged to the *latter*, so neither doth the *former* concern us; and as for *that* we have another *Sacrament*, so for *this* we have *another Day* to honour God with our Worship. Moreover, it is not the *Day*, but the *Service* of the Day on which the Sanctification depends; and tho' the Ordinance of God set apart that *particular Day*, and made a difference between it and the rest of the *Week*, yet 'tis the *Duties* of the Day make it *holy*; and if the *Jews* had no respect to *these*, the *other* hallowing had signified little; and notwithstanding the sanctification of the Day, it had gone without the Blessing. And in a word, if this way of arguing has any force, it is only in behalf of the *Sabbatarian,*

butarian, to conclude for that *Seventh-Day* called the *Sabbath* ; but is ill apply'd by those
who consent to a change from the *last Day* of
the Week to the *first* ; and makes as much for
the rest of the *Jewish Feasts, Sacrifices, Offerings,* and other *Legal Ceremonies* which were
made the *means* of Blessings, as well as the *Sabbath* ; and by *this* Argument we ought to retain them *all,* or else we hazard the Heavenly
Benediction.

B. To detain you no longer in a Point on
which you have said enough to make it *doubtful,* we will advance forward, and propose
some Reasons, which, I think, are not liable
to any exception, and they are such as these.
This Law about the *Sabbath,* is ranked with the
others confessedly *Moral,* and partakes of all
the honours and privileges in common with
them ; it was *written with the Finger of God,*
and not in Paper or Parchment, or upon the
Leaves of Trees, but in *Tables of Stone,* as the
rest were, to denote the *perpetuity* of them (as
the *Gentiles* used to ingrave their Laws in *Brass,*
to show they would always have them inviolably kept) and thereupon it is called the *Eternal* and *Everlasting Sabbath* : It had the same
glorious *Promulgation,* the same *Majesty, Terrours,* and all the Circumstances of the other
Nine ; such as *Thundring* and *Lightning, Sound
of the Trumpet, Fire and Smoak* ; and pronounced by God's own immediate voice in the Au-
dience of all the People. Nay the Emphasis of
remember (you just now mentioned) is a Note
of special observance, requiring more than ordinary attention and care ; and as the (35)
Hebrews say, *we are bound for ever to remember*

(35) *In primis memoria tenendum est.* Vid Mr. *Ainsworth*
in Gen. xiii. 3.

it.

it. 'Add, that *this Law* is no where *repealed* no more than the *others*; and as for that Text of *Paul*, which is the great Proof to lay it by, it fpeaks of the *other* Feſtivals of the *Jews*, not *this*, and therefore faith in the plural [σαββάτων,] *Sabbaths*, meaning the *Seventh* (36) *Month*, the *Seventh Year*, and the *Jubilee*; not *this Sabbath* of the *Moral* Law, about which we are now difcourfing. On the contrary, *Chriſt came not* (as himfelf declares) (37) *to deſtroy the Law, but to fulfill it.* And it is very obfervable, that foretelling the deſtruction of *Jeruſalem*, which was not to be till a great many years after his *Aſcenſion*, he bids his Difciples pray that (38) *their flight be not in the Winter, nor on the Sabbath-day.* And the Reaſon was, becauſe if fo timed, they might be tempted or forced to fome Action tending *to prophane the Day*, which there was no fear of, if it was not to continue *Sacred*, as before. And according to this notion of it, we find our Lord himfelf obferving the *Sabbath-day*, and it was his *cuſtom* to do fo. And after this Example, when he was dead, the *Holy Women*, tho' they had prepared *Spices* and *Ointments* to imbalm his Body (a Work of Piety as any Man might think) yet they would not then do it, becauſe it was the *Sabbath*; and therefore.(39) *they reſted on the Sabbath-day according to the Commandment.* They were Difciples to the Lord, and without doubt well inſtructed in the Duties of Religion after the way of the Gofpel; yet they underſtood nothing to the contrary, but they were to keep *this Day*, as heretofore, in obedience

---

(36) *Quibus nomen Sabbati aliquando in Scriptura tribuitur.* Curcellæus, *de eſu ſanguinis.* (36) Mat. v. 17. (38) Matth. xxiv. 20. (39) Luke xxiii. 56.

to

to the Law : They did fo, and the *Holy Ghoft*
commended 'em for it; and not only *they*, but
the *Apoftles* many years after had it in great
efteem, and *Pray'd* and *Preach'd* on it.   Even
Paul himfelf who feems to call it a *Shadow*, was
conftant on that Day *in the Synagogues* or *in the
Temple.* (40) *He reafoned in the Synagogues
every Sabbath-day*; and He fo religioufly obferved it, that for want of thefe Conveniencies
we find him Praying (41) by the River fide,
becaufe it was the Sabbath.   And long after his
deceafe, a Man muft be very ignorant in the
Hiftory of the Church, if he does not know
that it was folemnly honour'd and fpent in
holy Duties for many years, when there was
no Apoftle in the World who could pretend
Divine Commiffion to repeal and void it.   All
which either concludes for the morality of the
Sabbath, or condemns thofe who fo carefully
minded it a long while after our Saviour's departure, even when *Jerufalem and the Temple
were deftroy'd*; and fo, if ever, there was a
full end of what was *Ceremony* in the Jewifh
Religion.

A. What you now propofe has weight in
it; yet I am convinc'd in my felf, that you
lay no great ftrefs on thefe proofs, becaufe
the ftrength they have ferves only to confirm
the *Jewifh Saturday Sabbath* which you are
ready enough to difmifs; as a thing not very
confiftent with your *Chriftian Liberty.* So
that your *own practice* confutes what you have
faid; and your obferving the *Lords-Day*, is a
demonftration to me, that you have effectually
confider'd thefe Objections already. However

(40) Acts xviii. 4   (41) Acts xvi. 13.

for

for Diſcourſe ſake, I will a little examine the ſeveral parts of your Argument, and ſee how far the expreſſions go to eſtabliſh a *perpetual Sabbath*; and the rather, becauſe you ſeem to borrow 'em from the Authority of the two Houſes of Parliament, who ſent 'em by *Sir James Harrington* to King *Charles the Firſt*, in anſwer to that *Query* his Majeſty made 'em concerning *Eaſter*; which in the King's Opinion, had the ſame Power for its Eſtabliſhment with that of the *Lords-Day*, as you heard before.

1. You ſay then, That the *Fourth Commandment*'s being rank'd with the others evidently *Moral*, inferrs the *Sabbath* to be *Moral* likewiſe, or elſe it was ill placed among thoſe that were ſo. This concludes nothing; For in reading other paſſages of Scripture, we may diſcover the ſame intermixture of *Natural* and *Ceremonial* Precepts, as (42) where *Peace Offerings* and *things ſtrangled* and *blood* are put with *Fornication* and *Image-worſhip*; yet I dare ſay no body will go about to make theſe Duties ſtand upon the *level*, and aſſert 'em *all Moral*, tho' in the ſame Verſes they are *joyn'd together*.

2. That *this Law*, as well as the reſt, was *written in Stone*, inforces not the *perpetual* obligation of it, no more than do the other Ordinances of *Moſes*, all which *Joſhua* (43) *writ on Stones in the preſence of the Children of Iſrael*. Among theſe a great number were *Ceremonial*, as is agreed on all hands; and by this Argument of yours, *theſe* alſo were to be *Eternal* as well as the others. But the truth is, This was

_____

(42) Levit. xix. 4, 5. Acts xv. 29.   (43) Joſhua viii. 3².

by

by way of *Emblem*, (44) To fignifie the *hard hearts* of the *Jews*, who were heavy and dull, as the Prophet informs us, *Ezek.* xi. 19. And the infinuation was that they fhould not immediately forget what he fet before 'em, but fhow a careful and confcientious obedience to thofe Laws, which for their better (45) remembrance he had ordred to be ingraven in Tables of Stone, that the fight might affect 'em, and make an impreffion on their *Hearts* anfwerable to thofe *lafting Characters* they found in the *Marble.*

3. And this was all the *Thunder* and *Lightning* aim'd at, To create the greater Awe and Reverence to what was then delivered, and induce 'em to fhew more refpect to thefe Laws, becaufe of the Solemnity then ufed to divulge and proclaim 'em. But then a great many Precepts, befides thefe of the Two Tables were publifh'd at the *fame time*, and with the *fame Ceremony*, which yet are not infifted on, nor is that *Solemnity* thought fufficient to make them *Moral.*

4. As for *God's fpeaking thefe words*, fo he fpake the *others* which followed, and probably might have done it with the fame kind of Voice, but that the People's fear made 'em requeft *Mofes*, that God would be pleas'd to do it rather by his Mediation. And yet perhaps *God* himfelf fpake in *neither* place, but ufed the Miniftry of *Angels*, if St. *Stephen* faith true, *Acts* vii. 38, 53. Where that Martyr giving

---

(44) *Ad fignificandum cor lapideum judæorum qui erant ftupidi, hebetes & lapidei*, Ifidor.   (45) *Dedit eam* [*legem*] *fcriptam lapideis tabulis ad oblivionem evertendam.* A Lapid. in Exod. xxxi.

an account of *Mofes*, declares of him, that *this is he that was in the Church in the Wildernefs, with the Angel that fpake to him in Mount Sinai.* And tho' it is faid *God fpake thefe words,* it is, (46) as when a *Judge* may be faid to pronounce the *Decree,* tho' he does it by the *Cryer*; yet it is not taken for the *Cryer's* Decree, but the *Judge's,* who bids him Proclaim it.

5. And in this fence may be underftood the Two Tables being *written with the Finger of God*; not fo *ftrictly,* but by God's *Spirit,* by *Mofes,* or an *Angel,* at his *Order.* As where St. *Luke* reprefents *Chrift* fpeaking, (47) *If I by the Finger of God caft out Devils.*— St. *Matthew* explains it thus: (48) *If I by the Spirit of God*—as if it were the *fame thing*; and this a *Man infpired* may do, and *Chrift,* as Man, did it. In Reading Scripture therefore we are to confider many things fpoken in a way of *accommodation,* or elfe we fhall run our felves iuto grofs abfurdities by adhering too much to the Letter, as in thefe inftances we are upon: *God fpake* and *God writ with his Finger*; which muft not be rigoroufly taken after the found of the Expreffions, becaufe God has neither *Finger* nor *Voice* in that fence which we apply to Men; yet when God makes ufe of Inftruments for *Speech* or *Action,* his Commiffion Intitles him to what is *faid* or *done,* whether *Mofes* or any other Holy Man be the *Organ* to make it known.

6. The fame care is to be ufed in the examining of the importance of that word *Eternal* which you fix on the *Sabbath,* and by virtue of

---

(46) Auguft. adv. Manic.   (47) Luke xi. 20.
(48) Matth. xii. 28.

which

which you conceive it was to laſt for *ever* ; becauſe it is ſaid, *the Children of Iſrael ſhall keep the Sabbath throughout their Generations for a perpetual Covenant.* But the word in the Hebrew is variouſly tranſlated according to the nature of the matter in hand. For ſome-times indeed it ſignifies an *abſolute perpetuity,* but in many caſes no more than ſome *remarkable pe-riod,* which not being come, there was to be no alteration of the thing, whatever happen'd to be the ſubjeƈt of the Queſtion. Thus the *Truth of God is to endure for ever. God is everlaſting, eternal,* and the like. And theſe places mean *a perpetual duration* without *bounds,* without *end* ; not ſo much from the bare *propriety* and *ſound* of the word it ſelf, as from the *neceſ-ſary exiſtence* of the *Divine Nature* to which it is applied. But where it is ſaid, (49) *Circum-ciſion is an everlaſting Covenant,* and (50) *the Land of Canaan ſhall be an everlaſting Poſſeſ-ſion.* Here *one everlaſting* muſt explain the *other,* and *both* are to be no otherwiſe under-ſtood than for *a certain term* of years, at the expiring of which *Circumciſion* was to have an end as well as their *Poſſeſſion of the Land of Ca-naan,* which we know the *Jews* have loſt for many Ages. And ſo God promiſes *David* and *Solomon,* (51) *in this Houſe and in Jeruſalem which I have choſen out of all the Tribes of Iſrael will I put my Name for ever.* And yet now what is become of *this Jeruſalem,* and *this Houſe,* this Temple ? So in the former ruines of that City in the days of *Nebuchadnezzar* it is called a (52) a *perpetual deſolation,* yet *that perpetuity* was reſtrain'd to a *few years* ; this

(49) Gen. xvii. 7.   (50) Gen. xvii. 8.   (51)
2 Kings xxi. 7,   (52) Jerem. xxv. 9, 11,

N   *whole*

whole Nation shall be a desolation and astonish-ment, and these Nations shall serve the King of Babylon Seventy years. In the Law it was di-rected that the Servant should have his (53) *Ear bored with an Awl, and then serve his Master for ever.* Which *ever* could extend it self no farther than the (54) *Jubilee*, when all sorts of Service had its utmost period. And with this limitation is that purpose of *Hannah*, that *Samuel* her Son (55) *should abide before the Lord for ever:* *i. e.* as she a little before expresses her self, *all the days of his life*, or to his (56) *fiftieth Year*, after which the *Levites* were to serve no more. And after this manner the (57) *Poets* speak and *Schoolmen*, who say, *That God will punish the wicked during his Eternity, for sinning against him during theirs*; *i. e.* they who are impious all their Life time, shall be damned *for ever.* So that hereby we see, that the same word is differently applied according to the *capacity* of the matter treated of, and that the Epithet *Eternal* is often joined to things very *short* of *Eternity*, and intends sometimes *fifty*, sometimes *seventy years*, and more fre-quently *not so many*, in case a Man does not live so long. And thus the *Rabbins* themselves qualifie the term as appears by their way of *computation*, wherein they make *three* Epochas, *before*, *under* and *after* the Law or Govern-ment of *Messias*, and to each of these they assign *two thousand years.* And they are of Opinion that when *Messias* doth come, there will immediately thereupon ensue a wonder-

---

(53) Exod. xxi. 6. (54) Levit. xxv. 41.
(55) 1 Sam. i. 22, 11. (56) Numb. viii. 25.
(57) *Serviet æternum qui parvo nesciet uti*——Horace.
Non potest in æternum absolutè servire, cujus vita qua servit æterna esse non potest. A Lap.

ful change in the ſtate of things, and a *new*
ἀιὠν commence, which will put a period to
many Services they hitherto retain, and which
we, on *their Principles*, have thought fit to ſet
aſide, becauſe we believe that *Revolution* and the
Meſſias already come. All which gives us
light enough to ſee what is propoſed to us
in the *Eternity of the Sabbath*, which can ſignifie only a *certain period*, as *Circumciſion*, the
Temple, the *Jews poſſeſſing the Land of Canaan*
had, *whoſe everlaſting* was to continue for *ſuch
or ſuch a time*, and then to have *an end*.
And this way, that ſeeming contradiction of
ſome Chriſtian Doctors may be eaſily reconciled, who call the Sabbath both *Temporale &
Æternum*, being ſo far *Eternal* as to laſt its
time appointed, but not to be *for ever*.

7. As for the *remember* in this Commandment, it admits of an interpretation quite different from what you make, and ſeems to
leſſen the dignity of the Precept inſtead of *advancing* it to the condition of the other Nine.
(58) For whereas *naturally* the Conſcience is
well inſtructed in the matter of the other Duties, and thereupon no occaſion to inſert any
caution or reaſon why they ſhould not *Kill*,
nor *Steal*, nor *Commit Adultery*, nor *Covet*, the
obligation of theſe Precepts and the neceſſity
of obſerving 'em being always obvious to the
underſtanding of every Man : The *Law* of the
Sabbath was of *another* quality, and had ſo little power to ingage the Conſcience *before this
Inſtitution*, that had it not been for the *Authority of the Law-maker*, and the *Penalties* on

---

(58) *Sabbati præceptio non eſt à naturæ neceſſitate ut re-
liqua præcepta quæ menti inſita, ut per ſe, cognita ſunt, ſed
κατὰ ſυνθήκην ex voluntate dei.* Synopſ. purioris Theol.

the breach of it, we had no more heard of the Sabbath *after Moses* than we did *before* him. And therefore becaufe *this Law* was not written *in their hearts*, as were the *others*, that defect was fupplied with *remember the Sabbath Day.* And to faften it in their memories, two Reafons were fubjoin'd, *one* concerning the *Creation*, as fet down in the Commandment it felf, the *other* in the *Preface* concerning their *deliverance* out of the *Egyptian* Bondage; otherwife it might have took up no more room in their *brains* now, than it did in their *hearts* before, but ran a great hazard of being forgotten. And this I take to be the moft proper inference to be made from the word, which befpeaks this Precept to be a *pofitive Law*, and not, like the reft, *an eternal Law of Nature.* But to proceed :

You argue that *this Law* is no where *repeal'd*; and confequently, fuppofing it a *pofitive Precept*, yet coming immediately from God, it came with an *unalterable Obligation*, unlefs the *Law-giver* himfelf does in as evident a way *cancell*, as he did once *eftablifh it.* And for the proof of this *Non-repeal*, you alledge, that what St. *Paul* calls a *fhadow*, is not *this Sabbath*, becaufe *there* he fpeaks in the *plural.* And Chrift declares folemnly before his Auditory (59) that *he came not to deftroy the Law, but to fulfill it*; and as an illuftration of this his intention, he obferved the *Sabbath-Day* during the whole courfe of his Life; and after his death, the *Holy Matrons* and *Apoftles* kept it Sacred, as fome Chriftians do to this day.

To which we Anfwer,

8. Firft, St. *Paul's plural* [Σαββάτων] is

---

(59) Matth. v. 17.

conform-

conformable to the Language of Scripture in many other Texts, where there is occasion to mention *this Sabbath. Jesus went on the* [Sabbaths] *Matth.* xii. 1. *And straitway on the* [Sabbaths] *he entred into the Synagogue——Mark* i. 21. *Luke* iv. 16. *Acts* xiii. 14. In all which and more places, the *Plural* is used, and they still mean the *Sabbath-day* (as we translate it in the *Singular*) or every *Seventh-day* at the end of the Week, and therefore this way of Speech can be no objection.

9. That *Christ* observed the *Sabbath*, and on that day frequented the *Synagogues*, cannot be denied; and he did it for the reasons you give, because *he came not to destroy the Law but to fulfill it*; which *Law* he could not be said to *fulfill*, unless he had *kept the Sabbath* as a very considerable branch of it. He was not, tho' sometimes charged with it, any Enemy to the Law of *Moses* under what distinction soever. (60) Nor would he be thought to pull asunder that former Fabrick under the Old Testament, but to improve and make it *better* than it was before. The alteration he intended was only to *reform*, not to *take down* the House, but to *repair* and beautifie it. His design was *amendment*, to give 'em *Substances* instead of *Shadows*, and set before 'em the signification of all the *Types* under the *Oeconomy of the Jews*, which in reality he no more destroy'd, than a *Painter* may be said to destroy the *first Lineaments* of a Face which he doth not *erase*, but add more strokes to *perfect* the Picture. This is seen in his *Divine Sermon* on the Mount, wherein he not only corrects the abuses of the Law, and recovers it from the dangerous

---

(60) Vid. Dr. *Hammond's* Annot. in loc.

Glosses

Gloſſes of the *Scribes* and *Phariſees*, but he furniſhes it with a more. (61) Noble and ſublime ſence than it had hitherto been taken in, and propoſes more ſuitable Rewards to *invite*, and more proper Puniſhments to *frighten* 'em to Obedience. And both ways inſtead of *Temporal* Motives He preſcribes *Eternal.* Thus when the *Ancients* ſaid, *thou ſhalt love thy Neighbour and hate thy Enemy*; He ſaith, *Love your Enemies, bleſs them that curſe you,* &c. And whereas it was written, *thou ſhalt not kill.* He ſaith, *thou ſhalt not hate*, becauſe even that is murther in the *intention.* It is ſaid *thou ſhalt not commit Adultery,* but he extends the Precept further, *thou ſhalt not luſt after a Woman,* becauſe as to thee that very thought defiles her. So that he calls for not only *clean hands,* but *pure hearts,* and will not ſuffer ſo much as a ſinfull *deſire.* In a word, the *Old Teſtament* made Laws for the *hands,* the *New* for the *heart;* That regulated the *Actions,* *This* the *Thought.* And therefore this Superſtructure or Addition to the Law of *Moſes* ſufficiently clears our Lord of the Article of Innovation, and we find him ſo far from deſtroying the Law, that according to the Metaphor in the word he *fulfils* it, or gives it better meaſure than it had before.

But beſides this *refinement* of the *Moral Law,* there were many paſſages in *Moſes's* Writings, and in the *Prophets,* and in the *Pſalms* which related to Chriſt, (62) and *theſe muſt be accompliſhed* or *fulfilled,* ſaith he himſelf, and then adds, that this being *done, they have an end.*

---

(61) *Explicatius & perfectius docuit.* A Lap. in loc.
(62) Luke xxii. 37. & xxiv. 44.

(63) Indeed

(63) Indeed moſt things of the Law of *Moſes* were *Prophetical,* and either in *word* or *figure* imported ſomewhat concerning *Meſſias* to come. Now a *Prophecy* or a *Prophetick-Law* is accompliſhed, when that is done which either *expreſly* or *covertly* foretold what ſhould happen. And therefore our Lord appearing and actually making good all thoſe inſtances which were the matter of ſuch Predictions, either in his Life-time, or *at* and *after* his death: This may be underſtood a plain *repeal* of all thoſe *Ordinances* which had an eye to him, and *implendo veritatem,* or doing the things foretold, he made the *Figure* for the future of no effect. And to this agrees that Saying of his, (64) *Not one jot or tittle ſhall paſs from the Law till all be fulfilled, ?till all be done,* but then when *done,* or *fulfilled,* that Law, you ſee, was to continue *no longer; and when theſe things were accompliſhed, they were to have an end.* (65) *Not to deſtroy* them does not mean, *not to abrogate* the Law, but *not to tranſgreſs it.* And to void it at the *time* unto which it was made a Law, this is no violation or injury done it, becauſe it was the intention of the Law-Maker it ſhould be in force *to that Date,* but *not after.* So that *Chriſt* fulfilling all the righteouſneſs of the Law of *Moſes,* and accompliſhing every particular in his own Perſon which the Law required, or the Prophets foretold of him: Here are two things for the annulling of Laws (66) firſt the *rea-*

---

(63) *Tota lex & ceremoniæ leviticæ figuræ fuerunt Meſſiæ:* Chemnit. Harm. c. 51. (64) Matth. xv. 18. *Non dicit, hæc non tranſibunt ſimpliciter, ſed non tranſibunt donec omnia fiant.* Alex. Hales. (65) *Qui implet non deſtruit.* Chemnit. vid. Suarez de leg. (66) *Cauſæ ceſſatio & tempus.* Juſtinian.

ſon

son of the Law ceaseth; and secondly, the *time* of it is expired, which are look'd upon to be warrants enough to neglect any *Decree* or *Statute* for the time to come, tho' there should be no *formal* and express mention of such *repeal.* Moreover there was to be at Chrift's Coming (67) [*Nova Conftitutio*] a *new Covenant,* for *behold the days come,* faith the *Lord, that I will make a new Covenant with the Houfe of Ifrael, and the Houfe of Judah—and I will put my Law in their inward parts, and* [inftead of Tables of Stone] *write it in their hearts.* This was a *Prophecy* of the State of Religion under the Gofpel, wherein there was to be another Condition very different from that which *Mofes* made at the Peoples departure out of *Egypt,* and when they were to be govern'd by fuch Laws, as were not written on *Skins,* or fuch materials then in ufe, but on the *Minds* of Chriftians by the Spirit of God, as it afterwards fell out on the Day of *Pentecoft.* From hence therefore the Apoftle argues, (68) *in that he faith a New Covenant he hath made the firft old;* and that *which waxeth old is ready to vanish away, i. e.* to be *abrogated* and *exploded* when the *Covenant* was eftablifhed of which he there fpeaks.

For this End, faith *Bucer,* he cites the Teftimony of *Jeremy,* to fhew *That the Legal Prieft-hood with all its Ceremonies and Rites were now abolifhed; becaufe when a new Covenant commences, the old of confequence muft take its leave of us.* The fame Apoftle further proves this, where he thus delivers

---

(67) Jerem. xxxi. 31.   (68) Heb. viii. 13.

himfelf;

himfelf ; (69) *The Priefthood being changed, there is made alfo a neceffity to change the Law,* (70) becaufe the *Priefthood* is fuited to that *Law* : and that Office being before limited to the Tribe of *Levi*, but now tranflated to the Tribe of *Judah*, is a *fign* that the Law of *Mofes* is become *void* ; for as much as by that Law none of the *latter Tribe* were to be admitted to the *Priefthood* ; and confequently, either *Chrift* was not an *High-Prieft* (which this Author faith he was, *Ch.* vi. 20.) becaufe he was of the Tribe of *Judah, of which Tribe Mofes fpake nothing concerning* · *Priefthood,* or elfe the obligation of that Law is over, feeing we have no longer the *Levitical Priefthood,* but do affert *Jefus* the *Mediator of a new and better Covenant,* and far more excellent than what concern'd the *Jew.*

10. Now becaufe (71) the Apoftle faith, and Experience fhews it, That no Teftament is of force *till the death of the Teftator,* and that our Lord did no otherwife *deftroy* the old Law, than by *fulfilling* it, and putting an end to the *former* Covenant by introducing a *new.* Therefore if the Holy *Women* on the death of Chrift *refted on the Sabbath-day according to the commandment,* it is not to be much admired. Becaufe the Law of the *Sab-bath* not being *repealed* by any (72) *Publick Act* or plain Sentence of the Law-maker, they could not prefently tell whether they were

---

(69) Heb. vii. 12. (70) *Quia Sacerdotium legi proportionatum & cum ea indiffolubiliter connexum.* A Lap. in Heb. (71) Heb. ix. 16. (72) *Legis regula tunc demum civibus applicatur quando per publicationem venit in eorum notitiam.* Aqui. Q. 90. Art. 4. & in Jacob. 5.

ftill

ftill obliged to keep it or no. This was the very next day after our Lord's Crucifixion. The thing was *New.* They had not time to confider. The impreffion of the *ancient Sabbath* was kept in their Hearts and Memories. Their veneration for it great. The Laws for not keeping of it very fevere. So that hitherto *fear and Confcience* called for their compliance, efpecially the *declaration* of its *repeal* being not yet made, or at leaft not fo full and clear, as to perfwade 'em to abandon an *Old Holy Cuftom* which they had found their Mafter always refpecting, and which they were bred up in ever fince they were Children.

11. As for thofe words of Chrift, *pray that your flight be not on the Sabbath-day* ; which feems to continue the obligation of it 'till the deftruction of *Jerufalem* about 40 years after, or elfe why not take their flight on *that Day* as well as any *other* without offence to Confcience? (73) The general Opinion is, that our Lord's Difcourfe was directed to the *Jews,* who on *that Day* would not *fight* or *flie* in any Cafe whatever, as we fee in 1 *Mac.* i. 34. But fuppofe the utmoft, That he fpake of *fuch* who were *Converts* to Chriftianity, and who living at *Jerufalem* when the City was deftroy'd, might ufe the fame Prayer for this reafon, becaufe, tho' their own Principles did allow 'em to flee on the *Sabbath-day,* (74) yet confidering that moft of the *Jewifh Nation* were of another mind, and made it an abominable fault and Prophanation of the Feftival,

---

(73) *Chriftus loquitur de Judæis.* A Lap. *Loquitur de Judæis.* Gerhard. and fo St. *Chryfoftom.* (74) *Religione publica impediebantur longius abire.* Arctius.

to attempt and execute any such thing, even·
these must needs be involved in the *common
Calamity,* because should they go about to flee
out of the City, or in their flight exceed a
Sabbath-days-journey, (75) consisting of two
Miles or thereabouts, the *Jews* would certainly
look on 'em as Transgressors of their Law,
and thereupon stone 'em in case they could
avoid the *Besiegers Army.* And therefore this
Text no further proposes the notion of the
Sabbath, than to make it an *unhappy Circumstance* to aggravate the miseries of those Days,
wherein the *Jews* would neither flee themselves on a nicety of Conscience, nor suffer
the *Christians* to flee, tho' without injury to
their *Principles.* So that I conclude this with
the words of Dr. *Prideaux;* (76) " That *'tis*
" *ridiculous for any to argue for a confirmation*
" *of the Sabbath from these words which Christ*
" *foretold as an inconvenience that would arise*
" *from the Superstition of the Jewish People.*

12. But the last part of your Argument
seems to oppose this; Because you have observed out of Ecclesiastical History, that Christians both *before* and *after* the destruction of
Jerusalem, have kept the Sabbath in a very solemn manner, and it may be supposed done on
a *Principle* too. It concerns us therefore to
examine that *Practice* and the *Reasons* they
went on to continue the Custom, so many years
after the date of our Liberty. The practice is
undeniable; For so (77) *Socrates* tells us ;
" *That all Churches over the World, excepting*
" *those of* Alexandria *and* Rome, *set apart as*

---

(75) *Vid.* Selden *de jure natural.* l. 3. c. 9.
(76) *De Sab.* Orat.　　(77) Lib. 5. c. 22.

" *well*

" *well* Saturday *as* Sunday *for Religious Uses,*
" *even the Egyptians, and those who dwelt at*
" Thebais *Borderers on* Alexandria *complied,*
" *and had on both* Days *Prayers and Collections.*
(78) Sozomen has the same exception of *Rome*
and *Alexandria,* but " *all or most of the other*
" *Churches carefully observed the* Sabbath. And
so great stress was laid on keeping it, that
Gregory Nyssen expostulates thus ; " *With*
" *what Eyes can you behold the* Lords-Day,
' *when you despise the* Sabbath, *do you not per-*
" *ceive they are* Sisters, *and that in slighting*
" *the* one, *you affront the* other ? And as *Sisters,*
we find 'em go hand in hand in the Ecclesiastical Canons. (79) " *If any Clergy-Man be*
" *found Fasting on the* Lords-Day, *or the* Sab-
" bath, *let him be suspended.* And in the 6th
Council in *Trullo,* (†) the Canon obliges all
People to Fast throughout Lent, *except on the*
Sabbath *and the* Lords-day. And so they are
joyn'd together in the 49 and 51 Canons of
the Council of *Laodicea.* But the words of
St. *Ignatius* are very severe ; (80) " *If any*
" *one fasts on the* Lords-day *or the* Sabbath,
" (unless *that before* Easter, *which* Balsamon,
" *Aristenus and others call the great Sabbath*)
" *he murders Christ again.* And no wonder
it was so strictly observed, seeing we find it
among the Constitutions of the Church (81)
in St. *Clement,* that we " *Celebrate as Festivals*
" *the* Sabbath, *and the* Lords-day ; *because, as*
the reason follows, *this is done in remem-*
brance *of the* Resurrection, *and that of the*

---

(78) Lib. 7. c. 19.   (79) Canon. 66. Apost.
(†) Can. 52.   (80) Ep. ad Philip.   (81) L. 7.
c. 23. & L. 8. c. 33.

Creation.

Creation. And elfewhere the fame Author makes *both*, Days of *Reſt*, that *ſo Servants may have opportunity to repair to Church to hear and learn the Duties of Religion.* And in ſumm, *The Holy Fathers* ſaith *Balſamon, made the* Sabbath *and the* Lords-day *to ſtand on the ſame ground, and they were equally reſpected in Ancient times.* And tho' in the Weſtern-Church eſpecially, this Cuſtom wore off by degrees, and is now altogether laid by, yet ſtill there are ſome marks of it in other places, as among the *Æthiopians, Melchitæ* and *Abyſſins,* as (82) as *Brerewood* informs us ; and (83) *Scaliger* ſaith, they call *both days* by the Name of *Sabbath,* the *firſt* and the *latter Sabbath*; or in their Language, the *one* Sanbath Sachriſtos, *Chriſts-Sabbath,* the *other* Sanbath Judi, the *Jews-Sabbath.*

We muſt yield therefore that the *Primitive Chriſtians* had a great veneration for the *Sabbath,* and ſpent the *Day* in Devotion and Sermons. And 'tis not to be doubted but they derived this Practice from the *Apoſtles* themſelves, as appears (84) by ſeveral Scriptures to that purpoſe ; who keeping both *that Day* and the *firſt of the Week,* gave occaſion to the ſucceeding Ages to join 'em together, and make it *one Feſtival,* tho' there was not the ſame reaſon for the *continuance* of the Cuſtom, as there was to *begin* it. The Church had to do with two ſorts of People; and her Edification did much depend on their Converſion, *Jews* and *Gentiles*; and therefore ſuch a me-

---

(82) Tract. Div. Lin. & Relig.　(83) De Emend. Temp.　(84) Acts xiii. 14. xvi. 13. xviii. 4.

thod

thod was to be taken, as would be, in all appearance, moſt ſerviceable to that *End,* and
conduce to ſave 'em. That then *both* theſe
might have good opportunities to hear the
Doctrine of the Goſpel, 'twas found neceſſary the Apoſtles ſhould Preach on *both thoſe
Days*; and being to deal with the *Jews* on the
one hand, they aſſembled with them on *that
Day* which · *they* dedicated to the reading of
Moſes and the *Prophets*; and being willing on
the other to oblige the *Gentiles,* they pitched
on a *Day* more ſafe for *them,* (85) becauſe it
was Capital for *Greeks* and *Romans* then to
ſhow any regard to the *Jewiſh Sabbath,* or any
other of their Ceremonies; and ſo by reaſon
of that heavy Penalty, tho' they might be
tempted on *other Days* to be preſent at their
Meetings, yet to be ſure they would not be
on this.

B. If this be true, that it was ſo great a
Crime for the *Gentiles* to ſhow any conformity
to the way of Worſhip among the *Jews,* and
that it was as much as their Lives were worth
to reſpect the *Sabbath,* then how comes it a-
bout we read in the *Acts of the Apoſtles,* xiii. 42.
that the Gentiles beſought *Paul* and *Barnabas*
to Preach to them the *next Sabbath*?

A. The word [ἔθνη] *Gentiles,* is not in
ſome *Greek* Editions; and accordingly the old
Latin Tranſlation ſaith only [*rogabant*] *they
beſought*; ſo do the *Syriack* and *Æthiopick* Ver-
ſions, meaning the *Jews* before-named; and
thereupon the *Arabick* ſaith expreſly, *ſome of*

---

(85) *Satis notum eſt capitale eſſe Græcis & Romanis
Sabbatum celebrare vel ſuſcipere ritus judaicos.* Calvin in
Acts xvi. 13.

the

the Synagogue of the Jews besought 'em. But letting it keep its place, the word signifies *multitude*, and is explained by the other Greek
word [τὰς ὄχλες,] *ver.* 45. Yet, if we must
make it a term of distinction, it means only
such of the *Gentiles* as were (86) *Converts* to
the Jewish Religion, and are called *Religious
Proselytes*, ver. 43. and who as *Jews* now, rather than *Greeks* and *Romans* might consort and
Pray with 'em. However that it was done
with great *caution* and some *concern* we find
by the matter of the request, which was, That
the Apostles would Preach to 'em *some Day
between this and the next Sabbath*, for that is
the strict translation of the Greek (87) *some
time between the Sabbaths*, suppose the next day,
or other day after; all which days among
the Jews were called *Sabbath*, as well as the
day on which they Worshipped. Which not
only expounds this verse, but may be the
sence of the 44*th*, that *almost the whole City the
next Sabbath*, *i. e.* the day following *came together to hear the word of God*. And this might
well cause so much Envy in the *Jews*, in *v.* 45.
not only because vast *Companies* came to
hear the Apostles Preach, but because it was
on such Days as brought some disrespect to their
famous *Sabbath*, on which and no other Day
of the Week, they would have such Meetings.
to be held. But to proceed to the Reasons the
Apostles went upon to observe the *Sabbath-
Day*.

It was an ordinary Charge against the *Apostles*, that they were *Innovators* and the Authors

---

(86) *Eos nimirum è gentibus qui judaizabant ideoque
cœtus judaicos frequentabant.* Beza.　(87) 'Εις τὸ
μεταξὺ σάββατον, or ἐν τῷ μεταξὺ σαββάτων χρόνῳ.

or Abettors of a *New Religion.* Upon this account therefore the Holy Men thought it expedient to deliver their Sermons *openly* at *stated times,* and in those *Publick Places* where the *Jews* assembled, to clear themselves of that accusation, and to show the whole World, and the *Jews* in particular, that the Doctrine they taught was able to abide the Test, and that *they said no other things than what Moses and the Prophets did say should come.*

Nor is it to be omitted, that they could do no less in point of (88) *decency,* to shew thereby some reverence to the *Law and the Fathers,* with whom they had dealt a little too familiarly, had they dismiss'd *them* and that *constitution* too *suddenly,* which God himself made with so much *Ceremony,* and frequently confirm'd by variety of *Miracles,* and other instances of his Power; and therefore if it was now at last *Dead,* it certainly deserved from them a very honourable *Burial.*

And the Motive was great in point of *Charity,* and that tenderness we ought to have for *weak Brethren*; who not so soon nor so well apprehending the reason of laying aside the *ancient way* of Worship, would have taken prejudice against the Apostles, and hindred the advancement of the Gospel; and is the true cause of that compliance St. *Paul* every where shew'd in the discharge of his Ministry. For, as he speaks, *tho' I be free from all Men, yet have I made my self Servant unto all, that I might gain the more. Unto the*

---

(88) *Cæremoniæ veteres sepeliendæ erant cum aliquo honore.* Calvin. in Acts xv.

Jews

Jews I became a Jew, &c. (89) *I am made all things to all Men, that I might gain some ; and this I do for the Gospels sake.* Thus he personates all sorts of Men, to win some of 'em to Christianity.

And lastly, the Peace of the Church was the better preserved by this means; for the *Jews* were naturally a sowre and turbulent People, and could ill bear a *Change* in any of their *Rites*, much less in *this* of the *Sabbath*; and rather than have seen it hurried out of the World in haft, (as the Apostles might have forthwith rejected it by virtue of their Christian Liberty) they would have been all in an uprore (even those who were in other respects well-wishers to the Gospel) ; and so instead of bringing some over, and confirming others in the Christian Religion, this unseasonable and *indiscreet Zeal* had certainly made 'em more prejudiced and bitter against it, and the Gospel had been preached in vain.

Upon these *Prudential* Reasons the Apostles and their followers went in indulging their Brethren the *Jews* by observing the *Sabbath*. But then in all these respects they made it only an *indifferent thing*, which they had power to *use* or to let *alone*. The Legal force of it they consider'd gone, and if they still kept it; it was by discretion for *Peace* and *Charity*'s sake, to keep fair with their Countrymen in order to save 'em. But all this was occasional. It was not *their own Day*, not the *Set Day* of their Devotion, not the *Day* which *they* Dedicated

---

(89) *Omnium infirmitatibus se accommodavit.* A Lap. in loc. 1 Cor. ix. 19.

to the use of their Religion ; not their *Lords-Day*, tho' they made it a *Day* of Worſhip and an opportunity to teach the People then aſſembled by *Cuſtom*.

And this helps to explain that paſſage of St. *Luke* concerning St. *Paul*, (90) *who haſted, if it were poſſible for him, to be at Jeruſalem the Day of Pentecoſt.* (91) " *What means this* " *haſte,* ſaith St. *Chryſoſtom, did he lie under* " *any obligation to keep that* Feſtival, *that he* " *ſhew'd ſo much earneſtneſs and zeal to get* " *timely to* Jeruſalem? *No, it was not ſo much* " *becauſe of the* Feaſt, *as becauſe of the multi-* " *tudes of People reſorting thither, and for their* " *ſakes he haſted that he might be able to Preach* " *the word to 'em.* In other reſpects *Jeruſalem* to him was no more than *Athens*, nor the *Temple* than *Areopagus* or *Mars's-Hill.* With the fame mind he frequented the *Synagogues* of the *Jews*, and the *Schools* of the *Gentiles.* In the *one* he incountred the *Scribes* and *Phariſees*, and in the *other* the *Stoicks* and *Epicureans* ; and in *both* he diſputed about *Jeſus* and the *Reſurrection.* So that it was not the bare Celebration of the *Feſtival* it ſelf, but *their Converſion* who came to Celebrate it, made the Holy Man *haſten* to *Jeruſalem.* And while he had hopes to ſucceed in this good deſign, he was conſtantly preſent at all their Meetings both in the City and elſewhere. But this hope failing, and that he found the *Jews* hardned, and (92) making it their buſineſs to blaſpheme and ſpeak evil of that way before the multitude, he departed

---

(90) Acts xx. 16. (91) Homil. in Act. Vid. Maſlorat. in loc. (92) Acts xviii. 6. xix. 9.

from them, and feparated the Difciples, *fhaking his raiment, and faying unto them, your blood be on your own heads, I am clean,* from henceforth *I will go unto the Gentiles*——they are his own words; and 'tis fuppofed from that time forward he was never feen in a Synagogue.

But for the further illuftration of this Point, we will take a view of the Article of *Circumcifion*, and then apply the *Sabbath*.

How much St. *Paul* cries down *Circumcifion* we every where fee in his Epiftles. (93) *Behold, I Paul fay unto you, that if you be circumcifed, Chrift fhall profit you nothing*; the Reafon follows, *becaufe he that is Circumcifed becomes a debtor to the whole Law.* Which *Law* being oppofed to *Grace*, to be obliged to the *one* by the act of *Circumcifion*, was to render the *other* of no effect; as he fpeaks a little after. But tho' this St. *Paul* out of his great Zeal and fervency of Spirit threatens *Thunderbolts* to the obfervers of *Circumcifion*, he himfelf for all this will have (94) *Timothy Circumcifed*, and by that compliance feemingly contradicts and confutes his own Doctrine. But then, as *Tertullian* excufes it, *he had regard to Times and Perfons*; and therefore he thought fit to *Circumcife Timothy, becaufe they all knew his Father was a Greek*; fo that this was done for *conveniency fake*, left otherwife the *Jews* fhould reject his Miniftry, knowing on his Father's account that he had never been Circumcifed; and not being fa-

_____

(93) Gal. v. 2, 4. *Circumcifio eft quædam proteftatio legis implendæ.* Aqui. 3d. Q. 40. A. 4. (94) Acts xvi. 3.

tisfied

tisfied; yet that the obligation of it was at an end.

But then this *Circumcifing of Timothy* was not reputed *neceffary*, tho' the prefent ftate of things made it *expedient* to be done. There was no ftrefs laid on the *Ceremony* any further than that it prevented *fcandal.* (95) It was not received as a *Sacrament* by *Timothy*, nor fo propofed by St. *Paul.* It was only to make *way* for the Gofpel, which *Timothy*, as a *Minifter* was to Preach unto 'em, but which they had flighted, had he not been thus qualified and provided for that Function.

And that *Circumcifion* was now brought to that *indifferency*, that it might be *done* or *let alone*, as moft tended to *Edification*, is very evident from what afterwards fell out in the Perfon of *Titus* who was a *Greek* as well as *Timothy*: yet tho' St. *Paul* would have the *one Circumcifed*, he would not give way to *Circumcife the other*. And the reafon was, becaufe the *fcandal* he avoided by *circumcifing Timothy*, he had now run into by fuffering *Titus to be Circumcifed.* For there were (96) *falfe Brethren*, as he fpeaks, who much prefs'd the doing of it, on purpofe and with defign to accufe him before the *Gentiles* for Preaching one thing and doing another; or that he *recanted* what he had taught before. This being the Cafe, and that thefe Men urged *Circumcifion* with more vehemence and earneftnefs than comported with the nature, of *an indifferent thing*, fuch as He now took *Circumcifion for*,

---

(95) *Non fpe falutis fed pace Ecclefiæ.* P. Mart. loc. com. *Non fuit Sacramentum quale datum Abrahæ.* Calvin. (96) *Improbi exploratores.* Bulling. in Gal.

this made him as *zealous* on his fide to oppofe
it ; and tho' at *another time* and on *another occafion* he was ready to do it, yet as matters
now ftood, he did not think it proper to give
way to his Adverfaries, *no not for an hour,
that the truth of the Gofpel might continue.*

He *Circumcifed Timothy* therefore to *avoid
fcandal*; and he would *not fuffer Titus to be
circumcifed to avoid the fame fcandal.* The End
was *one* and the *fame*, tho' he exprefs'd himfelf differently, but both refulted from his
Chriftian Liberty; and he was neither way
obliged, but as it confifted with *Prudence and
Charity.* For hitherto all thofe *Legal Rites,*
(97) tho' *mortua*, they were not *mortifera*;
and as they were *dead* Ceremonies they might
be laid by, or be *buried*, yet not being *deadly*,
and bringing at this time no danger to *Chriftianity*, they might be ftill ufed, and were
ufed by St. *Paul* and the other Apoftles, as far
as they contributed to Edification and Peace.

It was from this *Liberty* the Apoftles ufed
the *firft Day* of the Week out of *Choice*, and
retain'd the *laft* out of *Charity.* They kept
the *Sabbath* as they would do any *other Feftival*
of their own making, wherein they might have
a good opportunity to teach and propagate the
Gofpel. They ufed it as they did *Purifying*
and *Circumcifion*, to prevent diforder, and to
keep a good underftanding between them and
their Brethren.

Thefe were their *Reafons* for obferving the
Sabbath; this was their fence of it; and in procefs of time, thefe Reafons ceafing, yet the

---

(97) A Lap. ex Auguft.

Authority and *Practice* of thofe Great Men became a *Reafon* to the following Generations ;
and thence it was we have the account before
given of it in the ancient Writers. However this is obfervable, that due care was taken to keep the Church from *Judaizing* in *this*
or any *other* particular, as appears in that reafon *Conftantine* the Great gives about the alteration of *Eafter-Day;* (98) " *That we may have*
" *nothing to do in common with that fpightful*
" *People* the Jews. *For how can they have one*
" *good thought who flew* Chrift, *and after that*
" *murder are like Madmen acted with Frenzy*——
" *You ought to take heed never to imitate that*
" *People. For in fo doing* (as *Valefius* com-
" ments on the place) *you make your felves par-*
" *takers of that villany which the Jews did on our*
" *Lord*——(99) This is the reafon *Juftin*
Martyr gives, why the *Gentile* converts obferve not the *Sabbath,* " *left thereby they fhould*
" *be thought to be* Jews *under another name.*
(100) This made the *Ecclefiaftical Canons* twice
forbid this compliance. (101) And tho' the,
Council of *Laodicea* permits *Chriftians* to affemble on the *Jewifh Sabbath* to hear the word
of God, yet they muft do it *as Chriftians,* o-
therwife they are liable to Excommunication ;
fo dangerous correfpondence is with fuch Men
who are mortal Enemies to us and our Religion. And that our Fathers look'd on the
Sabbath as an *indifferent thing,* we may partly
guefs from the ufage they gave it, making it as

---

(91) Eufeb. de vit. Conftant. l. 3. c. 18. Can. 11.
Conc. Sexti in Trullo.   (99) Dialog. cum Trypho.
(100) Can. vii. 70.   (101) Can. 16. 29.

they

they faw occafion fometimes a *Faft* and fome-
times a *Feftival* (as at that time when the
Church .put a check to the *Marcionifts* · who
Fafted on that Day) and fo' it continued with
this difference in the Eaftern and Weftern
Churches.

B. I ftand much obliged, that you have been
fo full in . clearing the Objections I put you.
But to be ingenuous, what I at firft intended
by the *morality* of the fourth Commandment
with refpect to time, was, That *one Day in
Seven* ought to be fet apart for the Worfhip of
God ; not that I infifted on the *Legal Sabbath,*
or *that Seventh Day* obferved by the *Jews,* but
any· one Day of the Week, any Seventh Day,
which I confider determined by that Precept,
and to be accounted *Moral.*

And here I take the word *Seventh* for the,
genus, wherein I place its *Morality*; · but look
on *this* or *that Seventh Day* in the nature of a
Species Ceremonial and alterable at the Churches
pleafure; fo that fhe may make it the *firft* or
laft Day of the Week, as it beft anfwers the
defign of being the *Memorial* of fome very
great Bleffing, fuch as was the *Deliverance* out
of *Egypt,* with refpect to the *Jews,* or *Chrift*'s
Refurrection, to which we *Chriftians* acknowledge our Redemption to be owing.

And of.this mind is (102) *Junius,* who declares it a *Law of Nature* that the *Seventh Day*
be confecrated to God. (103) So *Curcellæus,*
more than once, calls it *Moral.* (104) Bifhop
Babington fubfcribes and fays, " *to have fome*

---

(102) Prælect in Gen. (103) Rel. Chrift.
Inftit. L. vii. Cap. xxxi. Sect. 14. *& de efu fang.* (104)
On the 4*th* Command.

" *Day*

" Day in the *Seven* is Moral, *and remaineth still*
" *obliging us*; tho' *to have precifely* Saturday,
" *and to reft as the Jews did, is Ceremonial*
" *and a Shadow, and therefore now abrogated by*
" *the coming of the Body of Chrift.* And,
who probably in your opinion, includes a
great many Authorities : (105) Mr. *Hooker*
fpeaks of it after this manner. " *The Moral*
" *Law,* faith he, *requiring therefore a feventh*
" *part throughout the age of the whole World*
" *to be that way employed, altho' with us the*
" *Day be changed in regard of a new revolu-*
" *tion begun by our Saviour Chrift, yet the fame*
" proportion of time *continueth which was be-*
" *fore, becaufe in reference to the benefit of*
" *Creation, and now much more of renovation*
" *thereunto* added by him *who was Prince of the*
" *World to come,* we *are bound to account the*
" *fanctification of* one Day in Seven *a Duty,*
" *which* Gods *immutable Law doth exact for*
" *ever.* And this is confonant to what *Igna-*
tius afferts in his Epiftle to the *Magnefians*;
wherein tho' he denys the Patriarchs to *Sab-*
batize or keep the *Jewifh* Saturday, yet he declares they obferved a *Seventh day,* and calls it
the *Dominical* or *Lords-Day,* the *fame* we now
Celebrate. And fo Bifhop *Ufher, Pearfon* and
Voffius tranflate him. " *That the Divine Pro-*
" *phets well verfed in ancient Cuftoms, attained*
" *to newnefs of hope and did not* Sabbatize, *but*
" *did Celebrate the* Lords-Day, *whereon our*
" *Life arofe, and victory over death was ob-*
" *tained by him.* And this, I think, may help
" to clear that of *Paul,* in making the *Sabbath*

---

(105) Ecclef. Pol. L. 5.

a *fhadow*;

a *shadow*; his word in the *plural* sometimes meaning that which *Weekly* occurrs, as in those Texts you produced, but then it is to be considered, that he intends the *Ceremonial Saturday-Sabbath*, prescribed the *Jews* in *Deuteronomy* v. 14, 15. and was peculiar to them; not the *Patriarchal Sabbath* commanded *Exod.* xx. *now* observed by us, which is *Moral.* and to last for *ever.* And by way of Corollary, (106) The quality and force of the *Septenary Number*, which you were mentioning, very observable in the Book of God and Works of Nature, is a kind of Lesson to us, that we should dedicate *this proportion* of time to Piety and Rest rather than any other, which the Creator has not made so remarkable on any account whatsoever. And of this sort is the River between *Arcas* and *Raphanae* (107) which *Josephus* and (108) *Pliny* take notice of, and which had this Miraculous quality, that
" *tho' when it flowed it was very full of water,*
" *and ran with a swift stream, yet having thus*
" *flowed six days together, on the* Seventh Day
" *it was so dry that you might see the bottom.*
" *Thus it always continued its course, and for*
" *this Cause the Jews called it the* Sabbatick-
" River, *taking its Name from the Jewish* Sab-
" bath, *which is on every Seventh-Day.* — So
Josephus, which seems very strange, and might well be construed into an Argument of Nature, to prove the Creator's will, that this

---

(106) *Septenarij numeri vis & facultas in multis naturæ rebus animadversa.* Curcel. *de esu sang.* (107) Joseph. de bell Jud. L. vii. c. 24. (108) Nat. Hist. L. 31. c. 2. *In Judæa Rivus Sabbatis omnib. siccatur, respondit Rabbi. Fluvius Sab. hoc ostendit qui per totam hebdomadam lapides trahit & in Sabbato quiescit* — apud Galatin. L. xi. c. 9.

Seventh-

Seventh-Day fhould be kept *holy* in the performances of Religion. As accordingly we
find it kept by feveral (109) Perfwafions,
tho' on different Days, and in divers manners.
For the *Mahometans* obferve the *Sixth*, the
Jews the *Seventh*, the *Indians* the *Fourth*, they
in *Guinea* the *Third*, the *Chriftians* the *Firft*,
yet all of them *one Day of the Week*, as a Doctrine taught by Nature. And fo *Philo* the
Learned *Jew* fpeaks. That " *Nature delights*
" *in the* Seventh ; *and therefore*, faith he, *you*
" *need not ask me, why God chofe the* Seventh-
" Day *and eftablifhed it as a Law* for a Day
" of Reft, *fince both Phyficians and Philofophers*
" *have often declared, of what great Power and*
" *Virtue that Number is*, as *in all other things*,
" *fo efpecially in the Nature and State of Man.*
And thus you have the reafon of the *Seventh-
Day*, and let me add, an evidence of that
Morality we afcribe to it.

A. As for the *Myfterioufnefs* and *perfection*
of the Number *Seven*, it is to be acknowledged that God and Nature have made it a
very fignificant and *remarkable Number*, yet
the *others*, as I fhow'd you, are not without
credit ; and the Numbers *Three* and *Ten* in
particular are *naturally* very eminent, and ftand
on a level, if they may not be advanced a-
bove it. So that by this kind of Argument
fuch proportions of time might be well call'd
for, and efteem'd as proper as *this*. But in

---

(109) *Chriftianorum Septimanæ initium eft à die Do-
minico Græcorum & Alexand. à die Lunæ. Jefnargit. feu
Perfarum, à die Martis. Nebuchadonazar feu Babyloniorum,
à die Mercurij. Ethnicorum, à die Jovis. Elhigerá feu
Mahumedis æra, à die Veneris. Hebræorum à die Sabbati—*
Cufan. de reparat. Kalend.

truth,

truth, thefe Infinuations conclude nothing ; and there muft be a much clearer and more audible voice than what they fpeak with, to give Being to *Laws* , and frame *Rules for Practice.*

And for that Account you give of the Sab-. batick-River, allowing the ftory true, (as *Pliny* and *Jofephus* tell it) and that the Water flowed *Six Days*, and made an unaccountable ftop on the *Seventh*, to recommend, as it was thought, the obfervation of the *Sabbath* ; yet *confidering*, faith (110) *Galatine, that there is no fuch River now in the World fubject to that condition*, we may argue on the contrary, that the *Jewifh Sabbath* is now ceafed, becaufe thefe extraordinary qualities of the Water have an end, which were *weekly* feen in thofe times, to countenance and inferr it. And yet were there fuch an *ebbing* and *flowing* of any Sea or River (as there is certainly great variety of Motions in that Element in feveral places of the World) they might proceed from the influence of the *Moon*, or fome other Natural Caufe, which though not comprehended, is not immediately to commence *Miracle*, nor extend to Matters of Religion.

The Authority then of the *Sabbath* is from *Scripture*. But every thing in *Scripture*, as revealed, is *pofitive* ; and fuch the *Seventh Day* is in this Queftion, which had never been known to be the *Reft-day* of God, if by another Infpiration it had not been difcovered to us. And if God on that reafon fanctified and made it a *Sabbath* to the *Jews*, it obliges no further than

---

(110) *Figmentum & Mendacium*, l. 11. c. 9. *Vid.* Selden *de Jure Nat.* l. 3. c. 13.

a *pofitive*

a *positive Law*, grounded on that *Revelation.*
And though we have not impiety and confidence enough to affert with *Leviathan*, *That
no Precept of the Gospel can be looked on as a Law,
until enacted by Civil Authority*; there being, according to this Hypothefis, no other Law, but
only the *Law of Nature*, and Civil Laws: yet
" (111)*it is a point ought to be taken for granted,*
" *That no part of the Law of* Mofes *doth bind*
" *Chriftians under the Gofpel by virtue of that
Delivery, no, not the Ten Commandments themfelves, but leaft of all the Fourth, which all confefs to be in fome refpect Ceremonial.* And *Zanchius* (112) faith, " *As neither the Judicial nor
" Ceremonial, fo neither the Moral Law con-
" tain'd in the Decalogue, doth any way affect us
" Chriftians, but only fo far forth as it is the Law
" of Nature, which bindeth all alike, and after-
" wards was confirm'd and ratify'd by Chrift our
" King.* His Reafon is, *becaufe if the Decalogue
" as given by* Mofes *to the Jews did concern the
" Gentiles, then the Gentiles had been bound by
" the Fourth Commandment to obferve the* Sab-
" bath *in as ftrict a manner as the* Jews : *But
" it is manifeft, the* Gentiles *never were obliged
" to obferve the* Sabbath ; *and therefore it fol-
" lows, they neither were nor poffibly could be
" bound to any of the refidue, as delivered by*
Mofes *to the Jews.* Which partly appears in
this, That *Mofes* calls the Decalogue *the words
of the Covenant between God and the Jews,* Deut.
iv. 13. *And he declared unto you his Covenant
which he commanded you to perform, even Ten
Commandments, and he wrote 'em on two tables of*

---

(111) Sanderfon. *Prælect.* 4. N. 28. de Caf. Confc. & de
Sabbato. (112) Zanch. de Redempt.

ftone.

ſtone. Conſequently, as we do not take our
ſelves obliged to that *Covenant,* ſo neither are
we bound to the *Terms* of it which make up
the Precepts of the Two Tables. Plainly, though
*to worſhip God ; to forbear Idols ; not to murther,
ſteal,* or the like, are originally *Laws of Nature ;* yet *Moſes* reducing 'em to that Body of
Statutes which he was framing for his Subjects,
makes *Theſe poſitive* as well as the reſt. And
if we reſpect *ſome* of 'em more than *others,* it is
on the ſame reaſon they went ; becauſe they
become *Laws* of our *own conſtitution,* and thereby are *poſitive* again ; and we ſhow 'em Obedience *not* as the *Laws of Moſes,* but as the
Laws of Nature, the tranſgreſſion of which has
ſuch or *ſuch* Penalties, as the wiſdom of our
Governours think moſt conducible to anſwer
the end they were made for. However, ſince
we find by Revelation that God *reſted on the
Seventh Day, and ſanctified it,* and that by *Divine Appointment* it was made an Holiday to
the People of the Jews, and ſince we are
taught by *Nature to worſhip God,* and to worſhip him *on certain. times,* for better Edification
and Order, we have pitch'd on the *Seventh-
Day* as congruous and convenient from the
analogy, equity and *reaſon* of the Fourth Commandment, as *a proportion of time* more proper
than any *other ;* becauſe *Revelation* has ſet a
mark on it in *God's Example,* who alſo inſpired
and directed *Moſes* to make that Limitation.
Not that there reſults any neceſſity for ſuch a
time on the account of that Revelation, (becauſe ſuch Diſcoveries are always *poſitive*) but
being *naturally* inſtructed to diſtinguiſh and determine Times for Sacred Actions, the *reaſonableneſs* of the *Seventh Day* got the ſtart,
and appeared ſo inviting, that our Fathers
could

could not but preferr it before any other, out of veneration to the Divine Example of God, who *rested on that Day,* and *whose Rest* we consider now in the quality of an *Eternal Law* ; because there cannot be a *better reason* for another Day, to keep it holy. And in this sence we understand some of those Authors you name, who call it a *Moral* and an *Immutable Law,* from this *lasting application,* we Christians are and shall be ready to make, from what, as to this matter, hath been discovered to us in Scripture, upon a Reason which must needs have its due influence, and, without rival, to continue for ever.

And as to the *Mahometans* and others who celebrate a *Seventh Day* as well as we, this is not to be imputed to any impression of *Nature,* but what they have learn'd from *us* or the *Jews,* or taken from the *Bible,* to which, we are well satisfy'd, they are no strangers, from the many passages we find in their *Alcoran* so agreeable with Scripture.

What you offer out of St. *Ignatius,* will admit this Answer ; That the main design of his Epistle to the *Magnesians,* is, to persuade those who profess themselves the Disciples of Christ to live as becomes *Christians.* And for a motive to this, he affirms to 'em, that the *Old Prophets* did the same, and on that account were persecuted by the People of those times. And so he makes this inference ; " *If therefore* " *they who were well versed in the works of ancient* " *days came to newness of hope,* (Bishop *Mountague* (113) saith, *communion of hope,* or the same hope common to them and us) " *not Sab-*

---

(113) Κοινότητι ἐλπίδ᾽⊙⟩, *Exercit.* 1. *sect.* 1.

" *batizing*

" batizing, but living according to the Dominical
" life : Then let us not be insensible——   Now
as *Sabbatizing* not only signifies keeping the Sabbath, but retaining all the Ceremonies and *Rites*
of the *Jewish Religion*, of which the *Sabbath* was
chief, (and therefore that People were called
Sabbatarij, as by a known distinction,) so by
Dominicam viventes is meant no more than
what he before said, (114) *that they lived according to Christ Jesus our Lord.* Thus it is
worded in the two Translations of *Ignatius*,
found by that *Primate* you named, *one* in the
Library of *Gunwell* and *Caius* College in *Cambridge*, the other in the Study of Bishop *Mountague*, printed 1644. But I take the holy Man's
sence to be, that we should live a life suitable
to the Example of Christ in the Gospel, and
(115) no longer continue in *Judaism*, which is
another word for *Sabbatization*, the *latter* being
an *Ecclesiastical* term, and the former *Civil.*
I must confess, the Latin Translations render
the place doubtful, and the Substantive to
Dominica may be *Day* or *Life*, as the Reader
pleases ; but the *Medicean* Copy, the best and
most like that of *Eusebius*, leaves no scruple,
because ζωὴ is exprest and determines the
word *Dominical* to the *Person* of Christ, and
not to the *Day* of his Resurrection. Neither
does this supplement disturb the sence, seeing
that what follows may be turned thus, *living up
to the life of our Lord, in which is included our
life and victory over death by him.* *Juxta Christum* or *Secundum Dominicam vivere*, inforces

---

(114) Κατὰ χριστὸν ἔζησαν Ἰησοῦν. *Juxta Christum vixe-
runt*, saith Archbishop *Usher.*   (115) *Non amplius Sab-
batizantes, sed secundum Dominicam viventes.*

this

this conftruction, that *Chrift* is propofed as an *Example* or Pattern which the divine Prophets had an eye to, and we ought to follow them in it, acquitting our felves not (116) *Judaically* but *Spiritually*, as the Primate gloffes in his red letters. So that all to be drawn from this paffage is, That *Ignatius* denies the Patriarchs to *Sabbatize* or have any regard to the *Jewifh Sabbath*. But that they kept a *Seventh-Day* or *Lord's-Day* now in ufe, I cannot fee how this teftimony proves it, when we have fo much reafon to fufpect whether it be faithfully reprefented or no. And herein the Primate concurrs: For he thinks the three firft fyllables of ἑορτάζομβυ wanting in the *Greek* of that Latin Manufcript found in *Caius* College, and on that reafon came in *Viventes* inftead of *Celebrantes*, which had been a better word to ferve your notion. But for my own part, I look on this defect with the fame eye as the redundance of ζωίω in the *Florentine* Copy, and take *both* as a matter of meer conjecture, and therefore unfit to fupport the Doctrine of the *Lord's-Day*; or to fhow that the *Patriarchs* kept it.

As to the *double* notion of the *Sabbath*, which you were propofing, I would defire you to explain your felf a little more, before I offer at an Anfwer.

B. Thus it is. The Law was given at two feveral times; *Once* from Mount *Sinai*, which was to oblige *all* People; *Then* fome years after reinforced for the *particular* ufe of the *Jews*, which, with their Government, was to have an end. And for the *Sabbath*, though mention

---

(116) Οὐκ Ἰσδαϊκῶς ἀλλὰ Πνδματικῶς.

is made of it in both places, yet we may
difcover a great deal of difference between
them, and fo many marks as fhew 'em *not the
fame*, and therefore we ought not to confound
'em together. For Inftance : In the *Moral Law*
of *Exod.* xx. the Reafon given why we are to
Remember to keep holy the Sabbath-Day, is, becaufe *in fix days the Lord made heaven and earth*—
But in *Deuteronomy*, chap. v. where the *Sabbath*
is made a *Sign* to the *Jews*, the Reafon is particular and proper to them, *ver.* 15. *And remember thou waft a fervant*—— So that here
their *Deliverance* out of *Egypt* was the motive, without one word of the *Creation*, or
God's *Reft* on that Day : And this Reafon
is the rather fet down, becaufe it is fuppofed
that on *this Day* their Redemption began, and
they entred on their Journey towards the Land
of *Canaan* ; Providence fo ordering it, that the
Day might be the better retained, becaufe it
was the *term* of their Deliverance. Moreover,
the *Law* of the Two Tables deliver'd from
Mount *Sinai*, were put *into the Ark* by God's
own Direction, *Deut.* x. 2, 5. But the *other
Laws* wrote by *Mofes* were placed in the *out-
fide* of the Ark, as it is the common opinion,
grounded on that Text, *Deut.* xxxi. 26. *Take
this book of the law, and put it in the fide of the
ark*—— Add further, that it is faid, *Ezek.* xx.
10, 11, 12. *I brought them into the wildernefs,
and gave them my ftatutes, and fhewed them my
judgments* —— *Moreover alfo I gave 'em my
fabbaths* ——. Where, if the Prophet had not
diftinguifh'd between thefe Laws, as *Ceremonial*
and *Moral*, he would have faid thus, *judgments,
ftatutes* and *fabbaths*. And, to conclude, 'tis not
reafonable to think, that God, who is a God
of Order (and who forbid *plowing with an Ox*

P   *and*

and an Afs, or wearing of *Linfey-woolfey,* and took care that Men and Women fhould not be feen in the fame Apparel) would fhuffle a *Ceremonial Law* among the *nine Moral* ; which is as ridiculous to the full as the yoaking of an *Ox* and an *Afs* together.

A. The whole *Pentateuch* was anciently one *Book* : But in procefs of Time, according to the variety of its Subjects, it was divided into *five parts,* the *laft* of which the *Greeks* call *Deuteronomy* or the *Second Law,* or rather, after the way of the *Rabbins,* an *iteration* and *repetition* (117) of the Law given at *Horeb.* And the Reafon of it was, becaufe *thofe* who lived when the Law was firft delivered were many of them (118) now *dead,* and a new generation of Men fucceeded, who did not *hear* nor *fee* with what Ceremony it was before publifh'd. And therefore *Mofes* being ready to leave the World, he thought it his duty to have the Law read to *thefe* before his death ; that making it a kind of *Teftamentary* and *Farewel-Speech* to them, they might remember it the better. The Laws therefore were not *new,* though *newly* recited before Men who had been ftrangers to the former Promulgation of it. Particularly, the *Decalogue* was the *fame* as before, only *another Reafon* is added to what is exprefs'd in *Exodus, i. e.* their *Deliverance* out of *Egyptian* Bondage ; that fo, on a *double* account, they might be perfuaded to worfhip God on *this Day,* as they were *Men,* and as they were *Jews* whom God had created and brought from a place in which they had been for many years under great Oppreffion. And yet in reality I cannot fee why this fhould

---

(117) *Non quafi nova & alia —— fed repetitio & explicatio.* A Lap.   (118) Deut. 2. 16.

be

be called a *New Reason*, fince we find the very fame thing in the Law of *Exodus* ; only what is there made a *Preface* to the *whole Law*, is here inferted as a *Motive* to *one* of 'em. However, this we are fure of, that both in *Exodus* and *Deuteronomy* the *Law* is the *fame* ; becaufe it is faid, (119) *Thefe words the Lord fpake unto all your affembly in the mount, out of the midft of the fire.* And again, *Keep the fabbath-day, as the Lord thy God commanded thee* —— meaning the *fame Sabbath* and the *fame Day* as was before appointed in *Exodus*, otherwife the expreffion would not have looked backward, neither could he have faid, *hath commanded thee*, if there had been intended a *new Inftitution* and a *new Reafon* for it.

As to the Place where the Two Tables were put, the expreffions of Scripture make fome difference ; becaufe in one Text it is faid *they were put in the Ark*, in another (120) *in the fide of the Ark*, or more critically in the *out-fide of the Ark* ; or *in a Cheft* by it felf *on the right fide of the Ark*, faith the *Targum* of *Jonathan*. And fo we read, (121) that *there was nothing in the Ark, but the Two Tables which Mofes put there at Horeb, when the Lord made a Covenant with the children of Ifrael at the time they came out of Egypt.* But in *Deuteronomy* (122) we find it commanded that the *Book of the Law* be put in the *fide*, perhaps the *out-fide* of the *Ark*, in a little Box made for that purpofe. What can we draw from thefe two paffages, but that the *Ten Commandments*, as *principal Laws* written by God,

---

(19) Deut. 5. 12, 22.   (120) *ex latere Arcæ*, Æthiop: & Gr. *ad latus Arcæ*, Arab. *in finu ejus vel prope eam*, A Lap. *Una cum virga Aaronis & urna continente Manna*, Abul. (121) 1 King. 8. 9. & 2 Chron. 5. 10.   (122) Deut. 31. 26.

were

were to have so much honour as to be kept *in the Ark* it self; whereas the rest, as soon as collected and brought into a Volume (called thereupon the *Book of the Law*) were to be set *near the Ark* in some convenient place, from whence, upon occasion, they might take it out to read it to the People. *That Book* in the *side* of the *Ark* contain'd *all* the Laws belonging to the *Jews,* and among them the *Decalogue* it self : But *in the Ark* was only the *latter* on *Tables of Stone,* which not being so fit for common use, they *transcribed* and inserted 'em into the *body* of their Laws, yet without altering the nature of 'em, or making 'em by this means a *new Institution.* For they were *all* or *most* of 'em deliver'd from the *Mount* ; and all of 'em, without distinction, made up the Volume which is called in the Text *the Book of the Law.* So that whether kept *in* or *out of the Ark,* the Laws were the *same,* made by the *same Law-giver,* and a little before *Moses's* death publish'd *a-new,* and read to the Assembly, that they might not be ignorant of their Duty to God and their Neighbour.

What you say out of the Prophet *Ezekiel,* supposes *Statutes* and *Judgments* to be different from the *Law* of the *Sabbath,* otherwise they had been linked more closely together, and the same Privileges equally bestowed on them *all,* that *if a man do 'em he shall even live in 'em.* And admitting this difference, then your own proof makes the *Sabbath,* what St. *Paul* calls it, *a shadow,* and so at *Christ's* appearance to vanish away. But indeed there is not, to my thinking, any such *distinction.* For as (193) by *Statutes* and *Judgments* are for the most part meant *such Laws*

---

(123) *A Lapide in* Levit. xviii. 1.

among

among the *Jews* as more immediately refpected
their *Government* in Church and State; (and the
Reward for Obedience to them Mr. *Ainfworth*
calls *legal*, and of another kind · than the
Promifes of the Gofpel) fo 'tis the way of
Scripture to fpeak of things in *general*, and then·
add one *particular* Inftance more eminent than
the reft, to engage and employ our Meditations.
As in *Mark* xvi. 7. when the Women came to
the Sepulchre after Chrift was rifen, an Angel
appeared to 'em, and bid ·'em *go tell his difciples*
and *Peter*.   *Peter* was a Difciple, and therefore
in ordering them to go and tell the Difciples,
Peter muft be included ; and the Women, to be
fure, had not omitted him, had he not been
named ; yet named he was in particular, and
'tis conceived the hint was intended to encourage that Difciple to accompany the reft into
Galilee ; or elfe perhaps confidering how lately
he had denied his Mafter, he might have been
afraid to appear before him. And thus *Act.*i.14.
St. *Luke*, fpeaking of the Apoftles and others after
Chrift's Afcenfion, informs us, that *thefe all con-*
tinued with one accord in prayer and fupplication,
with the women, and Mary the mother of Jefus. The
Women and *Mary*.   So here *Statutes* and *Judg-*
ments are named in the *general* ; but then, as it
prefently follows, they are all determined and
explain'd by one remarkable part, the *Sabbaths*
to which the *Jewifh Law* related, and which, of
all others, bore the Emphafis. The *Sabbath* (124)
was the great Subject of their *Law* ; and if it be
here particularized, it was not in oppofition or
to diftinguifh it from what goes before, but to
illuftrate what the Prophet defign'd, and charge

· (124). *Qui negaverit Sabbatum fimilis eft ei qui negaverit*
totam legem, a Saying of the Talmudifts.

'em with the breach of all the Laws of God, without defcending to every inftance, unlefs one, which becaufe of its dignity ought not to be pafs'd in filence. I prefume what *Ezekiel* aim'd at may allow this Comment, That by him God upbraids the *Jews* of grofs ingratitude; becaufe notwithftanding he had given 'em *Statutes* and *Judgments*, fuch as made the World believe 'em *a Wife and Underftanding People*, and fuch, as if obey'd, would make 'em live in a Flourifhing and profperous Condition; nay tho' he had among other Favours, afforded 'em *his Sabbaths*, as a *Sign between him and them*, and whereby he diftinguifhed them from all Nations, and rendred 'em his *peculiar People* and Children; yet fenfelefs as they were, they regarded not thefe Bleffings, but thofe wife and wholfome Laws they daily violated, and thofe indearing *Sabbaths* which were the Teftimonies of the Divine Goodnefs; thefe they alfo polluted, and inftead of ferving him at fuch times, they fix'd *their eyes on their Fathers Idols*. Hereupon, fometimes in vengeance he gave them *Statutes that were not good, and Judgments whereby they could not live*, ver. 25. i. e. (125) fevere Punifhments and Calamities; fuch as are Recorded *Numbers* xvi, xvii, xxi, xxv. Chapters. And in order thereto, *he gave 'em up to their own hearts lufts, and let them follow their own imaginations*, as the *Pfalmift* faith, *Pfalm* lxxxi. 12.

As for the *mixture* of *Moral* and *Ceremonial Laws*, that's not rare, as I noted before to you. But for your conjecture that the *Sab-*

---

(125) *Quæ fententias mortis continerent—Ipfis incommoda noxiaq; ut fuerunt hiatus terræ & ignis, plaga peftilens, ferpentes,* &c. Jun. & Trem.

bath commanded from Mount *Sinai,* and the
other in *Deutronomy* had feveral Days ; and
that the *Jews* kept the *one* and we the *other*,
as the very fame the Patriarchs and this very
People obferved before, This feems to beg
too much : For it doth not yet appear, but
that the Law was the *fame* in *both places*, tho'
repeated in *Deuteronomy* for the further inftruction of the People. Neither is there the
leaft *innuendo* of the alteration of the Day,
tho' it was an Article of too great confequence to be omitted. Nor am I convinced
that it was truly the *Day* they took their
farewell in, when they left the Land of
Egypt.

Your diftinction of *genus* and *fpecies* of the
Seventh-Day looks fomewhat like *Fancy.* For
if we muft have a *Seventh-Day Moral,* it
ought to be *that Seventh-Day* mention'd in
the Commandment, or elfe there is no correfpondence between the *Precept* and the *Reafon*
of it, *i. e.* the *Reft* of God. And therefore
that particular Day is to be diftinguifhed on
which it is Recorded he actually refted :
and accordingly the Precept begins, *Remember the Sabbath-Day,* then follows the Motive,
becaufe God refted on the Seventh-Day, — and fo
concludes, *wherefore the Lord bleffed the Seventh-Day, and hallowed it :* or more exactly
after the *Hebrew, he bleffed the Sabbath-Day,*
and made *that Seventh* the *Sabbath* to the *Jews,*
in which himfelf *refted,* and that *reft* was the
reafon why he *blefs'd* it. The confequence is,
That if the Day be kept on the account of the
Bleffing, then *that individual Day* ought to
take place, which God Sanctified, and Dedicated to his Service. And fo far the *Jews* are
in the right, that if the *Seventh-Day* be *Mo-*

ral,

ral, it muſt be their *Sabbath* or the *laſt of the Seven,* which on that ſuppoſition is *unalterable.*

.*B.* As far as I can gather from your Diſcourſe hitherto, you incline to the Opinion of the *Rhemiſts,* To make the obſervation of this Day a *Tradition* and *Cuſtom* of the *Church,* grounded more on the *reaſonableneſs* of the practice, than any *Divine Authority,* propoſing and requiring it. And of this mind was *Tindal,* who looked on it with ſo indifferent an eye, that he declared in his Anſwer to Sir *Thom. More,* that we are *Lords of the Sabbath, and may change it to Monday, or any other Day,* or appoint every *Tenth Day,* or *Two Days in a Week,* as we find it moſt expedient. And ſo *Barclay* faith of *Calvin,* that he once deſigned to tranſlate it to *Thurſday,* as an inſtance of Chriſtian Liberty; eſpecially being the Day, whereon might be Commemorated the moſt Triumphant and Glorious Act of our Lord, his *Aſcenſion* up into Heaven. But if you go this way to work, and allow the Decalogue to contain *Ceremonial* Laws, as well as *Moral,* you give a fair opportunity to the *Papiſt* to interpret the *Second* Commandment as you do the *Fourth,* and ſo may diſmiſs it as a Temporal Law prohibiting Images as dangerous things to the *Jews,* but are innocent and uſeful in theſe latter days for the better information and inſtruction of the ignorant.

.*A.* The Doctrine of *Images* is exploded by the Law of *Nature,* and the better reaſon of Mankind, which looks on it as a thing very abſurd and inconſiſtent with the Notion of an *Infinite Spirit,* an *Almighty, Eternal, Immortal, Inviſible* and *Wiſe* God to be repreſented in

that

that grofs manner, and what might make a
Sober Man laugh to fee the Carpenter, Smith,
or Painter, adoring the works of his own
hands. A matter found of fo ill confequence,
that (*) St. *Auguftin* reports it a Saying of
Varro a wife Heathen, That had *Rome* continued without Images as they had done for 170
years together, the Gods had been ferved
much better. And the firft who made thefe
Images for the Gods, difcharged the fear due
to them, and were the caufe of many Errors.
And as a *Sin of Nature*, the Holy Prophets re-
buked the Heathen for it, *Ifaiah* xliv. 9.
Habak. ii. 18, 19. *Deut.* xii. 3. whereas we
never find them charged with the breach of
the *Sabbath*, as they had often certainly been,
had that been a *Law of Nature* and affected
them as it did the *Jews* whom a multitude of
Scriptures blame for their ill keeping it. As
for the opinion of *Calvin* and *Tindal* about
changing the Day, I anfwer, it is a diftinction
of *Suarez*, that the alteration of the Lord's-
Day is *abfolutely* neceffary, but not *practically*;
he means, that it is needful *fuch a power* fhould
be in the Church, tho' not convenient to put it
in *execution*. Upon this Foundation *Calvin*
and *Tindal* built; and the *Sabbatarian Tenet*
breaking out in a fierce manner at the *Reformation*, was the reafon they fpake fo highly of
their *Chriftian Liberty* in this particular, to put
a check to that Doctrine. Yet in prudence
and *difcretion* the alteration was not made tho',
as to *Principle* they thought it not amifs to make
the Adverfary fenfible of the *Authority* of the
Church in a thing which they confidered of *an
indifferent Nature.* Not that it was a *fet Day*

(*) De Civ. Dei.

which

which the *Law of Nature* requires for the Service of Religion, but as *one* was pitched on rather than *another*, and they would have *that Day* changeable to prevent all *Superstition.*

B. How does this agree with the Judgment and Doctrine of the *Church* of *England* in her *Liturgy* and *Homilies?* For in the *First* she has appointed *this Precept* as well as the *rest* to be prononounced in the 2*d* Service. And at the conclusion of it her Children are taught to beg Gods Grace *to incline their hearts to keep this Law*; keep it as it is there worded in the plain sence according to the understanding of those who are ingaged in the Service. And then in the *Catechifm*, the same Law is again repeated, and in the Charge given the Godfathers and Godmothers, they are required to take Care the Children be taught the *Creed*, *the Lords-Prayer*, *and the Ten Commandments in the vulgar Tongue*, and undoubtedly in the *vulgar sence*, as most fit for the Capacities of young People, who are not able to penetrate into *Figures*, but take every thing in the *common* acceptation of the words laid before 'em. And then in the *Homily* of the *place* and *time* of Prayer, she hath these words: "*God has given* " *exprefs Charge unto all Men*, *that upon the* Sab- " bath-Day *which is now our* Sunday, *they fhould* " *ceafe from all weekly and work-day labour*; *to* " *the intent that like as God himfelf wrought* " Six Days *and refted the* Seventh, *and blefsed* " *and fanctified it*; *and confecrated it to quiet-* " *nefs and reft from labour*; *even fo Gods obe-* " *dient People fhould ufe the* Sunday *holily*, *and* " *reft from their common and daily bufinefs*, *as* " *alfo give themfelves wholly to Heavenly Exer-* " *cifes of God's true Religion and Service.* So that God does not only command the obfervation

tion of this Holiday, but alfo by his own example doth ftir and provoke to the diligent
keeping of the fame. And therefore either
this Law is ftill in force, and has the fame vigour and obligation with the other *nine,* or
elfe the *Church* feems to me to equivocate, and
may be well thought to impofe on her Children.

A. The Doctrine of the *Church of England
is,* that *fome times* be fet apart for the honour
and worfhip of God, which is what we are directed to by *Natural Reafon,* and is called the
Moral of the *Fourth Commandment.* But that
the Commandment obliges no further than in
the *Equity,* appears by that *Homily* you referr
to, as may be eafily difcovered, if we carefully
read it, for it fpeaks to us thus. " *Albeit this*
" *Commandment doth not bind* Chriftian People
" *fo ftraitly to obferve and keep it as it did*
" the Jews, *as touching the forbearing of work*
" *or labour in a time of great neceffity, and as*
" *touching the precife keeping of the* Seventh-
" *Day after the way of the* Jews ; *yet notwith-*
" *ftanding, whatever is found in the Command-*
" *ment appertaining to the Law of Nature, as a*
" *thing moft godly, moft juft and needful for the*
" *fetting forth of Gods glory, ought to be retain'd*
" *and kept of all good and Chriftian People* ;
" *and therefore by this Commandment we ought to*
" *have a time,* as one in Seven, *wherein we are*
" *to reft, yea from our lawful and needful*
" *works.* So that fhe referrs to this Commandment, no otherwife, than as it contains a
Doctrine exhibited by the *Light of Nature,*
that *fome Days* fhould be confecrated to Divine Ufes. And if fhe pitches on the *Seventh,*
it was not that fhe thought a Seventh *neceffary,*
or that the Commandment binds us to *that*
Day ;

Day; but being *a Day* once commanded on the account of God's refting upon it, fhe was willing to *determine* the equity of the Precept, and take *that Day* rather than any other, in conformity to the Example of God, who, in the Commandment, is faid to reft on *that Day.* And fo the *Homily* faith, that " *this Exam-* " *ple and Commandment of God, the godly Chri-* " *ftian People began to follow after Chrift's Af-* " *cenfion, and to chufe them a ftanding Day of* " *the Week to come together in, not the* Seventh- " Day, *which the* Jews *kept, but the* Lord's- " Day, *the Day of his* Refurrection. ' *Since* " *which time Gods People hath always, in all* " *Ages, without any gainfaying, ufed to come* " *together on* Sunday. So that *after Chrift's Afcenfion* the *Piety* of Chriftian People *began* this *Cuftom*, and the *fame Piety* has continued it to the prefent time. And tho' the *Homily* mentions the *Seventh-Day* in feveral places, fhe doth not count this period a part of the *Law of Nature*, but as a *time* that *God* once determined under the Law, and the *Church* ftill keeps to it, as a decent and proper Day, becaufe of the Divine Precept and Example. And accordingly fpeaking of this Commandment, fhe faith; " *By this Commandment we* " *ought to have a* time, *as one Day in the* " *Week*, or *as one Day in Seven*, having recourfe, for illuftration fake to the Day fixed among the *Jews*, which tho' fhe was not obliged to, yet fhe was bound to fome *ftanding Day*, as *their one of Seven* to adore and worfhip God in. And truly tho' the *Seventh-Day* be not of the Law of Nature, " Yet (126) " when God had thus determined it, Nature

---

(126) Stillingfleet's Iren. P. 1. C. 5. §. 3.

cannot

" cannot but affent to that particular deter-
" mination ; that in confideration of the
" works of God, it is moft reafonable that ra-
" ther *one Day* in the *Week*, than *one* in a *Month*
" fhould be dedicated to God's Service; that
" the *Seventh-Day* of the Week upon God's
" refting on that Day and fanctifying it,
" fhould be the precife Day, unlefs fome rea-
" fon equivalent to that of the firft inftitution,
" and approved by God for that end, be the
" ground of its alteration to another of the
" *Seven,* which is the reafon of the change
" under the Gofpel. And as fhe thought fit
to determine thus the *time* of Worfhip, as in
the Precept, fo fhe fets forth the *manner* of it,
and how fhe would have the worfhip exprefs'd ;
and here fhe thought fhe could not do better,
than to take the directions of the fame Commandment, as far as, in this refpect, it appertained to the *Law of Nature.* (127) So that
it being *natural,* while we worfhip God, to
forbear *all* other things, fhe ufes the *fame
words* prefcribed in the Commandment, and
alfo the *fame motive* from the Example of God
to require the *Jews* and invite *us* to adjourn all
forts of work but fuch as might be reconciled
to the Service of the Day. And fo come in
thofe expreffions of the *Homily* you now cited
to admonifh us to fanctifie the Day, as God did,
and reft from all our Weekly and common
Bufinefs.

And this being the meaning of the Fourth
Commandment in the Judgment of our
Church, we may very fafely fubjoyn that Eja-
culation *Lord have Mercy,* &c. without being

---

(127) *Naturale eft quod dum deum colimus ab alijs ab-
ftineamus.* Tofta.

made

made a prop for the *Sabbaths-Morality.* For tho' the Commandment be not *intirely* a *Law of Nature,* yet there is somewhat in it which *appertaining* to the *Law of Nature* makes it neceſſary to be read, to ſignifie to the Congregation the Will of God, that ſome ſet times are to be devoted to his Service, and that the times ſo determined muſt be piouſly and ſolemnly kept, and therefore we *beſeech* him to give us Grace to do it. But then tho' we ſend up ſuch a Prayer at the end of each Precept every *Lords-day,* yet we do it on *other Holidays* too, which ſhows we have no ſuperſtitious conceit of the 7*th Day* in particular, only as it is a Law of the Church to obſerve it, but withal to obſerve *other Holidays* with it. And tho' we Reverence the 7*th Day,* as the *Jews* did, yet the *Homily* ſaith " *We do it out of choice after the Example of* " *Chriſtian People who began this Cuſtom from* " *the Aſcenſion of our Lord.* And if *out of Choice,* to be ſure they had *Liberty* to let it alone. And as they had power to *change* the Day of the Week from *Saturday* to *Sunday,* ſo they had the ſame power either to *contract* or *inlarge* the time as they ſaw reaſon for it.

And that this is ſo doth further appear in the Act of Parliament made by King *Edw.* VI. where it is thus worded. **Neither is it to be thought that there is any certain or definite number of Days preſcribed in Holy Scripture, but the appointment both of the** Time **and alſo of the** Number of Days **is left by the Authority of Gods Word unto the Liberty of Chriſt's Church to be determined and aſſigned orderly in every Country, by the diſcretion of the** Rulers and Miniſters **thereof, as they ſhall judge moſt expedient to the true**
ſetting

ſetting forth of God's Glory, and Edification of the People. Be it therefore
Enacted, that all Days hereafter mentioned, ſhall be kept, and are Commanded to be kept Holidays, and none
other ; *i. e.* all Sundays, Circumciſion,
Epiphany, &c. And I the rather take notice
of this Law, becauſe ſome of thoſe *Prelates*
who compoſed the *Liturgy*, were Members of
the *Parliament* which made *this Law* ; and ſo
by conſequence the *Liturgy* and *this Law* explain one another.

The Summ is this. The *Fourth* Commandment is ſo far forth a *Law of Nature*, that it
requires *ſtanding Days* to do God Service in.
The *Church* has thought fit to *determine* thoſe
Days, both as to their *Annual* and *Weekly* returns. The moſt Famous of theſe is *Sunday*,
the Firſt Day of the Week, on the account of
Chriſt's *Reſurrection* : And it is *one Day* in *ſeven*, in conformity to what God was pleaſed
to preſcribe the *Jews*, upon the reaſon of his
own reſting on the *Seventh-Day*. And we
look on it a *good Motive*, tho' not *neceſſary*,
that we on the *Seventh-Day*, ſhould reſt likewiſe from all ſervile Works, the better to contemplate the Almighty and Wiſe Creator.
This therefore being the determined time, and
manner of Worſhip, according to our conſtitution, ſeeing that it is requiſite that the *Laws
of Nature* be read to the People, and that *this
Law* about *ſet times* of Worſhip, be repeated
as well as the other *nine*, what need is there to
alter the form we find it in ? and reject *words*
given by God himſelf, which as fully expreſs
our ſence, as any we can offer of our *own* ? And
ſince our Governours and Guides have pitched
on a *Seventh-Day*, why ſhould not the Congregation

gregation be admonifhed, *to remember the Se-. venth Day to keep it holy?* and as an inftance of fo doing, to *do no manner of work,* i. e. no common work on that Day which might hinder or difturb the Service of God? and becaufe the motive of this reft from ordinary Bufinefs on the *Seventh-Day,* is on the account of God's Example, *who in Six Days,* &c. ——May not this be delivered very well in *Mofes's Language*; and may not God be befeeched to affift us in all this, without the charge of *Judaifm* on the one hand, or without making the Commandment wholly *Moral* on the other, which is what you aim at in this Objection?

And if this be the fence of our *Church* in the *Second Service,* the fame fence muft be in the *Catechifm* where Children are taught, what as to this Point, the *Law of Nature* is, and how the *Church* of which they are Members underftand it. But you fay, This diftinction in the Fourth Commandment between what God requires, and the *Church* calls for, is not difcernible by fuch Capacities as are in *Children,* who will be apt to take all the Ten Commandments, and every claufe in 'em, as purely Laws of God, and in the *literal* and ordinary meaning. To which we anfwer; That *this Precept* is in no more danger of being miftaken than are the *others* which will want the Catechift's pains to explicate and make 'em eafie. As for example. It is faid in the Second Table, *Honour thy Father and thy Mother, that thy days may be long*—Now thofe who reflect on the miferies of Life, have no reafon to take *length of days* for a Blefling, or efteem it an *adequate Reward* for our Obedience and the Refpect we fhow to *Father* and *Mother*; and therefore it is look'd upon as a favour done to good King

Jofiah,

Joſiah, that God was pleas'd to take him from the *Evil to come.* And yet it is a *Bleſſing,* conſidering the *longer* we live, the *more* opportunity we have to ſerve God, and thereby be able to get in the end to an *higher Manſion of Glory.* For the main *Reaſon* why we were made, being to do the Creator honour, the *more Years* we have, the *better* we may anſwer this Deſign ; and in proportion to the Service we do, we ſhall be rewarded hereafter. Or if we expound this Promiſe as belonging to the *Jews,* whoſe felicity depended and was thought to depend on *long Life,* to be able to propagate and fill their Country ; then why may we not argue, That if a *Ceremonial Promiſe* had room in the *Decalogue,* why ſhould it be wonder'd that a *Ceremonial Precept* be found in it ? and where is the inconvenience, to believe it ſo in one reſpect more than in the other ?

Again, *Thou ſhalt not kill* —— yet we are to make a difference between a *legal Execution* and a *ſinful Murther* ; for the one *complies* with the *Law,* and the other *tranſgreſſes* it. It is forbid in the Firſt Table *to make any graven Image* —— Perhaps the Boy that learnt this, has never read that of the Poet, *Qui colit ille facit,* and cannot without his Maſter diſcern the difference between *drawing a Picture* and *making it the Object* of his Worſhip. And ſo in this Fourth Commandment, *God reſted the ſeventh day* —— yet ſtrictly, God can no more (128) *reſt* than be *weary,* but he *reſted* when he *ended* his Work. Nor doth he, or ever did *ſimply reſt* ; becauſe he is always doing, by his *Providence,* for the conſervation of thoſe Species he produced at the Creation. I mention theſe things, to let you ſee, that *other* Precepts as well as *this* are ſo worded as to need *explanation,* and in particular,

---

(128) Chryſoſt. *Hom. in* Gen.

Q   the

the reafon of the Fifth Commandment, tho' we can well enough apply it now under the Gofpel, as in what I took notice of to you, yet without doubt it was chiefly meant for thofe ancient Times, when *many Years* were accounted a *Mercy* by People who in a great meafure were influenced by *Temporal Bleffings*, and a *long Life* to enjoy 'em. However, we ufe the fame motive to perfuade *Obedience* to Parents, as we do what we read in the Fourth Commandment for keeping the *Seventh Day holy*.

B. I find no Argument will take with you ; But yet once more. What think you of the *Refurrection?* Did not (129) Our *Lord* fet a particular mark on *this Day*, by his rifing from the Grave? And is it not a fufficient difcovery of his Will, in having this Day *celebrated*, by his fo often appearing on it to his Difciples? And that thofe Difciples fo conftantly met on *this Day*, can we imagine it *cafually* done, and not rather by the *appointment* of their Mafter, who made it *folemn* by frequenting thofe places where at *fuch times* they were got together? And afterwards, was it not the *Day* whereon was that plentiful Effufion of the *Bleffed Spirit*, foretold by the Prophet *Joel*, on purpofe to fanctifie and diftinguifh it from all others? Accordingly we find it the Day on which the Apoftles affembled, and prefcribed it to their Converts for holy Ufes, as we fee by *Paul's* Firft Epiftle to the *Corinthians*, (130) *Upon the firft day of the week let every one of you* ―― *As I have given order to the Churches of Galatia* ―― ὥϚες διέταξα, as I have *ordain'd* ; which is an *Inftitution*, ὅτω ϗ ὑμεῖς ποιήσατε, *fo do ye*, which amounts to a *Command*. And fo elfewhere, *Upon the firft day of the week, when the difciples came together to break bread*, *Paul preached* ―― This declares the *Practice*,

_____

(129) Athanaf. *Hom: de Sem.*   (130) 1 Cor. 16. 2.

and

and ſhows it to be [*dies ſacri cœtus & dies panis*]ʳ an *appointed Day* for the People to *hear Sermons,* and *receive* the *Sacrament* of the *Lord's Supper,* a time well known to be ſet apart for ſacred Performances. And upon theſe and the like Authorities it is that (131) *Hoſpinian, Eſtius, A Lapide,* with many others, ſpeak peremptorily of it, that *it is not to be doubted but the Inſtitution of the Lord's Day* (Name and Thing) *is owing to the Apoſtles,* who, as (132) *Baſil* and *Auſtin* alſo ſay, decreed it to be ſolemnly and religiouſly kept ; and from that time to this it has been devoutly obſerv'd by all Chriſtian Churches throughout the World.

A. The *Motives* you propoſe are good, and a Man muſt be very ſingular and peeviſh not to accept 'em. And their influence is ſo powerful, that there is no likelyhood to think of an *Alteration.* However, as I conceive, you ſtrain the point too much, to call it an *Inſtitution of Chriſt* or his *Apoſtles,* when the Scripture is ſilent as to any ſuch thing. It was indeed *Calvin's* opinion, (133) that
" *at firſt the Apoſtles for a conſiderable time kept on*
" *foot the* Old Day, *which had prevailed with the*
" Jews *for ſo many Ages. But afterwards, being*
" *compelled to change it, becauſe of the many Abuſes*
" *which the Superſtition of their Countrymen brought*
" *upon it, they did ſubſtitute the* Firſt of the Week,
" *in remembrance of Chriſt's Reſurrection* ; *which*
" *put a period to all the* ſhadows of the Law, *and*
" *admoniſhes us Weekly of our* Chriſtian Liberty —
But then this ſubſtituting of *one* Day in the room of *another,* was not in the way of *Doctrine,* but *Practice* ; nor did they *enjoin* the Obſervation of the Firſt Day of the Week, though 'tis evident themſelves *obſerved* it. And ſo Mr. *Calvin* con-

---

(131) *Hoſp. de Feſt. Chriſt.* c. 8. *Eſtius & A Lap. in* 1 Cor. xvi.
(132) *De Sp. Sanct.* Aug. *de Temp.* (133) *Calv. in* 1 Cor. xvi.

ſiders

fiders it, as perhaps the Apoftles did, *an inftance of Chriftian Liberty,* wherein they left us fo free, that in that Author's judgment we may ftill change the Day, and fubftitute another. Certain it is, there was *a change,* even in the Apoftles times, from the *laft Day* of the Week to the *firft,* but (134) *when* precifely, or *by whom* it was made, does not appear from Scripture. And if the Apoftles made it a Rule, as you would have it, yet we have this account only by *Tradition*; and fo, not the *Rhemifts* alone, but *Irenæus* and others call it, as well as they: *We following their Tradition, have dedicated the* Lord's-Day *to holy Affemblies*—(135) *A Lapide,* whom you named, treats it in the fame manner, and makes it an Argument for *unwritten Doctrines*; *Becaufe,* faith he, *we no where find the Scripture commanding the* Lord's-Day *to be obferved inftead of the* Sabbath. And for *Hofpinian,* notwithftanding thofe words of his, (136) *the Apoftles ordained and fubftituted it,* he declares in the fame Chapter, that though 'tis true the *Lord's-Day* was very folemn in the days of the Apoftles, yet we cannot difcover that the Apoftles made any Canon of that kind, but left it to the Church's liberty to ufe what Day fhe pleafed, moft ferviceable to the good of her Children; and accordingly *other Days* were made religious, as St. *Auguftine* and *Epiphanius* witnefs. (137) *Socrates* is pofitive, that *neither* Chrift *nor his Apoftles made any Law concerning Feftivals, but their main End was, to perfuade Chriftians to lead a godly and vertuous life.* And therefore until (138) *Conftantine's* Reign there was no

---

. (134) *Quàndo facta fuit hæc mutatio in Sacris literis non habemus,* Mufcul.P.Mart.*Loc.Com.in* Quar.Præcept. (135) *Neque enim ufquam Scriptura jubet Dominicam fervari pro Sabbato, in* 1 Cor. xvi. (136) *Subftituerunt & ordinarunt* — yet, non *invenitur.* (137) Lib. 5. c. 22. (138) Eufeb. *de Vit.* Conftant. *l.* 4. c. 23.

Conftitution

Conſtitution touching theſe Matters, though *then* and *afterwards* the Empire growing *Chriſtian,* care was taken to obſerve Days by *Law,* and Penalties were inflicted on thoſe who refuſed to keep 'em.

As for Our *Lord's Appearing* on that *Day* to his Diſciples, it was not ſo often done, as to lay any great ſtreſs on't. For though it cannot be denied but that on *this Day* he ſhow'd himſelf to *Mary* and the *two Diſciples going to Emaus,* and the ſame night to the *reſt* aſſembled together ; yet that his ſecond Appearance, intended for the conviction of *Thomas,* before abſent, was on the *eighth day* after, is not ſo clear, but we may ſafely queſtion whether on this Day he was ſeen or no. The Goſpel ſaith expreſly [μεθ᾽ ἡμέρας ὀκτὼ] *after eight days,* therefore not on the *eighth* from his former appearance, but ſome Day (what is uncertain) when the *eighth* was expired and gone. However, he diſcover'd himſelf to his Diſciples on other Days as well as this, as at the (139) *Sea of Tiberias,* where ſeveral of 'em were fiſhing. And St. *Luke* ſaith, (140) *he was ſeen of 'em forty Days,* without exception or diſtinguiſhing one day from another. And it is very obſervable, that the moſt ſolemn manifeſtation of himſelf that he *ever* made *after his Reſurrection* was on the *Fifth Day* of the Week, when in the preſence of an Hundred and twenty Diſciples he went up to Mount *Olivet,* and from thence to *Heaven.*

The deſcent of the *Holy Ghoſt* on *Sunday* or the *Firſt Day of the Week* was *caſual,* and too uncertain to make it commence a *Rule.* For *Pentecoſt* was a *Moveable Feaſt,* and depended on the *Paſſover,* as the *Paſſover* did on the Motion of the *Moon.* So that the Paſſover *this* Year falling on the *Sabbath,* it followed, that the *Feaſt of Pentecoſt,* upon the

---

(139) John xxi. 2. (140) Acts i. 3.

Q 3 revolu-

revolution of so many Weeks, was to be the Day after; and tho' at this time it happen'd to be *Sunday*, the *Day* must alter in another Year. The true Reason then why *this Day* was pitched on for that miraculous effusion, (141) is given by St. *Chrysostom, because Pentecost* was a very famous *Festival*, at which all the *Jews* were to be present at *Jerusalem*, according to the Law; and among others, those who had an hand in shedding our Redeemer's Blood, or at least consented to his Crucifixion and Death; therefore God was pleased to take this Opportunity, that *these Men* might receive publick censure for that bloody Act, and so bear record to the power of the Gospel. It might be added, that some respect was had to this time on the account of the Law, which was proclaimed from Mount *Sinai* in an illustrious manner at the same time of the year. (142) " *So* " *that the thing being* casual *as to the Day, and* " special *as to the business then by God intended,* " *it will afford us little proof either that the* Lord's " Day *was as then observed, or that the Spirit Se-* " lected *that Day for so great a work, to dignifie* " *it for a* Sabbath.

That the Disciples met on *this Day* we believe, because St. *Luke* affirms it, *Acts* xx. 7. but there is more frequent mention made of the *Sabbath* as a *Day* they assembled in, and yet that *Practice* has not the force of (143) an *Institution*, nor can it be called a *Command* to preferr this Day before another.

That St. *Paul* Preach'd on the *first Day of the Week* the same Text saith; but what is this to

---

(141) In Act. '(142) *Heylin's* Hist. of Sabbath. P. 2. c. 1. n. 5. (143) *Ex facto & exemplo legem facere iniquum est. Nunquam licet à facto ad jus argumentari,* Zuinglius.

near twenty places in the fame Author, where
we find him Preaching on *Saturday*, for the Reafons (144) St. *Chryfoftom* and *Calvin* give; *becaufe* then the *Jews* met, and by that means he
hoped to Convert 'em by his Preaching.

Again, St. *Paul* writes to the *Corinthians*, to
make their Collections for the Poor on *this Day*.
The reafon of it is, faith St. *Chryfoftom*, becaufe
at fuch times the *Mind* being free from the in-
cumbrances of other bufinefs, fhe is more inclinable to pity than fhe would otherwife be; and
the rather, becaufe then the thoughts are intent
on the ineftimable bounty of God beftow'd on this
Day in the refurrection of our *Redeemer*; a confideration which will invite a Good Man to be
bountiful and kind to thofe who want him. I do
confefs the Motives great and preffing for our
Charity to the neceffitous, becaufe God has been
gracious and compaffionate to us in our wants,
yet I queftion the validity of this proof, that either the *Corinthians* always met on *this Day*, or
that St. *Paul* means it the particular Day on which
thofe Contributions were to be made. St. *Chryfoftom* indeed feemingly affirms it, but (145) dif-
fents, and elfewhere afferts it to be the *Sabbath-
Day*; and he has (146) a great many to bear
him company, whofe Authority muft fo far prevail at leaft, as to render it a *queftionable* Cafe;
and feeing the Greek κατὰ μίαν Σαββάτων or Σαβ-
βάτε, may indifferently fignifie either the *Firft
Day* or *one Day of the Week*, and in ftrict Gram-
mar more efpecially the *latter*, therefore this
can do you but little Service in the prefent
Difpute, becaufe when the proof looks *both ways*,
it concludes for *neither*.

(144) Hom. in Act. Calv. in Act. (145) Inftitut.
(146) *Singulis Sabbatis* Strigel. Areti. Arab. *per unam Sabbati*, Vulg. Lat. Heming *&* Magdeburg.

And

And laftly for thofe words *as I have given or-der, fo do ye,* which feem you think to import an *Inftitution* and *Command*; they do not referr to the *Day it felf*, but *what was to be done* on the Day ; namely their *benevolence* towards the fup-port of the *Saints in Judea*, which he prefs'd in all places where he Preached, at *Macedonia, Achaia, Galatia,* as alfo *here* according to the Agreement the Apoftles made between them-felves on this occafion, *Gal.* ii. 10.

But the Night draws on ; and therefore to give you my opinion in this matter, which is what you defired, I fay, (147) " That *the ob-
" fervation of the* Lords-Day *among Chriftians
" inftead of the* Jewifh-Sabbath *is not grounded
" upon any* Commandment *given by* Chrift *to his
" Apoftles. Nor yet 'upon any* Apoftolical Con-
" ftitution *given to the* Churches *in that behalf.
" But that it was taken up by the fucceeding
" Church, partly in imitation of fome of the* Apo-
" ftles *who ufed, (efpecially in the Churches of the
" Gentiles, for in the Churches of Judea the Old
" Sabbath was ftill obferved,) to Celebrate their
" holy Affemblies upon the* firft Day of the Week
" *in the honour of* Chrift *and his* Refurrection ;
" *and partly for the avoiding of* Judaifm *wherewith
" falfe Teachers in thofe firft times, were ever and
" anon attempting to inthrall the* Chriftian Church.
And herein that *Homily* confidered before, is my Warrant. For it faith, " *after the Afcenfion,
" Godly Chriftian People, taking the 4th Command-
" ment not for a Law but an Enfample, began to
" fet apart a ftanding Day for the worfhip of God,*
and they chofe the *firft Day of the Week,* as the beft Day to celebrate the Refurrection. So that

---

(147) Dr. *Sanderfon's* Cafe of the Sabbath. *Rivet* in *Exod.* xx.

the

the *Lords-Day* had no Command that it should be sanctified, but it was left to *God's People* to pitch on *this* or *that Day* for the Publick worship. And being taken up and made a Day of Meeting for Religious Exercises, yet for 300 Years there was no *Law* to bind 'em to it, and for want of such a *Law*, the Day was not *wholly* kept in abstaining from common business; nor did they any longer rest from their ordinary Affairs (such was the necessity of those times) then during the *Divine-Service*. And therefore (148) St. *Jerom* makes it a particular Circumstance of the *Egyptian Monks*, that *on the Lords-day they did nothing else but Read and Pray*. And for a proof of this *imperfect Celebration* of the Day, the same Father proposes the Example of *Paula* a Devout Lady, whose Custom it was with the Virgins and Widows attending her, to repair to the Church every *Lords-Day*, and returning home again they sate down to their Work, which was to make Garments for themselves, and others who needed 'em.

B. With your leave, Sir; may not that Author's meaning be, that (149) when *Paula* and her Company were not at *Church* serving God, they were then so employ'd as you represent 'em? For the words do not necessarily conclude for Work on the *Lords-Day*, but seem to me rather to say, that she kept both that Day *intirely*, and all *other Days*, when there were opportunities of Worshipping God; and when there was no such opportunity, she diligently attended her Household-Affairs, and such business as became her Condition and Sex, because she would never be idle. This better agrees with what *Jerom*

---

(148) Ad Eustochium. (149) *Dies Dominica*, Lib. i. Cap. 20.

writes elfewhere; that namely *on this Day,* (150)
Men are to do only fuch things as relate to the
welfare of their *Souls.* So that either *Paula* did
no work at all on the *Lords-Day,* or it was no
other (after *Dorcas's* Example) than what *fuited
the Day,* *i. e.* Works of Charity, whereby fhe
made provifion for her felf in the Eternal State
hereafter. And to this fence is that of *Chryfoftom,*
who in his Tenth Homily on *Genefis* tells us, that
" *God blefled the Seventh-day, and has taught us
" that in the compafs of a Week we fhould fet apart
" one whole Day for* the practice of Religion.
And in his fifth *Homily* on *Matthew,* he cautions
his Auditory, not (upon their return from
Church) to refume their common bufinefs, but
to take the Holy Bible, examine what had been
Preached to them, and fee that their Families
fhared in the Inftructions given 'em. Yet were
it fo, as you take it, that even on the *Lords-day,*
at her coming home from the publick Worfhip,
Paula betook her felf to her ordinary Task whatever it was, (151) yet *Cyprian's* Rule in this cafe
is to be heeded, *That we are not to follow any
Cuftom, untill we are fure it is a fafe one.* And
therefore fuppofing this to be her practice on the
Lords-day, it doth not follow, that others *then*
did, or that we *now* fhould imitate her in it.

A. That St. *Jerom* fpeaks of the *Lords-day,* is
without gain-faying, for he faith, (152) " *Paula
" with the Women, as foon as they returned home on
" the Lords-day, they fate down feverally to their
" work, and made Cloaths for themfelves, and
" others*—fo that both belong to the *fame Day,*
their *return home,* and their *return to work,* which

---

(150) *Sabbato ea tantum faciant quæ ad animæ falutem
pertinent. In Ifai.* (151) Cypr. Epift. (152) In
Epitaph. Paulæ ad Euftoch.

was to make Garments, but whether all of 'em intended for *Charity* may admit some doubt. To be sure what was made [*sibi*] for *her self* and *them* will not allow that interpretation; and as for the [*cæteris*] this consideration will not excuse her, because in case she design'd 'em for *Charity*, yet there was no necessity for her to work on *that Day*, but might put it off safely to the next Morning. The Rule of St. *Cyprian* is necessary, *That we are not to imitate an ill Custom.* But this *Rule*, if applied here, charges St. *Jerom.* with a very great oversight to propose *Paula* for an *Example*, and insert this passage in the commendation of that excellent Lady; " *that she* " *with her Women returned to their work as soon as* " *Church-time was over*—in case it had not been the *innocent* practice of that Age, and was part of the Character of a good Woman. As to what you produce out of St. *Chrysostom*, I wish you had read on in that *Homily*, and then you had met with these words immediately following. *And when these Lessons are well fixed in the Mind, then he* gives 'em leave to *proceed to other Matters relating* to this Life. So that the fault was not to *do* any *common work* on that Day, but they made *too much haste* to it, because without giving themselves leisure to reflect on what was Preached, they *forthwith* ran to their Employments and Trades, which tho' harmless enough in themselves, ought to have been deferr'd 'till the Instructions given 'em in the Church were throughly setled in their memories. And therefore these Exceptions do not weaken what was before asserted, That tho' the *Lords-day* had respect shown it, and was distinguish'd by the exercise of holy Duties, yet it was not *fully* confecrated to the Worship of God, but was *part* of it spent on those ordinary works which humane weakness and their daily wants required to be done. *B.* Do

B. Do you allow Work to be done on this Day?

A. By no means, excepting such as pure *Necessity* or *Charity* calls for, which are not so much the works of *Men* as of *God.* For the (153). *Law of Nature* requires, that *Sacred times* Dedicated to Divine Services, should not be *Prophaned* or polluted by business not suiting that name. And the *Laws of the Church* determining these *Sacred Times,* they ought to be spent in the worship of God without the interruption of our *Secular* Concerns. And this *Paula* and the rest did, as far as they were then obliged to it. And if we read they did any work on the *Lords-day,* it is to be remembred that this application to their daily tasks, was not 'till the worship was quite over, when they might with innocency enough resume 'em, because the *length of time* or the *number of hours* assign'd for Piety was not then so well explained as in after Ages. The State of the Church is vastly different from what it was in those early Days. *Christians* then for some Centuries of Years were under *Persecution* and *Poverty*; and besides their own wants, they had many of 'em severe *Masters* who compel'd 'em to work, and made 'em bestow less time in *Spiritual* Matters than they otherwise would. In St. *Jerom*'s Age their Condition was better, because *Christianity* had got into the Throne, as well as into the Empire. Yet for all this, the *intire* Sanctification of the *Lords-Day* proceeded slowly; and that it was the work of time to bring it to perfection, appears from the several steps the *Church* made in her *Constitutions,* and from the *Decrees* of Emperors and other Princes, wherein

---

(153) *Nisi quod necesse est, nefas habetur facere,* Fest. *Vid.* Macrob. Saturn. l. 1. c. 16. & Servium in Virg. Georg.

the prohibitions from *Servile* and *Civil* Bufinefs, advanced by degrees from one fpecies to another, 'till the Day had got a confiderable figure in the World. Now therefore the Cafe being fo much altered, the moft proper ufe of Citing thofe old Examples, is only, in point of *Doctrine*, to fhow, that *Ordinary Work*, as being a compliance with *Providence* for the fupport of *Natural Life*, is not *finfull* even on the *Lords-Day*, when *neceffity* is loud, and the *Laws of* that *Church* and *Nation* where we live, are not againft it. This is what the *firft Chriftians* had to fay for themfelves, in the works they did on *that Day*. And if thofe Works had been then judged a *Prophanation* of the *Feftival*, I dare believe, they would have fuffered Martyrdom rather than been guilty. But where this Plea is wanting, what was *no Sin* in *them*, may be *a Sin* in *us*, when we have not only opportunities and liberty to fanctifie the Day wholly, but not to do it, is a *tranfgreffion* of our Laws, which command and oblige the Confcience to a thorough obfervation of it, inflict Temporal Penalties on Offenders, and which to obey (efpecially in thofe inftances wherein God is concern'd) is what the Gofpel requires, and muft needs be underftood a piece of true Piety. And *this appeal* to the Primitive Times, is not to be taken as if thofe Authors would warrant us, by what our Fathers did in *former Ages*, to do the *fame* in *this*, but only to maintain the *Argument*, That *common work*, when it is no *hindrance* to Devotion, is not *Criminal* even on the *Lords-Day*, were our Circumftances fuch as our Anceftors labour'd under. But becaufe our Condition is better, as it would be an Overt Act of high *Ingratitude* to God to let our *Secular* affairs interpofe and intrude into his Service, now there is no fuch neceffity for it: So it would be withall a

Difobedience

Difobedience to our *Laws* and *Magiftrates* to do
any thing of that kind ; and the Apoftle faith,
they that refift fhall purchafe to themfelves Dam-
nation.

.*B.* Well, Sir, to come to your *Notion.* Were
the *Lords-Day,* as you hold, an *Humane Inftitution,*
what an ill influence might this Doctrine have on
the minds of Men, who will be ready to think
that they may make bold with a thing which has
not the Authority of Divine Appointment to fettle it, and fo be induced to further *prophanenefs,*
except in fuch notorious inftances of irreligion,
where the *Law* terrifies them, and yet in the Punifhing of which, the *Magiftrate* is almoft as remifs as themfelves. Whereas on the other fide,
where the contrary Principle prevails, " *It not*
" *only brings Men to Church to worfhip God, but*
" *alfo obligeth them in Confcience, to do fomething*
" *extraordinary in their Families on* the Lords-Day,
" *towards the Educating them in the nurture and*
" *fear of the Lord, beyond what they think them-*
" *felves bound to do on the* Week-Days ; *fo that if*
" *this were an error, it would be an happy error, as*
" *being the occafion of bringing Men to the worfhip*
" *of God, and knowledge of the truth. And truly,*
" *if I were perfwaded that the other Opinion* [*that*
" the Sanctification of the Lords-Day hath no
" other ground than Ecclefiaftical Conftitution]
" *were a Truth; I fhould think it a Truth not ne-*
" *ceffary to be publifhed.*

A. (154) *The Queftion is not what is fit to be*
Preached, but what is Truth, (155) which is able
enough to defend it felf. (156) and St. *Chryfo-*
ftom pronounces that Man a betrayer of it, who

---

(154) *Hobs* againft *Bramhall.* (155) *Magna eft*
vis, veritatis. Et facile fe per feipfam defendit, Senec. Ep.
(156) In Matth.

takes

takes refuge in indirect Means to uphold it. (157)
And if People will be fcandalized at the *Truth* becaufe
it is not juft *fuch* as they would have it, it is much
better to let the fcandal continue, than to let Truth
be modelled to their humour. It is the Apoftles Rule
that we fhould *not do evil that good may infue.* Nor
can it be prudent and fafe, to make that a *Divine
Doctrine*, which is *not* fo, for fear it becomes a *Reafon*
to call in queftion *thofe* which really are. That the
Lords-Day ought to be ferioufly and folemnly kept,
is agreed on all hands; but if Men will ufe fuch Arguments for the obfervation of it, as cannot abide
the trial, in this cafe inftead of inforcing it, they do
but tempt Prophane Perfons to neglect it the more,
who will be apt to judge the *Day* it felf to be as
weakly grounded, as their *Reafons* are weak, which
they offer to maintain it by, and procure it a greater
veneration. We cannot therefore admit the *Lords-
Day* to be an *Inftitution* of *Chrift* or his *Apoftles*, becaufe the proofs to make it fo, are very infufficient,
and give occafion of *fcandal*. Yet tho' it will not
bear that Character, a Character fo *ftrictly Divine*, as
many would have it, yet we are not deftitute of very
folid Reafons to recommend it, fuch as are not fo liable to exceptions, but if well examined may be very
forcible to ingage us to keep it. For we fay it is a
Law of Nature to fet apart fome *particular Times* for
the worfhip of God; and it is a *Law of the Church*
and *State* that *Sunday* fhould be the *Set time* to do
him Service in; and therefore on this account it obliges the *Confcience*, and a Man certainly Sins in tranfgreffing it. It was refolved before, that no Law in
the two Tables obliges a *Chriftian*, as a *Law of Mofes*, but *as a Law of Nature*, which binds all Mankind of what Nation or name foever. And fuch I
take the *Lords-Day* to be, a *certain time* which *Nature*
has *fix'd* for Divine Worfhip, and which the *Church*
has *determined* to the *Seventh*, and to the *firft of the
Seventh*, or the *firft Day* of the Week. I fay, the
Church (which the Gofpel injoyns us to hear) from

---

(157) *Si de veritate fcandalum fumitur, utilius permitti-
tur fcandalum nafci quàm veritas relinquatur.* Aug. de lib. Arb.

the

the beginning of *Christianity* to this present time has made this comment on Nature, and our *Civil Governours* press it, whom we are commanded to *obey not only for wrath but Conscience sake.* So that tho' 'tis not expresly said, *keep Sunday* (or the *Lords-Day,* or the *first Day of the Week*) *holy*, yet seeing *Nature* proposes some *set time*, and the Church of God requires *such a set time* for our Service, is not this the same thing, as if God himself had said these words from Mount *Sion* which he said by *Moses* from Mount *Sinai, Remember to keep holy, &c.* I conclude therefore thus, That if neither the *Law* of *God* nor *Man* did require this Day to be celebrated as it is or should be, yet considering that my natural understanding tells me, that God ought to be worshipped, not only in a pious and vertuous Life, but also on *stated times*, in a formal and set Devotion ; and remembring what I read in the Holy Book, that God heretofore appointed a *Seventh-Day* to be adored in, I would of my self pitch on *this proportion of time*, i. e. a *Seventh Day*, in deference to that All-wise Example ; and the *first of the Seven* in memory of my *Saviour*'s Rising : And I should have been well pleased, had this proceeded from my own *private choice* to make it a voluntary oblation. However since I find in the same Sacred Volume that *Obedience is better than Sacrifice*, I am not the less pleas'd for having this opportunity to show my obedience and conformity to my *Superiours Will* in what they command so agreeable to my *own*. And I do wish with all my heart that the opposite Opinion doth not proceed from a Principle of *Pride* and *Disaffection* in some Men, who will strain hard for *new Reasons* to support the grandeur of the *Lords-Day*, because they would not be beholding to the Piety and Industry of those to whom in reality the *Institution* is owing. Whereas for my part, I should think my self obliged to bless God that I live in subjection to a *Christian Government*, where this and other Duties are proposed, and *whose Laws* tend so much to the better execution of 'em.

And so I take my leave for this time.

The End of the Second Dialogue.

The Third DIALOGUE.

The CONTENTS.

The Design and Service of the Lord's-Day.

THE Contemplation of the Works of Nature leads to the Worship of the Creator, which was the business of the Sabbath. The Sabbath an Emblem of God's Rest to the Jews. A sign or badge to distinguish them from other Nations, and a Declaration that they Worshipped the Maker of Heaven and Earth who rested that day. The Sabbath not for idleness, but meditation and hearing of the Law. Synagogues not till after the Captivity. Psal. 74. 8. is no Objection. Nor what Josephus Reports. Nor what Philo saith Nor 2 King. 4. 23. Several Councils, Imperial Decrees, Laws and Canons, both Foreign and English, for the Observation of the Lord's-Day. Judgments for the contempt of it; yet no Arguments for Divine Institution. God to be adored in the Church. Acts 7. 48. Is no Objection against Meeting in Publick Places. Reasons for Publick Worship. Absolution the notion, necessity and comfort of it. SS. Chrysostom, Jerom, and Gregory's Opinion of it. The power of the Keys in John 20. 22. not Personal to the Apostles; but given to a standing Ministery. Sermons heard in the Church better

R   than

than read at home. The Reasons. The necessity of receiving the Sacrament of the Lord's Supper. St. Paul's unworthiness, in 1. Cor. 11. 28. examined. No Plea to keep others from the Holy Table.

B. I Have almost loft my Breath, *Sir*, by endeavouring to overtake you; For feeing you at a little diftance and walking gently, I was invited to mend my pace, out of the Ardent defire I have to enjoy your Company; But truly had you not ftopt, as you did, at this Place, I had not been able to reach you.

A. Your long confinement to your Chamber and Chair caufes this feeblenefs. For not only the *Diftemper* has contributed to it by abating the Animal Spirits, the want of which brings a faintnefs on you, but the *Difufe* of your Legs has given a great check to the motive faculty, which putting you to more pains than ufual at other times, you now walk with greater difficulty. Pray therefore reft your felf on this Rail for fo much time at leaft as to recover your Breath, otherwife I confefs it will little eafe you. [*A paufe for fometime.*]

B. What means, *Sir*, this filence and *Serioufnefs* which I have obferved ever fince I came to you.

A. I thank you for your humanity to give my *Silence* that Name, which according to the way of the World, might have been conftrued into *Sullennefs* and want of humour. For People no further confider *Man* than *as a converfible Creature,* whereas he has a *reflexive* as well as *communicative faculty,* and ought to *think* before he *fpeaks,* which being rarely done, this Precipitation and hafte in venting our conceptions before we take time to form 'em, tho' it be generally called *agreeablenefs* and *freedom,* yet is the reafon why our Ordinary converfation is fo frothy and vain. But without complement, my for-

forbearance to fpeak had fome regard to *you* and *your condition.* For I know one word begets ano-her, and to ingage you in Difcourfe before you had well recovered your felf, I thought 'twould be unkind, becaufe perhaps I might by that means caufe a greater decay of Spirits than your coming hither had brought you to.

B. Indeed I remember 'twas a Leffon the *Phy-ficians* taught me and thofe about me during my illnefs, that I fhould *talk* little, and I ftand obliged to you that you thus confult my Condition.

A. The reafon is, Becaufe the *Spirits* iffue out with the *Voice,* and are conftantly employ'd to form it. And if this be continued for any time it makes a Man as *faint* and *feeble,* as any other Work or Motion whatever. So that this was truly *one* reafon of my filence, though I cannot fay it was the *only One* ; and not to give you the trouble of asking me, it is this. You fee the Glories of this Evening; and can we fee and not Admire, Love, and Adore the Almighty Wifdom of our *God,* which gave *Being* to all thofe things which concurr to make it fo. Behold what Beauties; what Fi-gures, what Colours thofe little *Clouds* in the Air reprefent, by the Reflection of the *Sun-Beams,* which according to their quantity and bulk, more or lefs affect 'em, *what Painter,* what *Paint* can imitate 'em ? How wonderfully and varioufly do they move, and fhape, and furnifh that Region ? But how much more wonderfully and varioufly does that *Flaming Globe* (that has juft taken its leave of us) fhow it felf, which caufes and with fuch difference inlightens 'em ? With what Pride do thofe *Trees* fpread abroad and fhake their *Leaves* ? And how do the *Fields* fmile in their va-riegated *Greens,* which the Gayeft fteal from them to make themfelves wantonly fine ? Thofe *Sheep* ; and thefe *Cattel* here feeding ; the *Birds* which

with

with such *sweetness* and *variety* of note have so
often entertain'd you and me, in and near this
place, *whence* had they all their beginning? Could
Atoms by their diversity of *Sympathies* produce
these Kinds? Could they digest and hook themselves into these manifold forms, and after an E-
ternal motion cling into such or such Bodies, as we
now see 'em? But how came these *Atoms* by their
own Being? Did *Chance* do all this? 'Tis as ridiculous to say it, as to avouch that the *Timber* of
yonder House hew'd and framed it self, and that
the *Stones* and *Mortar* luckily conspired to make that
building.   To talk of *Nature,* is to affirm that the
Virtues, Inclinations and *Tendencies* of the Creatures
produced themselves. Or if we mean by *Nature,* that
Efficacy and *Power,* which gives 'em their different
Operations, under *another Name* we signify *God.*
Can a Man, my Friend, see these mighty Works
and not think, and not reverence the *Divine Artist*
that made 'em? It was this, for sometime before
and since you came, which caused my Meditation.
For I was willing to make my Diversion profitable,
and while in my walk I pleased my *Eye* with this
variety of Objects, I was desirous they should
impress my *Heart*; and beholding, as I went along,
these several Works, (*a*) I consider'd 'em as invi-
tations to magnify the *Creator.*

B. This ought to be done by us all, and 'tis
the proper use to be made from beholding the
Works of God. But alas, generally speaking,
Familiarity, and the continual sight of the Creatures have weakned this Reflection.   *Nature*
grown common is lessen'd in her Beauty; and because she is now tied to Laws and *Rules,* for that
reason she is become less venerable. The constant

(*a*) *Wisd.* 13. 4, 5.

courfe of *fecond Caufes* has almoft defaced the notion of the *Firft* ; And we are at length arrived
to fuch a pitch of *Infidelity*, that we more admire
that *Carver* or *Painter*, who can *imitate Nature*
well, than that *God* who *made* both *Her* and *Them.*
But I have a better example now before me ; and I
am well pleafed that you have given me fo fair an
Opportunity to renew the Difcourfe on our late
Subject——I mean , the *Sabbath* or *Lord's-Day*,
the *names* and *notion* of which have been fully explain'd, and there remains now no more than to
fpeak of the *end* and *defign* of it, and what we are
to do to obferve it well, which indeed is the principal part of this Religious Queftion.

You fay, *Sir,* you have been contemplating the
Works of *God*, and making fome Pious Reflections
on the particulars of the Creation. And was not
this Day fet a part to be a (*b*)*Memorial of the Creati-*
on, and a *fign* by which might be known when the
Creation was finifht ? I fpeak in the general, without the diftinction of *Jew* and *Chriftian*, and thofe
particular Obligations they lie under *as fuch* to Celebrate the *Seventh-Day.* As we are all the Children of *Abraham*, this is our *common reafon* ; And
we adjourn all *civil bufinefs* till *this* Day be over,
that fo we may have leifure to reflect on the Creatures, and ufe 'em as fo many fteps or links to get
to the *Chair* of our *Jehovah*, and there fee thofe
Divine *Attributes* of *Wifdom*, *Power* and *Goodnefs*,
which gave 'em *Being*, *Motion* and *Life.*

A. He who employs his Thoughts about the
Creation, ought to advance his fpeculation and
end in what you mention, or elfe he opens his *Eyes*
barely to ferve his fanfie, but his *Heart* will be

(*b*) τὸ μὲν δημιουργίας ὑπόμνημα κὴ σημεῖον τῶ εἰδέναι τὴν
τῆς κτίσεως ἡμέραν. Clem. Conftit. l. 7. c. 23. & Athanaf,
de Sab.

as *cold and cloſe ſhut* as it was before. When I would be ſaid to admire the Creature, 'tis not to be ſuppoſed I terminate there or fix my ſelf wholly on that Object, but I look on this as an *effect* of a much more Excellent *cauſe.* And if I wonder at the *Act,* in an higher degree I admire the *Power,* and while my *Senſes* and *Underſtanding* are thus engaged, my *Affections* grow warm, and at length I *Love* what I find reaſon to *Admire.*

B. Undoubtedly the ſtudy of *Nature* ſhould conclude with *God.* And this I take to be the *Inſinuation* of that ſtrict *Reſt* among the *Jews* on this *Day,* wherein (c) *every Man was to abide in his Tent, and not go out of his place,* which tho' ſuperſtitiouſly abuſed afterwards to that degree, that in whatſoever (d) *Habit, Place* or *Geſture,* they were on the *Sabbath,* in the ſame they continued until the *Evening;* yet their true meaning was, that they were not to divert their Thoughts from the great Buſineſs of the *Day,* which referred to the *reſt* of *God* after the *Creation,* by going forth to act in their *Ordinary Affairs,* as in the gathering of *Manna,* or making the like Proviſion for *Secular* Life. Otherwiſe to my thinking, their walking abroad did not a little contribute to the *deſign* of the *inſtitution,* if ſecurity could have been given that they would employ their Eyes, as you have done this Evening, to behold the *Creatures,* and be thence ſummoned to conſider the *Maker.*

A. The *Reſt* of the *Jews* was a ſignificant *Emblem* of the *Reſt* of *God:* And the keeping of the Day in that manner was a *Profeſſon of their Faith,* and a kind of Declaration to the *Gentiles,* that *their* 'God' was he *who made Heaven and Earth,* and that they

---

(c) *Exod.* 16. 29. (d) 'Origen, Π εει, ἀεχῶν l. 4. Selden de Jur. Nat. l. 3. c. 9.

adored

adored him *as fuch.* (e) "*For all Nation had fome-*
" *thing in their Ceremonies whereby they fignified the*
" *God they worfhipped.———In the Revelations the*
" *worfhippers of the Beaft receive his mark; and the*
" *worfhippers of the Lamb carry his and his Father's*
" *mark in their Foreheads. And hence came in the ufe*
" *of the Crofs in Baptifm, as the mark of Chrift, the*
" *Deity to whom we are initiated, and was ufed in all*
" *Benedictions, Prayers and Thankfgivings, in token*
" *they were done in the name and Merits of the crucified*
" *Jefus. Agreeably to this Principle and Cuftom of all*
" *Religions, of all Nations, of all Vaffals, the Lord*
" *Jehovah Creator of Heaven and Earth, ordain'd to*
" *his People this Obfervation of the Sabbath-Day, for*
" *a fign and cognizance, that he and no other fhould be*
" *their God; it is a fign between me and you, that I* Jeho-
" *vah am your God;——as if he had faid it is a fign that*
" *the Creator of Heaven and Earth is your God. And by*
" *fanctifying the Seventh Day, after they had laboured*
" *Six, they profeft themfelves Vaffals, and worfhippers of*
" *that only God who had made Heaven and Earth. And*
" *who having fpent Six Days in that great Work, refted*
" *the Seventh-Day, and therefore commanded them to*
" *obferve this futable diftribution of their time, as a Badge*
" *and Livery, that their Religious Service was Appropri-*
" *ated to him alone.* Thus Mr. *Mede,* and he has
the Authority of St. *Cyril* for it, who gives the
fame account of the *Seventh-day,* " *Becaufe,* faith
" he, *the Jews became infected with the Idolatries of*
" *Ægypt, which worfhipped the Sun, Moon and Stars,*
" *and the Hoft of Heaven* (as is infinuated Deut. 4.
" 19.) *therefore that they might underftand the Hea-*
" *vens to be God's Workmanfhip, he willeth them to*
" *imitate their Creator, that refting on the Sabbath-*
" *Day, they might the better comprehend the reafon of*
" *the Feftival. Which if they did, and refted on that*

(e) Mr. Mede on *Ezek.* 20.

" *Day,*

" Day, wherein *God* had rested, it was an open Con-
" fession that all things were made by him, and confe-
" quently that there was no other besides him. So that
the *Ceremony* carried with it the Nature of an *Argument* to prove the true God, and silence the *Philosophers* in their several *Hypotheses,* concerning the
Eternity of the *World,* or the manner of making it.
And if the *Jews* rested, it was in imitation of *God*
whose they were, and who resting that *Day* taught
them by his Example to do so too. Neither can I
imagine *their* rest to be simply *idleness,* or no more
than a *cessation* from *servile labour,* which was understood in those Days, as it is thought, a piece of
Divine Worship, because done in Obedience to the
Precept, but that rather they minded, in some
proportion the *sence* of that *vacation.* And, as
God's rest was a reflection on what he had done the
Six Days before, and as the *Psalmist* speaks (*f*) *A
rejocing in his Works,* so they may be allowed to
spend the *Day* or *Part* of it in some such Holy Meditations. And examining into the several Benefits
and Blessings, which accrued to themselves by it,
they were invited to Praise *God,* who had been so
much a *Father* and *Benefactor* to them. And thus
Maimonides, expounds that of Exodus 20. 8.
Remember the Sabbath-day to Sanctifie it. (*g*) " It is
" commanded, saith he, to *sanctifie* it with words,
" both at coming in and going out. At the coming in,
" to bless *God who hath given his Sabbath for a remem-
" brance of the Creation of the World,* a remembrance
" of the coming out of *Ægypt,* and who of his love
" hath chosen, and sanctified his Church above all Peo-
" ple. And at the going out, to bless him again, for
" making a separation between the holy and prophane,
" between light and darkness, between Israel and other

(*f*) Ps. 104. 31. (*g*) Tract. de Sab.

" Nations,

" *Nations, between the Seventh-day and the other Six.*
So that 'tis no ill glofs that of *Ferus,* on Exod. 16.
29. *Let every Man abide in his place;* (*h*) Let every
one retire within himfelf and examine his Confcience, otherwife he is a very ill obferver of *this reft,*
who makes no difference between *Good Works* and
common labour, but equally refrains *both,* when the defign of forbearing the *latter,* was only for an opportunity to attend the *other.* The *reft* of God
himfelf is not ftrictly fo. *My Father hitherto
worketh and fo do I,* faith Chrift, *John* 5. 17. He
ftill goes on in the Works of *Providence,* to preferve and govern the World, and do fuch things
as tend to his Glory. And thus we are to apply
(*i*) his reft to our felves, not in a literal laying
afide *all* Work, but only *fuch* as are *impediments* to
the proper Work of the *day,* which is to *think* of
God and *adore* him. And this is indeed the (*k*)
τὸ ἴδιον τῦ Σαββαῖυ, and we ufe it as a *means* to lead
us to the Knowledge of God, and by meditating on
the *Hiftory* of the *Creation* be moved to magnifie
him.

And it may be Credited, that the *Jews* themfelves fpent the *day* in thefe *exercifes of the Mind,*
or elfe what occafion had they for that vaft number
of *Synagogues* we find among 'em! For there were
in *Jerufalem* befides the *Temple,* no lefs than 460.
as *Rabbi Phinehas* reckons 'em, though others fay,
480 and 481. (*l*) from an Hebrew word, in *If.*
1. 20. whofe Numeral Letters, being put together amount to that fumm. And that they conftantly atrended 'em, appears from that faying of

---

(*h*) *Maneat apud fe & confcientiam fuam fcrutetur.*
(*i*) *Lex Sabbati Opera' humana non divina prohibuit.*
Tertul. ad uxor. *Omne opus tuum non facies——de humana
Opere definiit,&c.——Adv. Marcion. (k)*Athan. de Sab.(*l*) Stil-
lingf. Iren. p. 2. c. 6 §. 5.

their

their Doctors, *(m) He who lives in a place where a Synagogue is, and will not go to it must be accounted a very ill Neighbour.* Now the use they put their *Synagogues* to, is partly discovered from the two Apartments they gave 'em. The One was the Room *(n)* for *Canonical Scripture,* where the *Law* and the *Prophets* were kept and read, *(o)* the *Other,* the room of *Traditions,* where the *Sayings* of the Fathers were expounded and taught the People. So that their business there was *One* while to hear the word of God as they had it *written*; and *another,* to be instructed in some things *not Recorded* in the other Book, yet required attention, as being *taken* (so it was pretended) *from the mouths of the holy Men,* in a way of *Supplement* or comment on the other, yet not deserving equal veneration, because we see the *Repositories* were not the same.

And that the *Law* was read, and expounded in their *Synagogues* on the *Sabbath-day,* is evident from St. *Luke* 4. 16. where the *Custom* of our Lord shows the *Practice* of the *Jews,* and gives us an account of what was done at such times. There we find (according to the several Stages we meet with in the *Arabic* Version) that they divided the Scripture into several *Portions,* one of which they read every *Sabbath,* and then Preach'd on it. That of *Isaiah,* happen'd to be the Lesson of *this Sabbath,* the Evangelist speaks of above,*(p) The Spirit of the Lord is upon me*——Which when *Christ* had read *standing* (being a Gesture always used out of reverence to the holy Book) he returned the Book to the *(q) Minister,* and then *sate down* (which every Teacher

***

(m) Maimon. in Tephil. c. 8. *(n) Domus libri..(o) Domus doctrinæ——*vid Dr. Lightfoot Hor. Hebr. *(p)* If. 61. 1, 2. *(q) Ministro Synagogæ——qui legenti adstitit summa cura observans ne quid falso aut incongrue legeretur, revocansq; corrigensq; si quid lapsum.* Dr. Lightfoot, on Matth. 4. 23.

was

was allowed for his eafe) to clear and apply it. This is further confirmed by St. *James*, Acts 15. 21. *Mofes in old time hath in every City them that Preach him, being read in the Synagogue every Sabbath-day*, read and preach'd ; and this for *many Genera-tions* before, to fhow it the *ufage* of their Ancestors and no *new-thing*. And it is not to be thought that their *Sermons* wanted *Auditories*, for in that paffage of St. *Luke* it is exprefly faid, That *all wonder'd at the gracious words that proceeded out of his Mouth.* And elfewhere, *the common People heard him gladly.* And this not out of Levity or principle of *Novelty*, but as it was the *old way*, and in compliance with their *Conftitution* and Duty, or elfe it had quickly commenced an *Article* againft him and them ; fo rigorous were the *Jewifh* Priefts in the moft minute parts of their Religion.

B. I think they fay, the *building* and *ufe* of *Syna-gogues* commenced *after* the *Captivity*, when the *Jews* returning from *Babylon* wanted Places for the Divine-worfhip, and therefore the *Temple* being deftroy'd, they erected thefe Conveniences for meeting together, as fome little Monuments and *refemblances* of it. And the Priefts finding 'em neceffary for the Peoples edification, continued them *afterwards* when the *fecond Temple* was quite finifhed, as *places* for Prayers and Sermons, but referved the *Sacrifices* as a Privilege peculiar to the *other* as the *Mother-Church*.

A. This is the general Opinion. For though St. *James* fpeaks of *Ancient times*, yet it muft be underftood only of fome confiderable time, *fome time before* very fhort of *Antiquity*. And whereas it is threatned, Levit. 26. 31. *I will bring your San-ctuaries into defolation*, by which the *Hebrews* would fignifie their *Synagogues*, yet after the way of Scripture in feveral Places, where for found-fake the plural number is ufed, it means no more than

than (r) the *Tabernacle* or *Temple*; which from the
diverse rooms or Divisions of it, *i. e.* the *Court*, the
Quire, and the *Holy of Holies*, was called *Sanctu-
aries*, though they were only *one structure* or house.
That which gives the utmost probability of their
being *older* than the Babylonish-Captivity, is, because *Asaph* Co-temporary with King *David*, faith,
(s) *They have burnt up all the Synagogues of God in
the Land.* But here the Hebrew word is of greater
extent; and because in the general it intends somewhat *certain* and definite, therefore 'tis variously
applied to *things, times,* and *places.* And if we consider it under those Limitations, the most credible
translations give it, it will hardly disprove the received Opinion. (t) For the *Syriac, Arabic, Chaldee, Æthiopic, Greek,* and Vulgar Latine render
it *Festivals,* and St. *Jerom* backs 'em with this reason, *because before the Temple at* Jerusalem *was built
the Divine worship consisted chiefly in* (u) *tranquillity
and mental Devotion.* And he adds, that the drift
of this malice in taking away those distinctions of
time, was, that *the honour due to God's Name might
cease in the earth,* the observing of *certain days* being great *helps* to the Memory, and do not a little
conduce to keep in mind *God* and his *Blessings.*
And therefore with respect to this project of the
Enemy, the stifling of their *holidays* was more
effectual to make them forget God, than the burning of their *Synagogues* could be, because in this
last Calamity, their Assembling only was hindred,
but as to the *former,* it had its effect on 'em, even
within their Houses. (w) *Calvin* will have this

(r) *Puta tabernaculum vel templum,* A Lapide, Ainsworth
in loc. (s) Pf. 74 8. (t) *Perdamus omnes festivitates Dei.*
Syr. and Chal. *Abrogemus dies festos de terra,* Arab. *Quie-
scere faciamus solennitates dom.* Æth. Vulg. Lat. κατατπαύσω-
μεν τὰς ἑορτὰς Κυρίου, Sept. (u) *In mentis tranquillitate & devo-
tione--* in Pf. (w) in Pf.

complaint

complaint of the *Pfalmift* to refer to the Days of *Antiochus*. And if his conjecture be good, the words contain a *Prophecy* of Perfecution in future Ages, and therefore having no relation to the days of *David*, in and near whofe Reign we do not read of any fuch Defolation, they do not prove the *Antiquity* of thefe *Synagogues*.

Yet (x) *Jofephus* hath thefe words. "*It was* "*the will of* Mofes *our Law-maker, that we fhould not* "*only once or twice or ofner hear the Law, but every* "*week, omitting other bufinefs, we all fhould come to* "*learn the Law*——And for this reafon he pre-fers *Mofes* before all other *Law-givers,* who did not take the like care to have their People inftructed. But I queftion whether this Teftimony infers ma-ny places, or only the *Temple,* where *Mofes* did command the Law to be read at *certain folemn times,* (y) as at the *year of releafe.* But to make this the Duty of every *Sabbath,* not one word is recorded in the Law to that purpo neither in the *Temple* nor elfewhere. 'Tis not unlikely, but that *Jofephus* (as alfo *Philo,* who has the fame paffage) might have an Eye to the practice of *later Ages,* and apply the precept of *Mofes* about reading the Law, to the interpretation made of it, *at and before* his own times, when the extraordinary ways of inftruction ceafing, they more frequently read the Law and made Difcourfes on it, for the information of the People. And for further confirmation, I muft not omit what the Bifhop of *Ely* hath noted on a Paffage that fell out in the Days of *Jofiah* (y) "*It is a thing,* faith he, *to be admired, that if the* "*reading and expounding the Law, had been in conti-* "*nual ufe among the Jews every Sabbath-Day, there* "*fhould be found in the days of King* Jofiah, *one copy*

(x) Adv. Apion. l, 2. (yy) Bifhop *White* on the Sabbath.

only

" only or Book of the *Law* in the most solemn place of
" God's worship, i. e. the *Temple* at Jerusalem. *And*
" that Hilkiah the Priest should find this Book hid in a
" Corner, and present it to the King as a very great
" rarity. *Every Man may in reason conceive, that if*
" the Law had been commonly read and expounded eve-
" ry Sabbath, either in the Temple or other Publick As-
" semblies of the Kingdom of Judea, there could not
" have been such a scarcity of Bibles or Books of the
" Law.

The Question proposed by the *Shunamite's Hus-*
band (when she desired to have an Ass Saddled to
ride to *Elisha,* for the recovery of her dead Child)
is brought as an argument to support the other
Assertion, because he asks her, To what end she
should give herself that trouble, since *it is neither
the new Moon nor the Sabbath,* meaning the stated
times for such Applications, and the ordinary
Days, (z) saith *Junius,* to consult God and hear
his word. For in the Kingdom of *Israel,* where
Religion was much corrupted, the more Pious
sort of People ran hither and thither to advise with
the Prophets, and no sooner heard they of such a
Person as *Elisha* was *, but by Flocks they immediately resorted to him, especially on *Days* Consecrated
to Religion; but we are now speaking of the *Ordi-*
nary Ministry, and the *Ordinary places,* of Divine
and Publick Worship, as were the *Synagogues* afterwards, and I conceive this Passage about the *Shuna-*
mite no proof of that Point, and yet the whole
Scripture before the Captivity affords no better.

Be it so or otherwise. That which concerns us
to remember is, the *Use* they were put to rather
than *when* they began. And as to this, the very

(z) In loc. (*) *Lyra* in loc.

Name shows the defign of 'em, for they were intended for Conveniencies for People to *Meet* and Pray in. And fo (a) *Maimonides* defines 'em, and faith, " That *where-ever there was a competent num-* " *ber of Jews, and ten Men learned in the Law, and of* " *fufficient leifure to give their attendance, there 'twas* " *neceffary an Houfe fhould be built, whither every Bo-* " *dy might betake himfelf to fay his Prayers in, at the* " *Hours of Prayer.* And this *House is called* " *a Synagogue.* Which no Man was to pafs by during the Service, but all were required to come to it, and not to Pray at home when they might do it with the Congregation. Women and Children all went thither, the *One* fort to hear the Law, the *Other* to be Catechized in the principles of Religion, and this fo Univerfally that they were ftigmatized and look'd upon with an ill Eye, who did not thus Affemble with their Neighbours and Brethren. 'Twould be too tedious to prefent you with the many *infcriptions* on the Walls of thefe Houfes, as on fome of our Churches, to be fo many *Leffons* for *Silence, Attention, Humility,* &c. to put the *Votaries* in mind, what behaviour and zeal was required from 'em while they made their appearance there. Nor will I go about to give you every particular Prayer which the *Minifters* ufed, and to each of which the Congregation faid, *Amen.* 'Tis *very well known,* (b) faith Dr. *Lightfoot, that fuch holy addreffes to God, with fome Portions of the Law and the Prophets, were the integral parts or chief ingredients of their Sabbath Service.* And in all this their Worfhip was folid and grave.

And on our *Lord's-Day,* it calls for imitation and comformity, as in thofe times when the *Chri-*

(a) In *Tephil.* (b) *Horæ Hebraicæ.*

stian Sabbath was Celebrated in the Observation of
the same particulars, " *In forbearing secular Work*
" *and minding Spiritual,* saith *Origen, such as meet-*
" *ing in the Church, and there hearing those Divine*
" *Lectures, and Lessons publickly read and explained to*
" *the People.*——To whose words I shall add those
of a Provincial Synod held at *Mascon* in *France,*
which shows *what* Anciently *was,* and *should be al-*
ways done on this *Day.* (*c*) " *We ought to observe*
" *carefully the Lord's-day, which hath given us a New-*
" *Birth, and delivered us from our Sins.* Let no *Man*
" *therefore presume to attend his Suit, nor plead causes,*
" *nor pretend necessity to yoke his Cattel, and Plough on*
" *this Day : But spend the time in Hymns and the Praises*
" *of God.* And *if the Church be not at too great a*
" *distance, let him be sure to hasten thither, and pour forth*
" *his Soul in Tears and Prayers, making both Eyes and*
" *Hands share in the Devotion.* It is *the Everlasting*
" *day of Rest insinuated to us under the shadow of the*
" *Jewish Sabbath.* And *'tis very meet we should cele-*
" *brate this day with one accord, whereon we are made*
" *what we were not.* For *we were the Servants of Sin,*
" *but are now become Children of Grace by his Resurrecti-*
" *on, whose Righteousness is imputed to us.* Let us give
" *our Lord a free and chearful Service, by whose Good-*
" *ness we are ransomed out of the dark dungeon of Er-*
" *rour, and Impiety.*——*And if any Man neglects,*
" *and sets at naught this our wholesome Advice,* let
" *him be well assured, that God will punish him as he de-*
" *serves, and he shall be also subject to the Censures of*
" *the Church.* If *he be a Lawyer he shall lose his cause;*
" *if Husbandmen or Labourer, corporally suffer; but if*
" *in Holy Orders, we command him to be suspended for*
" *the space of Six Months.*—— Thus, or to this

(*c*) Concil. Matiscon. Canon. 1. Apud Caranzam sub Gun-
thrano Rege.

effect

effect that *Canon.* And there are a great many other *Canons, Decrees, Edicts,* and *Laws* to the same purpose; which perhaps it may not be loss of time to present you with, to let you see the *Piety* of all *Ages* in this particular, and the care they had to have the *Lord's-day* kept.

B. If the trouble be not too great, I shall be glad 'to hear 'em collected.

A I begin with the Emperour *Constantine,* who, as soon as he had espoused the interest of *Christianity,* made it his particular business that his subjects should reverence this *Festival,* and so issued out this *Decree:* (d) " *Let all Judges, Citizens and* " *Tradesmen rest on the venerable Lord's-day. But as* " *for such as live remote in the Country, they may* " *have licence to attend their husbandry, because it of-* " *ten falls out that there is no better day for sowing their* " *Seed or Planting the Vines ; and therefore let them take* " *the advantage of the Weather, left otherwise they run* " *the hazard of losing those Blessings which the Divine* " *Bounty bestows upon us.* Thus runs the *Edict* in the *Justinian* Code, about the Year 321. Wherein it seems the *Farmer* might work on the *Day,* for fear the community should suffer by neglecting the Opportunity of *Sowing* or *Planting.* Yet *Eusebius* who lived in that Emperour's Reign, and was Privy to all his Counsels of this kind, doth not mention the *Exception,* but saith, (e) " *He invited and stir-* " *red up Mankind to observe the day ;——particularly,* " *the whole* Roman *Empire was obliged to it.——* And in his *Panegyrick* on that Prince, he affirms, That *Constantine* " *Commanded all the World, as well* " *Islands as Continent, to meet every Week, and Cele-*

(d) *Omnes Judices,* &c ——Dat. Non Martij Crispo 2. & Constant. 2. Cols. Cod. Justin. l. 3. t 12. de feriis. (e) de Vit. Const. l. 4. c. 18. & de laud. Const c. 17.

S

brate

"brate the *Lord's-day* (f). And *Sozomen* giving an
"account of the same *Edict*, saith, that *He*, (the
"Emperour) *required every Body, both Judges, and*
"*others, to forbear on the day all manner of busi-*
"*ness* —— However, 'tis not unlikely but there
"might be such an indulgence granted the *Hus-*
bandman, because *Leo* afterwards takes notice of
the reason, and thinks it not strong enough to excuse the Country People.

A while after he sent out another *Proclamation*
on this subject ; intended both to *quicken*, and *ex-*
plain the *Law* foregoing ; And in this (*g*) *Manu-*
mission or giving Liberty to Slaves and Servants
was made *another Exception*, as being a work of
Charity, and done in imitation of the *Lord Jesus*
who *lived, died*, and on this *day rose* for our Redemption, to rescue us out of the Tyranny and Bondage of the Devil. Besides it did not a little contribute to the honour of the *Church*, and the encrease
of *Christianity*, because this *Act* of discharging
Bondmen, being to be done by or in the *Bishop's*
Presence, they who had the benefit of it, could
not but respect them on this account, and were more
easily brought to embrace the same Religion.

About the Year 381. *Gratian, Valentinian* and
Theodosius, being Emperours , an *Edict* came forth
to prohibit all *shews on the Lord's-day*. And it did
not only hinder the *Judges from sitting in open Court
on the day*, but it also forbid all *Arbitrations* (hitherto allowed as means of Peace) and the taking Cognizance of any pecuniary business. To which *Va-*
lentinian and *Valens* added, that *No Christian should
on that day be brought before the Officers of the Ex-
chequer, as being a vexation not to be reconciled to the
Notion of our Christian Sabbath.*

(f) Eccl. Hist. l. 1. c. 8. (g) *Emancipandi & manumit-*
tendi die festo cuncti licentiam habeant, &c. Vid. Niceph.
Hist. l. 7. Sozom. l. 1. c. 8.

Five years after, This Law was revived by *Va-lentinian*, *Theodoſius* and *Arcadius*, (*h*) and ſome o-ther days added for the like Obſervation, as the Emperour's *Birth-day;* and the day whereon the Empire began, with a *Week before and after Eaſter*.

In the Year 425. a Petition was preſented *Theodoſius the Younger*, by the Council of *Carthage*, praying, *That the Law made by Gratian* (much neg-lected*) againſt Publick Sights, might be re-inforced*. Accordingly that Prince renew'd the *Edict*, and Commanded, (*i*) *That the Cirques and Theatres in all Places ſhould be ſhut up on the Lords's day, and ſome other Feſtivals* which he named, That ſo all *Chriſtian* People might wholly bend their minds to the Ser-vice of *God*, to which thoſe diverſions were very prejudicial, the multitude at ſuch times flocking more *thither* than they did to the *Churches*.

But the *Edict* of the Emperour *Leo* in the Year 469. *Zeno and Martian* being Conſuls, is much fuller and ſtricter for the Obſervation of this great day! (*k*) " *It is our will and pleaſure*, ſaith he, *that* " *the holy days dedicated to the moſt high God, ſhould* " *not be ſpent in ſenſual recreations, or otherwiſe propha-* " *ned by ſuits of Law. Eſpecially the Lord's-day, which* " *we decree to be a venerable Day, and therefore free* " *it of all Citations, Executions, Pleadings and the like* " *avocations. Let not the Cirque or Theatre be open'd,* " *nor Combating with Wild Beaſts ſeen on it. And if* " *either our Birth-day or Inauguration-day happen to* " *fall upon it, we require it to be put off till the day* " *following——— If any will preſume to offend in the* " *Premiſes, if he be a military Man, let him loſe his* " *Commiſſion; if other, let his Eſtate or Goods be confiſca-*

(*h*) Timaſio & Prom. Coſs. Cod. Juſtin. l 3. t. 11 (*i*) Cod. Theod. (*k*) *Dies Feſtos Majeſtati altiſſime dedicatos,* &c. Cod. Juſtin. l. 3. t. 11. de feriis.

§ 2 " ted,

" *ted.* And whereas before in the Law of *Conftan-tine* the *Farmer* was permitted to attend his Work on *this day,* which might fometimes fall out to be more proper, and feafonable than the reft of the *Week, this Emperour* would not continue the *Indulgence,* but orders *them* to forbear as well as their Fellow-Subjects. (t) " *For,* faith he, *As to the pretence, that by this reft an opportunity may be loft----
This is a poor reafon, confidering that the fruits of the Earth do not fo much depend on the diligence and pains of the Men, as on the efficacy of the Sun and the blefling of God. We command therefore all, as well Husbandmen as others to forbear work on this day of our Reftauration. For if other People (meaning the Jews) *keep the fhadow of this day in a folemn reft from all fecular Labour on their Sabbath, how much rather ought we to obferve and celebrate the fubftance, a day fo ennobled by our Gracious Lord who faved us from deftruction.----*Thus he. Yet he difpenfed with People's meeting on *Sunday* in Order to *compofe differences,* as *works* tending to *Charity,* and the reconciling of Neighbours, and therefore thought it not unbecoming the *day* confecrated to him, who came into this World with *peace on Earth, and good will towards Men,* and who died, arofe and afcended into Heaven to confirm, and feal a lafting *peace* between his *Father* and *Us.*

In the Year 588. *Gunthrum* King of *Burgundy,* and about two Years after *Clotair* King of *France ;* And two Centuries forward, *Pepin,* another King of *France,* made *Laws* to the fame effect ; but being confider'd as the Acts of three *Councils,* by them called, *Mafcon, Auxerre* and *Friuli,* we will chufe rather to take notice of 'em there.

(l) *Quanquam fructuum præfervatio prætendi poffe videatur,* &c. *Statuimus,* &c. Novel. Leon.

Charles

Charles the Great, following the Example of his Father *Pepin*, convocated the *Clergy* in five feveral Places, to make *Canons* for the keeping of the *Day*; and withal publifhed this *Edict*: "*We do ordain (as* " *it is required in the Law of God) that no Man do a-* " *ny fervile work on the Lord's-day. i. e. That they* " *employ not themfelves in the works of husbandry, in* " *drefling their Vines, ploughing their ground, making* " *hay, fencing or hedging, grubbing and felling trees,* " *digging in the mines, building houfes, planting or-* " *chards; and that they do not go a hunting in the* " *fields, or plead in the Courts of Juftice; that Wo-* " *men weave not, or drefs cloth, do no needle-work,* " *or card wool, nor beat hemp, nor wafh linen openly,* " *nor fheer fheep: But that they come all to Church,* " *to magnifie the Lord their God, for thofe goods things* " *which on this day he beftowed upon 'em.* This Law was, as I faid, back'd with the Authority of the *Church*; Yet in a little time, by the remifsnefs of *Lewis* his Succeffor, it became very *feeble*; and thereupon an Addrefs was made to the Emperours (*Lewis* and *Lotharius*) that they would be pleas'd to take fome care in it, and fend out fome *Precept* or Injunction, more fevere than what was *hitherto* extant, to ftrike terrour into their Subjects, and force 'em to forbear their *ploughing, pleading,* and *marketting,* then grown again into ufe. Which was done, about the year 853; and to that End a *Synod* was called at *Rome* under the *Popedom* of *Leo* IV.

In this Century the Emperour *Leo,* firnamed the *Philofopher*, reftrained the works of *husbandry,* which according to *Conftantine's Toleration,* was permitted in the *Eaft*. The fame care was taken in the *Weft*, by *Theodorius* King of the *Bavarians*, who made this Order, That, " *If any perfon on the Lord's day,* " *yoked his Oxen, or drove his Wain, his right fide* " *Oxe fhould be forthwith forfeited; or if he made* " *Hay, and carried it in, he was to be twice admonifhed*

S 3 " *to*

" to *defift*, which if he did not, he was to receive no *lefs*
" than *fifty ftripes.*

About the Year 1174. The Emperour *Ema-
nuel Comnenus,* confirmed the decrees of his Prede-
ceffours, and forbid *all accefs to the Tribunals, where
no Judge was to fit except in very extraordinary and
neceffary cafes.*

Thus the *Civil Power* proceeded. Nor was the
Church backward to affift in a point which fo much
concern'd her own Well-being. And therefore
we find a great many Conftitutions, and *Canons* on
the fame fubject.

(*m*) At *Eliberis* a Town in *Spain*, a Synod met,
where it was decreed, that " *If any Citizen or other
" Perfon living in or near a City, abfented himfelf from
" the Church three Lord's-days together, he was to be
" kept fo long from the holy Sacrament---* In thofe days
it feems a fhameful punifhment.

Some Years after, about 368. fate the Council
of *Laodicea,* which (*n*) " *required Chriftians not to
judaize in keeping the Sabbath, but prefer the Lord's-day
before it; and thereon reft from labour, if they could,
but ftill as became the Profeffours of Chriftianity.*
Here it feems the claufe in this Canon (*if they can*)
makes it not neceffary to forbear *all* manner of
Work, unlefs they could *well* do it. And fo *Zonaras* explains the place, as a mitigation of the *Civil
Law,* which demanded an *Univerfal Ceffation* of
bufinefs on *Sunday,* excepting the *Husbandmen* who
might go on in their way, for fear they might
not have another day fo favourable for their purpofe. But here *other People* came under the fame
exception : And *Balfamon* inftances fuch whofe Po-

(*m*) Circa annum 307 Can 21 Apud Caranzam. (*n*) Canon 29 Ου δεῖ χριστιανὸς ἰουδαΐζειν, &c. Τὴν δὲ κυριακὴν——
ἄγε δύναιντο ——

'verty, and wants juftified their Labour even on the *Lord's-day* , without offence to the *Law* or their *Confciences*. I fuppofe thefe words refpect the *times* in which the *Council* met, and that was before the Empire became *Chriftian*, when great numbers of *Men and Women*, who had entertain'd the *Gofpel*, and were willing to fubmit themfelves to the Difcipline of the *Church*, being in the Service of *Infidel* Mafters, they could not do it. So that the *Bifhops and Fathers* then Affembled, took their Cafe into confideration, and for the eafe of their Minds declared, they did not expect impoffibilities from 'em. And if their *Mafters* or *Miftreffes*, would not fuffer 'em to *Reft*, and go to *Church* on the *Lord's-day*, they might proceed in their *Common-work*, without fear or fcruple.

About the Year 401. was held the fourth Council of *Carthage*, (*o*) which punifhed thofe with " *Excommunication, who neglecting the folemn Worfhip* " *of God on this and other facred times, fpent the day* " *in Plays and the like Diverfions*— (*p*) And in another Council, in the *fame* City, not long after, it was the requeft of the *Bifhops* to the *Emperours* then in being, " *That all fights and fhows fhould be laid afide* " *on the Lord's-day , and other folemn Feftivals, on* " *which the People ran more to the Theatre than the* " *Church, renouncing their Devotion when thefe vanities came in their way.*

Under *Clodoveus* King of *France*, met the Bifhops in the firft Council of *Orleans*, (*q*) where they obliged themfelves and their Succeffours , to be always at the Church on the *Lord's-day*, except in Cafe of *Sicknefs* or fome great *Infirmity*. And becaufe they

(*o*) Can. 88. *Qui die folenni*, &c. *Excommuncetur*. (*p*) Can. 64. circa an. 408. (*q*) *Epifcopus fi infirmitate, &c Ecclefiæ die dom. deeffe non liceat*. Can. 31. circa 507.

with

with fome other of the Clergy in thofe days took Cognizance of Judicial matters, therefore by a Council at *Arragon*, about the Year 518. in the Reign of *Theodorick* King of the *Goths*, it was decreed, that (r) " No Bifhop or other Perfon in holy Orders fhould " examine or pafs judgment in any civil Contro- " verfie on the Lord's-day.

In the Reign of King *Childebert*, met the third Council of *Orleans* in *France*, and then the Fathers took fome pains to clear the notion of the *Chriftian-Sabbath*, and to keep People from *judaizing*, as many did in that Age. Yet they all agreed in this and refolved, that (s) " Men fhould reft on " that day from Husbandry, dreffing Vines, Sow- " ing, Reaping, Hedging and the like, that fo " they might have leifure to go to Church, and " fay their Prayers. Wherein thofe who offended " were to be punifhed by the Clergy. And about feven Years thence, in honour of the *Day*, and as a *Work* well becoming it, a *Conftitution* was made by the fame *Prince* in a fourth Council at *Orleans* : That " The Arch-deacon or fome other Digni- " tary of the Church, fhould take fpecial care that " all Prifoners, every Lord's-day, might be well " relieved in what their neceffities called for—— And herein he followed the Example of the Empe- rour *Honorius*, who by a formal Edict, and under (t) a great penalty commanded the Judges " To " fuffer all forts of Prifoners to go abroad on the " Lords-day, with their Keepers, to ask the Cha- " rity of well difpofed People, and by no means " hinder 'em to do the Duty of the Day. And withal " permit 'em, to go to the Baths on thofe days to " cleanfe and refrefh themfelves.

(r) Concil. Tarracon. Canon 4. (s) Concil Aurel. Can. 21. circa 540. apud Garanz, (t) *Aurt* 30. *libra*. Baron. ad annum 409.

Not

Not above feven Years after this, the fame *Childebert*, had another *Conftitution*, which forbid (*u*) " *Banfatrices*, to ramble from Village to Village on " the *Lord's-day.*

And becaufe, notwithftanding all this care, the *Day* was not duly obferved, the Bifhops wei e again fummon'd to *Mafcon*, a Town in *Burgundy*, by King *Gunthrum*, and there they framed this Canon. (*w*) " Notice is taken that Chi iftian Peo-
" ple very much neglect, and flight the Lord s-
" day, giving themfelves, as on other days to com-
" mon Work, to redrefs which Irreverence for the
" future, we warn every Chriftian who bears not
" that·name in vain, to give Ear to our advice,
" knowing we have a concern on us for your Good,
" and a Power to hinder you to do Evil. Keep
" then the Lord's-day, the day of our New Bii th,
" whereon we were delivered, *&c.* as before.

About a Year forwar
Narton, which forbid
" Country or Quality foever, to do any fervile
" Work on the Lord's-day. But if any Man pre-
" fumed to difobey this Canon, he was to be fined if
" a freeman, and if a Servant, feverely lafhed.
Or as *Surius* reprefents the penalty in the Edict of King *Recaredus*, which he put out, near the fame time, to ftrengthen the decrees of the Council,
" Rich men were to be punifh'd with the lofs of a

(*u*) Apud Siimond. A. D. 554. *Banfatrices, morrice-dancer*, or fome fuch People, who wandred up and down at all Hours and lead very lewd lives. *Du Frefre* thinks the woi d miftook for *Danfatrices*, from *Danfer Saltare*, and perhaps it may have a *French* Etymology, *Childebert* uling it in the Epiftle he wi t for the rooting out the relicks of idolatry. (*w*) Concil. Matifc. 2. Can. 1. A. D. 587. (*x*) *Omnis homo*, &c. Can. 4.

" Moiety

" Moiety of their Eftates, and the Poorer fort
" with perpetual banifhment.

In the Year of Grace 590. Another Synod was
held at (y) *Auxerre* a City in *Champain*, in the
Reign of *Clotair* King of *France*, where it was decreed, or rather a Canon renew'd, made by his Pre-
deceffor *Chilperic*, twelve Years before, that " No
" Man fhould be allowed to Plough, nor Cart, or
" do any fuch thing on the Lord's-day.

Afterwards, about the Year 627. as *Caranza*
dates it, was affembled the third Council of *Toledo*,
intended chiefly againft the *Arrian Herefie*, which
had got footing in *Spain*, and with it a great neglect
of the *Lord's-day*, which they took notice of Canon
22*d.* (z) " An irreligious Cuftom has prevail'd a-
" mong the Common People, to give themfelves
" up to lafcivious dances on the Feftivals of the
" Saints, and other Solemn times, when they
" fhould attend at the Divine Service, and not
" only fing unfeemly Songs, but thereby
" difturb and Poifon others, who are better dif-
" pofed; which mifchief that it may be removed out
" of all the Provinces, the Council leaves it to the fi-
" delity, and care of the Minifters and Judges----
Accordingly *Recaredus* took great pains to fee it
executed, and great punifhments were inflicted on
the Contumacious. This Canon indeed with fome
others, mean for the moft part [*Obſcænas Voluptates*]
immoral, and *unwarrantable Pleaſures*, becoming
neither the *Lord's-day*, nor any other day of the
Week, fuch as *Women's Dancing Naked*, and *Men
Fighting* till they killed 'one another, yet the reafon reaches *all diverſions* whatever, fo far forth as
they are found *injurious* to the honour and worfhip

(y) Antifiodorenfis Synod. (z) *Irreligioſa conſuetudo*, &c.
Conc. Tolet. 3. Can. 22.

of the *Day*, while People make it no more than an
Opportunity to indulge their Sins, and as our Homily
fpeaks, *ferve the Devil*.

At *Chalons* a City in *Burgundy*, about the Year
654, there was a Provincial Synod, which confirm'd what had been done by the third Council of
Orleans(*), about the Obfervation of the *Lord's-Day*,
namely, That (*a*), " *None fhould plough or reap, or do
any other thing belonging to Husbandry, on pain of the
cenfures of the Church*. --Which was the more minded, becaufe back'd with the fecular Power, and
by an Edict menacing fuch as Offended herein,
who, if *Bondmen*, were to be *foundly beaten*, but if
free had *three admonitions*, and then if faulty loft
the *third* part of their Patrimony, and if ftill obftinate were made *Slaves* for the future.

And in the firft Year of *Eringius*, about the
time of Pope *Agatho*, there fate the 12th Council of *Toledo* in *Spain*, (*b*) where the *Jews* were forbid to keep their own Feftivals, but fo far at leaft
obferve the *Lord's-Day*, as to do no manner of work
on it, whereby they might exprefs their contempt
of *Chrift* or his *Worfhip*.

In the Year 692. was held the 6th General
Council at *Conftantinople*, where were prefent
125 Bifhops, the Emperor himfelf, *Conftantinvs
Pogonatus*, being Prefident. The great queftion
in it was concerning the Actions and Wills of
Chrift; which being throughly difcufs'd, they condemned in the Iffue *Sergius*, and his Adherents,
who in the defence of *Eutychianifm*, pleaded that
there was but *one Will* in Chrift. But before they
broke up, they made two Canons relating to the
Subject we are upon ; The firft refpected the An-

(*) Concil. Aurel. 3. Can. 21. (*a*) Concil. Cabilonen. Canon.
18. apud Caran. (*b*) Concil. Tolet. 12. c 9. apud Binium circa 681.

niverfary of the *Lord's Refurrection*, which they would have to confift of a full Week, and to be fpent in Attendance at the Church , *In finging Pfalms and Hymns, and Spiritual Songs, in a con-ftant reading of the Holy Scriptures, in frequenting the B. Sacrament, with the like Teftimonies, and evidences of celebrating that great Feftival* , which that it might be the better kept, they prohibited *All Horfe-races and other fights, apt to draw People afide from thofe Divine Services.* And then for the *Weekly* Commemoration of that great Miracle of Chrift's rifing out of the Grave, which makes the *Lord's-day* fo folemn among us, they further added, *That if any Bifhop or other Clergy-man, or any of the Laity abfented himfelf from the Church three Sun-days together, except in cafes of very great neceffity, if a Clergy man he was to be depofed, if a Lay-man debar-red the Holy Communion.*

At *Dingofolinum*, a Synod met about the Year 772. *Taffilo (c)* being Duke, where a *Conftitution* was made , to inforce the Obfervation of the *Lord's-day, According to the directions of the Civil Law, and the Decrees of former Councils. And if any offended in this kind, they were to be punifhed in the fame manner, as the Law and thofe Councils had ap-pointed. (d)* Or as *Avicen* fpeaks, *Let every Man abftain from prophane employments and be intent on God's Worfhip, if any Man fhall work his Cart on this day, or do any fuch common Bufinefs, his Team fhall be prefently forfeited to the publick ufe, and if the party perfifts in his folly, let him be fold for a Bondman.*

Some time after, difputes arifing concerning the Doctrine of the *B. Trinity*, and the *Incarnation*

(c) D. of the *Baiorians* [*Bavarians*] Cap. I. (d) Hift. l. 3.

of the fecond Perfon, (*e*) *Charles the Great*, fum-mon'd the Bifhops to *Friuli* in *Italy*, where *Pauli-nus* Patriarch of *Aquileia* being Prefident, they de-creed, " That all People fhould with due reve-" rence and devotion honour the Lord's-Day, be-" ginning on the Evening of the day before, and " that thereon they more efpecially abftain from " all kind of Sin, as alfo from all Carnal Acts " and fecular Labours : And that they go to " Church in a Grave manner, laying afide all fuits " of Law and Controverfies, which might hinder " 'em to praife God's Name together.

Under the fame Prince, another Council was called at (*f*) *Frankford* in *Germany*, about three Years after the former, and there the Limits or Boundaries of the *Lord's-day*, were determined from *Saturday Evening*, to *Sunday Evening*, that fo. there might be Uniformity in the time of their Worfhip, and the Confcience made eafie by the *certainty* of the Hours, when they were to *begin* and *end* that days Service.

The fame Emperour made a Conftitution, (*g*) " That there fhould be no Markets on the Lord's-" day, but only on fuch days as were alotted for " fervile Bufinefs. And this he the rather did to Countenance what was decreed by the Bifhops, in Five Councils at *Mentz, Rheims, Tours, Chalons* and *Arles*, which he called together the fame Year [81 3.] all which forbid Markets, and other World-ly matters to be done on this day.

(*h*) " We forbid (faith the Council of *Arles*) " publick Markets, civil Difputes, and pleadings

---

(*e*) Circi annum Chrifti, 791. & Temp Hadriani, a Paulino Aquileienfi convocat. in caufa Trinitatis c. 13. (*f*) Can. 2 . anno 794. (*g*) Capitul. Ecclef. C M. 21. (*h*) Conc Arel. 4. Can. 16. apud Bin.

" on

" on the Lord's-day; as alſo Husbandry, and all
' manner of Work, except ſuch as is proper for
" the day, and becomes the Divine Worſhip.

"(*i*) Let there be no Markets or Pleadings on
" the Lord's-day(ſaith the Council of *Tours*)which
" Chriſtians' ought to ſpend in the Praiſes of God,
" and Thanks for his Bleſſings, and to continue in
" ſo doing untill the Evening.

(*k*) " We have decreed (ſaith the Council of
" *Mentz*), that the Lord's-day be obſerved with
" all due Veneration: And that People to this end
" forbear all common work, from buying, ſelling
" and the like ; And that no Criminal cauſes be
" heard, in order to puniſh Malefactors by Death
" or otherwiſe.

(*l*) " In conformity to the Lord's Command(ſaith
" the Council of *Rheims*) let no Perſon preſume to
" do any ordinary Work on Sundays, nor proſe-
" cute Law ſuits, nor go to Fairs or Markets ; nor
" in a publick way to diſtribute doles, though in
" it ſelf a work of Humanity and Charity.

Thus *four* of the aforeſaid Councils ſpake; but
the *Fifth*, that of *Chalons* taking notice, that notwithſtanding the induſtry of the Church in ſeveral
Aſſemblies before, the *Day* was much neglected,
they entreated the help of the ſecular Power, and
deſired the Emperour by ſome Decree or Law of
his to provide for the ſtricter Obſervation of it.
Which he accordingly did, and left no Stone un-
turned, to ſecure the honour of the *Day*, and reſtrain his Subjects from abuſing it.

His care ſucceeded ; and during his Reign the
Lord's-day bore a conſiderable Figure. But after

(*i*) Conc. Turon. 3. ſub Car. Mag. [813]Can. 40. (*k*)
Conc. Mogunt. ſub. Car. M. Canon. 37. (*l*) Canon 35 ---
ſub Car. M. apud Binium:

his

his deceafe, it put on another Face. And thereupon Pope *Eugenius* in a Synod held at *Rome*, about
the Year 826. obferving, that there were certain
Perfons, efpecially Women, who fpent their time in
Dancing, Singing, *&c.* he gave directions "That
" the Parifh-prieft, fhould, from time to time, ad-
" monifh fuch offenders, and wifh 'em to go to
" Church and fay their Prayers, left otherwife
" they might bring fome great calamity on them-
" felves and Neighbours.

But thefe Paternal Admonitions turning to little account, a Provincial Council was held at (*m*)
Paris about three Years after, under *Lewis* and
Lotharius then Emperours, [829] wherein the
prelates complain that " The Lord's-day was not
" kept with that reverence as became Religion,
" and the practice of their Forefathers, which was
" the reafon that God had fent feveral Judgments
" on 'em, and in a very remarkable manner punifh-
" ed fome People for flighting, and abufing it. For
" (fay they) many of us by our own Knowledge,
" and fome by hear-fay know, that feveral Coun-
" trymen following their Husbandry on this day,
" have been killed with Lightning, others being
" feized with Convulfions in their joints, have mi-
" ferably perifhed---Whereby it is apparent, how
" high the difpleafure of God was upon their neg-
" lect of this day. And at laft they conclude,
that " In the firft place the Priefts and Minifters,
" then Kings and Princes, and all faithful People
" be befeeched to ufe their utmoft endeavours,
" and care that the Day be reftored to its honour,
" and for the credit of Chriftianity more devout-
" ly obferved for the time to come.

(*m*) Conc. Parif. Can. 50.

And

And although *Matrimony* be an *holy Sign*, and *Emblem* of the ſtrict *Union*, that is between *Chriſt* and his *Church*, and therefore no undecent or improper Work for ſuch a day as this, ſequeſtred, and conſecrated to the uſes of Chriſtian Religion, yet for as much as at ſuch a time, there is more *Lightneſs* and *Vanity*, than well comports either which the *Thing* it ſelf or the *Feſtival*, it was decreed about ſeven Years after in a Council at *Aken* (*n*) under *Lewis the Godly*, that " Neither Pleadings, nor " Marriages ſhould be allowed on the Lord's-day-- And it was added, that " As far as it was poſſible, " there ſhould be laid aſide that ill Cuſtom, then " prevailing, of communicating ſeldom; and care " was to be taken to have the Sacrament Admi- " niſtred every Lord's-Day, for fear it might " happen, that the long abſence from the Holy " Communion might indiſpoſe People for Salva- " tion.

(*o*) Three Years after this, another Synod was called at *Rome*, by the aboveſaid Emperours, and Pope *Leo* the Fourth, where it was ordered more exactly, that " No Man ſhould from thence forth " keep or frequent Markets on the Lords-day, no " not for things to be preſently eaten, nor to do " any work belonging to Husbandry.

(*p*) *Herardus* Archbiſhop of *Tours* took theſe Precedents, and as far as his Juriſdiction went, forbid all ſervile Works, obſcene Language, and Marketings on the *Lord's-Day*, which he required to be religiouſly kept *from Evening to Evening*. And this was about the Year 858.

(*n*) Conc. Aquiſgran. ſub Ludovico pio. 836. Ca. 3 n. 18. 22. apud Sirmond. de Concil. Galli. (*o*) Canon. 30. circa 852. (*p*) De die Dom. *à veſpere ad veſperam celebretur.* Capitula Herard. Archiepiſcopi Turon. Temp. Nicolai Papæ & Carol. Calvi circa 858. c. 2. apud Sirmond. Tom. 3.

(q) In the fame Year, the *Bulgarians* fent fome Queftions to Pope *Nicholas*, to which they defired Anfwers. And that which concern'd the *Lord's-Day*, was, *That they fhould defift from all fecular Work, and Carnal pleafures, or whatever contributed to defile the Body, and do nothing but what agreed with the day.* The Lord's Work on the Lord's-day.

This care ufed in the *Weft*, to keep up the Dignity of our Weekly Feftival, invited the Emperour *Leo*, furnamed the *Philofopher*, to fend out the Edict in the *Eaft* I before mentioned. Wherein taking notice of *Conftantine's* Indulgence to *Husbandmen*, he cenfures it, and faith, "It is our "Will and Pleafure, according to the true mean- "ing of the Holy Ghoft, and of the Apoftles by "him directed, that on the Sacred day whereon "we were reftored to our Integrity, all Men "fhould ceafe from Labour, neither *the Husband-* "*men*, nor others putting their hand to prohibited "Work. For if the *Jews* did fo much reverence to "the *Shadow*, ought not we to honour the *Sub-* "*ftance*, I mean *the Day*, which the *Lord* ho- "noured, by refcuing us from the Captivity of "Death? Are not we bound to keep it inviolably, "and be contented with the liberal Grant we have "of all the reft, without encroaching on this one, "which God hath named for his Service ?—*&c.* This was towards the Conclufion of the Ninth Century. (r) About which time *Riculfus* Bifhop of the *Sueffones* formed an Ecclefiaftical Conftitution, wherein complaining that fome ill People made no Confcience of going to Market and doing fuch other things on the *Lord's-day*, which all

---

(q) Nicolai I. refponfa ad confulta Bulgarorum, 858. (r) Conftitutio Riculfi Ep. Sueffonum anno 889.

Laws,

Laws, divine and humane, forbid 'em to do, he decrees that " All imaginable care was to be " taken· to redrefs, and put a ftop to thofe un- " godly Courfes, as being a great folly and fhame, " that any Chriftian fhould fo overlook *the day*, " which is the Memorial of Chrift's Refurrection " and our Redemption by him, and fo eagerly pur- " fue his fecular gain at a time, when he ought to " be employed in holy Offices for God's Honour, " and the Good of his own Soul, and theirs belonging to him.

(*s*) Six years forward was the Council of *Friburgh* in *Germany*, under Pope *Formofus*; and there according to the decrees of the Father's a Canon was made, " To forbid even thofe of higheft " Quality to go themfelves, or to compell others " to attend at the Courts of Juftice on the Lord's- " day, which they were to fpend in Prayers, and " Devote wholly to the Service of God, who o- " therwife might be provoked to Anger.

(*t*) To the fame purpofe was there another Canon at *Erfordt*, " To prohibit all Law-fuits and " Pleadings on the Lord's-day, and other Fefti- " vals according to the Ancient Conftitutions.

(*u*) And in the middle of the next Century, a Council was held at *Coy* in *Spain*, under *Ferdinand* King of *Caftile*, in the days of Pope *Leo* IX. where it was concluded, that " All Chriftians fhould be " admonifhed every *Saturday-Evening*, to go to " Church, by way of preparation to the *Lord's-* " day following, which was to be intirely confe- " crated to the hearing of Mafs. And no Perfon " was to prefume to Travel thereon, unlefs for " Devotion fake, or to bury the dead, or to vifit the

(*s*) Conc. Tribur. ca. 35. apud Binium, 895. (*r*) Ca. 2. apud Bin. 932. (*u*) Sub Ferdin. M. 1050. apud Binium.

" Sick,

" Sick, or carry expresses for the security of the
" State, against the attempts of the *Saracens.*

(w) Pope *Gregory* IX. in the Year 1228, reckoning up the days to be kept holy, concludes that "No
" process should hold good, nor Sentence be of force
" if pronounced on those days, though both parties
" agreed to it.

The Council of *Lyons* sate about the Year 1244.
and it restrained the People from their ordinary
Work on the *Lord's-day,* and other Festivals, on
" pain of Ecclesiastical Censures, unless in cases of
" very great *Necessity,* and wherein *Charity* was
" concern'd.

(x) Thirty eight years forward was the Council of *Angeirs* in *France,* (called by *Ptolemy Juliomagus*) in *Anjou,* which forbid *Millers by Water,
or otherwise to grind their Corn from Saturday Evening, till Sunday Evening,* and it was further *order'd,
that* at such times the *Barber also should desist from
his Trade.*

In the Year 1322. a Synod was called at
Valladolid in *Castile,* and then was ratified what

"
" any Mecha-
" nick employment on the *Lord's-day,* or other *holy-*
" *days,* but where it was a Work of Necessity or
" Charity, of which the Minister of the Parish
" was to be judge.

(y) At a Synod at *Sens* in *France,* 1524. the
Bishops complaining that the Devotion of Christians waxed cold, and that idle and vain People on
these days gave themselves up to surfeiting and
drunkenness, plays and wantonness, rather than
to Prayer, and the like Divine exercises, they

(w) Decret. l. 2. de feriis, c. 5. (x) 1282. (y) Apud Bochellum.

there-

thereupon order, that " The Rectors of Churches
" shall Admonish their Parishioners, to frequent
" holy Places on such days, and there to Wor-
" ship of God with a Pious Mind, and ardent af-
" fection, and attentively hear the Word of God,
" and what is Preached from it."

(2.) But Monitions of this kind being found too
weak to restrain the People from prophaning *these
days*, by pleasures or common business; it was
further decreed in a Synod two Years after, that
" On Holidays all matters of Judicature, Sales,
" Merchandize, Luxury, Drunkenness, Plays and
" Fairs should cease.   Those who offend, let 'em
" be cited before us or our Official.

(*a*) And because on the Anniversaries of the
Saints, many sports and diversions were in use,
which were too *light* and *vain* for the *Lord's-day*,
and great impediments to the service of it, when
they happen'd to fall out on that day, therefore
a few Years after, in a Canon made at the Council
of *Mentz*, there was a proviso made, That those
Festivals of the Saints which fell on the *Lord's-day*,
should be removed, that so all due respect might
be preserved to the Lord of all Saints———And
that the Glory of God might not suffer, and the
Devotion of the Faithful be hindred, " We decree
" that on the Lord's-days, and the more Eminent
" Festivals, Merchandize, Dances, Morrices,
" which the Council of *Toledo* condemned, are not
" to be tolerated.

(*b.*) The same thing was decreed in a Council at
Paris, about eight Years after, that " Christians
" devote themselves to Prayer, not to plays and
" idleness——Therefore let Ministers teach their

(*z*) Synod. Carnotenf. 1526. apud Bochel. (*a*) Synod.
Mogunt. 1549. apud Surium. (*b*) 1557 apud Bochel.

" **People**

" People to go to Church on the Feaſt-days, to
" hear their duty and worſhip God ———— And
" let Plays, Dances, Drinking, idle Diſcourſe,
" or whatever elſe may offend God, be laid aſide—

(c) A Council was held at .*Cologn*, almoſt 20
Years before this of *Paris*, and there an *Injunction*
was formed ——— Requiring Miniſters :" To ad-
" moniſh and inform their People, why Holy-
" days, (*the Lord's-day eſpecially*, which hath been
" very Famous in the Church from the Apoſtles
" times) were inſtituted, to wit, that all might
" aſſemble the better on thoſe days to hear God's
" Word, and receive the Holy Communion ;
" that they might apply their Minds to God a-
" lone, and ſpend this Day in Prayers, Hymns,
" Pſalms, and Spiritual Songs. For this is to
" ſanctify the Sabbath. Wherefore we deſire
" that all Plays ſhould be prohibited on theſe
" Days, Victualling-Houſes ſhut, Riotting, Drink-
" ing, Indecent Recreations, Dancing, Impious
" Communication, and in a word, all Luxury
" be avoided. For by theſe things, and (which
" for the moſt part follows) by Blaſphemies and
" Perjuries, the name of God is prophaned, and the
" Sabbath (which teaches us to ceaſe to do ill, and
" learn to do well) is groſly polluted.

(d) At *Milain*, in a Council met about the
Year 1565. the Biſhops mutually ingage themſelves to uſe their utmoſt endeavours, that *theſe
Sacred days*, ſet apart to celebrate the Praiſes of
God ; be not abuſed by doing things which diſ-
pleaſe him and injure the Soul. And accordingly
they came to theſe Reſolutions. That " No Me-
" chanick or ſervile Work be done on theſe Days ;
" no buying or ſelling, unleſs Proviſion and what

(c) 1536. (d) Conc. Provinc: Mediolan. I. apud Binium.
T 3　　　　　　　　　　　" was

" was neceſſary for Sick People; no Shops open'd;
" no Fairs or Markets.---Wherein if any body
" offended, he was to be puniſhed at the diſcre-
" tion of the Biſhop, if a Son or Servant, then
" the Father or Maſter was to ſuffer for 'em. That
" there be no Cirque-ſports, Combates, or other
" Paſtimes or vain Shows exhibited; no Morrice-
" dancings allowed in Cities, Suburbs, Towns,
" Villages or any place whatever. But the People to
" be taught to Dedicate all this time to Holy Offices,
" hearing Sermons, ſaying Prayers, and reflecting
" on the Divine Bleſſings.

(*e*) And in another Council held in the *ſame City*, about eight Years after, they not only ratify
what was here decreed, but proceed to ſome particularities before omitted, and wherein they had
obſerved diverſe perſons very faulty——— " We
" expreſly forbid, *ſay they*, on theſe Days, Fairs,
" Markets, and all ſorts of Sales, all contracts and
" bargains, executions and proceſs, but wherein
" the Law it ſelf makes exceptions; all Collecti-
" ons of Money by way of Cuſtoms, or Taxes in
" in any Town or Village, eſpecially at the hours
" of Service and Sermons; we require that no
" Books, Pictures or the like things be expoſed
" to ſale; no diſguiſes hired out, no proviſions
" ſold or Shops open'd; no Barbers, Bakers, Tai-
" lors, Shoo-makers or Men of like Occupation
" follow their Trades on theſe days.

(*f*) In the ſame Year, as I think, there was one
Council at *Cracow*, and another at *Petricow*, five
Years after in *Poland*; and in both Places it was
decreed, that " The Lords and Gentlemen of the
" Country, ſhould not on the *Lord's-day*, permit
" Fairs or Markets, in any of the Towns belong-

(*e*) Conc. Mediol. 3. 1573. (*f*) 1573. 1578.

" ing

" ing to them ; nor on that Day, employ their
" Tenants in carriages or such servile Works——
" And they further concluded, that "There
" should be no meetings at the Tavern, no drinking
" matches, Dice, Cards, Consorts of Musick,
" Dancing, or any such Pastimes, especially at that
" instant when they ought to be at Church, to hear
" Sermons and do God Service.

(*g*) About which time we find this Constitution in another Council. "God as we see in Scri-
" pture has appointed *Holidays* for Monuments,
" and Remembrances of his benefits, that Men
" might acknowledge and give him thanks————
" Because *Festivals* were introduced from the be-
" ginning of the World for this end, that the
" Mind and Body, being free from ordinary cares
" and concerns of this Life, might be more intent
" in Recognizing their kind Benefactour; but find-
" ing no Age more negligent in this point, than
" ours is ————We command, that the Door-
" keepers of the Church, at these *sacred times*,
" narrowly observe, and note, which of the Pres-
" byters and Parishioners be absent from the pub-
" lick Service, and make report thereof, that en-
" quiry may be made, what the cause of their ab-
" sence was, and whether they were not at Ale-
" houses, Taverns or Plays.

(*h*) The Council of *Bourges*, much Laments the
abuses of the *Lord's-day* in these words. " Al-
" though *the Lord's-day and other Festivals* were in-
" stituted for this purpose, that faithful Christi-
" ans abstaining from *External Work*, might more
" freely, and with greater Piety devote them-
" selves to *God's-Worship* ————Notwithstanding
" a contrary Custom prevails among us, and

(*g*) 1575 Apud Bochel. (*h*) 1582. Apud Bochel.

T 4   *these*

" *thefe Days* are fpent in unlawful, and *fecular Af-*
" *fairs*, and which is yet worfe, in *rioting*, *drink-*
" *ing*, *playing*, and other *execrable Wickedneffes.*——
Thereupon they enjoined all Magiftrates and Of-
ficials, to put a ftop to thefe Courfes, by not only prohibiting, but cenfuring thofe who fhould
be found refractary.

(*i*) And fo did the Council of *Rheims*, which
fate the next Year after, command the People on
the one fide to refort, on *thefe Days*, to holy
Places for the Performance of their Duties to God,
and thofe in Authority on the other to fee that
they did it. " Let the People affemble at their
" Parifh-Churches, on the *Lord's-day, and other ho-*
" *lidays*, and be prefent at Mafs, Sermons and
" Vefpers. Let no Man on *thefe Days* give him-
" felf to Plays or Dances, efpecially during Ser-
" vice. And the Magiftrate fhall be admonifhed
" by the Minifter of the place, to fee that nothing
" of this be done. We utterly prohibit Stage-
" plays, and other filly Paftimes under the pre-
" tence of Cuftom, by which means the honour
" and fanctity of the Church, doth not a little
" fuffer in the Feftivals of Chrift and the Saints.
" Thofe who act contrary to what we here di-
" rect, it is our Pleafure, that they be punifhed
" by their Superiours.————

(*k*) In the fame Year another Synod at *Tours*, order'd the *Lord's-day*, and other holidays to be reverently obferved, under pain of Excommunication.——" Since, *fay they*, according to the pre-
" cept of St. *Paul*, thofe who are *Chrift's*, ought
" alway to follow fobriety, *efpecially on the Lord's-*
" *day*—This Synod prohibits under the pain of
" Excommunication, all Riotting, Publick-feafts,

(*i*) 1583. Apud Bochel (*k*) Synod. Turon. 1583. apud Bochel.
" Dancing,

" Dancing, Morrices, Hunting and Hawking,
" Sales of Wine, or Victuals in Inns, or Cooks-
" shops, excepting to Strangers and Travellers,
" all Prizes or other Plays (*especially at the stated*
" *hours of Prayers, and other Divine Services*) all
" Stage-Plays, Comedies, and other irreligious
" Spectacles of this kind. *And* we enjoin all, and
" singular Rectors of Parishes, to cite those be-
" fore the Bishop who obey not this Decree, that
" in his name they may be denounced and pro-
" claimed Excommunicate. For it is very absurd
" that Christians *on these Days* intended to appease
" the Anger of God, being allured by the tempta-
" tions of Satan, should be drawn away from Di-
" vine Offices, religious Addresses, and holy Ser-
" mons.

(*l*) And in a Synod held the next Year else-
" where, " The People are prohibited prophane
" Assemblies, Riotous-feasts, Dances, Plays and
" Disguises on the *Lord's-day* ; as also all Shows,
" Musick-meetings, and the Noise of Tabrets, and
" other Instruments in the Procession of Images
" through the Streets ; all going to Publick-houses,
" and the doing of any thing that doth not favour
" of Piety —— *And again*, " Let all Christians re-
" member that the *Seventh-day* was Consecrated
" by God, and hath been received and observed,
" not only by the *Jews*, but by all *others*, who pre-
" tend to Worship God, though we Christians
" have changed *their Sabbath* into *the Lord's-day*. A
" Day therefore to be kept, by forbearing all
" Worldly business, Suits, Contracts, Carriages,
" *&c.* and by sanctifying the rest of Mind and
" Body, in the contemplation of God and things
" Divine, we are to do nothing but Works of

(*l*) Synod Bituri 1584 apud Bochel.

" Charity,

"Charity, fay Prayers, and Sing Pfalms —— *And as it is worded in another Council.* " Lay afide all fe-"cular matters; frequent the Church, and there " learn what is to be done, and how we are to "behave ourfelves all the Week after. (*m*) Or in the Language of *Gregory the Great*, long before, "Expiate on *the Day of our Lord's-Refurrection*, "what was remifsly done for the *Six Days* be-"fore.

The like care was taken in the Synod of *Dort*, anno 1618. where it was concluded to entreat the Civil Magiftrates, That by their Edicts and Pro-hey would reftrain all fervile Works, the Works of Ordinary days, and efpecially Games, Drinking and other Prophanations of the *Sabbath*, wherein the *Afternoons on Sunday*, chiefly in fm Towns and Villages, had before been fpent, that fo the People might repair to Catechizing. ——

There have been other Councils and Laws to the fame effect, which do not at prefent occur——But by *thefe* already named, we may eafily per-ceive how all the Nations and Religions in Chri-ftendom have confpired in the *Obfervation of this Day*; and what care they have ufed by the *Edicts* of their Princes, and the *Decrees* of their Bifhops to have it reverently kept by the People under 'em, all of 'em concluding, that as *a certain Day*, and *one in Seven*, is to be fet apart for the Wor-fhip of God, fo being Sequeftred and Confecrated to that Bufinefs, it ought to be reverently and con-fcientioufly obferved, and no Work to interfere, but what may well Anfwer the Name, Dignity and Defign of it. I have hitherto omitted our own Country, but by what follows, you will find that

(*m*) Greg. Ep.

our Governours in Church and State, have not been backward and cool in this Affair, but have from time to time, look'd on the *Lord's-day* with the same Eye, and treated it with the same respect, as those before.

(*n*) *Ina* King of the *West-Saxons*, by the advice of *Cenred* his Father, and *Heddes*, and *Erkenwald* his Bishops, with all his *Aldermen* and *Sages*, *in a great assembly of the Servants of God, for the Health of their Souls, and common preservation of the Kingdom* made several Constitutions, of which this was the *third*, " If a Servant do any Work on Sunday " by his Master's Order, he shall be free, and " the Master pay thirty Shillings; but if he went " to Work on his own head, he shall be either " beaten with Stripes, or ransom himself with a " price. A freeman if he Works *on this Day*, shall lose " his freedom, or pay sixty Shillings; if he be a " Priest, double.

(*o*) Five Years after a Synod was held at *Berghamsted*, under *Bertualdus* Archbishop of *Canterbury*, and there they resolved on these Canons ——— " If any Person whatever doth any manner of com- " mon Work on *Saturday, or Sunday-Evening af- " ter Sun-set*, if a Servant and by order of his Ma- " ster, the Master shall be fin'd eighty Shillings. " If a Servant travels *on these days*, he shall pay six " Shillings to his Master, or be beaten. If a Free- " man be faulty, he shall be put in the Pillory or fin- " ed, and half of the fine be given to the Informer.

In the Year of our Lord 747. a Council was called under *Cuthbert*, Archbishop of *Canterbury*, in the Reign of *Egbert* King of *Kent*, and this Constitution made. " It is ordered, that *the* " *Lord's-day* be celebrated with due veneration,

---

(*n*) Leges Inæ c. 3. anno Christ 691 (*o*) Anno 5 Withredi regis Cantij, 697. Can. 10 11, 12.

" and

" and wholly devoted to the Worſhip of God.
" And that all Abbots and Prieſts, on this *moſt*
" *holy;Day,* remain in their reſpective Monaſteries
" and Churches, and there do their Duty accord-
" ing to their Places ; and omitting all ſecular
" Works and Journeys, (unleſs on very urgent
" occaſions, and ſuch as will not admit delay)
" teach their People the rule of Religious Conver-
" ſation, and good-living, by Preaching the holy
" Scriptures to them. And it is further required,
" that on *this day and other great Feſtivals*; the Peo-
" ple always get together, to hear from their Mi-
" niſters the word of God, and be more frequently
" at the Sacraments than in times paſt.

(*p*) *Egbert* Archbiſhop of *York*, to ſhow poſi-
tively what was to be done on *Sundays*, and what
the Laws deſign'd by prohibiting ordinary Work
to be done on ſuch Days, made this Canon, "Let
" nothing elſe, *ſaith he*, be done on the *Lord's-*
" *day,* but to attend on God in Hymns and Pſalms,
" and Spiritual Songs. Whoever Marries *on Sun-*
" *day* let him do penñance for ſeven-days. On all
" *Feſtivals and Sundays,* let the Miniſter Preach to
" the People the Goſpel of Chriſt.

(*q*) *Alfred the Great,* was the firſt who united the
Saxon Heptarchy, and it was not the leaſt part of
his care to make a Law, that among other Feſtivals
this Day more eſpecially might be ſolemnly kept,
becauſe it was *the Day* whereon our Saviour Chriſt
overcame the Devil ; meaning *Sunday,* which is
the Weekly Memorial of our Lord's Reſurrection,
whereby he overcame *Death, and him who had the
Power of Death,* i. e. *the Devil.* And whereas before the *ſingle* puniſhment for Sacrilege committed

---

(*p*) Excerpt. Egbert. n. 104. 106, Aⁿn 784. (*q*) Leg.
Eccl. Aluredi, c. 5. anno 876.

on any *other Day*, was, to reftore the value of
the thing ftoln, and withal lofe one hand, he added,
that if any Perfon was found guilty of this Crime
done on the *Lord's-day*, he fhould be *doubly* punifhed.
He further ordained, that whoever prefumed
on the *Lord's-day* to act in any Bufinefs, by way
of Merchandize or fale, he fhould not only forfeit his Goods, but alfo be fined, if a *Dane* twelve
* *Oræ*, if an *Englifhman* thirty Shillings. *A free-*
man if he did any Work on Holidays, *was to lofe his*
Freedom. If a Servant to be beaten, or to redeem him-
felf with Money. And if a Mafter, whether Englifh or
Dane, *compelled his Servant to work on fuch a Day,*
he was himfelf to anfwer for it, and be *punifhed by*
mulct, or otherwife as the Law directed. And if pof-
fible, no Criminal was to be then executed, but kept in
fafe Cuftody till the Feftival was over. Which Laws,
at the League between *Gunthrum* King of the *Danes,*
and *Edward,* Son and Succeffour to the faid *Alfred,*
were again ratified in the Year [905] or foon after, and the penalties inflicted as mention'd before.

(r) King *Athelftan,* followed the examples of
his Father and Grandfather, and in the Year
928. made a Law, *That there fhould be no Market-*
ting or civil pleadings on the Lord's-day, *under the*
penalty of forfeiting the Commodity, befides a fine of
thirty Shillings for each offence. ————

And in a *Convocation* of the Clergy, (s) a *Con-*
ftitution was made, *forbidding all forts of Merchan-*
dize, and keeping of Courts upon Sunday, *all kinds of*
ordinary Works, all carriages whether by Cart, Horfes
or otherwife ———— *And whoever tranfgreffed in any of*

---

* A Danifh and Saxon coin, valens 16 Denariorum. 15
Oræ libram faciùnt, 20 Oræ, valent 2 argenti Marcis Vid.
Gloffar. Spelman. & du Frefne. (r) Conc. Grateal. ab Athel-
ftano rege Angl. ca. 6. (s) Leges Prefbyter. Northumbrenf.
ca. 49.

thefe

thefe inftances, if a freeman, he was to pay twelve Oræ, *if a Servant be feverely whipt, unlefs he. were a Traveller neceffitated to it, either through hunger or fear.* Yet in the *Eves* of Feftivals, it was permitted in cafes of great *neceffity,* to travel from *York* to any place *fix Miles* diftant from it, and fo to *York* again——

(*t*) About theYear 943, *Otho* Archbifhop of *Canterbury* had it Decreed, *That above all things,* the Lord's-day *fhould be kept with all imaginable caution, according to the Canon and Ancient practice.*

(*u*) Somewhat above 20 Years after this, King *Edgar* not only prohibited *buying and felling* on *Sunday,* with all legal procefs or attendance on Courts, but a fcruple arifing about the *Terms* of this Chriftian Sabbath —— (*w*) he further commanded, that the Feftival fhould be. kept *from three of the Clock, in the afternoon on Saturday, till day-break on Monday,* under. pain of what the Laws prefcribed, for the punifhment of thofe who mis-behaved themfelves on the *Lord's-day.* Here is no mention made of *Recreations*; but it is very likely they alfo were prohibited, if it be true what *nftan,* Archbifhop of *Canterbury,* that he forbid King *Edgar* to go a hunting. And if the *King* had not his liberty, it cannot be expected but it was denied the *People.*

(*y*) King *Ethelred the Younger,* Son of *Edgar,* coming to the Crown, about the Year 1009, he called a general Council of all the *Englifh* Clergy, under *Elfeagus* Archbifhop of *Canterbury,* and *Wolftan*

(*t*) Odonis Conftit. (*u*) Ca. 19. dat. fub Edgaro, 967. (*w*) Edgari Eccl. Leg. ca. 15. (*x*) Anno 980 Dunftanus Archiep. Cant. prohibuit regi ne ulterius in die dom. venatum pergeret *Anton. Chron.* T. 16. c. 6. §. 3. (*y*) Conc. Ænhamenf. pananglic. c 15.

Archbiſhop of *York*——And there it was required, *That all Perſons, in a more Zealous manner, ſhould obſerve* the Sunday, *and what belonged to it, forbearing in the mean while all Marketting or publick meetings,* (*unleſs on the ſcore of Religion*) *and laying aſide both common Works, and common diverſions,* as hunting &c.

(y) This Conſtitution was afterwards confirmed, by a Law made by King *Canutus,* who forbid all publick *Fairs , Markets , Aſſemblies, Hunting,* and all ſecular Actions, on the *Lord's-day,* unleſs ſome urgent *neceſſity* ſhould require it—— And according to King *Edgar's* rule, he *began the Feſtival on Saturday, at three of the Clock, and ended it on Monday Morning.*———

——And in a Book of an uncertain date but very Ancient, we find this Decree ———— (z) *As to* the Lord's-day, *for as much as it is* the Day, *on which God created Light, and whereon he began the rain of* Manna *in the Wilderneſs,* &c.——*Although on it, if* neceſſity *calls for it, leave may be granted, to ſet ſail or take a Journey, yet let it be conditionally, that no opportunity be omitted to ſerve God at the hours of Maſs and Prayer. And while the Congregation is got together at the Church for this end, let no cauſe be pleaded, no diſputes be made, but let all People reſt to God in the celebration of holy things, in beſtowing Charities, and Feaſting Spiritually with their Friends, Relations and Strangers, and ſetting forth the Glory and Praiſe of God.——*

(a) As ſoon as *Edward* the Third, was well ſetled in the Throne, (commonly called from the Holineſs of his Life, *Saint Edward,* and *Edward* the Confeſſour, a Prince firſt indued with a Power

———

(x) Canuti Leg. Eccl. c. 14. 15. Anno 1032. (z) Capitula incertæ editionis. (a) 1054.

to cure the Difeafe going by the Name of the *King's Evil*) he made a Collection out of the *Danish*, *Saxon*, and *Mercian* Laws, and what he found moft ufeful both for the *Civil* and *Ecclefiafti-cal* Government, he felected and confirmed; and from hence they have the ftile of *King Edward's Laws*, though he did not fo much *make* as *collect*, and fee them put in execution. —Among thefe the *Obfervation of the Lord's-day* was not forgotten, but according to the way of Elder times, he took care to difcharge it of all *litigious difputes* and *fecular bufinefs*, and to determine the *bounds* of it, *from three a Clock on Saturday Afternoon, till Munday Morning.*—— During which time, no Chriftian was to be molefted going to Church for his Devotion-fake, or returning thence, or travelling to the Dedication of any new Church, or to the Synods, or any publick Chapter.——

b) This was afterwards ratified in the Reign of *Henry* the Second, who entred on the Government about the Year 1155. and of him it is reported, That he had an Apparition at *Cardiff* (a Town of *Glamorganfhire* in *South-Wales*) which from St. *Peter* charged him, that *upon Sundays throughout his Dominions, there fhould be no buying or felling, and no fervile Work done, except what concerned the Provifion of meat and drink, which thing if he obferved he fhould fucceed in all his Affairs.* But the ftory faith, the King took little notice of it; and being afterwards very unfortunate in many inftances, it was charged on the neglect of the Sabbath.——

In the Year, 1201. (in the beginning of King *John's* Reign) *Hubart Walter* being Archbifhop of *Canterbury*, *Euftachius*, Abbot *de Flay*, (whom I

(b) Acts and Monuments.

took notice of before) returned into " *England,*
" and Preaching the Word of God from City to
" City, and from Place to Place, he forbid *Mar-*
" *kets to be held on the Lord's-day.* Accordingly the
People forbore all fale of Goods, but Meat
and Drink to Paffengers; and fome were fo zealous, as to difturb the Markets of thofe who affented
not, and overthrew the Booths and Stalls, where
the Commodities were lodged on thofe Occafions,
which coming to the Ears of the King and Council,
(without whofe Licenfe it feems all this was done)
they were cited and fined for their diforderly pro-
ceeding. But to confront their Authority, and
keep up the People's Spirits, the Abbot produced
a Divine Warrant, or *Mandate* from Heaven,
for the ftrict obfervation of the Lord's-day, in
the Words following.

(c) *An holy Mandate touching the Lord's-day, which
came down from Heaven unto* Jerufalem, *found on
St.* Simeon's *Altar in* Golgotha, *where* Chrift *was
Crucified for the Sins of all the World, which lying
there three Days and three Nights,* ftruck *with fuch
terrour all that faw it, that falling on the ground they
befought God's Mercy. At laft the Patriarch, and*
Akarias *the Archbifhop, ventured to take up with their
hands the Letter of God, wherein it was thus written —
I am the Lord who Commanded you to keep* the Lord's-
day, *and you have not kept it, neither repented of your
Sins — I caufed repentance to be Preached unto you,
and you believed not ; Then I fent the Pagans among
you, who fpilt your blood on the Earth, and yet you
believed not ; and becaufe you did not obferve* the
Lord's-Holy-day, *I punifhed you a while with Famine :
But in a fhort time I gave you fulnefs of bread, and then
you behaved your felves worfe than before. I again*

(c) Apud Spelman. & Binium.

U *charge*

charge you, that from the Ninth hour on Saturday, until Sun-rising on the Monday , *no Man presume to do any work, but what is good, or if he do, let him repent for the same, verily, I say unto you, and Swear by my Seat and Throne, and by the Cherubims which surround it, that if you do not hearken to this my Man-date, I will send no other Letter unto you, but will open the Heavens, and Rain upon you stones, wood and scalding water by Night, so that none shall be able to provide against 'em.————— I say, ye shall die the death for the* Lord's-day *, and other Festivals of my Saints, which you have not kept; and I will send among you beasts with the heads of Lyons, and the hair of Women and the Tails of Camels, which being very hungry shall devour your flesh. And you shall desire to flee to the Sepulchers of the dead, and hide your selves for fear of those Beasts. And I will take the light of the Sun from your Eyes, and send such darkness that not being able to see, you shall destroy each other.—— And I will turn my face away, and not in the least pity you, I will burn your bodies and Hearts, and of all them who do not keep the* Lord's-day. *Hear then my words, and do not perish for neglecting this Day. I swear to you by my right hand, that if you do not observe the* Lord's-day, *and Festivals of my Saints. I will send Pagan Nations to destroy you.*———— Thus that Paper, whose credit I leave with you ; yet it shows how industrious Men were in those times to have this *great day* solemnly observed. And to that end it was again produced and read in a Council of *Scotland,* held under *Innocent* III. (*d*) about two Years after, *viz.* 1203. in the Reign of King *William,* who with the consent of his Parliament, then assembled, past it into a Law, *That Saturday from twelve at Noon ought to be accounted Holy,* and that no

(*d*) Hector Boet.

Man should deal in such Worldly business, as on Feast-days were forbidden. As also that at the *Toling of a Bell,* the People were to be imployed in holy Actions, going to Sermons and the like, and to continue thus until *Monday-Morning,* a penalty being laid on those who did the contrary.

About the Year 1214. which was eleven Years after, it was again enacted, in a Parliament at *Scone,* by *Alexander* the Third King of *Scots, That none should fish in any Waters, from Saturday after-Evening Prayer, till Sun-rising on Monday,* which was afterwards confirmed by King *James* I.

(*e*) In the Year 1237. *Henry* III. being King, and *Edmund de Abendon* Archbishop of *Canterbury,* a Constitution was made, *requiring every Minister, to forbid his Parishioners the frequenting of Markets* on the Lord's-day, *and leaving the Church, where they ought to meet and spend* the Day *in Prayer, and hearing the word of God.* And this on pain of *Excommunication.*

And eighteen Years after, in the same Prince's Reign, *Walter* Bishop of *Durham* had a decree past, wherein he strictly prohibits all Marketings in holy places and on *Lord's-days*——

And the better to understand the Nature of the Festival, (*f*) a Declaration was made by *Peckam* Archbishop of *Canterbury,* in a Synod at *Lambeth,* 1281. in these words. " It is to be " minded, that the obligation of rest on the *Legal* " *Sabbath (as was required in the* Old Testament) " is altogether expired with the other Ceremo- " nies. And it is now sufficient under the *New* " *Testament,* to attend God's Service on *the Lord's-* " *days,* and other holidays appointed by the Church

---

(*e*) Sub . Episcopo Anonymo, apud Spelman. (*f*) Conc. Lambeth. 1281. Edw. 1. Tit. de inform. simpl.

  " to

" to that end. The manner of fanctifying all
" which days is not be taken from *Jewifh Superftition*, but from the *Canons of the Church.*

(*g*) Six Years after this, Peter *Quivil*, in a Synod at *Exeter* by him called, ordered his Clergy
to take fpecial care, that throughout his Diocefs,
the *Day* fhould be celebrated in fuch a way as might
anfwer the defign of it. " Both the *Old and New*
" *Teftament* (faith he) have affign'd *a Seventh day*
" for a Day of Reft, whereupon the Jews obferved
" *their Sabbath* according to the Letter, but we the
" *Lord's-day* in the true fence and meaning of it.
" For whereas *they* underftood it kept in the for-
" bearance of ordinary Work, *we Chriftians on this*
" *Day* are to go to Church to hear holy Duties,
" and learn the rule of living well, and the more
" the bufinefs of this World diverts People on o-
" ther Days, and will not fuffer 'em to be pre-
" fent at Divine Service, fo much the more on
" *thefe Days*, are they obliged to make their ap-
" pearance there, that as all the Week they have
" been labouring for the meat that perifheth, fo
" they might now on this Day be refrefhed, with
" that meat which endureth to Everlafting Life---
" Wherefore we require all Minifters to teach
" their Parifhioners, and perfwade 'em to refort
" to the Church at *fuch times*, to affift at the Di-
" vine Offices, and be inftructed in their Duty.
" And if any through the prevalence of an ill Cu-
" ftom do keep away, let fuch be punifhed by
" their refpective Ordinaries. And that all Co-
" lour for abfence may be prevented, we prohi-
" bit Markets on the Lord's-day within our Dio-
" cefs on pain of Excommunication, or the felling
" of any goods whatever, except neceffary Provi-

(*g*) Synod. Exon. à Petro Quivil Congreg. 1287.

" fion,

" fion , and that not during the hours of Ser-
" vice. They who offend in the premiſſes, let'
" 'em be ſeverely.puniſhed.——

But in the Century following, under King *Ed-*
ward III. ·1358. *Iſlippe* Archbiſhop of *Canterbury*,
with very great concern and zeal, expreſſes himſelf thus. (*h*) " We have it from the relation of
" very credible Perſons , that in diverſe Places
" within our Province, a very naughty, nay dam-
" nable Cuſtom has prevailed, to hold Fairs and
" Markets on the Lord's-Day, wherein, not only
" Proviſion is bought and ſold, but many other
" matters tranſacted, which can hardly be done
" without cheating one another. And which is
" worſe , Rioting and Drunkenneſs, with other
" ſhameful Practices follow'd, to the great diſho-
" nour of God and ſcandal to Religion. By whieh
" means Men are apt to proceed to Quarrels and
" revilings, threats and blows, and ſometimes to
" murder, and bloodſhedding, the Devil every
" moment gaining upon 'em, while they run in
" Troops to the aforeſaid Places: ——Wherefore
" by virtue of Canonical Obedience, we ſtrictly
" charge and command your Brotherhood, 'that if
" you find your People faulty in the Premiſſes, you
" forthwith admoniſh or cauſe 'em to be admo-
" niſhed, to refrain going to Markets or Fairs *on*
" *the Lord's-day.* And all thoſe who are arrived
" at Years· of diſcretion, let them conſtantly at
" ſuch times reſort to their Pariſh-Churches to do,
" hear and receive what the *Day* requires , as
" Prayers, Sermons, Sacraments and the like. And
" as for ſuch who are obſtinate and·ſpeak, or act a-
" gainſt you in this particular, you muſt endea-

(*h*) Conſtit. Archiep. Cant. Iſlippe. **Tit.** *De exorando pro*
Rege, & de obſerv. Dies Dom. 1358.

" your

" vour to reſtrain 'em by Eccleſiaſtical Cenſures,
" and by all Lawful means put a ſtop to theſe ex-
" travagances.

Nor was the Civil Power ſilent, (*i*) for much
about that time King *Edward* made an Act that
Wool ſhould not be ſhown at the ſtaple on Sundays, and
other ſolemn Feaſts *in the Year.*

In the Reign of King *Henry* VI. Dr. *Stafford*,
being Archbiſhop of *Canterbury*, 1444. it was decreed, that *Fairs and Markets ſhould no more be kept
in Churches, and Church-Yards* on the Lord's-day,
or other Feſtivals, *except in time of Harveſt.*

(†) And *Catworth*, then Lord-Mayor of the
City of *London*, with the aſſiſtance of the Com-
mon-Council, iſſued out an Order, that "No
" manner of Commodities be within the Freedom,
" bought or ſold on *Sundays*, neither Proviſion
" nor any other thing. And that no Artificer
" ſhould bring his ware unto any Man, to be worn
" or occupied *that day*, as Tayler's-Garments,
" Cordwainer's-Shooes, and ſo likewiſe all other
" Occupations.

(*k*) And. ſeven Years after, 1451. it pleaſed
King *Henry* to ratify what was before Ordered by
Archbiſhop *Stafford*, and a Law was made, a s fol-
" lows, Conſidering the abominable Injuries and
" Offences done to Almighty God——by the occa-
" ſion of Fairs and Markets, upon the high and
" Principal Feaſts——*On Trinity Sunday, and other*
" *Sundays*——accuſtomably, and miſerably hol-
" den, and uſed in the Realm of *England*——
" Our Soveraign Lord the King hath ordained,
" that all manner *of Fairs, and* Markets on the
" ſaid Principal Feaſts, *and Sundays*—— ſhall
" clearly ceaſe from all ſhewing any Goods and

(*i*) 28. Edw. III. (†) Fabian. Chron. (*k*) 28. K. Hen. VI.

" Merchandizes, neceſſary Victual only excepted,
" upon pain of forfeiture of all the Goods afore-
" ſaid, to the Lord of the Franchize or Liberty,
" where ſuch Goods be or ſhall be ſhowed contrary
" to this Ordinance.

And in the Fourth Year of his Succeſſour *Edw.*
IV. 1465.it was again enacted , " Our Soveraign
" Lord the King, hath Ordained and Eſtabliſhed,
" that no Cordwainer or Cobler, within the Ci-
" ty of *London,* or within three Miles of any part
" of the ſaid City———do upon any *Sunday in*
" *the Year*, or on the Feaſts———ſell or Com-
" mand to be ſold any Shooes,Huſeans or Galoches,
" or upon *the Sunday or any other of the ſaid Feaſts*,
" ſhall ſet or put upon the Feet or Legs of anyPer-
" ſon any Shooes, Huſeans or Galoches, upon pain
" of forfeiture, and loſs of twenty ſhillings, as of-
" ten as any Perſon ſhall do contrary to this Ordi-
" nance.

And in the ſeventeenth Year of his Reign, there
was another Act of Parliament complaining, that
many ſpent their *Holidays* in Dice, Quoits,Tennis,
Bowling, and the like, which if any Perſon was
found chargeable with for the future, and proved
upon him, this Law puniſhed him on a double account, Firſt, For his contempt of the *Day* , and
Secondly, For uſing ſuch *Diverſions* on it, as were
unlawful Games , and forbidden by the Laws of
the Realm.

(*l*) In this King's Reign,*George Nevil* Archbiſhop
of *York,* in a Provincial Synod , renewed the Conſtitution of Archbiſhop *Peckam* , and by way of
expounding the fourth Commandment, declared
the general Obligation of keeping the *Seventh-day,*
and the *manner* of keeping it, to avoid the notion
and ſuperſtition of the *Jews.*

(*l*) Ann. 1466.

To

To which end the Bishops, under King *Henry* VIII. in the Year 1540. set out a Book concerning the *Sabbath*, wherein they call the Sabbath *ceremonial.* Yet they require rest from Sin, from carnal Pleasures, and Command attendance on holy duties.

So did Dr. *Hooper*, in his Treatise on the Ten Commandments, printed in the Year 1550. *For to this end God did sanctify the Sabbath-day, not that we should give ourselves to idleness or heathenish pastimes, but being free that Day from the travels of this World, we might consider the works and benefits of God with Thanksgiving; hear the word of God, honour and fear him, then to learn who, and where be the Poor of Christ that want our help.*——But to insist on private Doctors would be an endless labour. To proceed therefore to our Laws and Constitutions,

Under King *Edward* VI. *To the honour of Almighty-God*——It was thus enacted——(m) *Forasmuch as Men be not at all times so mindful to laud and praise God, so ready to resort to hear God's holy word, and to come to the holy Communion, as their bounden duty doth require, therefore to call Men to the Remembrance of their duty, and to help their infirmity, it hath been wholsomly provided, that there should be some certain times, and Days appointed, wherein Christians should cease from all kind of Labour, and apply themselves only, and wholly to the aforesaid holy works, properly pertaining to true Religion. Be it therefore enacted, that* all the Days *hereafter mentioned shall be kept, and are* Commanded *to be kept* Holidays, *and none other,* i. e. all Sundays *in the Year.* On which all People for the aforesaid ends in the preamble, (namely to do their duties to God) are to abstain from Bodily labour.——

(m) § Edw. VI.

Thus that Prince in his *Civil* Capacity ; and as the fupreme Governour of this *Church*, he fent out an *injunction* in thefe Words ⸻ *(n) Like as the People be commonly occupied the* Wor k-day *with bodily labour, for their bodily fuftenance, fo was the* Holiday *at the firft beginning Godly inftituted, and ordained that the People fhould that Day give themfelves wholly to God. And whereas in our time God is more offended than pleafed, more difhonoured than honoured upon the* Holiday, *becaufe of Idlenefs, Pride, Drunkennefs, Quarrelling and Brawling, which are moft ufed in fuch days, People neverthelefs perfwading themfelves fufficiently to honour God on that Day, if they hear Mafs and Service, though they underftand nothing to their edifying. Therefore all the* King's *faithful and loving Subjects, fhall from henceforth celebrate and keep their* Holiday, *according to God's holy Will and Pleafure* ⸻ i. e. ⸻ *in hearing the word of God read and taught, in private and publick Prayers, in acknowledging their offences to God, and amendment of the fame, in reconciling themfelves charitably to their Neighbours where difpleafure hath been, in oftentimes receiving the communion of the very body, and blood of Chrift, in vifiting the Poor and Sick, in ufing all fobernefs and godly Converfation.*

The very fame *Injunction* was given by Queen *Elizabeth*, and publifhed 1559 concerning both the Clergy and Laity of this Realm. N. 20. *All the Queen's faithful and loving Subjects, fhall from henceforth celebrate and keep* their Holiday, *&c.* ⸻ verbatim as before.

And in a Statute made by the fame Princefs, the Year before, called the *Act of Uniformity*, it is Commanded, that *(o) From and after the Feaft of the Nativity of* John the Baptift *next coming, all*

(n) 1547. (o) 1 Elizab.

a'd every Perfon, and Perfons inhabiting within this Realm, or any other of the Queen's Majefty's Dominions, fhall diligently and faithfully (having no Lawful or reafonable excufe to be abfent) endeavour themfelves to refort to their Parifh-Church, or Chappel accuftomed, or upon reafonable Let thereof, to fome ufual place, where Common-prayer and fuch Service of God fhall be ufed in fuch time of Let, upon every Sunday and other *Days ordained, and ufed to be kept as* holidays, *and then, and there to abide orderly and foberly, during the time of the Common-prayer, preaching or other fervice of God, there to be ufed and miniftred, upon pain of punifhment by the cenfures of the Church. As alfo upon pain, that every Perfon offending fhall forfeit for fuch offence twelve pence, to be levied by the Church-Wardens of the Parifh, where fuch offence fhall be done, to the ufe of the Poor of the faid Parifh, of the Goods, Lands, and Tenements, of fuch offender by way of diftrefs.*———

(p) And it was one of the *Articles* of *Vifitation,* in the fame Year, *Whether any Inn-holders or Ale-houfe Keepers, do ufe commonly to fell Meat and Drink in the time of Common-Prayer, Preaching, Reading of the Homilies or Scripture.*

Three Years after, the *Book of Homilies* was Authorized by the faid excellent Queen; and in (q) one of them our Church delivers herfelf after this manner. *Although we ought at all times*———*to have in Remembrance, and to be thankful to our Gracious* Lord———*yet' it appeareth to be God's Will and Pleafure, that we fhould at* fpecial times———*gather ourfelves together, to the intent his name might be renowned, and his glory fet forth in the Congregation and Affembly of his Saints. As concerning* the time, *which Almighty-God hath appointed his People to affemble together*

———————————————————————

(p) Ann. 1559. (q) Of the Place and Time of Prayer.

folemnly,

folemnly, it doth appear from the fourth Command-ment of God [Remember, *&c.*] *, that we ought to have a time,* as one Day in the Week, *wherein we ought to reſt, yea, from our Lawful and needful Works. And as by this Commandment no Man in* the ſix days *ought to be ſlothful or idle, but diligently to labour in that State, wherein God hath ſet him : Even ſo God hath given expreſs charge to all Men, that on the* Sab-bath-day, *which is now our* Sunday, *they ſhould ceaſe from all weekly and work day labour, to the intent, that like as God himſelf wrought* ſix Days *, and Reſted the* ſeventh, *and bleſſed and ſanctified, and conſe-crated it to quietneſs and reſt from Labour: Even ſo God's Obedient People ſhould uſe the* Sunday *holily, and Reſt from their common and daily buſineſs, and alſo give themſelves wholly to Heavenly exerciſes of God's true Religion and ſervice. So that God doth not only Command the obſervation of this* holiday, *but alſo by his own Example doth ſtir, and provoke us to the dili-gent keeping of the ſame. This Example and Com-mandment of God, the godly Chriſtian People began to follow immediately after the Aſcenſion of our Lord Chriſt, and began to chooſe them a* ſtanding-day *of the Week to come together in; yet not the* Seventh-day *which the Jews kept, but the* Lord's day, *the Day of the Lord's-Reſurrection, the day after the* Seventh Day, *which is the* firſt Day of the Week. *Since which time God's People have always in all Ages without any Gain-ſaying, uſed to come together upon the* Sunday *to honour, and celebrate the Lord's bleſſed Name, and carefully to keep that* Day *in holy Reſt, and quietneſs, both Man, Wo-man, Child, Servant and Stranger. For the tranſ-greſſion and breach of which* Day, God hath declared himſelf much to be grieved, as it may appear by him, who for gathering of ſticks on the Sabbath-Day was ſtoned to Death. But alas ! All theſe notwithſtand-ing, it is lamentable to ſee the wicked boldneſs of thoſe, who will be counted God's People, who paſs nothing at*

all

all of keeping and hallowing the Sunday. *And these People are of Two sorts; the One sort, if they have any business to do, though there be no extreme need, they must not spare for the* Sunday ; *They must drive and carry upon the* Sunday ; *They must Row and Ferry on the* Sunday ; *They must ride and journey on the* Sunday ; *They must buy and sell on the* Sunday ; *They must keep Markets and Fairs on the* Sunday ; *finally, They use all days alike, Work-days and Holidays, all are One. The other sort is worse, for although they will not travel nor labour on the* Sunday, *as they do on the* Week-day, *yet they will not rest in holiness, as* God *Commandeth, but they rest in ungodliness and filthiness———in excess and superfluity, in gluttony and drunkenness, like rats and swine ; They rest in brawling and railing, in quarelling and fighting, they rest in wantonness and toyish talking, in filthy fleshliness, so that it doth too evidently appear, that* God *is more dishonoured, and the Devil better served on the* Sunday, *than upon all the Days of the Week besides. Wherefore O ye People of* God , *lay your hands upon your hearts; repent and amend this grievous and dangerous Wickedness ; stand in awe of the Commandment of* God ; *gladly follow the Example of* God *himself ; be not disobedient to the godly order of* Christ *s-Church, used and kept from the Apostle's time to this day. Fear the displeasure and just Plagues of Almighty* God, *if ye be negligent and forbear not labouring, and travelling on the* Sabbath *or* Sunday, *and do not resort together to celebrate and magnify* God's *Blessed Name in quiet, holiness and godly reverence.*

(r) In the Year 1580. The Magistrates of the City of *London,* obtain'd of Queen *Elizabeth,* that Plays and Interludes should no more be Acted

---

(r) Field's Declaration, &c.

on the *Sabbath-day*. And to make fure Work, at the motion of many Godly Citizens, and well difpofed Gentlemen, they alfo máde fuite to the faid Queen, and her Privy-Council, that they might have leave to expel the Players out of the City, and fo pull down all the Play-houfes, and Dice-houfes within their Liberties. Which was accordingly effeded, and the Play-houfes in *Grace-Church-Street*, *Bifhopfgate-Street*, and the others near St. *Pauls*, on *Ludgate-Hill*, and in the *White-Fryers*, were pulled down and repreffed by the care of thofe Religious Men.

King *James* upon his Acceffion to this Crown, iffues out a Proclamation, dated at *Theobalds*, *May* 7. 1603. " Whereas, *faith he*, we have been " informed, that there has been in former times a " great negled in keeping *the Sabbath-day*. For " better obferving the fame, and for avoiding all " impious Prophantion of it, we ftraitly charge " and command, that no Bear-baiting, Bull-bait-" ing, Interludes, Common-plays, or the like " diforderly or unlawful Exercifes, or Paftimes, " be frequented, kept or ufed any time hereafter " upon any *Sabbath-day*.

(*s*) And in the fame Year, by a Synod begun in *London*, a Canon was made, requiring " All " manner of Perfons within the Church of *Eng-*" *land*, from henceforth to celebrate and keep the " Lord's-day, commonly called Sunday, and o-" ther Holidays according to God's Will and " Pleafure, and the Orders of the Church of *Eng-*" *land*, prefcribed in that behalf, *i. e.* in hearing " the Word of God read and taught; in private " and publick Prayers, in acknowledging their Of-" fences to God, and amendment of the fame; in

(*s*) Can. 13. Jacobi.

" reconciling

" reconciling themfelves Charitably to their
" Neighbours where difpleafure hath been ; in of-
" ten receiving the Communion of the Body and
" Blood of Chrift; in vifiting the Poor and Sick,
" ufing all godly and fober Converfation.

(*t*) Twelve Years after this, in *Ireland*, when
his Majefty's Commiffioners were employ'd about
the fetling of the Church, there paft this Article.
(*u*) " The firft Day of the Week which is the
" Lord's-day, is wholly to be Dedicated to the
" Service of God ; and therefore we are bounden
" therein, to reft from our common and daily bu-
" finefs, and to beftow that leifure upon holy exer-
" cifes, both private and publick.———

(*w*) King *Charles* I. as foon as he came to the
Crown, paft a Law, intituled *an Act for punifhing
diverfe abufes committed on the Lord's-day called Sunday.*. " Forafmuch as there is nothing more ac-
" ceptable to God, than the true and fincere Wor-
" fhip of him according to his holy Will; and
" that the holy keeping of the Lord's-day, is a
" principal part of the true fervice of God, which
" in many Places of this Realm hath been , and
" now is prophaned and neglected by a diforderly
" fort of People, in exercifing and frequenting
" Bear-baiting--and the like Exercifes, and Paftimes
" upon the Lord's-day : And for that many
" quarrels, bloodfheds, and other great inconve-
" niences, have grown by the refort and concourfe
" of People, going out of their own Parifhes to
" fuch diforder'd , and unlawful Exercifes and
" Paftimes , neglecting Divine fervice , both in
" their own Parifhes and elfewhere.———Be it En-
" acted,———That from and after forty Days
" next after the end of this Seffion of Parlia-

(*t*) Ann. 1615. (*u*) Art. 56. (*w*) 1 Caroli, 1625.

" ment,

" ment, there shall be no Meetings, Assemblies, or
" Concourse of People out of their own Parishes
" on the Lord's-day, within this Realm of *Eng-*
" *land*, or any the Dominions thereof, for any
" Sports or Pastimes whatever. And that every
" Person or Persons offending in any of the Pre-
" misses, shall forfeit for every Offence three Shil-
" lings and four Pence, the same to be employed
" and converted to the use of the Poor of the Pa-
" rish, where such Offences shall be committed---
" to be levied by way of distress, and sale of
" the Goods, of every such offender. And in
" default of such distress, that the party offending
" be set publickly in the Stocks by the space of
" three Hours———Which Statute being to be
continued unto the end of the first Session of the
next Parliament only, was recontinued by the
Statute of third *Caroli*, and so remaineth in
force.

And in this Third Year of the said King, another Act was made against Carriers, Butchers, &c.
" Forasmuch as the Lord's-day commonly called
" Sunday, is much broken and prophaned by Car-
" riers, Waggoners, Carters, Wain-Men, But-
" chers and Drovers of Cattel, to the great dif-
" honour of God and reproach of Religion.———
" Be it Enacted ——— that no Carrier, &c. shall
" travel on the Lord's-day, upon the forfeiture
" of twenty Shillings for every such Offence———
Which was confirm'd and made perpetual 17
Caroli.

'Tis true, after the Example of King *James*,
his Father, *Anno* 1618. and by the advice of some
about him, he was prevail'd on to set out a *Decla-*
ration, wherein he allows his *dutiful Subjects* Innocent Diversions, or *Lawful Recreations* on the *Lord's-*
day, *so that the same be had in due and convenient*
times, without impediment or let of divine Service, and

that the People had first done their Duty to God — But as the former *Declaration* was not well taken, which probably occasioned this Prince to make the aforefaid Law, for the ftricter keeping of the Day, fo to be fure this could not be rellifhed notwithftanding its Cautions; and upon the fatal breach between him and many of his Subjects, by the Concurrence and confent of the Parliaments in both Kingdoms, it was one Article in the *Propofitions* of 1644. that *an Act* fhould be made *for the obfervation of the Lord's-day* ——Meaning a New Act for greater reverence to be fhown the Day, and more for the Honour and Service of God.

April 20. 1629. Sir *Richard Dean*, being Lord Mayor of *London*, he iffued out the following Order, "Whereas I am credibly informed, that "notwithftanding diverfe good Laws for keeping "of the Sabbath. holy, according to the exprefs "Commandment of God Almighty, diverfe in- "habitants and other Perfons of this City, and "other Places having no refpect of duty towards "God, and his Majefty or his Laws, but in con- "tempt of them all, do commonly and of Cuftom "greatly Prophane the Sabbath-day in Buying, "Selling, Uttering and Vending, their Wares and "Commodities on that Day for their private "gain. Alfo Inn-holders fuffering Markets to "be kept by Carriers, in moft rude and Prophane "manner, in felling Victuals to Huckfters, Chan- "dlers and all other Comers. Alfo Carriers, "Carr-Men, Cloth-Workers, Water-Bearers, "and Porters carrying of burdens, and Water- "Men plying their Fares, and diverfe others "Working in their Ordinary callings. And like- "wife, that I am informed that Vintners, Ale- "Houfe-Keepers, Tobacco, and Strong-Water- "Sellers, greatly Prophane the Sabbath-day, by "fuffering Company to fit drinking and bibbing

"in

" in their Houfes on that Day ; and likewife diverfe
" by Curfing and Swearing, and fuch like behaviour,
" contrary to the exprefs Commandment of Al-
" mighty God, his Majefty's Laws in that behalf,
" and all good Government. For the Reformation
" whereof, I do hereby require and in his Ma-
" jefty's Name, ftraitly Command all his Majefty's
" Loving Subjects whatfoever, and alfo all Con-
" ftables, Headboroughs, Beadles, and all other
" Officers whatfover to be aiding, and affifting to
" the Bearer hereof, in finding out & apprehending
" all, and every fuch Perfon and Perfons, as fhall
" be found to offend in any of thefe Kinds, and
" them and every of 'em, to bring before me or
" fome other of his Majefty's Juftice, of the Peace,
" to Anfwer to all fuch Matters, as fhall be object-
" ed- againft 'em, and to put in good fecurity for
" their good behaviour, whereof fail you not,
" as you will anfwer at your Peril.

Ten Years after, *Auguft* 29. 1639. an *Act* was
paft by the *General Affembly*, held at *Edinburgh* in
Scotland, anent the keeping of the Lord's-day.
" The General Affembly recommendeth to the fe-
" veral Presbyteries, the Execution of the old Acts
" of Affembly againft the breach of the Sabbath-
" day, by the going of Mills, Salt-pans, Sal-
" mon-fifhing, or any fuch like labour, and to
" this end revives, and renews the act of Affem-
" bly holden at *Halirood-houfe*, 1602. Seff. 5.
" Whereof the tenour follows ——

" The Affembly confidering the Conventions of
" People, efpecially on the Sabbath-day, are very
" rare in many Places by diftraction of labour, not
" only in Harveft and Seed-time, but alfo every
" Sabbath by fifhing, both of White-fifh and Sal-
" mon-fifh, and in going of Mills. Therefore
" the Affembly difchargeth, and inhibiteth all
" fuch labour of fifhing, as well White-fifh as

X " Salmon-

" Salmon-fish, and going of Mills of all forts upon
" the Sabbath, under pain of incurring the Cenfures
" of the Kirk, and ordains the Commiffioners of
" this Affembly to mean the fame to his Majefty,
" and to defire that a pecunial pain might be en-
" joined upon the Controveners of this prefent
" Act.

In the Year, 1644. *Jan.* 3. an Ordinance of
Parliament was made, *That the Directory for publick*
Worfhip fhould be ufed, purfued and obferved in all ex-
ercifes of the publick Worfhip of God, in every Con-
gregation, Church, Chapel, and Place of publick Wor-
fhip, within this Kingdom of England *and Dominion*
of Wales; *which directory for the publick Worfhip of*
God, with the Preface thereof followeth ———

Of the Sanctification of the Lord's-day—

The Lord's-day *ought to be fo remembred before-*
hand, as that all Worldly bufinefs of our Ordinary
callings may be fo Ordered, and fo timely and feafon-
ably laid afide, as they may not be impediments to the
due Sanctifying of the Day, when it comes.

The whole day is to be celebrated as holy to the Lord,
both in publick and private, as being the Chriftian Sab-
bath, To which end, it is requifite, that there be an ho-
ly Ceffation or Refting all the Day, from all unnecef-
fary labours, and an abftaining not only from all fports
and paftimes, but alfo from all Worldly Words and
Thoughts.

That the diet of that day be fo ordered, as that nei-
ther Servants be unneceffarily detained from the publick
Worfhip of God, nor any other Perfons hindred from the
Sanctifying that Day.

That there be private Preparation of every Perfon or
Family, by Prayer for themfelves, and for God's af-
fiftance of the Minifter, and for a bleffing on his mi-
niftry, and by fuch other holy exercifes, as may fur-
ther

ther difpofe them to a more comfortable Communion with God in his publick Ordinances....

That all the People meet fo timely for publick Worfhip, that the whole Congregation may be prefent at the beginning, and with one heart folemnly join together in all parts of the publick Worfhip ; and not depart till after the Bleffing.

That what time is vacant, between or after the folemn meeting of the Congregation in publick, be fpent in reading, meditation, repetition of Sermons (efpecially by calling their Families to an account of what they have heard) and Catechizing of them, holy conferences, prayer for a Bleffing upon the publick Ordinances, Singing of Pfalms, vifiting the fick, relieving the Poor, and fuch like Duties of Piety, Charity and Mercy, accounting the Sabbath a Delight.

In the 13 *Car.* 2. An Act was made for the Eftablifhing Articles, and Orders for the regulating and better Government of his Majefty's Navy, whereof the firft was, that " All Commanders, " Captains and Officers at Sea, fhall caufe the pub- " lick Worfhip of Almighty God, according to " the Liturgy of the Church of *England* Eftablifh- " ed by Law, to be folemnly, orderly and reverent- " ly performed in their refpective Ships ; and that " Prayers and Preachings, by the refpective Chap- " lains in holy Orders, in the refpective Ships be " performed diligently ; and that the Lord's-day " be obferved according to Law.

Somewhat like this, the Earl of *Effex* fet out for the better behaviour of his Army, 1642. (*x*) " All thofe who often and wilfully abfent them- " felves from Sermons and publick Prayers———— Shall undergo Cenfure.

(*x*) Laws and Ordinances of War. Art. 3.

X 2

And King *James* II. 1685. took the fame care
for his Forces. " All Officers and Soldiers (not
" having juft impediment) fhall diligently fre-
" quent Divine Service and Sermon — under pe-
" nalty that every Officer not doing fo fhall be re-
" prehended at a Court Martial, and every pri-
" vate Soldier *toties quoties*, forfeit twelve Pence :
Which is to be underftood more efpecially of the
Lord's-day, though not named, becaufe on other
Days there were no Sermons.

In the 29 *Car.* 2. a Law paft *for the obfervation of
the Lord s-day called Sunday* — (*y*)*Be it Enacted* —
" That all the Laws enacted, and in force con-
" cerning the Obfervation of the Lord's-day,
" and repairing to the Church thereon, be careful-
" ly put in Execution, and that all, and every
" Perfon and Perfons whatever , fhall on every
" Lord's-day apply themfelves to the Obfervati-
" on of the fame, by exercifing themfelves thereon
" in the Duties of Piety and true Religion, pub-
" lickly and privately, and that no Tradefman,
" Artificer, Work-man, Labourer, or other Perfon
" whatfoever fhall do or exercife any Worldly
" labour, bufinefs or work of their ordinary cal-
" lings upon the Lord's-day or any part thereof
" (Works of neceffity and Charity only excepted)
" and that every Perfon being of the Age of
" fourteen Years or upwards offending in the
" Premiffes, fhall for every fuch offence forfeit the
" fumm of five Shillings, and that no Perfon or
" Perfons whatfoever, fhall publickly, cry fhew
" forth or expofe to fale any Wares, Merchan-
" dizes, Fruit, Herbs, Goods or Chattels whatfo-
" ever, upon the Lord's-day or any part thereof,
" under pain that every Perfon fo offending fhall

" forfeit

" forfeit the fame Goods, fo cried or fhew'd forth
" or expofed to fale, excepting Milk, which
" may be cried and fold, before Nine a Clock in
" the Morning, and after four in the Afternoon.
" And it is further enacted, that no Drover,
" Horfe-Courfer, Waggoner, Butcher, Higler,
" their, or any of their Servants fhall travel or
" come into his or their Inn or Lodging, upon
" the Lord's-day or any part thereof, upon pain
" that each and every fuch offender, fhall for-
" feit twenty Shillings for every fuch offence. And
" that no Perfon or Perfons fhall ufe, employ or
" travel upon the Lord's-day with any Boat,
" Wherry, Lighter or Barge, except it be upon
" extraordinary occafions, to be allowed by fome
" Juftice of the Peace, upon pain that every Per-
" fon fo offending fhall forfeit, and lofe the fumm
" of five Shillings for every fuch offence. And be
" it further enacted, that if any Perfon or Perfons
" whatfover, which fhall travel on the Lord's-day,
" fhall be then robbed, no Hundred nor the Inha-
" bitants thereof fhall be charged with, or be an-
" fwerable for any Robbery fo committed, but
" the Perfon or Perfons fo robbed, fhall be barred
" from bringing any Action for the faid Robbery,
" any Law to the contrary notwithftanding. And
" that no Perfon or Perfons on the Lord's-day,
" fhall ferve or execute, or caufe to be ferved or
" executed any Writ, Procefs, Warrant, Order,
" Judgment or Decree (except in cafes of Felony,
" Treafon, or breach of the Peace) but that the
" Service of every fuch Writ, Procefs, &c. fhall be
" void to all intents and purpofes whatfoever.
" And the Perfon or Perfons, fo serving or exe-
" cuting the fame, fhall be as liable to the fuit of
" the party grieved, and to anfwer damages for
" the doing thereof, as if he or they had done the

X 3　　　　　　　　　" fame

" same without any Writ, Proçefs, Warrant,
" Order, Judgment or Decree at all.

This Law is fo full, that in the fucceeding Reigns, there was no Occafion to make a Supplement, but only to fee it put in Execution. Accordingly King *James*, in the Year 1685. after his Brother's example 1662. Writ a Letter to the two Archbifhops, *Straitly charging and commanding them, to ufe their utmoft care and diligence, that among other things, for the better obferving of the Lord's-day, too much neglected of late, the Clergy of their Provinces fhall, as by often and ferious Admonitions and fharp reproofs, endeavour to draw off People from fuch idle, debauched and profane Courfes as difhonour God, bring a fcandal on Religion and contempt on the Laws and Authority, Ecclefiaftical and Civil, fo fhall they very earneftly perfwade them to frequent Divine Service on the Lord's-day, and other Feftivals appointed by the Church to be kept folemn, and in cafe any Perfon fhall refort to any Taverns or Ale-Houfes, or ufe any unlawful fports and exercifes on fuch Days, the Minifter fhall exhort thofe who are in Authority, in their feveral Parifhes and Congregations, carefully to look after all fuch Offenders in any kind whatever, together with all thofe that abett, receive and entertain them, that they may be proceeded againft according to the Laws, and quality of their Offences, that all fuch diforders may for the time to come be prevented.*

The two *Metropolitans* purfued the *King's* Directions, and tranfmitted his Commands to the feveral *Bifhops* within their Provinces, and the *Bifhops* to the Inferiour *Minifters*, particularly the *Lord Bifhop of London*, called his *Clergy* together, and had a long Conference with them, on the Subject of the *King's* Letter, and afterwards writ to them to remind 'em, of what had been faid, *Dec.* 10. 1686. " The laft Article, faith " he, is that which at all times you ought to be
" concerned

" concerned for : To fee that the folemn Day, of
" our Religious Worfhip be obferved, as becomes
" fincere Profeffours. But more efpecially. at
" this time it lies upon us to apply double dili-
" gence. For this indulgence the King has granted
" upon the notion of having a difpenfing Power in
" himfelf, has been fo little confidered in reference
" to the abufe wicked and prophane Men will
" make of it, that it hath laid the Lord's-day o-
" pen to all contempt imaginable. We have al-
" ready the fad experience of it. Worldly Peo-
" ple ftay at home on that Day, and attend their
" fecular Affairs. The loofe and debauched lie at
" the Ale-houfe, and every one that fears not God,
" takes an occafion to be an Offence to thofe that
" do. As to what remedies we fhould ufe to prevent
" thefe mifchiefs, as much as may be, I think,
" we fully confidered in our laft Conference before
" this, whither I refer you.

Feb. 13. 168⁸⁄₉₀. The prefent *King* fends his
Letter to the Right Reverend Father in God,
Henry Lord Bifhop of London, to be communicated
to the two *Provinces* of *Canterbury and York.* Wherein the *Clergy* are directed *to Preach frequently againft
thofe particular Sins and Vices, which are moft prevailing in this Realm ; and withal on every of thofe Lord's-
days, on which any fuch Sermon is Preached, they do
alfo read to their People fuch Statute, Law or Laws,
as are provided againft that Vice or Sin, which is their
fubject on that Day, as namely againft Blafphemy,
Swearing , and Curfing , againft Perjury, againft
Drunkennefs, and againft Prophanation of the Lord's-
day, all which Statutes we have ordered to be Printed
together with thefe our Letters , that fo they may be
tranfmitted to every Parifh within this our Realm.*

Hereupon the aforefaid *Prelate*, not only takes
care to difperfe the *Letter* above written, with
the feveral *Laws* there mentioned, and annext to

X 4 it,

it, but also writes another to his *Own Clergy*, bearing date, *April* 24. 1690. wherein he presses 'em, *To put their People often in mind of the importance of the Word Reformed Churches, which import that as our Doctrine and Worship, are by the blessing of God reformed, so our Lives ought to be reformed, otherwise all the advantage we have of Light and Truth, beyond other Churches will rise up in judgment against us, if we do not live suitably to them. But above all things they were to study to possess those committed to their charge with the deep sense of the Duty, that they owe to God their Maker, and to Jesus Christ their Saviour, that so they may apply themselves to the exercises of Devotion in secret, to the frequenting the Publick Worship, and chiefly to the receiving the Sacrament with that serious disposition of mind, as becomes such holy Performances, that so they may delight in going together to the House of God. And in order to their doing this aright, infuse into 'em a great reverence for the Lord's-day, as a time separated from the common business of Life, for their attending on the Worship of God, and such other Religious exercises, as may both increase their Knowledge and their Sense of Divine matters; and that therefore they ought not to satisfy themselves with going to Church, and assisting publickly in the Service of God, but that they set themselves more to Prayer on that Day, and to the reading of Scripture and other good Books, both apart and together in their Families, that so they may grow up in Grace, and in the Knowledge of our Lord and Saviour Jesus Christ. These things, saith he, you must open to your People frequently, in Season, and out of Season, both at Church and from house to house. And I charge you by all the Authority I have over you, by the zeal you bear to the Church of England, and as you desire to have from your labours, and your People a Crown of rejoicing in the day of the Lord, and as you bear a due regard both to your own Soul, and the Souls committed to your Care, and to that precious Blood*

Blood by which they were redeemed ; *as you desire to be faithful to your Ordination vows, and to have a share in those blessed Words* [well done good and faithful Servant, enter thou into the joy of thy Lord] *that you will give your selves wholly to these things, that you will account no labour great in advancing that Work, for which our Saviour spared not his own Life, and that you pursue all the parts of your Ministry, with a zeal suitable to the importance of them,* &c.——

July 9. 1691. The *Queen* writ a Letter to the *Justices of the Peace in Middlesex,* to this Effect. *Trusty and Well-beloved, we greet you well.* "Con-"sidering the great, and indispensible Duty in-"cumbent on us——we think it necessary——"to recommend to you, the putting in Execu-"tion——those Laws which have been made, and "are still in force against the prophanation of the "Lord's-day, and all other disorderly Practices, "which by a long continued neglect, and conni-"vance of the Magistrates and Officers, concerned, "have Universally spread themselves to the disho-"nour of God and scandal of our holy Religion—"we do therefore hereby charge and require you, "to take the most effectual Methods, for putting "the Laws in Execution against the Crimes, Sins "and Vices abovementioned, &c——

In the Year 1695. a Book of Injunctions was given to the Two Archbishops, and by them to the rest of the Clegy, wherein it is commanded [*Art.* 12.] that "They use their utmost endeavour, that "the Lord's-day be religiously observed, that "they set a good example to their People, and "exhort 'em frequently to their Duty herein.

And *Feb.* 24. 1697. a *Proclamation* was issued out, at the request of the House of Commons, to require "All, both Magistrates and Ministers, "to be very vigilant and strict in the discovery, "and effectual Prosecution and Punishment of all "Persons,

" Perfons, who fhall be found guilty of exceffive
" Drinking, Blafphemy, Prophane Swearing and
" Curfing, Lewdnefs, Prophanation of the Lord's-
" day——as they will Anfwer it to Almighty
" God, and upon pain of the King's Higheft dif-
" pleafure.

. And in the Year, 1698. Sir *Francis Child* being
Lord Mayor, an Order was iffued out bearing
date *March* 1. in thefe words, " Forafmuch as the
" general corruption and depravation of Manners,
" within this City, and the Liberties thereof; in-
" ftead of being amended and reformed by the
" many good Laws provided, and defign'd for
" that purpofe, and the feveral Orders publifhed
" by the Court of Lord Mayor and Aldermen, to
" inforce the Execution of them, feems rather
" to prevail, and increafe, and daily manifefts it
" felf in the groffeft and boldeft Acts of de-
" bauchery and licentioufnefs.

" The Right honourable the Lord Mayor, be-
" ing deeply fenfible of the unhappy prevalency
" and dangerous confequences of fuch Practices, and
" being convinced, that nothing can put a ftop to
" the further growth and increafe, of fuch im-
" pieties but a refolute, and vigorous Execution
" of feveral Laws by a ftrict, and impartial in-
" flicting the feveral penalties and punifhments by
" them appointed on all Offenders.

" His Lordfhip therefore, out of a due fenfe of
" his Duty to God, and regard to the honour and
" welfare of the Government of this City, com-
" mitted to his care, being refolved to effect the
" fame, doth (with the advice of his Brethren the
" Aldermen) hereby renew and command the
" obfervance of all former Orders and Precepts;
" and doth ftrictly charge, and command all Con-
" ftables, Church-Wardens, Over-Seers of the
" Poor, in their refpective Parifhes, and all o-
" ther

" ther Officers, and Ministers of Justice within
" this City and Liberties, to put the said Laws in
" Execution. [which Laws, Offences and Penal-
" ties, are recited in the Order.]

"; And forasmuch as the keeping holy the Lord's-
" day, commonly called Sunday, is a principal
" part of the true Service of God, and that all
" Persons on that day ought to apply themselves
" to the Duty of Piety and Religion, both pub-
" lick and private; and the keeping open of Ta-
" verns, Coffee-Houses and Ale-Houses; on the
" said Day, and the receipt and entertaining of
" the People, as well in time of Divine Service, as
" out, is a great means of Prophaning and abusing
" the same, his Lordship doth strictly charge and
" command, that no Vintner, Coffee-Man, or o-
" ther keeper of publick Houses, do keep open
" his or their Houses on that Day, nor permit
" any Person to Drink or Tipple therein,
" either in time of Divine Service or after-
"; wards, upon pain to be prosecuted, not only
" as Offenders against several of the Laws afore-
" mentioned, but also to be proceeded against
" by such other Methods and Punishments, as
" the greatness of the said Offence requires. ——

And Order carefully issued out very frequently
by the *Lord-Mayors* of this City.

An in a Word, our Church takes so much
care in this particular, that it is an Ordinary (z)
Article in our Episcopal Visitations, *Whether any in
our Parishes do prophane the Lord's-day, or on any pretence abstain from coming to Church or the publick
Places, where there are Prayers or Sermons, and spend
their time in Ale-Houses, or Houshold Affairs.*

(z) Articles of Visitation and Enquiry, &c. In the 4. Episc.
Visit. of *Henry* Lord Bishop of *London*, Octo 3. 1700. tit. 4.

B. The

B. The account you have given of so many *Laws* and *Canons,* doth indeed show what care hath been taken to see the Day observed: But surely they are People of little Religion, who will be influenced by such Motives , and serve God purely for the sake of *Man.* As for *Christians* who submit to *Principle,* and have any degree of Vertue and Goodness in 'em, the *very Day* and *what* we remember on it, are inducements so Powerful, that if at any time we think of another World, we must needs bless him who has given us the ravishing prospect of being for ever happy in it. He that believes his Condition to have been once desperate, must needs be brought to acknowledge the kindness of his Deliverer. And since we read, that God *on this day first visited,* and *then Redeemed* the World, and made it as it were the same date of the *Old* and *New* Creation, can any Man live, and not call to mind this *Double* Blessing? And as soon as he is brought to *think,* will he forbear to adore God, both as his *Maker* and *Saviour?* I consider therefore, no Law of this Nature otherwise, than in the *reason* of it, and this to me is more than all the terrours of *pecuniary Mulcts,* or *bodily penalties,* for I have learn'd, and hold good that Lesson of my Redeemer, *fear not them which kill the Body, but are not able to kill the Soul, but rather fear him who is able to destroy both Body and Soul in Hell, yea, I say, unto you fear him*——And if any thing is terrible to me in this World, it is what you spake of out of a *Council* at *Paris,* and what Mr. *Field* relates, happen'd at the *Bear-Garden* on the *Lord's-day,* Feb. 13. 1533. where the loss of so many lives and limbs are sufficient indications of God's Displeasure against those who make no Conscience of observing this Day.

A. Why

A. Why truly, we may well conftrue thefe *Judgments* of God, into fo many *Laws* againft the contempt of *that*, on the account of which thefe, and the like punifhments are inflicted. Some have taken pains in making (*a*) *Collections* of fuch remarkable Paffages; and though there are thofe in the World, who much queftion the truth of fuch relations, and that *others* confider 'em as the *ordinary events* of Providence, which fall out *indifferently* any Day, without fpecial Application, yet for my part, as I am not very credulous on the one hand, to accept all reports of this kind, fo neither on the other, am I hard of belief to admit none. But remembring the cafe of the *Man* in the *Wildernefs*, who by God's immediate Command was *ftoned to Death, for gathering a few fticks on the Sabbath-day*, (though probably there was no wilful contempt of the Feftival in what he did, but feemingly a compliance with his prefent Poverty) I cannot be perfwaded, but that God is and will always be jealous of his Honour; and where People are more fully and clearly informed, than I conceive *that Man* was, in the Nature of our *Chriftian Sabbath*, and yet will venture to tranfgrefs, it may provoke the divine Juftice to punifh fometimes this contempt in a very extraordinary way; and becaufe our *Laws*, or the *Execution* of 'em are ftill *Defective*, he may be pleafed by his feverity on a *few* upon this account, to give warning to the *Reft*, to behave themfelves better.

B. Is not this an *Evidence*, that the *Day* is of *divine appointment*, feeing God fo much intereffes himfelf in the *Breach* of it?

A. It is an Evidence of his high difpleafure a-

(*a*) *Spelman's* Engl Councils in the Chapter of the *Mandate*, &c. *Prynns Hiftrio-maftix*, Theatre of God's Judgments. Preface to the Practice of Piety. Mr. *Merfton* againft Immorality, &c.——

gainſt ſuch as preſumptuouſly abuſe *any Day* dedicated to his Service. To have *ſet-times*, and *ſet-
places* to Worſhip God ; *To ſwear* by his name, and
the like, is certainly of *divine inſtitution*, but for
the *particular times*, or *places*, or *manner* of Worſhip, and *forms* of Oaths, theſe things are left to
diſcretion, yet being by us appropriated to God's
Honour, they are very fitly ſtiled *his Day*, *his
Houſe*, *his Worſhip*, *his Oath*, and according to this
Relation to him, he often deals with thoſe who
tranſgreſs in theſe particulars, as if he himſelf
had expreſly appointed them.

    B. Well ; The *Worſhip* of the Day is no
doubt to me, though I ſomewhat queſtion the
manner of the Worſhip. And as to this, that
practice of the *Jews*, you reported out of *Jerom*,
which I take for the *moral* of the *Sabbath-Reſt* (and
which ſome ſuppoſe to laſt to the Captivity) *Contemplation*, and *mental* Devotion, or *Devotion at
home*, ſeems very good and ſutable to this deſign.
For as to the *Publick-places* ſet a part for this uſe,
there are ſo many Temptations, ſuch variety of
objects to ingage the Senſes, diſtract the Thoughts,
and alienate or withdraw the mind from ſacred
Reflections, that the numbers of People there aſſembled, do ſeem to me to *hinder* Devotion, inſtead of *helping* it. And whereas our going *thither* is look'd on, and pretended to be an invitation for each other to ſerve with Emulation, our
common-Lord, it falls out quite otherwiſe, and
'tis found by woful Experience, that our *Habits*,
Geſtures, and a thouſand inſtances of Peoples *irreverence*, conſtrain us to mind every thing more
than what we meet there for, ſo that this *publick
Service* of God becomes little leſs than a *Publick diſhonour* to him. But at home and in our Cloſets,
there are none of theſe interruptions, and which
is certainly a very neceſſary quality in our Prayers,

                                        they

.they are made in *fincerity* and *Truth*, without the
fufpicion of Hypocrify or thofe little Arts Men
and Women, moftly ufe to deceive the Congregation rather than ferve God: Here we may be
devout without impediments; and the contemplation of God's Attributes, with the effects and
emanations of 'em for our good, cannot but have
its utmoft vigour and extent, becaufe the *Eye* and
the *Ear*, are then fecured from all temptations of
Treachery, nor have they opportunities to let a-
ny thing in to difturb and divert the Soul.

   A. Can you fhow me any good in the World
but what is or may be *abufed*? Yet is it the lefs
good for having this Entertainment? All that we
can honeftly fay, is, that the *Men* are to blame
for giving it this ufage. *Meat, Drink*, and *Clothes*,
are the neceffaries of Life, and to what excefs do
we ftrain 'em? Yet no *Logick* can difpute nor *Rhetorick* diffwade us from *Meat, Drink and Apparel.*
All the Arguments we offer this way, are but
fo many *cautions* againft *Surfeiting, Drunkennefs and
Pride*. Nor is it the *Creatures* of God we cenfure,
but the *Vices* of thofe Men who do not treat 'em as
they fhould. The *wantonnefs* of fome People in
the Church, the *coldnefs* of others, and the *irreverence* of moft are too obvious to every Eye, that
will lofe fo much time as to look and examine them,
and it muft be lamented, that *Chriftians* are fo fupine,
and unmindful of what they come into that place
for, and fo daring as thus to affront God in his
own Houfe, and at thofe very minutes, wherein
they would be thought to do him Service. Yet all
this concludes little againft the true end of our
Meeting together; and this advantage the Pious
Man has, that the Honour he doth God in his ferious
Devotion, is made more remarkable amidft a multitude of light and vain Perfons about him, and as
his fober and grave deportment pleafes God better,

                            and

and gains him a greater refpect from fuch as himfelf, fo 'tis a mighty check to fuch of the Congregation as are otherwife difpofed, and who beholding
his behaviour, may be happily brought at length to
reflect on their *own*, and by his *example*, grow more
referved, and careful in what they fay or do ;
fo that at the fame time he ferves *God* and his
Brother, and while he pays his Duty to the *one*,
he becomes an inftrument to fave the *other*.

Nor is it to be forgotten, that God has been
pleafed to afford *thefe places* the ftile of his *own Houfe*;
fo that it is a piece of holy Manners to give our
attendance *there* ; and we may be fufpected we are
proud or indifferent in his Worfhip, when we are
found to ftay away. For although God is indeed
every where, and fills all parts of the World with
his prefence and power, yet plainly he is not every where *alike*, not in the fame *Manner*, nor in
the fame *degree* in one place as in another. He is
in *Heaven*, as a glorious *King* upon his Throne of
Majefty, receiving conftant Honours and Hallelujahs, from an innumerable Company of Angels.
He is in *Hell*, a *Judge*, punifhing the Souls of the
Wicked, for their many Sins againft him. He is
all over the *Univerfe* by his ordinary *Providence*,
managing *Nature*, and giving efficacy to the
Earth, *Air and Sea*, to accomodate us in our feveral neceffities. But in the *Church* he is a gracious
Father, defcending from above to meet his Children, and receive thofe Addreffes they make him,
either for the obtaining the Bleffings they want, or
averting thofe Calamities they fear, or removing
thofe they already lie under. And this is agreeable
to fuch Texts of Scripture as call the Church,
*the Houfe of Lord, the Courts of his Holinefs, the Ha-
bitation of his Houfe, the Place where his Honour Dwelleth,* &c. All which infers a more immediate refidence of God in fuch a Place, efpecially when we
folemnly

folemnly Affemble to tender him the refpects of our Prayers and Praifes.

B. Doth not this contradict what *Steven* avoucheth, that (*b*) *The moft high dwelleth not in Temples made with hands,*——and he fetcheth his proof out of the Evangelical Prophet, (*c*) *Heaven is my Throne, and the Earth is my Footftool, what Houfe will you build me,* faith the Lord, *or what is the place of my Reft ? Hath not my hand made all thefe things ?*

A. True ; we muft not look upon *God* fo comprehended or confined to the Church, as the *Idols* of the Heathens were wont to be, who called their Temples the *inclofures of the Deity,* and who conceited, that if they could keep their Gods within thofe Walls they were fafe enough, and needed not to fear any Enemy, which made him in *Menander,* fay, that *he liked no God, that would be gadding abroad, and was never contented to ftay at home;* God is not fo grofly limitted to *this* or *that* place, as to dwell *materially* in it, which is fufpected to be the vain imagination of fome among the *Jews,* upon all occafions boafting and crying out, *the Temple of the Lord, the Temple of the Lord,* as if having the Temple did inforce the Confequence, that they muft by that means have the Lord of the Temple too. No, his refidence is not fo *literal* and neceffary there, but he will withdraw upon the mifdemeanours of his People ; yet during their Devotion and Obedience to his Will, the *Temple* then, and the *Church* now has eminently his Prefence, and is up and down the holy Book called, *His Reft, and Refting Place* ——as a particular Manfion, and thofe words declare him *certainly,* and more efpecially *there.*

(*b*) Acts 7, 48: (*c*) If. 66. 1, 2:

. But to proceed to some other confiderations. It is to be underftood, that our Applications to God, are not only for the *relief of our Wants*, (with refpect to which we might pray in any place, be-caufe God is every where and ready to hear us) but in a great meafure they tend to *his Glory*, to whom thefe Addreffes are made. For every votary brings with him to the *Church*, an open Declaration and Confeffion of his dependance on God; and the greater therefore the Company is, the greater is the Honour that accrues to God by it. So that becaufe our Chriftian Service has a double refpect, partly *to God*, and partly *to our-felves*, it naturally follows, that the more publick (as in the Church). we exprefs this Service, the more compleat and full it is: And herein it out-does a *private* Devotion, in as much as we mani-feftly, and *openly* celebrate the Power and Mercy of our Heavenly Benefactour, and in the face of all the World, own and adore him.

. Add to this, that our Meeting in publick, An-fwers better the notion we ought to have of *Chri-ftian Communion*. For with refpect to God, we are *all one*, as he would have us be, and we feem to be fo while we Affemble in the Church, and unanimoufly fend up our Prayers to Heaven. To be devout at *home*, when there is no *publick Service*, is pious and neceffary: But to pray in *private* at *Church hours*, favours of *fingularity*, and may be Thought to be *the defpifing of the Church of God.* — I do not intend cafes of *neceffity*, as under Confine-ment or Sicknefs, yet even under thefe Circum-ftances we are fo to pray in our *Chambers*, or *Beds*, or *Prifons*, as to have our Defires and Hearts with our devout Brethren, when we think 'em met toge-ther. The primitive Chriftians, as they had *one Heart and one Mind*, fo they met in *one Place* to exercife their Religion in, as the moft fignificant

inftance

.inftance, of their being all Members of *one Body*, and as fuch Members they had a common concern for the *Whole*, and mutual Charity for one another.

Moreover in the *Church*, our Prayers are for the *Publick good*, and therefore better faid in a *Publick way*. (*d*) Here the wants of a People, *as a People,* or Society of Men and Women are fet before God: And as it redounds more to his Honour to beftow *General* Bleffings, fo it tends more to the good of the *Common-Wealth*, which is of greater concern than any *private Man*'s Condition; and yet every *individual* is therein obliged and fome way or other has a fhare of the Benefit. For which, and the like Reafons, our appearance at Church is the moft acceptable way of doing our Duty to God. And though probably you may object the Promife of our Lord, that *where two or three are gathered, together in his Name, he will be in the midft of 'em* —— this was not faid to *leffen* the *Church*, but was a word of *comfort* to them, who had not nor could have the benefit of the *Temple*, or fuch like Buildings, and therefore fhould not fuffer for what they could not help; but provided they met together *any where elfe* in his Name, it fhould be the fame thing as if they met in the *Church*, with a greater number of the Faithful. But then tho' this is faid to *thofe* who might be deprived of the Conveniency of ferving God in publick Places, yet the Promife reaches not *them* who have thefe good opportunities, yet neglect or flight 'em. God heard *Job* on the *Dunghill*, *Daniel* in the Lions *Den*, St. *Paul* by the *Water-fide*, and St. *Peter* in the *Prifon*; yet though we prefume not to con-

---

(*d*) *Quando oramus, non pro uno oramus, fed pro toto populo,* &c. Cypr. in Orat. Dom.

fine

fine his Majesty, within those few Places where
·Publick Service is done, nor so limit him, as not to
be elsewhere, when two or three are met in his
Name, however, *humanely* and *comparatively* speaking, the Devotion is not so Powerful of *two*, as of
many People ; nor can we well expect, for the
reasons foregoing , that God will vouchsafe the
same attention to Prayers, said at our *Houses*, as
what we offer at his *own*, when we have sufficient
means and opportunity of going thither, to make
·up the Congregation.

But besides the inducements and motives before
proposed, there are many advantages, this absence from the Church deprives us of, especially in
most instances of the *Ministerial Office*, such as
Absolution, *Sermons*, and *Sacraments*, the loss of all
·which the Conscience of a Good Man, cannot easily digest ; and in each of which there is unspeakable comfort and benefit to the Soul. Not but
Ministers are still *Men*, and have many infirmities
incident to Humane Nature, notwithstanding the
sacredness of their Function, yet they are withal
what the Scripture calls 'em, *Men of God*, such as he
has been pleased to make *Intercessors*, between him
and his People. Sometimes they are the *Mouths* of
the Congregation, to send up their Prayers and
·Praises. Sometimes again, they are the *Voice of
God*, to publish and explain his Will. And both
ways they Act with Authority and Power, as *Ministers*, and not barely as *Men*.

That a few illiterate *Fishermen*, whose cunning
lay in their *Nets*, and strength in the *Cable*, should
be able to Work such a change in the World on a
·sudden, by confounding Philosophers, and bringing
inveterate bigotry into a dislike of its old Errours,
this cannot be owing to the *parts* of the Men, to
their Education in the Schools, or Proficiency in
Learning, but to their *Mission and Apostleship*, on
which

which God beſtowed a Bleſſing, and whereby he choſe to manifeſt his own Power, by making *weak things to confound the things that are mighty, and baſe things, and things which are deſpiſed, and things that are not, to bring to nought things that are, that no fleſh ſhould glory in his preſence.*———

We can do nothing without God. We want his help in the diſcharge of our Duties, and he is willing to afford it us, and has appointed thoſe Methods he thought beſt to convey his Grace into our Hearts. And therefore though *Water* in *One Sacrament*, and *Bread and Wine* in the *Other*, be ordinary things in their own Nature, and may ſeem to carnal Men ſomewhat ſurprizing to be told, that the *One* or *Other* can benefit the Soul: Yet ſo it is ; and how contemptible ſoever theſe *Creatures* are in themſelves, yet by Virtue of the *Ordinance* they are the *means* of Salvation to Chriſtian People. The meaner things are, the greater is the Power which gives 'em efficacy, and ſuch things are purpoſely uſed to move us to admire that Power.

The ſtóry of *Naaman* and *Eliſha*, may ſerve for illuſtration. *Naaman* being all over a *Leper*, comes to *Eliſha* for cure. The Prophet bid him go to *Jordan*, and waſh *ſeven times* in that River. *Naaman* is angry, and asks whether *Abana* and *Pharfar* Rivers of *Damaſcus*, *were not as good as the Waters of Iſrael*? Perhaps the *Waters* might be the ſame, but not the ſame to *him*, becauſe *Eliſha* bid him go to *Jordan*, and he expected Obedience, and that *Obedience* was to cure him. With much ado he went to *Jordan*, and was made clean. To argue rationally, *Naaman*'s Objection was not trivial. Why to *Jordan*, why to any *River* at all ? In a *Bath* there might be ſome Virtue, ſome good quality in this *Fountain*, or that *Spring* immediately iſſuing from *this* or *that Mineral*. But for *Rivers*,

which

which are the concourfe or drain of all forts of Waters, what Medicine could be expected from them?
Or if fo, why not the Rivers of *Damafcus*, as well as
a River in *Ifrael*? But then the ftronger the Argument was againft the *River*, the greater was his
Power who by that River cured him. There was a
Miracle to be done on this *Syrian*; and therefore the
more repugnance there was between the *Means* and
the *Cure*, the more difcoverable was the hand of God
in reftoring his flefh to him. 'Twas hard to bring
him to hearken to the Prophet; but he complied,
or he had returned again a *Leper* to his own Country. Where God ordains things, the *Cavils* we
make, do not fo much difpute the *things* themfelves, as his *Power* which prefcribes 'em. There
the reflection ends whatever we think of it. Becaufe we either queftion his *Wifdom* in appointing
fuch means; or we fcruple his *Faithfulnefs*, whether he will indeed blefs 'em; or we doubt his
Omnipotency, and fear he cannot go through with
his Defign.

It pleafed the Lord for the good of his Church
to fet a part a felect Company of Men, to Baptize
and Preach the Gofpel. *And when he afcended up
on high*, faith *St.* Paul, *he gave fome Apoftles, fome
Prophets, fome Evangelifts, fome Paftors and Teachers* —— (to what end?) *For the perfecting of the
Saints, for the work of the miniftry, for the edifying of
the Body of Chrift, till we all come into the Unity of the
Faith, and the Knowledge of the Son of God, to a perfect Man* —— What thefe Men were in themfelves,
you heard before: However this *Seal* gave 'em the
pre-eminence: And as they were made the Keys,
to open the Door of Knowledge to others, fo
their *Ordination* was the Key to open it to themfelves, and furnifh 'em with Abilities to carry on
that great Bufinefs.

This

L. This then being made an *Ordinance* to edifie and teach his People, (which is the reason they are often called *Builders, Master-builders, Stewards of the mysteries of God,* &c.) we are to have the same notion of these *Men,* as if God's other appointments, not purely on their own score, but *relatively* and with regard to him, whose *Ministers* they are. And because of this Relation a slight on them reflects on God himself,(e)*he that despiseth you, despiseth me*——'tis so by interpretation *(f),* because the *Messenger* borrows his Name, from the party *sending him,* and thereupon it is, that the ill treatment of a *Servant,* is an affront to the *Master,* whom we are understood to abuse in the Person of the other. Considering then the *Ministry a Divine Appointment* for the good of the Church, it is to be presumed, that the same Wisdom which gave it being will take care to qualify and bless it, and make it serviceable to such a Christian, as uses the opportunity and frequents those places, where it is daily and publickly exercised in those particulars I before mention'd.

B. I have no disrespect to Men of that Profession. But as for those instances you named, *Absolution,* the *Word* and *Sacraments,* the two first especially, their Ministry in these Matters doth not appear so necessary. For as to *Absolution,* we take it to be the *Application of the Promises of God in Scripture, to the case of a wounded Conscience,* or as some think, *a Declaration of the Priest, to let the Sinner know that God forgives him, upon the Condition of his Repentance.* Now in either of these respects, a Man may serve himself Effectually *without* the Ministers help, because if he repents seriously, he may, *by applying* God's Promises to his present

_____

(e) Gal. 4. 11, 12. (f) Vid. Chrysost. Hom. in Gen.

Y 4 case,

case, ease himself under the weight of his Sins, and the *Minister* can do no more by making the same Application.

Then for *the word of God*; it lies before us, the Book is open, and no Person that sets himself about that holy Study, needs fear success, but may expect that God will send his Grace to inlighten and assist him. However in cases of difficulty, we have many Expositions and Sermons, almost on every Text of the Bible, which-being published and exposed to the Censure of the World, are commonly more *pertinent* and *elaborate*, than what are in Course delivered from the Pulpit, and therefore more likely to give satisfaction.

The *Sacraments* indeed depend on their Office; and as we are all beholding to them for our *Baptism*, so would we gladly accept their kind Tenders of the *Lord's-Supper*, but that for our *unworthiness* we dare not, lest in so doing, *we Eat and Drink our own Damnation*. And 'tis with no little concern, we see so many running to this Sacrament, without thinking what they do, as appears *afterwards* from their lives and practices, so little answerable to those holy resolutions, Men are supposed to make before they approach that Table.

A. The *Ministers*, whom you say you have respect for, are so much the more obliged to you, since you seem of Opinion, that the *Dignity* of their Function doth not challenge, nor its *usefulness* invite you to it. But I have better hopes of your perswasion, and consider what you said as the Representation of *other* Peoples Judgment rather than your Own. However, to say somewhat to your Objections; and first as to *Absolution*. 'Tis true, *Absolution* applies the Divine Promises of Pardon to that Sinner, who is sorry for his Sin, and

and refolves to live better ; but who can do this fo well as the Minifter of God, whofe Commiffion Seals to him this Power of Pardon ? An hearty penitent may hope to find Mercy ; and his contrition and tears, are very good *figns* not only of his *Repentance,* but they are withal *Teftimonies* of the *Grace* of God, working in his Confcience and preparing it for his Pardon : Yet ftill he cannot but hefitate and doubt his State, till this publick *Officer* comes and declares him fafe ; which if done, he takes courage and rejoices , becaufe he knows God muft be juft to his Ordinances, and having given the *Minifter* a Power to *abfolve,* he will ratifie what is pronounced *in his name,* from the mouth of an *Officer* Commiffion'd by himfelf. This Commiffion we have , John 20. 22. *Receive ye the holy Ghoft* (faith Chrift to his Difciples) *whofe Sins ye remit, they are remitted, and whofe Sins ye retain, they are retained.* —— And that it amounts to a Power of binding and loofing, we find by St. *Matthews* words, 16. 20. *Whatfoever ye fhall bind on Earth fhall be bound in Heaven, and whatfoever ye fhall loofe on Earth, fhall be loofed in Heaven.* ---Which the Learned Ancients expound, to be not barely a *Declarative* but *Judicial Power,* who were Men too pious to be Thought to fpeak *Blafphemy,* and too old to be fufpected of *Popery.*

B. I fuppofe thofe words, *Whofe Sins ye remit,* &c. mean the forgivenefs of Sin, obtain'd by *applying the word* they Preach'd, or by vertue of the *Sacrament of Baptifm,* which they Adminiftred to the converts of Chriftianity.

A. We can't fay but *both thefe* may be *means* and *helps* to take away Sin, but this is not what is intended in that place of St. *John.* Becaufe as to

---

(g) Math. 16. 20.

the *Preaching-Part* and Baptizing, the Diſciples had this faculty (*h*) long before. But this Authority and Power of *remiſſion*, was not had till *after the Reſurrection*, for though promiſed while they were on the Coaſt of *Cæſarea Philippi*, yet 'twas done at *Jeruſalem* at that time, when he breathed on 'em, and by that Ceremony ſignified ſome further *Addition* of Power, than they *hitherto* had, and therefore muſt be more than what belong'd to *Baptizing* or *Preaching.*

B. We believe the Apoſtles might have ſuch an extraordinary Power, but it was *Perſonal* and limited to them.

A. That cannot be the ſence of their Commiſſion. Becauſe it was a *ſtanding Miniſtry* our Lord now intended ———— for he tells 'em, he *will be with them to the end of the World;* which can no otherwiſe be than in their *Office,* and the *Succeſſion of Miniſters,* whereby he makes good this promiſe, and will continue it till the Day of Judgment. And thus we underſtand the Prieſtly Power, in the Office for the Viſitation of the Sick, where the *Abſolution* is *Authoritative,* and prefaced with the Reaſon why the *Miniſter* takes this upon him—— *Our Lord Jeſus Chriſt who hath left Power in his Church, to abſolve all Sinners which truly repent, and believe in him, of his great Mercy forgive thee thy Offences, and by his Authority committed unto me, I abſolve thee from all thy Sins,* &c.——'Tis true, this is not ſimply *Arbitrary;* but you may call it, if you will, a *Conditional Power,* upon the *ſuppoſal* of *Repentance;* but then be it remembred, that ſuch *Conditions* were neceſſary even to the *Abſolution* of the Lord *Jeſus.* For impenitency and *Unbelief,* were *Bars* to the exerciſe of *his Miniſtry,* neither did he cure the

---

(*h*) Matth. 10. 7. John 4. 2.

Sick,

Sick, but with such cautions as these; *be it unto thee according to thy Faith.*——So that though it be confest, that the reason of *Our*, nay of *Chrift's Abfolution* depends on the *Faith*, and *Repentance* of a Sinner, yet the efficacy is owing to the *Minifterial Office*, and that *Commiffion* our Lord has left with the Church, and who has fent us, as God fent him, *to be able Minifters of the New Teftament, and Stewards of the myfteries of God.*

But ftill fome Man will fay, *this Man Blafphemeth, who can forgive Sins, but God only?* How dares one like ourfelves, perhaps as bad as ourfelves, ftanding in need of that Abfolution he pretends to give, ufurp thus upon God, and fuppofe himfelf able to remit Sin, which being a Crime againft God, he alone, who is offended, can effectually Pardon? Thus we difpute againft the *Perfons* of Men, without regard to the *Commiffions* that are given 'em. But we forget, that whatever *Equality* there is otherwife between Man and Man, yet the *King's Seal* makes a vaft difference. Neither is it good Manners to queftion any Man's Merit, or enquire boldly, how the King came to prefer him. 'Tis fufficient in fuch cafes, the thing is actually fo, and 'tis our Duty to fubmit with modefty and patience to this delegated Power. Every Sin is a Crime againft God; and God alone can forgive it, and fo far the Doctrine of the Scribes and Pharifees was found and true; tho' no Objection againft Chrift, who was the *Meffias*, and fent from God. That *Miffion* was *his Power*; and it is *Ours*, becaufe as the *Father* hath fent *him*, fo hath *he* fent *us*: So that 'tis no Blafphemy, or Ufurpation of God's Prerogative of Pardoning Sin, becaufe his *Minifters* Pardon 'em too, no more than it pinches on the *King's* Greatnefs, that others Act by *Commiffion* under him. We forgive Sins by *appointment and delegation* from God;

we

we abſolve in *his right* and confeſſedly *in his Name*, we acknowledge our Power derived from him, and we own that without his *fiat* and ratification, all we ſay ſignifies nothing. But then we are ſure he doth confirm it, becauſe in the very inſtitution it ſelf, he tells, that *whoſeſoever Sins ye remit*, &c. which are words rehearſed at every *Prieſts Ordination*, and are not ſaid in vain.

(*i*) Yet I know, God can do what he deſigns as well *without* means as *with* them. He can ſave *without Baptiſm* and the *Euchariſt*. He can Pardon *without the Miniſters Abſolution*. But theſe are *extraordinary Caſes*; neither do we pretend to tie *him* to Rules, though *we* are tied to 'em. With reſpeſt then to *theſe Rules*, and the beaten way of Salvation God has put us in, there is no ſafety without theſe means where they may be had, and it is fatal to negleſt 'em, becauſe God who makes Ordinances expeſts we ſhould keep them; and he therefore makes 'em to try our Obedience which is the main end of all his Appointments. And if we ſlight 'em, the contempt refleſts on the Ordainer, who made 'em Rules for us to walk by, and *as ſuch*, we ſhould not venture to tranſgreſs 'em.

And this being allowed, it clears the *ſecond exception* againſt going to Church, becauſe the *Bible*, and ſome diſcourſes on it extant in print, may be as well, if not better read at home. (*k*) For admit the Scripture to be the ſame on the *Publick desk* and on our *Private Tables*; and that it is *as much* the word of God, in *one* place as in the *other*, yet conſidering that God has a regard to the *Circumſtances* of his Service, as well as the *ſervice* it

---

(*i*) *Gratia dei non alligatur medijs.* (*k*) Vid. *Jewel's* Anſwer to Dr. *Cole's* ſecond Letter.

ſelf;

felf; and that he calls for *holy Convocations,* and *Religious Assemblies* for the *hearing, reading* and *learning* of his Will; upon this account the ufe of the Scripture is *not the fame* at *home,* and in the *Church,* becaufe in the latter our Obedience to the Ordinance weighs down the Scale. And fo as to *Sermons* ; grant fome printed Difcourfes better in your Sence, becaufe of the *Author*'s Name ; the fublimenefs and ftrength of his *Matter,* the politenefs and fweetnefs of his *Language,* and other Flowers, which Charm fuch Readers, as in exercifes of this kind propofe to themfelves no more than pleafure ; yet *thefe* fall very fhort of what we may hear from the *Pulpit;* nor are they, as to religious Edification, in any refpect comparable to it. Becaufe in going to the *publick places* of Worfhip to hear the word, we do it in *Obedience* to a *Divine Ordinance;* and therefore how weak foever in common Opinion, the *Sermon, as preach'd* may feem to be, yet 'tis more likely to benefit him, who comes to it with due attention and care. For the *Bleffed Spirit,* that came down from Heaven at firft *in a found,* many times in the *fame manner* enters the Hearts of Believers; and while the *Voice* affects the *Ear,* it pleafes God to let the inftruction fink into the *Heart* to engage the affections, and make 'em at once both *wifer and better.* The weaknefs of the *Preacher,* is not for the moft part fo great a Bar to Edification, as want of Faith in the *hearer.* Alas ! In ftrictnefs, 'tis neither Voice nor Language can move the Confcience, let 'em be never fo fweet, and *Charm they never fo wifely.* That is *God*'s Work by the Minifters mouth. And while we foberly and dutifully attend, as to the *fenfible* inftrument of an *invifible Power,* we feem not fo much to hearken to *him,* whofe Voice it immediately is, as to *God* himfelf who ufes that Voice, for the information of his People.

The

The Sermons, the Apoſtles Preach'd were ·very
Lcm, and wanted that *Stile* and *Elegancy,* which might
·be read in the ·writings ·of *Philoſophers,* yet God
converted Thouſands by the *baſeneſs,* by the *fooliſh-*
neſs of their Preaching. Their words were with
·Power, becauſe they had a Bleſſing; and, how
mean ſoever· their *Perſons,* and their *way of Speech*
were, how-*rude*·ſoever they:appear'd in their *Dia-*
lect or Delivery, yet ſtill·they prevailed over the
moſt accompliſhed. *Orators,*·who became their
Proſelytes and· ſubmitted: to Chriſtianity. And
indeed. in *their weakneſs* God manifeſted his ,own
ſtrength,·and the *Power of* ·his Spirit. His Commiſſion was ·enough to give their Diſcourſes efficacy,
whatever their· Education or Abilities were, and
in all this he conſulted his own honour. For where
·the *Miniſter* is a *Learned* or Eloquent Man , we
·ſhould ·be· tempted, perhaps, to give·the·inſtru-
ment that praiſe which belongs to ·God who· uſes
him. As ſome magnified *Paul,* and *Apollos* and
Cephas, ·who forgot *Chriſt* who ſent 'em. But the
unaptneſs of the *Tool,* more recommends the *Art* of
the *Workman*; and ·where God thinks fit, to employ ſuch ·as are made remarkable for their, want
of Knowledge, it is· that·thereby we may be convinced that the *Energy and Power,* is ·purely from
himſelf, and thereupon we are lead to give¯him
the ·Glory.

I have no deſign in what I have ſaid to diſpa-
rage, much leſs cry down, *private Reading,* I only
blame the ill timing of it, and ſhow that it ought
not to interfere, or ſtand in competition with the
publick Leſſons we have in the Church at the hours
of Prayer and Preaching. ·And in this I, apply,
that of Chriſt, *this is to be done, and the other not left*
undone. ·

But there is one inftance wherein ,you allow the neceffity of the Miniftry, and that is the *Sacraments, one* of which you have already received, and would be glad to have the benefit of the *other*, but that the fenfe of your *unworthinefs* keeps you away. And truely who is *worthy* the leaft of all God's Mercies, much lefs of this, if *Merit* be properly and ftrictly taken ? Yet fince God is gracioufly pleafed to accept us as we are, and affectionately calls us to this holy Table, is it not ftupidity and Ingratitude to flight the invitation ; indeed is it not a piece of *unworthinefs* to reject the Offer ? This is a very ftrange Contradiction, that this *Sacrament* fhould be called *the Bread of Life*, and yet we fay, that *in the day we eat thereof we fhall furely die.* The State of Chriftianity is vaftly different from what it was in *former Ages*, when they came fo frequently to it, that it was called [ἡμεϱινὴ θυσία] the *daily Sacrifice*, becaufe every Day they received it ; and in fuch *Multitudes* , and with fo much *eagernefs*, that we muft confefs their *earneftnefs and hafte* degenerated into a *fault*, and though their *attendance* was *conftant* and *dutiful*, yet their *zeal* was intemperate and wanted *knowledge*, and that was the reafon of St. *Paul's* caution, (*l*) *He that eateth and drinking unworthily, eateth and drinketh Damnation to himfelf* ——words never intended to *frighten* us from the Communion, on the account of that Unworthinefs we cannot avoid, but to oblige us to *come* to it with greater reverence, by not being guilty of *that kind of Unworthinefs*, which becomes *good manners* as little as *Religion*, and is no more to be indured at our *Own* than at the *Lord's-Table*. But we catch at any thing, and take fo much of the holy Writer as ferves our turn, omit-

---

(*l*) 1 Cor. 1 : 29|

ting

ting that wherewith the Apostle explain'd his *Unworthiness*, which was in truth nothing else but *inadvertency* and *want of Thought*, for the sentence runs thus. *He that eateth and drinketh unworthily, eateth and drinketh Damnation to himself* —Οὐ διακείνων, *not discerning the Lord's Body.* There lay their *unworthiness*, that they did not *consider* what they were eating and drinking. They employed their *Senses* only in that sacred Action. They went no further than *tast and sight ?* (m) They eat it as *Bread,* and they drunk it as *Wine*, without remembring that now it was *more* than *Bread and Wine*, as being *consecrated* to the uses of Religion, and or-dain'd to feed the Soul.

But to discharge this place of St. *Paul*, from the sence you put on it, let us examine the reason why the Apostle thus exprest himself, and whe-ther we deal fairly with him, to wrest his Autho-rity for abetting our neglect, and coolness in this great duty of Christianity.

It appears then, that at the Church of *Corinth*, when People came to the Sacrament, there were great feuds and heats among 'em on the account of their several *qualities and degrees* in the World, as the place is (n) generally understood ; for the *rich* despised the *poor*, look'd big, and thought it disgrace to communicate with 'em : the Apostles words are, *When you come together in the Church, I hear there are divisions among you, and I partly believe it* —— *v.* 18. so that hereby one great end of the Sacra-ment was lost, for not considering it the *Lord's Body*, given and thus administred to *unite* 'em all to *him*, and engage their affections to *one another*, whatever their *fortunes* and *conditions* were. For tho'

(m) *Indignè dicit acceptum ab ijs qui hoc non discerne-bant à cæteris cibis*—— Aug. ad Jan. (n) Vid. Piscator. Estium. A Lapid. Calvin.————

riches and *honour*, are very great Advantages and Comforts here, yet they are merely *accidental*; neither do they make the Soul better, nor prefer one before another in the fight of God, who invites us without diftinction, and teaches us to make no difference in thefe cafes, becaufe he himfelf hath made none. This the *Corinthians* it feems were guilty of, and he blames 'em for it, and the rather, becaufe they did it at a *time*, and in a *place*, where they were receiving fo great a *Teftimony* of God's *Condefcenfion* and *Love* to them, and therefore they ought to have been more humble, and charitable towards one another.

Nor was this all. For they came with fo much *irreverence and diforder*, that it was not to be born at any *Common Table*. They crowded in with fuch *Violence* and *Appetite*, that they had neither patience nor manners to ftay for one another, but the *firft Comer*, firft ferved himfelf, and in fuch *quantities*, that they not only confulted their *natural hunger and thirft*, but *debauch'd* themfelves with it to intemperance and *Drunkennefs*. *Is this to eat the Lord's-Supper,* faith the Apoftle, *for in eating every one taketh before other, and one is hungry, another is drunken. What, have you not houfes to eat and drink in? Or defpife you the Church of God,* &c. So that we fee St. *Paul's unworthinefs,* is oppofed directly to *this behaviour* of the *Corinthians,* which was not tolerable at *any* Feaft, or before *any* Company whatever. I think any fober Man, who has no prejudice nor wilfulnefs, nor affectation in his arguing will eafily difcover this to be the true meaning of that frightful expreffion; efpecially if he cafts his Eye on the laft verfe of that Chapter, where it is faid, *if any Man hunger, let him eat at home, that you come not together into Condemnation.* By which we find that their approach to the Communion with carnal defires, as to the ordinary

Z food

food of humane Life, was *that unworthiness*, the holy Man reflects on, and the charge against them was, that they did not discern the *Bread* and *Wine*, to be *Sacramentally* the *Lord's Body and Blood*, during the sacred Action.

And if this was St. *Paul's* notion of *Unworthiness*, how miserable, and unjust is the construction we put on't, and how vain the objection we draw from these *Occasional* words to keep us from receiving? We dare not come, because *unworthy*, and we are afraid of Damnation. But it would better sute our Christianity to argue the other way; And because the *unworthiness*, the Apostle speaks of, is *not discerning the Lord's-Body*, then the consequence is, that *to discern*, and consider it in that manner, I proposed, will be a *Sacramental capacity* to fit us for the holy Communion.

How this is to be done, the Apostle in that Chapter partly shews us. For after he had reproved the *Corinthians* for coming to the Sacrament, as to *common Bread and Wine*, he proceeds to instruct 'em in the *nature* and *end* of the holy mystery, by an *Historical* account of its *Institution*. And first he tells 'em, as to the *thing it self*, that when Christ had finished the *Paschal Supper*, *he took Bread and Blessed it, and gave it to his Disciples* to eat, and called it *his Body*, as he did also the *Cup* which he styled his *Blood*. So that after Consecration, they were to look on those *Elements*, not altogether what they seemed to be, but somewhat *more* now, in the sacred use of 'em, the *Bread* as *the Body*, and the *Wine* as *the Blood* of their crucified Redeemer. Then as to the *end and design* of it; it was to remember Christ—*do this in Remembrance of me*———How Remember him? In his *Passion and Death*; for in *eating this Bread*, and *Drinking this Cup*, *ye do shew forth the Lord's-Death till he come.*——— For want of weighing these two things, *what*

what they were receiving, and to what *purpofe* it was done, the converts at *Corinth*, run themfelves into that danger the Apoftle warns 'em of, I mean *Damnation.* And therefore the *caution* given *them*, and which concerns *us* on this occafion is, that we do not approach the Sacrament without *difcerning the Lord's Body*——And what that means , and how thereby we may be fafe in the difcharge of this Duty, were it not late, and that I could per-fwade my felf it might be ferviceable to you, I would not grudge my pains to lay it before you ; and if defired, fhall be ready to do it at our next Meeting, whenever Providence gives the oppor-tunity and brings us together.

B. I wifh this Evening would have born it ; but I make it my requeft that it may be to *Morrow.*

A. I know nothing to the contrary, but it may be fo. At prefent,

FAREWELL.

The

TheFourth DIALOGUE.

The CONTENTS.

A continuation of the former Subject.

WHAT it is to difcern the Lord's Body. To difcern it, is a Sacramental capacity. The Church of England vindicated from over eafy Admiffion of People to the Holy Communion, as appears by her feveral Exhortations. Two Objections againft the Churches way of Adminiftration. Firft, The Minifter's diftributing the Elements to the feveral Communicants. Secondly, The Communicants taking it kneeling. Thefe two points explain'd by the practice of the Jews at the Paffover, to which the Sacrament alludes. Two Suppers at the Paffover. Two Wafhings. Chrift Wafhed his Difciples Feet, at the Conclufion of the fecond or common Supper. Whether Judas received the Sacrament. Authorities againft and for it The Objections. Thofe Objections Anfwered. Ill Men muft not be fuffered to Communicate. St. Chryfoftom's Refolution in that Cafe. St. Auguftine's Method. The example of St. Ambrofe, how he dealt with the Emperour Theodofius on this occafion. Prefumptions of a Man's being Wicked, are not fufficient for the Minifter to bar him the Holy Communion. St. Auguftine's Judgment. The Sacrament Judas took, was not the Sop. The Agapæ of the
Primitive

the

the Sacrament. *An Objection from the practice of the Church; standing at Prayers between* Easter *and* Whitsuntide, *and every Lord's-day, whereon to be sure the Sacrament was Administred. The Objection Answered.* Honorius's *Decree about the Adoration of the Host considered.* St. Chrysostom's *standing at the Altar cleared.*

A. I Doubt I disturb you in your Reading.

B. No, good Sir, The *Subject* I am upon will quickly convince you, that I expected and desired your Company. For this *little Book* you see, are *the Epistles* of the Apostle *Paul*; and I was examining what you were setting forth *last Evening,* concerning the *behaviour* of the People at *Corinth,* while they were *Communicants* at the *Lord's-Supper*; and I find your interpretation warrantable from the Passages of that Chapter, and that the notion of their *unworthiness,* was, the *not discerning the Lord's Body,* i. e. They looked on the *Elements* with an ordinary and carnal Eye; they did *Eat* the *Bread,* and *Drank* the *Cup,* without the relation they had to the *Body* and *Blood* of *Christ,* and so not regarding them, as the *signs* of something more Excellent, than what their *Senses* presented them with, they were disorderly and intemperate in their *Eating* and *Drinking.* However, Sir, for further explanation of this weighty point; I must entreat you to renew your Discourse, according to promise, and make me understand *that,* which you called a *Sacramental capacity,* or such a kind of *worthiness,* as will give us a *safe* admittance to the holy Communion : Or, in the Scripture Language, What it is to *discern the Lord's Body,* for want of knowing which, a Man Eats and Drinks *unworthily,* and in so doing, *he eats and drinks Damnation to himself.*

A. To

A. To proceed then where we left off———
We are to confider the *Bread* and *Wine* in the
Bleffed Sacrament, to be the *Body* and *Blood* of
Chrift ; not in that fenfe of the People at *Capernaum*, mentioned in *John* 6. 52. but according
to our *Lord's* own interpretation of it, *Spiritually*
and *by Faith*. (o) For *to eat the Bread of Life, is
to believe in him* —— and fo it is obferved, that
Chrift had no fooner called himfelf the *Bread from
Heaven*, but he immediately adds, *he that cometh
to me, and he that believeth on me, fhall never hunger, and fhall never thirft* —— fo that *believing* in
him, is *the eating him to eternal Life*, as the eating
of the *fign*, or *Bread*, is for the fupport of *temporal* Life. To *difcern* therefore the *Body* and *Blood*
of *Chrift* in this holy Ordinance, we muft imploy
the *mind*, rather than the Eye ; and while we
grind the *Bread* with our *Teeth*, we are to eat the
Body of *Chrift* by *Faith*. If we think the *Eating* of
the *Bread* fufficient, we then conclude it his *real
Flefh*, and are content with the *Opus Operatum*, or
bare act of receiving. And as to this, our *Lord*
is pofitive, *the Flefh profiteth nothing*. But if we
eat the *Bread* by way of *Emblem*, and as it *fignifies*
a more durable and noble food , which concerns
the *Soul*, then we confider the two parts of that
Sacrament ; and though we fwallow the Bread *as
Bread*, yet we difcover fomewhat *more* than *Bread*
in the facred *myftery* ; and by acknowledging the
ftrict relation between the *fign*, and the *thing* (I
mean the *Bread* and the *Body* of *Chrift*) in taking
the *one* reverently, we by confequence receive effectually the *other*. And by this means, we keep
our felves from thofe *two Errours*, on this Subject,

(o) *Manducare panem iftum eft credere in eum*——Aug. in
Johan. 6.

recorded

recorded in the Gospel ; becaufe on the *one hand,* we confefs the *Bread* and *Wine,* to *continue* fuch, even *after* Confecration, with refpect to their own Nature (which probably was the miftake of thofe at *Capernaum*) and on the *other hand,* we find the *Elements* to be *more* than *Bread* and *Wine,* in the ufe and Application, which thofe of *Corinth* did not Remember, and through that inadvertency indangered their Condition, by abufing the *Bread* and *Wine,* which in the *myftery* referred to the *Body* and *Blood* of *Chrift,* and thereupon, as he himfelf was pleafed to tell his Difciples, *he that defpifeth you, defpifeth me ; and he that defpifeth me, defpifeth him that fent me* ——Though they that flighted *Man,* did not think to reflect upon *God,* yet certainly fo it was, becaufe of that ftrict *Union* between *God* and *Chrift ;* and between *Chrift* and his *Difciples :* So he that either neglects, or carries himfelf *irreverently,* at the holy *Table,* while he *eats* the *Bread* and *drinks* the *Wine,* may be faid to defpife or difhonour, even *Chrift's Body* and *Blood,* becaufe the *Bread* and *Wine* relate, and are the *figns* of 'em at the Moments of receiving ; and therefore on this account, that Perfon (whoever he be) indangers his Salvation.

Again, *to difcern* well the *Lord's Body,* in the holy *Sacrament,* we are withal to confider the *reafon* of that facred action. *The reafon of the Sacrament* is, *to put us in mind of Chrift's Paffion and Death,* and *to fhow* that his *Body* was once *broken* on the *Crofs,* and his *Blood fled* for our *Redemption.* A thing which ought never to be forgotten. And in order to help our frail Memories, this *Myftery* was appointed, wherein the *broken Bread* is an *Emblem* of his *torn Body,* and the *Wine poured out,* a *Reprefentation* of the *fhedding* of his *Blood* to become the *Saviour* of Man. So that barely to *Eat* and *Drink* is not enough, without confidering,

why

why we eat and drink, that our Hearts may be imprest with the unfpeakable *Mercy* fhown us in the *Sacrifice* and *Death* of *Chrift*. In a word, this confideration, not only fets before us the *Bread* and *Wine*, as the *Body* and *Blood* of *Chrift*, but further reprefents the *Body broken*, and the *Blood fhed* for the Remiffion of Sins.

Nor is this all. We confider moreover, that *in this Action* we not only remember *Chrift's Body* Sacrificed for us, but we eat his *Flefh* with *full Affurance*, that though *Chrift's Body* was *Dead* and *Buried*, yet it *arofe again, afcended* to a Life Immortal, and is made the *Seed of Eternal Life* to every *Chriftian*, who rightly applies, and faithfully eats it at the B. Sacrament. For we argue thus, that if *this Body*, by the Power of the *God-head* joined to it, raifed *it felf* to a Life of Glory, therefore *every good Communicant*, who receives this *Body*, fhall be, by the fame Energy, *rais'd up* with him to the like Condition. And this is the reafon, why our *Lord* called himfelf the *Living-Bread*, becaufe he who *eats his Flefh* and *drinks his Blood fhall live for ever*, it being impoffible for that *Body* to mifcarry, which has well entertained this powerful *principle of Life* and *Immortality*.

It muft be added; That in the performance of this holy Duty. We not only look on the *Sacrament* in the way of *myftery*, and as an *Emblem* or *Signification* of the *Death of Chrift*, in his *Body broken*, and his *Blood fpilt* for us, but, as was faid, we further inquire into the true *Occafion* of thofe Sufferings, or *Why* his Blood was fpilt, and his Body broken. And as on the *one* fide, we find therein, that this was done out of Mercy and Pity to us; fo on the *other* we may eafily difcern thofe neceffities of ours, which called for this miraculous Affiftance, without which we could not be recovered. Now a ferious Meditation on thefe two points,

points, muſt needs have on us a double influence;
Firſt, To make us *thankful* to God, and move us
to *love* him, who *ſo loved* us: And *Secondly*,
When we call to Mind, that *our Sins* were the
Cauſe of that Bloody uſage towards the Body of
our Redeemer, which at the *Sacrament* we repreſent in the *broken Bread* and the *Wine poured out*,
ſuch a reflection may invite us to abandon our *Sins*,
and not think on 'em, but with amazement and
horrour, leſt we ſhould be thought *Acceſſory* and
conſenting to his Death, nay, *Crucifie him a freſh and
put him to an open ſhame.* Beſides; we go to the *Sacrament*, as a *Pledge* of our Pardon, and as a *means*
to apply the Merits of *Chriſt's Body given* and *broken*; and we conclude after this manner; That if
the *Sacrifice* of *Chriſt's Body* on the Croſs, was in
the *general* a ſufficient *Atonement* for the Sins of the
whole World, Therefore the *particular* application of
it, as in the *Sacrament*, will certainly do for my Sins.
in the *individual*, if I ſincerely and heartly take
it. Which if a Man doth, and approacheth the
Holy Table, with an humble earneſtneſs to be rid
of his *Sins*, for which *Chriſt* died, and whoſe
Death is *there* commemorated, he will be induced
to do what he can to leave his *Sins* behind him,
when he goes to the *Communion*, and not only
ſuſpend but renounce them for ever.

In all which, you ſee the *Sacrament* is a *Subject*
which calls for our moſt *diſcerning Thoughts*, and
a very ſerious Application. A Chriſtian before
he goes to it, is to take all the ways he can by *Advice*, *Book*, *Meditation*, and by the help of *all* of
them together, to inform himſelf, *what* he is going to do, and *whither* he is going. Not to approach it, hand over head, as we ſay, with little *Zeal* and leſs *Knowledge*; for want of which
Knowledge, I cannot ſee, how a Man can be, in a
Religious ſenſe, *Zealous* at all. *Firſt*, We examine

mine *what* the Sacrament is *in it self*, we indeavour to *difcern that*; and *then* we examine *ourfelves*, whether we fo confider it. We find the food *Myftical* and *Spiritual*; we go therefore to it with *Spiritual Appetites*, with the hunger and thirft of the *Soul*, and with a *full perfwafion*, that though the *mouth* receives, yet the *Spirit* is fed in it; we *difcern* therein the great *condefcenfion* of Almighty *God, firft* in taking, and *then* in giving his *Body* and *Blood* for us; and fo confidering the debafement of the *God-head* under this veil of Flefh, upon a little further inquiry, we cannot but difcover, that exceeding *Love*, which inclined and ingaged him to it. This thought will oblige our affections to him, as alfo to one another, as the moft intelligible and vifible teftimony of our being devoted to him. And in a word, finding it a *Feaft of Love*, we fhall be induced to Love God and our Neighbour.

And to come to a Period. The Religious enquirer is made fenfible that the *Sacrament* is an *Holy-Feaft*, and thereupon as to what concerns him, he thinks it his bufinefs at that time to make, it *Holy*, which is not rarely the meaning of the word δακείνων. He puts a great difference between *this* Table and his *own*, between *this Bread* and his *own*; and he futes his Appetite to the *Meat*, and his refpects to the *Company*. The *Bread* is the *Body* of *Chrift*; The Company is *God*, and his Holy *Angels*, lefs *Vifible*, but not lefs *Prefent* than thofe who Communicate with us. This is the Difference we do and ought to make of the *Lord's Body*, for fo we call *this Sacrament*, from the ftrict Friendfhip between the *fign* and the *thing*; fo that, as I faid, the contempt fhown the *one* will reach the *other*; as on the contrary, the refpect we give *it* will redound to our good, to *whom* it is indeed the *Flefh* of *Chrift*, and *the Bread which came down from Heaven, and which if a Man eat, he fhall never die.——* B. It

B. It is to be feared, Men go not to the Communion with these Thoughts ; becaufe, if they did, they could not be guilty of thofe many *Enormities,* we daily find 'em chargeable with almoft as foon as the *Sacred Action* is over.

A. (p) Secrets belong to God, and he alone *Searches the Heart,* we cannot dive into the Confciences of People ; and although in God's fight Men *appear* what they *are,* yet on our parts it becomes us to take them for what they *appear.* Their carriage then at the *Holy Sacrament* being *outwardly* fober, our *charity* Commands us to believe them *inwardly* pious, and to hope what is fo far well done, they do it by *principle,* and not out of any Worldly or *carnal defign.* If their *after* practice contradicts this Opinion, yet that is no warrant for us to judge them Hypocrites *before.* For *good Thoughts,* and a *remifs carriage* have too often their *Turns* and Succeffions. The *Spirit* is fometimes *willing,* when the *Flefh* is *weak.* And a vertuous refolution is frequently run down by an impetuous, vicious Habit, efpecially when the tempter puts on double diligence, and ufes his utmoft efforts to reduce them, when he finds 'em in fo fair a way to renounce him, and his intereft for the future. No *Cuftom* is eafily broken. And therefore though Men may be fenfible of their Errours, are willing to leave them, and do fome part of the Duty they owe *God* and the *Soul,* if they continue not, without fome excurfions, in that good way they are entred on, the reafon is, becaufe it requires no little time to *undo* ill *Habits,* as well as to *make* 'em. And if they can be perfwaded, to be conftant at the *Sacrament,* and in order thereto, confider and provide for it, it is not to be much doubted, but in

---

(p)*De occultis non judicat Ecclefia,*&c. *Bucan.Loc.Com.* 48.

due time a better Habit may ſucceed, and notwithſtanding ſome *relapſes* or intervening failures,
the *Grace* of God, which *left* them by Degrees,
may in the ſame Method *return* again. However
the *Parable* of our *Lord* tells us, there will be
Tares, among the *Wheat*; and it is the Work of
the *Angels at the laſt day,* to *make a ſeparation* and
diſtinction between them. But let the worſt be
granted ; there can be in the mean while no reflection on the *Church* or *Miniſters*, upon this account ; becauſe where Sins are committed, and
yet have not reached the *Miniſters* Knowledge,
he gives thoſe *ſecret Offenders* ſuch warning as this;
(*q*) That their *danger is great if they receive the
ſame unworthily, for then they are guilty of the Body
and Blood of Chriſt their Saviour, they eat and drink
their own Damnation, not conſidering the Lord's Body.
They kindle God's Wrath againſt 'em ; they provoke him
to plague them with diverſe Diſeaſes and ſundry kinds
of Death*——He exhorts 'em therefore, out of *St.*
Paul, to *try and examine themſelves, before they preſume to eat of that Bread and drink of that Cup*——
(*r*) and ſaith he,. *If any of you be a Blaſphemer of
God, an hinderer or ſlanderer of his word, an
Adulterer, or be in malice or envy or any other grievous
crime, repent you of your Sins, or elſe come not to this
Table, leſt after the taking of the holy Sacrament the
Devil enter into you as he entred into* Judas, *and fill
you full of all iniquity, and bring you to deſtruction both
of Body and Soul* ——— This is the care taken in
caſe of private Offences, induſtriouſly concealed
from the Eye of the World ; and what can the
Church do more, in theſe inſtances, than to ſet before them the *Divine-vengeance*, if they venture to
come with ſo much *guilt* to the ſacred Table. But

(*q*) 3. Exhort before Com. (*r*) 1. Exhort.

where

where Sins are *open* and scandalous, another Method is used ; and the (*s*) *Canon* requires, that *no Minister shall, in any wise, admit to the receiving of the holy Communion, any of his Cure or Flock, which be openly known to live in Sin notorious, without repentance, nor any who have maliciously and openly contended with their Neighbour , until they shall be reconciled.* Agreable to what is in the Rubrick before the Communion——(*t*) *And if any be an open, and notorious evil liver , or have done any wrong to his Neighbour, by word or deed, so that the Congregation be thereby offended , the Curate having knowledge thereof, shall call him, and advertise him that in any wise he presume not to come to the Lord's Table, until he have openly declared himself to have truly repented, and amended his former naughty Life , that the Congregation may thereby be satisfied, which before were offended ; and that he hath recompenced the parties, to whom he hath done wrong, or at least declare himself to be in full purpose so to do, as soon as he conveniently may———* (*u*) *The same order the Curate shall use with those, betwixt whom he perceiveth malice and hatred to Reign, not suffering them to be partakers of the Lord's Table, until he know them to be reconciled——* (*w*) So it was ordered in the injunctions given by King *Edward* VI. *Also, forasmuch as variance and contention is a thing, which most displeaseth God and is most contrary to the Blessed Communion of the Body and Blood of Christ our Saviour : Curates shall in no wise admit to the receiving thereof any of their Cure and Flock, who hath maliciously and openly contended with his Neighbour, unless the same do first charitably and openly reconcile himself again, remitting all rancour and malice , whatever Controversy hath been*

(*s*) Can. 26. (*t*) Second Rubr. (*u*) Third Rubr. (*w*) Ann. 1547.

between

between them : *And neverthelefs, their juft Titles and Rights, they may charitably profecute, before fuch as have Authority to hear the fame.* ————

All which *Orders* and *Rules*, if neglected by fome *Minifters*, the fault you fee, is not in the *Conftitution*, but *Men* : Yet *many* punctually obferve 'em ; at leaft in *fuch a way* as the perverfenefs of the Age will bear, I mean, the *Admonition* is managed with prudence and *tendernefs*, fo as the Offender may not through too much rigour and fhame be tempted, to add *Obftinacy* to his Sin, and being roughly handled, grow much more incorrigible, than otherwife he might have been.

But to fay, what you have obferved, that moft Men are wretchedly impious, even upon the moft extraordinary Acts of Religion ; and *after* the *Sacrament* relapfe to their old Courfes ; what can a fober Man infer, but the general decay, whereby *found Principles* and *good Manners*, yield to *corrupt Nature*, and People are hurried in this Manner, to what will end in their Eternal difgrace and pain. A Man that is fenfible of this *Univerfal degeneracy*, is bound to blefs *God* that his Circumftances and Temper is better than what *others* have ; but then his *Charity* inclines him, to Pity and Lament the Condition of his *Neighbour*, (*x*) and the more carelefs he finds the *other* in the difcharge of his Duty, the more diligent *he* will be in doing of his *own*, that by his *example*, at leaft, God may be glorified in the midft of a perverfe generation.

'Tis furely a very odd way in me to forbear Religion, becaufe others refrain it ; and at the fame time to find fault with my Neighbour for *his* neglect, and yet *my felf imitate* him in it. Moft *Chri-*

(*x*) Vid. Lactant. de cultu vero, c. 18.

ftians

ftians either come not at all to the *Holy Communion,* or if they do, it appears plainly, they live
not *anfwerably* to it.   Is this an excufe to keep me
away, who perhaps have better Thoughts, and
Grace enough to fee the common mifcarriages, and
withal do abhor 'em ? Shall I neither *eat* nor *drink,*
becaufe others *furfeit* in fo doing ? And mvft I never approach the *Sacrament,* becaufe of my Company, whofe goodnefs I fufpect, and think them
not fincere enough in that facred Application ?
This is too much *like* the *Pharifee;* nay 'tis fomewhat *worfe* than he, becaufe, though he bragged
of a way of Life much before that of the *publican,*
yet 'twas no fcandal to him to find *that Sinner* in
the Temple; Nor was the *Publican's* being *there*
any reafon that *he* fhould *ftay away.*

I intend no reflection on you, whom the Senfe
of your *unworthinefs* keeps from the Sacrament, and
who blame others, for not being as fenfible as you
are. Yet let me take the liberty to add this,
That even *thofe* you fpeak of, *comply* with a *Divine Ordinance* by their outward appearance at the
Holy Communion, which is a piece of *Homage*
done to *Chrift,* and fo far they own him to be
their *Lord* and *Redeemer.* And though their behaviour is amifs *afterwards,* yet 'tis not fafe for us
to Condemn what they did *before* (z) *If a Man fay*
(as the Church fpeaks) *I am a grievous Sinner, or I
am not worthy, and therefore am afraid to come,
wherefore do you not repent and amend ? When God
calleth you, are you not afhamed to fay you are not
ready ?*

(z) Second Exhort. poft. Com.

It

It is obfervable in the *Parable*, that when the Men *excufed* themfelves, for their non-attendance at the *Wedding-Feaft*, the *King* was very Angry; and pronounced them all *u worthy* ; and upon no *other* account, but *becaufe* they would not come: (*a*) Their *Apologies* incenfed him ; and becaufe they *flighted* his Supper , on that account they made themfelves unfit for it. And we muft take notice further, that when the *Servants*, (according to their Lord's Order) went out into the *High ways*, and gathered together all, as many as they found both *Bad* and *Good*, whereby the wedding was furnifhed, yet of all this *mixt* multitude, *One only* Man had not on a *Wedding-Garment.* So gracious was the *King*, not fo much to confider the People themfelves, as their *cheerful regard* to the invitation he fent 'em. I need not tell you this *King* was *God*. The *Feaft* he made may be well conftrued into the Holy *Sacrament.* How he underftood the *unworthinefs* of his guefts, is plainly difcovered from the difpleafure he took at their abfence, tho' their feem'd fomething of *good Manners*, in the excufes they returned him. And with what a favourable Eye he beholds our Obedience, is it not feen in this , that out of fuch a *number*, and fuch *variety* of Men, he rejected but *One*, for being impudent and a floven. Remember, my Friend, what the word faith, *To obey is better than Sacrifice.* And where is that *unworthinefs* you and others alledge, when the *Will* is good, and the *Heart* willing ? He that fhows this good difpofition, and *prepareth his Heart to feek God, the Lord God of his Fathers*, it is not to be doubted, but that Prayer will be heard, which King *Hezekiah* once

***

(*a*) *Qua, fci. illam contemnendo eadem fe ficere nd gnot.* A *Lap.*

A a   offered

offered up on the like occasion, namely, That the *Lord* will *Pardon* him, *though he be not cleansed, according to the Purification of the Sanctuary.*

  B. I must confess the *Parable* inviting. And if that *Marriage-Feast* be applied to this *Religious Supper,* it bespeaks a great *unworthiness, not to accept the invitation.*

  But if a Man were disposed for that *Ordinance,* the *Manner* of Administring it, is no small *Obstacle* or hindrance. For the *Method* being *altered,* which the *Lord* himself was pleased to use at the time of *Institution,* it is apt to create offence to the Conscientious Communicant, to see no regard had to what he *did*; and when he finds the *Church* taking such *liberty,* as makes it quite another thing than what it at *first* was, he thinks he may venture on the same *liberty* to stay away, out of a reasonable distrust, that the efficacy of the *Sacrament* is utterly lost, by such an affected and *needless change* in it. I instance in two things; *One* is the *Ministers delivering the Bread and Cup to every Communicant,* and using a *form of words,* to each of 'em, when he delivers it, whereas our *Lord* said in the *Plural* (b) *Take, eat and divide it between you* — leaving it to the *Disciples* to serve themselves with Bread and Wine, set before 'em for that purpose on the Table. The *other* is, that we are obliged to eat and drink, *Kneeling,* expresly against the gesture of the *Text,* which represents it *sitting.* For so *Matthew, Now when the even was come, he sate down with the Twelve:* And *Luke — He sate down, and the Twelve Apostles with him*; which is indeed a *Table gesture,* and better suits the notion of a *Feast,* and the *Fellonship* supposed to be among those, who eat and drink together.

(b) Matth. 26 26. Luke 22. 17.

A. In the Ecclesiastical Rites, † faith Origen, *There are many things requisite to be done, though every Body doth not apprehend the reafon of them;* and among the reft, he inftances the *Ceremonies* ufed at the Holy *Euchariſt.* Of which though we fhould not be able to give a precife account, yet that's no ground for us to quarrel with 'em. Without doubt the *Church* of God hath a very great Power in her hands; to make *Rules* for *decency*; and as to the *particular* we are upon, you fee we celebrate the *Sacrament* in the *Forenoon*, not in the *Evening*; and *Faſting*, not *after Supper*, though it is evident that at the *firſt inſtitution* it was quite otherwife. And this St. *Auguſtine* calls an *Apoſtolical Tradition*, which though fome *African Churches*, in his time, did not intirely obferve, but (according to the Canon of a Council at (*c*) *Carthage*) upon the *Thurſday* before *Eaſter*, gave the *Sacrament* at *Evening* and *after Supper*, as the livelier Reprefentation of what *Chriſt* had done; yet the *Council* (*d*) *in Trullo*, took away the exception, as a Deviation from the Ancient Practice, and ordered the Sacrament to be taken *Faſting*, as well on that day as the reſt. *We, following the Traditions of the Apoſtles and Fathers, Decree, that they ſhall not break their faſt on the fifth day at the end of Lent——* (*e*) *Tertullian* indeed faith, the *Euchariſt* was given ordinarily [*Tempore Victus*] *at Meals*; and the practice in all likelihood was grounded on St. *Paul*'s Language, who calls it *Supper* in his time, 1 *Cor.* 11. But *St. Chryſoſtom*'s Judgment on the place is, that the Apoſtle did not name it *Supper*, becaufe adminiſtred *in the Evening*, but with refpect to the *time* of the *inſtitution*, which the *Goſpel*

---

† In Num. (*c*) Conc. Carthag Can. 44. (*d*) Concil. Conſtant. Can. 29. (*e*) De coro. Mil.

faith

faith was *after Supper.* Yet *Chriſt* in this *Inſtituti-*
on, as afterwards St. *Paul*, had more regard to
the *thing* it ſelf than the *manner* of it —— *Do this*
in Remembrance of me. ——— And when that end
is anſwered, the *Sacrament* is *Well* Adminiſtred.
And therefore though we ſtill do, and muſt retain the *breaking of Bread*, and *giving* it to the *Com-*
municants, and after it the *Cup*, as a (*f*) *form* ſo
neceſſary to the *Sacrament*, that without it
'twould very much ſuffer, (*g*) yet for other Circumſtances, as the *Upper-room*, the *Number Twelve*,
and the like, we look on them as *indifferent things*,
which may be *omitted* or *changed*, as tends moſt to
Conveniency.——— For Chriſt did not ſay, *do*
this after Supper, or *ſitting*, or being ſo *many* together, neither did the *Apoſtles* ever ſo underſtand
him.—— but *do this* —— and the reſt he left to
diſcretion.

In reverence then to the *Sacrament*, the *Prieſt*
diſtributes *ſingly* the *Bread* and *Wine* to the Company, the better to avoid that confuſion, which
would certainly follow, if they were left to themſelves, as in the caſe of the *Corinthians*, which
the *Apoſtle* obſerved, and the diſorder moved
him. Again, it is Adminiſtred to Communicants *Kneeling*, as being a proper geſture, to *ſig-*
nifie the great ſenſe they, to whom it is handed,
have of the Bleſſing ; and to *teſtifie*, with what
humility of Soul and *Thought* they take it from the
Miniſter, whom *God* hath made the inſtrument to
convey it to them.

(*f*) Vid Forbes. Iren. l. 1. c. 3. (*g*) Chamier l 7 c 15.
de Euchar. & l 8. c. 3. Synopſ. purioris Theol. Diſp 45.
Muſcul. de cœna Dom. Calvin Inſtit. l. 4. c. 17. n. 43. Biſhop
Jewel's reply to *Harding* Art. 2.

But

But becaufe you objeƈt our *Lord's* Method, which we feemingly negleƈt, let us confider *that* a little; and the better to underftand it, we fhall be forced to examin *what* the *Cuftom* of the *Jews* was at the celebration of the *Paffover*, which the aƈtion of *Chrift* in a great meafure refers to, and after *which Supper*, he appointed his *own.*

At the *Paffover* then there were (*h*) *Two Suppers,* The *one* confifted of a *roafted Lamb, an unleavened Cake* and *bitter Herbs* ; and *This was Sacramental.* The *other,* was ordinary and in the way of fupply, to make up a full meal, the Lamb of it felf, not being fufficient for the Company, if the number was not fmall. At the beginning of the *firft,* they had a *Cup* of Wine, which went round the Table; and *this* is it St. *Luke* fpeaks of——— *He took the Cup and faid, take this and divide it among your felves* —— or hand it round till you have all drunk, but was not the Evangelical Cup, for that he was not yet come to, as appears *v.* 20. the new inftitution, not commencing till *after* Supper, whereas this was *before* it. This done the *Pater-Familiâs,* or Governour of the Feaft, faith to thofe at Table—*This is the Paffover we are going to eat, the Memorial that the Lord paft over the Houfes of our Fathers in* Ægypt, (*i*) *when he flew the firft born of* Pharaoh, *and all his Subjeƈts.*—Then lifting up the dish of Herbs, he adds, *We eat thefe to fhow how the* Egyptians *made the lives of our Anceftors, uncomfortable, and bitter.* After this, holding up the *unleavened cake,* he proceeds, *We eat this, in remembrance of the hafte our Fathers were in, when they left* Ægypt, *having not time enough to leaven*

(*h*) *Gerhard* Harm. Evang. c. 179. Scalig. de Emend. Temp. A Lap. in Matth. Arias Mont ex Rabbinis, in Matth. 26. (*i*) Maimonid. apud *Lightfoot,* Hor. Hebr. in Matth. 26. 26.

their

their dough——*Let us therefore praise the Lord,* &c. in the words of the 113, and 114, *Psalms.* And having thus, or in some *Catechetical way,* instructed the Persons present in the *Nature,* and *use* of the *Passover,* (on which account this Night was called the *Night of Annunciation,* and from hence St. *Paul* borrowed, and applied the word to our Sacrament, wherein *we do shew forth the Lord's Death till he come,* 1 Cor. 11. 16). He takes the Bread and breaks it (whence he was stiled the *Breaker*) and Blesses it in this form. *Blessed art thou O Lord God of the World, who bringest food out of the Earth* —— and then eating one Morsel of it himself, (*k*) he distinctly hands and distributes the remainder to the rest of the Company one after another in the like Proportions, or quantities, not less than an (*l*) *Olive* , nor bigger than an *Egg* —— Sometimes before he gave it, he dipt it in the *Charoseth* or *Sauce* made of Dates, Raisins, Figgs, and Vinegar, as thick as *Mustard,* and with the Colour of *Clay,* to put them in mind how their Fathers wrought Clay in *Ægypt.*——

And this is the (*m*) *Sop* the Evangelist mentions, which *Christ* gave to *Judas,* and after which *the Devil entred into him.*————This done, he takes the paschal Flesh, and saith, *Blessed art thou, O Lord God, the Eternal King, who hast sanctified us by thy Precepts and Commanded us to eat.* Then he falls to eating with the rest of the guests, but in small Portions, suited to Religion and not Appetite. After this they proceed to the (*n*) *Second Course,* as we may Term it, or the *Vulgar Supper,* which was made up of what might please the Palate or

———————————————————————

(*k*) *Singulis dat seu distribuit.* Camero. Bucer. (*l*) *Quanta est Oliva distribuit singulis accumbentibus*—— Tremel. (*m*) John 13. 16. (*n*) *Protrahit cænam hoc & illud edens prout libet.* Maimonid.

satisfie

satisfie Hunger. Of which when they had plentifully eaten, the Master of the Family concludes *(o)* *This Night I will eat no more,* which explains that Expression of *Christ, I will not any more eat thereof, until it be fulfilled in the Kingdom of God.* ——— Supper being ended, he takes the *Second Cup,* and saith over it, *Blessed art thou, O Lord, King of the World, who hast made the fruit of the Vine.* ——— This they all drank of, and then *Sung an Hymn,* (as *Christ* also did *Matth.* 26. 30.) which was called the *great Hallelujah,* beginning at *Psalm* the 115, and ending at 118. And hence this *Cup* was *(†)* named the *Cup of Praise,* and from the insuing Grace, the *Cup of Blessing,* which St. *Paul* alludes to, *the Cup of Blessing which we Bless, is it not the Communion of the Blood of Christ?* 1 Cor. 10. 16.

As soon as the *Pater-Familiâs* had drunk of this *Cup,* he said, *This Night I will. drink no more* —— and this occasioned that Declaration of our Lord, *I will not drink of the fruit of the Vine, until the Kingdom of God shall come* —— i. e. not till after his *Resurrection,* for it is evident, he did eat and drink with his *Disciples,* after he arose from the Dead, though not for *Hunger* sake, or upon any *Legal consideration,* but to satisfie them as to the *reality* of his *Body,* and the *Truth* of his being *Risen.* It doth not appear when this Addition of the *Cup* was made. *(p)* In the Institution of the *Passover* there is not a word of it. Yet the *Talmudists* ground it, on that of *Moses, (q) Deut.* 8. 10. and the *Rabbins,* call it *an Ancient Tradition (r);* and the design of the *Fathers* in this practice was to in-

---

(o) *Et exinde nec quicquam cibi gustat omnino ut gustus maneat in Ore ipsius.* Idem (†) ποιήσιον ὑμνήσεις. (p) Exod. 12 (q) When thou hast eaten and art full, then shalt thou Bless the Lord thy God, &c. —— (r) Bucer in Matth.

gage

gage themſelves, and the People to love God who both ways bountifully fed 'em. The reaſon the *Jewiſh Doctors* give is, becauſe *a Man is obliged by the Law to make his Family merry upon all the Feſtivals,* according to that in *Deut.* 16. 14. *And thou ſhalt rejoice in thy Feaſt, thou and thy Son---* but *how can this be done without Wine* (s) *which cheereth God, and maketh glad the Heart of Man.* But 'tis not material, as *Calvin* ſaith, nor worth while to enquire when the Cuſtom commenced, or on what occaſion it began. 'Tis plain, our *Lord* complied with it, and referred to *this Cup* in his *own holy Inſtitution,* and has made it an integral, and eſſential part of our Chriſtian Sacrament, and indeed if a compariſon may be uſed, the moſt *lively* repreſentation of his Sufferings in the ſhedding of his moſt precious Blood. And in this very inſtance we may diſcover the *Power* of the *Church* to make ſome Additions even to the *Ordinances* of God, when they have a *pious Signification,* and are warranted by their *uſefulneſs,* tho' not expreſly Commanded in *Scripture,* no more than *this Cup* of the Paſſover, which yet was well accepted, and approved by Chriſt who drank it, obſerved the Ceremonies of it, and has made it neceſſary now in the times of the Goſpel. But to return. At the *cloſe of this Supper,* it is ſuppoſed *Chriſt* aroſe and Waſhed his Diſciples Feet, according to that of St. *John,* (t) *Supper being ended, he riſeth and layeth aſide his Garment*——by which *Supper,* moſt likely he intended the *Second* or common-*Supper,* or elſe it might be Thought he would have treated it with more reſpect, and added *Paſchal,* or ſome other word for a Mark of Honour and Diſtinction. The Ceremony being over,

---

(s) Judg. 9. 13　Pſ. 104. 15.　(t) John 13. 2. 3.

he

he fitteth down again ; and having finifhed the *Inftitution* of the *Evangelical Supper*, he difmiffeth *Judas*, and then defcends to that excellent *Sermon* of Confolation to his Auditours, we read in 14, 15, 16, 17. Chapters of St. *John :* And after it goes to the *Garden*, whither the Traitor came with a band of Soldiers to take him;, Chap. 18. 3.

B. (*u*) I fhould rather think this wafhing *Antecedent* to the *Jewifh Supper*, becaufe that was the way both of the *Hebrews* and *Gentiles*, to wafh their Feet *before* difcumbency, left otherwife the *Beds* on which they lay at their Meals, and alfo the *Guefts* might fuffer for want of it.

A. You fay well ; and fo it is in the *Jewifh Ritual*, directing them to Wafh their Feet *before* they fate at *Table*. And without doubt our *Lord* did fo in conformity to their *Rule*, and upon the reafon you mention. And their *fitting* or *lying* after the Fafhion of thofe Days, muft needs fuppofe fuch *Wafhing*. But the *Pafchal Canon* required *two Wafhings*, the *one* according to the ordinary Cuftom, the *other* out of Reverence to the *Paffover*, which was called *Lotio Pafchalis*, and which Chrift improved, to recommend humility to his Difciples, as appears from the Application he makes of it, *John* 13. 13. to 17. (*w*) And though *Peter* feems to wonder at this Wafhing , *v.* 6. Yet the furprize did not proceed from its being a *new thing*, but he was confounded to fee the *Mafter* do this to the *Servant*, and *God* to *Man*. *Lord doft thou wafh my Feet*, faith *Peter*, amazed at the Condefcenfion. *Jefus anfwered, what I do, thou doft not know now, but thou fhalt know hereafter*——— meaning that he fhould by and by more fully un-

---

(*u*) Gerhard. loc: cit. (*w*) Sca'ig. de emend. temp.

der ftand

derftand it, as he did, when Chrift fate down a-
gain, and began the Difcourfe on what he had
done. And the infinuation was good, faith *(x)*
St. *Bernard*, for by this *Wafhing* of their Feet,
before the *Inftitution* of the Bleffed *Sacrament*, is
fignified and taught, the *Preparation* we ought to
make by ferious Repentance, when we put on a defign of going to the Holy Communion, *(y)* that
fo by *purifying* and cleanfing of the *Heart* from all the
Pollutions and filth of Sin, we may with *innocency*
approach to the *Altar*, and *worthily*, and with benefit receive that Sacred *Myftery.*

B. The intimation is wholefome and ufeful.
But if the *Inftitution* of the *Lord's-Supper* was *after*
the *wafhing* of the Difciples Feet, and that *wafhing*
when the *Second Courfe* was over, how came *Mat-*
thew and *Mark* to fay, *(z) while they were eating,*
or when they were at Supper (for this is the proper *Englifh* of what they fay, *the Act continuing*
and not ended,) then Jefus took Bread, i.e. the
Bread he was going to Confecrate. *(a) Auftin*
times the *wafhing* of the Difciples Feet, *previous*
to the *Sacrament, before* the conclufion of Supper.
The Pafchal Supper, faith he, *being finifhed, and the*
other begun; as they were eating, Chrift arofe and wafh-
ed their Feet.——And again, *(b) You muft not un-*
derftand the Supper over, for they were ftill eating.
And whereas *(c) Luke* and *Paul* word it, *after*
Supper, and when he had fupped [μιτὰ τὸ δειπνῆσαι], this
doth not contradict the other Evangelifts, who
fay, ἐδιόντων δὲ αὐτῶν, as they were eating, or as they
did eat, *(d)* becaufe the one fide mean the *Pafchal*

(x) De cœn dom *(y) Pedes, i e aff. Actus animæ & affectus*
ablutione indigent. Ferus. *(z)* Ἐδιόντων δὲ αὐτῶν, Matth.
26. 26. Mark 14. 22. *(a) Illis cœnantibus.* De confenf.
Evang *(b)* Tract. in Joh. *(c)* Luke 22. 20. 1 Cor. 11. 25.
(d) Vid. Maldonat.

Supper, which was *over ,* and the other, the *Vul-gar or Second* part of it which was juſt *begun.* And to this inclines that of *John, he aroſe from Supper,* not *after* it, to ſhow it laſted till both the *waſhing* and *Sacrament* were finiſhed ; *about the cloſe of Supper,* ſaith *Piſcator, but before Supper was done.*

1. When a Man ſaith, Supper is done, or *after Supper,* though the *Supper* ſhould conſiſt of *ſeveral Parts* or *Courſes,* he muſt needs be underſtood to mean the *whole.* The *Paſchal Supper* of the *Jews,* being attended by a *common Meal,* though diverſly conſidered , yet made *one Supper*; and when the Holy Writers declare it *over,* there is no Room left to divide the *one* from the *other,* unleſs there had been ſome ſpecial and particular mention made of *either* to infer the diſtinction. St. *Paul* therefore, and St. *Luke* ſaying μετὰ τὸ δει-πνῆσαι, it muſt either ſignifie *both parts* of the Supper, which becauſe of their Contiguity or quick Succeſſion, were looked on as *one,* or at leaſt *that courſe,* more properly and vulgarly called the *Supper,* and which the other *Evangeliſts* ſpeak of, or elſe the reverence which they muſt be ſuppoſed to have for the *Paſſover,* and the Cuſtom of the *Jews,* wherein they had been bred, had made them uſe other Language, as *Paſch* or the *Paſchal Supper,* and not barely *Supper* as a common, indifferent Meal. That St. *John* ſaith, (e) *Chriſt aroſe* [ἐκ δείπνυ] *from Supper,* i. e. as you interpret it, while Supper continued, or while they were eating. (f) All the Latin Tranſlations render it, either with Elegancy, *à coenâ,* or more flatly, for Explanation ſake, *poſt coenam,* and *cum coenaſſent,* the true *Engliſh* of all which is, *after Supper.* And if St. *Matthew*

(e) ἐκ τȣ δείπνȣ, John. 13. 4. *Sub illius coenæ finem:* Piſcat. in Matth. (f) Vid. Maldonat. Janſen. A Lap. Ferum, &c.

and St. *Mark*, deliver the Paſſage by *Participles*
[ἐϑιόντων] we ought to place them in the *ſecond in-*
definite, and make them ſpeak in [*Præterito* or]
the time, not only preſent, but perfectly *gone*.
For theſe *two Tenſes* are often confounded, and
thoſe Authors in this very word will juſtifie the
aſſertion. St. *Matthew*, giving an account of the
Miracle of the Loaves, (g) tells us, *and they that*
had eaten, were about five thouſand Men. The very ſame words are uſed, Chap. 15. 28. and ren-
dered, *they that did eat*, (h) and ſo St. *Mark* treating of the ſame Miracle, writes in the ſame manner, changing only the ἐϑιόντες into φαγοντες, *and*
they that did eat of the Loaves, &c. In which Places
you ſee theſe holy Pen-Men, whom you object,
repreſent by thoſe participles *what was done*, and
not *what was doing*; for the multitude had all fed
and were filled; and as an evidence and ſign of it,
the fragments were collected, and put into ſeveral Baskets; and then after all this, they proceed
to give us the number [τῶν ἐϑιόντων] *of thoſe that*
had eaten. (i) However, it is not improbable, but
that though the *ſupper* was *ended*, and the *eating*
over; yet the *Table* was not *removed*, nor the
Diſciples gone from it, when our *Lord* aroſe to
waſh their Feet, and then *inſtituted* the *Euchariſt*.
For though he would not intermingle or confound
the *Old and New Sacrament*, by introducing his
own, until *that* of *Moſes* was punctually obſerved,
and the ſolemnity quite *finiſhed*, yet it was his mind
to let the *one* immediately ſucceed the *other*, as the
Antitype of the *Paſſover*, and the *ſubſtance* of all
thoſe Rites he had juſt now uſed, but yoided for

_____

(g) ὁι δὲ ἐϑιόντες, &c. (h) κὴ ἦσαν ὁι φάγοντες——Chap.
6. 44 (i) *Poſt cœnam ſed menſa nondum remota*--Ger-
hard, Eſtius, Hammond, Aſſembly, Calvin.

the

the future. (*k*) It may be added from *Epiphanius*, that in point of *Conveniency* the Table was not cleared, becaufe his time was fhort, and the *Bread* and *Wine* neceffary for *that* Supper, he was going to *begin*, as the moft proper things he could propofe for the *figns* of his *Body* and *Blood*, the *Sacrament* being intended *for the ftrengthening and refrefhing of our Souls by the Body and Blood of Chrift, as our Bodies are by the Bread and Wine*——Thefe *Elements* therefore being already on the Table, upon the former occafion, he took the opportunity to Confecrate and Dedicate them to a Nobler ufe, than they had hitherto been put to, either in the *common* or *Pafchal Supper*.

This is a fhort, (*l*) and according to the current of interpreters, a likely account of the *Order* obferved in thofe *three Suppers*, without intruding or difturbing one another, as they make 'em, who fet the Bread and Cup, at a mighty diftance and confider the *Bread* a part rather of the *Pafchal*, and *ordinary Supper*, than a diftinct, and *feparate Ordinance* appointed to *follow* it : And all this to reconcile the *Evangelifts*, who better underftand one another in *that Order* I gave before.

B. The account is plaufible. Yet let me offer this againft it : It is faid that *Judas* having received the Sop, went immediately out to execute the defign of betraying his Mafter. Either therefore *Judas*, was not at the *Sacrament*, which is generally afferted and fuppofed he was ; or that *Sop* Chrift gave him was the *Sacrament*, which I cannot admit, though it has been fometimes in practice, and is retained in the *Greek Church* to this Day to give the *Sacrament* in that or the like manner ; or elfe this *Sop* was given at the *Pafchal*, to be fure *before* the other *Supper* was over, at which time,

---

(*k*) Ancorat. (*l*) Vid. Luc. Brugenf. in Luke 22.

according

according to Cuſtom, the *Pater-Familiâs* or his deputy diſtributed the Bread, dry or dipt, to the Company.

A. Whether *Judas* received the Sacrament or no, is a Queſtion *variouſly* decided by learned Men, who giving an Anſwer to it, directly and plainly contradict one another. (*m*) *Hilary* ſaith, *The New Paſſover was inſtituted without him, as unworthy the Participation of the Eternal Sacrament. When, in* Judas's *abſence, he had delivered, to us the myſteries of his precious Body and Blood,* (*n*) ſaith *Clement, he went out to the Mount of Olives*——(*o*) *Some may think* Judas *was there, but if we ſearch diligently, what the Evangeliſts and Doctors ſay, you will perceive, he was not preſent at the Holy Sacrament. It appears,* cries (*p*) Innocent 3. *That* Judas *went forth before our Lord gave the Sacrament to his Diſciples.*———*Tatianus* and *Ammonius* place it *after his departure.* And ſome do make *Dionyſius* the *Areopagite* of the ſame Opinion, but his words are obſcure. However 'tis certain his interpreter and Scholiaſt affirm, that the Sacrament was Adminiſtred *after Judas was gone.* Of the *Romaniſts Turrianus, Barradius* and *Salmeron :* And among *Proteſtants Danæus* and *Muſculus* ſay the ſame thing :——*And in my mind,* Judas *was not at that Supper,* are the words of *Piſcator* (*q*).

On the other ſide, (*r*) St. *Cyprian* ſpeaks thus : *As ſoon as he* [Judas] *had touched the holy food, and the Conſecrated Bread put into his Mouth, the perfidious Wretch, not able to bear the Powerful Operation of the holy Sacrament, like Chaff blown away by ſome ſudden and impetuous Wind, in a precipitate manner, he got out of the Houſe and ran to execute his Treaſon.*

(*m*) In Matth. (*n*) Conſtit. l. 5. (*o*) Rupert in Jöh. (*p*) De myſter. Miſſæ. (*q*) In Matth. 26 26 (*r*) De Cœn Dom.

Becauſe

Becaufe Judas *drank of the fame. Cup with his Fellow Difciples, fhall he therefore lay claim to the fame worthinefs?* It is (s) St. *Jerom's* queftion; and that he meant the *Sacramental Cup,* appears from what goes before, where he calls it the *Blood* of the *Lord,* and the *Blood of Chrift.*

(t) St. *Auguftine* difputing againft *the Donatifts,* who objected to the *Catholicks,* That they could be no *true Church,* becaufe they wanted *Excommunication,* makes Anfwer, that the charge was falfe, becaufe they had both *that,* and *other* inftances of *difcipline;* and likewife ufed it, when there was no danger of a *Schifm:* But otherwife he thought it better to let it alone. And he produces in his behalf the Authority of St. *Cyprian;* who in his Sermon [*De Lapfis*] complains, that *there were Bifhops in his time, fo unchriftian, as to talk of nothing elfe but new purchafes, even while the Poor were ftarving; and to grow rich on a fudden, they did not ftick at any extortion* or fraud. Yet that Father durft not hazard a feparation, nor *unchurch Carthage* for not *Excommunicating* them. On this occafion he introduces the *Parable* of the *Tares,* which *Chrift* would by no means fuffer to be plucked up, for fear of pulling up the *Wheat* with 'em. And to prefs home the Argument of *Tendernefs* and *Charity* between Men, in this and the like cafes, he propofes the example of *Chrift,* who bore with *Judas,* and let him *Communicate* with his Fellow Difciples, although he knew him to be a *Devil.*

Leo, in one of his Sermons about the Paffion, *Accofts Judas* in this Language, *How canft thou difturft his goodnefs, who did not thruft thee back, when he gave thee the Communion of his Body and Blood?*

(s) Adv. Jov. (t) Vid Aug. adv. Fulg. Ep. 162. in Pf. Tract. in Joh.

And

And elſewhere, *Even* Judas *was not removed from the Myſterious Eucharist, to ſhow ; that no Provocation or injury done him, but purely his own malice tempted him to the Sin.*

(*u*) *Oh !* The blindneſs *of this Traitor, who though a partaker of the ineffable myſteries, continued the ſame* Wretch *; and when he had been a Gueſt at the Holy Table was ſo far from amendment, that he became a much worſe Man.* And again ; *Oh !* The clemency *of Chriſt !* Oh the madneſs *of* Judas *!* Judas *Bargains to ſell Chriſt to the* Jews *for Thirty pieces of Silver, and Chriſt offers* Judas *that very Blood which he had thus ſold, to be a means to obtain Pardon for his Sin, if he would be wicked no longer.* Thus St. *Chryſoſtom.* And without troubling you with their words, *Bernard,* Haymo, Remigius, Theodoret, Euthymius, and of the School-Men, Lombard, Aquinas, & reliqui fere omnes, *as alſo* Baronius, Bellarmine, Pererius, Janſenius, Maldonate, A Lapide, *with* Calvin, Beza, Bucer, Peter Martyr, Et ex noſtris qui aliter ſentiat nemo mihi notus, *ſaith* Gerhard, *for himſelf and Country-men —— Whitaker, Lightfoot, Hamond, Stillingfleet,* and others who all affirm *Judas* to be a *Communicant,* injoying all the *Privileges* of other *Diſciples,* and *this* on purpoſe to aggravate his Crime, that though there was no partiality on *Chriſt's* ſide to provoke him to it, yet he ſtill went on to contrive and execute that villainous deſign.

B. It is an unequal match, as you have muſter'd the Men. Yet it muſt be confeſt, the *Evangeliſts* have delivered *this part* of their Hiſtory, with ſo much *perplexity* that there is colour enough on both ſides, to juſtify their Opinion.

A. The ground the firſt go on is this. Chriſt tells his Diſciples, (*w*) *I will not drink henceforth of this fruit of the Vine, until that day I drink it new with you in my Father's Kingdom*——from whence they argue, that *thoſe* to whom he gave his *Body* and *Blood,* were to *drink* again with him *after his Reſurrection,* which is meant by his *Father's Kingdom.* But *Judas* did not then *drink* with them, nor could, becauſe he hang'd himſelf before his Maſter died, therefore neither did he *partake* of the holy Communion. Beſides it cannot be ſuppoſed, but whatever *Doctrine* our *Lord* taught, he who is ſaid *to fulfil all Righteouſneſs,* obſerved it to a tittle in his own Perſon. Becauſe then it was his directions, (*x*) *not to give that which is holy unto Dogs, nor caſt Pearls before ſwine.*——He knowing *Judas* to be a *Traitor,* 'tis not credible he would vouchſafe him his *Body* and *Blood,* and ſo by his *example,* invite us to that which in his *Doctrine* he forbid us to do. St. *Paul,* who without doubt well underſtood the mind of his Maſter, requires *Timothy not to be a partaker of other Mens Sins.*——But knowingly and willingly to admit a Sinner, as in this caſe, to the holy Communion, may it not be conſtrued into a *partaking* of his Sin, and letting him *eat and drink his Damnation?*

To which the *others* make Anſwer. That in the words of their firſt reaſon there is a *Synecdoche ;* and the promiſe of Chriſt to drink with his Diſciples in his *Father's Kingdom* (however underſtood) ought to be taken as that *other* is where he ſaith, (*y*) that when *the Son of Man ſhall ſit in the Throne of his Glory, then ſhall ye alſo ſit on twelve Thrones, Judging the twelve Tribes of* Iſrael ——. meaning them in *general,* and as they were a *Col-*

(*w*) Matth 26. 29. (*x*) Matth. 7. 6. (*y*) Matth. 19. 28.

B b   *lege,*

lege, not every *individual* Perfon, becaufe it is e-
vident *Judas* was not to be *one* of thefe *Judges,* and
yet the words infer it, if rigoroufly taken, and
with refpect to each of thofe to whom he fpake 'em.
He did not fay, that *after* his *rifing,* he would
drink with (z) *all of 'em,* but *with them,* or with fuch
of 'em as did not put themfelves out of a Capacity
to do it, as *Judas* did both by his *Treafon* and *violent Dying.* As to the fecond Argument. 'Tis
readily owned, that we are not to *encourage Wickednefs,* nor partake with ill Men in any of their
Follies, and where a Sin is *notorious,* we dare not
admit the *guilty* party to the Holy Communion.
St. *Chryfoftom's* Refolution in this point was, that
*rather than fuffer a flagitious Man to eat and drink at
the Holy Table* (if he knew him fuch) *he would be
torn to pieces.* And fpeaking to the Clergy at *Antioch,* he faith, that *if they did not put by offenders,
it would be as heavily revenged on them, as if themfelves had fhed Chrift's Blood.* (a) St. *Auguftine* was
very wary, and therefore always earneftly perfwaded his People at *Hippo, to examine their Confciences, and if they found themfelves guilty of fuch Crimes
as rendred them unfit for the Sacrament, he wifhes 'em
to withdraw, till by Prayer, Fafting and Alms they had
qualified themfelves for it.* But the moft remarkable inftance in this kind, and a very exemplary
Care and Courage, is that of (b) St. *Ambrofe,*
who hearing that the *Emperour Theodofius,* after
the flaughter of 7000 *Men* at *Theffalonica,* without
any *legal Procefs,* was coming to *Milain* where he
was *Bifhop,* and to the *Church* where he was *prefent,*
the *Father* meets him at the Door and forbids him

(z) *Gerhard Harm.* Evang. (a) In anniverfario Dedicati-
onis Eccl vel Altaris, Serm. 1. de Temp. 152. (b) Theodoret, Eccl. Hift. l. 5. c. 17, 18.

entrance;

entrance ; and though the *Prince* fent *Ruffinus* to the *Bifhop* to intercede for him, and came afterwards in *Perfon* with all the *humility* and *concern* imaginable, yet he perfifted in his repulfe and would not admit him, till by a publick inftrument or *Edict* he declared to all the World his repentance for what was done.

Such was the Religion of thofe times, fuch the *Prelates* of the Church and fuch its *Princes*, who in the caufe of God were not unwilling to fubmit their *Crowns* to the *Mitre*, and think it no fhame to retract an Error, as foon as the honeftPreacher told 'em of it. Methinks I can never enough admire the *boldnefs* of St. *Ambrofe*, but the *forrow* of *Theodofius* charms me more. Hear what *Theodoret* faith of him. Upon the Bifhops refufing him entrance into the Church, he returned to the Palace *fighing and weeping*——and there fate down *lamenting himfelf, and pouring down a fhower of Tears*—— *groaning, wailing and reflecting on his miferable cafe*——and going to the *Archbifhop* in a dejected manner vehemently and earneftly begs *Abfolution*. Which being at length obtained, and admitted to come to the *Church* and *Communion*, attempting to go *within the rail* at the *Altar*, (as he was wont to do at *Conftantinople*) the Bifhop ftop'd him and order'd him to *ftand without*, for, faith he, *the purple makes Emperours but not Priefts*, and this is the place for them Whereupon the good Prince withdrew and ftood *without the rail*; and was fo far from taking it ill, that at his return home, he *reformed* this indulgence and faid, *I know* Ambrofe, *who alone deferves to be called a Bifhop*.——And having borrow'd fo much of the *Hiftorian*, let me add further, that fo great vertue fhining in the *Prince* and *Bifhop*, I cannot but admire *Both*. Him for his Liberty of *Speech*, and the *other* for his Submiffion, St. *Ambrofe's Zeal*, and *Theodofius's Faith*.

You

You will excuse me for being so long on this *Example*, wherein you see the *vigilancy* of the *Church*, not to admit those (though of greatest quality), who themselves put a Bar in the way by some open and scandalous Sin. And if *Ministers* now a Days, have not Courage answerable to the Dignity of their Office, let *them* be blamed and not their *Ministry*. I must confess they stand too much in awe of every Body above 'em, and seem to forget God who is above all, and from whom they have their *Commission*; a *Commission* to reprove and *censure Men*. But they have St. *Ambrose* for a precedent, whom an *Imperial Crown* did not dazzle, or *Sceptre* terrify to make him cool in a matter of Religion. No, the sight of the *Emperour* did rather improve the *Idea of the King of Kings and Lord of Lords, Theodosius's Soveraign and his Master*. Their *Commissions* were *both* from Heaven. And as it might have cost the *Bishop* his Life, had he meddled in matters belonging to the *Emperour*; so 'tis reported of *Theodosius*, that (c) *He knew very well what appertain'd to the Priest, and what to the Prince.* And in Spiritual affairs, he durst not so much hazzard his own Soul, as to exceed *his Commission*, and intrude on the *others*. He would not contend with the *Priest*, for fear of *God* who made him so.

I believe not *many Princes* in the World would bear this usage, though *all* in this and the like case should patiently do it. Less *Zeal* than this of St. *Ambrose*, might tempt them in Power, to pull any *Bishop's Mitre* from his Head, and tear his *Body* from the *Altar*, though the meaning of such reproof is not, thereby to bring the *Prince* into contempt, but to put him in mind of the reverence he owes his *Maker*. And truely, the greatest poten-

---

(c) ἤδει σαφῶς τίνα μὲν τ̄ ἱερέων, τίνα δὲ τ̄ Βασιλέων ἴδια. Theodoret supra.

tate on Earth, fhould confider it an inftance of the higheft policy to teach their Subjects *obedience* to *themfelves*, by their *own* obedience to *God*. Otherwife what fecurity can Governours have, unlefs it be in the *Confciences* of thofe under 'em, and how fhall that point be gain'd without the Power of *Religion ?* Which if the *People* find *they* have no regard for, they will quickly follow fuch an *Example*; and growing by degrees as *loofe* as themfelves, in words and behaviour, *they* may at laft be tempted to do by their *Rulers*, as thofe *Rulers* do by *their God* to whom *they* have folemnly fworn Allegeance, and who by fuch hands often dethro ies them.

But as we find in St. *Ambrofe*, an excellent *Prelate*, fo we have in *Theodofius* an Admirable *Emperour.* A great Prince he was, becaufe he would not be wedded to his humour and fancy. He was guilty of *Paffion*, but he will not be a *flave* to it. *Paffion*, another word for *weaknefs*, which he blufh'd at and wept for, as foon as it was reprefented to him. On that occafion we have his *Tears, Humiliations, agonies of Spirit*, in the *Palace*, on the *Church Floor*, and at the *Altar*. Certainly he deferved to govern the World, that grieved thus for his Infirmities; and confidering he took fo much pains to get the maftery of himfelf for his *own Good*, it was reafonable to expect he would govern his People to no other end, than to do *God honour* and make *them Happy.*

Well; to fay no more of him, the drift of all this, is to fhow, what a Man is to do to reconcile himfelf to God upon the Commiffion of Sin; which if not done, the party offending ought not to come, nor the *Minifter* to admit him to the holy Communion. Yet this concludes nothing againft what *Chrift* did to *Judas*; and his fuffering that Difciple to partake of the *Sacrament*, doth not in the leaft prejudice the foregoing Doctrine.

For

For as St. *Augustine* sets the Rule, *we are to de-bar no Christian this Privilege, until by his own Confession or the sentence of the Court he forfeits, and deprives himself of it.*For (d) *Presumptions are no evidence; and though we may think we have reason to suppose an ill Man. yet that suspicion doth not make him so.* Judas was a *Devil*, and *Christ* knew him to be *such*, yet it was a *secret* to his fellow-Disciples; and though Christ (e) *as God* knew this, yet hitherto there was no *open overt act* or Testimony of his malice, or plain evidence to scandalize his Brethren. And therefore our Lord himself considered, as a *Priest* or *Minister* of holy Things, not understanding *Judas*'s design, let *him* also take the Sacrament, (f) in order to leave *us*, an *example* and *warrant* to do the same. Because therefore St. *Matthew* and St. *Mark*; declare that *Christ sate down with the twelve*——or with all the *Disciples* without exception; and it being taken for granted, that at this time the *Sacrament* was *instituted*, it is concluded against the Objections before mentioned, that *Judas* did *receive* at the Holy Communion(g), though because of his Crime, it was *without benefit.*

Yet, though it passes among most, that *Judas* took the *Sacrament*, it cannot be supposed, that the *Sop* meant it; because though it was and is the practice of some Churches, to moisten the Bread in the Administration of the Sacrament, yet in the Opinion of the most judicious, it ought to be *dry* for decency and signification sake, as better representing the *Body* of Christ distinct from the *Blood.* Yet the Greek word [ψωμίον] is rather in the abstract, and signifies no more than the *broken*

<hr />

(d) *Beza* de Presbyt. (e) P. Mart. Loc. Com. cl. 4. c. 5. n. 13. (f) Tho. P. 3. Q 8. (g) *Reliqui panem dominum, manducarunt,* Judas *panem domini*——Aug. in Joh.

piece

piece of a Loaf, a (*h*) fragment or morſel of Bread; and ſo the Eaſtern Tranſlations render it, [*Panis,* or] a *bit of dry Bread.* However, finding it ſaid, (*1*). *To whom I ſhall give a piece of Bread, when I have dipped it* ―― the tranſlation is good, to con‑ traƈt the Periphraſis, and call it *Sop* or a bit of Bread moiſt'ned, or dipt in the Sauce or Wine.

But whether *wet* or *dry*, it affords no room for your inference, namely, That this muſt be either *at* or preſently *after* the *Paſchal Supper*, and *before* the concluſion of the *other.* Becauſe, though *both Suppers* were over, yet neither was the *Table* nor the *Diſhes* removed, (*k*) the Lord deſigning to make uſe of the *remainder* of the Bread and Wine, without loſing time or cauſing a new Trouble to fetch more. And as for the *Pater-Familias*, his diſtributing Bread to the gueſts, this was done, not only *at*, but *after Supper*, to ſignify the Cha‑ rity, which ought to be among them, and this was the meaning of the *Agapæ*, afterwards in the *Chriſtian Church*, to anſwer the *poſt-cœnium* among the *Jews*, and was continued many Years after the Communion, till ſeveral abuſes attending theſe Feaſts, made our Fathers think it convenient to lay them aſide.

B. *Tertullian* I think, gives us a very fair ac‑ count of them, and ſhows the Nature of 'em by their (*l*) *Name.*

A. So doth (*m*) St. *Chryſoſtom*, and calls 'em *teſtimonies of Love, the comforts of Poverty, the ſub‑ ject of the beſt Philoſophy, the Doƈtrine of humility*, &c. ――yet he complains, that, in his time, this good Cuſtom began to decay, although, not above

<hr>

(*h*) τᷠ ἄρτε ἀπόθερυσμα, Heſych. (*1*) John 13. 26. (*k*) A Lap. in Joh. 13. *Gerhard* Harm. Evang. c. 171. (*l*) *Cæna noſtra*—*vocatur Agapæ, id quod dilectio penes Græcos eſt.* Tert. Apol & ad Uxor. (*m*) Hom. in 1 Cor. 11.

sixty Years before, the Council (*n*) of *Gangra*, excommunicated such as slighted 'em, being intended for God's Honour and the relief of the necessitous. And indeed for some time they answered their Name, in promoting Charity and feeding the Poor. Nothing *obscene* or immodest was heard or seen at 'em. Before Christians sate down to Table, they bestow'd some time on *Prayer*. Then they did eat as much as was Convenient, and drank as became sober People; and in *both* they remembred, that *these Nights* were set apart for *Prayer* and *Watching*. Their *Discourse* was such as became Men, who were perswaded that *God* heard 'em. After they had *Wash'd*, they challenged one another to Sing *Hymns*, to the Honour of God, either of their own composing, or out of the Book of *Psalms*. Which being over and the Table clear'd, they went again to *Prayer*, and so departed, (*o*) but not till they had taken some care of their indigent Brethren in sending them *Fruits*, *Meat*, or *Money*, as every Man was able. But the Scene being changed, and these Feasts made the opportunities of diverse *irregularities*, the Council of (*p*) *Laodicea* first, and afterwards that in (*q*) *Trullo* expelled 'em the *Churches*. *Let 'em not on the Lord's-day or in the Church make those Feasts they call* Agapæ *——and they who presume to do so, let 'em either forbear or be excluded*, i. e. excommunicated. (*r*) And so the third Council of *Carthage*, forbids *Bishops* and *Clergy-men*, to be present at these Feasts, and hinder the People as much as they could, Strangers and Travellers excepted, who perhaps otherwise could not be provided for. St. *Augustine* was at this Council, and no doubt gave his Vote to

(*n*) C̀an 11. apud Caranz. A. D. 324. (*o*) *Agapæ nostræ pauperes pascunt, scs. frugibus, carnibus———*——Aug. adv. Faustum... (*p*) Can. 28. (*q*) Can. 74. (*r*) Can. 45.

dismiss

dismiss 'em, herein following the Judgment of his Master St. *Ambrose*, by whose means *Africa* was rid of 'em, and in a little time most *Churches* removed them into *Private-houses*.

But to return to the *Paschal Supper* ; some *Bread* and [*Embamma* or] *sweet sauce* then in use, being still on the Table, as soon as *Christ* had *ended* the Sacrament, his Agony *began :* And being much troubled in Spirit, he tells his Disciples, that *one of them should betray him.* Hereupon with great surprize and astonishment they look'd one on another, doubting of whom he spake ; and being very desirous to know who it was, *Simon Peter* beckon'd to *John*, who sate next his Master, to ask his Name. *John* accordingly *Whispers* him ; and *Christ* as privately Answers, *(s) It is he to whom I am going to give a Sop,* — which in a few moments after he reached to *Judas*, as the most secret way to discover him. For had he immediately named him, *John* had not forbore looking on the Traitor, and such a look had publish'd the *secret*, as much as if he had pointed at him. Whereas by this means, *Christ* Answer'd the Question of his beloved Disciple, and the rest never the wiser, who though they saw the *Sop* given, yet did not put that interpretation on it, but supposed it the effect of an *Old Custom* without special Application.

B. But what need so much *industry* and *care* to conceal *Judas*, when *Christ* himself (upon the Question put by all the Disciples, and by *Judas* among the rest, *Is it I* ?) Answered, *Thou sayest*, or, *It is as thou hast said :* An expression plain enough to let the Company know that he was the *Traitor*.

(r) John 13. 21, 22, 24, 26.

A. We

A. We find the *Evangelists* very much differ-
ing in the *Order* of this report. Some place it
before the *Sacramental Supper* and some *after* it:
(*t*) Particularly St. *Luke* having given on account
of the *Institution*, and Administration of the Eucharist, subjoins immediately, *but behold the hand
of him who betrayeth me, is with me on the Table*——
To reconcile the Holy Writers, *Jansenius* will
have the *first* to speak by a *Prolepsis*, whereby they
Anticipate or prevent the Declaration of *Christ*,
and represent it *already said*, what was to be *afterwards said* when the Sacrament was *over*. Because had this Passage fallen out *before*, it had caused
a great disturbance among the Disciples, and by
that means rendred 'em, at those minutes, incapable to *receive*. (*u*) *Baronius*'s Opinion is quite
contrary to this, and he conceives the words uttered *before* the Sacrament, supposing St. *Luke* to
post-pone the account, and set it *after* the Supper,
when according to the other *Evangelists*, it should
have gone *before* it. But likely it is, that this
complaint of *Christ*, or prediction of *Judas*'s
Treason, was (*w*) *twice* given at the Table, our
gracious *Lord* taking all opportunities both to *prepare his Disciples*, and *bring* Judas *to reflect on his
Crime*, and the villainy he was contriving against
him. *Once* when he had the *Sop*, after which he
went to confer with the *Priests* about the *Terms* or
price of his *Treason*, and *again*, at the conclusion
of the *Sacramental Supper*, when he impudently
ask'd his Master, *Is it I*? And when our *Lord*'s Answer was forced to publish what the delivery of
the *Sop* concealed before, and kept it a secret from
all but *John*, inraged at the discovery, he leaves the

(*t*) Luk. 22. 21.. (*u*) Ad ann. 34. (*w*) A Lap. in Matth. 26.
and John 13.

Room, and runs to his *Chapmen;* to put in *execution* what they had agreed on.

This will more fully appear, if we can learn that St. *John's Supper*, which juft now I fpake of, and where thefe words concerning betraying Chrift were faid, is *not the fame* with that *Supper*, which the other *Evangelifts* treat of, and where they reprefent the *fame words* fpoken, as I think it will be no very hard task to do.

You muft know then, that though I have hitherto walked in the beaten way, and followed a multitude of Authors in explaining this Paffage of the Gofpel, yet I cannot fay I am fatisfied with it. Nor do they perfwade me to accept St *John's Supper*, after which *Chrift Wafhed* the Difciples Feet, and gave *Judas* the *Sop*, for the *Pafchal Supper*, after which he was pleafed to *inftitute* the Sacrament.

It is indeed reprefented thus. That upon the firft day of the Feaft of Unleavened-bread, the Difciples came to Jefus, faying, *(x) where wilt thou that we prepare for thee to Eat the Paffover? And he faid, go into the City, &c.* ——And when they had provided, he came to the place, *and fate down with the Twelve.* In this all the Evangelifts agree, that *thofe words* were faid, and the *thing* done *on the Day* of the *Paffover.* At the *Evening* of this Day, according to St. *Matthew* and St. *Mark*, while they were at Table, *Jefus began to be very forrowful, and faid unto his Difciples, one of you fhall betray me.* And when it was demanded *who* the Traitor was, he Anfwers, *he that dippeth his hand with me in the difh* (as 'tis fuppofed *Judas* did at that moment) *the fame fhall betray me.* All which agreeing with what St *John* faith in his

(x) Matth. 26. 17.

Gofpel,

Gofpel, *(y)* where the *fame* expreffions are found, it is concluded that in all thefe places of Scripture it muft needs be *one* and the *fame Supper.*

But if we look carefully into what St. *John* hath written, we fhall perceive it quite *otherwife.* For although it is faid by this Author, that *Supper being ended,* he arofe and wafhed his Difciples Feet, and having done fo, fate down again, and inftructed them in the ufe and moral of that action (which was, to teach 'em humility, and fince he their Lord and Mafter wafhed their Feet, they ought alfo to wafh one anothers Feet) the difcourfe being finifhed, *he was troubled in Spirit and teftified, faying, one of you fhall betray me ;* and *John* asking him who it was, that fhould do this wicked thing, *(z)* he told him in his *Ear,* that it was *be to whom he fhould give a Sop, and he gave it to* Judas Ifcariot, *the Son of* Simon. Though, I fay, all this was faid and done *at* or *after Supper,* yet *this Supper* could not be the *Pafchal,* becaufe the Chapter begins thus, *now before the Feaft of the Paffover*—*fo that 'twas before the Feaft,* before the *Lamb* was eaten, nay, before the *Day* was come. And in all probability *this Supper* was at *Bethany,* and not at *Jerufalem,* though he went thither from *Bethany,* two days after to eat the *Paffover.*

The Circumftances of the ftory warrant this conjecture. For firft, after *Judas* had taken the Sop, *Jefus* faid unto him, *that thou doeft do quickly. Now no Man at the Table knew for what intent be fpake this unto him, for fome of 'em thought, becaufe* Judas *had the Bag, that* Jefus *faid unto him, buy thofe things we have need of againft the Feaft,* or *that he fhould give fomewhat to the Poor.* What abfurdities

---

(y) John 13. 21. *(z) Admovet Johannes*———*ut fibi in aurem indicaretur proditor*——— Pifcator in Joh. 13 25.

muft

muft Men run themfelves into to reconcile this to the *Paffover?* For how could it enter into the Difciples minds, that their *Mafter* meant either that *Judas* fhould *give fomething to the Poor*, or provide *neceffaries for the Feaft*, if it had not been *fuch a time*, wherein the *Poor* might have been *found* or the *Markets furnifh'd with goods* upon this occafion? But on the *Day* of the *Paffover* it was ridiculous to feek for either; becaufe the *Poor* as well as *Rich* obferved ftriċtly *this folemn time*, and were, under *penalties*, obliged to it, either at their *own* or their *Neighbours Table:* So that there was no likelihood of finding them at their *ftands* or places where they were wont to beg *relief*, being *this Night* well provided for *without it:* But if not, it was very dangerous to be found abroad tranfgreffing the *Law* in that open manner. Then as for the *Market*, could fuch a thing be expeċted *on that folemn Day, on the Night of that Day?* And is it reafonable to believe the *Jews* would be fo giddy and unfurnifhed, nay, fo irreverent as to rife from the *Pafchal-Table* to go to fuch a *Market?* No, if the *Peafants*, or Country People had fhow'd themfelves negligent, and cool in the Performances of Religion by reforting to the City, and bringing their Wares with 'em, yet the zeal and rigour of the *Priefts* had never endured it. They would have feverely punifhed fuch Offenders, and made both *Buyers and Sellers* pay very dear for this contempt of the *Paffover*. But indeèd the Text exprefly faith, that the Difciples fuppofed their Máfter bid *Judas* to buy thofe *neceffaries againft* or *for* the *Feaft*. And therefore the *Feaft* was *not* yet *come*; for it is unfeafonably faid, *provide for fuch a Day*, when the *Day* is already *gone*. And this agrees with the firft verfe of the Chapter, *before the Paffover*; for it was proper enough at a Day or two's diftance to give fuch inftruċtions for the

procuring

procuring of things Cuſtomarily uſed by 'em on that occaſion.

But you will ſay, the *Diſciples* were miſtaken in the words of their Maſter, who intended no ſuch Proviſion, but only bid *Judas* be quick and haſten what he had contrived againſt him. And without doubt, this was our *Lord's* meaning; and to this end *Judas*, after the *Sop* went out with impatience, and eagerneſs to *conſult* with the *Jews* about the *reward* and *manner* of betraying him. However, this could not be done in that hurry; the Method which the holy Pen-men repreſent him taking was a Work of time. For St. *Matthew* tells us, [*Chap.* 26. *v.* 14.] *He went out to the chief Prieſts.* St. *Luke* goes further [22. 4.] *He communed with the Captains.* St. *Mark* adds, [*Chap.* 14. *v.* 43.] that the *Sanhedrim*, or whole Conſiſtory were applied to, *the Chief Prieſt's, Scribes and Elders.* ——— How is it poſſible for *Judas* to do all this *that Evening* of the Paſſover, ſeeing, as St. *John* ſaith, 'twas *Night* before he left his Maſter ? Were the Chief-Prieſts, Scribes, and Elders all *at Supper in one houſe*, that he did ſo readily meet 'em ? This could not be, becauſe the *Law* required 'em to be at *Home*, every Maſter *this Night* with his *Family*, for the more punctual celebration of the Feſtival. But had *they* been together, how came the *Captains* to be in their Company ? Did theſe *Romans* Sup with 'em too ? No, that was an *Abomination* to the *Jews*, to admit ſuch *Aliens* to this Sacred Supper. Did *Judas* go from Houſe to Houſe, to ſummon them to the Hall or Council-Chamber ? Let a Man conſider the time for this, which did not conſiſt of many hours between *Judas's Departure*, and *Chriſt's* going to the *Garden*, where he had not long been, before that Diſciple came to apprehend him. It is not an eaſie matter to bring Perſons of that figure and

'and fo many of 'em into one place. And when affembled, the *debate* muft be ferious and long, becaufe it was a cafe of Blood, and his Blood whom the *People* refpected, and they feared to put the People in an Uproar. The *manner* therefore of feizing him with fafety to themfelves; the *Propofals* and Conditions of this piece of Service, and what they were to give the Traitor for difcovering, and delivering him into their hands and the like, could all this be done *that Evening*? 'Tis hard to think it. Yet all this and more muft be granted, and fuppofed done in thofe few minutes (as we may call 'em) between *Judas*'s rifing from the Supper, and his meeting Chrift at *Gethfemane.*

Befides, we may obferve that after the promife, and bargain made by the Chief-Priefts to give him thirty Pieces of Silver, *from that time* Judas *fought an opportunity to betray him——he fought an opportunity*; but in the Evening of the Paffover he *had* it. And therefore the Natural fence of the words is, That *before* this *opportunity* he *fought* for *others*; but till this hour he could find none proper to betray him in, and hereupon it follows in the next words, *now the firft day of the Feaft of unleaven'd Bread* —— or in other terms, *after this confultation*, after fo much *deliberation* and *contrivance*, of ways and means to deliver him up, *began the Paffover.* So that apparently this fell out *before*, and not *on* the Evening of the Paffover.

'Tis eafie then to conceive, that *this Supper* St. *John* mentions, was at *Bethany*, at the Houfe of *Simon* the Leper, and *two Days* before *that* of the *Paffover*, as St. *Matthew* faith, [*Chap.* 26. *v.* 2] *You know that after two Days is the Feaft of the Paffover, and the Son of Man is betray'd to be Crucified* —— and this he might fay in the prefent tenfe, as doing

ing

ing or done [περαξι´ωλαι] becaufe *Judas* was now gone to debate and contrive about it. Accordingly we find in the next verfe, *then affembled together the Chief-priefts, and Scribes, and Elders of the People, unto the Palace of the High-Prieft, and confulted how they might take Jefus by fubtlety , and kill him, but they faid, not on the Feaft-day, left there be an Uproar among the People.* ———It feems their *firft* refolution was to feize him on the *Day of the Paffover*, being well affured he would then be at *Jerufalem*. But the great concourfe of People *that Day* in and about the Temple, made it hazardous to lay hold on him in that *open manner*. But then the expreffion fignifies that the Feaft was *not come*, becaufe defigns look *forward*, and their intending to do it on *that Day*, was an intimation, that the Day as yet was not in being.

Allowing therefore *this Supper* to be two Evenings before, we may frame the Hiftory after this Manner. While Chrift was at the Houfe of *Simon* the Leper, *two Days* before the Paffover, as he there fate at meat, there came a Woman having an Alabafter-Box of Oyntment , of *Spikenard* very precious, and fhe brake the Box and poured it on his Head. The Difciples feeing this profufenefs, as they thought it, had indignation and faid, *To what purpofe is this waft?* Particularly *Judas Ifcariot, Simon's* Son, who was to betray him, faith, *Why was not this Oyntment fold for three hundred Pence, and given to the Poor?* Jefus excufing the Woman, and declaring it a *good work* done by her, and fuch as fhould be recorded to her honour, *Judas* grew more Angry , and took a prejudice againft his Mafter for this Declaration, and Satan was active enough to improve any ill motion in him. *Before* Supper was quite over, Jefus arofe and wafhed the Difciples Feet, and fitting down again, out of the fenfe he had of the wild

Thoughts

Thoughts, which began to be tumultuous in the villains Heart, which neither his Masters gracious countenance, nor late condescension could in the least melt, unwilling yet that he should be lost for want of warning, he enters on a discourse concerning one of the Company's betraying him, to the end, that by this *private hint Judas* might be alarm'd, and being at once informed of his own *guilt* and his Lord's *Omniscience* he might be brought to recollect himself and repent before it was too late. But nothing will do; as soon as the *Sop* was eaten, (which had in shew some particular *Mark* of Christ's Favour, but was withal a *Testimony* of his black attempt, and a means to shew. *John* who the party was that would be guilty of the treason) out he goes, though dark, gets to the *Priests* and *Captains*, sells his Master for thirty pieces of Silver, then returns back to *Bethany* to see how Christ would bestow himself on the Day of the Feast, goes with him to *Jerusalem*, continues with *all him Day*, eats with him in the *Evening* both *Passover* and *Sacrament*; and finding by his discourse that he was to pass over *Cedron* to *Gethsemane* (a little Village at the foot of mount *Olivet*, where there was a Garden to which *Christ* for privacy-sake frequently resorted) *thither* he comes with a band of Men, apprehends *Jesus*, carries him first into the *High-Priest*, then to *Pilate* the *Roman* Deputy who examined, scourged, condemned and crucified him.

But to return from this digression and consider, the *Passover* in those instances wherein our Sacrament referrs to it. We see the *Bread* was divided into several Morsels; and that the *Cup* was used in both Suppers, and in both called *the Cup of Blessing*. As soon as the Master of the Family had eaten, he said, *I will eat no more this Night*,— and so Christ, *I will not eat any more thereof, until it be fulfilled in the*

E e

King-

Kingdom of God——The *Pater-Familiâs* when he had drunk, adds, *This Night I will drink no more---* and our Lord makes the fame Declaration, *I will not drink of the fruit of the vine, until the Kingdom of God fhall come.* The *Pater-Familiâs* lift up the *Bread,* and told the Company what it meant *:* So Chrift took the *Bread* and holding it up, faid, *This is my Body*——*fo* his Body, *as* the unleaven'd Bread in the *Pater-Familiâs* hand, was *that* which the Fathers did eat when they left Ægypt, i. e. the *one* was a *Symbole* or reprefentation, and fo was the *other,* yet neither of 'em to be *ftriɛɛly* but *Sacramentally* taken; And in both the whole aɛɛion, is called, *Haggada,* for fo the *Jews* ftile the *Paffover,* as St. *Paul* doth the *Sacrament,* wherein we do *fhew forth the Lord's Death till he come.* And when all this was finifhed, the *Jews* Sung an *Hymn,* as Chrift and his Difciples did, *And when they had Sung an Hymn they went out into the mount of Olives,* Matth. 26. 30.

And now to clear your Objeɛɛions. Firft, The *Pater-Familiâs divided* the Bread, and gave a *piece* of it to *each of the guefts* ; and it is not to be much queftioned, but as in the other particulars, fo in this Chrift conformed to what was ufually done, giving each Difciple *(z)* a Portion out of *his* hand into *theirs,* as did the *Pater-Familias* at the Paffover. Nor doth the word [*take*] deny it ; for a thing is as properly reach'd from *anothers hand,* as from a *Difh* or *Patin.* Nor doth the *Minifters* delivering either the *Bread* or *Cup,* offer the leaft violence to the *Communicants taking it,* any more than at *common Meals,* where the *Mafter* or *Miftrefs* of the Houfe Carves for the Company,

---

(x) Vid. Mufcul. de cœn. dom. Bucer. & Camer. in Matth. 26. Bez. in eundem loc. *Per partes & fingulis diftribuit*——*figillatim & ordine difcumbentibus.*——

without

without any prejudice to the *Freedom* of the Table, and the *guests* do not think themselves the less welcome, because they are sav'd that trouble: Chrift faid, *Take, Eat* —— The *Minifter* ufes the very *fame words* ; and if this be faid and done *feverally*, and in a particular manner, it has the example of the *Jews* in the like cafe ; and moreover 'tis apt to make a deeper impreffion on every Man's Heart, when he hears the words diftinctly and *directly* pronounced to him.

And that this was the practice of the Ancient Churches, we find by (c) *Tertullian*, and (d) *Juftin Martyr*, who declared it the Office of fuch Clergy, as prefided in the Church, *to diftribute to each Man prefent the Bread and Wine at the Sacrament.* And in that paffage between *Theodofius* and St. *Ambrofe*, (of which you had a large account) the *Bifhop* asks the *Emperour, how he could reach out his hand to receive Chrift's Body and Blood* —— i. e. receive the Elements from the Minifters hand ; for otherwife it was impoffible to take the Bread and the Cup, all the Communicants being *without the rail*, and at a great diftance from the *Table.*

As to your other Exception, that the Sacrament was Originally adminiftred to the Communicants *fitting*, becaufe the Evangelifts fay, *he fate down with the twelve*, and *as they fate and did eat*—— you remember what was faid, that the *Jewifh* Supper at the Paffover confifted of *two Courfes* or parts, the *Sacramental*, and the *Vulgar*, befides, *this* of our Lord which made 'em three. It is not therefore unreafonable to think , that as the *Suppers* differ'd, fo might the *geftures* : And whereas the *firft* was *Religious*, and the *other common*, *this* might be eaten with *difcumbency* or *fitting*, and the *for-*

(c) De coron. mil. (d) Apolog.

mer more reverently *ftanding.* And thus St. *Chryfoftom* expounds thofe Places; for having asked the Queftion, whether indeed Chrift and his Difciples did eat the Paffover, and how they came to eat it contrary to Law, becaufe by Law they were not to eat it *fitting* or *lying*, he anfwers thus, *after they had eaten the Paffover ftanding, they fate down to Supper.*——The fame fcruple, and the fame refolution *Theophylact* makes, that they finifhed the Legal part *ftanding*, and then they *fate down.* The Law in this point referr'd to, is *Exod.* 12. 11. *Thus fhall you eat it* [the Paffover] *with your Loins girded, your Shooes on your Feet, and your Staff in your Hand, and you fhall eat it in hafte.* Here is indeed no mention of *ftanding* (e) but the circumftances of the Text prove it, for they were to eat *in hafte*, and fo no leifure for difcumbency or *fitting*; they were to *gird themfelves*, as Men ready to depart, loofe Garments being for eafe, and repofe, but unfit for Work or a Journey; they were to have on *their Sandals*, or Shooes which they always put off while they lay on their *Beds or Couches*, becaufe otherwife they had dirted or defiled them: And therefore we may obferve, that the Angel intending to lead St. *Peter* out of Prifon, bid him firft *gird himfelf and bind on his Sandals. Acts* 12. 8. Neither can we well conceive 'em in any other gefture, while they held their *Staves* in their hands, which were a conveniency and fupport in a *Journey*, but very cumberfom and improper, when they were eating and drinking at *Table.* The words of St. *Paul* confirm this Habit of Body, where he alludes to this Cuftom among

---

(e) *Quorfum enim baculos tenentes manibus, fuccincti lumbos & calceati, fi non ad iter expediti ftabant.* A Lap. in Exod 12.

the Jews, *(f) Stand therefore having your Loins girt about with truth, and your Feet shod with the preparation of the Gospel*———— Borrowing his phrase from the *Ceremonies* used at the eating of the *Passover,* and beginning with *standing* as a fit posture to show a Man to be upon his *Guard,* and in a *readiness* to *Fight* or *Travel ;* which the Apostle applying to his *Christian,* he exhorts him to do the same. *(g) Philo* the Learned Jew, and out of him *Pererius* understands this to be the gesture of the Jews at *that Supper. Arius Montanus* reports it so from the old *Rabbins, (h)* and *Euthymius* takes it for granted, and supposes that from hence Christ and his Disciples did eat in *that Manner.* And of this Opinion are *Maldonate, Lucas Brugensis, A lapide, (i) Beza, (k) Gerhard* and many *others.* Because then the Law about the *Passover* required *standing,* and was accordingly the practice of the *Rabbins,* and other Jews to eat it in that manner, it cannot be well suspected, that Christ and his Disciples would break that Law, and not eat *this Passover,* much more his *own* in that form ; Though as to the *ordinary Supper,* it may be well enough said, that he *sate* or *lay down* to eat, as more conducible to *ease* and *pleasure.*

Now *standing* was a *praying-gesture,* as appears from *(l)* Scripture, *Abraham stood before the Lord, (m)* i. e. he stood in Prayer. *And the Publican stood afar off and pray'd*———And it is a proverbial saying among the Hebrews, that *(n) without Prayers made standing, the World would fall* ————and

---

(*f*) Eph. 6. 14, 15. (*g*) De Sacrif. *Cain* & *Abel* (*h*) In Matth. 26. (*i*) In Matth. (*k*) Harm. c. 169. *non sedentes, sed stantes——a stantibus—stantes manducarunt Pascha——* (*l*) Gen. 18. 22. 1 Chro. 23. 30. Nehem. 9. 5. Rev. 7. 9, 10. (*m*) *Stabat in O: atione.* Targ. Onkelos. (*n*) *Sine stationibus non subsisteret mundus.*

because

becaufe in thofe days, and by the Cuftom of that People, thefe holy addreffes to God were delivered *ftanding*, therefore they give out that [*Gnamuda*] *ftanding* is one of the *Names of Prayer*.

And fo under *Chriftianity* it was the way of the Church to *ftand* at their Prayers every *Lord's-day*, and all *the time between Eafter and Whitfuntide*, according to the twentieth Canon of the Council of *Nice*, in honour of Chrift's Refurrection. *Becaufe there are fome who kneel on the Lord's-day and during Pentecofte*, (the fifty Days between Eafter and Whitfunday) *That there may be uniformity in every Parifh, it feems good to the holy Synod, that People fhould offer up their Prayers to God ftanding*. And thefe Prayer Days are called, *dies Stationum*, becaufe hereon [*Stamus ad Orationem*] *we ftand at our Prayers*, faith St. *Cyprian*. This ufage is mentioned by (o) *Tertullian*, who accounted it an heinous matter to *faft* or *kneel* on thofe Days. Yet it was a bare *Tradition*, as (p) St. *Jerom* ftiles it: But fuch as was obferved, faith *Epiphanius*, by the whole Catholick Church. And if we ask the reafon why the Cuftom was introduced, the Anfwer is, that it was [συμβολον της αναςασεως] *tha Symbol of the Refurrection*, that fo we may take notice as of our fall by Sin, fo of our Refurrection by the Grace of Chrift. *(p) Six days we pray upon our knees, in token of our fall, but on the Lord's-day we bow not the knee in token of the Refurrection, by which according to the Grace of Chrift we are freed from Sin, and the Power of Death.* ____It fhows, faith *Balfamon* on the Canon, *that we are rifen with Chrift, and that now we feek thofe things that are above.*—The fame reafon *Zonaras* gives out of *Bafil the Great*,

---

(o) De coron. Mil. (p) Adv. Lucifer. (q) Quæft. & Refp. ad Orthod.

telling us, that herein the Church teaches her Children to raise their Thoughts to the contemplation of that Life which will never have an end. And hence he calls the whole time an *Advertisement*, or lesson of our Resurrection to that State, and considers it as one continued Festival, or in *Balsamon*'s words, *one Lord's-day*, and the *standing* on it, an *emblem* of our rising from the Grave to Heaven. Which is a Thought must needs create us a great deal of joy, and therefore we use a gesture answerable to it, and forbear *kneeling*, while these Days last, because such a *bowing* or *bending* is a testimony or *sign* of dejection and sorrow, inconsistent with that delight, and satisfaction every good Man is ready to entertain upon the belief and assurance he hath of his after Condition above.

It doth not clearly appear how long this Custom lasted, but we see it continued by a Decree of Pope *Alexander* III. about the Year 1160. at which time it seems it begun to decline, and is now worn out in latter Ages, the Church finding she had outlived those *Hereticks* on whose account it commenced. And I wish there was no need now to *revive* it on the same reason.

But all I aim at, is, only to show it to be a *Religious gesture*, and of the same importance with *Kneeling*, though it had an additional signification in the first Ages of the Church, to set forth the honour of *Christ's Resurrection*, and give us an assurance of our *Own*. And this was but for *certain times* of the Year, the *remainder* being spent in a more humble way of adoration. (*r*) Whether

---

(*r*) *Æthiopes semper stantes non de geniculis collectæ intersunt, sed die Pentecostes ingeniculant* —— Arndii *Lexicon.*

the

the Chriſtians in *Æthiopia* are influenced by the practice and motives of the *Fathers*, is not certain, but to this Day they generally *pray after that manner*, and have *Poſts* or *little Pillars of Wood*, made on purpoſe to lean againſt, and thereby reſt themſelves, while they *ſtand* at their Prayers, becauſe their Liturgy is long.

And if Chriſt and his Diſciples did this, much more doth it become us to uſe a geſture of *humility* and Reverence : And becauſe *they ſtood*, *we* ought to *kneel*, if not, as (s) *Gorgonia* did, [*Nazienzen's* Siſter] *proſtrate* our ſelves at the Table. By this outward and viſible debaſement of himſelf, the ſupplicant expreſſes the *lowlineſs* of his mind 'His *bended knee* beſpeaks a *broken Spirit*, and while he Bows down towards the ground, in the very act he confeſſes himſelf to be Originally *Duſt and Aſhes*, and that it is purely owing to the Mercy of a gracious God, that from this mean beginning he has now got a better Figure. In a word, a *Zealous knee*, charitably ſpeaking, always ſuppoſes an *affectionate-prayer*. Indeed an *humble prayer and kneeling* are but *two words* for the ſame thing ; and where we ſee other geſtures, it may be reaſonably thought that ſuch a Man is *not worſhipping*, not praying at all.

B. (t) By the general conſent of the Learned in the Jewiſh Rites, that *geſture* intended and commanded in the Law belong'd only to the *Night*, wherein the *Iſraelites* were to leave *Ægypt in haſte*, but was not to continue when they came into *Canaan*. So that there was no neceſſity for Chriſt to eat the Paſſover *ſtanding*, and then to *ſit down* at the common Supper.

(s) Greg. Naz. Orat. 25. (t) Aſſembly.

A. I deny

A. I deny not, but Men of note both Jews and Chriſtians, favour what you ſay. Such as *Tremellius,* who will not allow thoſe *four circumſtances,* the *Loins girt, the Shooes on, the Staff in Hand, nor the eating in haſte,* to go further than *Ægypt,* becauſe in *Exod.* 12. 14. where it is made a formal inſtitution, *to be kept as a Feaſt by an ordinance for ever,* there is mention only of the Paſſover it ſelf, *without any of the* Ceremonies or Rites uſed, and expreſt occaſionally before, *v.* 11. (*u*) *Scaliger* believes the ſame thing in the main, but dates the alteration from the *Babyloniſh Captivity.* (*w*) *Beza* admits a change, but differs from them *both,* for he rejects no more than the *Blood on the two ſide Poſts, and the upper door Poſt of the Houſes,* ſo that by making *this* exception he confirms the *Reſt.* *Cajetan* and *Baronius* are of this number. And of our own Countrymen, *Willet, Godwin, Babington, Ainſworth,* and ſome *others,* explode *all* the Ceremonies, particularly that of *ſtanding,* upon the warrant they have from ſome *Canons,* and *Speeches* of the *Rabbins* in theſe Terms. (*x*) *We are obliged to eat ſitting or lying, that we may eat like Princes and Great Men——We ſit eating as a Memorial of our Deliverance—— the Bread of affliction is to be eaten, but in a way that declares our Liberty——'Tis the manner of Servants to eat ſtanding. We uſe another geſture to let the World ſee we are in ſlavery no longer— Let not the Pooreſt* Iſraelite *eat otherwiſe than ſitting* — And in thoſe interrogatories made on this occaſion, we find a diſtinction obſerved between this Night and all others, (*y*)*Becauſe all other Nights we waſh but once, in this twice. In others we eat leavened or unleavened Bread, in this only unleavened.*

(*u*) De Emend. Temp. (*w*) In Matth. 26. (*x*) Maimonid. R. Levi. (*y*) Lib. Peſach.

In other Nights we eat any sort of Herbs, in this none but bitter Herbs. : In all other Nights we eat and drink sitting or lying, but in this altogether lying————
And it passes for an Ancient Tradition in the *Talmud*, that this *discumbency* at the eating of the Passover was a testimony of their Liberty.

But put. the case that the Jews of the latter Generations, altered the Custom, and changed the gesture from *standing* to *sitting* or *lying down*, either *before* or *after* the *Captivity*, to signifie thereby the *Redemption* they had got from *Ægypt* and *Babylon*; and that now they were to eat and drink as a *free* People, and *Lords* of those Places, where the Passover was kept by 'em, yet it is not likely, that Christ, who came to ~fulfil and did *fulfil all Righteousness*, and show an impartial, (*z*) and intire obedience to the Law of his Father, would prefer this indulgence, before what was expresly written by *Moses*, not only at the time of *Institution*, but as it was after ratified when they were got far enough from a State of Bondage. For in *Numb.* 9. 3. *Moses* repeats the Command about keeping the Passover *at the appointed time according to all the rites of it, and according to all the Ceremonies of it*————And what *rite* more material and significant then *standing*, in conformity to that veneration they show'd at the institution of this ordinance, when at the bare mention of it, (*a*) *The People bowed the head and worshipped* ——nay, which bespeaks a more Religious and Sacramental gesture, (*b*) *They kneeled, and yet further; (c) They fell flat on the ground and adored the Lord.*

(*z*) *Gerhard* Harm. Evang .c. 169. (*a*) Exod. 12. 27. (*b*) Genuflexerunt. Syr. (*c*) Prostratus. Arab.

And besides this Obedience which Chrift was to
fhow in every tittle; at this particular time the
Gefture hád a fpecial fignification, and a *reafon*
not much unlike that at the firft appointment of it,
. (*d*) Becaufe *hereby*, he declared, that he was going to leave or *pafs* out of this World, according
to that of St. *John, when Jefus knew that his hour
was come, that he fhould depart out of this World to the
Father —* (*e*) he inftituted this Chriftian-Paffover
in remembrance of this *departure*; and in all probability did it *ftanding*, to fignifie his *readinefs* to
be gone to the *Celeftial Canaan*, as the Jews expreft theirs, in the fame gefture upon their Journey to the *other*. So that allowing the *Jews* to
make this *alteration* at the Paffover, (as in truth
we know they added and diminifhed, and changed
many things, and faid, and did almoft what they
pleafed, without regard to the Law, which was
fo loud in their mouths) yet it is not credible that
the *Lord Jefus* would fubmit to any of thofe a-
bufes; And though he did comply with diverfe
inftances in the Jewifh Worfhip of *humane appointment*, where the Law did not fuffer by it, yet
where the Law was plainly contradicted or eva-
ded, (as in this cafe,) to be fure, he would by no
means difpenfe with it himfelf, nor give an ill example to future Generations, to do by *him* as he by
Mofes, and thereupon fruftrate all divine inftitutions, becaufe of the little refpect he might feem
to give them.
. *B.* But if Chrift and his Difciples did eat the
Paffover, and perhaps the Sacrament *ftanding*, why
do not we conform to their examples? And feeing

(*d*) *Se jam ex hoc mundo tranfiturum.* Joh. 13. 1. (*e*) *In
memoriam tranfitus fui ex hoc mundo ad patrem.* Synod.
Trid.

neither

neither our Lord in the *institution*, nor *Paul* in the *recital of it*, prescribed any Ceremonies to be used on that occasion; would it not be safest for us to *stand* likewise, as a gesture which *Christ* cannot take amiss, because it was his *own*. And methinks, as to this, our *dissenting* Brethren are so far in the right, Because, reading in the Gospels, that Christ *sate down with the twelve* — they *literally* submit to that Custom, and receive the Sacrament *sitting*. If *they* are mistaken in the gesture, it is an Errour of the *Understanding*, and not the *Will*; And I dare say, in their behalf, that were they perswaded, our Lord and his Disciples used any *other* gesture, they would cheerfully comply with it, and take the Sacrament, either *standing* or *kneeling*.

4. The *silence* of *Christ*, and his *Apostles* leaves it to discretion. And their prescribing *no* gesture at all, makes us consider it within the number of *indifferent things*, comprehended under the general Rule of *Order* and *Decency*. And as for our conformity to their examples, we see no warrant for it; because the only gesture the Scripture takes notice of, was *sitting*, which being at a *common-meal* or that *part* of the *Paschal Supper*, which consisted of *ordinary food*, it is no sufficient precedent for us to apply it at a *Banquet* confessedly *Divine*. And though it is no more than probable from what has been alledged, that they did eat the Passover *standing* (*f*) yet we are not sure, whether that gesture was *continued* in the Sacrament, or changed into *kneeling*, as more becoming the dignity of this *new* institution: And in this uncertainty, we can frame no rule to our selves on that consideration.

(*f*) Forbes Irenicum, l. 1. c. 4. *unde scis an non mutato gestu acceperint Eucharistiam*, &c.

However, *Standing,* *Kneeling,* and *proftration* are all *fupplicatory geftures,* and uſed over the whole World in the Adoration and Worſhip of God, but ſtill they have their *Degrees* of Reverence ; And as the *firſt* better ſuited the Jews, becauſe it was preſcribed 'em, and ſignified withal their departure out of *Egypt* : So the Church thinks the *two* latter more proper for our Circumſtances, not only becauſe ſhe has a great care that her Children do not *judaize* in any particular (and therefore muſt not *ſtand* at the *Sacrament,* as the Jews *ſtood* at the *Paſſover*) but moreover, becauſe in the Sacrament we offer up a *Memorial* of the Sacrifice of Chriſt, for the Pardon of our Sins, and we ought certainly to preſent it in the *humbleſt way* imaginable ; And if ſhe prefers *Kneeling* before the other, it is not becauſe ſhe thinks *Kneeling* ſubmiſſive enough, but becauſe we cannot with any manner of Conveniency, take the Elements or eat and drink with *Proftration.*

As for the way of our *Diſſenting Brethren,* who eat and drink at the Sacrament *ſitting* ; if they do not ſubmit to the diſcipline of the Church out of a ſcruple of Conſcience, my Mouth is ſtopped, I Judge no Man. *Conſcience* is tender, and 'tis a dreadful thing to act againſt it ; nor dare I incourage an hard thought againſt them in their caſe, for fear by a Revolution of Providence it may ſome time or other be my Own. Yet this ought to be done ; I would check all motions which would tempt me to be *ſingular.* To do nothing out of *Affectation* or *Pride* ; Not to break the *Unity* or Peace of the Church of God, if it can be avoided : To indeavour all Chriſtian-ways to clear my doubts ; and be well perſwaded at laſt, that I am in the right, before I ſeparate from *that Communion,* wherein I had my *Baptiſm,* and all the advantages of pious Education. And when

this

this is done, to convince the World I have no o=
ther end, than the fafety of my *Confcience,* in this
withdrawing my felf, I would not be induftrious
to *Propagate* my fenfe of things, left it fhould afterwards be made appear, that I was *miftaken*;
(g) And this I would be fure of, to have no more
of my Errour to anfwer for, than what immediately concerns my felf. Nothing of *malicious
diligence* fhould be charged upon me ; nor would I
expofe my Soul to the hazard of bearing the burdens of other People, who will be ready to plead
the Contagion of my example, and ufe the reafons
I gave, to lead them aftray. In a word, whatever my principles were, they fhould be always
attended with *Sobernefs and Modefty* ; I would ufe
my beft care to avoid contention ; Never lofe my
Charity, nor my *Manners,* towards thofe, who
differ in Opinion from me, becaufe fuch eagernefs
and intemperate Zeal favours of *defign,* and makes
a *party,* but *unchriftians* Men. My Ear and my
Heart fhould be conftantly open to wholefom advice ; and for Peace fake I would yield as far as I
well could, rather than be a means to diftract my
Neighbours, and bring all to Confufion. And
God forbid any fuch Article fhould be made a-
gainft me, that as much as in me lay, I have been
one of thofe who Studioufly reform Religion to
nothing. Mr. *Baxter* was of this mind, if we may
believe his words, for he fpeaks thus, though
*I differ from many in feveral Doctrines, yet if I fhould
zealoufly prefs my Judgment on others, and feek to
make a party for it, and difturb the Peace of the
Church, and feparate from my Brethren, I fhould fear
left I fhould prove a Fire-brand in Hell, for being a
Fire-brand in the Church.*

(g) *Errare poffum, hæreticus effe nolo.* Aug.

Now

Now as for the point in hand: Our *Brethren*
fhould be very fure, that the *gefture* of Chrift and
his Difciples at the Sacrament was *fitting*, becaufe
otherwife the Argument of their practice is loft,
and they will have no manner of Divine warrant
for that *habit* of Body, at the Lord's-Table. How
Chrift's *fitting* is to be underftood, and at what
part of the Pafchal Supper, you had before. So
that either they muft have a very mean conceit of
that facred Meal, or they fhould ufe a *gefture* anfwerable to the notion of it, to be fure no worfe
than *that* at the Paffover.

But what if it be demanded, why they take it
fitting? Why not rather *lying* or *leaning down on
one fide,* which was the way in thofe Days, and
'tis very plain, (*b*) the *Greek* word fpeaks it fo.
*When the even was come, he lay down with the twelve.
And as they lay down and did eat. When his hour was
come, he lay down with the twelve.* And St. *Matthew* calls a *gueft* (*i*) [ἀνακείμενον] *And the wedding
was furnifhed with guefts.* So we tranflate it, but
in the Original it is, the Marriage-Feaft filled with
People *to lie down.* And therefore to be critically
rigorous in making *Chrift* and his Difciples our
Patterns for a *gefture* to be ufed at the Holy *Communion,* we ought to *lie down,* as they did in the
Greek, and not *fit,* as in our *Englifh Tradition,* and
the rather, becaufe the word (*k*) [ἀνακείμενος] has
a Religious fignification, and means one *Confecrated* or devoted to God, *it becomes thofe who are devoted to God, and who lift up their Eyes to him alone,
to be thus religioufly difpofed* — So that keeping clofe
to the Letter of the Text, we find *difcumbency* the

(*b*) Matth. 26. 20. Mark 14. 18. Luke 22. 14. (*i*) ϰ
ἐπλήσθη ὁ γάμ☉ ἀνακειμένων. Matth. 22. 10. (*k*) Δεῖ γὸ τὰς
ἀνακειμένας θεῷ ϰ πρὸς αὐτὸν βλέποντας μόνον ὅτας διακεῖσθαι
εὐλαβῶς. Chryfoft.——

gefture;

gesture ;.(*l*) and if Men will be very *exact*, they
should not *sit*, but *lie down at this Table*, as Christ and
his Disciples did, being a gesture more warrantable on the account of their example, and of near
kin to religious *Prostration* or falling flat on the
ground.

B. We and they know, that the word in strictness signifies *leaning* or *lying down* ; but *discumbency*
and *sitting*, is by interpretation the *same* ; and
therefore though the *Jews* and *we* seemingly differ
in Table-gestures, yet we all mean but *one thing.*
And consequently our English [*sitting*] is very
proper, because, though it was the Custom then
to *lie down*, yet now, in our Nation at least, the
way is *to sit*, when we eat at Table.

A. Fashions among *Men* must not extend to the
Ordinances of *God.* And if our *Brethren* are perswaded, that the *gesture* of Christ and his Disciples should influence us, to use the *same* at the Holy Sacrament, it is not safe for us to vary from it
upon the consideration of a Country Custom. We
might as well by this Argument take *Beer* and *Sy-
der*, or some such Liquor instead of *Wine*, because
they are naturally the product of this *Northern Cli-
mate*, and as much used by us, as *Wine* by the *Romans* and *Jews.* But though there were formerly
a sort of Hereticks (*m*) (called *Hydroparastatæ*)
who used *Water* for Wine, yet I think neither *that*
nor any thing like it, has yet entred into our
Thoughts, though there seems a great *Latitude* in
the *Institution*, which mentions barely the *Cup*,
but no *Wine.* But we have sufficient reason to believe that the *Cup* contained nothing besides *Wine*,
both from the *Custom* of that Country ; and from

***

(*l*) Vid. de hac Quæst. plura in Saundersoni Prælect. Oxon.
de Conscientia Prælect. 3. N. 16, 17, 18, 19, 20, 21, 22.
(*m*) Can. 30. Conc. 6. in *Trullo.*

the *Declaration* Chrift then made, that *thenceforth he would drink no more of the fruit of the Vine.*

And it is to be further noted, that this *Difcum-bency* or lying down on Beds and Carpets, was not the common *Table gefture* among the *Jews*, though without doubt they did fometimes ufe it in com-plaifance to the *Romans*, their Lords, and other Nations; with whom they convers'd, and among whom that Cuftom prevailed. For it is faid of *Joſeph*'s Brethren, וישבו which the *feventy* and the other verfions, except the *Syriac*, render by *fitting*; *and they fate before him.* So again, the Peo-ple murmuring in the Wildernefs, faid — *Would to God we had died in the Land of* Egypt, *when we* (n) *fate by the fleſh-pots* — again, *It came to paſs, as they fate at Table* — And in the Prophet *Jeremy*, *Thou ſhalt not go into the houſe of feaſting, to fit with them to eat and drink.* — In which three laft places the *Syriac* confents, and all the tranſlations agree; only in that of *Jeremy*, the *Targum* of *Jonathan* faith, [*Ut difcumbas*] to lie down, though the word ישב, properly fignifies *to fit*, and when lying down is intended, another *Hebrew* word is ufed, as in *Amos.* 2. 8. and they laid themfelves down upon Clothes, יטו *declinare fecerunt*, as Dr. *Walton* turns it. And in thofe *Queſtions* and *Anſwers* at the Paſſover, *this Night* is diftinguifhed from all *other Nights*, on the account, that, *in other Nights*, the Jews did eat *fitting* or lying down, but in this only *lying*; from which it is evident, (o) that the fafhion of *fitting* at Table, was both more Anci-ent and more practifed, even among the Jews themfelves; and therefore if they, for diftincti-

---

(n) Exod. 16. 3. 1 Kings 13. 20. Jer. 16. 8. (o) Hinc *patet morem fedendi in menſa eſſe antiquiſſimum : Mos enim accumbendi vel difcumbendi longè poſterius cepit* —A Lapid. in Gen. 42.

on fake, *lay down* at the Paſchal Supper, and that, as is urged, our Lord did the ſame, this *Emphaſis* calls for a more exact conformity; becauſe, tho' they indifferently *ſate* or *lay along at other times*, yet at the *Sacramental Supper*, the latter, (on a particular reaſon) was obſerved by them in a more formal and ſolemn manner.

I muſt confeſs, I am not in love with this way of diſputing; yet it is *Argumentum ad Hominem*, as they call it, and concludes againſt Men, who are ſcrupulous and nice, in adhering to a geſture then in Faſhion. But for my own part, I lay no mighty ſtreſs upon what Chriſt *ſaid* or *did* at the Paſſover. And unleſs it could be well proved what *geſture* he was pleaſed to require from the Diſciples, at the Adminiſtration of the Sacrament, my Conſcience is affected with nothing but what I find clearly expreſt at that Sacred inſtitution. And ſeeing there is a profound ſilence concerning this Circumſtance, I ſafely believe it left to the Piety and Wiſdom of the Church, who Chriſt foreſaw would preſcribe ſuch a *Geſture* as might be very *ſignificant* to expreſs that *humility* and reverence we ought to approach with to the *Divine Table*.

B. Well, laying aſide a precedent liable to Cavil, and following the Conduct of that diſcretion, and reaſon you appeal to in this point, what *Geſture* can there be more proper, and more agreeable to the Nature of the thing than *ſitting*? Becauſe the *Sacrament* being an holy Banquet and *Feaſt*, (as you ſometimes call it) the Privilege of a gueſt, and the *freedom* of a Table, expect ſuch a geſture as beſpeaks the ſenſe we have of God's reconciliation, who to teſtify his Good-Will towards us, admits us to eat and drink in his preſence as Friends and Children, or in the words of the Prayer after the Communion, *as very members incorporate*

incorporate in the myſtical Body of Chriſt, which is the Bleſſed company of all faithful People, and heirs, thro' hope of God's everlaſting Kingdom, by the Merits of the moſt precious Death and Paſſion of his dear Son. And therefore in full aſſurance of his favour, we come to this Table with great ſatisfaction and joy, not in a *Suppliant, dejected manner,* and diſtruſtful of the Clemency and Mercy of the inviter, as they ſeem to come with, who uſe *proſtration or kneeling.*

A. 'Tis true, this action hath the ſhew of a *Feaſt,* and ſo it is, but 'tis (*p*) a *Sacred Feaſt* made for Divine Worſhip. And though it be a *Table,* it muſt be remembred that it is the *Lord's-Table,* and the Lord's-Body and Blood, which ought to be diſcerned well, as St. *Paul* ſaith, and not treated as *vulgar food* which periſhes in the uſe, whereas this is the Bread of Eternal Life, and he that eats of it, ſhall live for ever. As therefore the *Bread* is not *common,* ſo neither is the *behaviour* to be as at ordinary Tables. The Scripture indeed ſaith, it is a (*q*) *Table,* but withal calls it an (*r*) *Altar;* and though the *firſt* Character of it encourages *freedom,* ſuch as Children may take, yet the *other* demands (*s*) *reverence;* and while we are with him as a *Father,* we ought to adore him as *God.* And as the *one ſtile* may *cauſe joy,* ſo may the *other trembling* without any incongruity or contradiction, if *David* knew what he ſaid, *Pſ. 2. 11: Serve the Lord with fear, and rejoice to him with trembling*——And ſo it is reported of the Women, that they departed from the Sepulcher with *fear and great joy*————with *fear,* becauſe of the won-

---

(*p*) *Hæc actio habet ſpeciem convivii, imò eſt convivium, ſed Sacrum & divini cultûs cauſa*——Piſcator in Matth. 26. (*q*) 1 Cor. 10. 21. (*r*) Heb. 13. 10. (*s*) τϱάπεζα φοβεϱά. τϱάπεζα ἱεϱά. τϱάπεζα μυςική.

ders

ders they had feen; and with joy for the good news which was told 'em,' *Matth.* 28. 8. (t) And fo in the Sacrament, we approach to it with *joy*, upon the confidence we have of the Divine goodnefs, but ftill we behave our felves with a reverential and Godly *fear*, becaufe of the idea we ought to have of his Majefty and Power; and although we are fure that for Chrift's fake our Sins are Pardoned, yet we are never to forget them, efpecially when we prefent our felves before the Infinite and gracious God, who has been pleafed to remit 'em. A fatisfaction it muft needs be to a wounded Spirit, that he is going to *Offer* up the *Memorial* of the great Sacrifice *once* made in his behalf; but then while he doth this, 'tis fit he fhould be feen in a *Sacrificing geflure*; and confider fuch a time to be what it is, a time of (u) *Mourning*, a time of *fighing*, a time of *weeping*, a time of *confeffing*, and *begging of Pardon*. For the *Apoftle* tells us, that in the *Sacrament*, we do *fhew forth the Lord's Death*; and the fight of what is there done fhould equally affect us, as if we faw Chrift hanging on the Crofs. And therefore fhall a Man come to fuch a fight (x) *Pompatice & gloriofe*, as St. *Cyprian* fpeaks? Shall he fit as a *Judge*, or be a *Spectator* of this *Tragedy* in a way of *diverfion*, and without any other concern than barely to *fee* it, and then go away? Surely a Communicant hath other Thoughts of this Religious Act, and remembers that at fuch an hour he is Offering up a Propitiation, or Atonement for his many Impieties, and thereupon doth it with all *humility*, for fear his unfeemly carriage

---

(t) *Ad domos ftatim Dominicas currimus, corpora humi fternimus, mixtis cum fletu gaudiis fupplicamus.* Salvian. de Prov. (u) *Tempus lugendi, tempus gemendi, tempus flendi, tempus confitendi & deprecandi* —— Aug. in Pf. (x) *De cœna dom.*

should

fhould provoke God inftead of pleafing him; (*y*)*outward irreverence being the fure fign of a Prophane mind*, as St: *Paul* tells the *Corinthians*, *That they did not difcern the Lord's-Body*; *becaufe they did not deal more refpectfully with it in the holy Supper*, *than in their meals at the common Table*.

. The *Mofaic Sacrifices*, as in *other* particulars, fo in *this*, will help to inform us. They then were confidered in two refpects. *Firft*, As dedicated and *Offered* up to God ; and *Secondly*, As *eaten* by, thofe Men who offer'd 'em. So it is in the Sacrament. We *Offer* and we *Eat*. And as on the *latter*, account we may call it a *Feaft*, fo on the *other*, it is a *Sacrifice*, and in *both an act of Religion*, and therefore to be done in a *Religious way* : Efpecially if it be remembred, that our Neceffities call for it under the notion of a Sacrifice, (*z*) *In the offering of which we prefent alfo our Sins*, *faying whether we will or no*, *we have finned*. *Pardon us*. i. e. *We mention them firft*, *and then we beg Pardon*——And in this refpect we are to look back on that Ceremony among the *Jews*, who always put their hand on the head of the burnt Offering, not only to fignify that they made over all the right they had in the Beaft , to the ufe of God (fomewhat like the *Manumiffion* among the *Romans*, when renouncing their intereft in the *Slave*, they laid their hand on his head and faid, *Let this Man be free*) but moreover (*a*) the *Offerer* transferred the *Punifhment*, due to himfelf on the *Beaft* ready to be Sacrificed, and thereby owned that he himfelf deferved to be flain, but that by a gracious difpen-

---

(*y*) Chemnit. Exam. Conc. Trid. *Externa irreverentia fignum prophanæ mentis* . &c. (*z*) Chryfoft. Hom. in Heb. (*a*) *Hac ceremonia fignificat Offerens fe peccata fua imprecari, & quafi imponere victimæ immolandæ eamq; pro fe Offerre.* A Lap. in Levit. 1.4.

fation,

fation , God was pleafed to accept of the *Beaſt*
for *him.* (*b*) And ſo *Euſebius* underſtands the
impoſition of the hand as the *Symbol* of an Offering, and a Teſtimony of that *Guilt* they diſ-
charged themſelves of, and laid on the Sacrifice,
For the *hands* are the inſtruments ofSinful actions;
and as by them they did many ill things to provoke God, ſo by them they laid their Crimes
on the oblation,in whoſe Death they thought their
own Puniſhment over, as Men acquitted and by interpretation reſtored to their former Innocency.

And this I take to be one meaning of the *Miniſters* laying his hand on the *Bread* and *Cup* at the
Communion, not barely to *Conſecrate* and Bleſs
the Elements, but withal to ſhow that in behalf
of *himſelf* and the *People;* he ſets *his* and *their Sins*
on that *Sacrifice,* they are going to Commemorate
and Tender to God at that time. Foraſmuch
therefore as every Communicant is before this *Altar,* as a *Condemned Man,* and muſt ſuffer for his
Sins, either in his own Perſon or ſomething elſe,
if there continues ſtill a Law of *Redemption* and
Exchange, whereby Puniſhments are *transferred*
from one Creature to another, and from *us* to
our Saviour Chriſt *Jeſus,* yet certainly (as Crimi-
nals are wont to do in the like caſes) we ſhould
receive our acquittal or diſcharge in a very *humble
manner ;* and ſo treat this holy Oblation (*c*) with
great *Religion and Reverence according to the Cuſtom
of every Church, with a comely Habit, modeſt behaviour, ſoberly and devoutly with the head uncovered,
and with a bended knee* ——— After the Example of
Chriſt, when he was juſt going to be made this
Sacrifice, *He kneeled down and pray'd* —— (*d*) *To teach*

(*b*) Demonſt. Evang. l 1. c. 10. (*c*) Hoſpinian Hiſt. Sacra.
(*d*) Roffenſ. de Geniculat.

all

all Spiritual Sacrificers, to use the same kneeling in their devotion and prayers, which he began in the Propitiatory, and all sufficient Sacrifice for Sin.

Nor is this the only oblation we make at the Holy Communion. For therein we *set forth our Prayers as the incense, and the lifting up of our hands as the Evening Sacrifice*——We tender the Sacrifice of Praise and Thankſgiving, and therefore the Communicants eat and drink *(e) kneeling, as a ſignification of their humble and grateful acknowledgment of the benefits of Chriſt, therein given to all worthy Receivers.* And then alſo *(f) we preſent unto God our ſelves, our Souls and Bodies to be a reaſonable, holy and lively Sacrifice unto him* ——And in what geſture can this be better done than what the Saints in Heaven uſe , *(g)* for they fall before the Throne on their faces and worſhip, ſaying, *Bleſſing and Glory, and Wiſdom, and Thankſgiving, and Honour, and Power, and Might be unto our God for ever and ever.*

B. But we ought to have a great regard to the *Conſciences* of our *Brethren,* who are ſcandalized at this geſture; and who ſeeing us kneel before the Table, may ſuppoſe we *adore* the Elements, and give too much countenance to *Tranſubſtantiation* , which yet in point of Doctrine we declaim againſt, as a *Romiſh* invention brought into the Church, more for the Honour of the *Prieſt* than the Glory of God.

A. Our kneeling at the Sacrament would be no offence, if Men did but ask what the Church meant by it. Her words are theſe. :——*(h) Whereas it is ordained in this* [Communion] *Office, for the Ad-*

(e) At the cloſe of the Rubrick, Poſt Commun. *(f)* Prayer, Poſt Communio. *(g)* Revel. 7. 12. *(h)* Declarat. poſt Communion.

miniſtration

miniſtration of the Lord's-Supper, that the Communicants ſhould receive the ſame kneeling--yet leſt the ſame
kneeling ſhould by any Perſons, either out of ignorance
and infirmity, or out of malice and obſtinacy, be miſ-
conſtrued and depraved, it is here declared that thereby
no Adoration is intended, or ought to be done either unto the Sacramental Bread and Wine, there Bodily received, or unto any Corporal preſence of Chriſt's Natural
fleſh and blood. For the Sacramental Bread and Wine,
remain ſtill in their Natural ſubſtances, and therefore
may not be adored (for that were idolatry to be abhorred
by all faithful Chriſtians) and the natural Body and
Blood of our Saviour Chriſt, are in Heaven and not here;
it being againſt the truth of Chriſt's Natural Body, to
be at one time in more places than one——(i) We
adore God in the myſteries, but not the *myſteries* ;
in the Sacrament, but not the *Sacrament*——*We*
will worſhip in the place where his feet ſtood. Well ſaith
Chamier, *In the place, but not the place its ſelf* : So
we worſhip *in* the *Euchariſt,* but we worſhip not.
the *Euchariſt.* We kneel *before* the Table, but
we *adore* neither the *Table* nor any thing on it,
though we have from that Table ſuch teſtimonies
of the divine Favour, as move us to worſhip God
who is ſo gracious to us. The *Papiſt* adores the *Bread*
and *Wine,* yet not *as Bread* and *Wine,* but as their
ſubſtance is ſuppoſed changed and made the very
Body and *Blood of Chriſt,* that *Body* which he had
here on Earth, and which the Diſciples literally.
Worſhipped. But it is hard to charge us with
what they think or do. Let the abuſes be to
themſelves. And if they will adore the Sacrament, we cannot help it. Our care is to Worſhip *God* alone, while the *Sacrament* is Adminiſtred.

(i) Chamier Lib.7. de Euch. 6. 2 §. 9. vid. Morney de Miſſa.

If

If Men were to be frightned from holy things, becaufe they are ill-ufed, we fhould not lay by the *Euchariſt* alone, but rejeét *Baptiſm*, throw away the *Bible*, and in fhort, have no *Religion* at all. For heretofore on the one hand, a very great ftrefs was laid on *trinal Merſion* in *Baptiſm*, and by this means fome crafty heads defign'd to prejudice the *Unity* of the Godhead. (*k*) *Eunomius* on the other hand, introduced *ſingle Merſion* to deftroy the *Trinity*, (*l*) or as *Zonaras* fpeaks, *to coñfound and contraƈt the holy Trinity intó one Perſon*--- Muft we therefore not Baptize at all? Then, as to *Scripture*, what Book, what Chapter of it is there, which *this* or *that Heretick*, has not rejeéted or blafphemed or wrefted, muft we therefore throw it by and never read it? And laftly, for *Religion* in general, what a fair fhew do fome Men make of it, who yet in reality have no Religion at all? But fhall we therefore lay it afide, becaufe they are Hypocrites? Shall we not fay our Prayers, becaufe others never Pray, or Pray only out of Wordly defign? In all thefe and the like cafes, we are to reform the abufes and mind the thing. And though in particular, the holy *Euchariſt* hath been all along expofed to this misfortune, fome believing it barely *Bread* and *Wine*, without relation to what they fignify, others making it the *very Body* and *Blood* of Chrift, and accordingly adore it, as the *Romaniſts* now, yet thefe are no reafons for us to renounce it, but going between the two extremes, we treat it with *decency*, as becomes a *Sacrament* ; and if we *kneel* while we continue Communicants, we do it purely in reverence to Chrift, who made it an *Ordinance*; and we no

---

(*k*) Sozom. Eccl. Hift 1. 6. c. 26. (*l*) In Can. 7. Conc. Conftant.

more Worfhip it, than we do the Wood or Stone on which it is placed, or the Minifter from whofe hands we receive it.

B. But to *adore,* or to ufe an adoring gefture in this action, though it be immediately directed to God himfelf, can we underftand it otherwife than a more fubtile, or more *refined piece of Idolatry,* or as *Durandus* foftens it, a *relative Worfhip,* innocently enough expreft before an Image, without adoring the Image it felf? The Old *Pagans* had this Evafion, who were not fuch Fools as to Worfhip *inanimate matter,* but only, as they pretended, thofe Deities the things *refembled.* Yet the Ancient Doctors for all that call 'em *Idolaters;* nor could the *inward intention* of the mind fanctify their vifible applications to the Idol, nor excufe the charge againft 'em, of being impioufly devout.

A. We are to diftinguifh between a *Negative Precept* forbidding Images, (as in the Decalogue), and a *pofitive inftitution* commanded in the Gofpel. The fame action may be good or bad diverfely confidered: And though to *kneel* at the Communion, as an holy Appointment, is decent and pious, yet to kneel *before* an Image *forbidden* in Scripture is *Idolatry* and Will-worfhip. We read in the Book of *Leviticus,* that God was wroth with *Nadab and Abihu,* for *Offering incenfe,* yet he was not angry, that incenfe was *Offered,* but becaufe it was offer'd *by them, with ftrange Fire before the Lord, which he commanded them not;* ———for in the words before *(m)* he accepted that *which* Mofes *and* Aaron *offered,* becaufe it was done according to the Precept. It was a Sin in *Ahaz* to Worfhip before the *Altar,* made in the Fafhion of that he had feen at *Damafcus,* or to facrifice on it,

(m) Lev. 9. 24,

yet

yet 'twas a Duty in *Solomon* to do both at the *Lord's-Altar* at *Jerusalem*. We have no need of *Subtleties* in what we do : Nor do we flee for refuge to the *intention* of Men to secure us from Idolatry. They who adored the *Golden-calf* or the *Brazen-Serpent*, did not terminate their Devotion *there*, yet it excuses 'em not ; and the charge of false Worship is not unjustly fixt on them, though they might pretend those Objects no more than the sensible representations of God their Deliverer. We declare the Bread and Wine at the Communion *sacred Mysteries*, sanctified for *use*, but not *Adoration*. They are an *Ordinance* of Christ, and so we consider 'em, and come to 'em as *such* ; we eat and drink in *Obedience to the Ordainer*, and as in them we *remember* him a *Sacrifice*, so on that account we *adore* him as a *Saviour*. We kneel before the Creatures ; true, and where shall we kneel without 'em ? (*n*) *Solomon* on his knees pray'd before the *Altar*. *David* addrest God before his Footstool. *Elias* pray'd before the People, before the *Altar*, before the *Sacrifice*. In what place soever we are, we lift up our Eyes and Hands to Heaven, yet we do not Worship it, no not as the Throne of God. We go to Church with our Neighbours to Worship, but we Worship, neither the Church, nor the People. (*o*) It is the Custom of those, who do Penance to *kneel* before the Minister from whom they receive *Absolution*. And when Men are *Ordained*, it is in the same gesture, and yet without the charge of doing this piece of Divine homage, to the *Bishop* or the *Minister*. Though then it be a sound Proposition, That it is an idolatrous Act to Worship before a

---

(*n*) 1 King 8. 54; Ps. 99. 5. 1 King 18. (*o*) Vid. Forbes Iren. l. 1, c. 1.

Creature, with such Thoughts as to make that Creature the *term and object* of our Worſhip, and limit our Devotion to it, either for its *own ſake*, or as it is the *Symbol* of ſomething adorable, as when the Apoſtatizing *Jews* offer'd incenſe to the *Brazen Serpent*; or the *Romaniſts* to their *Images, Reliques, Croſs* and the like, yet it is not Applicable in this caſe, becauſe, though we kneel at our Prayers, while the Bread and Wine are on the Table, and take 'em when conſecrated, as an holy Sacrament, or *mean* for God to convey his Grace into our Hearts, and as a *Pledge* of his Love to us, yet we conſider 'em no further than as a *Teſtimony* of the Divine favour; and we no more Worſhip 'em, than we Worſhip a Ring, Jewel or Goblet, the *King* might beſtow upon us, and which *as from the King* we receive *kneeling*. And though the *Papiſts* in general have another Notion, yet ſome particular Men among 'em are not aſhamed to own the truth, and ſay, *That in the* Euchariſt *Chriſt is to be diſcerned by the mind from the viſible ſign, and he is to be adored, and not the Sacrament, becauſe, the Elements are things created and without Life, and conſequently incapable of Adoration: For it is not enough that Chriſt is under 'em, becauſe God is alſo in the Soul of Man as in his Temple, and and yet God is Worſhipped, and not the Soul:* —— So *Suarez.*

Briefly: Our going to the Sacrament we look upon as a Religious Act, and one diſtinguiſhing inſtance of our Chriſtianity; and ſo we call it in the Prayer after the Communion, *our bounden Duty and Service.* And thereupon, as in all the reſt, ſo eſpecially this, we take our ſelves obliged to do it in a very *reverent and humble way*, and upon this reaſon we *kneel*, not *to* the Sacrament, but *at* it or *in* the time of it, as a ſacred Ordinance, which with our Prayers and Praiſes make up the

Service of *that Day*, or that *part* of the Day dedicated to his Service?

And in this the (*p*) *reformed Churches* agree with us, treading in the steps of all the Churches before 'em. And though they look on the gesture as an *indifferent thing*, within the Liberty and Power of the Church to alter or retain, yet to *sit* at the Sacrament, they take for such an *overt act of inward irreverence*, that they cannot but think, either the *Pagans* who adored their Images *sitting*, (according to a Law fathered on *Numa*, requiring *Ut Adoraturi sedeant*) or the *Arians* who denied the Divinity of Christ, must be Godfathers of this innovation. So speak (*q*) two Synods in *Poland*, which call these Men *Arians*, (or in the new stile *Socinians*) *Perfidious deserters, unbelieving runnagates, who place Christ on the same bench with themselves, and deny the Lord that bought 'em. And who under pretence of imitating Christ and his Disciples, encourage an evil practice to the scandal of Religion: And change that decent gesture approved, and used throughout all* Europe, *and over the whole World.*

B. I must crave leave to dissent in that: For I cannot believe this Custom of *kneeling* so *Catholick*, on the account either of *place* or *time*, as is commonly said, because not only in these our Days the Church of *Scotland*, many in *England*, in the *United Provinces*, and elsewhere use sitting, (as I think they say, the *Pope* doth when he *receives*) but in Ancient times the Communicants *stood* at the Sacrament, as *Dionysius*, Bishop of *Alexandria*, informs us upon this occasion. (*r*) There was a certain Person who had been Baptized by the *He-*

(*p*) *Veterem Ecclesiam in hoc imitantes*, &c. Forbes Iren. l. 2. c. 16. n. 1. (*q*) Concil. Ulodislaviens. Can. 6. Concil. Petricoviens. Art. 4. (*r*) Euseb. Eccl. Hist. l. 7. c. 9.

reticks, and who afterwards discovering how much it differed from the way of the *Orthodox,* in comparison of which he found the other(s) full of impiety and blasphemies, he comes to *Dionysius* (t) weeping, and lamenting his hard fortune, and desiring the *Bishop* to baptize him. It was a nice point, and *Dionysius* durst not depend on his own Judgment, but writes to *Xystus* Bishop of *Rome,* and desires his advice. But withal lets him know his own Opinion; that for his part, he had hitherto denied the Man for this reason, *Because,* saith he, *he has been partaker of all the instances of Christian-Worship, and,* among the rest, (u) *he has often stood at the Altar, and received the Sacrament of the Body and Blood of Christ* ——— Whereupon (w) *Valesius* (as well he might) makes this inference, That *heretofore the Communicants went up to the Altar, and there received standing, and not kneeling,* as is now in practice. ——— This is confirm'd by that Canon of the *Nicene* Council you cited, and which for Uniformity sake, required all Churches to *stand* at their Prayers, between *Easter* and *Whitsuntide,* as also on every *Lord's-day,* whereon the Sacrament being always Administred, they must be supposed to Communicate *standing,* because the *Canon* makes no exception. And it is to be suspected, that this Custom is in a great measure owing to the Decree of *Honorius,* for the Adoration of the Sacrament, *this gesture* being very proper for their Doctrine of *Transubstantiation,* but ill becomes those who explode that notion. The Language of

---

(s) ἀσεβείας ἐκεῖνο κỳ βλασφημῶν, &c. ———(t) κλαίνων κỳ καταβρήνων ἑαυτόν (u) κỳ τεαπέζη παεϱsαῦ]α. — (w) *Fideles communicaturi ad altare accedebant, ibiq; corpus Christi de manu Presbyteri stantes, non ut hodie, flexis genibus, accipiebant.*——Val. in loc.

Chrysostom

Chryfoftom concurrs, with what I am saying ; for he complains thus of the remiffnefs of the People; *In vain we ftand at the Altar:* ——where you fee, though he calls the *Table* an *Altar,* yet the Sacrificers, *i. e.* the Communicants *ftood* at it. *Homil. ad pop. Antioch.*

A. Your Objection is plaufible. But to Anfwer it in its parts, and firft for *Dionyfius,* who calls it *ftanding,* and fo a Critick muft needs tranflate it. Yet moft likely the *Bifhop* intended no more than the parties *prefence* at the Sacrament, and not his *Gefture.* And his queftion to *Xyftus,* may be fhortned thus. *Whether he who had been Baptized by an Heretick, but had lived a great while in the Communion of the Church, and eat and drunk at the Holy Table, ought to be rebaptized?*

Now that the word *ftanding* is not always to be ftrictly taken, appears by feveral examples; for whereas it is faid , *the publican ftood afar off,* it means nothing elfe but that he was at a great diftance from the Pharifee in the Temple, yet probably on his *knees,* as better anfwering the *dejection* of his Spirits, and the great *confufion* he was then in, not daring to *lift up his Eyes to Heaven :* And accordingly the *Perfian* tranflation faith, [*In genua fe dabat*] *He fell on his knees.* And fo it is reported of *Mary Magdalene,* (z) *She ftanding at his feet behind him,* i. e. being behind him, and *kneeling,* for otherwife, how was fhe able *to wafh his Feet with her Tears, and wipe 'em with the Hairs of her Head.* 'Tis a common way of Speech, we do or we do not *ftand* upon this or that thing, when we mean no gefture at all, but that we will or will not continue our *Refolution* to proceed, or

---

(z) ςᾶσα. Stans, i. e. *præfens & genibus innixa ad pedes Chrifti.* A Lapide in Luc. 7. 38.

forbear

forbear what we defign. So that confidering the way of the Church to Adminifter the Sacrament to the People *kneeling,* (according to that rule of the Fathers, that *every Man muft adore before he eateth,*) by *Dionyfius's ftanding,* is underftood no more than that the party *had been a conftant Communicant* for fome time, that his Principles were found and good, and his inclination altogether for the way of the Catholicks, without any regard to his *fitting, kneeling or ftanding.* However, to make fome improvement of this part of your exception, I defire you to remember the words immediately following thofe you cited, *and ftretching out his hand to receive the facred food* —— which fhows, efpecally if you take *Valefius's* Comment (whofe Opinion is in credit with you) that it was the practice of *thofe days,* as now, for the *Prieft* to give the *Bread* and *Wine* into the hands of the People.

But you obferve the Council of *Nice,* required *ftanding* all the time between *Eafter and Whitfuntide,* and on the *Lord's-days,* whereon to be fure the *Sacrament* was Adminiftred ———— I cannot deny all this, yet am not convinced that they continued the *fame gefture* at the holy Communion, which they ufed at their other Devotion. Becaufe, though the latter was enjoined to be done *ftanding* in honour of Chrift's Refurrection, and as a token of our belief, that we are to rife again, yet it muft not be forgotten, that the *Lord's-Supper* is the *fhewing forth his Paffion and Death,* and therefore it calls for another gefture, as reprefenting a paffage which fell out *before Eafter,* and fo in Congruity it Challenged *another kind* of behaviour; And while they treated our Redeemer as a *Sacrifice, Bowing* or *Kneeling* was more fuitable, though under the ftile of a *Triumphant Conquerour,* and during the time of fuch a Reflection, the other well became

came 'em. However, this is not to be omitted, that the same *Canon* takes notice of another gesture, which People had been accustomed to, even between those two great Festivals; And if we restore that *more common*, and *more ancient* practice, there is no harm done. For as it then lay in the discretion and power of the Church to *make* that Constitution, so it is in the Power of the Church now to *alter* or model it, as she sees occasion.

As for Pope *Honorius*, I am apt to think you mistake the sence of the Decree. The words are these. *Let the Priest instruct the People, that whenever in the celebration of Mass, the hoste is elevated, they reverently Bow; doing the same when the Presbyter carries it to the Sick.* ———So that first this is to be done at all times when the hoste is lifted up; whether in the *Church* or *Street*; and every Body is to show it reverence, whether *Communicants* or *not*. And the gesture is *Bowing* not kneeling. And in a word, this is nothing to the purpose, as to our behaviour at the holy Table. The History, as I take it, is that after *Innocent* had made his Declaration, that the *Bread* was the *Body*, and the *Wine* the *Blood* of Christ, truly and strictly, and the Elements changed by the Divine Power, into what after Consecration we Sacramentally call 'em, then *Honorius* his Successour, decreed that the Sacrament should be adored, not only God *at* the Sacrament, but the Sacrament it self upon the reason of *Transubstantiation*, supposing it now the *very Body and Blood* of Christ, and no longer *Bread and Wine*, as in appearance they are. And this we may gather from their way of arguing in the Council of *Trent*. For as soon as it was resolved, that by virtue of Consecration, there is a *through change* of the whole substance of Bread into the substance of Christ's Body, and of the whole substance of Wine, into the substance of his Blood

E e

(which

(*which* Converſion, ſay they, *is aptly named Tranſub-*
ſtantiation) they ſubjoin as follows, *There is left*
therefore no room to doubt, but that all the faithful ac-
cording to the received cuſtom of the Catholick-Church,
will have the Sacrament in the ſame veneration as God
himſelf, and allow it, Latriæ cultum, *becauſe we believe*
the ſame God preſent, which the Eternal Father brought
into the World, and ſaid, let all the Angels of God
Worſhip him ———— *the ſame the Wiſemen adored,* &c.
Now for our parts, we no more regard this *De-*
cree, than we do the *Day* dedicated to the *hoſte,*
which they call the *Feſtival of Chriſt's Body.* However, notwithſtanding this abuſe of a Worſhipping geſture directed to a wrong object, we think
we have no more reaſon to leave it off in that ſence
we uſe it, than St *John* had to forbear *all kneeling,*
becauſe the Angel forbid him to *kneel to him.*

As for St. *Chryſoſtom,* a very few words will
explain him. *We ſtand at the Altar* ——— what
then ? *And no Man Communicates,* for ſo it immediately follows. It ſeems the People were grown
very cold in this duty, and the good Biſhop complains of it, becauſe he and other Miniſters *ſtood at*
the Altar, expecting 'em to come to the Sacrament,
but they declined it. However, had they gave
their Attendance, St. *Chryſoſtom's ſtanding,* is not
to be taken for a *Sacramental geſture.* For all Miniſters now *ſtand,* and muſt ſtand to give the Sacrament to others, though when themſelves receive, they do it *kneeling. His ſtanding* means an
invitation, or as the Sacrament is Adminiſtred to
the Congregation, and not the geſture they Communicated in. To conclude, were theſe Arguments of any ſtrength to diſprove *kneeling,* yet
they contribute nothing to juſtify *ſitting. Stand-*
ing and Kneeling, as I ſaid before, are both *Religi-*
ous ; and both *indifferent,* ſo that the Church may
preſcribe the *one* or the *other.* But as for *ſitting,*

to say no more, 'tis a very *irreverent*, unmannerly habit of Body, in the presence of the great God, at whose Table we then are; and we appear to have little value for the Divine favour, while we are seen to deal so *familiarly* with him.

But we are now come to the place where we must part for this Evening, and I believe by that time you get home, you will want a Conveniency for the gesture you have been pleading for, and which you may safely and innocently use in such a place; I wish therefore you were there to enjoy it, for I doubt I have tired you.

Good-Night.

E e 2

The

The Fifth DIALOGUE.

The CONTENTS.

A Reverent gesture becomes Prayer. Prayer one great work of the Lord's-day. Reasons for us to Pray. How we can be said to honour God. Forms of Prayer vindicated. The Lord's-Prayer twice delivered. The Liturgies of St. James, and some other Apostles illegitimate, yet Ancient, and in what sense they may be called Theirs, whose names they bear. The former Ages abounded with Liturgies. Their number reduced. The Councils of Carthage and Milevis, on that subject. Justin Martyr's ὅσν δύναμις explain'd. 1 Tim. 2. 1. a Rule for Liturgies. The nature of Prayer infers the usefulness of common-Prayer. Ministers absence from all or part of the Divine Service misunderstood. Their not reading the Prayers themselves excused. Readers Ancient. The notion of Edification, proves the necessity of forms of Prayer. The Minister the Mouth, but not the Mind of the Congregation. The import of Amen. St. Paul's praying with the Spirit cleared. Our Liturgy not Popish. Older than Popery. Agrees rather with the way of the Old Gallican-Church. The Book and the Compilers of it burnt by Queen Mary. The parts of the Common-Prayer examined. Short Prayers, and the same Prayers justified. Difference of gestures in the Service. Our Ceremonies vindicated. Romish censured: The reasons why the Reformers reain'd some. Bishop Hooper's scruple about Episco-

pal

pal veſtments reſolved by Bucer, *and* Peter Martyr. *His Opinion of the ſeventh-day. The reading of Leſ-ſons without expoſition. Such expoſitions introduced by* Ezra, *and the reaſons of it. The example and Prece-dent of our Sermons. The Fathers Preach'd every day. Short Sermons. Twice on the Lord's-day, ac-cording to the neceſſity of thoſe times. Reading of the* Apocrypha *excuſed. Repetitions in the Liturgy, and often repeating the Lord's-Prayer vindicated. What were the Heathen Battologies. Some other Objections conſidered.*

A. I Fear my moving this way hath occa-ſioned your Friend to leave you, if ſo, I am ſorry and beg your Pardon.

B. There's no need of it, Sir ; His buſineſs calls him away : And though I was unwilling, being alone, to part with him before, yet upon ſo good a change, I eaſily yielded to let-him attend his af-fairs elſewhere. I ſuppoſe you know him. He is a very induſtrious, honeſt Man, but of few words, and therefore not ſo agreeable or fit for Conver-ſation.

A. I remember his face, for he comes frequently to our Church, but as I have obſerved always *late*, which makes me ſuſpect him to be no great Ad-mirer of the *Prayers* ; and if I may judge of his *Principle* by his *behaviour*, he thinks it an *uſeleſs Ser-vice* : For his *geſture* contradicts the notion of a *Supplicant*, and he deals with the *Houſe of God* as with his *Parlour* ; Sits immediately down, and ſo continues till the Liturgy is over. *(a)* 'Tis true, St. *Auguſtine* tells us, that it is not preſcribed *how* the *Body* is to be managed in Prayer, provided the *Mind* diſcharges it ſelf well : ——And adds, That

---

(a) *Non eſt Præſcriptum, &c: ad Simplic.*

ſome

ſome Votaries *ſtood,* ſome *kneeled,* and others, *pro-ſtrated* themſelves on the ground. And ſo (b) *Juſtin Martyr*, and (c) St. *Cyprian* repreſent 'em *ſtanding.* (d) And *Clemens* of *Alexandria* ſaith, that when they pray'd they *threw themſelves on the ground.* So (e) *Arnobius,* that they did either *kneel* or *proſtrate themſelves* at Prayer; (f) as did the *Chriſtian* Soldiers in the Emperours Army. All which geſtures are *ſignificant* enough to ſhow their *concern* and *humility* : And a Man according to the ſtate and condition of his Body, may innocently uſe which he pleaſes to expreſs his Devotion by, where the *Church* and his *Governours* have left him at *Liberty.* But we never read of a Man s *ſitting* at his Prayers : *That's* a geſture too free and *familiar* to pretend Adoration and Worſhip ; and it is a piece of irreligion, ſome what worſe than not praying or not coming to Church, to be ſo *publick-ly irreverent,* when we would be thought *pious,* and thereby invite others to follow our Examples. For my part, as I look on the *Lord's-day* to be a *Day of Prayer,* ſo I take the *Church* to be the *Houſe of Prayer,* as the Scripture and (g) the Ancients call it, and therefore they who pray, ought to ad-dreſs God (h) with humility and tears, and not with a diſorderly and impudent carriage. When then on *ſuch* a *Day,* I come to *ſuch a Place,* I con-ſider my ſelf obliged to anſwer the end of my be-ing there, and not preſently *ſeat* my ſelf, and abide

---

(b) Apolog 2. (c) De Orat. Dom. (d) Strom. l. 7. (e) Contra gent (f) Euſeb. Eccl. Hiſt. l. 5. c. 5. (g) αἱ τῶ θεῶ ἐκκλησίαι ὄικοι προσευχῶν λέγονται. ————————Balſam in 75. Can. Conc. in *Trullo.* (h) μετὰ δακρύων ἡ ταπεινώσεως, ἒ μετα ἀταξία ἡ ἀναιδὲς σχήματος——ibid. *Intramus templa compoſi-ti—vultum ſubmittimus, in omne argumentum modeſtiæ fin-gimur.* Senec. Nat. Qu. l. 7. c. 30.

in

in that gesture during the Divine Worship, as if I had so much wearied my self in getting to the *Church*, that now I had nothing else to do but to ease me for an hour, and then recovering Breath and Spirits, return home again.

B. Surely there is more than that in it.

A. You mean the *hearing* of a *Sermon*. Which if done on a Religious score, and as an *Ordinance* of God, the carriage of a Man in the whole Service, would be Decent and Correspondent to such a Principle. But this being apparently otherwise, the Religion of such hearers, must be construed into what the *Athenians.* went to *Mars*'s-hill for, *to hear news*; wherein indeed they gratify Curiosity, and may serve *themselves*, but not *God*. But this *Christian-Sabbath* is intended for us to walk in *God's-ways*, not our *Own*. It is separated and sanctified for his Honour and Worship: And though the hearing of those *Divine Lectures*, (if so taken) are very necessary for our instruction and reproof, and thereby we show respect to the Author of these Holy Appointments, yet it should be ever remembred that our *Prayers* and *Praises*, are more properly the *Service*. And though we obey God in giving due attention to his word, yet then only we are said to Worship and Glorify, and do him Reverence, when we are seen on our knees, and in that humble manner acknowledge his *Soveraignty*, *Power*, *Wisdom* and *Mercy*; and on the sense of these Attributes make our Supplications, and zealous Addresses to him.

B. Undoubtedly, *Prayer* is one great work of this *Day*; And if *Paul*, saith, we are to *pray without ceasing*, and *Luke*, that *Men ought always to pray*, or be by a good Habit disposed to it, and ready to perform it *on all Days*, when our ordinary affairs permit; so more especially is this to be done on the *Lord's-day*, which is distinguished

from

from all others on that account, and whereon all *fe-cular* bufinefs is; adjourn'd & removed to a diftance, that we may be able to follow *this* the better.

A. Can any reafonable Man forget this inftance of his Homage, to the Lord of Heaven and Earth, when he reads fuch Scriptures as tell him, that *God made us and not we ourfelves* ; that *in him we live move, and have a Being* ; in a word, that he alone fubfifts of himfelf and hath every Creature, and every fecond Caufe link'd to his Chair, being altogether managed and directed by his Providence ? This, if we are once perfwaded of, we cannot but *apply* ourfelves to him for Life, Health and Protection ; and this *Application* being made by *Prayer*, is the reafon why we fhould *Pray* to him.

A Truth fufficiently clear'd to us by the Light of Nature: And therefore the Heathens had a God, to invoke for every thing they wanted, attributing all relief to the *Divine Power*, though they grofly erred in the notion of the *Divine Unity*. And of this the Magnificence and furniture of their *Temples* were plain demonftrations, for they confifted of prefents almoft numberlefs, promifed and vowed in their *Prayers* for *fafety, victory* or any other *fuccefs*. And we may obferve in the *Bible*, that the name of ill Men is rendred by this Periphrafis, *They feek not after God, they work wickednefs, they have not called upon God*——And pertinent is the remark of the *Chaldee* (*h*) Paraphrafe on *Gen.* 4. 26. fpeaking of thofe times when *Enos* was born, *then were Men fo Prophane, that they did not call on the Name of the Lord*———*Yet* it feems not fo Prophane as to call upon no God, but they miftook the object, *they did not call on the Name of the Lord.*

(*h*) *Tunc prophani erant homines ut non orarent in nomine domini.*

Briefly,

Briefly, to attempt the enjoyment of any *Good*, or to expect the removal of any *Evil* without God, and without thefe Addreffes to him, if it hath not fome fhare in the *Atheift's Creed*, That indeed *there is no God*, or of the *Epicure's*, That he intermeddles not with matters here below; yet to give it the fofteft turn, 'tis very great *ftupidity*, or Caufes a fufpicion, that we believe fome kind of independency in ourfelves, and that by our own ftrength, cunning or power, we can do very well without him. Whereas alas ! Should he be once provoked to withdraw his hand, which continually fupports us, down we muft fink, and in a moment moulder away to nothing For we are not in the leaft able *of ourfelves, to help ourfelves, but all our fufficiency is from God.* Nor can *we receive any thing, but it muft be given us from above.* In ficknefs he is our *Phyfician*; In diftrefs our *Deliverer*; In danger our *Refuge*; *A prefent help in Trouble.* But then it is required, that we fay, *Help, Lord, or we Perifh :— Mafter, Mafter, we Perifh : Help us now, O Lord:— O Lord, fave Us.—*

Yet it is not to be thought, but that without any formal reprefentation of our wants, God hath *Infight* and *Wifdom*, enough to underftand 'em, and as our Lord fpeaks, *He knows that we have need of all thefe things :—*Which is the reafon, the (*i*) *Adamiani* went on to deny the neceffity of Prayer; however, he requires us to fpeak of 'em, if only by that means to (*k*) imprefs our own *Hearts*, and bring us to a true fenfe of his *All-fuf-*

(*i*) *Deum à nobis precandum & orandum effe negant Adamiani, quia fcit ipfe per fe quibus egeamus.* Clem. Alex. Stro. l 7. (*k*) *Ad parandos animos ut ardentius oremus*——Aretius in Matth. 6. *Excitando non indicando*—— Grot. *Ut vires noftras*——*incitemus*, &c. Reuchlin. de Art. Cabal. l. 3.

ficiency to help us, and of our *incapacity* to help our-selves. He that is unwilling to own his neceffities, 'tis to be fear'd his *Pride* hinders him, and Pride ill becomes a *Beggar.* When a Man is in ftreights, 'tis a folly and a *fault* not to confefs it to a *humane Benefactour*, but 'tis a *Sin* to be fullen and filent be-fore him who is *Divine.* For altho' we may fuppofe *both* to know what his Condition is without fuch difcovery, yet *both* probably on the fame reafon will fhut their Eyes, becaufe it too often happens, that People do not value the relief which comes unfought, as a Jewel is quickly flighted that coft us nothing: So that this confideration makes Men not over forward to throw away *their* favours, much lefs is it to be expected that God fhould *His.* When we are in want and fure of fuccour if it be defired, would it not be an inexcufable madnefs to neglect asking it? Certainly he that is thus regardlefs of his own welfare, deferves the utmoft misfortunes that can befal him; and no matter if he continue *Poor* or *Weak* for ever, if he will not be at the ex-pence or uneafinefs of a Prayer to befeech God to pity him. And thus you fee, intereft invites to Ad-drefs that Almighty Power, which alone is able to do us good. And becaufe we are perpetually wanting fomething, in fome way or other, which we cannot help ourfelves to, without his affift-ance, therefore on this reafon we are always to Pray to him. But ftill 'tis a Duty on another fcore, becaufe in thefe Addreffes we fet forth the *Ma-jefty* and *Goodnefs* of God, and at the fame time *both* Pray to him for our *own benefit,* and alfo exalt, and *do him honour;* by declaring before him and all the World, that without him we *are* and can be *nothing.* So that fhould a *Mental Prayer,* in any Room or in any gefture, be offered, and fo well taken as to gain relief to our own wants, yet with refpect to God and his Glory, *publick Places,* and another

fort

fort of behaviour muſt be much more requiſite and proper. For the Holy Scripture requires us, *To let our Light ſhine before Men, that they may ſee our good Works, and* be invited to glorifie our *Heavenly Father* ; And we are to *confeſs Chriſt before Men,* that *he may confeſs us before the holy Angels* : And therefore for theſe ends, it is very neceſſary to appear in the *Church* on *theſe Days,* alotted the Divine Worſhip, and acquit ourſelves there in ſuch a manner, as may convince all the beholders of the Awe and Reverence, we have for God, which we teſtifie by our *modeſt* and *humble carriage* , and of our *dependance* on his Providence ; which we ſignify by *Praying* to him.

Nor doth this in any degree Contradict the Notion of God's Being perfectly happy and per-

though in ſtrictneſs of Perſon ſuppoſes his Station capable of improvement , and preſumes a Power in us to give it, as *Honour* is ſaid to *depend on the Honourer,* it being in every Man's Breaſt to value his Neighbour as he pleaſes) yet this is not God's caſe, who is infinitely great, and whoſe Glory will not admit *more* or *leſs* from his Poor Creatures. No, his Majeſty is *Eſſential,* not leaning on the fancy, and will of thoſe under him, like the *Grandeur* of Princes , which ſtands wholly on the People's *Obedience* : But as for God, 'tis impoſſible to *Eclypſe* his greatneſs, nor are we able to give it *more Luſtre* than what it already hath. So that the words vulgarly underſtood imply an abſurdity, and we ſeem to forget the Nature of God, when we talk of magnifying him. And truly to look *upwards,* the Language is improper, the *Greatneſs* of God, like his Nature, being ſimply unalterable. Yet to look *downwards,* and about us, it may very well paſs; and conſidering the humour and practice of the World, with reſpect

spect to *them*, we may be said to give Honour to God, though as to *himself* he can receive no Addition, becaufe, whether we will or no, *he is*, and muft be *God bleffed for ever.* However, we *magnify* him, when we *acknowledge* his *Power* to do all things; his *Wifdom* to Order all things for the beft; his *Omnifcience*, or Univerfal knowledge to fee and underftand very Thought, Word, or Action, though never fo filently faid, or fecretly done; his *Mercy* to pity, and receive an humble penitent; his *Juftice* to reward or punifh, as Men fhall deferve in this Life; his *Veracity* or faithfulnefs to make good all his Promifes; his *Providence* to manage the Univerfe, and take care of thofe who rely upon him.———And therefore as on the one fide, he that *diftrufts* or doubts thefe Attributes, as much as in him lies, *leffens* the Deity, fo on the other we *glorify* God, when we both *believe*, and do him this piece of right, which fuch a one refufes to give him. And when we are found on our knees applying ourfelves to him in an open manner, then more efpecially we proclaim him great, and we fhow all our Neighbours the Opinion we have of him.

B. What you fay is very good. And without fcruple the many *neceffities* we lie under, call for our *Prayers :* And I am convinced 'tis more for God's Honour, when thefe Prayers are *publickly* faid. And I conceive it hard, to find a Man having fuch a fenfe of Religion, as to think it a Duty, to go to the publick Service; but muft be perfwaded that *Prayer* and *Humility* become the place. Yet poffibly thofe Prayers, to which you give the Name of Divine Worfhip, are not fo well rellifh'd by tender People, who yet meet and join in what they can, to avoid the danger of *Divifion*, which weakens the intereft of the *Proteftant Religion*, and therefore come to *Church*, though they diflike fome things, and wifh for Amendment. *A.* So

A. So far well. This was *Beza's* Judgment, who look'd on it Sinful to separate from a Church, wherein *found Doctrine*, an *Holy Life*, and the *use of the Sacraments* is kept up. And so said not only *Bullinger, Zanchy*, and others *abroad*, but our own old *Puritans* at *home*, who asserted in their Writings, that *they* were bound in Conscience to Communicate with the *Church of England*; and to preserve *Union*, go as far as they were able. I wish our *Modern Dissenters* were of the same mind, and follow'd that rule. And the rather, because, I have a Charitable thought, that such Men who comply in *some* particulars have no prejudice against the *Rest*, but are ready to yield as soon as with safety they can. This *partial conformity*, tho' some are apt to call it *interest*, seems to me to be a very good *sign*, for I take 'em to be such as will not lose the opportunity of better information, but are willing to hear what the *Church* can say for herself. And if they find her reasons convincing they may hap'ly at length submit to the *whole*, as hitherto only to some *few points*, more agreeable to their present perswasion.

B. Your sense of these Persons is fair and just. And I am the better pleas'd with what you say, because (to be sincere) I myself have an interest in it. For though ever since my Infancy I have, and will continue in the Communion of the *Church*, wherein I was *Baptized*, yet since my arrival to riper Years, and been able to discern Good and Evil, I have taken liberty to deal with *Her*, as with my *Nant*, whose Milk I sucked, though I can't approve of all her Conduct, yet Duty and Gratitude oblige me to respect her as my *Mother*.

A. What is it offends you? Do not the *Ministers* answer their Character, and perform what might be expected from Men of that *Order*?

B. I object nothing againſt 'em, but own this to their Credit, that their Writings teſtify both their Abilities and Courage, in ſtemming *Popery*, when like a flood it was coming on us, while *Others* (as I took notice) were more *cautious* and *ſilent*, and would not run the hazard of having their *hands*, and Names produced againſt 'em.

A. Thoſe who know their *Hiſtory*, and have honeſty enough to acknowledge it, cannot but be ſenſible, what Streams of Blood they have ſhed ſince the *Reformation*, to ſecure us from thoſe Errours, which however, ſome People diſingenuouſly charge 'em with, and call 'em *Popiſhly affected*, when weighing the matter without prejudice, they are found to be our *ſtrongeſt Bulwarks* againſt *Popery.* And I am almoſt perſwaded, that theſe Men wrong their own Conſciences by ſpeaking otherwiſe of 'em, for which we not only forgive 'em *ourſelves*, but deſire *God* to forgive 'em.

B. The little inſight I have in the controverſie between 'em, makes me look on 'em with another Eye, though perhaps ſomethings may be uſed in the *Church*, which ſeem to tend *that way.* But as for the *Men*, I muſt confeſs, as far as I am Judge, they *Preach* and *Pray well*, and all I except againſt, is, that where there are ſuch excellent *gifts*, 'tis great pity any preſcribed *form* ſhould ſo much hinder, as it doth, the exerciſe and uſe of 'em.

A. I cannot ſee how the *form*, you mean, is any way injurious to the *Miniſters gifts*; or why what is read in the *Desk*, ſhould be thought to exclude the *Pulpit Prayer*, when in an orderly manner they ſucceed one another in the Service, which one might think ſhould be better accepted, becauſe carried on with ſo much *variety.* And here by the way, let us take notice of the indulgent temper of the preſent Church, in ſuffering her *Miniſters* to turn *that* into a *Prayer*, which originally was

and

and ought to be, no more than a piece of *instruct̄i-on*, to let People understand *what they are to Pray for*, and *how well* our *Liturgy* answers that *End.* This the *Preacher* insinuates by his *standing* till he comes to the *Pater-Noster*, which in strictness is all the *Prayer* he should say in that place, and which he delivers *kneeling*. All this I say, and more the Church winks at, to invite those who make a shew of tenderness in joining with her, that we might all of us serve God, *in the Unity of the Spirit and the bond of Peace.* But then (*l*) though *I am not against a Grave, Modest, Discreet, and Humble, use of Minister's gifts, even in* Publick, *the better to fit and excite their own, and the Peoples affections to the present occasion, yet I know no necessity, why* Private *and* single Abilities *should quite justle out, and deprive the* Church *of the* joint Abilities, *and concurrent gifts of,* many Learned and Godly Men, *such as the composers of the* Service-Book *were, who may in reason be thought to have more gifts and graces, inabling them to compose with serious deliberation, and concurrent advice, such forms of Prayers, as may best fit the Churches common wants, inform the hearers understanding, and stir up that fiduciary and fervent Application of their Spirits (wherein consists the very Life and Soul of Prayer) than any private Man by his* solitary Abilities *can be presumed to have.* Thus the Royal Martyr, according to the piety and judgment of all Ages and Churches, which out of their great care to have God gravely and mannerly served, have used the like prescriptions, that so their Children might in *sound words* express their Devotions. A Man might say a great deal in behalf of these forms in *general* and of *Ours in particular*, but that I am prevented by *others*, who have so well, and so ful-

---

(*l*) Ἐικὼν Βασιλικὴ. c. 16.

ly difcourfed on this fubject, that now we can only
repeat their words: And I wifh you had read and
confidered their reafons.

Perhaps you might think the Argument weak, if
drawn from the Practice of *Heathens*, who
had their *certain Modes* and Rules of Worfhip, as
appears from *Homer* and *Herodotus.* And whofe very *Sacrifices* (in which they obferved a conftant
Order) were but the *Hieroglyphicks of Liturgies*,
thofe *unbloody Sacrifices* (*m*) [εὐχαῖς ἂν αἱμαχ]αῖς]
which we make the true God who is more pure
than to be pleafed with thofe Abomiñations. Nor
did they look upon the *repetition* of thefe Offerings daily done in the fame manner, any way un-
acceptable to their pretended Deities, but was
rather a kind of *Confeffion*, that they thought 'em
conftant and *unchangeable*, always the *fame* to confider their wants and anfwer 'em upon thefe Addreffes. So were *they* taught by the Light of Nature, and fo far the reafon holds good with refpect to us.

And this was the meaning of the *Jewifh Oblations*,
and Rites of Supplication, whereby they who come to
God, would by that means befpeak his favour and
acceptance ; or rather as fo many *deprecations* or
forms of Prayer to God, to avert or remove
their Calamities ; According to that of *Jofephus*
concerning *Noah*, (*n*) *who fearing left God determi-*
ning deftruction to Men fhould in every Age drown the
World, he offer'd Sacrifices, befeeching him that all things
might continue in their firft Order———— which laft
words explain what *Noah* intended by his *Sacrifices*,
and that was to beg the Divine Favour. And
without doubt in all fuch cafes, as the *Mode* of the
Oblation was always the *fame*, fo a *certain form of*

(*m*) Sozom. lib. 2. cap. 14. (*n*) Jofeph. Antiq. l. 1. c 4.

words attended the Action, though till the Days of *Mofes*, we are left in the Dark, and can only guefs at 'em. But afterwards when that People, like other Nations, came to live under *Conftitutions and Laws*, we find 'em directed almoft in every thing, and a more efpecial care was taken, to fet 'em *Rules* or *Canons*, to guide 'em in matters of Religion. And among the reft (as the weightyeft of all) *Prayers and Bleſſings* were prefcribed 'em, as we find in (*o*) feveral places of Scripture. And it is exprefly faid of the whole *Book of Pfalms*, that it was delivered by *David* into the hands of *Afaph*, and his Brethren to this end, (*p*) *to give thanks unto the Lord, and call upon his Name.* About the incarnation of Chrift, the Liturgy of the Jews (befides *Pfalms* and Leffons) confifted of *eighteen Prayers*, the three *firſt* and three *laſt* of which concern'd *God*, and the reft *themfelves*, and their *Wants*. And thefe they fometimes faid in *full length*, and fometimes *contracted* into a leffer bulk, and to all of 'em, the Congregation either fubjoin'd their *Amen*, as in the *Synagogues*, or as in the *Temple*, (*q*) *Bleſſed be his glorious name for ever and ever.*

Our Lord followed the *Cuſtom* of his Country in *this*, as in many *other things* relating to Worfhip. And as the *Jewiſh Doctors*, befides the Common-Prayers, had a particular form to diftinguifh them, and their Scholars: So he was pleas'd to propofe that Comprehenfive, fhort Prayer called by his Name, as a form for his Difciples to Pray by. And it was accordingly ufed by 'em at the Adminiftration of the *Euchariſt*, as *Gregory*, and (*r*) *Pla-*

(*o*) Lev 16. 21. Num 6 23 Deut 21. 8. and 25. 13. 1 Chro. 29 30 Joel 2 17. (*p*) 1 Chro. 16 7 (*q*) *Lightfoot's Hor Heb* (*r*) *Petrus ubi confecraverat, pater nofter orationis ufus eſt.* Plat. in vita Xyfti.

find

tina inform us, though in thofe times infpired, and directed immediately by the *Bleffed Spirit.* And all Churches in the feveral Ages of Chriftianity continue it, and look on it as a proof of *their* Liturgies, as we for what is now in practice among us.

B. The Lord's meaning was, to exhibit in thofe words, the *fubjects* and *matter* of all our Prayers, and to fhow *what* we are to Pray to God for, not that we are to be fuperftitious, and adhere fo ftrictly to the *Phrafes themfelves.* For we read in *Matthew,* where he explains himfelf, that he fpeaks thus, [ὅτως] *Pray in this wife, pray thus,* not in thefe words, but as we well tranflate it, *after this manner* ———— (s) fo *Calvin,* and others underftand the Text, that therein Chrift did not command his Difciples to pray in thofe very 'terms, but only fet before 'em a *model of Prayer,* to which all their defires and petitions were to refer.

A. The word [ὅτως] hath not always that latitude, but frequently fignifies fo much *exactnefs,* that there is no room left for the leaft variation. As in *Numbers.* 6. 23. [ὅτως εὐλογήσετε] *Thus or in this wife you fhall blefs the People* ———— not by imitating that form of Bleffing there fet down, or rather taking the matter, and expreffing it in words of your own, but you fhall blefs the Children of *Ifrael* [λέγοντες αὐτοῖς] faying unto them in thefe words, *The Lord blefs thee,* &c. as the *Jews* took 'em, and we retain the fame benediction in our Office for the Vifitation of the Sick; And I believe, fhould we bid a Child or Servant *do,* or *fay thus,* we undoubtedly mean, that he muft *precifely do or fay,* what we enjoin him, to the leaft circumftance or tittle.

(s) *Non jubet fuos conceptis verbis orare,* &c. ———— Calv A Lapide, diesdom. l. 2. c. 10. *Liberam eft aliis atque aliis verbis eadem tamen in eo modo petere* ———— Aug. ad Prob.

However,

However, allowing that expreſſion in St. *Mat-thew* liable to Cavil (as indeed I cannot deny it to be one interpretation of the words) and that it ſignifies *praying to this ſence,* this effect or purpoſe, (ſo that keeping this Rule in the ſubſtance of our Prayers, we may be thought to anſwer what Chriſt deſign'd in it, though enlarged and worded as our-ſelves ſhall judge convenient) yet St. *Luke* repre-ſents it in other Language and ſhows, that not on-ly the *Contents* of the Prayer, but even the *Phraſe* its ſelf is to be followed; becauſe it is ſaid, *When you Pray, ſay our Father* — i e. not only *Model* all your Prayers according to this I now give you, or not only *Pray after this Manner* — but when you Pray, *uſe this very Prayer,* the very words of it, and ſay — *Our Father* — I think, the directions are ſo poſitive and clear, that to endeavour to e-vade 'em, were to call in queſtion, the obligation and force of all other precepts in Scripture, which cannot be more plainly worded than this, *ſay, Our Father* — or when you Pray, *ſay theſe words, Our Father* —

I ſuppoſe the miſtake might proceed from hence. They who think Chriſt's meaning, to be no more than that *our Prayers* ſhould be *directed by his,* in the ſence and ſubſtance of 'em, leaving us to the li-berty of our own Language) do take it for gran-ted, that St. *Matthew* and St. *Luke,* as they ac-count for the *ſame Prayer,* ſo they ſpeak of the *ſame time and occaſion.* Whereas by comparing to-gether theſe two Evangeliſts, we ſhall be able to diſcover, that this Prayer was *twice* delivered, in *diverſe Places,* at *ſeveral times,* and on *different rea-ſons.* Once it was propoſed on the *Mount,* and by way of *Sermon.* Afterwards, not while he was *Preaching* to his Diſciples, but as ſoon as he ended *His Prayer* for himſelf. In St. *Matthew,* he ſaid it *freely,* unasked and of his own accord, conſequent

to

to the cautions in his Sermon againſt the Hypocri-
ſie of the *Jews*, and the vain repetitions and bablings
of the Gentiles; But in St. *Luke* it was at the motion, and requeſt of one of his Diſciples, who ſeeing his Maſter pray, deſired a form for them, that
they might pray the better. Morever, according
to the circumſtances of each Goſpel, the one was
in the *ſecond*, the other in the *third* year of his
Baptiſm. All which makes interpreters conclude,
that the Prayer was *twice* given, both for the confirmation and fuller underſtanding of it. And a
modeſt Man would thereupon be apt to infer, That
becauſe it was delivered at *ſeveral times*, but *to the
ſame Perſons* (for in that both Writers agree)
therefore the *laſt* account muſt needs be the *Plain-
eſt*, as intended for the ſatisfaction of ſome one
particular Diſciple among 'em, who probably had a
ſcruple on him before concerning its true meaning. And it is not unlikely but the Diſciples
might think at firſt, that Chriſt propoſed it in
the way of imitation or in oppoſition to the Heathens, *whoſe* Prayers were after *this* or *that manner*, but *yours* ſhall conſiſt of theſe or the like petitions. This I ſay, might be their former conceit; and calling to mind afterwards, what St. *John
Baptiſt* had done for his Followers, in compoſing a
form of words for them as well as *matter*, to pray
by, that they might not be the *only Sect* or Party
of Religious Men, deſtitute of ſuch an help to Devotion and Piety, they entreat *their Maſter* to do
that for them, which every *Rabbi*, and which the
Baptiſt had done for his Diſciples, *Lord teach us to
Pray* —— ſo that for fear they ſhould miſtake
him again, by any ambiguous or doubtful expreſſion, he was now reſolved to ſpeak very intelligibly, *When you pray, ſay, Our Father*——

But

But suppose these two holy Writers had consented in the time and occasion of this Prayer, their difference of Phrase is no warrant to reject one of 'em. In this case we follow the Rule of safety; And because the Prayer was *both ways* proposed to the Disciples, we ought to admit it in *both* sences, and consequently *pray after this manner*, in the Prayers we make ourselves or are made for us according to this Model, and withal when we pray *after this manner*, say also, *Our Father*, to sanctify and bless the others. For our parts, we do not so nicely adhere to St. *Luke*, who bids us say, *Our Father*, as to exclude St. *Matthew's, After this manner, pray ye* — for if so, we should use nothing but the *Lord's Prayer*, as you know we do, and others have done before us, though all of 'em reducible to this *manner*, so much insisted on. And why our Brethren should take the liberty to pass by the positive words of St. *Luke*, and resolve only on the *manner of* St. *Matthew*, and call our practice *Popish* and *Superstitious*, because we say, as Christ bid us say, *Our Father*—, we know no solid reason for it: And I should be glad to hear any thing from 'em, to satisfy me in this Question. To my thinking, if if the *Method* be holy, because Christ set it, and such Prayers be Authentick and Sound, which close with this *Pattern*, Our *Lord's Words*, surely do not *unsanctify* the Prayer, and render the sence less holy than it would otherwise be. On the contrary, because we use both his *matter* and his *words*, such a Prayer seems most agreeable to his own mind; And being sent up to God, not only in his *Name*, but in his *Language*, we may be sure 'twill find acceptance with him. And this appears to be their own meaning, when themselves call that *Speech* the best, which hath most of *Scripture* in it: So that we argue upon their own Principles, that *no Prayer* whatever, can be comparable to the

Ff 3

Lord's,

Lord's, becaufe all that belongs to it proceeded from the Wifdom, and unerring Spirit of God, and on this account carries with it an *irrefiſtible Eloquence*, to charm and move him to grant our defires. Sure I am, to wave all other commentatours, on this place, their *Affembly of Divines* accord with us, in the interpretation of this Faſſage, and do fay, that *Chriſt did* twice *at leaſt teach this very* Form of Prayer. *And hence it appeareth, that as this is the moſt* abfolute and compleat Pattern of Prayer, *comprehending all that we muſt ask, ſo it is the moſt exact and ſacred* Form of Prayer, *indited and taught the Diſciples, who where to teach the whole World the Rules and Practice of true Religion, by Chriſt himſelf who is beſt able to teach his Servants to Pray* —— Again, *Chriſt preſcribed his Diſciples this form of Prayer to be uſed by* 'em, *not rejecting others, which his Spirit taught or teacheth, but to abridge all neceſſary petitions into this one ſumm* —— You hear what they fay, it was to be a *Pattern* according to St. *Matthew*, and a *Form* as St. *Luke* makes it; it was preſcribed the Diſciples and uſed by 'em, yet not reſtrain'd to their Perſons, but as they were to teach the whole World, the Rules and Practice of true Religion. And indeed for this end chiefly, they were taught the Prayer. For as to themfelves, there was not that neceſſity, becaufe, they were infpired, and the *Spirit of Supplication* conſtantly affiſted 'em, but for the *Churches ſake*; it was made 'em; And not fo made as to exclude all other Prayers, which the Spirit taught or might teach, but as the *brief* of all neceſſary Petitions, and the ſumm of what we are to fupplicate for, that God may be glorified, and we finally faved.

Incouraged by this *Form*, we find in the Church the Liturgies of feveral Apoſtles and Evangeliſts, as of St. *James*, St. *Peter*, St. *Matthew*, St. *Mark*, and St. *Andrew*; And of many Fathers, St. *Clement*,

ment, St. *Bafil,* St. *Chryfoftom* and others. (*t*) It
is recorded of *Conftantine the Great,* that he made
Prayers for his *Army.* And in thofe Apologies
the Ancients offer'd to the Heathen Emperours,
in behalf of Chriftianity, they had fometimes occafion to fet before thofe Perfecutours the *particulars* they tender'd God in their *daily Prayers;*
Which is a proof that their *Prayers* were *certain,*
otherwife it had been a ridiculous reprefentation,
and what might provoke their Governours, if
they had infifted on the innocency, and goodnefs
of their *Prayers,* and the Prayers not known to be
always the fame. (*u*) *It was not then thought, that*
praying by the Spirit confifted in the inventing of new
words, and uttering them with warmth. And it feem'd
too great a fubjection of the People to the Priefts, that they
fhould make 'em join with 'em, in all their heats in
Prayer, and would have proved as great a refignation
of their Devotion to 'em, as Superftition fince hath
made of their Faith. And on this account as well as
for many other reafons, it was refolved at our Reforma-
tion, to have a Liturgy, and to bring the Worfhip of
God to a fit mean, between the Pomp of Superftition and
Naked flatnefs.

(*w*) *Calvin* himfelf, was fo far perfwaded of the
truth of this point, that he durft not difpute a-
gainft the neceffity of Common-Prayers, though
the conftant practice of his Romifh Adverfaries,
but ingenuoufly owns, that as for *Forms of Prayer,*
and *Ecclefiaftical Rites, he did highly approve 'em, to*
help the ignorant, and *reftrain the inconftancy of fuch*
who affect novelty. All the *Reformed Churches* abroad,
unanimoufly fubfcribe to fuch a Rule ; and though
they leave the Preacher fo much liberty, as to fuit

(*t*) Eufeb. de vit. Conft. l. 4. c. 20. (*u*) Hift. of the Reformation. (*w*) Ep. Protectori Angl.

his

his Prayer to the occafion, yet ftill they have their
fet-forms, from which they will not fuffer their
Minifters to vary. And in a word, fuch hath e-
ver been the notion of thefe Books in the Catholick Church, that fome have been fo bold to affirm,
that the *Ceffation of Liturgies*, would be a Principal (x) *fign* of the coming of *Antichrift*; and if
fo, fome People have brought him very near
us.

B. You were fpeaking of the *Liturgies* of *Peter*,
James and fome others. Do you take them for
Legitimate, and compiled by thofe whofe names
they bear, feeing, as I am informed, they are
chargeable with very grofs miftakes, as to *Do-*
ctrine and *Chronology*, and contain in them an account
of *Perfons* and *things*, not to be reconciled to that
Age they lived in?

A. I am not a Man of an hard forehead, nor
dare I affert any thing for *truth*, when I have not
pretty good grounds to believe it fo. And therefore to anfwer roundly, I much doubt their Authority for the reafons you mention, and to examine them feverally (†).

In the Liturgy of St. *James*, we read the word,
[όμοέσιθ] *one fubftance*, often repeated, which
was never heard of till after the Third Century,
and then brought into the Church to make a diftinction, between the *Orthodox* and *Hereticks*, who
denied the Son to be of the *fame fubftance* with the
Father. And certainly had the Term been of Ancienter date, than the Council of *Nice*, it had
much advantaged the *Catholick Caufe*, and the Fa-

(x) *Pretiofum corpus & fanguis non extabit, Liturgia*
extinguetur, pfalmorum decantatio ceffabit, Scripturarum
recitatio non audietur.—Hippolytus de Antichrifto & Con-
fummat Seculi. Vid Hieron. in Daniel. (†) De his vide Rivet Crit. Sacr. l 1.——Tom. 6. Bibl. PP. & Arndii Lexicon-
thers

thers there affembled, had without fcruple offer'd
this Apoftles credit, to affirm the Queſtion fo ſtifly
oppoſed by *Arius*, and his party. In this Book we
have likewife the [τρισάγιον or χερυβικὸς ὑμνὸς] *Holy, Holy, Holy*, and the *Gloria Patri* — of younger
ſtanding than the Apoftolick times, and in a
great meaſure introduced, to aſſert and explain
the notion of the Bleſſed *Trinity*. And here the
word [ΘεοτόκΘ] *Mother of God*, is put for the
Virgin ; *(a)* which though fome plaçe no higher
than the Councils of *Epheſus* and *Chalcedon*, to confute *Anaſtaſius* and *Neſtorius*, who propoſed
[ΧριςοτόκΘ] *Chriſt's Mother*, that ſhe might not be
accounted the *Mother of God*, (there being about
that time, *(b)* faith *Evagrius*, a controverſie in
the Church, whether ſhe ſhould be called ['αιθρωπο-
τόκΘ or ΘεοτόκΘ] the *Mother* of *Man* or *God)* yet
it is evident from *(c) Origen*, that the ſtile was
uſed before, though not fo eaily as to fix it on St.
James. The *ſame* may be faid for the word [*Con-
feſſours*] there mention'd, and recommended in
its Prayers, but which had its Birth long after
the Death of the Apoftles. Which with the like
exceptions, gives reaſon to ſuſpeĉt the Antiquity
of that Book. And tho' *(d) Balſamon* ſpeaks of it,
as a *Form of Prayer* held in great Veneration by the
Chriſtians of *Jeruſalem*, and *Paleſtine* on the higher
Feſtivals, yet, faith he, it is not own'd by us —
and for a very good reaſon, *becauſe*, as *Bellarmine*
objeĉts, *all things in that Piece, have not our Lord's
Example, nor precept to ſupport it.*

As for St. *Peter's* Liturgy, we have in it the
Names of *Linus, Clemens, Xyſtus, Cornelius, Cyprian, Lucia, Agnes, Barbara, Juliana*, and fome

---

(a) Socrat. Eccl. Hiſt. l. 7. c. 32. *(b)* Lib. 1. cap. 7.
(c) Ep. ad Rom. *(d)* In Canon. 32. Conc. Trullani.

other

other Saints, who fome of 'em, lived two hundred Years after St. *Peter* was Martyr'd. And which favours little of an Apoftolick Spirit, it begs God's Protection *through the interceffion, and for the Merits of* Peter *and* Paul, who cannot be thought to forget themfelves fo far as to infert fuch a claufe in the common Liturgy, and let People addrefs God in their Meditations and Names. They therefore who treat of thefe fubjects take little notice of it. *Binius, Bellarmine,* and *Baronius,* neglect it, and though *Genebrard* fpeaks of it, yet he charges it with many *interpolations,* or *amendments* in the *beginning, middle* and *end* of it, and thereby makes it a very corrupt and fictitious piece.

St. *Matthew's* is called the *Æthiopian Liturgy.* And in this we have the Names of *Bafil, Chryfoftom,* and *Gregory the Great,* the two *firft* of which lived in the Fourth, the *laft* in the Sixth Century, It mentions likewife the Councils of *Nice, Conftantinople,* and *Ephefus,* with the *Epact,* and *Golden Number,* invented many Years after the Apoftles Death. It prays for the *Pope, Patriarchs, Archbifhops,* &c. *Diftinctions* and *Orders* in the Church, a long while after St. *Matthew,* and of which there was not one Syllable during his Life.

St. *Mark* was the Apoftle of the *Ægyptians,* and having fetled a Church at *Alexandria,* he is fuppofed to frame this Book of Devotion, called by his Name. But though the *Alexandrians* had it in great efteem, (e) as *Balfamon* tells us, yet the Catholicks in general rejected it, as a *Spurious Book,* and forbid the *Patriarch* of that City to ufe it, *who promifed,* faith he, *to lay it afide for the future.* In this Book, as in that of St. *James,* we

_____

(e) In Canon. 32. Concil. in Trullo,

have

have ὁμοὐσῐΘ̄—τρῐσᾴγιον, and Cônfeſſors ; as alſo
Sub-deacons, Singers, and the like, unknown to the
Apoſtles, and which the Church in thoſe days
was not furniſhed with : And which is very remarkable, there is a Prayer to God, *That he would
be pleas'd to protect their City, for the ſake of his Evangeliſt, and Martyr St.* Mark, *who taught 'em the
way of Salvation.* So that plainly St. *Mark* was
dead, becauſe he had been a *Martyr,* before this
Prayer was made.

The Liturgy of St. *Andrew,* depends much on
the credit of the Authors who mention it, and
therefore let us ſee how it is with them. One is
Abdias, ſuppoſed to be a Diſciple, and within the
number of the *ſeventy,* a Follower of SS. *Simon*
and *Jude,* when they went to Preach the Goſpel
in *Perſia,* and there by them made *Biſhop of Babylon.* A Man ſo much valued by *Faber,* eſpecially,
by *Wolfangus Lazius,* who brought him to Light,
that he did not ſtick to ſay, it was a doubt with
him, *whether St.* Luke *borrowed from him, or he from
St.* Luke, ſo well they agreed in the ſeveral Paſſages of the Goſpel. He is ſaid to write *in Hebrew*
ten Books, of the *Acts* of the Apoſtles, tranſlated
into *Greek,* by *Eutropius,* and rendred Latin by
Julius Africanus. But were he a Perſon of ſuch a
Figure, and ſo Ancient as is repreſented, 'tis
ſtrange that neither *Euſebius,* nor St. *Jerom,* nor
any other of the old Hiſtorians, ſhould give us an
account of him. And 'tis as odd, that *Julius A-
fricanus* ſhould turn him into Latin, whom (†) *Euſebius,* and others make a *Greek-Writer.* But moſt
of all it is to be admired, that he ſhould pretend *to
ſee Chriſt in the Fleſh,* and yet commends *Hegeſippus*
the Hiſtorian, (f) who was Co-temporary with

(†) Eccl. Hiſt. l. 6. c. 31. (f) Euſeb. Eccl. H. l. 4. c. 22.

Juſtin

Juſtin Martyr, *Dionyſius* Biſhop of *Corinth,* *Irenæus,* *Apollinaris* and *Theophilus,* Biſhop of *Antioch,* *Aurelius* and *Verus* being Emperours. He ſaith, that a Temple was built at *Epheſus,* to the honour of St. *John* the Evangeliſt, yet the Church *then,* and many Years after was under Perſecution, and I think it was not leſs than two hundred Years, when *Celſus* asked *Octavius* the Queſtion, (*g*) *Why Chriſtians had no Temples nor Altars?* And 'tis equally incredible what he reports, that there were ſo early in one Province, ſeventy five Churches erected for the Chriſtian Service. Theſe things with ſome ridiculous ſtories concerning *Gondofer,* a King in the *Indies,* occaſion'd *Paul* fourth to reject him as Suppoſititious. *Salmeron* calls him (*h*) *Apocryphal,* and ſo doth *Poſſevin,* and *Bellarmin,* and *Baronius.* So that we can beſtow little Authority on the Liturgy of St. *Andrew,* upon this Writers account, who himſelf ſtands on ſuch ill terms in the Opinion of the judicious.

'Tis true, it is again named in another Book, called *the Sufferings of* Andrew *the Apoſtle,* written, as is given out, *by the Presbyters, and Deacons of the Churches of* Achaia. And which *Petrus Damianus* owned to be *Authentick,* but is rejected by *Epiphanius, Philaſtrius,* and *Innocent* I. as compoſed rather by the Philoſophers *Nexochorides,* and *Leonidas,* or ſome *Manichee* to whom *Philaſtrius* attributes it, as a piece eſteem'd by Men of that hereſie.

But then though theſe exceptions diſprove the *credit* of thoſe Liturgies, yet we cannot deny them their *Grey-Hairs,* and ſome of the Arguments produced againſt 'em, make 'em very *Ancient.*

(*g*) Minutius Fœlix. (*h*) Vid. Sixt. Sen. Bibl. Poſſev. in Apparat. Bellar. de Scrip, Eccl. Baron. ad an. 44.

And

And to give you my Thoughts concerning their *Names.* It is not unlikely, but that some part (at leaft) of thefe Prayers may be owing to thofe *Apoftles,* who are reported to be the *Compilers.* Not that *they* tied themfelves to a form of words (excepting that of the *Lord's-Prayer*) becaufe, as their Mafter promifed, they were immediately directed by the *Holy Ghoft,* yet *their Difciples* and Converts, hearing what was faid by thofe Good Men, *in their publick Devotions,* and digefting it afterwards as well as they could, they thought it prudence and fafety to make it a form to themfelves, and their Succeffours, and fo gave it the name of *this* or *that Apoftle,* from whom they derived the *matter,* and as far as they could remember the *Method* and *Language.* But in procefs of time, *thefe Prayer Books* might (as did the Liturgies of *Bafil, Chryfoftom,* &c. of later Ages) receive great *Alterations,* and many things be *inferted, added,* or *changed* by Pofterity more agreeable to their circumftances. And from hence proceeded the objections before offer'd, which however, to fpeak fairly, fhould not call the *whole* into queftion, feeing the like *variations* and *amendments,* are frequently made in our *Englifh Liturgy,* yet without any reflection on the *firft Compilers* of it.

But whether fo or no, this is evident, that the Primitive Ages fo abounded with Liturgies (as well the *Hereticks* as *Orthodox*) that the Fathers were at length forced to reduce their number, and fome of 'em worded with fo little Care, that the Third Council of (*i*) *Carthage,* and that (*k*) of *Milevis* (at both which St. *Auguftine* was prefent (*l*) who complains, that fome pray'd *contrary to the*

(*i*) Canon. 23 (*k*) Canon. 12. (*l*) Adv Donat.

rule

rule of Faith) decreed, *That no Prayers should be used but what were first seen and approved by the Governours of the Church, left through inadvertency or ignorance, some thing might be spoken to the disgrace, and damage of the Christian Religion.*

B. May not these Councils be said to begin the practice, because the words infinuate, that before that time Men were left to their Liberty, to use what Prayers they pleafed, or as *Justin Martyr* fpeaks, fend up their fupplications and thanks, *(m)* according to their *Abilities.* But for fear any thing fhould be faid amifs, (however under that pretence) the Bifhops then affembled made thofe *Canons* to reftrain 'em.

A. Were it fo, the reafon holds good. For it is the duty of the *Prefidents*, and *Paftors* of the Church to take care, that nothing (efpecially in publick) efcapes the Minifter's or People's mouth, which may offend the Ears of God, when they are Praying to him. But *their* cafe was otherwife. For we cannot find that the Chriftians of thofe Days attempted fuch a Liberty, but Perfons of all perfwafion agreed in the *ufefulnefs*, and *decency of fet forms* in Prayer, becaufe the want of 'em, faith Mr. *Baxter*, *is apt to breed a giddinefs in Religion.* And to this purpofe we find *(n)* in a Canon of the Council of *Laodicea*, many Years before either of the 'former, that the fame Prayers ought always to be faid, both in the *Morning* and *Evening Service.* And *Balfamon* faith on the Canon, that the meaning of the Decree was, *That it should not be in the Power of every Minifter* [εὐχὰς ουντιθέναι] *to compofe the manner of the Service:* Or as *Zonaras* repiefents it, it was not allowed him, *to make* [ἢ

(m) εὐχὰς κὴ εὐχαριςείας ὅση δύναμις ἀναπέμπειν. Apolog. 2. (n) Canon. 18.

ταύτας

πάν]ας λέγειν ἐν ταῖς σύναξιν] *and read 'em in the face of the Congregation*——Which plainly befpeaks a *fet form*, becaufe they did not deliver them *Extempore*, but firſt compofe, and then read 'em before the People. Yet thefe Prayers were not liked,but the *Council* required every Congregation to clofe with *thofe*, which had been of a long continuance in the Church, and were handed to 'em **B**y their Fathers. And if it was found by Experience, a thing very unfafe to admit the Prayers *contrived*, and *digeſted* as well as the *Miniſters* could, who were thereupon forbid to pray in that manner for the future) the Argument concludes ſtronger againſt *fuch Prayers*, as are made at *random*, when Men, 'tis to be fear'd, fometimes fpeak what will not bear the Teſt, if called to an account for it. However here we fee, that though the *zeal* of the Miniſters, and the earneſt defire they had to *excel* one another in the Bufinefs of Religion, invited them to thefe pains of making and ufing feveral *forms of Prayer* in, and for their refpeſtiveChurches(and to be fure ufed great *induſtry*, and *caution* to *model*, and *word* 'em well) yet the more *Grave* and *Learned* among 'em, did not approve the *way*, becaufe it tended to diſturb and diſtraſt the *Church* of God, and upon that reafon thought fit to recal them to the *Old* Method,which their Anceſtours had ufed before 'em,

• As for *Juſtin Martyr*'s [ὅση δύναμις] it means no more than that the *Biſhop* or *Miniſter* did, what every Chriſtian ought to do in the like cafe, pray *with all his Might*, with the feveral Powers and Faculties of his Soul, with a becoming Zeal, and all the earneſtnefs imaginable. For as we aie to *love* God *with all our Heart*, *with all our Mind, and with all our Soul*, and *with all our Strength* ; So we are to *Worſhip* him in the *fame Degree*, of ferionf-nefs and feivency. And to this end we ufe a

form

form of Words prepared to our hands, that we may have then nothing to do, but raife our Affections, and apply our Thoughts to what we are faying, the *firft* of which would grow very cool, and the *laft* be much diverted, and otherwife employ'd, were we put to the care and trouble of *inventing* Language to exprefs ourfelves in, to the great hindrance and prejudice of true Devotion. This is what *that Father* meant, or elfe he had weaken'd the proof of *Loyalty*, which *he*, and the *other Apologifts*, offer'd in the remonftrances they made to the Heathen Emperors, wherein they would take off the fufpicion of being Male-contents, or difaffected to the Government they lived under, fince [ἐν τῇ λατρείᾳ τῇ καθημερινῇ, faith St. *Chryfoftom*] they formally pray'd for 'em, *Morning and Evening*, that God would be pleafed to give 'em *a long Life, a fecure Empire, valiant armies, a faithful Senate, good Subjects*, and *a quiet World* ——— and all this [(o) *Sine Monitore*] without being directed or frightned to it by others, faith *Tertullian*, but purely out of *a Principle* of Chriftianity, *not for Wrath but Confcience-fake*, and in purfuance of that *model*, St. *Paul* left *Timothy*, whom he enjoin's to make publick Offices, for the ufe of his Province, confifting of thefe four Particulars, *Supplications* to avert evils, *Prayers* for Beneficial things, *Interceffions* for others, and *Thanks* for Bleffings received, as Dr. *Hamond* Paraphrafes on the Place. And fo SS. *Chryfoftom*, and *Ambrofe* underftood it, who thereupon call it an *Ecclefiaftical rule, fet by the Doctor of the Gentiles, which our Minifters conftantly ufe*, and is obferved in our Liturgy to this Day.

_____

(o) T·rtull. Apolog.

B. I look on the Apostle's Words to be only a *Phrafe* ; and that he defigns no more in them, than that whenever we pray (whether by *form* or *otherwife*) we fhould take care to remember *other Peoples wants* as well as our *own*, and more particularly intercede for *fuch* as are in Authority, that God would either *convert* 'em, or at leaft *encline* their Hearts to be favourable to us, that fo we many be the better able to do him Worfhip without Perfecution, or any other let.

A. True ; That may be one fence of the Exhortation : For 'tis very ordinary to add the word [*make*] to diverfe Subjects whereon it has not the leaft influence or fignification, but what thofe Subjects give it, As to *make a lye*, is, *to lye* ; to *make excufe*, is, *to excufe* ; to *make ftrait*, is, *to ftraiten* ; to *make plain*, is, *to explain* ; and fo to *make Interceffion*, is, *to intercede* ; to *make prayer*, is, *to pray* ; as in St. Luk. 5. 33. *Why do the Difciples of* John *faft often*, [κỳ δεήσεις ποιȣ̃νται] *and make Prayers*, i. e. Pray ? However, the Propriety of the word befpeaks *Contrivance*, and a Man is faid to *make a thing*, when he gives it *Being*, or beftows on it a *Condition* it had not *before*, as [ποιεῖν τὰ 'αγάλμα]α, and ποιεῖν βδ'ελυγμα κỳ ψεῦδος] *to make an abomination, and make a lye*, i. e. make an Idol or Picture, engrave, paint or form it, either for Ornament or Adoration. And fo [ποιη]ὴς] is a Creator, Artift, Poet, or fuch a one who not only *loves* and admires the Art of making Verfes, but *Compofes* or *Practifes* in it himfelf, and endeavours by fomething new to improve that pleafant invention. In the Holy Scripture we find great variety in expreffing this inftance of Religion , *I pour out my Prayer*, faith David. *While I was fpeaking in my Prayer* ; fo *Daniel.* But more commonly in the Hebrew, *Pray in Prayer*, or avoiding the repetition, *To fay our Prayer* and the like. And as for [ποιεῖν δεήσεις]

G g   the

the Periphrasis seems to carry an Emphasis, and signifies either a *Prayer* then *Composed*, or brought to a Birth when the Supplicant utters it, or rather, because the word insinuates *Care, Pains, Time,* &c. it means a *Prayer*, made for a *standing* rule in the Church, as St. *Paul* here intends it, if the Ancients took him right, who on that warrant compiled their Liturgies, and made what he mentions, the several parts of 'em throughout all Ages, *Supplications, Prayers, Intercessions, and giving of Thanks.*

But waving these Authorities, were we only to consider the *Nature* of Prayer it self, we should find *Liturgies* highly *useful,* if not *necessary* to answer the design of it. For the reason why we pray is, to set our case before God, humbly beseeching him to pity and ease us. But then it must be remembred, that this *Representation* of our Condition is made not to *inform* God what our necessities are, but that the formality and care we use in this Declaration, may make in our *Hearts* the deeper sense of our wants, and frame in the Mind a more perfect *Idea* of that *Goodness* and *Power*, we apply to for our relief. Were God to be *taught*, or that his Knowledge of the state we are in depended on our Information, and that he was to be more or less gain'd according to the *Rhetorick*, and *Skill* of our Addresses, then Peradventure the *Eloquence* of the (*p*) Heathens might Charm, their *Battologies* importune, their *variety* please, and a *fine strain* of Words over-reach him. But alas! He with whom we have to do, under-

---

(*p*) *Ethnici habuerunt quasdam preculas verbis picturatis, & rhetoricis flosculis tam eleganter & artificiose ad persuadendum adornatas, ut existimarent eleganti illa facundia deum ad exauditionem permoveri*—Chem. Harm. Evang. c. 51.

ſtands both our Neceſſities, and our Thoughts
long before, nor doth he need *our Mouths*, or the
Mouths of *Mediators*, to make him ſenſible of what
we ſuffer, neither do we pray to *tell him*, but to
ſhow that we ourſelves are convinced of what our
caſe is, of being *Poor*, *Sick*, or in *Trouble*. Yet we
outwardly expreſs this in words (and he expects
we ſhould do ſo) that we may be *inwardly* more affected, our deſires more inflamed, and that the
ſenſe of our Circumſtances might make us to value
the help the more, when God thinks it ſeaſonable,
and fit to give it us.

And this may be called, *praying with the Spirit*,
when he inſpires us with *fervency* and *zeal* ; when
he *ingages our Spirits* in that ſacred Work, that we
may not fall under the Prophets Cenſure, to be
near God with our *Lips*, but *far* from him with
our *Hearts* ; Contrary to *David's* way, *whoſe Heart*
[Firſt] *burnt within him, and then he ſpeak with his*
Tongue. For this good Office it is, namely, becauſe of the aſſiſtance he gives us in our Prayers
(which through the weakneſs of our Nature, and
by the force of many Temptations would be much
impeded) that the *Holy Ghoſt* is called *the Spirit of*
Prayer, and Supplications in the Prophet : Becauſe,
as St. *Paul* ſpeaks, *He helpeth our Infirmities* ; and
whereas we know not what we ſhould pray for as
we ought, *He himſelf maketh Interceſſion for us.* But
then how this is done, he immediately ſubjoins,
With Groans that cannot be uttered. So that this Prayer doth not ſhow it ſelf in the *Utterance*, and *Nim-*
bleneſs of the *Tongue*, nor in the *Elegancy* and *Neat-*
neſs of *Expreſſion* (which an Hypocrite may do as
well as the beſt Man in the World) but in the *mo-*
tions of the *Heart* and *Soul*, which is beyond the
Power of the fineſt Phraſes, *Groans* being *Imper-*
fect ſounds from within, ſhowing indeed the *concern*
of the Mind whence they come, but *not declaring*

in

in the leaft *what* that concern is, nor can they be underftood but by the Searcher of Hearts, who knows our Meditations and Thoughts long before, without the help of Words to reprefent them.

'This then confirms the benefit of *Liturgies.* For feeing the ftrength, and *efficacy of Prayer* confifts in having the *Heart concern'd* ; and he is faid to *pray beft* who *prays moft affectionately,* therefore for this end we make ufe of a *form,* becaufe in this cafe the votary has nothing elfe to do, but to Compofe his *Heart,* and apply his Thoughts to the Words before him. Whereas were he at the trouble to make his Prayer , and invent Language to exprefs it in, he would by this means certainly *abate,* if not altogether *lofe* the vigour of his Devotion, his *Mind* being all the while chiefly employ'd in *Compofing,* and digefting his Words, which after all can be no more than the *Shell* and *Body of Prayer,* or indeed rather the *Clothes,* than the *Spirit* and *Life* of it.

Thus as to the *Minifter* : But for the *People,* their Condition appears worfe : Becaufe, being altogether ignorant of what the Minifter intends to fay, they are obliged to give the ftricter *attention* to him, and fo the *Ears* alone being engaged in the reception of what is faid, the *Tongue* in the interim has nothing to do, but is *filent,* and *ufelefs* till the Service is over. And for the *Heart,* it has no further bufinefs than to examine, fentence after fentence, whether what the Minifter delivers, be *found* and *proper* or no. Which every Man muft do, if he has Religion enough in him to confult his own fafety. And yet if he does it in any low Degree of care and pains, he muft of neceffity lofe fome part of the Minifter's Prayer, who ftill goes on, and proceeds to *new matter,* while the Congregation is perpetually *halting,* to weigh what in their behalf has been offer'd already.

ready. And provided fuch a Man be fo apprehenfive and quick, that no tittle of that Prayer efcapes him, yet this amounts to no more than the exercife of the *underftanding*, and can have no other effect on him than the *Sermon* afterwards has, to better perhaps his *Knowledge*, but wants that which makes it a *Prayer*, at leaft a Prayer to *him*. 'Tis true, this is much help'd by *Implicite Faith*; But that Doctrine, as it is not fafe in *it felf*, fo it has no Credit with *thofe* who make the Objection. And yet methinks this reliance on *anothers Prayer* favours of that *Principle*, and is fuch an overt-act of the confidence we have of the Minifters being infallibly guided, that no *Romifh Prieft* can demand more from the greateft Zealot under his care.

B. In my Opinion, this way of Devotion is very edifying. And I find by experience fo much *vigour* and *warmth*, in a Prayer affectionately delivered by the *Minifter*, that the other comparatively fpeaking, is *cold* and *flat*, and fo little touches the *Heart*, that it fcarce enters the *Ears*, or invites to any Degree of attention or concern while the *Reader* faith it. And truly, Sir, to be free with you, this is the reafon, I generally come *fo late* to the publick Worfhip, not out of defign thereby to affront my Neighbours, who benefit by the *Service-Book*, but becaufe it hath not that good effect on *me*, as on *them*, who yet (if I may fay it without offence) notwithftanding their zealous Profeffion, and adherence to that Mode of Prayer, are very *tardy*, and many of 'em enter *as late* as I. But that which moft furprizes me, is, (what I have often obferved) that the *Minifters themfelves* are very backward in the ufe of that, which they fo much prefs to the People, and whereby they would be diftinguifhed from the *other Teachers* of God's Word. For they not only forbear reading

the

the Prayers in their own *Perſons*; but moſt of them go directly to the *Veſtry*, and appear not in the *Church*, till the *Pſalm* and *Sexton* give notice, they muſt be moving; which makes me ſuſpect, that the *Prayers* you recommend, are not ſtrictly the *Service of God*, or that *they* think them ſo, becauſe they deny themſelves an intereſt in *that Service*, and are voluntarily withdrawn till it be quite over.

A. You judge uncharitably. But ſuppoſe ſome *few* fall under your Cenſure, yet we ought not to make the neglects of *Men*, the faults of a *Conſtitution*. Nor are *their* remiſſneſs any Plea, to abate *our* Piety and Zeal at ſuch times. *Some*, you ſay, do not read: *Others* remain in the *Veſtry* during the Service, yet *neither* are chargeable with the contempt of the Prayers, as you imagine. For, as to the *former*, they are, it may be, *infirm* and *weakly*, and thereupon unable to go through the *whole Duty*. And in this caſe, we are to remember, that God is *for Mercy, and not Sacrifice*, and they ſo ſerve God, as to keep themſelves in a Condition to ſerve him long. Or they are willing to *divide* their *incomes*, and make the preferment they have, a kind of *Nurſery*, to train up the Younger ſort, in the Miniſtery of the Church. And at leaſt, to take off *that reflection*, which I have often heard made on them, for *graſping all*, and parting with nothing. It may be added, that there hath been in the Church a difference of *Clerical-Officers* throughout all Ages, among whom the *Readers* had a ſpecial Figure, who were the *Deacons* of the Primitive times, and to whoſe *Voices* a particular regard was had by the Biſhops, and other Miniſters, that ſo what was delivered out of the Book of God, might be *diſtinctly* heard by all the Congregation. To this *Juſtin Martyr* bears

testimony,

teſtimony, who ſaith, (q) *Upon the Day called Sunday, all the Chriſtians, whether in City or Country, aſſemble in the ſame place, wherein the Memoirs of the Apoſtles, and the writings of the Prophets are read, as long as the time will permit.* Then the Reader *ſitting down,* the Preſident *of the aſſemble ſtands up, and makes a* Sermon *of inſtruction and exhortation to the following of ſo good examples.* In a word, becauſe the *Divine Service* conſiſts of *diverſe parts,* and is of a very conſiderable *length* every *Lord's-day,* therefore the Miniſters uſe theſe helps, that each, in his Station, may acquit himſelf better, and more to the ſatisfaction and benefit of the aſſembly. And as for thoſe of the latter kind, you ſhould diſtinguiſh before you cenſure; For it is not the *incumbents* themſelves, or very few of 'em go to the *Veſtry*, but ſuch *Gentlemen* as come from remote Places, to let us partake of their pains, and who, becauſe of the diſtance cannot but be late, and are on that account very unwilling by an unſeaſonable entrance to diſturb our Devotion. Or probably the length of their Walk *diſorders* and *heats* 'em, and therefore may want the conveniency of a *cloſer Room,* both to *cool* and *recollect* themſelves before they go to the *Sermon.* In any of theſe reſpects they are very pardonable; and the rather, becauſe in that retirement, they are often found *as attentive,* and as warmly ingaged in the Common-Service, as the reſt of the Congregation, with whom they join, though not ſo *openly* as in their own Churches at *home.*

But you ſpeak of them as you find it in your own Caſe; and becauſe the *little haſte* you make to the Prayers proceeds from your *indifferency,* and the low conceit *you* have of their goodneſs, you

---

(q) Apolog. 2.

ſuppoſe

suppose, *other* *Peoples* absence to be altogether grounded ,on the *same reason*.　But the *rule* of *judging others by ourselves*, will not *at all times*, and *in every case* hold; and you cannot but be sensible, how fallacious the Argument is from *one* to *all* or from *few* to *many*.　Yet it imposes on your Charity, and makes you think hard of them, who have a great deal to say for themselves, in those seeming Omissions you mention to their disadvantage.

And I am afraid you are as much deceived in that comparison, you made between the two kinds of Worship.　For if your affections grow warm at the *Minister's Prayer*, it, is Peradventure, not because there is more *Holiness* in what he saith, but you are taken with the *Novelty*.　I must confess *things extraordinary* are commonly very *surprizing*; But let me tell you, they have frequently that Character, not because they are *more excellent* than what are daily seen, but because they are more *unusual*, as when we neglect the *Sun* and admire a *Meteor*.　The words of the Minister mightily affect you, not because they are *more pious*, and Proper to signify what he means by 'em, but either their *variety* Pleases, or their *sound* Charm you, because you hear *without prejudice*.　But would you with as little pre-engagement or pre-possession of Mind consider the difference, I am bold to say, you would discover so much *Holy Elegancy*, so much *Majesty*, such a *close Correspendence between the Language, and the wants we express* by it, in those *forms* we use, that if you have any reverence, (as without doubt you have) for the *Scripture it self*, you cannot dislike or retain a mean Opinion any longer of what is for the most part borrowed from it.　'Tis not in my Thoughts to disparage any *Good-Man's Prayer*.　I have always a *Veneration* for the *Gifts* of God *where-ever* I find 'em.

'em. I hear our *Minister* with as much Devotion as the thing will bear; And because *his Prayer* is now become a *form* by his conftant repeating it, I fincerely and heartily join with him. Yet I venture not to fay, that the two Prayers equally move me; and I am fure, if he heard me fay fo, he would not be Angry. But admit the Scales were even, why fhould we be byafs'd and parcial, and flight *one fort* of Prayer more than the *other* ? Why not clofe with the Minifter in the *Desk*, as well as in the *Pulpit*, and let our Hearts have an intereft in *Both* ? Good Children may without offence have a great liking for an honeft, diligent and difcreet *Servant*, yet I hope none of us have fo little fenfe of Duty, and the refpect we owe to the ftile of a *Mother*, as to flight the food fhe provides, purely on the account, *becaufe fhe* provides it. The Minifters own Prayer *may be good*, but the other is *certainly* fo, and therefore 'tis the beft way to attend *both*, but defpife *neither*.

But they do not equally affect you, the *one* being *languid* and *flat*, in comparifon of the *other*. And I believe it true, but the reafon is *in ourfelves*, and not *in the Prayers*. Our perfwafion makes the difference, and we come, as was faid with *prejudice*, and coldnefs to the *one*, and with a refolution not to be concern'd till the *other* begins, and fo becaufe of this *partiality*, the impreffions are very *unlike*; for the *inclination* draws the *judgment* afide, and where we have no kindnefs for a thing, it muft be underftood that the thing did not deferve it. The Minifter's Prayer is very *edifying*; And it ought to be fo. For his appearing in the *Pulpit*, is on purpofe to better us. And as in other Duties he gives us inftructions how to difcharge 'em well, fo as to this of Prayer, he never forgets to put us in Mind of it, as an inftance of Religion, wherein God's Glory has an Eminent fhare. And if,

if his words commence a *Prayer*, it is to quicken
his Exhortation, and show by *his Example* what
we are to do, and how to acquit or behave ourselves in it.

But I conceive your Language of *Edification* is
not well examined, for though it be intended an
Objection against the Liturgy, it rather confirms
and proves the *use* of it. It is a *Metaphor* borrow'd from *Building*, and as it is or should be *applied* to Prayer, it is the *conspiring* or *consent of several Persons in a Congregation*, to *send up a Petition
to Heaven, and with one Heart, and one Mouth glorify God.* Now though a *form of Prayer* may be
very convenient at home, in our Chambers or Clo-
sets to express our Thoughts by, in case we do
express 'em, (because having no care to order the
Words, our *inward concern* may be so much the
greater) yet in a *Publick Meeting* this is much
more necessary, because if we know not what the
Prayer is the Minister offers, how shall we be able
to give our *Suffrage* to it? But if we differ, and
say each Man a *several Prayer* for himself, then
the notion of *Edification* is utterly lost, or very
ill applied, when there is not that *Union of Souls*,
(as of many stones or Bricks in an house) in that
Address we send up to God. This is very far
from that Holy Violence, the Scripture mentions,
of laying Siege to Heaven, and the force must be
very little when the Spirits of the supplicants are
distracted, and weak'ned for want of agreeing better together. But by *Edification* you mean *Improvement*; and the Minister's Prayer adds to
your Devotion. And here I wish you be not mistaken. For suppose *his Prayer* should cause some
Motions in your *Soul*, and that you are much pleas'd
with what you see and hear from him, yet consider, that though the *Minister* may in this manner
do *his Duty* well, and serve God to the Admiration

on of thofe who are *Witneffes* of his *Zeal*, yet where is *your Worfhip* all this while, and how do *you* ferve God in your attention to *him*? The con-cern you are work'd to at fuch a time, is an *effect* of the *Minifter's Prayer*, but not, as it ought to be, a *quality of your Own*. Devotion is active. When we pray we make a Speech to God; and that it may prevail, we deliver it decently, and as zealoufly as we can. But how can this be applied to you, who are purely *paffive* while the Minifter Prayeth? For though it fhould happen he ftirs your affections, yet that is all; and you are in the Condition of Men under *furprize*, who are ravifh'd with fome *uncommon object*, yet at that inftant have no room for *reflection*, and the fight makes 'em neither *wifer* nor *better*. In fhort, the moft that can be faid of your warmth is, that thereby you fhow you like the *Minifter's praying*, but what is this to yourfelf, and how in his Devotion do you ex-prefs your *Own*?

B. That is eafily Anfwered; Becaufe, the *Mi-nifter* is the *Mouth* of the Affembly, and for that reafon *his Prayer* is ours, and the *Amen*, which concludes it doth *fign* our confents.

A. The *Amen* at the end of the Prayer is not fufficient of it felf to entitle us to it, unlefs the *Heart* throughout the whole exercife has bore it Company, the beft ingredient of Prayer confift-ing in the *inward defires*, and affections of the Soul, Befides, when we fubjoin *Amen*, we thereby af-fert the truth of what has been faid; we declare, that our Condition has been *faithfully reprefented*, and we wifh it may fucceed and be anfwered ac-cording to what is faid in it. And how can this be fuppofed in a long *Extempore* Prayer, where the hearers *Memory* muft be very extraordinary to retain all the parts of fuch an Addrefs, the *appre-henfion* quick, and the *judgment* ripe to determine

the

the goodnefs of it. Moveover we fay *Amen,* not to convince God of our concurrence in fuch a Prayer, but for a *Teftimony* to one another, that we have been all the time bufied in the publick Devotion, *minded* it as we fay, and made it our *own* by a filent and mental repeating it. For tho' it is not Convenient that every fingle Votary fhould be as *loud* as the *Minifter,* which is the reafon we only fay *Amen* to avoid noife, confufion and diforder, yet the very Word implies, that our *heart* has pray'd with the *Minifter* all the while ; and if not, neither *his prayer,* nor *our Amen* is of any benefit to us. The Minifter is the *Mouth* of the Congregation ; True, but be it remembred that the Office and Duty of a *Mouth,* confifts in uttering *Audibly* and *Faithfully,* what the *Mind* has conceived within ; and to make the Language proper; there muft always be a clofe Correfpondence between 'em. So that this Character therefore fhows that the *Minifter fpeaks* no more than the *People's Thoughts,* and what themfelves would declare with their *own Voice,* if they might not be troublefome to one another. And here I muft not omit the danger of confiding too much in the *Minifter's Prayer,* for fear by the *fame imputation,* whereby we would make what is good in his Prayer, our own, we may be forced to own likewife what he faith *amifs.* For let his *Office* be never fo *Holy,* there can be no fecurity of his *Perfon.* *Judas* was *one of the twelve,* but he was a *Devil.* If you think your felf fafe from the experience you have both of the *Man and his Prayer,* this I confefs a folid Anfwer, but then it prefumes you have not only known the *Minifter,* but heard his *Prayer* often before, (there being no other way in this cafe to fatisfy Confcience, than to ground its fafety on fuch an *Experience*) and if fo, you give up the Caufe, *his Prayer* fo repeated being made a *form* to the Congregation that hears him.

him. So that the *Question* is reduced to this,
Whether a *Prayer* made and revised by *many*, is not
much better, than what is composed by *One* ? For
if it be true, that *in the multitude of Councellors there
is safety*, can we imagine but that the *publick Liturgy* must needs have the precedence, when there
has been so much care, and all other likely means
taken for its sufficiency and goodness?

· *B.* How can this form of Worship be reconciled to the Apostle's *Praying by the Spirit* ?

A. You have the Phrase from St. *Paul,* 1 *Cor.*
14. where though he gives two interpretations of
those Words, yet neither of 'em contributes to
your Objection. The *first* is, *praying in an unknown Tongue*, a faculty bestow'd on the Disciples
of Christ, for the publication of the Gospel by
immediate Revelation from Heaven ; And therefore
those who prayed in that manner, were said to
pray by the Spirit : A way of praying if not *opposed*
to, yet very much *distinguished* from praying with
the *understanding*, as we may see, *v.* 15. *What is
it then? I will pray with the Spirit, and I will pray with
the understanding also*—but more plainly, *v.* 2.
where *speaking in an unknown Tongue*, and *speaking
by the Spirit*, interpret each other. A sort of
praying or preaching so little edifying, that St.
Paul declares, he had rather speak *five words* o-
therwise, than *ten thousand* such to the People.
v. 19. The other meaning of *praying by the Spirit*,
is, when his Heart was engaged, and his Spirit
prayed, *v.* 14. *I will pray with the Spirit, and my
Spirit truly prayeth*——i. e though he pray'd in
an unknown Tongue, his *Spirit* prayed, and did it effectually as to himself, because he knew what he
said, and his Soul and Spirit join'd in the Service.
But still with respect to others this way was un-
fruitful ; and being altogether for *Edification* in this
Chapter, he was clearly for that kind of Prayer,

to

to which all the People could say *Amen*, and in which the Congregation might be as much concern'd in *their Spirits*, as he was in *his*, while he pray'd in an *unknown Tongue* So that the Authority of this Text, is of little use to support your notion ; Becaufe as to the *firft* way of praying, it ceafed long ago, as being by Miracle and the infufion of Tongues. And the *latter* being yielded makes nothing againft us, becaufe we hold, that in every Prayer *our Spirits* muft have an intereft, or elfe we are fure to pray in vain.

It is to be wifhed, that the Spirit we fo much fpeak of, and pretend to pray by, be not miftaken. For there is a Spirit of affectation and pride, which is apt to delude and make us believe the *Gifts of Nature* to be *the fruits of Grace*, and habits divinely infpired, and if a Man has affurance enough with a plaufible faculty to vent his conceptions, he is prefently endow'd with a *Prophetick* Talent, and all he fpeaks muft be underftood, as if he was moved by the *Holy Ghoft* : When perhaps an *Atheift* or an *Hytocrite*, may deliver himfelf in a dialect full as holy, and yet have fo little intereft in the Spirit of God, as not to deferve the Chriftian Name.

To me it appears not only *modeft* and humble, but *prudent* and fafe to diftruft ourfelves in a thing of this confequence ; and remembring how many and great our Infirmities are, and what the Majefty of God is whom we Addrefs to after this manner, 'tis better furely to ufe the found words wife and good. Men have furnifh'd us with, than to offer fuch as (though never fo carefully compofed by ourfelves,) muft make us doubt, whether we pray well by 'em or no. For the Doctrine we profefs denies *infallibility*, or *private infpiration* in thefe Days : Yet this we are pretty well perfwaded of (God having engaged his Word for it) that

the

the Holy Ghoſt ſhall never ·fail the *Body* of his Church ; and therefore what that *Body* preſents to us, falls under the leſs ſuſpicion of being erroneous.

B. The *Papiſts* talk thus, and make their Church the *Pillar and Ground of Truth* ; And thence take occaſion to obtrude upon us, what they pleaſe on pain of Damnation. And to deal above·board with you, though for the reaſons you have given, I was never very averſe to a *form of Prayer* in the Publick Worſhip of God (and therefore am not angry at what our Miniſter ſaith, though conſtantly the *ſame*) yet the Common-Prayer we daily uſe being fetch'd from a Church, which all Parties among us confeſs full of Corruptions, is indeed an offence to me on the account of what our Lord ſaith, *Of thorns, Men do not gather·Figs, nor of a bramble Buſh, gather they Grapes. A good tree bringeth forth good fruit, but a corrupt tree bringeth forth evil fruit. A good tree cannot bring forth evil fruit, neither can a corrupt tree bring forth good fruit---* So that our Service-Book being little more than a Copy· of *theirs,* whoſe Communion we reject for their manifold Errors, how can it be·ſuſpected, we ſhould Heartily join in ſuch a piece of Devotion, and ſay the Prayers, ſuch ill Chriſtians have made to our Hands?

A. The *Corruptions* of the Church of *Rome,* we call *Popery,* are of a low date in Compariſon of the times, when Liturgies began in that Province, and other Places of the World, where the Goſpel was ſetled. It was the care and piety of our *Fathers,* at the *Reformation* of Religion in this Kingdom, not to *Deſtroy* the Church of *Rome,* but *reſtore* her to that purity, which ſhe retained for ſeveral Centuries, and was ſo much commended·by St. *Paul* , who thanks God , *through Chriſt Jeſus, that her faith was ſpoken of throughout the World* ⸺

And

And this Apology we of this Church have for ourfelves in what has been done, that the fault and
charge of Schifm is fimply, and altogether her
own, becaufe fhe left herfelf, and not we her, the
Church of *England* continuing what fhe once was,
and what in honour, and fafety to herfelf fhe ought
to be again. And as in diverfe *other* inftances, fo in
this of the Liturgy, our *Reformers* corrected what
they found amifs ; and feparating the *Gold* from
the *Drofs*, they expunged what was fpurious and
novel in the fervice, and retaining the ufeful and
wholefom part, they tranflated it into our own
Tongue, that as we were no longer to *believe*, fo
neither to *pray implicitely*.

But what if it be proved, that our Liturgy has
another Original ? For we find in a *Cotton*-Manu-
fcript, that *Germanus*, and *Lupus*, brought into
the *Britifh-Churches*, *Ordinem curfûs Gallorum*, by
which Archbifhop *Ufher* underftands the *Gallican
Liturgy*, which very much differ'd from the *Roman*, as we may conclude from that Queftion,
Auftin the Monk put Pope *Gregory*, Which of 'em
he fhould follow ? and anfwer was made, That he
fhould chufe what he thought moft proper for the
Englifh Church. Accordingly the *firft* was prefer-
red ; and the rather ; becaufe, the *Queen* was a
Chriftian before *Auftin* came hither, and had been
ufed to the *French* Liturgy (which fome Authors
derive from St. *John*, by *Polycarp* and *Irenæus*) fo
that fhe, and her Bifhops being *French*, it had given great offence, to take that form of fervice a-
way, which they had brought along with 'em,
and which the *Britifh* Church had now for fome
time been accuftomed to. As to the feveral parts
of it, I refer you to Bifhop *Stillingfleet's* Book, called *Origines Britannicæ*, c. 4. All which are retain'd in the Offices of our Church; not from
Rome as our Diffenters imagine, but from the confent

fent of all the Ancient Churches, which fhe alfo follows by putting them into a Language under-ftood by the People. The agreement between *this* and the *Gallican* Liturgy, you will find in that Author; From whofe difcourfe it appears, that our *Church of England,* as it introduces nothing *New,* fo it hath omitted none of thofe Offices, wherein all the *Old Churches* agreed; And in cafe of difference, we adhere to the *Gallican,* and not to *that* from *Rome.* But grant it otherwife, that fome of the materials came from the *Roman Miffal;* why fhould not this be confidered, as it really in it felf is, a Teftimony of that prudence and good temper our *Reformers* fhow'd in compiling it, who, to draw the *Papifts* into their Communion (then the only Diffenting party, and whofe Converfion they defired) they kept as near 'em as they fafely could, and by that means brought many of 'em o-ver, and had better fucceeded, but that the *Pope* fent a *Bull* hither to feparate 'em from us. But ftill 'tis the *Mafs-Book* a little refined. This is an objection may make a great noife among unthink-ing People; But can ferious and judicious Men lay any ftrefs on it? (a) *Whatever the Pagans them-felves,* (as St. *Auguftine* fpeaks) *had in their Doctrine divine and juft, our Saints refufe it not;* nor is the confideration of any force to frighten *Catholicks* from doing a thing, becaufe *Hereticks* have done the fame——(b) *A Novatian prefumes to do it; what then, muft we therefore forbear it? He hath ufurped the honour of the Chair, fhall we therefore a-bandon it? He hath againft all right and reafon fet up an Altar, and would do Sacrifice on it, are we there-fore to lay afide ours both Oblations and Altar? It is a foolifh and ridiculous conceit, that, becaufe a Novatian*

(a) Adv. Donat. Ep. 154. (b) Cypr Ep. 73 n. 3.

challenges

challenges to himself the shadow of Truth, we must therefore reject the Substance, and take leave of the Truth; that we may not in any respect appear like him. ——Truth is of God, though utter'd by *Balaam* or a Sibyl. *(c)* Nor is a Diamond or any other Jewel less precious, though it be smear'd over with dirt, or found on a dunghil. What admirable pieces of Morality and Politicks do we hourly read in the Writings of *Pagan Greece* and *Rome*? Are these Books to be burnt, because *Plato* and *Aristotle*, *Cicero* and *Seneca*, or the like penned 'em? Surely 'tis no Crime to use the Light of the *Sun* and *Moon*, though our Ancestours adored them. And for my part, I should no more scruple to speak to God in a good *Prayer*, made by a *Dominican* or a *Jesuit*, than according to your Metaphor, to eat the *Fruit* of a Tree, planted by a *Moor* or a *Mahumetan*. We do not find King *(d) Solomon*, unwilling to send to *Hiram* King of *Tyre* for Cedars and Workmen, for the building of the Temple at *Jerusalem* ; nor that the structure was accounted less holy, because the materials and Builders were *Heathen*. Many of our Churches in this Nation we owe to the Zeal and Purses of our Popish Predecessours, yet we safely Worship in 'em : And herein we follow not only the Judgment of *(e)* St. *Augustine*, who declares, that *even the Idol Temples, when devoted to the Honour and Service of the true God, may be as well used and accepted, as Infidel People converted to Christianity*; but even the *(f) directory* warrants us in this particular, and saith, that *whatever the builders of our*

(c) *Quasi aurum non sit aurum quod in luto quærimus.* Reuchlin de art Cabbalist. lib. 2. (d) 2 Chro. 2 7, 8. (e) Epist. 154. (f) An Appendix, touching Days and Places for publick Worship.

Churches

Churches were, yet the places are not subject to such pollution by any superstition formerly used, and now laid aside, as may render 'em unlawful or inconvenient for Christians, to meet together therein for the publick Worship of God. And therefore we hold it requisite, that the Places of publick Assembling for Worship among us, should be continued and employ'd to that use———
The *Water* of Baptism, and the *Bread* and *Wine* of the Eucharist were Elements prophaned by the Gentiles, yet they are the signs and *matter* of our Christian Sacraments, and made the ordinary means of Salvation, notwithstanding those abuses. A Man might abound with these illustrations to remove the Calumny But after all, prejudice is clamorous, and Persons otherwise bent are apt to let go truth, rather than be supposed to have been in an Error. So that we must still be told, that our Liturgy is the *Mass-Book* in *English*, a New Edition of the *Breviary*, and all their *Rituals* reduced to a lesser Volume. And were there any truth in this charge, the compliance is not Sinful; Because, we take from the *Papists* no more than what they had from others, who never knew what *Popery* was. And as in common we *Both* receive the Scriptures of the Old Testament from the hands of the *Jews*, notwithstanding the Additions, and corruptions of the *Scribes* and *Pharisees:* In like manner, we have the matter and model of the Service of God by their conveyance. But as for the excesses of *Ave-Maria's, Prayers for the dead, Addresses to the Saints,* &c. these we have separated from what is *Old* and *Legitimate,* and curing the *Diseases* of the Church and Service, our *Reformers* have restored 'em to the features, and vigour of the *ancienter* and *purer* times. And if this answer be not sufficient, we shall be hard put to it to defend the practice of reading the Bible it self;

which

which we enjoy from, and by *their means*, and which *they* retain, and ufe as well as *we*.

We do not beg all this. Let the *Book* be examined, and fee what there is in it of any affinity with that *Popery*, wherewith it is vulgarly charged, and which you think deferves your Cenfure. The *Sentences*; The *Pater-Nofter*; The *Venite exultemus*, or *Pf.* 95. The *Pfalms*; The *Leffons*; The *Benedictus*, or Song of *Zachary*; The *Jubilate*, or *Pf.* 100. The *Magnificat*, or *Virgins* Hymn; The *Cantate Domino*, or *Pf.* 98. The *Nunc Dimittis*; or Song of Old *Simeon*; The *Deus Mifereatur*, or *Pf.* 67. The *Decalogue*; The *Epiftles* and *Gofpels*; And the *Bleffing*——Thefe are every one of them *literally* Scripture. The *Te deum*, has Author, a Divince piece, and above 200 Years older than *Popery*; And near his time lived St. *Chryfoftom*, whofe Prayer goes before the *Benediction* of St. *Paul*. The *Creed* was framed either by the *Apoftles* or Apoftolical Men; To be fure the feveral *Articles* and Heads of it, are fuch as to Merit that name, and are without gain-faying the *Apoftles Doctrine*. And to explain *this*, were added, the *Athanafian* and *Nicene*, occafionally penned to affert, againft the Hereticks, the God-Head of Chrift, and the Bleffed Spirit; And it favours too much of *Socinianifm*, to be fo loud in crying 'em down. The remainder of the Worfhip confifts in grave *Exhortations*, *Confeffions*, or in the *Gallican* ftile, *Apologies*, *Prayers*, *Supplications*, *Interceffions*, and *giving of thanks for all Men*, efpecially thofe of the *Catholick Church*, or the Houfhold of Faith, for *Kings*, and *thofe who are in Authority*, whether in Church or State, according to St. *Paul's* Directions, and the Prayers fo well compofed, that we give 'em the name of *Collects*, meaning the *Collection*, and joining together Phrafes of Scripture orderly digefted,

gefted, to set our neceffities and defires before God, as near as we can in his own Language. And when that is wanting, we fupply ourfelves out of the Devotions of thofe Fathers, whom envy it felf cannot deny to be both *Ancient* and *Pious*. Our *Litany,* our *Refponfes,* our frequent fpeaking to the Affembly, to quicken their attention, thefe and the reft, have the venerable examples of the firft Ages of *Chriftianity,* to juftify our Practice. And the *Apologifts* for it, are fo able and numerous, that if the Adverfary is not convinced, it muft be malice, or becaufe he is a Stranger to their Writings. And certainly in *it felf,* and *from them* it appears to be *g) a form of Divine Worfhip of fo good quality, as that fince the Holy Apoftles Days, the Chriftian World never enjoy'd a more reverend and religious*————And though all Churches had their refpective Liturgies, yet *none was ever Bleffed with fo comprehenfive, fo exact, and fo inoffenfive a compofure, fo judicioufly contrived, that the wifeft may exercife at once their Knowledge and Devotion, and yet fo plain, that the moft ignorant may pray with underftanding ; fo full, that nothing is omitted fit to be ask'd in publick ; and fo particular, that it comprizes moft things which we would pray for in private ; and yet fo fhort, as not to tire any that have true Devotion. Its doctrine is pure and primitive ; Its ceremonies fo few and innocent, that moft of the Chriftian World agree in 'em. Its method is exact and natural ; Its language fignificant and perfpicuous, moft of the words and phrafes being taken out of Scripture ; And the reft are the expreffions of the firft and beft Ages. So that whoever takes exceptions againft thefe, muft quarrel with the Language of the Holy Ghoft, or fall out with the Church in her greateft Innocence.* In a word, 'tis

***

(g) Dr. Comber's Preface to his Companion to the Temple.

so little a Friend to Popery, that fair and judicious Men consider it as a Wall of defence against the Superstitions of that *polluted Church.* And were it not really so, what made the *Priests* in Queen *Mary's* Days give it that hard usage, as not only to burn (b) *those* who made this Book, but to Martyr the *Book it self,* and throw both *it,* and the *Compilers* into the Fire? To this end, a *Proclamation* was set out by the King and Queen, *June* 13. 1555. for the restraining of all Books and Writings, tending against the Doctrine of the Pope and his Church————*Whereas by the Statute, made in the second Year of King* Henry IV. *concerning the repressing of Heresie, there is ordained and provided a great punishment, not only for the Authors, Makers and Writers of Books, containing wicked Doctrine and Erroneous, and Heretical Opinions contrary to the Catholick Faith————The King and Queen, our Soveraign Lord and Lady, therefore————straitly charge and command, that no Person or Persons presume to bring, or cause to be brought into this Realm any Books, Writings and Works hereafter mentioned————Containing false Doctrine contrary, and against the Catholick Faith————Also that no Person or Persons presume to Write, Print, Utter, Sell, Read or Keep, or cause to be Written————any Book or Books written or printed in the Latin or English Tongue, concerning the Common Service, and Administration set forth in English, to be used in the Churches of this Realm, in the time of King* Edward VI. *commonly called the Communion-Book, or Book of Common-Service, and ordering of Ministers, otherwise called the Book set forth by Authority of Parliament, for Common Prayer and Administration of the Sacraments——but shall within* 15 *days*

(b) This Book was penn'd by those that shed their Blood, and Sealed it with their lives—Lord Keeper *Finch's* Speech to the Judges, *Feb.* 13. 1639.

after

after publication of this proclamation bring or.caufe to be brought the aforefaid Books, to the Ordinary of the. Diocefs,or his Chancellor, or Commiffary ——— to be burnt. Such were the Men that formed this Excellent Work, and *fuch* the Ufage *this* and *they* had from thofe Papifts whom we are fufpected to imitate in this way of Service. Yet it is the *Mafs-Book* in *Englifh, Rifum teneatis?* Methinks I .am concerned that any *proteftant* fhould fo zealoufly. efpoufe and carry on the caufe of the common Enemy by thefe groundlefs furmifes, and honour *Popery* fo much as they do, by attributing to fo corrupt a Church that admirable Service, which *Calvin* liked fo well, and *Grotius* among other. Foreigners, fo highly commended as the beft *Copy* of the Old and beft Liturgies.

B. I cannot but own, thofe hardfhips you fpake of are good teftimonies, that neither our *Reformers*, nor the *Service-Book* were welcome to the *Papifts.* And truly it doth not feem very credible they would treat the Common-Prayer-Book in that rough manner, if it had been their proper iffue. I'll give you no further trouble therefore on that fcore to add to its vindication, nor will I offer thofe exceptions many have made in my hearing, and which tho' they have fome weight are not powerful enough to induce me to condemn it. As for example, *The applying of the Hymns* we find in the Gofpel, efpecially the *Magnificat* and the *Nunc dimittis* they think very improper; The refponfe after the Creed, when we pray for Peace in our time, *becaufe there is no other fighteth for us but only thou, O God,* feems an odd reafon for God to grant our petition,as if his help and protection were not fufficient under any Circumftances; but becaufe in War he alone Fighteth for us,therefore we beg of him to fend us peace. Then they complain that the Prayers are, *fhort* and conftantly the *fame;*

, That

That the *variety of gestures* during the worſhip
ſhow light and comical ; That the reading of
the Leſſons without expoſition is altogether unedi-
fying ; and that the whole Service being tranſacted by theMiniſter in a *Surplice* ſavours of Superſtition. That which more offends me, are thoſe
Tautologies always uſed and ſaid in defiance of our
Lord's prohibition, when inſtructing his diſciples
how to pray well, he bids them(i) *not uſe vain repeti-*
tions, as the heathens do, who think they ſhall be heard
for their much ſpeaking ;---which agrees with the
better ſenſe of mankind, as we read in the Book
of Eccleſiaſticus, (k) *Uſe not,* ſaith that Author,
many words in a multitude of Elders, and make not
much babling when thou prayeſt ; (l) nay it is in the
Greek *do not ſay the ſame words twice in thy Prayer.*
But with more authority the preacher admoniſhes, (m)
Be not raſh with thy mouth and let not thine heart be
haſty to utter any thing before God; for God is in Heaven
and thou upon earth, therefore let thy words be few.--And
truly as it looks unmannerly to be thus trouble-
ſome in the preſence of ſober men ; So in my judgment, the preſumption is greater to addreſs God in
this manner ; to whom we ought to ſpeak in few,
and proper Words, and not tire his Wiſdom and
Patience with what would be very (n) *nauſeous*
and unpleaſant to Men. And to this may be reduced the often ſaying of the Lords-Prayer. *For*
tho' I know it neceſſary to Pray and pray often, and
tho' I know that in a few Words it is impoſſible for any
man to frame ſo pithy a Prayer, and that the Church
doth well to join the Lords-Prayer to her own ;----yet I
ſtand upon this, That there is no neceſſity to uſe it

(i) Matth. 6 7. (k) Ecclu. 7. 14: (l) μὴ δευτερώσῃς
λόγον εν προσευχῇ σου——(m) Eccleſ. 5. 2. (n) *Quod mo-*
leſtum eſt & tædioſum coram Deo ſicut battologia eſt eruditc-
rum auribus.——Chemnit. Harmon. Evang.

so frequently in that small proportion of time we dedicate to God's service, and the so much insisting on it seems to me to tend to Superstition:

And as these *reiterations* in Prayer insinuate to the World a great barrenness in us to expressDevotion, and withall infer with what difficulty our petitions are heard, which must be said over and over again, to make God understand them: So the custom of some Churchs sounds very odd by *Voice*, and *instrument* to chant the Service; even those parts of it, wherein we confess our Sins, and supplicate for pardon. This does not only make the worship *unintelligible* to the Votaries themselves, but perswades us to believe, that God is more taken with the *harmony* of Prayers than the *matter* of them, and supposes that we must *charm* him with the *Musick*, before he will be brought to hear, and relieve us in those wants we set before him. If a *common beggar* in the street should accost me in that Sort, I might be apt to think his greatest *want* to be in the *Brain*, and consequently the best instance I could give of my Charity would be, to have him to *Bedlam*. Men in Prayer are under this notion; And therefore, *Sir*——I need not many Words to apply it; you may guess my meaning.

A. I do guess what you intend; and am very sorry to hear you. But to consider your Objections as they lie in order: And first for them which you report from others, and which, tho' not in the same degree as those lastly proposed, yet still have an influence on you, and ought therefore to have some share in the answer. But before I begin, let me tell you a short Story. Once upon a time, it fell out, that a Friend of mine dined with a Wealthy Citizen, not long after *Sheriff* of *London*: Part of the Table-Discourse was concerning the Liturgy; against which he produced this exception; That in the Deprecations 'tis said,

from

from Fornication, *and all other deadly-Sin, Good Lord deliver us,*----as if, faith he, *Fornication* were not *a deadly Sin.* Yes, anſwer'd my friend, the expreſſi-on calls it ſo, *from Fornication* and all *other* dead-ly Sin, ſo that Fornication is one of the deadly Sins, and the only one named ; and being ſo named puts it out of Queſtion. He ſaid it was ill Word-ed and ought to be mended. I perceive you ſmile at the Objection, and ſo did I when I firſt heard it, but it yielded Matter for a very ſerious reflection: And we hereupon concluded, That it muſt needs prove a fruitleſs attempt to alter our way of Service, becauſe it ſeems an impoſſible thing to pleaſe every body. For whether this was a defect in the *Underſtanding* or Will of that Gentleman I know not, but no doubt he would ex-pect that *his Exception* ſhould be taken notice of, as well as *other* Peoples ; Otherwiſe you incenſe him the more and confirm him in his Error, wherein we may ſuppoſe he was not alone. To tell him his ſcruple was groundleſs, he will anſwer, That in other mens opinion the reſt are ſo ; and if *they* are indulged, why not *he?* So that plainly, as there would be no end in finding faults, ſo not to re-dreſs them *all,* is to do *nothing.* And if every Cavil ſhould be minded, farewell the whole Litur-gy. Yet I am not againſt doing any thing in rea-ſon, to gain over our brethren, that we might all ſerve God in the *ſame way.* But firſt I wiſh they could *all* agree in the exceptions, which hitherto was never done, and perhaps will never be till *Elias come.*

B. But was not the Gentleman miſtaken, who probably intended no more than to find fault with the Word [*deadly*], as favouring too much the Popiſh diſtinction, between Sins *Venial* and *Mor-tal,* as if *every Sin* was not deadly, and expoſed a Man to Damnation ?

A. There

A. There was no mention of this; and though it be objected by some, who thereby would reduce us to the *Mafs-Book*, yet 'twas omitted by him, who perhaps thought that exception as frivolous as you and I take the other to be. For what faith St. *John*? *there is a Sin unto Death and a Sin not unto Death*, *John.* 5. 16, 17. And 'tis evident, that some Sins are not so bad and desperate as others. In this place *deadly Sins* mean *presumptuous ones*; and as in the Petition before we beseech God to deliver us from more secret Sins and such as more immediately respect the Heart, as *Pride, Uncharitableness*, and the like, so here we pray against open and scandalous Crimes, and such grofs acts of wickednefs, as show the Sinner harden'd in his way, and which ending for the most part in an impenitent State must bring him to damnation at last. Of this kind *Solomon* reprefents *Fornication*, Pro. 2. 19. *None that go unto her return again nor take hold of the paths of life*——So that though *all Sins* are in their own nature *Mortal* without repentance, as being violations of the Divine-will, yet there are degrees in our difobedience; and Repentance is not fo difficult of fome Sins as of others, and we befeech God to deliver us from the latter.

And here fince I am fo near it, let us not pafs by the next petition which fome People condemn, and wherein we pray against *fudden Death* as a very fad Event to endanger the Soul. For tho' we ought all of us fo to live as if every minute were to be the laft, yet who of ten thoufand takes this care and in perfect health, ftrength and other enjoyments of *this* world, fo thinks of *another* as to be always provided for it? Alas no; the influence of thefe temptations are fo powerful, that they too much ingage the Heart, to let us prepare for futurity. But when Sicknefs comes, it puts us us on thinking ; Then we begin to consult the after Peace of our Families, and settle our Affairs both with respect to God and Man. And though we feel the *pain* of our Disease great, yet we consider the *Torments* of Hell greater, and *those* we take for warnings to avoid the *latter*. *Sudden-Death* may be thought an easie *exit*, if we had nothing to do but to die (though after all, what Wiseman would wish it before his House be set in Order, and who does that till he has one foot in the Grave?) Yet remembring there is another World ; that there is *after Death the Judgment* ; that Death is not so much the leaving of this Life, as the entring into another: He, I say, that calls these things to Mind, may easily Credit, that the Church knows his case, and takes more care of him than he does of himself, by beseeching God not to let him be hurried out of this World, either by an untimely Death, or violent Death, or an unprepared Death, which will in all likelihood end very dismally in that to come.

1. But to return to your Objections: And first for the *Hymns* you proposed. They are always used after the Lessons, wherein having heard God say to us, something relating to Salvation, we think it our Duty to show our *gratitude*, and joy in some *Hymn of Praise* ; And if we use *those words*, the Holy Ghost composed, and wherewith good People heretofore Praised God on the same occasion, where is the harm ? 'Tis true, the *Magnificat* was said by her, who was Christ's Mother, and it more immediately refers to *her Person*, and the favour done her, yet the same Hymn saith, that *the Mercy of God is on them that fear him throughout all Generations.* We are concern'd in it as well as she ; And tho' the Virgin bore him *literally* in her Womb (which was an honour the greatest Matrons in *Israel* expected, and call'd for her

acknow-

acknowledgments that had it) yet if St. *Paul* speaks properly, *Chrift may be formed in us likewife*: Nay, our Lord has told us, That he who hears the word of God, (as he fhould) is *his Brother, Sifter and Mother*: So that being brought under the *fame relation* with her, why may we not ufe the *fame form* of words, to magnify the Blefling? The like may be offer'd for the *Nunc Dimittis*, which was faid by old *Simeon*, when he faw Chrift with his Eyes, and held him in his Arms, and then was contented to go immediately to that Salvation, which by this means he was enfured of. What he did in a *fenfible way*, we may do *by Faith*, and when we ufe the Language of the Spirit, we ufe it in a way applicable to us. A Man that is fure of his Salvation, and defires to enjoy it, why may he not pray with *Simeon* to *depart*, or with St. *Paul* to be *diffolved*, and *be with Chrift, which is much better* than living here. It favours not a little of what we call *Carnal*, when a Chriftain is not willing to utter fuch a Prayer. However, this Hymn need not give offence, becaufe the words do not import a requeft to die, but teftifie our belief, that if God thinks fit to let us

that we go to an happier State.
deed fomewhat of Refignation to the Will of God, and the confidence we have in his Mercy, that when we die we hope he Will make us Happy, but it does not imply that at all fuch times we folicite for Death, though I know no reafon why we fhould not do it, if we have a fair profpect of E-ternity.

2. In the *Verficles* we pray for Peace, *becaufe there is no other that fighteth for us, but only thou, O God*——— which is underftood as a difparagement of the Power of God, that we pray for Peace, becaufe he alone fights for us, as if that were not
fufficient

fufficient to do our bufinefs. But this [*becaufe*] does not fo much refer to *God* as *Man*, in whom we can have no affurance of fafety, though he promifes well, and will fight for us, And therefore becaufe there is no other that fighteth for us, with certainty of fuccefs, unlefs God is on our fide and fights our Battels, we befeech him to fend us Profperity and Peace, which are the ends we defign by War, and which if God pleafes we would have without it. This is the meaning of the refponfe, and where the fence is fo full, I know not how it can be Worded, with more concifenefs than it already is in the Liturgy.

3. That the Prayers are *fhort*, is, left they fhould naufeate, and make Devotion languid or faint through the tedioufnefs of the Service. And every Prayer being made for a particular want, the Spirits are fixed, and all the motions of the affections determined to one Point. So that were our Memories never fo bad, we cannot well forget what we are about, and we come to Church with a very low degree of Piety, if it keeps not its warmth till we fay *Amen*. This motive the *Brethren* in *Egypt* had, who are reported to have very frequent but fhort Prayers, and thofe in the Nature of fuddain Ejaculations,(*o* left the intention of the Mind, which is neceffary to him that prayeth, fhould grow dull and heavy through a longer continuance in their Devotion.

4. As to their being every Day the fame, (*p*) *I could never fee any reafon,* faid King *Charles* I. *Why a Chriftian fhould abhor, or be forbidden to ufe the fame forms of Prayer, fince he prays to the fame God, believes in the fame Saviour, profeffeth the fame truths,*

(*o*) *Ne per moras evanefcat & hebetetur intentio.* Aug. ad Prob. Ep 121. c 9. (*p*) Ἐικὼν Βασιλικὴ. c. 16.

reads

reads the fame Scriptures, hath the fame Duties upon him, and feels the fame daily wants for the moft part, both outward and inward, which are common to the whole Church. Sure we may know beforehand, what to pray as to whom to pray, and in what words, as to what fence; when we defire the fame things, what hinders that we may not ufe the fame Words? Our appetite and digeftion too may be good when we ufe, as when we pray for our daily Bread——*I make no doubt but a Man may be very formal in the moft Extemporary variety, and very fervently devout in the moft wonted Expref-fions. Nor is God more a God of variety than of con-ftancy. Nor are conftant Forms of Prayer, more likely to flat and hinder the Spirit of Prayer and Devotion, than unpremeditated and confufed variety to diftract and lofe it.*

5. The difference of *Geftures*, they find fault with, is very agreeable to the parts of our Serv ice. For the Wifdom of the Church has fo order'd, that all the Worfhip of God fhould not be *Prayer*, (*q*) left too much intention weary the Soul, as too long bending weakens the Bow, and makes it unferviceable: Nor yet muft it wholly confift in *reading*, left the Soul, as the Bow ftand-ing ftill unbent, becomes unable at length to fhoot up one Arrow to Heaven. But *reading* and *pray-ing* have their turns, and relieve each other; And as the *one* teaches us to adore God, fo the *latter* makes that knowledge practical, and we actually adore him. While therefore we *read* or *hear*, we *fit* down for the refrefhment and eafe of the Body, but when we *pray* we *kneel* as Suiters to God, be-fore whom we ought to behave ourfelves with all imaginable humility. When we fay our *Creed* we

---

(*q*) Roffenf. de geniculat.

deliver

deliver it (*r*) *ftanding*, as Confeffours and Souldiers who fight the good fight of Faith, and in the ftrength of which we hope to *ftand* firm in the Prefence of God, and be enabled by it to tread our Spiritual Enemies under our Feet. And fo we *ftand* at the reading of the *Gofpel* in the fecond Service, as the gefture of thofe, who expect the glad tidings of what the Gofpel propofes, fuch as the remiffion of Sins, and the confequent of it, Eternal Glory. A Cuftom fo general, that (*s*) *Sozomen* reckons it peculiar to the Church of *Alexandria*, that the Bifhop did not rife up at the Gofpel: (*t*) Contrary, faith *Nicephorus*, to the practice of all the Churches. Yet it is not to be underftood, as if this portion of Scripture calls for this refpect, as being more holy than what we read before, but we give it this reverence in the name of the *whole*, which deferves and demands the fame gefture, but that the Church is indulgent and fatisfied with thus much, as a fignification, and witnefs of our willingnefs to pay our acknowledgments, if required, to all the Leffons of the Bible in the fame manner. And if the *Gofpel* hath the preference, and is rather pitch'd on than any other part of the divine Writings, the reafon is, becaufe generally fpeaking it reprefents fome *Sermon*, or great *Action* of Chrift, either of which we

---

(*r*) Some Ceremonies are ufeful, give me leave to fay, I hold it neceffary —— that at the repetition of the Creed, we fhould ftand up to teftify the refolution of our Hearts, that we will defend that Religion we profefs, and in fome Churches, it is added, They did not only ftand upright with their Bodies, but with their Swords drawn. Sir *John Elliot's* Speech in Parlia, 1628 (*s*) L. 7. c. 19. (*t*) L. 12. c 34. *Dum SS. Evangelia recitantur in Ecclefia facerdotes & cæteri —— non fedentes fed venerabiliter curvi in confpectu SS. Evan: Stantes —— Epift. decret. An ftafii.*

ought to entertain in a solemn way, as more immediately relating to his own Person.

Sixthly, As to Ceremonies. The Liturgy tells us, That though our Church, becaufe of the excefs, and abufes of 'em, hath laid by a great many Rites, which before fhe labour'd under, yet *confidering, that without fome Ceremonies it is not poffible to keep any order or quiet difcipline in the Church,* therefore for this Order and difcipline-fake, fhe has been content to retain a few, but fuch only as are apt *to ftir up the dull Mind of Man, to the remembrance of his Duty to God, by fome notable and fpecial fignification, whereby he may be edifyed* and taught. And herein other Proteftant Churches confent, That *fuch Rites and Ceremonies ought to be retained, which do advantage Faith, the Worfhip of God, Peace and good Order, whoever be the Author whether Council, Pope, Bifhop, or any other*——(*u*) faith the *Bohemian* Confeffion. (*x*) The *Auguftane* admits 'em on the fame confideration, having an Eye to St. *Paul's* Rule, That *all things be done decently and in Order.* And to this end, *every Church may prefcribe what means fhe in her Wifdom thinks proper,* faith (*y*) the *Gallican* Church, *So that they affect not the Confcience, and are not abufed to Superftition.* And fhe calls them *heady and obftinate Men,* that will not comply with 'em. As for the Reformed Churches in *Poland, Lithuania, Ruffia,* &c. *It makes not much,* fay they, *what Rites are obferved*——and *every Chuch is left free to take what fhe pleafes, as far as they conduce to edification and ufefulnefs.* (*z*) *Melanchton* on this reafon, doth not only affert the Liberty and Power of the Church, but makes it the Duty of thofe in Authority, either to intro-

---

(*u*) Art. 15. (*x*) Cap. de difcrim. cib. (*y*) 1562. apud Calv. (*z*) In refp. Prot. 1541.

I i

duce

duce or continue fuch Cuftoms, fo that they be grave and *useful, and help to admonish, and inform the ignorant:.* (*a*) *Calvin* calls 'em the *Bonds of Order and Comeliness,* and *without which the Church connot subfift.* (*b*) And therefore he declares, that taking 'em for no other than *External Rites,* he was not againft 'em. (*c*) And *Bullinger* owns, and commends this temper in him, *I know,* faith he, *you have never been ftiff and peevish in things of this Nature* —and then adds his own Judgment for the Churches Liberty, to appoint what fhe thought convenient for her Childrens good. But *Calvin* is very large, and conftant to himfelf on this fubjeft, (*d*) "Becaufe, *faith he,* as to out-
"ward difcipline and ceremonies, our Lord would
"not punftually fet down what we are to do (fore-
"feeing thefe things much depended on the Con-
"dition of the times, and judging one form not
"proper for all Ages) we are to have recourfe to
"the Apoftles general Rule, of expediency and
"comelinefs. And the Church may fafely, either
"alter the Old, or appoint New, as her necef-
"fity fhall require. And in the foregoing Seftion he defines or defcribes, what we may call *decent* and *comely.* "Not that, *faith he,* which has no-
"thing in it, but what may pleafe the Eye of the
"beholder, whereof we have many inftances in the
"Stage like-Pomp, which the Papifts ufe in the
"Adminiftration of holy things: But that we ac-
"count comely, which contributes to the Reverence
"of the Holy Myfteries, is apt to ftir up to the
"exercife of Piety, inftructs the faithful with what
"Modefty, Religion, and good Behaviour they
"ought to handle holy things, contributes to De-

(*a*) Inftit. l. 4. c. 10. (*b*) Anglis Francoford. Lib. Epift. (*c*) *Scio te nunquam fuiffe morofum* ——Ep. ad Calv. (*d*) Inft. l. 4 c. 10. n. 30.

"votion,

" votion, and leads us to Chrift — And therefore
he concludes in one of (e) his Epiftles, That as
to what belongs to Ceremonies, his Opinion was,
*That none of his Brethren ought to infift fo much on
that point, as on this account to leave their Churches——*
An advice fit for thofe to follow, who pretend to
have a great veneration for the Memory of Mr.
Calvin, but whofe Judgment it feems they no farther regard, than as it clofes with their own Spe-
culations. But elfewhere he is fharper, and (f)
faith, That *if any Perfon is clamorous and troublefom
in this matter, and will be wifer than becomes him, let
him fee how well he will be able to approve and juftify
this frowardnefs hereafter before the Lord.*—All the Reformers were of this mind. And if ever they
fpeak againft the Rites of the Church, it was, *when
by their multitude they clouded the light of the Gofpel ;
when they did not edifie, but were rather for diverfion
than Piety ; when they were made ferviceable to ava-
rice and fordid Gain ; when they were obferved with
much difficulty ; when they were look'd on as matters of
Confcience, and declared neceffary to Salvation———*
And for thefe reafons, and in this cafe the *Auguftane* Confeffion excepts againft 'em, when they
are propofed as *means to obtain remiffion of Sins,* when
they are thought *neceffary,* and made the *Worfhip of
God.* Thefe are indeed *impious Doctrines, dangerous O-
pinions. But otherwife they are helpful to the Miniftry of
the Gofpel. And therefore whoever proudly, and with
fcandal offer violence to thefe, and thereby hinder the fervice of the Gofpel, we adjudge fuch Men to be guilty of
Sin.*——*Zanchy* recommends 'em with the fame
caution, that they be *not contrary to the word of God,
nor clog Confcience, but be ufed to edifying* ——And
this Limitation our Church has fet herfelf in the

(e) In refpo f ad duo certa capita, in lib. Epift. (f) Inftitut. loc. fupra cit. N. 31.

Book of Articles (*g*), where she claims the Power of *adding, taking away,* or *altering* these Matters, *so that all things be done to edifying,* as *Zanchius,* saith in the Apostle's words before.

This then being the general reason for all the Ceremonies in use among us, because namely, they not only have a *natural comeliness,* but an *useful significancy,* and are very conducive both to help the *understanding,* and excite the *affections* of Men, I cannot see why we may not innocently continue 'em, especially being so *few* as well as proper, that were St. *Augustine* himself now alive (who was a Man of a very tender and Scrupulous Conscience, and (*h*) who complain'd of their excess in his time) he could not but commend and justify us, in what we have done. I know the Church of *Rome* has another notion of 'em : She spoils the Beauty of Christianity, by Muffling it up in Superstitious Observations ; she gives 'em a *purifying* and *cleansing faculty*; makes 'em effectual to help the Soul, and asserts 'em, Able *ex Opere Operato, To blot out Sins, and drive away Devils.* But what is all this to us, who have no such Opinion of 'em, and between whose Ceremonies and ours there is a vast Difference ? For whereas the number of *theirs* is intolerable, as appears by their *Rituals* and *Ceremonials,* and the bulky Volumes writ in explication of 'em, *ours* are *few,* and so very plain and easie, that it requires almost as great skill not to understand 'em, as it doth to understand *theirs.* Then *they* place *holiness* in those they use, as appears by the forms of Consecration of their *Water, Oil, Salt,* &c. but we allow no such thing, but use and declare 'em appointed, only for *order* and *decency,* which is all the Virtue and Efficacy we give 'em.

(*g*) Art. 34. (*h*) Ep. ad Jan. 119.

They

They make their Ceremonies *neceſſary* parts of Divine Worſhip, but we look on 'em as things of *indifferent* Nature, even after they are determined ; And all the ſtreſs we lay upon 'em, is thereby to ſhow our Obedience to Lawful Authority. This and the like diſparity there is, between the *Roman* Church and ours, with reſpect to theſe Ceremonies; And no Man can pretend otherwiſe, that is not either groſly *ignorant*, or doth not *wilfully* miſunderſtand the State of this controverſie between them and us.

B. Well ; but what neceſſity was there for our Reformers to retain any of theſe Ceremonies, which were then diſtaſtful to ſome Proteſtants, and were like to prove the occaſion of future contentions ?

A. The *Reaſons* our *Reformers* went upon to keep or appoint thoſe few Ceremonies we have in our Church, were ſuch as theſe. *Firſt,* A due regard to *Antiquity.* They would hereby convince the Papiſts, that they put a difference between the groſs and intolerable *Superſtitions* of Popery, and the *innocent Rites* and Practices, which were obſerved in the Church before it: Otherwiſe it muſt needs have hard'ned thoſe of *that* Communion, to find no diſtinction made between the one ſort and the other. It is an unſpeakable advantage ſome Men give the *Romaniſts*, to be reforming 1600 Years backward; And when they are pinched with a teſtimony of *Antiquity*, preſently cry out, *The myſtery of iniquity was working in the Apoſtles times,* as if every thing they diſliked were a part of it. This unreaſonable humour of innovation was it, that gave a check to the progreſs of the *reformation* in *France,* where many great Men were inclinable to receive it, till they found ſome Preachers too hot in oppoſing the *undoubted* practices of *Antiquity,* and putting 'em on the ſame level,

with

with modern Corruptions. But our *Reformers*, though they made the *Scripture* the only *Rule of Faith*, and rejected all things repugnant thereto, yet their defign was not to *transform* the Church, but reduce it, as near as they could, to that State it was in under the firft Chriftian Emperours, who were found in Religion: And therefore they retain'd thefe few Ceremonies as Badges of the refpect they bore to the Ancient Churches. And this they did, *Secondly*, To manifeft the *Juftice* and enquity of the *Reformation*, by letting their Enemies fee they did not break Communion with 'em, for *merely indifferent* things. For fome of the Popifh Bifhops of that time were fubtile and Learned Men; And nothing would have rejoiced them more, than to have found our *Reformers* Boggle at fuch Ceremonies as thefe; And they would have made mighty advantage of it among the People. Of which we have a clear inftance in the cafe of Bifhop *Hooper's* Scrupling the *Epifcopal Veftments.* Peter *Martyr* tells him plainly, that fuch needlefs fcrupulofity would be a great hindrance to the Reformation. "For, "faith he, fince the People are with difficulty e-"nough brought to things neceffary, if we once "declare things indifferent to be unlawful, they "will have no patience to hear us any longer. "And withal hereby we condemn other reformed "Churches, and thofe ancient Churches which "have hither to been in great efteem. *Thirdly*, 'Twas thus order'd, to fhow their confent with other *Proteftant* Churches, which did allow and practife the fame or more Ceremonies, as the *Lutheran* Churches generally did. And even *Calvin* himfelf, as you heard before, declared for 'em, both as being *Decent* and *Symbolical*. So did *Oecolampadius, Bucer* and others. So that feeing fo many *Proteftant* Churches ufed the fame Ceremonies, and

that

that the chief leaders of the Reformation abroad thought 'em not unlawful, (i) therefore for this and the foregoing reasons, our *Reformers* thought it fit to continue 'em in this Church, and I see no cause why they may not be still continued, seeing they are so *few*, and so *easily understood*.

And to be particular in the *Surplice*, the attire which the Minister of God is by order to use at the time of Divine Service : Which being but a matter of mere formality (yet such, saith (k) Mr. *Hooker*, as for *comeliness* sake, hath hitherto been judged by the wiser sort of Men, not unnecessary to concur with other sensible notes, betokening the different kind or quality of Persons, and actions whereunto it is tied) as we think not ourselves the *holier*, because we use it, so neither should they with whom no such thing is in use, think us therefore *unholy*, because we submit ourselves to that which in a matter so indifferent, the Wisdom of Authority and Law have thought comely.——Actions of Royalty and Justice, are made more solemn by such Ornaments as these. For though *Princes* Robes do not in the least raise their Power, nor the *Judges* Habit infuse new Principles of Justice, or give 'em more insight in the Laws than they had before ; though neither the *Scarlet*, *Violet*, nor *Fur-gown*, are qualifications in themselves to set one Citizen above another, Yet these *Ornaments* are good *Testimonies* of their several ranks and qualities ; They are marks of those Privileges and Authority which some Men injoy ; They are notes to discern, and distinguish Persons, who ordinarily have one and the same Figure, and lively express those Dignities and Stiles they are called to ; and in a word, we find by daily

(*i*) Vid. *Stillingfleet's* Unreasonableness of separation, P. 1. Sect. 5. (*k*) Eccl. Polit. l. 5. n. 29.

Ii 4　　　　　　　　　experience,

experience, that they procure awe and refpect to thofe, who are found to wear them, and who might be otherwife lefs regarded for want of thefe remembrances and fignifications of what they are. And herein I think few or none diffent from us, but are willing that themfelves or their Friends fhould be thus far *Ceremonious.*

Doth not *Decency* as well become the (*l.*) *Houfe of God,* as any Palace, *Court of Juftice* or *Hall?* And why fhould not the Veftments of *Minifters* be thought as convenient and proper, as what are ufed by Men of *another quality,* Society or Order? Efpecially being *Monitors* and *Emblems* of that innocency, good converfation, continuance in well-doing, purity and holinefs we ought to approach with into the prefence of God, and which the fight of 'em calls for from us.

The Surplice, as that judicious Author before fpeaks, " Suits that lightfome affection of joy, " wherein God delighteth, when his Saints " praife him, and fo lively reprefenteth the Glo- " ry of the Saints in Heaven, together with the " Beauty, wherein Angels have appeared unto " Men, that they who are to appear for Men, in " the prefence of God, as Angels, if they were " left to their own choice, and would chufe any, " could not eafily devife a garment of more decen- " cy for fuch a Service.

The Gentiles by the light of Nature difcovered this to be the fenfe of fuch Garments, and for *order* and *fignification*-fake, both ufed, and accounted them Reverend and Honourable. Thus Ha-

(*l*) *Indicat Sacerdotis fplendidam converfationem; figni- ficat perfeverantiam in bona actione, Ergo dicitur græcè poδηρης feu-talaris, quia ufq; ad finem vitæ hujus bonis operibus infiftere debet facerdos.*—Raban. Maur. de inftit. Cler. tom. 6.

bited.

bited, *(m)* He, in *Virgil*, Sacrificed. And *Herodotus* teſtifies, that the *Egyptian* Prieſts always wore 'em. The ſame *Philoſtratus* reports of *Apollonius*, that being charged for uſing this Habit, he excuſed himſelf by what the Garb repreſented, *Sincerity* and *Fairneſs* ; which made it valuable to *Phythagoras*, *Orpheus*, the *Indians*, *Egyptians* and others, and became a *diſputant* in the *School*, as well as *Prieſt* in the *Temple*. The Poet *(n)* *Ovid*, makes *White* the *Type* of Happineſs ; and by *White-Days*, another means *Halcyon-Days* ; and the, *Niveo ſignati lapillo*, were reputed very *Fortunate-Days*, to the *Romans* and *Scythians*. *(o)* And *White-Stones* among them (to which the Scripture alludes, *Rev.* 2. 7.) were *Symbols* of innocency, and *ſigns* of abſolving, or acquitting Men from the Crimes charged on 'em.

And when any were Competitors or *Suiters* for an Office under that Government ; they put on *(p)* *White-Coats* to recommend them to the People, intimating thereby *that integrity*, ſimplicity of Mind and Honeſty they would be ſure to uſe in the Adminiſtration of their Truſts ; and from this Cuſtom and Ceremony they were called *Candidates.*

It was the Ancient way, to put on *White Apparel*, at their Feaſts and moſt joyful Solemnities; as we may ſee, *Eccleſ.* 9. 8. *Let thy garments be always White* ──── Or in plainer words, I wiſh nothing may happen to thee, but what is delightful and pleaſing ; and may'ſt thou never have occaſion to wear the *Black Garment*, as a diſaſtrous, melancholy or mournful attire. And in the Eaſtern Countries eſpecially, to uſe *White Robes*

(m) *Puraq; in veſte ſacerdos. Æncad.* l. 12. *(n)* *Candidus & felix proximus annus erit.* *(o)* ──*Niveis atriſq; lapillis,* &c. *Metamorph.* *(p)* *Candidas togas*────*Candidati.*

Wa4

was looked on, as a fignification of *pre-eminence* and honour, *Efther* 8. 15. and thofe who were allowed to ride on *White Affes* were *noble* Perfonages, and fuch as were deemed worthy to fit in Judgment.

We muft be great ftrangers to the Oeconomy of the *Jews,* and manner of Worfhip among 'em, if we do not underftand that the Officiating *Priefts* and *Levites,* were always vefted with *Linen Coats.* or White linen Garments. And in this particular, they have been thought no ill precedents for the Church of Chrift to follow; And accordingly in her beft Days, we find it her practice, as to diftinguifh *times* and *places,* fo likewife to make difference of *Habits* for thofe, who attended at the Altar, and had any concern in the Adminiftration of Holy things. (*q*) So St. *Jerom* informs us, That *Religion has one kind of Habit in the Divine Worfhip, and another for fecular and common ufc.* And in a way of anfwer to *Pelagius,* (who was not it feems well pleafed with this Cuftom of the Church) he demands, What offence it could be, that the *Officers* of the Church in the exercife of their Miniftry, *appeared in White?* And for the Eaftern Communion, St. *Chryfoftom* puts the Clergy of *Antioch* in Mind, that they had greater inftances concerning their employments, to Glory in, than the honour of being feen at the Church in *White Garments.* But there needs no more Witneffes to prove what is not denied. For the *Novelty* of this habit is not fo much objected as the *abufe* of it; And the Papifts having been over-exact, and nice in *this* as in the *other Rites* of the Church, fome People think it neceffary, that it fhould be now

---

(*q*) *Religio divina alterum habitum habet in Minifterio, alterum in ufu vitaq; communi*——In Ezek.

laid

laid afide as a Monument, and relick of the old Superftition, or a practice too much favouring, and approving what we pretended to redrefs at the *Reformation.*

B. You fpeak plainly their Thoughts; For I have often heard 'em talk after that manner; And they inftance fome *Bifhops* to be of that Opinion.

A. One indeed we have an account of, and that was Dr. *Hooper*, I juft now named, who being called to the See of *Gloucefter*, in the Reign of King *Edward* VI. (r) "He had fome fcruples about the "Epifcopal Veftments, and thought that all thofe "Graments having been confecrated with muchSu- "perftition, were to be reckon'd among the Ele- "ments condemned by St. *Paul.* But *Ridley* jufti- "fied the ufe of 'em, and faid, The Elements "condemned by St. *Paul*, were only the Jewifh "Ceremonies, which though the Apoftle difal- "lowed, when they were impofed as neceffary, "becaufe that imported, that the Mofaick Law "was not yet abrogated, and that the Meffias was "not yet come, yet they themfelves ufed them "at other times, to gain upon the Jews by that "compliance. And if the Apoftles did fuch "things to gain them, fubjects ought much more "to obey the Laws in matters indifferent, and "Superftitious confecrations was as good an An- "gument for throwing down all the Churches, as "for laying afide thofe Habits——Hereupon he writes to *Bucer* at *Cambridge*, and *Peter Martyr* at *Oxon*, (two able Foreigners invited into *England*, to affift at the Reformation) to defire their Judgments. And the fumm of his Letter confifted in thefe two Pofitions. *Firft*, That this attire is re-

(r) Hiftory of the Reformation.

calling

calling the Aaronical-Prieſt-hood, to which this diſtinction of Veſtments appertained, and a practical denial of Chriſt's Being come in the Fleſh, whom in a great meaſure they prefigured and foretold. *Secondly*, That we could not with a ſafe Conſcience, retain theſe inventions of *Antichriſt*, ſeeing it becomes us not only to renounce the *Pope* but all *his Works*, and devices, among which this difference of Habits has not the loweſt Room —— To both which (without making one reaſon to deſtroy the other, for if they be inſtances of the *Legal-Prieſt-hood*, preſcribed and appointed by God himſelf, how can they be ſaid to be the *invention of Antichriſt*) we find *Peter Martyr* returning this Anſwer.

Firſt, To the firſt, (*s*) That in the Law and *Aaronical-Prieſt-hood*, ſome things were indeed *Typical*, and being ſigns of the promiſes of God concerning Chriſt, as ſoon as Chriſt came, they had their Conſummation and were repealed for the future. And *theſe* were the *Sacraments* of the Jewiſh-Church ; and our Lord having inſtituted and appointed *others* under the Goſpel, *thoſe* before are to be continued no longer. But beſides theſe, there were ſome things again purely *Ornamental*, having a natural comelineſs, and in the Judgment of all the World, not a little uſeful to keep order and help Devotion. And ſuch as theſe (and the rather being once of Divine appointment) we ought, at leaſt may, recal or retain. For did not the *Apoſtles*, for the peace and quiet of the Church, forbid the gentiles *ſtrangled Creatures and Blood*? Do not we keep on foot the Cuſtom of *Tythes*, for the maintenance of the Miniſtry? Have we not *Pſalms* and ſacred Hymns in the Church,

---

(*s*) Epiſt. Theolog.

nay,

nay, the very *same* as they had before us? And which is St. *Ambrofe* his note, Did not St. *Paul* derive his form of Preaching from the *Jewifh* Synagogue, which we all keep to this Day? Are not our Feftivals of the *Nativity*, *Paffion*, *Refurrection* and *Pentecoft*, the very *Foot fteps* of the Law? Nay, is not our *Lord's-day*, their *Sabbath*, in the fenfe and equity of it? A Man might fay more on this head. But thefe particulars fhow, that every thing ought not to be exploded, becaufe the *Jews* ufed it, whofe conftitution was *Divine*, and whom we need not be affraid to follow, but in what impairs our *Creed*, and denies *Meffias's* coming.

To the *Second*, he faith, That the Superftitions of the Papifts are no reafon to make void Cuftoms, not only innocent in themfelves, but very ferviceable to thofe ends they were intended for, when thofe abufes are taken away. Otherwife, how can our Anceftours anfwer it, to convert the *Temples* of Idols into *Chriftian-Churches*, and take the revenues and profits allotted *Veftal-Nuns* and *Pagan-Priefts*, and beftow them on *Gofpel-Minifters*? What think you? Thefe things were not Dedicated to the ufe of *Antichrift* alone, but the Devil himfelf was ferved by this means in Pomp and Grandeur : Yet now are confecrated to the Worfhip of the *true God*, and we ftick not to enjoy their Eftates and Privileges, without offence to our Confciences. The Verfes compofed by Infidel Poets, and Sung in honour of their Mufes and other feigned Deities, how often do the Ecclefiaftical writers cite and appeal to them? And they have St. *Paul's* warrant, who thought it not below him to produce the teftimony of *Menander*, *Aratus* and *Epimenides*, and though Originally prophane, infert their words in his *Canonical* Writings, and make 'em ferviceable to the Gofpel. Befides

fides this, who is there of any reading, but knows,
that our *Wine* was once confecrated to *Bacchus*, our
Bread to *Ceres*, our *Water* to *Neptune*, our *Oil* to
Minerva, *Learning* to *Mercury*, *Wit* to *Apollo*,
with many other particulars mentioned by *Tertullian*, which yet we ufe, and are not fcrupulous,
to let 'em have an intereft in the higheft points,
and moft myfterious parts of our Religion. You
call them the devices of *Antichrift* ; I muft crave
leave to diffent and be of another Opinion, becaufe we read in the Hiftories of the Church, that
St. *John* himfelf wore at *Ephefus*, Petalium or a
Pontifical Plate on his Breaft. And *Pontius* the
Deacon reports of St. *Cyprian*, that being ready to
fuffer Martyrdom, he gave his (t) *Tunick* to the
Executioner, his *Cope* to the Deacons, and he ftood
in *Linen*. St. *Chryfoftom* makes mention of a
White Garment, wore by the Minifters of the
Church. And the Ancients tell us, that it was the
way of thofe, who turned Chriftians to change their
Clothes, which, becaufe the Heathens ridiculed,
was the occafion of that excellent difcourfe of *Tertullian, de Pallio*. You cannot forget, how early
the practice was for thofe who were Baptized, to
put on *White Garments*, in token that now all their
defilements were wafh'd away, and that thenceforward they were to lead lives inoffenfive and
pure. This was long before the Papal Ufurpation and Tyranny ; and therefore this diftinction of
Habits cannot be well called the invention of Popery.

Yet grant it fo. Humane appointments even
in Religious matters are not fimply rejected. For
in the Adminiftration of the *Eucharift*, the *time*

(t) *Birrum carnificibus, dalmaticam veftem diaconis, &
fteterit in linteis.*

is

is changed from *Evening* to *Morning*; and we receive *fasting* what was first of all given the Disciples *after Supper.* The Feast of *Dedication* among the *Jews*, our Lord honour'd and solemnly kept, and yet it was not divinely instituted, which in part discovers the insufficiency of that Plea against what our Governours order, especially in things which have a grave signification, and do not a little conduce to instruct us. As in the case of a *Surplice.* For seeing the Ministers of the Church are stiled by the Prophet *Malachy*, *the Angels* or *Messengers* of God, and that the Angels thus alluded to, always appear in *White* Raiment, why should not the Church use her Liberty, to appoint such rites as may improve the Analogy, and represent as well as she can in her Temples and Oratories, the condition and qualities of those Angels in Heavens, of which these *Holy Places*, and their *Officers* are the constant figures and *Types.*

You will say, they should be Angels *indeed* and not barely signify 'em. I hear you. The same answer might have been made to St. *Paul*, when he order'd Women to be *covered*, and their Husbands *uncover'd*, but gives no other reason for it than that of *Signification*, it being not a fit thing for the Man to cover his Head, forasmuch as he is the Image and *Glory of God*, but the Woman the *Glory of the Man.* Now a captious *Corinthian*, might evade the Ceremony by telling the Apostle, that 'twas better for *both* to *do* the thing it self than to trouble themselves with the *signs*; and if the *Man* and *Woman* acquitted themselves well, and discharged the Duty of *Husband* and *Wife*, this is what the Ceremony meant, and this being mutually done, the Ceremony was of no use. But it seems the Apostle did not think it enough, that they lived as became 'em, for he was willing they should

should continue such Customs, as did fitly express the sense they had of their Duty to each other, and were a kind of remembrancers to put them in mind of it, and admonish others to do the like.

To alledge, that the Eyes of the votaries being employ'd in viewing the Pomp, and variety of this attire, their Thoughts are diverted from more serious matters, and while they consider the Ministers or Bishops *Formalities*, they will be apt to neglect the *Worship* it self; it may be rather affirmed on the other side, that where these Formalities are few, and the Habit grave and significant, they help attention and raise the Thoughts to an higher pitch, than otherwise they would be, if the Service were done in a Cheap, careless and slovenly manner. And to this end it is supposed the *Symbols* of the Sacraments were instituted as we have 'em, that the sight thereof might ingage the Heart and Work on the affections, with more vigour. Yet your reason holds good against them, who *abound* in these things; and where *Superstition*, and *Number* make 'em both burdensom and dangerous, you conclude beyond an Answer. But these reasons cease here, the Ceremonies now used being *few* and *proper*, and helpful to express the reverence we have for the Worship of God. We attribute nothing of *holiness* to 'em; We account 'em *indifferent* in their own Natures; We say, God may be well adored *without* 'em, but better *with* 'em under our present Circumstances, because, there not only is a *Natural Beauty* in the Service done after such a manner, but there is likewise *Obedience* to Authority, whose commands are so far sacred, that Conscience is obliged to yield compliance, where God is silent and the Gospel does not contradict 'em. This very consideration resolves all Proposals in matters of

scruple,

fcruple. Becaufe *Scruples* are *doubts,* and nothing
that is *doubtful* fhould ftand in competition with
Doctrines *certain* and plain, fuch as is Submiffion
to Authority ; And we *ought* not to ftruggle with
it, till our Objections are determined and commenced to the fame Degree of *certainty*, as our
Obedience to Governours is. In a word, every
Creature of God is good, and *to the pure all things
are pure.* The danger is within our own Power.
No former abufe can render an indifferent thing
unlawful ; 'tis fafe and innocent, if we ourfelves
do not abufe it.

Thus or to this purpofe, *Peter Martyr* to thofe
Objections of Bifhop *Hooper* ; and I have been the
larger, becaufe, that Prelate has been the *occafion,
upon which the heats concerning things indifferent, that
have fince his time fo fatally rent the Church, had their
firft rife and beginning.* Bucer's anfwer was much
the fame, which he fent Archbifhop *Cranmer* on
this Queftion. "He thought Ancient Cuftoms
"ought not to be lightly changed, and that there
"might be a good ufe made of thofe Garments,
"that they might well exprefs the purity and can-
"dour, which became all who Miniftred in holy
"things, and that it was a Sin to difobey the Laws
"in fuch a matter——And that thefe Doctors
might not be fufpected to be *time-fervers*, and give
their Opinions in fuch a manner, as might fuit *their*
Minds then in *Power*; Peter Martyr in particular
declares, that his Judgment on thefe points was of
Ancient ftanding, and that from the very Year he
betook himfelf to the ftudy of Divinity beyond
Sea, it was his fenfe, that there could be no harm
in the ufe of Ceremonies, as being things which
might be either continued or taken away, as they
thought beft whom we were fubject to. This is a
fhort account of that *Controverfie* fet on foot in
King *Edward*'s Days. And I wifh thofe among

K k

us,

us, who borrow Bishop *Hooper's Exceptions*, would likewise confider the *Answers* made 'em, in order to preferve peace and love among us.

Before we part with this Prelate, let me take the opportunity to fet before you his Opinion concerning the *Sabbath*; hoping his teftimony among fair Men, may have the fame effect in one point as in another. "We may not think, (*faith he*) "that God gave any more holinefs to the *Sabbath* "than to the *other Days*. For if you confider *Friday*, *Saturday*, or *Sunday*, inafmuch as they be "Days and the Work of God, the one is no more "holy than the other: But *that day* is always *moft* "*holy* in the which we moft apply ourfelves unto "holy Works. To that end he did fanctify the "*Sabbath-day*, not that we fhould give ourfelves "to idlenefs, or fuch paftimes as are now ufed a- "mong faithful People: But being free that *Day* "from the travail of this World, we might con- "fider the Works and Benefits of God with "Thankfgiving, hear the Word of God, Ho- "nour him, and Fear him, then to learn who, "and where be the Poor of Chrift that want "our help——So that the holinefs of the fe- venth-Day, depends chiefly on the fanctity of our actions, in the Works of Piety and Charity: And as to other refpects, it had the fame ftamp with the reft of the Week, they were all alike the Creatures of God, and not to be diftinguifh'd but by our Services. And in this belief he died a Martyr, under the Perfecution of Queen *Mary*.

But I am not much furprized, that fome People are offended at the *Ceremonies* in ufe, when 'tis thought a piece of Superftition, at leaft an unprofitable pains, to read any part of *Scripture* in the Church, but what is prefently followed with an *Exposition* or *Sermon* on it. And though 'tis true,

that

that fometimes they afford their Profelytes a Chapter or two in their Affemblies, yet the end of it *(as* I have fomewhere obferved*)* is only to *divert* fome Men and Women, that are earlier than their Neighbours, at the place of *Meeting*, and who otherwife might think the time long, before the Worfhip begins. But to judge in part of the Reverence they give this Book or what is delivered out of it, not only the *Precentor* or *Clark*, are Officers able enough for the difcharge of this Service, but fo little ftrefs is laid on the Work it felf, that as foon as the Congregation is full, and a better Oracle appears, then they enter, as they conceive, on the bufinefs of the Day, which they all meet about, and which the firft Comers, who have been hitherto *religiouſly idle*, have with no little impatience waited for. Surely 'tis not in the Mind of thefe *Teachers*, to abet the *Romiſh Doctrine* concerning the Scriptures being a dead-letter, unlefs they quicken and apply it. Is not this a fevere reflection on the goodnefs of God, who was gracioufly pleas'd to reveal to us his Divine Will, with Relation to himfelf and our Eternal State, yet has not done it fo fully and plainly, but that it needs a *Second Edition*, and a new infpiration for thefe Doctors to render it ufeful and edifying. And if fo, why do they prefs their Auditors to read it at *home*, where the Difficulties feem greater than in the Church, the Minifter reading it here *Ex Officio*, and who for the *Ordinance-fake*, may be well fuppofed to deliver it better, and with *better effect*, becaufe being prefumed to underftand what he reads, he on the account of the Accents, Stops, helps of the Voice, and way of pronunciation reads it more intelligibly, and becaufe of his Commiffion and Authority more beneficially to thofe who hear him ———— *This* (as our *reverend Diocefan* fpeaks) *is a Comment or Pa-*

raphrafe

raphrafe on the Text to read it fenfibly, and with a due Emphafis. [Bifhop of *London*'s feventh Letter, 1686.] (*u*) And this is a fort of *Preaching* too, when in this publick and folemn manner, the Minifters witnefs the truth of thofe facred Leffons, God has revealed to us, and declare to the World, they acknowledge and confent to them.   And the People hereby being well affured of this point, it makes the way eafier to the *Sermons* following, which wou'd in themfelves be of little credit, were there any fcruple concerning the Text or Foundation the Preacher builds on.   Which is that which ftuck with the *Beræans*, who could not be induced to yield their affent to what *Paul* and *Silas* faid, (though divinely infpired) until they had recourfe to the Holy Writings themfelves, to fee whether what they delivered were fo or no. (*x*) " So that a fecond kind of Preaching is the " reading of holy writ, *faith Mr.* Hooker; for " thus we may the boldlier fpeak, having the Au- " thority of St. *Paul,* who faith that *Mofes* of old " time had in every City them that Preached him, " being read in the Synagogues, every Sabbath- " day.   He was Preached in that he was read; " for fo of neceffity it muft be meant, in as much " as we know that the Jews have always had their " Weekly readings of the Law of *Mofes,* but that " they always had in like manner their Weekly " Sermons upon fome part of the Law, we no " where find. ———   •

And 'tis true, they had not *always* this Cuftom, yet to fay they *never* had it, goes I think a little too far, for we find in *Nehem.* 8. 4. that *Ezra the fcribe ftood upon, a Pulpit of Wood, which they*

(*u*) *Qui Scripturas legit eum quodamodo eas prædicare non diffiteor.* Diesdom. l. 2. c. 5. (*x*) Hooker Eccl. Pol. l. 5. n. 19.

made

made for the purpose—So they read the Book, in the Law of God distinctly, and gave the sense, and caused them to understand the reading.——-This *giving of the sense*, to make them understand what was read, was undoubtedly the same or very like our *Preaching* ; and there was great necessity *Ezra* should do this *now*, though it had never been in practice before : Because the Law being writ in *Hebrew*, and the Jews having been so long in the *Babylonish Captivity*, that their Native Language was much impaired and corrupted, by conversing with the Infidels, they could not comprehend the meaning of the Law as read in the *Original* ; and therefore their Governours, and Priests were forced to be at this pains to *explain* what was read to them, in other more familiar Words, and a Language then vulgarly in use among 'em. But then as this was (to say truth) little more than a *Metaphrase* at that time, occasioned by the People's loss of the purity of the *Hebrew Tongue*, so perhaps it might not be *Weekly* till the after Ages, as the Learned Man affirms ; though to me, I must confess, it seems more credible, that the Custom was continued ever after the Days of *Ezra*, and that the building of *Synagogues* began on that very reason, that there might be Opportunities for the People to meet, to have the Law read and expounded to them. Plainly it was so in the times of our *Saviour*, who as he constantly went to the *Synagogues on the Sabbath Days*, so according to the common practice, as soon as that Section or Portion of the Scripture appointed for the day was read by one of the Ministers, we find him expounding or preaching upon it; and he began to say unto them, (y) *This Day is this Scripture fulfilled in your Ears*——And that which contribu-

(y) Luke 4. 21.

ted

ted to this Cuſtom, was the Tyrannical Edict of *Antiochus Epiphanes*, wherein he made it Death to read the Law of *Moſes*; For this obliged the Jews to have recourſe to the writings of the Prophets, and at their ſtated times of Worſhip, to read ſo much of them, as in likeneſs of matter, came neareſt to each Section of their Law——And after-wards, when this Perſecution was over, and that they had liberty to read the Law again, the ſame Method, from the Prophets, continued ſtill, as a good Comment, and interpretation of the other. And this way of explaining Scripture by Scripture, was ſo well liked, that the Scribes were incou-raged to greater pains in it, and by Degrees in-troduced the mode of making *ſet diſcourſes* on both, to make them eaſier for the Peoples Capa-cities. All this was of *humane invention*, and by the Wiſdom of their Paſtours, well accommo-dated to the neceſſities of the *Jews*——And it took ſo well in the *Chriſtian Church*, that we find the Apoſtles, and particularly St. *Paul*, frequently conforming himſelf to that method of inſtruction; and as ſoon as the Ordinary Leſſons were read to the Congregation, he proceeded to give the ſenſe, in a Speech of his own compoſing. And ſo after-wards, the Fathers retained the ſame reading of the Law and the Prophets, but withal added a *ſecond* Leſſon, out of the Evangeliſts or Apoſtoli-cal writings, and on the ſame reaſon, the Jews had, for uſing the Prophets. For as *theſe* were now and then extraordinarily ſent, to expound *Moſes*'s Law, and may be called *Commentatours* on it, ſo are the Epiſtles and Goſpels in the *New* Teſtament, *Explications* of what we find in the *Old*, and *both* together make a compleat Body of Divinity, and include all ~~Doctrines~~ neceſſary to Salvation. For *what elſe is the Law but the Goſpel foretold, and what is the Goſpel, but the Law fulfilled.*

What

What the *Old* Teftament hath, the very fame the *New* containeth ; But that which lieth there under a *Shadow* is here brought forth, as in the *open Sun.* Things there *prefigured*, are here *performed*. And as in the *Old* Teftament , there is a dark comprehenfion of what is in the *New*, fo in the *New*, there is an *open* difcovery of what is in the *Old*——Thus the Ancient Doctors, and on this account we have the *two Leffons* in *our* daily Service, as we find our Forefathers had in theirs. That the Epiftles of the Apoftles were read in the Church, we find exprefly in feveral Scriptures. (*z*) And *Eufebius* out of *Clement* reports, that St. *Peter* commanded St. *Mark's* Gofpel to be publickly read to the Congregation. *Juftin Martyr* makes it a great part of the *Lord's-day-bufinefs*, to read the writings of the Apoftles and Prophets. *Origen* has his *Leffons* and *Lectures*, and he affirms, That the Apoftles ordained the reading of the Jewifh Hiftories. St. *Ambrofe*, and St. *Avguftine* affert the fame, that the Scriptures were read both of the Old and New Teftament. The Council of *Laodicea* fhows the practice in its nine and fiftieth *Canon*, requiring *nothing to be read in the Church, but only the Canonical writings of the Old and new Teftament*——The fame caution the Council of *Carthage* gives, but includes both Teftaments within its *Canon*, to be the fubjects of their publick Leffons.

Whether thofe *Ancient* Churches ufed felect portions of Scripture : Or after the manner of the *Jews* read it in order, fo much at a time till the whole was finifhed, doth not fully appear. Yet we find by (*a*) St. *Auguftine*, that the Book of the

---

(*z*) Eccl. Hift. l. 7. c. 4. (*a*) *Anniverfaria folennitate poft paffionem dom. Librum Actuum Apoft. omni anno recitari.* In Johan. tract. 6. *Et pfalmum* 21 *omni anno noviffima hebdomade imminente paffione Chrifti,* Tract. 13.

Acts

Acts of the Apostles was solemnly read every Year after the Lord's Passion, and the one and twentieth *Psalm* the Week before it. And *(b) some Lessons* were so *peculiar*, and so necessary to *some Festivals*, that they could not well substitute *others* in their Places. And therefore in all likelihood they had a kind of *Kalendar* or common Course of what Scriptures were to be read on each day, to preserve *Uniformity* and Peace in the Church; and that every Diocess at least might consent in a Rule, to prevent the distractions which must have unavoidably followed, if every private *Minister* had been his own *Ordinary* to appoint *what*, and *how much* was to be read when they met together,

But though 'tis certain, that it has been ever accounted a part of the Divine Service, the reverend and publick reading of the Old and New Testament, and that such reading was of great use to instruct the Congregation, yet in the same Monuments of Antiquity, wherein we discover this, we find also that after the Writings of the Prophets and Apostles were read, then the Πρόεδρος, or Bishop made an homily to the People. *Origen* calls it, *An exposition, by which the Auditory were exhorted to Piety towards God and to all Vertue.* Now saith, St. *Augustine* (after the Lessons) *I am come to my Sermon.* St. *Ambrose*, and before him St. *Cyprian* declare the same. And these *Preachers* were called *Tractatores*, and their *Sermons Tractatus.* At first they were *Bishops*, but afterwards *Presbyters*, and at last *Deacons* were not excluded, and as in other cases, so in *this*, gave their Assistance. Their Sermons were very *short*, choosing rather to Preach *often* than *long*, *(c)* because as the Father obser-

---

(b) *Ita erant annua ut, alia esse non possint.* (c) Ep. 11.

ved

ved, *a tedious Difcourfe tires the Underftanding.*
(*d*) And therefore St. *Bafil* tells his People, that
he will put an end to his *Morning Sermon,* for fear
he fhould make 'em dull againft the *Afternoon,*
(*e*) And St. *Chryfoftom*'s reafon for *fhort Sermons*
was, that they might be *better remembred.* That,
they were not to exceed an *hour* at a time, we gather from the words of St. *Bafil,* who faith, That
(*f*) *becaufe he could not finifh his Sermon the day before
within the hour,* he put it off — (*g*) And St. *Auguftine* confeffes, he *induftrioufly avoided fome forts of
fubjects,* becaufe he could not go through with 'em,
within the fpace of an *hour.* But whether *long* or
fhort, (*h*) they were to be attentively and reverently heard, and the Congregation were not to
ftir till the Sermon was over on pain of (*i*) Excommunication. We fee by (*k*) St. *Bafil*, and
(*l*) St. *Auguftine,* that thefe Difcourfes were *twice*
a Day. For the *firft* exhorts his hearers to blefs
God, and between themfelves repeat, and confider thofe things which they had heard that *Morning* and *Afternoon.* And the *other* in his Preface
to the Evening-Sermon, calls for his Peoples attention to the remaining part of the *Pfalm,* which
he Preach'd on in the *Morning.* Sometimes there
was a *third Sermon,* but very rare, and on occafions extraordinary, as we fee by the Apology,
(*m*) St. *Auguftine* makes for it to the *Brethren in
the Wildernefs.* And as to the *two* then in practice,
we are to confider the *neceffity* of thofe times, which
called for *frequent Sermons* to make way for the
Converfion of Men, who were either *Strangers,*

(*d*) Hexam. Hom. 8. (*e*) Hom. 15. in Gen. (*f*) In Pfal.
(*g*) *Verbis ad horam occurrentibus me poffe fufficere non
putarem.* Serm. 11. de Verb. Dom. (*h*) Concil. Carthag. 4.
Can. 24. (*i*) Concil Agath. Can. 31. (*k*) Hom. 7. (*l*) In
Pfal. 88. (*m*) *Serme ad fratres in Eremo.*

or not *well affected* to the Christian Religion, especially in Cities of great resort, whereby Opportunities were had to disperse the Gospel, and therefore *these precedents* make nothing for us, to continue the Custom in *these Churches,* where the Gospel and the Duties of it are very well known, and want only practice *to be doers of the word; and not hearers only,* which word however is constantly Preach'd to remember us of what we know. But I am gone further than I thought in *this way of* Preaching, which even our *Opponents* are fond of, when it was only my intention at first to offer Authorities for the other. Yet I repent not this Excursion; And I wish all our Neighbours would show so much Ingenuity and Candour, as to take the word in its full extent, and herein follow the examples of those before us, who were not so wedded to an Harangue from the *Pulpit,* but they could patiently hear a Sermon out of the *Desk,* wherein God in his own words was pleas'd to speak to 'em.

B. I condemn not this practice: And am therefore more easily reconciled to that Expression, in the Prayer for the Catholick Church (which displeases some;) wherein it is desired, that *God would give to all People his Heavenly Grace, especially to the Congregation then present, that with meek hearts and due reverence, they may hear and receive his holy Word* —— And in the *Letany, That it would please him to give to all his People increase of Grace, to hear meekly his word, and to receive it with pure affection—* For though on some Days there be no Sermon, when these Prayers are said, yet the Lessons read out of the Old and New Testament, may very well bear that Name, as being more truly and properly the holy word of God, and what the Ministers at other times Preach no otherwise so, than with *relation* to the Scripture those Lessons afford us,

But

But that which ſcandalizes me more than this is, That ſome things are read for holy leſſons in the Church which are ſo little the Word of God that they are rather as *Auſtin* ſomewhere calls 'em [*à ſutoribus fabularum ſcriptæ.*] *ridiculous forgeries*, and tho' in the title page they are term'd *Apocrypha*, as not being ſatisfied of the Original and Authority of theſe Writing, yet the reading 'em in the Church, ſeems as if we had a months mind to have emranked among the *undoubted Scriptures*, or Books without exception *canonical* and divine; a thing that very Council of *Laodicea* you lately cited forbids to be done.

A. A man muſt know little of the Bible if he cannot diſtinguiſh the *ligitimate* Books from thoſe which are not ſo, as ſoon as he hears them named : a thing the *Miniſter* always takes care to do, and the (n) Rubrick requires it before he begins the Chapter. *Wherein ſhould there happen by way of clauſe, ſentence or ſpeech, any thing to be read which leads to error, muſt the mixture of a little droſs conſtrain the Church to deprive herſelf of ſo much gold, rather than learn how by art and judgment to make ſeparation of the one from the other ?* You were contented that theſe Leſſons ſhould be accounted a kind of preaching to the People. And if ſo, why ſhould we any more quarrel with theſe Sermons than with what the preacher compoſes himſelf, and who for collateral evidence to what he ſets forth, very often introduces *Sayings* and *Examples* of Men borrowed from *Hiſtory*, whoſe authority is as *uncertain* as of the *Apocryphal Books*, which it muſt be confeſt the Jews themſelves did not look on with the ſame Eye as they did the Law and Prophets, yet they bare 'em re-

---

(n) *Note that before every leſſon the Miniſter ſhall ſay, Here beginneth ſuch a Chapter or ſuch Verſe of ſuch a chapter of ſuch a Book,* (o) *Hooker, Eccl. Pol. lib.* 5. *n.* 20.

fpect as written by perfons of no mean Figure a-mong 'em: and were by our (p) ancient doctors reputed *profitable* tho' not *divinely infpired.* And indeed what an excellent example of vertue and Chaftity, do we find in the perfon of *Sufanna,* who could not be tempted or terrified to that act of uncleannefs the two Elders propofed to her, tho' humanely fpeaking inevitable death was to follow the denial? And how do we, in the be-haviour of the *two Elders,* difcover the temper of the World in Charging innocence with a wick-ednefs, which that admirable Woman would not confent to, and for no other reafon, but becaufe fhe did not confent to it. But withall, we have, in this Story, a pregnant inftance of the protection and care *divine providence* hath over fuch exem-plary purity and a fignal teftimony of his Almighty Juftice, to let thefe Villains *fall into the pit they had dug for her, when their travail came on their own heads, and their wickednefs fell on their own pates*——— The Story of *Tobit* and *Tobias* fhows the conduct and kindnefs of Heaven, in letting the *angels* be the *guides* of good Men, who tho' not prefently fenfible of the affiftances given 'em, yet a little reflection would eafily lead them to the knowledge of thefe extraordinary means; and the Succefs they fometimes have, above their hope, cannot but inferr God to be the Author, and that all thefe events are purely owing to his Wifdom and fatherly care of them. The like application may be made of that paffage about *Bel* and the *Dragon;* Wherein the holy youth *Daniel* did not a little fuffer by the malice of the heathen priefts and their adherents; but his fufferings only made way for the utter deftruction of his adverfaries,

---

(p). *Vid. Chemnit. Exam. Conc. Trid.*

and

and were but means to advance his credit among the *Perſians*, and make an infidel prince give God his due glory, for preſerving *Daniel* in that miraculous manner, as the Narration informs us.

The Books of the *Maccabees* are pieces of *Hiſtory*, containing an account of the *Jews* both in Church and ſtate under the Tyrant *Antiochus* and others; and are a relation of the great actions of *Judas* and *John* (firnamed *Maccabæi* and from thence the Books are ſo called) which they did out of an heroick Love to their Country's liberty and Zeal for Religion. A conſideration of ſuch influence in the *ancient* times, that our Fathers appointed 'em a *Feſtival* and made Orations in their praiſe, as we ſee in *Gregory* of *Nazianzum. Orat.* 32. And here we have (what the ſame Author admires) the ſurprizing patience and conſtancy of a *Mother* and her *ſeven Children*, who rather than tranſgreſs the Law of their Anceſtors in *eating Swines fleſh*, as the King required, were barbarouſly tortured, and died in ſuch a manner, that the *Perſecutor* himſelf, tho' never ſo incenſed and harden'd in his cruelty, could not but wonder at 'em, and had they afforded the leaſt room for pardon, was inclinable to ſave 'em. As for the Books of *Wiſdom* and *Eccleſiaſticus* which of all thoſe Writings are moſt read in our Churches, none that takes the pains to peruſe 'em, can judge otherwiſe than that they are *pieces* of *great* (*q*) *piety and learning* and of high Eſteem even with thoſe who have made it their buſineſs to paſs cenſure on the *Apocryphal Writings*; and tho' not penned by immediate inſpiration, yet they are reckoned ſo exceeding profitable and good, that they are alotted the next place to the Scriptures them-

(*q*) *Pet. Galatin. de arcanis Catholicæ Verit.* lib. 1 *cap.* 3.

ſelves

felves and their authority cited with no little veneration. The reft of 'em, which I have not
named, have likewife their ufe and fervice to edification; and tho' perhaps you are ready to queftion the reality of many things reported in 'em,
yet without referring you to feveral of the old
Doctors, who have been at pains to vindicate what
is therein written, fhould we allow 'em merely
parabolical or pious inventions for the fake of fome
Doctrines in that manner reprefented and cleared,
which we fhould be apt to overlook or forget
without the impreffion of a Story; were, I fay,
the cafe thus, I do not fee the harm of reading
'em; And if this be a reafon to lay 'em afide, it
reaches divers Pages in the Old Teftament, and
more in the New, where Chrift ufually fpeaks
by *parables*, or things which never had a Being,
and *thefe* we muft reject upon the force of the
Same Objection. But here we think ourfelves
in no danger: Nor are we lefs fafe on the other account, efpecially when (*r*) our Church declares
in St. *Jerom's* words, that we read 'em only *for*
example of life and inftruction of manners, but not
to apply 'em to eftablifh any doctrine, nor admit
'em fufficient to build an Article on, if we have
not a plain proof of it in thofe Books confeft to be
canonical. And yet St. *Auguftine* whom you mentioned, reckons thefe as fuch. And the (*s*) Council
of *Carthage*, forbidding every thing to be read in
the Church under the notion of *Canonical*, but what
are truly fo, places *Tobias*, *Judith*, *Efther* and the
two Books of *Efdras* within the *Canon* of Scripture; But then it is to be taken in a *large fence*, and
as *Cajetan* explains it, not ftrictly as a *rule of faith*,
but *behaviour and manners*, as our Church takes

(*r*) *Article* 5. 1652. (*s*) *Canon.* 27.

'em

'em, and in which refpect they may be called *regu-lar* as they guide us in our *morals*, but not in our *Creed*. Thus the Council and St. *Auguftine* who was a member of it, muft be underftood. For tho' that Father ftiles 'em *canonical*, becaufe they were allow-ed to be read in the Church, yet he frequently makes St. *Jerom*'s *diftinction*, and alotts 'em their degrees of credit and certainty : For he tells us, that fome of thofe books contained in the *African* Canon were received by *all* the Churches, others not fo; and then infers, *that the Scriptures univerfally own'd ought to have the preference before thofe which fome particular Churches only accepted*———— And a-gain, *What the moft noted Churches both for Number and Figure, receive, ought to take place before what few Churches, and thofe inconfiderable ones, do think fit to read*————(t) And being a little puzzled with the example of *Rafis* (one of the Elders of *Jerufa-lem* who to avoid the infults of *Nicanor* flew him-felf) that Doctor neither being willing nor able to defend the felf murder, he takes refuge in this confideration, That the *Jews* have not the fame regard to this Book of the *Maccabees* as to the Law, Prophets and Pfalms, to which our Lord gave teftimony, yet confeffes 'twas allowed by the Church, not without benefit, if it be foberly read and heard, which was a caution needlefly made, had the Book been really *Canon*. (u) And fo having occafion to cite a Text out of the Book of (w) *Wif-dom*, concerning Enoch, that *he was fpeedily taken away left wickednefs fhould alter his underftanding, or deceit beguile his Soul* — which it feems was object-ed againft as no folid proof, becaufe not produced out of a *canonical* Book; He do's not go about to vin-

---

(t) *Contra Gaudent. c.23.* (u) *De prædeft. Sanct. c.14.* (w) *Wifd. 4. 11.*

dica te

dicate the authority of the Book confidered barely in itfelf, but infifts on the argument from o-
ther unqueftionable places, and thereupon appeals
to a Prophet and wonders the Exception fhould be
made againft thofe words in *wifdom,* feeing the Divine Writing faid the fame. But tho' this Father
did not take thefe *Ecclefiaftical Books* as precifely *Canonical* and *divinely written,* yet honouring 'em with a
Stile which looks that way, plainly fhows, that
thofe *Apocrypha,* (x) or fabulous ftories you cite
him for, do not mean the *Books,* of which we are
now treating, but *fuch* as fome Hereticks were the
Authors of, and which to fupport, they publifhed in the Apoftles name. Thefe indeed he calls
Apocryphal ftrictly, illegimate, falfe and exploded,
and they come under *Eufebius's* laft divifion of
the Books paffing for Scripture, *fome* whereof
(faith he, are genuine and *Catholick, others* are
doubted and *fome* are *abfurd, impious* and *counterfeit,*
which are they St. *Auguftine* brands as you faid,
but muft not be applied to thofe writings which
contain many excellent Truths and Examples of
Vertue, tho' their authority is difputed, nor
doth it well appear who they were that penned
'em.

As for the Council of *Laodicea,* we muft not
lay too great a ftrefs on this Canon in it, becaufe
*(y) as it forbids the reading of fome things which are
not canonical, fo it makes fome things not canonical
which are, fo that her judgment in this we may not, and
in that we need not follow* ——— In the *one* we muft
not, becaufe thereby we wholly exclude the Book
of *Revelations* which is not in that Canon; and as
to the *other* there is no neceffity but that our own

(x) Adv. Fauft. & de Civ. Dei. (y) *Hookers* Eccl. Pol.
lib. 5. n 20.

Church

Church may ufe her liberty to take the beft methods fhe can think of to inftruct and make us better, provided fhe goes not about to alter the nature of what is read, and as the Romanifts have done, make that *Divine* which was never fo efteem'd in the Catholick Church, whofe judgment we follow in this, as in other difputes between us. Yet the reafon of that Canon was good: For the Fathers were fenfible how the World was abufed by forgeries, bearing glorious infcriptions under the pretence of *Apoftolical Writings*; And therefore endeavouring to put a ftop to the frauds of *Hereticks*, they limitted the Canon of Scripture to fuch a number of Books, that fo there might be left no room for thefe additions.

I omit fetting before you the cuftom of the ancients to read the Epiftles of *Clement*; the Book of *Hermes*, &c. And among others St *Jerom* reports that one *Effrenus*, a Deacon of the Church at *Edeffa*, had rais'd himfelf to fuch a pitch of Credit, that after the reading of the Holy *Scripture*, *his works* were publickly read in fome of the Churches. But more (z) efpecially the *Book of Martyrs* was much in requeft, to keep up the Spirits of Chriftians under the feveral Perfecutions of the Roman Emperors, and which had fo good effect that no human means contributed more to make 'em fuffer with patience and cheerfulnefs. And hereupon it was, the Council of *Carthage* which prohibited the reading of any thing *befides* Scripture in the Church, concludes thus, That *not-withftanding what was decreed in that Canon, it fhould be lawful on the Anniverfary of the Martyrs to read the account of their Sufferings.* And in truth they did not forbid other Books to be read, (a) no

---

(z) Concil. Carthag. 3. Canon 47. (a) Concil. Carthag. 4. Canon. 16. *hæreticorum pro neceffitate & tempore*——apud Caranzam.

not

not the Books of *Hereticks* in what they were ufeful, provided they gave 'em not wrong *names* and Father'd 'em on the *Apoftles,* which was the artifice then in practice; Otherwife they might be read, as far as they ferved to edification; And with this caution we now-a-days fometimes read the *Apocrypha* in our Churches.

But to come to thofe inftances which you more infift on, *viz.* Some *repetitions* in our Service; the frequent faying of the *Lords Prayer,* and the *Mufick* in a few of our Churches.

Firft. Firft, as to the *repetitions.* Which I cannot fee to be fo faulty as you imagine 'em, fince we have fo many Examples in the Holy Book to affert the ufe of 'em. Thus in the Song of *Deborah,* fpeaking of *Sifera* flain by *Jael* the wife of *Heber,* the *Kenite,* fhe faith (b) *at her feet he bowed, he fell, he lay down: at her feet he bowed, he fell; where he bowed, there he fell down dead——*And again, v. 30. *Have they not fped? Have they not divided the prey? To Sifera a prey of diverfe colours, a prey of diverfe colours of needle work, of diverfe colours of needle-work on both fides——*And in *Pfalm* 24. 7, 8. *Lift up your heads, O ye gates,* &c. And again, v. 9, 10. the fame words. So, *Pf.* 42. 6. *Why art thou fo full of heavinefs, O my Soul,* &c. *v.* 14. the fame, as alfo in the next *Pfalm* v. 5. Again *Pfalm.* 46. 7. *The Lord of hofts is with us,* &c. and *v.* 11. the fame. And, *Pfalm* 107. 13. *So when they cried unto the Lord, he delivered them,* &c. and *v.* 19. 28. the fame. And *v.* 15. 21, 31. we have thefe words thrice repeated, *Oh that Men would therefore praife the Lord for his Goodnefs,* &c. But of all others the moft remarkable place is *Pfalm* 136. where the fame form of words is ufed, for 26. verfes

---

(b) *Judges.* 5. 27.

together,

together, *For his mercy endureth forever.* Nor is it otherwise in the Gospel; for we find our Lord himself in the Garden paſſionately addreſſing his Father *three times* in the very ſame expreſſions: (*c*) *He left 'em and went away and pray'd the third time ſaying the ſame words.* And in that affectionate prayer, he made for his diſciples and the Church, he delivers himſelf in this manner, (*d*) *Holy Father, keep through thine own name thoſe which thou haſt given me, that they may be one as we are*——*That they all may be one, as thou Father in me and I in thee, that they alſo may be one in us*————*That they may be one as we are one*-————*I in them and thou in me, that they may be made perfect in one.* ——So that you ſee *all repetitions* are not faulty; but may be uſeful for the quickning of devotion, eſpecially in Prayers publickly ſaid. And therefore the thing which Chriſt cautions againſt is moſt likely this,(*e*) That we ſhould not tumble out many inſignificant words, or the ſame words over and over again, as the heathens were wont to do, not out of *fervency of mind,*but to *lengthen* out the Prayer as long as they could, counting this length of Words, a good quality, or what makes it more powerful or more acceptable to God.

This will better appear, if we conſider the Word which the Evangeliſt uſes, and which he borrows from an Heathen Proverb to repreſent his Maſters meaning in this place[μὴ βαττολογήσητε] *do not battologize* (*t*) which among the Greeks ſignifies an *unprofitable trifling away time in words often repeated without Elegancy or any tolerable ſenſe in 'em.* In ſtrict Engliſh it muſt be rendred *the way of ſpeech Battus uſed.* Now there being *Two* of that

(*c*) Matth. 26. 44. (*d*) John 17. 11 (*e*) *Hammond's* Pract. Catech: (*f*) *Significat Græcis* βατ]ολογία *inutilem nugacitatem quando idem ſæpius*——*incondita verborum repetitione cum tædio inculcatur*——Chem. Harm. in loc.

name,

name, pretty remarkable on this account, it will not be eafy to determine *which* of 'em, or whether *both* may not be intended in that Text of St. *Matthew*. One was a Prince of the *Cyrenians* with a very fhrill Voice, who ftuttered much, and confequently was neceffitated to repeat his words very often before he could get to the period. And fo *Varinus*, and *Hefychius*, turn βατ⁊ολογΘ into ἰχνόφωνΘ and τεχυλίφωνΘ, *(g)* when the voice is *fmall* and with all *intercepted* and ftopt, fo that the party cannot, without much difficulty, bring forth what he intends to fay. So *Beza* and *Tremellius* tranflate the Word [*Ne blaterate*] *do not ftammer.* *Salmafius* fuppofes *Battus* to mean him properly *(h)* who cannot *pronounce plainly* what he has a mind to fpeak, but *often* falls on the *fame fyllable* before he can proceed. But becaufe thefe repetitions, tho' frequent in fuch cafes, are owing to the impediments and defects of nature, and are chargeable on the *Organs* or ordinary means of utterance, without any affectation or influence of the will, therefore 'tis more probable the term alludes to *(i)* a *Poet* of that name who abounded with *tautologies,* and was not worth taking notice of in any other refpect, than for his often repeating the fame expreffions; and from him *Suidas* derives the Word *Battology*: and fo *Ovid* reprefents him in

---

(g) *Qui habet, exilem, qu.* interclufam & interceptam vocem & linguam balbutientem——ibid (h) *Qui non poteft plane eloqui quod vult, uti funt qui dicuntur,* μογίλαλοι, *fæpe enim unam Syllabam multis vocibus iterant priusquam unam Syllabam queant integram; unde* Βατ⁊ολογεῖν, &c. (i) Βατ⁊ολογία ἀπὸ Βάτ⁊υ πρΘ μακρὸς κỳ πολυστίχυς ὕμνυς ποιήσαντΘ ταυτολογίας ἔχυτας——
——*fub illis*
Montibus inquit erant, & erant fub montibus illis
——*me mihi, perfide, prodis,*
Me mihi prodis, ait.

his

his *Metamorphoses,* as describing the way he took
in his hymns and poems. Some think it an Ap-
pellative, and will have *Battus* derived from (*k*)
Ba and *Bat* frequently heard from the mouths of
Infants before they can speak, and which they pronounce without any meaning, and from them the
Word is borrowed to set forth a Prayer, Poem
or Speech consisting of many unnecessary, flat,
empty and idle Words. St. *Chrysostom* was of
opinion that the censure of the Gospel concerning
repetitions reached only those prayers wherein
they desired not only *Spiritual* and Divine Blessings
but *riches, power* and such advantages as concern
the happiness and pride of this Life. And
of this mind was *Theophylact*; And *Epiphanius*
calls it [διὰ λεπτολογίας προσεύχεσθαι] when for
mean and *trivial* things we say (*l*) *Thine is the
might, the power, the honour, and glory,* &c. which is
a form of doxology not bad in it self, but ill applied to matters not deserving that Emphasis. What
the *Syriack* Word was which Christ himself was
pleas'd to use we cannot say; Nor is it to be dis-
puted whether St. *Matthew's* Βαττολογήσητε exactly answers it, and was the most proper to translate by what he heard from his Master: yet the
context sufficiently clears his meaning, where forbidding us to do as the *Gentiles* did and showing
with all, what their Prayers were faulty in, we
may easily infer that the *Battology* in this caution,
must needs intend these *two things, first a multitude
of phrases* altogether the *same,* or a very *little varied*
to lengthen out the Prayer: and *Secondly* a design
in these Words either by their numerous repeti-

(*k*) *Est autem* Βάττος κατὰ ὀνοματοποίίαβ *ἀba vel* bat
quæ syllaba crebro est infantibus in ore——Vid. Vosſ (*l*) Σή
ἐστιν ἡ δύναμις. Σὸκ τὸ κρᾶτϴ. Σή ἐστιν ἡ τιμή. Σή ἐστιν
ἡ δόξα, Σή ἐστιν ἡ εὐλογία. Σή ἐστιν ἡ ἰσχύς. Σή ἐστιν ἡ δύναμις——

tions

tions to inform and prefcribe or by their variety to charm and oblige their Gods to grant what they requefted of 'em. The former of thefe we have in *v*. 8. *When you pray ufe not vain repetitions as the heathens do, for they think they fhall be heard for their much fpeaking.* The latter in, *v*. 9. *Be not therefore like unto them, for your Heavenly Father knoweth what you have need of before you ask him*————— Where he oppofes his Father who knew all things to the *Gods* of the Heathens who where prefumed not to know their wants unlefs they fpake of 'em, and thereupon offer'd *many* and the *fame* Prayers to inform and prevail on 'em. Chrift's meaning was to teach his difciples what their Prayers were to be, not fuch as the Hebrew Doctors call [*labiorum elocutionem*] the bare found of Words, which was all the infidels took care of; but what came from the *Heart* and fhow'd the fenfe themfelves had of their wants, which God knew before they were expreffed, and had compaffion enough to eafe 'em, before he was asked, yet would be asked to make them know from whence their relief came. (*m*) Now that the heathens abounded in thefe unneceffary and barren *tautologies*, or as our tranflation has it in *vain repetitions*, both in their *Civil* and *Religious* Addreffes, we every where find. The latter of which we have an example of in the *priefts of Baal*, who called from morning to evening, faying, (*n*)*O Baal, hear us*, and,

---

(*m*) Φεῦ Φεῦ, Ἰὼ Ἰὼ————*paricida trahatur rogemus,* Augufte,=*paricida trahatur, hoc rogemus paricida trahatur*————*exaudi Cæfar delatores ad leonem, exaudi Cæfar, delatores ad leonem, exaudi Cæfar*————*Antonine Pie dii te fervent. Antonine Clemens dii te fervent, Antonine Clemens dii te fervent:* Lampr in Com.————c. 18: (*n*) 1 K. 18. 26. *Continuo fex horarum fpatio*——*iifdem vocibus*——*adclamarent*———— Selden de diis Syris Proleg. c. 3.

as the prophet jeers 'em for it, they cried in this loud manner, for fear he should be in a *sleep*, or on a *journey, or pursuing the enemy*, and so probably might not hear them, unless they were instant, clamorous, and using the same Words a long while, to make him understand what they expected from him. And so the *Ephesians for two hours together cried out in no other Words*, but (o) *Great is Diana of the Ephesians----*-----They did [κεᾀζειν] bawl aloud in the same tone like *crows*, from whom the Metaphor is taken, their whole zeal depending on those *Epiphonema's*, in commending and magnifying their Goddess with the same Words. (p) We may add, that it was the way of those *Pagans* to heap up in their Prayers the several *titles* of their Gods and Goddesses, out of a conceit, that this was an instance of their respect and that it mightily pleas'd 'em. So the Sun was called *Sol, Phœbus, Apollo, Hyperion,* &c. and the Moon *Luna, Isis, Diana, Trivia, Hecate,* and by many other names which gave her the Stile of μυειώνυμ☉, or the Goddess with a thousand titles; and after this manner are composed some *Arabick hymns* containing an hundred Words to the same purpose. Now tho' all repetitions are not forbid, whether consisting of the *same* or *Synonymous Words*, in case they are zealously and affectionately said, yet we are not to heap up Words before God, as if he measured our Prayers by the *length* of 'em, or valued more the *voice* which sounded, than the *Heart* which conceived 'em. This is a great fault in the *Papacy*,

---

(o) Acts 19. 34, (p) *Titulorum varietate capi deos, placari & ad vota suscitari, maximoque inde affici honore putabant, quod multiplex potestas & imperium imprimis ita agnosceretur ----Habes in Arabicis canticis---------ubi centum amplius nomina,* &c. Vid. Maimonid in more Nevoch.

where they lay so great a stress on the *Opus Operatum,* that they constantly use *beads* for fear they should fail in the number of their *Ave-Maria's* and other Devotions, how short soever they otherwise are in the qualifications of Prayer, and whether their Desires and Thoughts have any interest or no in 'em, and yet the Gospel saith that God will be worshipped rather *in Spirit and truth.* Briefly those Prayers which have vain and superfluous Words, as St. *Augustine* speaks, and (q) the *Persian* Translation so renders it : Or tho' made up of proper language are repeated by the mouth, but have no communication with the heart, and are at great distance from the mind of the votary, these are the *repetitions* in Prayer which do not become a Christian, *vain repetitions,* Heathen Battologies, and Words said over and over again, to make their Deities first hear and then grant their petitions.

What *repetitions* then occur in the *Liturgy,* a sober man should consider some of 'em at least, the very *ejaculations* and *sentences* of *Scripture,* and the rest correspondent to it in grave, proper and plain language, which if People were not indifferent and cold in, would certainly contribute to help Devotion and raise the affections which it ought to proceed from. And if not, they make 'em indeed such repetitions as our Lord censures [*otiosos sine mente sonos*] idle, heathenish and without effect, for want of ingaging the *Soul* and *Spirit,* whose earnestness and fervency is not a little discerned when we patiently and piously (after those patterns we have in the Holy Book) say over the same thing in our Prayers or Praises to God. These iterations so qualified are so many *testimonies* of

---

(r) *Multa vana ne proloquamini* Pers.

true

true *Zeal*, and *figns* that our *affections* and *hearts* go with 'em, which is what God expects in thefe words, and they no otherwife do or can inform and charm him. And if fome *Preachers* out of the pale of our Church, had not this Apology to offer for themfelves, I doubt they would be much to feek for reafons to juftify, not only the *length* of their Prayers, but which in a great meafure occafions that length, the *repeating* over the fame words to ingage God to attend to 'em.

· But of thefe repetitions, the recital of the *Lord's-Prayer*, is more particularly mention'd. A Prayer which the Ancients call, *the falt of all divine Offices, and without which thefe have no favour* (r). And truly, if we are Chriftians, we muft be perfwade that Chrift has taught us thofe things, which are moft edifying and ufeful, becaufe he is the only Author of our Salvation; and fo defirous of it, that he fuffer'd Death in order to accomplifh it; and therefore to be fure, if a better Prayer could have been thought on, our careful Mafter would not have omitted it. As much therefore as Chrift excels all the Prophets, all Men, ay and Angels, fo much is this Prayer beyond all others; Nor can it be fuppofed any other fhould be more acceptable to the (i) *Father*, than what his own beloved *Son* has fet us, a Prayer not to be denied, becaufe he made it, who is the Mediator between God and Man, our conftant advocate and interceffor. Hath not Chrift faid, *Whatfoever you ask in my Name*, &c.—— How much rather grant what we ask, when we not only ask in his *name*, but in his *Language* alfo. Efpecially when God has faid, *This is my beloved Son*—— *Hear him.* And if we hear him, he will the rather hear us, when we

---

(r) *Ferus* in Matth. (i) Cypr. de Orat Dom.

fpeak

ſpeak or pray tŏ him in that form of words
he has taught us, a form which in a very compre-
henſive way, contains all things needful for *Soul*
and *Body*; a form which comprehends all the
Prayers of Scripture and of the Holy Men in it, and
wants nothing to procure us *preſent* and *future* happineſs. " For this cauſe our Cuſtom is (accord-
" ing to the example of our Pious Anceſtors (both
" to place it at the (*k*) front of our Prayers as a
" guide, and to add it at the (*l*) end of ſome
" principal limbs or parts of our Service, as a
" Complement, which fully perfecteth whatſo-
" ever may be defective in the reſt. (*m*) Twice
" we rehearſe it ordinarily, and oftner as the
" Service requires ſolemnity and length, not mi-
" ſtruſting that any Man has reaſon to think our
" labour or time miſpent, and our Worſhip the
" worſe by repeating that, which otherwiſe would
" not be made ſo familiar to the ſimple ſort, for
" the good of whoſe Souls there is not in the
" Chriſtian Religion, any thing of like continual
" uſe, and force throughout every hour and mo-
" ment of their whole lives————The Church
" has preſcribed it therefore after the abſolution
" for repentance; after the word of God read,
" and the ſaying of the Creed, for aſſiſtance in
" holineſs and confirmation of Faith; in the Li-
" tany for deliverance from evil; in the Commu-
" nion Service to diſpoſe us for a penitent hearing
" of the Law of God; and for ſanctifying to us
" what we eat and drink in the holy Sacrament,
" never too often, never ſuperfluouſly, never
" with ſuperſtition. For how can we too often

(*k*) *Præmiſſa legitima & ordinaria oratione quaſi fun-
damento*——*Tertull.* (*l*) *Quam totam petitionem ferè omnis Eccleſia dom. Oratione concludit.* Aug. Ep. 59. (*m*)
Hooker Eccl. Pol. l. 5: c. 35.

" join

" join his moſt perfect Prayer to ours, that are ſo
" imperfect, ſince by him both we and our Pray-
" ers are alone made acceptable? Thoſe who pre-
" ſented Petitions to the *Roman* Emperors, drew
" them by the direction of ſome judicious Law-
" yer; but we have this ſacred Form from the
" wonderful Councellour, who came out of the bo-
" ſome of his Father, and knew his Treaſures, as
" well as our wants; he beſt could inform us, what
" was fit for us to ask and what moſt likely for
" him to grant; he was to go to Heaven to be
" our advocate there, and he hath taught us to
" uſe this here, that there might be an harmony
" between our requeſts and his. What zeal, and
" height of Devout affections are ſufficient to of-
" fer up this Prayer, which was drawn by the great
" Maſter of requeſts, and Orderer of all intercourſe
" between God and Man? How ſure is this of ac-
" ceptance, which is ſtampt with his Image, ſign'd
" with his hand and ſent in his name? His Power
" will make it prevalent, and God's love to his
" dear Son moſt acceptable. For what can pierce
" the Ears or melt the Heart of a tender Father,
" more readily than the Voice of his only and be-
" loved Son (*n*)? Are not theſe motives for us to
uſe it reverently and heartily? And do they not
well excuſe (if that word be proper here) the Piety
of the Church for repeating this Prayer ſo often,
which has the Royal ſtamp of divine Authority,
and which may make amends for our other Petitions, not ſo zealouſly put up by reaſon of many
intervening diſtractions apt to draw us aſide, and
cool us in our moſt intent and reſolved Devotion,

(*n*) *Comler's* Companion to the *Temple.* P. 1, Sect. 5
P. 2. Sect. 2,

B. What

B. What Rout is that yonder?

A. By the' noise they make and the disorder they go in, they seem to be Men who have drunk more than does 'em good.

B. Not unlikely. And therefore, Sir, I think it the best way to turn back, and mend our pace towards the Town, for it is a misfortune attends Men in drink, that they are not only quarrelsome, but they make no distinction between those who do, and do not offend 'em, and are sometimes very abusive without provocation.

A. Do as you please——And truly now I think on't, I promised to meet a Friend at the Coffee-House much about this hour, but I profess had forgot it but for this interruption.

B. I thought to have begg'd the Favour to spend a few minutes by the way at my habitation, but

hope you wil
I pray favour me so far as to make up this loss in the Afternoon to Morrow.

A. If nothing hinders, I shall comply with you, and till then

Adieu.

The

The Sixth DIALOGUE.

The CONTENTS.

Muſick *in the Church Vindicated. The Antiquity and Uſefulneſs of it in Devotion. What* Saul's *Spirit was, which* David's Muſick *allay'd. The effect it had on* Eliſha. St. Auguſtine's *Experience of it. Its Power ſhow'd by the fabulous ſtories of* Orpheus, &c. *How it compoſes the Paſſions. King* Charles's *Declaration about Recreations on the Lord's-day, and the Apologies of ſome Divines on that ſubject conſidered. The Doctrine of our Church, and the Laws of the Nation require the ſtrict Obſervation of the* Lord's-day. *The ſeveral Parties who abuſe it. The Office for it as to Devotion and Practice. The time when it begins and ends.*

A. I Have for ſome time obſerved your attention to this Conſort of *Muſick,* which to my thinking is very fine; Neither can I well tell, whether the *Inſtruments* or *Voices* excelled. They *both* deſerve their Praiſe. And I hope this lucky Adventure may ſomewhat contribute to ſoften your *Objection* Yeſterday, and make you leſs averſe to a thing, which if you ſhould any longer diſpute againſt, you muſt needs quarrel with your own *Senſes.*

B. My being alone caus'd me to ſtep aſide for this Entertainment; Not that I take any delight in hearing the *Muſick,* which I look upon as a ve-

ry

ry odd accomplishment in Young Men and Women, and bordering very near on *Vanity*, but being by my self, as I said, I was invited, as many others might be in the like case, ·to hearken to what I do not approve; yet was contented to bear with it for want of Opportunity to employ my-Senses better. However, this is understood to be the Diversion of *idle hours*, but my objection chiefly aim'd at what is done in the *Church*, and at such times when we pretend to be more *grave* and *serious*, and 'tis in that I crave your Answer.

A. Well, as to this kind of *Musick*, it is to be supposed you do not in all respects, and simply condemn the use of it, because then there must be laid aside a very essential part of *their Worship*, whom you so much favour in this Objection : And the *Psalms* in *Metre* must be heard no longer, which is Devotion in *Singing*. But you mean the more Artificial way we use by *Voice*, *Organ*, and other *Instruments*, beyond the capacity of every ordinary Man and Woman, and wherein they have no interest or share, but what relates to the matter, which the Members of the Choire so melodiously Sing, and in which they cannot join with 'em. *This* then we are to explain and justify, and we may the more easily do it, from the *Institution* of *David*——(*a*) *The Priests waited on their Offices, the Levites also with Instruments of Musick of the Lord,* which *David* the *King had made to Praise the Lord, because his mercy endureth for ever, and the Priests sounded Trumpets before 'em* —— So *Hezekiah* set the *Levites* in the House of the Lord with *Cymbals*, with *Psalteries* and *Harps*, according to the Commandment of *David*; nay more, of *Gad* the King's *Seer* and *Nathan* the Prophet, and further

---

(*a*) 2 Chro 29. 25, 27.

ftill, *So was the Commandment of the Lord by the Prophets*——'Tis true, *David* had no small skill in *Mufick* and *Poetry*, and thereupon perhaps you may think he introduced a Worship suitable to his *Genius*; But he had certainly other motives; for he found by Experience how neceffary *both* were for the Service of God to raife attention, to fweeten humane affections towards God, and make us (*b*) delight in his Worship. So that being inabled by the Spirit of God, he writ and left behind him many *Pfalms* for the benefit of the *Jewifh* Church, which they conftantly ufed in the *Tabernacle* and *Temple*. And as we ftill retain the *Hymns* themfelves, fo we do in a low degree the *manner* of expreffing 'em, and the other parts of the Worship, as far as it confifts with the ferioufnefs, and gravity of the *Chriftian* Religion.

Nor can you furely fufpect it an Article of the *Ceremonial Law*, which was to have a Period at the coming of *Meffias*, becaufe not only *before* the delivery of that Law, (*c*) *The Children of* Ifrael *fung unto the Lord with their Voices faying*, &c. *And* Miriam *the Prophetefs, the Sifter of* Aaron, *took a timbrel in her hand, and all the Women* (in the Nature of a *Chorus*) *went one after another with timbrels, and with dances, and* Miriam *anfwered, fing ye unto the Lord,* &c. but we alfo find the *Gentiles* taking the fame courfe; and as an inftance of the *Law* of *Nature*, they fet forth the Honour and Praifes of their Gods, both by Inftruments and Voices, as we fee in their *Janualia, Minervia,* and the like Poems and Verfes compofed by the Ancient *Romans*, and Sung to the Honour of thofe Gods, whofe names they bear. So the *Greeks* had their

---

(*b*) *Perfuadet autem quicquid fuave eft, & animo penitus dum dele[c]tat infidet.* Lactant. de Vero Cultu. c. 21. (*c*) Exod 15. 1. 20. 21.

solemn

solemn Hymns, some to their *Propitious Gods*, which they called κλητὺς ὕμνυς, and the Latins, *Indigitamenta*; Others to their *Vejoves*, or *hurtful Deities*, which they stiled ὕμνυς ἀπυτρορταίυς. The *Romans*, *Carmen averruncale*, appeasing Hymns, and for the removal of incumbent Calamities. Thus *Apollo* had his Παιὰν, *Ceres* her Ἴαλος, *Bacchus* his *Dithyrambus*, &c. which the Priests and People took care to Sing, with the greatest Zeal and the best skill they had in their respective Solemnities. So that if you will take it for a *Ceremony*, it was *such* as all Nations conspired in the use of And therefore as it had not its being from the *Law of Moses*, so neither is there any reason that the repeal of *that Law* should abrogate a Custom, practised indeed under that Oeconomy, but which had not its *Original* or *Institution* from it.

And yet were it so, why may not the *Christian-Church* by vertue of her Liberty recal some Expedients, for the better Worship of God, from the *Tabernacle*, *Temple or Synagogue?* And as we have borrowed several particulars of the *Judicial*, and *National* Law of the Jews, why not take some of the Ceremonial likewise, such as are serviceable to set forth the Grandeur of the Gospel? For my part, I am not angry to hear a *Psalm* of *David* sung in the Church, though set by *Sternhold* and *Hopkins*, and which, while they are singing it, is by me as little understood, as those *Anthems* made by better Masters, unless I have a Book in my hand; and that is an help that will make the other Hymns intelligible and easy. You would smile if I should call the singing of *Psalms* a piece of *Judaism*; And why is one way of Singing so named more than another, when they differ not in kind but degrees, and the only fault is, that there is not *less Piety*, but much *more skill* in the latter?

'Tis

'Tis evident our *Lord* uſed this Method of Deꞏ votion, (*d*) for *he Sung an Hymn* with his Diſciꞏ ples a little before his Paſſion. And I queſtion not, but it was with ſuch melody and ſweetneſs, as became that ſacred Mouth, which had no imꞏ perfection to give a check to the skill of the Singer. And St. *Chryſoſtom* in an homily on the place, ſaith, That *he therefore gave thanks and ſung an Hymn, to leave us an example to do the ſame* And elſewhere he Admoniſhes us, (*e*) to conſider what the Aꞏ poſtles did after the holy Supper. *Did they not return* (ſaith he) *to prayer and ſinging of Pſalms?* And on this reaſon (*f*) a Council of *Toledo*, Exꞏ communicates thoſe who preſume to reject theſe Hymns in the Churches. (*g*) 'Tis St. *Paul*'s Exꞏ hortation to the *Coloſſians*, that they ſhould *teach* [or edifie one another] *in Pſalms, and Hymns, and Spiritual Songs*——or to join the Words with what follows, *Singing with Grace to the Lord* in that manner. Yet if we refer it to the beginꞏ ning of the Verſe, the Apoſtle knew well enough that the expedient was good in Order to *Admoniſh, i.e.* mutually heighten each others Devotion, let the matter or ſubject of the Anthem be what it will, (*h*) whether concerning the Majeſty and Power of God , the make and order of the Creaꞏ tures, or Moral Leſſons for vertue and ſober living, as the Interpreters of the Text diſtinguiſh the Words. So again, he exhorts the (*i*) *Epheſians*, to ſpeak to themſelves in Pſalms , Hymns , and Spiritual Songs, ſinging and making melody in their Hearts, unto the Lord——where if the Apoſtle be thought to intend only *private ſinging* in their own Houſes,

(*d*) Matth 26. 30. (*e*) In 1 Cor. 11. (*f*) Conc Tolet. 4. Can. 12. Apud Caranz. (*g*) Coloſ. 3. 16. (*h*) Beza in loꞏ. (*i*) Epheſ 5. 19.

M m yet

yet without Controverfie, the fame was done in the *Church* or *Publick* , as appears from what we read in another Epiftle ———— (k) *How is it then, Brethren? When you come together, every one of you has a Pfalm* — The Church has from Age to Age followed this Pattern : And though probably at firft it was little more than a *melodious* kind of *pronunciation,* and after the manner of a *plain Song,* yet in procefs of time, and by degrees it became a more exact and artificial Harmony : And in St. *Auguftine's* Days it grew fo excellent, that it drew many to the Church, and gave opportunity to win 'em over to the Chriftian Religion.

As for its *Antiquity,* befides thofe Examples before cited ; (*l*) *Dionyfius* the *Areopagite* mentions, τῶν ψαλμῶν ἱερολογίαν, and faith, That *all the Priefts were required to fing Pfalms at the celebration of the facred myfteries*—and (m) *Socrates* reports, that *Ignatius* Bifhop of *Antioch,* faw a Vifion of Angels celebrating the Holy Trinity with alternate Hymns ; And thereupon introduced that way of finging into the Church of *Syria,* whence the Tradition was convey'd to other Churches. I muft confefs, I a little doubt the truth of this Paffage ; for though I have a refpect for the way, and confider it done by thofe Bleffed Spirits about the Throne of God, yet I cannot think it worth the while for a Choire of Angels, to defcend from Heaven to prefcribe it to us. And therefore (n) *Theodoret* contradicts the Tradition, and faith , that *Flavianus* and *Diodorus,* long after, were the firft who divided the *Choire* into *two parts,* and taught the *Syrians* to fing *David's Pfalms* interchangeably or *by turns,* which 'beginning at' *Antioch,* proceeded to other

---

(k) 1 Cor. 14 26. (l) De Hierarch. (m) Hift. Eccl. l. 6. c. 8. (n) Eccl Hift. l 2. c. 24.

Churches, and at length reach'd the utmost limits of the Earth, (*o*) yet neither can I affent to
this, if any credit may be given *Theodorus* Bifhop
of *Mopfueftia*, a City in *Cilicia*, co-temporary
with *Flavianus* and *Diodorus*, who faith, That
they indeed *firft* tranflated thefe Hymns, alternately Sung, from the *Syrian* Language into Greek ;
And from thence the miftake arofe of being *Authors* of this ufe, becaufe they appear'd fo to other
Nations on the account of the tranflation.' However long before *them*, (*p*) *Eufebius* informs us
from *Philo*, that the *Afcetæ* in *Egypt* (whom that
Author reckons among the converts to Chriftianity) not only gave themfelves up to a con-
templative Life, but they made *Songs* and *Hymns*
to the Praife of God, in all kinds of *Metre* and
Tunes, fuch as are wont to be Sung among us, *i. e.*
One began the *Pfalm* in a tuneable way, and the
reft affifted in the laft claufes of it.——The reafon whereof probably was, becaufe all the Company not being equally skilled in chanting the Service, they were not to be concerned till towards
the end of the Hymn , to avoid thereby thofe
confufed and difharmonious founds, which would
neceffarily be made from the great variety of un-
managed Voices. And this occafioned thofe two
Canons in the Councils of (*q*) *Trullo* and (*r*) *Laodicea*,
wherein the Fathers decreed, That *none fhould
fing in the Church befides the Members of the Choire,
and fuch as Sung by Book*. Not that the Congregation were forbid, faith *Balfamon*, to fing with the
others, provided they Sung by *Note*, and did not
(which was the fault) bawle, and with a rude
clamour drown the Voices of thofe who Sung bet-

(*o*) Vid. Valef. Annot. in Theodoret——(*p*) Eccl. Hift.
l 2 c 17. Vid Valef in loc . (*q*) Can. 75. (*r*) Can. 15.
M m 2 ter——

ter—Every Body might fing, as *Ariftenus* gloffes on the *Canon*, who could do it well, but if not he was by no means to difturb the Choire———So that thefe two *Councils* which regulate the form of finging in their Ages, prove it a Cuftom of very Ancient ftanding. But before them *(t) Pliny* II. in his Letter to *Trajan*, tells the Emperor, that Chriftians did *rife before day, and fing an Hymn to Chrift as God*——And this he faid was done [*Secum in vicem*] alternately. And fo in more words, *(u)* Bafil explains it. That *it was then the common Cuftom of the Churches to go very early, while it was yet dark, to the place of Meeting; and there having confeffed their Sins and pray'd, they all rofe up to fing a Pfalm, and dividing themfelves into two parts, they anfwered one another in courfe:* And after this the *Precentor,* or fome other Perfon qualified *for that purpofe, began an Hymn, and the reft followed him according to their parts: With which variety of Singing, fome Prayers being faid between, they fpent the Night*———Thus he: And becaufe *Sabellius,* and *Marcellus,* took occafion from hence to incenfe the Churches againft him, as the Author of a *New* device, in the Service of God, becaufe he had brought this way of *Singing* into his Church, before they of *Neocæfarea* ufed it, that he might avoid the charge of *fingularity and Novelty* (which is what they offer'd againft him) he vindicates himfelf by the Authority of the feveral Churches in *Egypt, Libya, Thebes, Paleftine, Phœnicia, Mefopotamia, Syria,* which did the *fame thing.* And he might well clear himfelf of Innovation, when the Council of *Antioch,* before his time, cenfured *Paulus Samofatenus* for exploding, as new things, thofe

---

(t) L 10. Ep. 101. A. Teftimony *Tertullian* makes ufe of in his Apology (u) Ep. ad Neocæfar———

Pfalms and *Hymns*, the Chriſtians of that Age ſung
to the honour of Chriſt. And *Eufebius* giving an
account of diverſe Authors, whoſe names he could
not learn, mentions *one* very Ancient, who diſputing againſt the errours of *Artemon*, (which *Paulus
Samofatenus* afterwards revived) among other arguments for the proof of *Chriſt's Divinity*, he propoſes this, That it was the doctrine of the Elder
times for this reaſon, (w) *Becauſe the Pſalms and
Hymns written long ago by the Faithful, did celebrate
Chriſt as God.*—Which indeed the very notion of
an Hymn ſuppoſes, if St. *Auguſtine* Judges right,
who makes it conſiſt of theſe three Parts. *Praiſe*,
(x) the *Praiſe of God*, and a *Song* ; and if any
one of theſe be wanting, it is not an *Hymn*. That
they *Sung* in the Days of *Gregory Nazianzen*,
appears in one of his Orations againſt *Julian*. And
becauſe the *Arians* made and Sung *Hymns* ſuited to
their Hereſie, and did it for the greater part of the
Night, (y) therefore St. *Chryſoſtom*, fearing leſt the
ſimpler ſort of People might be drawn away from
the Church on the account of this *Singing*, that he
might countermine the *Arians*, and confirm the
Catholicks in the Faith, which the others ſought to
ſhake by this Artifice, he appointed ſome of his own
Communion to *ſing* at the ſame hours ——— Not
that he *begun* this practice in the *Greek Church*, to
ſing after that manner, but he was forced to apply
this expedient at ſuch unſeaſonable times, as the
Hereticks uſed ; and might perhaps have ſome *new
Anthems* made, beſides what the Church commonly Sung out of the *Pſalms*, and other Books of
Scripture, in oppoſition to *thoſe* the *Arians* had to

(w) Eccl. Hiſt. l. 5 c 28. (x) *Hymni ſunt cantus conti-
nentes laudem Dei, ſi ſit laus & non ſit Dei non eſt Hymnus.*
In Pſalm. (y) Socrat. Eccl Hiſt. lib. 6 cap 8.

expoſe

expofe and leſſen the Doctrine of the *Trinity*, as
we may ſee if we carefully read the *Hiſtorian* in
that Chapter.

Thus in the *Eaſtern-Church*. But for the *Weſtern*
to which we belong, we do not find that
it had any firm footing till Pope *Damaſus* came
to the Chair, who writ a Letter to St. *Jerom* then
at *Jeruſalem*, to deſire him to *tranſmit to* Rome
the (*a*) *manner of ſinging Pſalms among the Greeks*;
Which he (*b*) accordingly did, and thereupon
the Tradition commenced, that *this Pope* firſt decreed, that *Pſalms* ſhould be alternately ſung, (*c*)
and the *Gloria Patri*——always added to conclude
'em. But St. *Auguſtine* refers it to his Maſter St.
Ambroſe Biſhop of *Milain*, who being perſecuted
by *Juſtina*, and the People forced to watch in the
Church, he thought it neceſſary to introduce the
Eaſtern Cuſtom of Singing Pſalms to keep up their
Spirits, and not let 'em ſink under that affliction;
and from thence the practice ſpread it ſelf over
all the Provinces of the *Weſt*——which does not
much thwart the report before concerning Pope
Damaſus, becauſe thoſe two Biſhops being *co-eta-
neous*; the *One*, on this occaſion, might begin that
at *Milain*, which the *other* near the ſame time had
done at *Rome*. Yet *Tertullian* in his Apology ſaith,
that the People in and before his time, were wont
to challenge one another to Sing Hymns to God,
either made by themſelves or taken out of the Bible : But then it muſt be conſidered, that though he
himſelf was a *Latin*, he ſpeaks [*De Chriſtianorum
cœtibus*] of *Chriſtians* at large, and ſo may mean the
Churches of the *Eaſt*, where this uſe had been of
a long ſtanding. And if this be doubtful, yet we

(*a*) *Pſallentium Græcorum.* Damaſ. Ep. ad Hieron. (*b*)
Platina de vit. Pontif. (*c*) *Stella de geſtis Pont.*

learn

learn that about the year 139. *Telefphorus* Biſhop of *Rome* writ a decretal Epiſtle, wherein he required the Clergy fix Weeks before *Eaſter*, to Sing the *Angelical Hymn*— as *Platina*, and *Stella* tell us ; which gives ſome colour to what *Baronius* aſſerts, That *this Cuſtom is as old as the* Roman See.

'Tis not eaſie to diſcover the date when this practice began in *England*, or (d) whether it came hither with the firſt Preaching of the Goſpel, *Bede* relates it of *Paulinus*, that when he was made Biſhop of *Rocheſter*, about the year 631. he left behind him in the North, one *James* a Deacon, a Man *excellent in Church Muſick*, who taught 'em that form of Divine Service he had learnt at *Canterbury*. And after, in the year 668. when Archbiſhop *Theodorus* made his Metropolitical Viſitation, the art of Singing Service, which was then only uſed in (e) *Kent*, was generally taken up all over the Kingdom. And whereas Pope *Vitalianus* added the *Organ* to that *Vocal Muſick*, which was before in uſe in the Chriſtian Church, in leſs then 30 Years after it was introduced into the Churches of *Britain*, and hath continued ever ſince without interruption. But more of this by and by. In the mean while we ſee by theſe teſtimonies what the practice of the Church was in her greateſt purity, and in times when her outward Circumſtances were ſuch, that ſhe had little reaſon to uſe any ſort of *Muſick* or Harmony, but what was adjudged ſuitable and neceſſary for Devotion, and wherein, (f) as St. *Auguſtine* ſpeaks,

---

(d) *Heylin's* Hiſtory of the Sabbath. Pa. 2. chap. 7. ſect. 2. (e) *Sonos cantandi in Ecclefia quos eatenus in Cantia tantum noverant, ab hoc tempore per omnes Anglorum Ecclefias difcere ceperunt.* Bed Eccl. Hiſt l.-4. c 2. (f) *De Hymnis & Pfalmis canendis ipfius Domini & Apoftolorum documenta, exempla & præcepta habere Ecclefiam* &c. Ep 119.

Sh3

She 'has her warrant from the Doctrine, examples and command of Christ and his Apostles. Sometimes, as St. *Basil* faith, *they all Sung together,* as if they had one Mouth as well as one Heart. *Sometimes they divided, and each side sung in his course. Sometimes one began, and the rest Sung after him. And sometimes again the Congregation did not put in, till towards the end of the Hymn*———This, I say, was *their way;* which the *present Church,* at her *Cathedral Service,* doth so exactly follow. And it is to be wish'd, we had that Harmony and Sweetness of Temper, that cheerfulness in Religion, that assurance of the joys of Heaven those holy People had, and of all which the *Musick* at their Worship was the signification and emblem. The hard usage they daily met with, could not make them despond or render 'em *sower* and *peevish* to one another. That Providence permitted ill Men to handle 'em roughly, could not prevail on 'em to be *sullen* in his Service; And though they were feemingly miserable in this World, and that the Condition they underwent, called for sighs and tears, rather than any instance of satisfaction and joy, yet they saw, with *Isaiah,* and heard what was done in Heaven, where the *Seraphims* stood before the Throne of God, and cried one to another, saying, (g) *Holy, Holy, Holy Lord God of Hosts, the whole World is full of thy Glory.*

Hitherto there was no melodious Service in the Western Church but what depended on the *Voice;* yet about the Year 653. or according to *Onuphrius* four Years after, when the State of the Church would better bear it, Pope *Vitalianus,* as I was just now saying, added the *Organ* to help the *Voice* in celebrating the Praises of God. For as he was

---

(g) If. 6. 3.

a Man

a Man very conftant in his attendance on the Worfhip of God, fo he made it his bufinefs to find out any expedient, which might invite other People to the fame diligence—*Platina* indeed fpeaks doubtfully of it, *As fome will have it* (faith he) and thereby feems to queftion the Tradition. And there are thofe who derive it from *Conftantinople*, as fent by one of the Emperors there to King *Pepin*. Others attribute it to *Lewis the Godly*. But the generality fix it on *Vitalianus*; Though it is not unlikely, but as the practice of *Singing* by *Voice* commenced *firft* in the *Greek Church*, and at length came to the *Weft*, fo likewife might the *Organ* be tranfmitted hither, as fome of thofe Authors conceive who draw the *Original* of it from *Greece* and *Conftantinople*. But whoever was the beginner of it, certainly the thing was not done without good advice; (h) *There being nothing more Powerful than melody, both Vocal and Inftrumental for ingaging the affections. Nor any thing wherein the Militant Church here on Earth, hath more refemblance to the Church in Heaven Triumphant, than in the facred and harmonious way of Singing Praifes, and Hallelujahs to our Lord God, which is, and has been long ufed in the Church of Chrift.*

I go not about to vindicate the abufes of this kind in after Ages, which ferved more to pleafe the *Ear* than help *Devotion.* The Ancients themfelves who practifed, and recommended this Cuftom of the Church had too often reafon to complain, and caution People what to do in it. God regardeth more the *affection of the Mind*, (i) as St. *Jerom* fpeaks, *Than the fweetnefs of the Voice*. (k) The Praifes and Hymns moft grateful to him, are not

---

(h) *Heylin.* P. 2. c. 5. § 12. (i) Ep. 4. aJ Ruftic. (k) De plant. Noæ.

such as an *Obstreperous Voice* sounds out, as what proceed from an *invisible* and *pure Soul*. So *Philo*. And therefore St. *Augustine* reflects on the *Donatists*, for singing Psalms of their own invention, and being *proud that they sung so well*. (*l*) And the same *Father* confesses with no little trouble, that he himself had *sometimes given more attention to the Notes, and Musical part of the Hymns sung in the Church than to the words and matter* ; which he thought a very great fault, and was much concern'd, that he, or any other should so much mistake the design of the Church in admitting these Notes, which was by this means to set off the matter of the Hymn, and not to make the Hymn for the sake of the Musick. This brought him one while to the Opinion, That the *Use in Alexandria*, under *Athanasius* appear'd safer, when the Minister was required so to order his Voice, that of the two it should more incline to *reading* than *singing*, and be rather *graceful* than *harmonious*. Yet he owns withal, he could not but approve the Custom of singing in the Church, *That so through the pleasure of the Ears the feeble mind might be raised up to an higher pitch of Piety*. However we find they went too far, more time and pains being spent in these composures than the Church at first intended ; (*m*) and at length the *Clergy* themselves became so busy and vain in it, that it gave great offence and (*n*) occasioned *Gregory the Great*, to prescribe [*Simplicem cantionem*] plain *singing* : And the *subject* to be (*o*) from *Scripture* ; And the form of words out of the Book of *Psalms*: And the *Organ* to be play'd to no other than these, and

---

(*l*) Confess. l. 19. (*m*) Vid. Zonaram in Can 22. Concil. Laod. (*n*) Greg M l 4. Ep 44. (*o*) *Extra Psalmos V. T. nihil poetice compositum in Ecclesia psallatur.* Concil. Bracar. l. Canon 30.

with

with such sounds and notes as became the *gravity of God's Service,* (p) Lest instead of Devotion it might be the cause of some other Passion———The fault of the latter Ages, and what is done commonly in the Church of *Rome,* is thus described, by *Cornelius Agrippa, The Musick and Anthems of the Church now,* saith he, *serve rather to excite lust than elevate the Soul of the Votary, while they sing out the Service, not so much with humane Voice as that of Beasts.* (q) *They bellow out the Tenour, bark the Counter point, roar the Treble, and grunt the Bass*———*i. e.* The strains are so different and surprizing, that what with the *shrilness* of some parts, the *hoarseness* of others, and *hideousness* of the whole, the Ears are possest with such violence and tumult, as serve only to distract the *Brain,* but ingage not the *Heart,* and in a word contribute to the hearer no benefit at all.

B. I am of his mind ; For I cannot see what benefit can be reaped from these *unintelligible sounds,* or what help they can administer to *Edification.*

A. 'Tis true ; If by *Edification* you mean the *Improvement of Knowledge,* and that the Understanding is thereby bettered, in this case *Musick* doth not *edifie,* because it doth not *teach.* Yet it cannot be said to be *unprofitable,* especially in Devotion, because it worketh on the *affections,* and makes Men more active and vigorous in expressing the matter of the Service. The reason before given, why it is thought most expedient to use a form of Words in our Prayers and Praises to God, is, because then we have nothing to do, but to apply our affections to what we are saying ; and if a

---

(p) *Ne lasciviam magis quam devotionem excitet*———Durant. de ritib. Eccl. Gath. l. 1. c 13. (q) *Hinniant Discantum, mugiunt tenorem, latrant Contrapunctum, boant Altum, frendent Bassum*———De Van. Scient.

Prayer be not *Zealous*, 'tis no Prayer at all, for that is a *Zealous Prayer* which is *affectionately* offered. So that any thing which will help to raise these affections in Prayer, must needs be understood to be a necessary adjunct of it; and he that denies *Musick* this effect, runs counter to the received Opinion, and common sense and experience of all Mankind. (*r*) *Plato* affirms, it penetrates to the most inward parts and recesses of the Soul; *Athenæus*, that it Charms the Mind; *Others* that there is no disposition or habit of the Soul, but what it manages and rules. And hence it is that *Pythagoras* judged the *Soul* it self, to be no other than *Harmony*, or as *Aristotle* speaks, of *near kin* to it. And certainly the force of it is such, and so pleasing effects it hath on that part of Man, which is the most Divine, that many have thereby been induced to think, that the Soul it self by Nature is or hath in it Harmony. (*s*) So *Cicero.* (*t*) *The reason hereof is*, saith *Mr.* Hooker, *That admirable facility Musick hath, to express and represent to the mind more inwardly than any other sensible means, the steps and inflections, the turns and varieties of all Passions which the mind is subject to.* And of this we have no better proof than that of our daily experience, when we find ourselves differently moved according to the *Musick* we hear. (*u*) *For some sorts of it settle the affections and others stir them, some render us grave, heavy and melancholy, others quick, brisk and aery, and put us in a kind of ecstacy, filling*

(*r*) De Rep l 3. (*s*) *Aut animam esse harmoniam, aut harmoniam habere.* Tuscul. Qu (*t*) *Omnes affectus Spiritus nostri prasuavi diversitate habent proprios modos in voce atq; cantu quorum occulta familiaritate excitantur.* Aug. Confess. l. 1c. Tho 22. Q 91. Art. 2. (*u*) *Ea vix est sonorum ut animum concitatum tranquillent, alii torpentem excitent & rebus magnis praparant;* &c, Horn. in Sulput. Sev, l 1.

the

*t*he mind with raptures of joy, and for a time, in a manner severing it from the Body. So that though we altogether set aside the consideration of the matter of what is play'd or sung, the very harmony of sounds fitly framed and convey'd from the Ear to the Spiritual faculties, is by a native puissance and efficacy greatly available to bring the Soul to a perfect temper in case of disturbance, compose and quiet all the disorders within; and as on some occasions it quickens the Spirits, so when too eager and violent it serves to allay 'em.

Thus it is said of *Clineas* the Pythagorean, that when he was angry he would always go and play on his Harp to subdue the fierceness of his mind. And it was the ordinary Custom of that Sect before they went to sleep, to take that or some *other Instrument* to compose the mind, in case any thing had happen'd to puzzle or disorder it. (*w*) The same means *David* used to recover King *Saul* to his right mind, and chase away the *Evil Spirit*, which being fundamentally nothing else but a *sowre* and distracted temper of mind (*a*) arising from *Melancholy*, grief and malice, wherewith he was at that time vexed, the proper cure of it was the *Harmony* and melody of *David's Musick*, which was therefore made use of to compose his mind, and to allay those turbulent Passions. But we have a very remarkable example of this kind in *Elisha*, when *Jehosaphat* came to him, and brought *Jehoram* with him, whose sight put him into such a fit of Passion, that he delivers himself thus, (*b*) *As the Lord of hosts liveth before whom I stand, surely were it*

(*w*) 1 Sam. 19.9. (*a*) *Hebræi, Josephus, Cajetanus, Delrio censent fuisse atram bilem sive melancholiam & μανίαν quæ in Saulo causabatur suspiciones, invidiam, mœrorem, furores, deliria*————*Hornius loc cit.* (*b*) 2 King. 3. 15, 16.

not· that I regard the presence of Jehosaphat *King of* Judah, *I would not look towards thee and see thee*————
However in respect to him he resolves to answer 'em; But before he was able to act the Prophets part, he called for a *Minstril*; and *it came to pass when the Minstrel play'd, the hand of the Lord came upon him, and he said,* &c.————It may be demanded, why so great a Prophet of God, going about that grave and serious work of prophecy, should require so youthful an expedient to qualify him for it? But it seems, it was very requisite at this time; And the *Rabbins* in the general make a free, cheerful and generous Spirit so necessary to a Prophet, that it has commenced a Proverb with 'em, *That the Holy Ghost never abides with a melancholy Man ——The Spirit of Prophecy never rests upon any but one whose Passions are allay'd. ——The Spirit of Prophecy dwells not with sadness ——— Every Man when he is in Passion, if he be a Wise-Man, his Wisdom is taken away, if a Prophet his Prophecy ——When a Man is disturbed through Anger or Passion, the Holy Spirit forsakes him*———— And for the Proof of this, they propose the example of *Jacob,* who all the while he grieved for *Joseph,* the *Shechinah* or holy Spirit did forsake him ——— So they say of this Prophet, that from the Day that his Master *Elijah* was taken up into Heaven, the Spirit of prophecy remain'd not with him for a certain time, for for this cause he was very sorrowful, and *the divine Spirit does not reside with heaviness.* Likely it is, that the sight of *Jehoram,* an idolatrous Prince, did not a little inrage him, but yet the compassion he had for *Jehosaphat,* and the People of *Israel* with him, in so evident a danger, wherein the Enemies of God threatned 'em destruction, this consideration exceedingly grieved him. What then could he do better than to call for a *Minstrel* to moderate these different Passions, and by an expedient so agreeable
ble

ble to the Soul, reftore it to its proper and former calmnefs. And not only fo, but being reduced to its Natural temper, it was then difpofed for the reception of thofe Images which the
Bleffed Spirit was to make on his mind, the expreffing or outward declaring of which is what we
call *prophecy*.

Some fuch effect the *Mufick* had on that Company of Prophets, 1 *Sam.* 10. 10. whofe Spirits being by this means elevated; they did compofe Hymns upon the place, by a Divine energy
inwardly moving their minds. So that there were
Holy raptures in fome of 'em, which tran-
fported them beyond the ordinary Power of fanfie
or imagination, in dictating fuch Hymns as might
be fuitable for the defign of celebrating the Name
and Power of God. (*c*) And thus much the very
Heathens attributed to the *Mufick* of their Priefts,
whom they often look'd on as Men *infpired*, while
they were performing this kind of Devotion to
their Gods, which probably was by Satan, as
many other things in the *Pagan* Worfhip, taken
up, in imitation of thefe infpired Hymns, and
Mufick ufed *by the Sons of the Prophets*. 'Tis
true, their Hymns were fo compofed, as to be
fit rather to *tranfport* Men beyond the Power of
their reafon, than to *fettle* and *fweeten* it. So their
Io Bacche was full of noife and din; And the *Cory-
bantes* are defcribed like madmen, dancing about
with their Cymbals and Drums——yet this *En-
thufiafm* feem'd to have a Divine touch with it,
and to come near to a *Prophetick Spirit*. However,
it explains the Power of *Mufick*, to frame this capacity of mind, either by raifing the Spirits to an
higher pitch than they ordinarily have, or making

(*c*) *Stillingfleet*, Orig. Sacr. l. 2. c. 4. § 6.

'em

'em fitter to receive thofe impreſſicns, which fome Spirit from without is ready to give 'em. And if it was not the Spirit of God, it was their unhappineſs, as not knowing the true Religicn. In a word, the *Soul* depending much on the temper of the *Body,* it muſt needs be, that according to the *right compoſure* or *diſorder* thereof, a Man is more or leſs diſpoſed to and fit for Divine Offices; which the ſubtile adverſary well knowing, that he may hinder us as much as he can from the due performance of our Duties in the Service of God, complies with all *Second Cauſes,* to diſcompoſe us by ſundry Paſſions and Perturbations of Mind; and during theſe ſtorms we cannot ſteadily diſcharge our parts. (*d*) Now ſolemn *Muſick,* becauſe of its Native affinity with the Soul, excellently accommodates it ſelf, by calming and appeaſing the tumults and tempeſts thereof with a pleaſing allay, gently drawing it to a ſweet Mediocrity, and ſometimes carrying it above it ſelf in an holy Rapture and Ecſtacy, like St. *Paul* in the third Heaven, to the contemplation of unutterable things. How St. *Auguſtine* was touch'd with it, we have in his Confeſſions. *I have often wept at the Hymns of thy Church, and the affections of piety being thereby inflamed, my Tears ran down my Cheeks* —— The cauſe of which he gives (and *Aquinas* out of him) from the correſpondence and familiarity, there always is between *Muſick* and the *Soul,* the affections of the *latter,* being more or leſs ſtirred up in Proportion to the variety and ſweetneſs of the *other.* And immediately after, Anticipating the Objection ſome are apt to make from the *untelligibleneſs* of this Service, (*e*) *Though,* ſaith he,

---

(*d*) Dr *Reading*'s Sermon, on 1 King. 3. 15, 16. (*e*) *Eſi. non intelligunt quæ cantantur, in elligunt tamen propter quid cantantur —— i. e. laudem dei.* Conf. l. 10. c. 33.

ſome

some hearers should not understand those things which are sung, yet they do understand at least why they are sung, namely to the honour of God, and this is enough to stir up Devotion.

I omit the influence it has upon all Creatures in the World, of which the naturalists give us diverse instances, as of the *Bees* which come to it; of the *Arabian-Sheep* that grow fat by it, of the *Dolphins* that cannot resist its Charms, and are by that means taken. Nor do I insist on what *Macrobius* asserts, That it cures many *diseases* of the Body; and *Bede* particularizes, the *pain of the Heart* and the *Head ach*; *Athenæus* the *Sciatica*, and *Aulus Gellius* the *Biting of Serpents*. That lasting and formidable disease, occasion'd by the bite of the *Tarantula*, which often mocks all other remedies, is by nothing so successfully oppos'd as by *Musick*: (*f*) The use whereof is so great, that *Kircher* informs us that the *Apulian Magistrates* gave stipends at the publick charge to *Fiddlers*, to relieve the poor by their *Playing*. *Jamblichus* tells us, that a Young Man of *Taurominium* being got drunk, *Pythagoras* plaid him sober, by a few tunes of grave *Spondees*: Which is not incredible, because we know how *Musick* composes the distracted mind, and forms it to holy attention, as hath been seen in the sudden lucid intervals, and abundant Tears of *madmen*, hearkening a while to the Churches melodious Service.

: It is reported of (*g*) *Aldelmus*, who first brought

(*f*) Vid. *Boyle's* usefulness of Nat. Philoso. p. 2. Essay 5 c. 25. Aul. Gell. Noct. Att. l. 4. c. 13. *Ferocientes animos mollivit Pythagoras, seditiones accensas inhibuit Asclepiades, Damon ebrios ac petulantes juvenes ad modestiam reduxit; lymphaticos morbo liberavit Xenocrates*——Hortius supra. (*g*) Lord *Clarendon's* survey of the Leviathan, out of *Harpsfield* Eccl. Hist. of *England*.

in ufe the compofition of Latin verfe into *England*, that befides his Eminent *Piety* he had fo great a faculty in *Singing*, that by the *Mufick* of his Voice he wrought wonderful effects upon the barbarous and favage humour of the People, in fo much as when they were in great multitudes engaged in a rude and licentious action, he would put himfelf in their way and fing, which made 'em all ftand ftill to liften ; and he fo captivated them by the melody, that he diverted 'em from their purpofe, and by degrees got fo much credit with 'em, that he reduced 'em to more *Civilty*, and inftructed 'em in the Duties of *Religion*, into which though they had been baptized, they had made little enquiry. *He* lived a little before the time of *Edward the Confeffor*, and the general teftimony of the fanctity of his Life, and fome miracles wrought by him (which it may be were principally the effects of his *Mufick*,) being related and believed by *Lanfranc* Archbifhop of *Canterbury*, he was admitted for a *Saint*. But enough of this. All I intend, is to fhow the Power *Mufick* has over the *Paffions* of Men. And this I take to be the moral of thofe fabulous ftories concerning *Terpander*, *Amphion*, *Orpheus*, *Arion*, &c. who are faid to tame WildBeafts, *i.e.* the unruly, brutifh affections of humane Nature, which being overcome by the fweetnefs of their *Melody*, they were managed as thofe Mafters pleafed, who thereupon reduced 'em to *Civility and Good Manners*. Neither am I fo much for all *Mufick*, but that chiefly which anfwers the end we defign by it, and which *Ariftotle* calls ἠθικὴν; *Boethius*, *Lydiam*, and others ftrictly ἁρμονίαν, fuch as *Elifha* is fuppofed to ufe, when he invited the *Spirit of Prophecy*, and was plaid by *David* before *Saul*, to drive away the *Evil Spirit* which troubled him. And of which fort was the *Church Mufick* of the Primitive Ages, fitted to

quiet

quiet the Paſſions and raiſe Devotion, that Men being taken by the *Ears* might be conducted at laſt
to the Heavenly Choire of Saints and Angels, and
there enjoy God and Eternal Glory.

I hope it cannot be ſaid, but that our *Muſick*
is *grave* and ſober, (*b*) ſuch as Queen *Elizabeth* who
was no enemy to the *proteſtant Religion* appointed
to be uſed. And therefore methinks, we ſhould
not be ſo forward to quarrel with a Church,
whoſe meaning is *& Delectare, & Prodeſſe,* as
the Poet ſpeaks; and gives us a convenient intermixture of *Pleaſure* and *Profit,* which is, looked upon as the higheſt teſtimony of humane wiſdom and
good contrivance. Nay St. *Baſil* places it higher (*ɩ*) "For whereas the Holy Ghoſt ſaw, that
"Mankind is hardly drawn to vertue; and that
"Righteouſneſs is leſs eſteemed by reaſon of the
"proneneſs of our affections to what is delightful,
"it pleaſed the wiſdom of the ſame Spirit to bor-
"row from melody that pleaſure, which mingled
"with Heavenly myſteries cauſeth the Smooth-
"neſs and ſoftneſs of that which touches the Ear,
"to convey, as it where, by ſtealth, the trea-
"ſure of good things into mans mind. To this
"end were thoſe Harmonious tunes of *Pſalms* deviſ-
"ed for us, that they who are either young in
"Years, or not grown ripe in the perfection of
"vertue, might at the ſame time they think they
"Sing, be alſo inſtructed. O the Wiſdom of that
"Heavenly teacher, who hath by his Skill, found
"out a way, that doing thoſe things, wherein
"we take pleaſure, we may alſo learn the things,
"which are uſeful.

(*b*) Injunctions, anno 1559. N. 49. (*ɩ*) In Pſalm.

I have no inclination to make reflections; and therefore will not venture to say, (*k*) That *he who is not delighted with Musick, is not regularly made,* but is either Senseless, or has a very disorderly and unquiet Spirit. I say only this, that tho' we have indeed some little *Musick* in our Churches, yet the places are very *few*, in Comparison of those, which have nothing but *plain Singing,* when the Prayers are over, and so may be well left to such persons who find themselves edified by it, and rendred more Spiritual, Lively and Cheerfull during the holy action. If all are not of this mind, yet, as our Church speaks, let us all follow the rule of Charity, prescribed by the Apostle, (*l*) *That they who use this way of Worship despise not them who use it not, and that they who use it not, condemn not those that use it.*

B. Well, Sir, I am so far satisfied with what you have said, that I wish the *Lord's-day* was spent in no worse manner than you have described the Service of it. But alas we find it otherwise; And as there is a general neglect in doing the *duty* of the *day* among most People who yet bear a Christian name, so I think, in particular, none more faulty in this respect than those of the Church *Communion,* and great *abetters* of the *Liturgy.* Not that *Charity* will allow me to believe them naturally more irreligious than others, but this indifferency is much owing to the Doctrines of your *Church-Men,* who not only *tolerate* but vigorously *defend* almost all sorts of *recreations*, and thereby draw the minds of Men from that veneration which is due and ought to be given it. And truly the notion of *Holiday* now is, that it is a *day of idleness*

(*k*) *Harmonia qui non delectatus est non est harmonice compositus* ——— Ficinus. (*l*) Canon —6. 1640.

and

and vanity ; a *day* set apart either for a literal *rest*
and doing nothing, or doing what ought not to be
done, and which People have not leisure to do on
any other. Great pains some *Bishops* and other
Doctors have taken to justifie a practice, which
by all their industry and learning they should
have put a Check to. But that which did the
most mischief was the *declaration of Charles the
first.* Wherein he Commands all the judges in
their several circuits to see that *no man trouble or
molest any of his Loyal Subjects and dutiful people in or
for their lawfull recreations, having first done their duty
to God, and continuing in obedience to him and his
laws;* and further, that *publication thereof be made
by order from the Bishops through all the parishes of
their several Diocefes respectively* ———— You find
what followed. And God only knows how
it is to be understood, and whether it was not
one sign of the divine displeasure to let the People be permitted to take so much liberty against
that excellent prince for giving them leave to
do as they did on that *Solemn day* assigned to his
worship.

'Tis true the Sabbath in strict translation is a
day of rest : but then as *(m) Chryfostom* explains it,
'tis no otherwise so, than as it rids us of the care of
temporal matters, that so there might be no avocations and interruptions to hinder us in our *Spiritual*
———— And to the same purpose *(n) Athanasius,* that
*the Sabbath no further fignifies rest, than as thereby
we are lead to the Knowledge of the Creator, which
Knowledge is more neceffary than our rest, neither are
we to rest for any other end*—— And yet in good truth,
to my thinking, bare *rest* would be much better
than the other abuses of the *day* ; and 'twere safer
to erre in the defect of not honouring the Lord,

(m) Homil de Lazaro. (n) De Sab. & Circum.
which

which might be Charged on infirmity, than active-
ly to dishonour him by forbidden *pleasures*, which
is a piece of presumption and too plain an overt-
act of inward *Atheism*, and tempts others to follow the example. If you say the express Words
of the precept is, *Thou shalt do no manner of work*;
————— This puts me in mind of an Ancient-Law
which prohibited *wooll* to be carried out of *Taren-
tum*; and to evade this law they carried the *sheep*
but were punished as transgressors, because he that
conveyed away the *sheep*, carried off the *wooll* by
consequence; (o) And *that which is forbidden one
way, we cannot come to it another*. Without doubt
the design of the fourth Commandment in forbidding all sorts of Common work, was that thereby
the People might have leisure and opportunity to
do the work of the Sabbath, that is, to meditate
on good things and mind the business of religion.
Whatever therefore hinders this design is under
the notion of *work*, altho' we give it another' name:
(p) And as for *recreations* which those *Apologists*
seem so much for, they appear to me greater
violations of the Divine Law than that which is
named and forbidden, because *work* in itself is not
only necessary for our present being, but some
Kind of honour redounds to God by it in case we
consider and declare ourselves the instruments
of his providence in what we do for the support of
ourselves and families. Whereas these Sports do
not only alienate the mind from those Heavenly
thoughts they should on this day be employ'd in,
but they often prove sinful in the very act and the
end is dismall.

(o) *Id quod non fieri potest directè, ex obliquo fieri non
debet*————Reg. Jurif. (p) *Vid. Stillingfleet's Ireniscum*
P. 1. Ch. 5. Sect. 4.

A. The

A. The *doctrine* of our *Church* is as found for obferving the *Lords-day* as you would have it. And as the *Laws* of our Nation punifh offenders of this kind, fo the *Ecclefiaftical Decrees* and Conftitutions ordain and teach that it ought to be folemnly kept by all her Children, as you have heard at large before. And as for particular Doctors, tho' of venerable Authority, yet their writings are no further accounted the doctrines of the Church than as they agree with thofe *Canons* and *Homilies* mention'd above. However as to thofe *Gentlemen* you point at, the *End* they propofed in what they faid on this Subject was to encounter *Judaifm*; Not by any means to encourage *prophanenefs*, but to ftop *fuperftition.* The main thing they drove at was, to difprove the *morality* of the fourth Commandment with refpect to that form of Words in which it is there fet down, and to fhew that tho' by the *Laws* of *God* and *Nature* a *Set time* was to be fequeftred for the Divine Worfhip, yet the Determination of *that time,* and the Modes of that *worfhip* was left to the Church and the Wifdom of thofe under whofe Government we live. This, I fay, was what they chiefly intended; And then the confequence which they proceeded to was, that *recreations* on that day were no Sin, provided they were not inftances of difobedience to our Superiors either with reference to *themfelves,* as lawful, or *thofe hours* alotted for 'em. *Some diverfions* are indeed *immoral* and vicious, and *thefe* ought not to be ufed on *any day,* much lefs on Sunday. *Others* have not *naturally* this contagion, yet may be *unlawful,* either becaufe the *Magiftrate* forbids 'em, or forbids 'em to be ufed at *this* or *that time*: and even *thefe* are *finful,* becaufe we difobey our *Governors* who require us to forbear 'em. But there are a *third fort* innocent in themfelves, as *Walking in the fields* or difcourfing with men of liberal Education and

legally

legally inoffenſive, as refreſhing the body and leaving little impreſſion on the mind, and ſuch King *James* I. declares *dancing, archery, leaping, vaulting* and the like to be, and which thoſe Authors, you mean, allow Youth, ſo far forth as they make 'em *(q) fitter for Gods ſervice the reſt of the day, and for the works of their vocation the reſt of the · week.* As for King *Charles* I. it appears plainly by the laws he made for keeping the *Lords-day*, that he had a very pious inclination to have it reverenced by all his People. But ſome *over-righteous* and nice *Miniſters* both in the Church and State, *miſtaking* the meaning of thoſe *Laws*, and putting a greater reſtraint on People than was intended at firſt, He ſets out that *Declaration*, you ſpeak of,. for the Eaſe of the Subject, to let him enjoy himſelf as far as Religion and the Statutes of the Kingdom permitted. And I queſtion not, but as this *Declaration* was no more than a *Second Edition* of what his Father had iſſued out before, ſo probably the reaſon was the ſame, Not only to put a ſtop to *Judaiſm*, but to countermine *Popery* which on this occaſion began to encreaſe becauſe of the preciſeneſs of ſome in power who, throughout ſeveral places of this Kingdom, hindring People from their innocent diverſions on *Sunday*, the *Papiſts* among us were thereby made to think that our *Religion* was *Sowre* and ſullen, and ſo not only refuſed to come over to us, but on the account of this rigour tempted others to renounce the *Reformation*. Which being noted by King *James* in his progreſs through *Lancaſhire* (a County abounding with thoſe of the *Romiſh* perſwaſion) he ſent out his *Declaration, That his good People after the DivineService ſhould not be diſturbed in · their lawful recreations·ſo as the ſame be had in due*

(*q*) Doctor *Saunderſon's* caſe of the Sabbath.

and

and convenient times without impediment or let of the *Worſhip of God.* Theſe as far as I can remember, were the words of the Declarations, "At his "[King *James*] firſt entry to this Crown and "Kingdom He was informed, and that too truly, "that his County of *Lancaſter* abounded more in "Popiſh recuſants than any County of *England*, "and thus hath ſtill continued ſince, to his great "regret, with little amendment, ſave that now "of late in his laſt riding throughout the ſaid Coun- "ty, he hath found both by the report of his Judg- "es, and of the Biſhop of the Dioceſs, that there "is ſome amendment now daily beginning, which "is no ſmall contentment to his Majeſty. The "report of this growing amendment among 'em "made his Majeſty the more Sorry, when with "his own ears he heard the general complaint of "his people, That they were barred from all "Lawful recreations and exerciſe upon the Sun- "day afternoon after the ending of all Divine "Services, which cannot but produce Two evils, "The One hindring the converſion of many whom "their prieſts will take occaſion hereby to vex, "perſwading 'em that no honeſt mirth and recre- "ation is Lawful or tolerable in the Religion the "King profeſſeth, and which cannot but breed great "diſcontentment in his peoples hearts, eſpecially of "ſuch as are peradventure on the point of turning--- "The Kings expreſs pleaſure therefore is, that "no lawful recreations ſhall be barred to his good "People which ſhall not tend to the breach of the "Laws and Canons of the Church———ſo as the "ſame be had in due and convenient time with- "out impediment or negleĉt of Divine ſervice. "Dated at *Greenwich May* 24 in the 16. Year of his "reign. Now ſaith his Son King *Charles*, out of "a like pious care for the Service of God and for "the ſuppreſſing of any humors that oppoſe Truth,

"and

"and for the eafe, comfort and recreation of his
" well-deferving People, his Majefty doth ratify
" and publifh this his Bleffed Fathers Declaration,
(r) *Octob.* 18· 1633. So that you fee in this the
reafons thofe *Princes* and *Divines* had to excufe
recreations on *Sunday* in the laft age. It was to
give a Check to the Errors of fome Preachers and
others then in being, whofe doctrines had fucceeded
better had not this *toleration* ftopt 'em. In difputes
and controverfies it is an eafie thing to ftrain a little too far, in oppofing an *Extreme* coming vio-
lently on us; (s) yet the Suppofition being true,
that the natural juftice of the Divine Law and
the pofitive precepts of Governors, commanding
no longer fpace of time for actual performance
of religious offices upon the *Lords-day* than 'fuch as
is both neceffary for God's folemn Worfhip and
for the fpiritual Edification of Chriftian People,
when that time is expired and the fervice over, if
Men for the refrefhment of their Spirits, betake
themfelves to thofe exercifes as the Law either
expreffly or filently allows, *thofe writers* cannot be
fo much blamed to let us both fee and enjoy our
Liberty (efpecially as their cafe then was with
refpect to the obligation of the fourth Commandment and *Sabbatarian Doctrine*) and if they produced many Authorities ancient and modern to
confirm the practice, it was not with defign to introduce *one Error* by baffling *another*, but to ftate
rightly and make good the queftion then no foot,
and to demonftrate that the Law of the two
Tables was fufficiently obferved, as long as nothing was done to injure it in its *Equity.* How-

---

(r) *Rufhworths* Collections. (s) *Bifhop* of *Ely* on the Sabbath.

ever

ever the Cafe is now altered; And as the *Conſti-* *tutions* of this Church and the *Laws* of the Nation are very ſtrict for the honour of God (and if not executed by thoſe to whoſe care they are intruſted, they muſt not bear the blame:) So neither *preſs* nor *pulpit* afford us any thing but what correſponds with 'em. And our *Miniſters* both in their *Writings* and *Sermons* are ſo tender in the [*caſus reſervati* or] *reſerved caſes* of neceſſity and charity, (which as *Tertullian* ſaith are rather the Works of God than *Man*) and ſo wary in explaining the *exceptions*, for fear they ſhould be ſtrained too far by People who are willing to indulge themſelves, and comprehend almoſt every thing with the Romaniſts *in ordine ad ſpiritualia*, that ſurely they cannot be ſuſpected to give 'em any incouragement for the neglect of this *day*, which in my hearing they have often threatned with the Vengeance and wrath of God.

B. I muſt confeſs I have heard many zealous diſcourſes on that ſubject, and it has exceedingly pleas'd me to find our Teachers ſo warm in their Maſters cauſe. Particularly the laſt *Lords-day*, after our *Paſtor* had explained the *notion* of the Chriſtian Sabbath (which has occaſion'd this trouble I have all this *week* put you to) he came at length to the *applications*, which were ſo pious and affectionate, that they eaſily made their way into my heart, and I hope, through Gods mercy, I ſhall never forget 'em. The drift of his words was *ſatyrical* enough and full of cenſure on our omiſſions this way; but his Language was *kind*, *ſweet* and *mannerly*, and his reproof was clothed in ſuch *paſſionate expoſtulations*, as at once both *chid* and *pleas'd* his Auditory. He demanded in the name of God, why they would be ſo ungrateful to the divine Bounty, who had reſerved to himſelf, ri-

gorouſly

goroufly speaking , but the *(t) seventh* part of time , when he might have justly claimed the *Whole,* or that proportion at least which he had given them for the concerns of this Life. He ask'd 'em, how they could carry themselves with somuch imprudence, as to let so strong an Evidence of an ill Principle escape 'em, of being so lavish of what was not *their own,* and thereby convince the World, that surely such Men must needs have very little *honesty* and *justice* (and consequently small confidence or trust to be put in 'em) who in this remarkable manner robbed God of his due, a God so *liberal,* so *good,* and withal so *wise,* that he cannot be over-reached by any of our pretences and so *powerful,* that his displeasure must needs be terrible. He desired to know, why of all the Days of the Week, *this* was pitch'd upon to begin a *journey,* and (as some prophanely abuse the Devotion of the Church) give this reason, because on the *Lord's-day* they should in all likelihood have better success, and more safety on the account of those Prayers, which the Congregation are then obliged to offer to God in behalf of them, *who travel by Land or by Water,* whereas the intercession means only *such* Persons who do it by *necessity* and constraint, which cannot be their *Plea,* who without this warrant act presumptuously and travel on this day otherwise, as they think, lost to 'em. He required a reason why this Day was set apart for the taking of *Physick,* which as it is mostly in its own Nature a *qualified poyson,* so it must prove Poison to the Body without God's Blessing, and they took an odd way to invite him to bestow it. He admired how they could so far mistake the notion of the Day, as to

---

(t) *Si voluisset deus absolutè uti dominio suo, potuit plures dies imperari cultui suo impendendos* —— Rivet Exod. 20.

ſleep out ſo much and *idle away* the remainder of it, as if they were not to be diſtinguiſh'd from the common *Beaſts* which do *reſt* that Day, partly to recover their ſtrength for the, following *ſix*, but chiefly that their owners might have leiſure to ſerve their great Creator. But his Blood roſe at the naming of them who *prophaned the day*, with thoſe *Vices* and *exceſſes* which became *no Day* and no Chriſtian, ſuch as *drunkenneſs*, *revelling* and the like. And when he had gone thro' theſe and ſome other Particulars, he put us the Queſtion how we would reliſh this behaviour from one of our own Servants, when we had furniſh'd him with ſufficient liberty and plenty, on condition that within the compaſs of ſo much time, he ſhould take care to ſeparate a very ſmall proportion to do us Service in, yet not only neglects the preſcribed Service, but every way defies and diſgraces us. I need not tell you, ſaith he, that we would take it very ill; and therefore let me beſeech you to bring it home to yourſelves, and conſider your Lord and Maker. The caſe is not indeed *Parallel*, goes he on, for what compariſon is there between *God* and *Man*? Yet thus we deal with God, though a Servant muſt not ſo deal with his *Maſter* or *Miſtreſs*. After this turning his diſcourſe from ſuch People who groſly *abuſed* the Day, to thoſe who make a ſhew of *keeping* it, he again expoſtulated, Whether their attendance at the publick Worſhip was out of ſerious intent to ſerve and honour God, or out of temporal and carnal ends? Did they not come rather to *ſee* and be *ſeen*, and uſe the Church as an opportunity either to ſhow their own Pride, or to diſcover how others expreſt it. Was it not to hear *News*; to pleaſe curioſity; to meet Friends and in order perhaps to tranſact ſome Worldly buſineſs? Was *Religion* any more than a *Collateral*, or *Secondary* motive for what they did, a reaſon to be given by the *Mouth*, but

but was the *Heart* intereſſed in it ? The humour of rambling abroad to *other. Churches,* ſaid he, and the partial coming to our *Own,* upon the rumour of *this* or *that* Man's Preaching, are too viſibly o-vertaɛts of our mind in this matter, and declare loudly enough that we have only the *form of Godli-neſs and not the Power*; or ſay rather, neither the *appearance* nor *reallity* of it.   In fine, he ſhew'd all parties the danger of abuſing the *Lord's-day,* and then, concluded with an affeɛtionate exhortation, back'd with a ſhort Prayer to God for his Grace to inable us all to ſpend it better for the future.

A. I am glad you have ſo ready a proof of what I have been propoſing.   The account you give of it invites me to preſent you with the ſight of an *Office ,* or a *Collection of Prayers* and directions made by a Friend of mine, calculated for the *Lord's-day,* and whereby we may be ſaid to ſpend the day, well , if we piouſly and carefully uſe it.   I will only read to you the *Rubricks* or Heads of it, which if you like I will lend it you home for ſome time to peruſe and conſider the Body of It.

The

The OFFICE.

At Waking, he saith,

Lighten mine Eyes, O Lord, that I sleep not in Death, O Blessed Saviour, who hast taught me that the Dead shall hear thy Voice, let me no longer lie in the Grave of sloth, but raise me as thou didst thy Servant *Lazarus*: Unbind my Hands and Feet; Set me in some good way, that I may glorifie thee, by serving thee this Day with a pure Mind and Humble Heart. Lord, as thou hast awaked my Body from sleep, so by thy Grace awaken my Soul from Sin; and make me so to Walk before thee this Day, and all the rest of my Life, that when the last Trumpet shall awake me out of my Grave, I may rise to the Life Immortal, through Jesus Christ. *Amen.*

At Rising.

IN the Name of the Father, Son, and Holy Ghost, I laid me down and slept, and now I rise again, the Lord sustaining me. Blessed be his Name, for ever and ever. *Amen.*

When Risen.

O Lord, by thy Mercy I am risen out of my Bed, where I might have slept in Death, but that Thou preserved'st me. Make it I beseech Thee a Resurrection to Grace in this Life, and to Glory in the Life to come, through Jesus Christ who Merited both for us. *Amen.*

At putting on Apparel.

CLoth me, O Lord, with the Ornaments of Thy Heavenly Grace, and cover me with the Robes of Righteousness, through Jesus Christ.

O my God, as I came into the World a Weak, Naked and Wretched Creature, so I continue still, if destitute of Thy Grace. Reach out therefore unto me the unspotted Robe of Thy Son's Righteousness; and so Cloath me with all the Graces of Thy Holy Spirit, that Thy Image may be daily renew'd, and Thy Name honoured by me for evermore. *Amen.*

At Washing.

O My dear Saviour, who hast opened a Fountain for Sin and for Uncleanness: Wash me throughly with those saving Waters, that being purified from the stains of Sin, and the guilt of my Natural corruption

corruption, I may with the more confidence draw near to thy Throne of Grace, and bow my self before thy Mercy seat.

O wash me throughly from my wickedness and cleanse me from my Sin: Make me a clean Heart and renew a right Spirit within me, a Spirit of cleaving stedfastly unto thee through Jesus Christ. *Amen.*

In his Closet.

O Most gracious God, whose Eyes have been open over me when mine were shut, and under the shadow of whose Wings I have past this Night in safety; I do with all possible thankfulness humbly acknowledge it, as thy great Mercy that thou hast not taken away my Soul this Night, as in Justice thou might'st have done, but hast given me respite and afforded me one Day more to call upon thy Name

O Lord, make me ashamed of my former unthankfulness, and wound my Heart with the consideration of my own dulness, whom so many favours have not wrought to more obedience: Give me Grace to confecrate this Day, and the rest of my Life, unto thy service, and to Redeem the time at least which I cannot recal.

And O thou, who turnest the shadow of Death into the Light of the Morning, inable me Powerfully to cast off all the Works of darkness, and to keep my Soul spotless and unblameable.

And as thou hast brought me to the comforts of this Day: So go along with me I beseech thee, through all the parts and minutes of my Life, that in all my ways being guided by thy Counsel here, I may hereafter be received into thy Glory, even for the Merits of my dearest Saviour Jesus Christ.

This Day by the Resurrection of thy Son my Redeemer, was made holy to us: Give me thy Grace, that I may keep it holy to thee, through Jesus Christ. And O gracious Jesu, since on this Day more especially, I am to humble my self at thy Feet, and to beg Mercy for my Soul, which ought to be dearer to me than a thousand Worlds. Be pleased not to suffer any Worldly Cares to divert or hinder me; Root out this Bed of Thorns, and Sow holy Thoughts instead of them. Let me not be like *Martha* troubled, about many things but fix me on the one thing needful, that so having chosen the better part, it may never be taken from me. Counsel me, govern me, lead me in the way I should go, or else I shall wander from thee into Infinite Errors!

O possess then all my bodily Senses, that my Sinful affections may find no place. Leave me no more to my own weakness whereof my frequent falls have given me many and sad Experiments.

Restrain

Reftrain thofe inclinations to which my Nature is chiefly prone, that their violence may never have Power over me to make me fwerve from thy holy will

Let not the corruption of thefe evil times prevail upon me, but keep me from the Flattering and lying Lips, the Prophane and Blafpheming Tongue; ftop my Ears and fhut up my Heart againft them.

Strike fuch an awful reverence into my Soul, that I may Watch over all my actions, and carefully avoid what ever may be dangerous to my felf, pernicious to others, or any way difpleafing unto thee, that fo living in thy fear I may die in thy favour, reft in thy peace, and reign with thee in thy Glory, world without end.

Or thus.

O Almighty and moft Bleffed God, Lord of Heaven and Earth, who makeft the out-goings both of Morning and Evening; By whofe alone bounty it is, that I have this Day added to my Life, and by whofe good hand upon me thy Creature, I am awaked out of my laft Nights fleep and being rifen prefent my felf before thee: I humbly bow to thee my knees, and therewith my Heart and Soul, and defire with all that is within me to adore thy Bleffed Majefty.

But moft unworthy, and of my felf moft infufficient, am I to perform unto thee any Worfhip or Service. What is duft and afhes (and fuch am I if I were innocent) to take upon me to fpeak unto the Lord? But, O God, I am a guilty Wretch, one whom it becometh to ftand afar off, and fhame covering my Face, to cry unclean, unclean. My Soul is naturally over run with Lufts, as with an Univerfal Leprofie: There is no found part in me. My Life is as corrupt as my Heart. My Childhood and Youth have not only been vanity, but Sin. I have done nothing elfe therein, but fulfill'd the defires of my Flefh and Mind. My corruptions have only grown with me: And my Sins fince become fo much the more Sinful, by how much the more knowledge I have had of thy Will, and Strength and Engagements to have performed it.

To this very Day, as indeed I ever have done, I daily break thy holy Laws in Thought, Word and Actions, by choofing what thou haft forbidden, and neglecting what thou haft Commanded. In all my ways I moft miferably Tranfgrefs. My very fleep it felf, O Lord, is not innocent. Nor is it thus only in the common, and more ordinary Actions of my Life. Thofe few good Deeds, which I do, have many, not only Infirmities, but Sins in them: And I have need to repent of my very Righteoufnefs.

Oo

Yet,

Yet, O Father of Mercies, thou art still kind to the unthankful and the evil. I acknowledge my self to have abundantly Experimented that gracious property of thine.

For notwithstanding my daily provocations against thee, thou still heapest Mercy and Loving kindness upon me. All my contempts and despising of thy Spiritual favours, have not yet made thee withdraw them, but in the riches of thy goodness, and Long-suffering thou still continuest to me, the offers of Grace and Life in thy Son.

And all my abuses of thy temporal Blessings thou hast not punished with an utter deprivation of them, but art still pleased to afford me a liberal portion of them. My Sins yesterday thou hast not repaid as, justly thou mightest, by sweeping me away with a swift destruction, and taking my Soul this Night from me, but hast spared and preserv'd me according to the greatness of thy Mercy.

What reward shall I give unto thee, O Lord, for all these thy benefits? What, O my God, am I able to offer thee? Yet let me say, Blessed be thy holy Name for ever. Let Heaven and Earth praise thee for all thy unspeakable Mercies. And be thou pleased to accept of that Praise, which thy Poor Servant, hereby returns thee (as well as he can for them all; and particularly for this last Nights refreshings,

together with the comfortable restoring him to the injoyment of Day) grant me thy special Grace, that I may spend my time to thy Glory, and may be all this Day long in thy fear. Keep me that I fall into no Sin nor run into any danger. And accept thou this my Morning Service, together with me, who here devote my self to thee, through my Saviour Jesus Christ, in whose name I further pray, as by him taught, when I pray, to say,

Our Father, &c.
Amen.

Then calling his Family together, he reads the Litany which he looks on, in it self a compleat piece of Devotion, inserting the Collect for the Day with the other two for peace and grace, which being over, he returns to his Closet, and bestowing some time in reading and meditation, he concludes with this Prayer.

O Lord, from whom the Preparations of the Heart are: The hour now draws near, which being holy unto thee, I am to spend in thy more solemn Worship. Let the effusions of thy Grace, both upon me and all the Congregation of thy People be very plentiful. Let my Heart be fixed, and none either vain or Worldly Thoughts lodge within

within me: Quicken me with thy holy Spirit that I may draw near unto thee with a true Heart, and be fervent in Spirit in thy Service; and with a good and honest heart receiving thy Word, may understand and keep it, and bring forth fruit with patience, and unto perfection. Remember thy Servants who are to difpence thy myfteries unto thy People: And efpecially him upon whofe teaching I am to wait. Pardon his frailties, open his Mouth, guide his Mind and Tongue, that he may deliver thy truths in the Demonftrations of thy Spirit: And let thy Work fo profper in his hand, that both he himfelf and we his hearers may be built up in our moft holy faith to the perfecting of thy Church, and the Eternal Glory of thy Name thereby, through our Lord and Saviour Chrift Jefus. Amen.

Going to the Church, he hath this fhort Ejaculation.

LOrd I love the Habitation of thy Houfe, and the Place where thine Honour Dwelleth——

Entring the Door, he faith.

HOW dreadful is this Place? This is none other than the Houfe of God, and this is the Gate of Heaven.

Getting to the Pew, he kneels and faith.

O Lord I am come into thine Houfe, even on

the multitude of thy Mercies, and in thy fear will I Worfhip thee; O Blefs me that I may; And grant that my attendance here may be for thy honour, and my own Salvation, through Jefus Chrift. *Amen.*

Before the fervice begins, while the Congregation is getting together, he either imploies himfelf in reading fome portion of the Bible, or in thefe Prayers.

O Lord God, I am come hither to Worfhip, to pray to thee. Stir up my Memory, to remember that Thou art prefent: Fix my intentions upon thee, upon thee alone: Awaken my underftanding, to confider what I am about, and who I am to fpeak to; But above all inflame my affections, that my Heart being fet on Fire with thy Love, my Prayers may participate of that fervency, and be accepted of thee for his fake, who came to fend this Fire on the Earth, even Jefus Chrift my Saviour.

O gracious Father, what thanks, what praife can I offer to thee for raifing me to this honour, of entring into thy prefence as a Son, and converfing with thee on the Earth, with the fame freedom, as the Angels do in Heaven. O grant me thy Grace, fo to make advantage of this Divine privilege, that my Sins may never make me forfeit it, but rather

ther

ther by a devout and humble ufe of it, acquire to my felf daily new degrees of thy favour, till thou haft brought me, thy unworthy Son to that incorruptible Inheritance, which can have neither increafe nor end

I confefs, O Lord, it is an excefs of boldnefs in me, that I fo poor a Worm, fo vile, fo contemptible a Creature fhould prefume to fpeak to thee: Yet be not angry with me for this; For it is not becaufe I value my felf more than *Abraham* did, (for if he were duft and afhes, what am I?) But becaufe I dare not undervalue thy Mercy, that I make my humble approaches to thee; Behold I am nothing in my own Eyes, O let me be fomething in thine: And difdain me not when I fpeak unto thee for Chrift his fake.

But O moft great God, what fhall I fay in thy prefence, when I pray to thee? By what title fhall I call thee? Or how fhall I fufficiently adore thee? If I ftile thee a Judge, I adore thy Juftice: If a Mafter I know my obedience: If I call thee my Saviour I acknowledge thy Mercy; whatfoever Name I ufe, I find caufe enough of reverence. And fince therefore now I appear before thee, to pay the tribute of Adoration, by a thoufand titles due to thee, let thy truth direct me, and thy Spirit guide me, that I may fo adore thee in Spirit and in truth, as thou requireft: And that all the inward facul-

ties of my Soul, may be fo many fiery Tongues to fet forth thy praife for evermore.

Moft mighty God, who haft not only permitted, but invited us needy and miferable Creatures, to prefent our Pititions to thee: Oh! Let me fet a true value on this moft ineftimable Privilege. I come unto thee, O Lord, as a worm to my Soveraign Maker; I come as an heinous Offender to a juft and fevere Judge: Let I pray thee my Addreffes in thy Houfe be with a reverence, fome way anfwerable to thine aweful Majefty; Give me an Hearty defire to pray, and fuch a pure intention and fixednefs of mind upon thee, that I may no more incurr the guilt of drawing nigh unto thee, with my Lips when my Heart is far from thee. But may fo ask that I may receive, fo feek that I may find, fo knock that it may be opened unto me; That fo from praying to thee here, I may be tranflated to the praifing thee Eternally in thy Glory hereafter, through Jefus Chrift our Lord

O Lord, who though thou Dwelleft not in Temples made with hands, yet haft promifed to meet and Blefs thy People, where-ever thou haft recorded thy Name; be pleafed to be gracioufly prefent to me thy Servant, and to the Congregation, which fhall here affemble themfelves this Day for thy Worfhip. Pardon every one, who hath not prepared himfelf himself according to the Preparation of the Sanctuary. Quicken us all for thy Name fake. Teach us to do thy Will, and build us up in our moſt holy Faith, through Jeſus Chriſt our Lord.

I am come, O Lord, into thy preſence upon Work, which no one hath more need to do than my ſelf. To conſider my ways, and repent of my Sins and turn to thee. But I have an hard Heart, not apt to relent; and dry Eyes, ſuch at leaſt which ſeldom ſhed Tears for my Sins; O that thou would'ſt bow thy Heavens and come down, and melt my Soul in ſuch Godly ſorrow which might Work repentance, not to be repented of. Open my Eyes and help me to ſee into my Heart. Bring my Sins to remembrance and ſet them in order before me, that an holy ſhame and confuſion may cover my face for them, and beholding my contrition may'ſt accept it, and both pardon me and aſſiſt me hereafter by thy Grace, that I may live more Godlily, righteouſly and ſoberly, in this preſent World, and attain unto Bleſſedneſs, with thy ſelf, in the World to come, through the Merits of Chriſt Jeſus, my Lord and Saviour.

O my dear and Bleſſed Saviour, who with ſo much zeal didſt drive out thoſe who turned thy Houſe of Prayer into a den of Thieves, clear at this time the Temple of my Soul; from vain and Sinful Thoughts, caſt out all wandering imaginations, leave nothing behind that may either diſturb or diſtract me in the performance of this my duty, that my Prayers may aſcend as the incenſe; And thy Grace, and Mercy may deſcend as dew to the ſaving of my Soul, and to the Glory of thy Name. *Amen.*

Service being begun, he leaves off his private Devotions, and joins with the Congregation, and as ſoon as the Miniſter Names the Leſſons, or the Epiſtles and Goſpels; He turns immediately to the places, and ſaith, as he always doth at home, when ever he applies himſelf to the Scripture.

OPen thou mine Eyes, O Lord, that I may ſee the wondrous things of thy Law.

O Lord give me a right underſtanding and an Heart to practiſe what I ſhall now read in this thy holy Book.

The Sermon being ended, if not prevented, by the Preacher, he ſaith,

GRant I beſeech, Almighty God, that the words which we have heard at this time with our outward Ears, may through thy Grace be ſo grafted inwardly in all our Hearts, that they may bring forth in us the fruit of good living, to the honour and praiſe praife of thy name, through Jefus Chrift our Lord. *Amen.*

If it be a Sacrament day, before he comes to Church to his other Devotions he adds this Prayer.

O Father of Mercies, who from the beginning haft been in Chrift, reconciling the World to thy felf, and to infure as well as compleat this reconciliation, haft called the Faithful to the Communion of the Body and Blood of thy Son, that true Paffover who tafted Death for every Man. With what holy hands, and pure and Heavenly heart, ought I to receive this food of Life which comes down from Heaven? Yet, Lord, how vile and polluted am I? My very preparations need Repentance, and my Tears forrow. And befides the infufficiency of my Repentance, which I befeech thee in the Blood of Jefus to Pardon, I have other miferable defects and diftempers, which, Lord, if thou wilt not remove, I am like to bring with me to thy Table. An exceeding dull Heart I carry very far from being unbroken for my Sins, unaffected too with that Zeal of Love, and thankfulnefs towards thee, of Charity and good will towards Mankind, which I ought to bring thither with me That truft and dependance which I exercife on thy Mercy in Chrift. I have reafon to fear may be too Prefumptuous. But, Lord, thou knoweft I have endeavoured to mourn

over and repent of my Sins: I have vowed to have refpect to all thy Commandments, and not to regard any iniquity in my Heart Thefe my vows of Holy Life, I have ready to feal at thy Table. O that thou by the Blood and Spirit of thy Son would'ft feal me to the Day of Redemption, pardoning all my paft Sins, and by the Power of thy Grace preferving me from future backflidings. Make this Bleffed Sacrament a Feaft of fat things unto my Soul. Vouchfafe me thereby larger communications of Grace and Comfort, than ever yet I received. And to that end at prefent thoroughly wafh me from the guilt of all my Sins in the Blood of my Saviour; from the guilt of all I know and have confeft, and from the guilt of all my fecret and unknown tranfgreffions.

O Lord, if there be any unfeen iniquity of mine, which is like to interpofe and hinder good things from me, reveal and difcover that to thy Servant, that by ferious repentance thereof, he may obtain the wafhing of it away, and may draw near with a true Heart fprinkled from an evil Confcience. And Lord let thy Spirit go along with me, impowering me from above, and at thofe inftants when I fhall receive that Bread of Life, and Drink of that Cup of the New Teftament in my Saviour's Blood, let my Heart fo relent for all my Sins, be fo inflamed
with

with fervour of Holy resolutions of Faith, Love, Gratitude
and moſt Chriſtian Charity,
that I may in nothing behave
my ſelf unworthily : Hear,
O Lord, and remember thy
Servant for good, through
that Blood which he longs to
be ſprinkled and ſatisfied with.
Amen.

*In the Church immediately
after Sermon, while the
non-Communicants are
going out, he kneels in
his Pew, and ſaith,*

ALmighty Lord, who
haſt of thine Infinite
Mercies vouchſafed to ordain
the Sacrament for a perpetual
Memory of that Bleſſed Sacra-
fice which once thou mad'ſt
for us on the Croſs; Grant
me with ſuch diligent remembrance, and ſuch due reverence
to Participate of that holy and
wonderful Myſtery, that I
may be made worthy by thy
Grace to obtain the vertue and
fruits of the ſame, with all the
benefits of thy precious Death
and Paſſion, even the remiſſion
of all my Sins, and the fullneſs
of all thy Graces, which I beg
for thy only Merits, who art
my only Saviour, God from
Everlaſting and World without end. *Amen.*

OLord, our Heavenly
Father, Almighty and
Everlaſting God, regard we
beſeech thee the Devotions of
thy humble Servants, who are
juſt going to thine Altar, to
celebrate the Memorial which
thy Son our Saviour hath Commanded, to be made in re-
membrance of his moſt Bleſſed
Paſſion and Sacrifice; that
by the Merits and Power
thereof, there to be now re-
pſented before thy Divine
Majeſty, we and all thy
whole Church may be made
partakers of all other the benefits of his moſt precious
Death and Paſſion, together
with his mighty Reſurrection
from the Earth, and glorious
Aſcenſion into Heaven, who
liveth and reigneth with thee
and the holy Spirit, ever one
God World without end.
Amen.

*The hurry being over, and
the way made clear,
he haſtens to the rail before the Table, and
kneeling down, ſaith,*

OMoſt Bleſſed Saviour,
who in the Bowels of thy
Mercy towards Mankind, didſt
not only offer thy ſelf a Sacra-
fice for the Sins of the whole
World, but didſt inſtitute
this Heavenly and holy Sacrament, as the means to convey
the benefits of thy precious
Death to all ſuch as with humility and repentance come
unto thee. I beſeech thee to
accept this my humble addreſs
who here preſent my ſelf a
woful Sinner, I confeſs, but
ſuch a one, who am heartily
ſorry for my Sins, and penitent for my Offences

Direct me therefore, O my
God, in this great action,
with ſuch a reverent and aweful

ful fear, that all the faculties of my Soul may be attentive rightly to apprehend, and joyfully to receive this wonderful Myftery of thy Body and Blood.

O my Lord, I am not worthy that thou fhouldeft come under my roof; let thy holy Spirit therefore before thy coming, prepare and drefs up a Lodging for thee in my Soul, cleanfing it from the Stains of Sin, and fuffering nothing to abide in it that may keep thee out; fo that being wholly poffeft by thee, all Sinful Thoughts and unclean Suggeftions, may not only prefently vanifh, but never find entrance more.

Grant this, O my Jefu, and fo this Day, receive me into thy favour, that I may with joy receive thee into my Soul, and being once united with thee, thy Grace may never depart from me; that fo thou maift live in me, and I in thee for ever. *Amen.*

At the Offertory, while the Minifter reads the Sentences, and the Church-Wardens gather the Alms for the Poor, he faith,

O Lord, whofe is the Earth, and the fullnefs thereof, I am willing to offer unto thee, out of what by thy gift and Bleffing I have, fome fmall teftimony of my thankfulnefs, and duty to be beftowed upon thofe wanting ones, whom thy Providence

has made the objects of our Charity; Be thou pleafed through the Blood of my Saviour to accept it and pardon all my vain expences.

And actually Offering, he filently faith,

BLeffed Jefu who didft accept the Poor Widows two Mites; Be gracioufly pleafed to accept this from thy unworthy Servant. *Amen.*

At the Confecration of the Elements he narrowly obferves every Paffage and Ceremony as having all of them their fignification and ufe.

And therefore when he fees the Minifter breaking the Bread, he remembers how Chrift's Body was torn with Nails on the Crofs, when he fees the Wine poured out, he calls to mind the fpilling of his Blood, and then confiders withal, that his Sins contribute to both. So that he finds by experience that the fight of thefe things worketh in him a great forrow, for thofe Sins, which caufed 'em, and that forrow begets an hatred and a firm refolution againft 'em for the future; and withal ingages him to thankfulnefs and Love, and perfwades him to exprefs it by an univerfal Obedience in his Converfation.

He obferves the People too, with what zeal and earneftnefs ness they take, and eat the Bread and take and drink the Wine. This to him signifies their particular laying hold on Christ by Trust and Faith; Their flying to and apprehending him as the means of their Salvation, and the pardon of their Sins tendered to them in this Blessed Sacrament, which ends in an holy Meditation.

Then he saith,

O Lamb of God that takeſt away the Sins of the World, grant me thy Peace.

O Lamb of God that takeſt away the Sins of the World, have Mercy upon me.

Grant me, gracious Lord, ſo to eat the fleſh of thy Son and drink his Blood, that my Sinful Body may be made clean by his Body, and my Soul waſhed, through his moſt precious Blood. *Amen.*

O Lord God, how I receive the Body and Blood of my moſt Bleſſed Saviour Jeſus Chriſt, the price of my Redemption, is the very wonder of my Soul, yet I firmly believe upon the words of my Saviour, that at this time they are graciouſly tendered to me; I am ſure it is ſo, though I diſpute not the manner: Lord make me a worthy receiver and partaker of all the benefits of this Bleſſed Sacrament. *Amen.*

Thou haſt ſaid, O my Jeſus, that he that eateth thy fleſh and drinketh thy Blood, hath Eternal Life.

Behold the Servant of the Lord, be it unto me according to thy word.

At eating the Bread, he ſaith,

BY thy crucified Body, O Jeſus, deliver me from this Body of Death.

Then he adds,

I Bleſs thee, O Father, for my Saviour and Lord, the Holy Jeſus. I adore thee O Lord Chriſt, with thy Eternal Spirit. I acknowledge and believe thy Body to have been Crucified, and broken by thy Father's Wrath for me; I beſeech thee, that through the ſame, this Body of mine may be ſealed to an Holy and Eternal Life; And withal I devote my ſelf to thee, by ſolemn vow, which by eating here at thy Table, I ſeal with all my Soul and ſtrength to ſerve thee all my Days. Let thy Grace, O Lord, be ſufficient for me.

At receiving the Cup, he ſaith,

BY thy Agony and Bloody Sweat, good Lord deliver me; O Let this Blood purge my Conſcience from
dead

dead Work, to ferve thee the living God.

Then Subjoins,

I Blefs thee, O Almighty Father, O Crucified Saviour, O Sanctifying Spirit, that my Soul is thus refrefhed I acknowledge and believe thy Blood, O holy Jefus, to have been fhed for my Sins; let it reit on me for Remiffion of them, and therein let all my Sins be wafhed away, and I fprinkled from all evil Confcience. Being now made clean, oh that I may Sin no more!

Moft Bleffed Redeemer, I do truly believe that thy Body was Crucified, and thy Blood was fhed out of thy Body, as verily as I have received this Bread, and this Wine fet a-part from the Bread. And that for the Remiffion of my Sins as well as any others: And I do believe alfo, that with this Bread and Wine I have really and Spiritually received thy precious Body and Blood, whereby my Sins are fully wafhed away, and my Soul purified and refefhed. This, O Lord, I believe, help thou my unbelief! *Amen.*

Lord, I have received the Sacrament of the Body and Blood of my dear Saviour. His Mercy hath given it me, and my Faith received it into my Soul. I humbly befeech thee fpeak Mercy and Peace unto my Confcience, and in-rich me with all thy Graces

which come from that precious Body and Blood, even till I be poffeffed of Eternal Life in Chrift. *Amen.*

Then giving way for others to come to the Rail, he retires to his Pew, and kneeling faith,

A Lmighty God, the Fountain of all goodnefs, from whom every good and perfect gift cometh, and to whom all Glory, and Honour fhould be returned, I do defire moft heartily to thank thee, for that thou haft vouchfafed to feed me, with the Spiritual Food of the moft precious Body and Blood of thy Son, our Saviour Jefus Chrift; and doft affure me thereby of thy favour and goodnefs towards me, and that I am a very Member incorporate in the Myftical Body of thy Son which is the Bleffed Company of all Faithful People; and am alfo an Heir through hope of thine Everlafting Kingdom, by the Merits of the moft precious Death and Paffion of thy dear Son, oh the height and depth of that unfpeakable Mercy of thine, who art pleafed to admit me a Sinful Wretch to have any part in thofe ineftimable benefits, which I have fo often defpifed and trampled under Foot. I am not worthy, O Lord, of that Daily Bread which fuftains the Body; but thou haft made me partaker of that living Bread, which came down from

from Heaven, which nourisheth the Soul, and of which whofoever eateth, shall live for ever: O grant that my Soul may relish this Divine Food with Spiritual Ravishment' and Love, great as the flame of Cherubims; and grant, that what thou haft given me for the Remiffion of my Sins, may not by any fault·become the increafe of 'em, that this holy Communion prove not to me the caufe of Judgment and Condemnation, but may fupport and preferve me in every Temptation; rejoyce and quiet me in every trouble, enlighten and ftrengthen me in every good Word and Work; comfort and defend me in the hour of my death, againft all oppofitions of the Spirits of Darkness, and further me in the attainment of everlafting Salvation, through Jefus Chrift. *Amen.*

O Lord, the only Spring and Fountain of all good, who haft this Day revived and quickened my poor Soul, by giving thy Self unto me after a wonderful way in this Bleffed Sacrament: I praife and glorifie thy Holy Name for this thine infinite Mercy; befeeching thee to Crown what I have begun by a continual fupply of thy Heavenly Grace, that I may never forget whom, or what I have received; but being purified by thy Blood, and ftrenthened by thy Body againft all future Temptations, I may conftantly run through all the parts of

an Holy Life to the poffeffion of thy gloriousKingdom, world without·end. *Amen.*

Worthy is the Lamb that was flain, to receive Power, and Riches, and Wifdom, and Strength, and Honour, and Glory, and Bleffing: Therefore Bleffing and Honour, and Glory and Power, be to him that fitteth on the Throne, and to the Lamb, for ever and·ever. *Amen.*

The remainder of the time, whilft the Minifter is giving the Sacrament to the reft of the Company, he fpends in faying the 103 Pfalm, and reading fome other parts of Scripture, or Book of Devotions, with Directions to an Holy Life, which he ufually carries in his Pocket, and at laft the Bleffing being given, he faith,

O Lord, pardon the wanderings and coldnefs·of my Affections and Heart in this thy Service; and deal with me not according to my Prayers and Deferts, but according to my Needs and thine own rich Mercies in Chrift Jefus, in whofe bleffed Name and Words I conclude thefe my imperfect Devotions and Prayers, faying,

Our Father, &c.

For thine is, &c. *Amen.*

Being

Being returned home, he re-
tires for a while into his
Closet, and meditating some-
time on what he had heard,
received and done in the
Church, he kneels and saith,

I Bless thee, O Lord, my
God, for the Comforts
of thy House, from whence
I now came; for thy awaken-
ing me to my Duty, for any
softnings of my Heart, and
sense of thy Love or hopes of
enjoying thee hereafter: Not
unto me, O Lord, not unto
me, who am a vain hard heart-
ed, sinful wretch of my self,
but to thy Holy Name be
the Praise. Now increase, I beseech thee, this thy goodness
to me, and confirm me in thy
Grace evermore: Let me grow
in the knowledge, fear and
love of thee; and any im-
pressions thereof, which I have
this day receiv'd, suffer me
not, to lose; but inable me
to bring forth Fruit unto Perfection, to the Glory of thy
Name, through Jesus Christ,
my blessed Lord and Mediator.
Amen.

My Soul and all within me,
blesseth thee, O Lord my God,
for that Bread of Life, and
Cup of Salvation, from which
I now come. What am I,
that thou shouldest feed me
from Heaven, and assume me
into so intimate an Union with
thine Eternal Son? I, who have
transgressed all thy Laws, a-
bused thy Mercies, slighted

thy Judgments; I who have
refused thy Calls, resisted thy
Spirits; broken all my former Covenants with thee:
What am I, that thou shouldest thus re-admit me into so
high a favour? It is, O Lord,
because thy Mercy is above all
thy Works, and the riches of
thy Grace most inexhaustible,
that Mercy and Grace I adore,
I admire; Oh, that I may e-
ternally magnifie! Nothing is
there, Lord, in me, but what
may provoke thy Wrath and
hinder my Happiness. How
gross were my unpreparednes-
ses for thy Table? How many
the wanderings, and how great
the dulnesses of my Heart,
even under my nearest ap-
proaches to thee there! These
may justly cause thee to hide
thy Face from me. And I cannot but bless thee, that thou
hast not more estranged thy
self, and instead of hopes of
thy favour, sent me home
with a sense of thy Wrath:
But, Lord, though I am not
worthy of those Joys and
Comforts of that hidden Manna, which thy choice and holier Servants taste, yet vouchsafe me this Benefit by the
Communion of the Body and
Blood of thy Son, that I may
receive such Grace and perpetual influences of thy Spirit,
as may enable me to perform
unto thee all my Vows; so
that I never, by revolting into any known Sin, unhallow
this Soul and Body of mine,
which the Body and Blood of
thy Son hath this Day Sanctified;

fied; but denying ungodliness and worldly Lusts, may live soberly, righteously, and godlily in this present World, and in that to come, obtain a blessed Resurrection, and some (though any means) share of an Inheritance with thy Saints in Light, through the Merits of my Crucified Saviour. Amen.

Then he goes to Dinner, and craves a Blessing on what he and his Family are going to eat: And according as the Company is, he has his [Menfarios Sermones] Table Talk on the Subject of the Sermon, or what the matter of the Meal may occasion tending to the Glory of the Creator.

Grace ended, he either pursues his Discourse as the Company invites him to it, or else composes himself

that the Meal being digested, he may be the more capable to discharge his Duty at the Evening-Service. The Bell Summoning him to Church, he goes and saith as in the Morning all the Prayers that are proper.

After Evening-Service returning home, he withdraws into the Closet for some time, to recollect what had been told him from the Pulpit; and giving God thanks as before at Noon.

Then calling the Family together, according to the advice of St. Chrysostom, St. Cyprian, and Origen, he makes them repeat what they can of the Sermon, helps their Memories and takes care to apply it, as they are able, and as he finds occasion.

THis being over, he proceeds to *Practice*; and his *Piety* being hitherto shown to *God*, he thinks it a Duty of near Kin to express *Charity* to his *Neighbour*; and this he doth two ways, either by *Visiting the Sick*, or by *relieving the Poor*. And if the same Party should happen (as it often falls out) to be both Sick and in necessity, then he concludes that such a ones Condition calls to him aloud for *double* Compassion and Care. If visited only with *Sickness*, then he thinks it expedient and seasonable to represent to him the gracious Design of God in sending this Affliction, which probably may be for a *Trial* of his *Patience* and Resignation to what *Providence* sends, and to work him to a persuasion, that whatever is done, is for the best; and that *God* being infinitely *wise* and *good*, has contrived and order'd it so, as a very proper means to benefit and save his *Soul*.

If he be a Man, whom he has observed to be *remiss* in his Duty, and regardless of God and his future welfare (in case his Condition will bear it) he puts such a one in mind of his former

mer neglects; admonifhes him to implore the Divine Pardon for the time *paſt*; and to put on holy Refolutions of taking up, and being better for the time *to come.* He tells him withall, that in all likelihood, this was the *caufe* of his illnefs, which God intended by way of *Summons* and *Alarm*, that the danger might reduce and ingage him to take refuge in that, which he had hitherto laid afide, *Repentance* and *Religion*.

If he be one who is found fenfible of all this already, then he imitates God's Example, *not to quench the fmoaking Flax, nor break the bruifed Reed.* Here he deals *gently* with him, commends and confirms him in his thoughts; perfuades him that God's end in this Sicknefs is anfwered; wifhes him to perfevere in the Notion he has got of the Divine Mercy, and conjures him when reftored to his former health and ftrength to make good thofe Vows of a *New Life*, which then he has, or ought to have made, *leſt a worfe thing fhould come upon him.*

Sometimes the Senfe of God's afflicting hand is drove too far, the *Rod* is turned into a *Scorpion*, and the Subtile Tempter difcovering an Inclination in the Patient, to be forry for his Mifcarriages and Sins, he *tranfports* a Pious thought, and makes it degenerate into *black Defpair.* So that, what at firft fet out for Mercy, is immediately forced back with the fad News of an *unalterable State*; that his Cafe will admit no pity; that his heart is hardened to impenitency; that he is already fentenced, and 'tis in vain to expect Pardon. Here my Friend thinks it enough to find the Perfon fo induftrious and curious to diffect the Sins he is chargeable with, and that the evil Spirit is fo active to abet and affift him in this melancholy work; for his part therefore he aggravates not; he accufes not; but if he allows the *leaſt* Sin to be *deadly without* repentance, fo he tells him the *greateſt* is pardonable He bids him remember, that he has an infinite Redeemer, whom he difgraces by thinking him unable to intercede with his Father effectually for him The fhedding of his Blood was price enough to ranfom Ten thoufand Worlds, for thefe have *limits*, but his Merits are *boundlefs* He fets before him *David's Adultery* and *Murder*; *Jonah's Difobedience*, and *Peter's Fall.* He cannot charge himfelf with Sins of this complexion; but if he could, *thofe* Men, thofe Sinners are faved, and he has the very *fame Saviour.* Thereupon he preffes him to anchor there; and though his *heart* condemns him, yet he must not forget that *God is greater than his heart*, and will imbrace the penitent Sinner. He exhorts him to fix his Eye on *Jefus Chriſt*; and if he doth not perceive the *Lord* prefently coming to him, it is becaufe he must call the more, *cry the louder* with the blind Man in the Gofpel: *Thou Son of David have mercy on me.* He tells him

him for his Comfort that his Remorse is one part of Repentance, but he must not stay there, and distrust the Almighty Goodness, whose *Grace* hath brought him thus far in his way, and who expects should pray, That he who has begun this Work in him would go further, and bring it in due time to a happy conclusion.

But if the Party has a greater sense of his *outward Pain*, than of the *Sin* which first caused it, and preferrs the ease of his *Body*, before the Peace of his Soul, and so repines and murmurs at his present Condition, then he judges it highly necessary to let him know, that what he now undergoes is far short of the Torments of the Damned; and for that reason, he ought not only to submit with Patience, but to be very thankful, that God so graciously sends *those* to put him in mind, and as it is to be hoped, to prevent the *latter*. It is not to be denied, but the Pangs and Tortures of a Fit of Sickness are very unwelcome to Flesh and Blood, sore Evils and heavy *Burdens* to those who are compelled to carry them. But would it not be a lamentable Instance of God's Favour, to let a Man be hurried to the other World, without the least Notice, without the shortest Opportunity to make his Peace with Heaven? These Agonies in Sickness are the Messengers of God to give him warning; and can he complain of a warning intended chiefly to keep him out of Hell?

Thus, and to this Effect, he discourses with his sick Brethren, according as he discovers the Temper of their *Mind*, and the State of their *Body*. And before he takes his leave, he earnestly desires them all to consult their *Minister*, who is an *Officer of God*, and who by virtue of that Office will be much more able to apply to their several Sores an effectual Cure.

If his Neighbour be *poor*, and such as he can go to, he lays before him the Uncertainty of Humane Affairs, and the common Events of Providence, which makes a Man a *Prince* to day, and to *morrow* a *Beggar*. Nothing, saith he, befalls us but by Divine Appointment; and therefore our wisest way is to relie on his Conduct, and be perswaded, that though our present Circumstances be very streight, yet God has something better in store for those, who humbly and patiently wait for it. However this is Matter of Comfort, that God has *two Places* to make his People happy in; and the *Poor* who has it not in *this World*, has a surer claim to the *other*, if they do not lay a block in the way, and render themselves incapable of what he intends them hereafter. *Blessed are the Poor*, saith the Gospel. Nor do their wants now contradict that saying, because their Names are already entered in the *Book of Life*, and 'tis but a little while, and they shall go to enjoy what this

Doctrine

Doctrine intitles them to. But then they muſt not be *par-tial*: They muſt remember the *intire* Qualification, *Bleſſed are the Poor* in *Spirit*. There may be *Pride* in *Rags*, and *Humility* in *Purple*. And to be *poor* and *proud* is a contra-diction too monſtrous to be reconciled —— For tho' God may be inclined to pity the Man, yet his Folly hinders it; and while his *Neceſſities* plead very powerfully in his behalf, his intolerable *Haughtineſs* diſobliges and forces God to let him continue in his low Condition. So that it ought to be the way of thoſe under Poverty to reduce their *Spirit* to their preſent *Fortune*, and be as humble in *Soul*, as they ſeem to be in *Eſtate* and *Body*; and then, beſides the many other Methods of Relief, this Frame of *Mind* will render their Caſe much more ſupportable. Thus, or after this manner, he applies himſelf to thoſe whoſe Loftineſs of Temper within is above the Senſe of their Wants, and will ſuffer rather than ſpeak out their Neceſſities, tho' loud enough in all reſpects, but from their own Mouths

But if their *Reſervedneſs* and *Silence* proceed from another Principle; and that through *Baſhfulneſs* and *Modeſty* they conceal what they undergo: Here he ſuppoſes it better to em-ploy his *Eye* to diſcover what may be ſerviceable to 'em, and then take ſome opportuity to convey it for their relief with-out forcing a bluſh from 'em And ſo he doth in the Inſtance before; otherwiſe, perhaps, the Party had rather loſe the *Cha-rity*, than underſtand from whence it comes, and to whom he is beholden for it. In both which Caſes, he follows the Dire-ctions of the Goſpel, to make his *Charity* a 'Secret; *That ſo God who ſeeth in ſecret may reward him openly.*

Where *Poverty* is *clamorous* (as it too often happens) and that he finds the neceſſitous Man, either murmuring at *Provi-dence*, or cenſuring the unconcern and neglect of his *richer Neighbours* Firſt, He checks him for his Impiety towards God, and then for his own *Uncharitableneſs* to Man, which in Juſtice calls for the ſame Uſage from other People. And (ſaith he) the reaſon peradventure, why your Neighbours are not ſo kind as you expect, may be, becauſe they find you do not deſerve it, as being too rough and ſurly toward them And as for God's dealing with you after this man-ner, it ought to be remembred, that he could have made your Condition *worſe*, and can yet make it much more miſe-rable. If he has been pleaſe to uſe you no better, it is becauſe your Notion of him will not bear it; and of this you give too plain a demonſtration, in that you accuſe his Goodneſs and Wiſdom for not complying immediately with your expecta-tions, and indulging your humour. It concerns you to be

con-

contented with your *Station*, and that is a sure way to mend it; for if you show your self satisfied with whatever God doth, it will not be long but he will provide for you *better*. Admit you were under the *Widow*'s Case at *Sarepta*, when she had only a *handful of Meal* to dress and eat, and then expected to die, because of the Famine; do you not read that *the handful of Meal did not waste, nor the Cruise of Oil fail, until the day that the Lord sent Rain upon the Earth*——We have the same God, and he has many miraculous ways to increase the *Loaves*, and feed those who depend on him. But then they must *depend* upon him, acquiesce in his Methods, believe him willing and able to relieve them, only the time is not yet come with respect to *their Good* and *his Glory*.

There are *other poor*, whose mind he may have no Opportunity to settle with *Discourses* of this Nature, yet these he takes care to ease with his *Purse*, and lets his *hand* speak seasonable Comfort to them. But then by *poor*, he means such needy Persons, as he *himself finds out*, rather than such as *find out him*. Those whom *Sickness, multitude of Children*, or some *Crosses of Providence*, make all their Industry, Care and Labour not sufficient to feed them; Those who if able, are very willing to take pains, but either have not *Work*, or the *Pay* is too little to support them, *These* ought to be encouraged, and God sometimes makes use of our Mediation to give them a Blessing in what they do. But as for them who make Begging a *Trade*, and spend as much time in publishing their Wants, as might serve to relieve them if they would employ those hands in *Work*, which they stretch out to receive an *Alms* with, these Mens Necessities my Friend suspects, at least thinks himself not much obliged to take notice of them, since their Hunger is their *Fault*, and not their *Affliction*. The *Charity* of the *Law* is great; and therefore he looks on an itinerant and common *Beggar*, with the same Eye as he sees a *disobedient Subject*, whom he must not countenance in an ill way, such as *Idleness* is, and which too often follows, *Lying, Stealing, and Murder*. So that tho' he well knows he is commanded to give, yet he is not to give blindly and rashly; he uses his Understanding to direct him in his Charity; and tho' as the *Steward of God*, he takes himself obliged to dispose of what he is intrusted with as God directs; yet he considers and weighs well what those Directions are, examines who are the proper Objects, and when he is to give, and in a word so contrives it that it may be *real Charity*; left otherwise, what might be well intended, becomes a means either to introduce or continue *ill habits*, and thereby prove a *Curse* instead of a *Blessing*.

And

And there is one Instance more of *Charity*, which he never omits, and that is, on all Opportunities to remember all such People in his *Prayers* and therein commend them to the Goodness of God, beseeching him that he *would be pleased to comfort and relieve them in all their Necessities, give them Patience under their Sufferings, and an happy issue out of all their Afflictions.*

This done; or when these Works of the Day do not occur, he refreshes himself either by *giving* or receiving of a Visit from his Friend or Neighbour, which he conceives to be another kind of *Charity*, and whereby we continue that Kindness and Love which God has made a Debt between us, provided our Conversations be *innocent*, and becoming the day : * Or else he takes a Walk into the Fields, where he not only inspirits and comforts the Body, but *beholding the glorious Light of Heaven, the passing Clouds, the verdant Earth, and smiling Face of all things, he is transported into new Raptures of Devotion; and being affected very much with the admiration of the Creator, he is induced to long for the time, when he shall dwell with him, and behold him face to face without these interpositions.*

At his return home he betakes himself to his *Closet*, and there spends some convenient time in *Meditation* and *Reading* ; but before he enters on that Work, he saith,

O Most Great and Gracious God, whose infinite Mercy it is, that I have this minute of my Life left me, I here appear in thy Presence, lamenting sadly that so much of my time is already lost either in doing ill, or doing nothing, or in doing that which hath been unprofitable and vain : O grant that I may redeem the hours that are past, and dispose of those that are to come in serving thee hereafter with a devout Heart, and earnest and passionate Affections; draw me off more and more from the Pleasures and Vanities of this Life, that I may the better settle my wavering and divided Soul upon thee alone. And since at this time I have here retired my self, that I might the more freely commune with my own Heart, and meditate on thine Holy Word, let thy Blessed Spirit assist me, that I may not only barely remember what I read, but digest it into the practice of an Holy Life, to the Comforts of my Soul, and the

---

* Such a Walk the Rabbins admit ——*Vid. Lyr. ex Judæis ad Act.* I.

the Glory of thy Name, thro' Jesus Chrift. *Amen.*

After a light and frugal Supper, he calls his Family to his Common E-vening Service, confift-ing of the Confeffion, fo much of the Abfolution as is fit for him to fay, the Lord's Prayer *the* Collect *for the day, the o-ther two following it for the Evening-Prayer, that in the Litany, We hum-bly, &c. one or more ta-ken from after the* Of-fertory, *one or more of the occafional Prayers, that for all Conditions of Men, with the other af-ter it, the general Thankf-giving, any particular one, as occafion requires, St.* Chryfoftom's *and the Bleffing.*

Then he goes to his Clofet, and faith,

O God my everlafting Keeper, bleffed be thy Name for ever-more; for thou madeft me when I was no-thing, thou redeemedft me when I was worfe than no-thing: Thou haft fo multipli-ed thy Mercies on me through all the Minutes of my Life, that the Sun has never yet rofe or fet upon me without new Blef-fings from thee. And as thou haft done fo much for me al-ready, for which I pour out my very Soul in Thankfulnefs,

fo in the fame degree of loweft Humility, I humbly befeech thee to continue thy Care of me this Night, and fo to fha-dow me under the Wings of thy Protection, that neither vifible nor invifible Enemies; neither Sin nor Danger may approach to hurt me. That fo when the joyful Light of the Day fhall return again, I may rife in Safety with an unfpot-ted Soul and a Body fitted to be the Temple of the Holy Ghoft: Even fo Lord Jefus. *Amen.*

O Moft Holy Father, the Searcher of all hearts, who feeft my down-lying as well as up-rifing, Darknefs and Light being both alike to thee, Let that Eye of thine which never flumbereth nor fleepeth; which hath been open upon me this Day, watch over me this Night: Let nothing di-fturb, or make me afraid. Let none of the Sins of the Day lie down with me, nor ever ap-pear againft me. Vouchfafe my Body due Refrefhment; and let my Soul have her Songs in the Night; keep both from all the Works of Darknefs, and let me be ever with thee, O Father, both here and hereaf-ter, thro' thy Son my Saviour Jefus Chrift, in whofe Name and Words I further pray,

Our Father, &c.

Amen.

At

At undreffing, he confiders the time coming when his Body muft return naked to the Duft. And this Thought confirms him more in his Refolutions of being humble and penitent ——

Jefus Chrift, who was crucified and laid in the Grave for me, I lay me down to reft, He blefs me and keep me! He fave me, and raife me up again, and bring me at laft to Life Eternal. *Amen.*

Lying down, he faith,

Ent'ring Bed, he faith,

Have Mercy on me, Lord, now, and at the hour of death. *Amen.*

In the Name of our Lord

The End of the Office.

THis is his Practice every *Lords-day*; and he reaps the benefit of it, for as he is a *Religious*, fo he is a *thriving Man*, God profpering his Concerns and Bufinefs all the *reft of the Week*, becaufe he is fo juft to him, and makes this good *beginning* of it.

B. I have one objection againft him, and that is, I find he begins the *Sabbath-day* from his *waking* in the Morning, whereas I expected fomething antecedent to that by way of *Preparation* to this great Day, and which ought to be done the *Evening* before; and fo much the rather, becaufe anciently the Day was reputed to begin at † *Saturday Evening,* and fo to continue to the *Evening* following, as appears from the *Canons* of divers *Synods,* and the Opinion of feveral old Doctors.

A. True; feeing the *Lord's-day* is to be kept Holy, that is, to be fpent in the Service and Worfhip of God, for which it is fet apart, it doth

---

† *Dies Dominicus à Vefpera ufq; ad vefperam fervetur,*&c. which is the fubftance of divers Councils. *Nos Dominicam à fpere Sabbati aufpicamur.* Aug. de Temp.

con-

concern us to confider, how we may fpend it in a
way moft complying with that its defign. And
we fhall eafily, upon the very confideration of the
nature of God's Worfhip, be convinced, that it is
in a manner impoffible for us to Sanctifie it duly,
if we come unto it hot and reeking from our
Worldly bufinefs. "For being we are to worfhip
"God in Spirit and in Truth with all our Mind,
"Soul and Strength, and in a word with our
"whole Man; evident it is, we fhall not be able
"fo to do, while our heart yet remains unempti-
"ed of the World: And being unfit to worfhip
"God, we are not, while fo, in a due ftate to
"fanctifie this Day. And therefore the Sancti-
"fication of the Lord's-day, is to begin with Pre-
"paration. And it depends much on thefe En-
"quiries. Firft, Whether there be not fome Sin
or fad Mifcarriage of the Week paft, which lies un-
repented of, and fo may blaft our next Days performances. And if there be, what are the aggra-
vations and nature of it? that fo we may be able
to exprefs our Repentance, and make *Reftitution,*
Reconciliation or the like, as we find there is need
of it: Then take care to empty our *Heads* and
Hearts of all worldly and diftracting thoughts, and
adjourn them to a Day better becoming them.
And in a word, fo to fettle our Affairs, that neither *our felves* nor *Families* may have any avocations or matters to call away our Minds from
the Holy Duties the next Day, to be expreft towards *God* and our *Brethren.* This indeed is to be done
by us every *Saturday Night*; and a good Man cannot
fafely go to Bed till all this is over. And if you will
have it rather a *looking forward* to begin the *New*
Week, than the *Recollection* of our felves, to fee how we
have fpent the other, and a *preparation* to the firft,
rather than cafting an Eye *backward,* for the fet-
tling of our Accounts, and for concluding well
the

'the _latter_, the thing is the fame; and as for its Name we will not quarrel about it: And if done in a way' of provifion for _Sunday_, the defign is Pious, and I very much commend it as a _Chriftian Duty._ And if my Friend has omitted it under that _Stile_, I am very fure it is not becaufe he doth not behave himfelf according to thofe particulars I mentioned, but he would not be fufpected to incline to Superftition, and lay too great a ftrefs' on that _Nominal Preparation_ fo loud from the Mouths of fome People, whom the _Sabbatarian Doctrine_ hath not a little engaged, and who herein follow that _French Prieft_, whom I had occafion to fpeak of before, and who according to a Law of _Canutus_ to the fame purpofe, began the Feftival from _Three in the Afternoon_ † on _Saturday_, and continued it to _Sun-rifing_ on _Monday Morning_: which was a flight beyond the _Jews_, who reckoned the Day _from Evening to Evening_,' Levit. 23. 32.

And no more doth the Letter of the Law of _Mofes_ call for, requiring the Sanctification of every _Seventh Day_, which if we underftand in the _Natural_ Senfe, as confifting of 24 hours whether it commences from _Evening_ with the _Athenians_ and _Jews_, or from _Sun-rifing_ with the _Chaldeans_; or from _Noon_ with the _Egyptians_, or _Mid-night_ with the _Romans_, (whom we follow, and thereupon begin the _Lord's-day_ immediately after 12 on _Saturday Night_,) provided we devote this proportion of time to the Honour of God, either _negatively_ in forbearing all Servile Work, or _pofitively_ in doing fuch things, as exprefs and fet forth the Service of the Day, we fuppofe _Sunday_ fully enough obferved, without exceeding the common limits of a Natural Day; nor do we think it in any wife

---

† _From Eight a Clock on_ Saturday Night, _to_ Monday Morning. L. C. J. _Hales._

neceſſary to borrow from the days *before* and *after*
it, to make it longer, than the Commandment it
ſelf has preſcribed: But it is not unlikely, but if
we, according to its *Equity*, take it for a *Civil Day*,
from *Morning* to *Evening*, from the *Riſing* to the
Setting of the *Sun*, or from the hour we *begin* to
work to *Bed time*, if we keep the Day with theſe
terms or bounds, it agrees very well with the
words of the *Precept*, which ſaith, *Six days ſhalt thou*
labour, but the ſeventh day is the Sabbath of the Lord
thy God ————So that the *Seventh Day* is to take
its meaſure from the length of the other *Six*; and
\s much of theſe as we ordinarily allot for World-
ły Buſineſs, ſo much of the *Seventh* we are to dedicate to God, and thoſe Holy Works he hath ſet
us to do

And being juſt to God in this proportion, the
Queſtion concerning *Climates*, and thoſe Places
where the Day is not diſtinguiſhed by a conſtant
Succeſſion of Light and Darkneſs, nor terminated by
the *alternate Changes* of the *Riſing and Setting Sun*,
but one Day continues for ſeveral Months together; This, I ſay, need not diſturb the Conſcience, no more than the gaining or loſing a Day in
compaſſing the World, which the *Geographers* obſerve, muſt of neceſſity happen to thoſe who ſail
from the *Eaſt* or from the *Weſt*. In theſe and the
like caſes, we are onely to conſider Time, in that
manner, as *Nature* or *Cuſtom* meaſures it, take
due care to let God have his *Share* in the Dividend;
and to let *his* part be as zealouſly uſed in Divine
Works, as the *others* are in common.

According to our *Lord*'s Rule, 12 *hours* are the
Extent and Complement of a Day; but in this we
conſider the *Sun* at the *Æquinox*; in other Seaſons
the days are much *longer* or *ſhorter*; and I conceive they
may be ſafely ſpent without regard to a preciſe
hour; and though in *Winter* the Dimenſion is *ſhort*

ęf

of what it is in *Summer*, yet as in our *Temporal* Affairs, so in our *Spiritual* too, one Season must make good the defect of *another*, that so the Seventh day may become intire.

As to the set hour of beginning the Day, the Church herein uses her Liberty. The Heathens by light of Nature, commenced *their* * *Festivals* about the *Rising of the Sun*, his appearance proclaiming the beginning of the Time for the Solemnity. And since the *Resurrection of Christ* is the ground and reason why we celebrate this Day, it better suits the Notion of this great Festival, to begin it near *the hour of his rising from the Dead*, though it be uncertain what hour exactly it was, otherwise we put the *Effect* before the *Cause*, and make the *Lord's-day* precede the *Resurrection*; which was the occasion of its Commencement.

But as to this, we need not trouble our selves with studying, when to *begin* or when to *end* this Christian *Sabbath*, whether at *Even*, *Mid-night*, or *Morning*; " He who having set his Secular Affairs " in such order, as they give no interruption to his " *Sunday* Devotion, goes to Bed with God on *Saturday* Night, and rises with him on *Sunday* " Morning, and spends the Day in such like Ex- " ercises, as have been mentioned, may after he " has commended himself and his Family to God, " go to his rest on *Sunday* Night, without danger " of prophaneness, at his usual time. But I doubt I have more than one way tired your Patience, and therefore the Night drawing on, I will detain you no longer, especially considering the Time *approaches* to prepare for the *Lord's-day* to morrow, if it be not, as you may think, already *begun*.

Good Night.

. * *Festa dies oritur, linguisq; animisq; favete,*
Hoc dicenda bono sint bona verba die.

F I N I S.

WS - #0003 - 190923 - C0 - 229/152/32 [34] - CB - 9780331662177 - Gloss Lamination